Econometric Society Monographs

The theory of general economic equilibrium
A differentiable approach

Econometric Society Publication No. 9

Econometric Society Monographs

Editors
Jean-Michel Grandmont, *Centre d'Études Prospectives d'Économie Mathématique Appliquées a la Planification, Paris*
Charles F. Manski, *University of Wisconsin, Madison*

Editor for this volume
Frank Hahn, *Cambridge University*

The Econometric Society is an international society for the advancement of economic theory in relation to statistics and mathematics. The Econometric Society Monograph Series is designed to promote the publication of original research contributions of high quality in mathematical economics and theoretical and applied econometrics.

Other titles in the series

Werner Hildenbrand, Editor   *Advances in econometric theory*
Werner Hildenbrand, Editor   *Advances in econometrics*
G. S. Maddala   *Limited-dependent and qualitative variables in econometrics*
Gerard Debreu   *Mathematical economics: twenty papers of Gerard Debreu*
Jean-Michel Grandmont   *Money and value: a reconsideration of classical and neoclassical monetary economics*
Franklin M. Fisher   *Disequilibrium foundations of equilibrium economics*
Bezalel Peleg   *Game theoretic analysis of voting in committees*
Roger J. Bowden and Darrell A. Turkington   *Instrumental variables*

The theory of general economic equilibrium

A differentiable approach

ANDREU MAS-COLELL
Harvard University

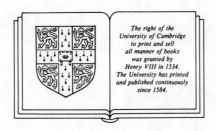

*The right of the
University of Cambridge
to print and sell
all manner of books
was granted by
Henry VIII in 1534.
The University has printed
and published continuously
since 1584.*

CAMBRIDGE UNIVERSITY PRESS
Cambridge
London   New York   New Rochelle
Melbourne   Sydney

Published by the Press Syndicate of the University of Cambridge
The Pitt Building, Trumpington Street, Cambridge CB2 1RP
32 East 57th Street, New York, NY 10022, USA
10 Stamford Road, Oakleigh, Melbourne 3166, Australia

First published 1985
Reprinted 1986
Printed in the United States of America

Library of Congress Cataloging in Publication Data

Mas-Colell, Andreu.

The theory of general economic equilibrium : A differentiable approach.

(Econometric Society monographs; no. 9)

Bibliography: p.

Includes index.

1. Equilibrium (Economics) I. Title. II. Series.
HB145.M38   1985   339.5   85-144
ISBN 0 521 26514 2

Als meus pares

Contents

Preface

The title of this book describes its content, as does the Introduction with more detail. In a sentence it could be summarized as a report on the theoretical developments that followed the publication in 1970 of the fundamental paper by G. Debreu, "Economies with a Finite Set of Equilibria."

I cannot pretend that this book does not assume anything. The economics is essentially self-contained, but it would not be sensible to attempt a systematic reading without a good grounding in the differentiable calculus of several variables and the basic elements of real analysis. Although they are not the central mathematical techniques of this book, it is nevertheless true that some background in topology, measure theory, and convex analysis can be of considerable help. This said, I wish to emphasize that a constant effort is made to facilitate comprehension. Thus, Chapter 1 is devoted entirely to the mathematics, different chapters and sections do not need to be read consecutively, and digressions are written so that they can be skipped. The same is true of proofs (their beginnings and ends are always clearly marked by, respectively, the term *Proof* and the symbol ■). Examples and figures abound, intuitive arguments are given often, essential results are proved leisurely and sometimes repeatedly. Even at the cost of an occasional pedestrian proof the use of comparatively sophisticated techniques is avoided.

This book was written over a period longer than I wish to remember. It was conceived and started at Berkeley, continued at the Universitat Autònoma de Barcelona, and concluded at Harvard. Each of these institutions provided a wonderfully supportive environment. It is only fair, however, to single out the very special contribution of Berkeley. After all, the book is an outgrowth of the intense research atmosphere on the differentiable approach to economics fostered there in the seventies by G. Debreu and S. Smale. My first attempt at a systematic presentation was a course taught in the Berkeley Mathematics Department in the spring of 1976. The typewritten notes for this course had a limited distribution and constitute the (very distant) antecessor of this book.

My debt to G. Debreu will be obvious enough through the book. Let me just say here that without his scientific work this book could not have been written, and without his friendly and kind encouragement it may not have been.

My ideas on the uses of the calculus in economics have been shaped by the interaction with many colleagues and coauthors. The fundamental roles of G. Debreu and S. Smale I have already mentioned. But I should also explicitly acknowledge A. Araujo, Y. Balasko, H. Cheng, E. Dierker, H. Dierker, W. Hildenbrand, T. Kehoe, W. Neuefeind, H. Scarf, S. Schecter, D. Sondermann, and H. Sonnenschein. In a sense this book follows in the tradition of the lecture notes by E. Dierker, *Topological Methods in Walrasian Economics* (1974). I only wish I could have kept the high standards of elegance and lucidity set by him.

I am grateful to a number of people who have helped me in one form or another to improve different parts of the book. Among them are B. Allen, R. Anderson, G. Chatterjee, H. Cheng, B. Cornet, G. Debreu, E. Dekel, D. Duffie, B. Grodal, F. Hahn, O. Hart, S. Hart, C. Langlois, J. Nachbar, L. T. Nielsen, C. Simon, N. Singh, W. Trockel, and D. Wells. Special thanks are due to J. Nachbar for his help with the references and the index. The figures were prepared by W. Minty. Finally, a word of thanks to the very able people at Cambridge University Press. A thought should also go to my wife, Esther, who has had to endure the process of writing this book to an extent larger than is fair.

Over the years I have enjoyed the financial support of a Sloan Fellowship and of the National Science Foundation. I am grateful for it.

The manuscript for this book has been prepared in the old and hard way, that is to say, by incessant typing and retyping. In this respect I have been fortunate to count at different stages on the able collaboration of I. Workman, K. Kraco, M. Bosco, and G. Cogswell.

Andreu Mas-Colell

Glossary

This is a glossary of symbols and abbreviations. For terms such as *manifold, rank,* and *kernel,* consult the analytical index (where the first page reference will usually provide a definition).

Mathematics

$\{a \in X : *\}$	the subset of X formed by the elements satisfying the property $*$
$\backslash$	set difference; for example, $A \backslash B = \{a \in A : a \notin B\}$
$\times$	product sign
$\#A$	number of elements in the set A
$\prod_{j \in J} A_j$	product of the sets A_j, $j \in J$
A^n	product of n copies of the set A
$f : A \to B$	function with domain A and range contained in B
$a \mapsto f(a)$	a is taken to $f(a)$ by the function f
$f \mid A$	restriction of f to the set A
$f(V)$	image by f of the set V
$f^{-1}(V)$	inverse image under f of the set V
f^{-1}	inverse function of f
$f \circ g$	composition of the functions f and g
∂X, Bdry X	boundary of the set X
cl X	closure of the set X
Int X	interior of the set X
$\mathcal{K}(X)$	space of nonempty compact subsets of X
$\mathcal{C}(X)$	space of nonempty closed subsets of X
$\to$	tends to
lim	limit
Ls, Li	see A.5

xiii

u.h.c.	upper hemicontinuous; see A.6
$\chi(X)$	Euler characteristic of A; see A.6
$B_\epsilon(X)$	ϵ neighborhood of the set X
R	set of real numbers
$[a,b]$, $[a,b)$, $(a,b]$, (a,b)	closed, half-closed, open intervals
ab	product of the real numbers a and b
sign a	$+1, 0,$ or -1 according to $a >, =, < 0$
a/b, $\dfrac{a}{b}$	quotient of the real numbers a, b
$\lvert a \rvert$	absolute value of the real number a
exp	exponential function
ln	natural logarithm
sup, inf	supremum, infimum
max, min	maximum, minimum
$o(a)$	$o(a)/a \to 0$ as $a \to 0$
$\displaystyle\sum_{j \in J}, \sum_{i=1}^{n}$	sum over the indices $j \in J$ or from 1 to n. If J or n is clear in context, it may be dropped.
$\displaystyle\int f(s)\,d\nu(s)$, $\displaystyle\int f\,d\nu$, $\displaystyle\int f$	integral of f with respect to ν
χ_A	indicator function of the set A
$\displaystyle\int_A$	integral over A
supp ν	support of the measure ν; see E.3
$\lambda \circ f^{-1}$	measure induced in the range of f by the measure λ in the domain; see E.2
λ	if used for a measure, it is always Lebesgue measure
dim	dimension
$L^{\perp}$	perpendicular complement to the subspace L
R^n	n-dimensional Euclidean space
$x = \begin{bmatrix} x^1 \\ \vdots \\ x^n \end{bmatrix}$	vector in R^n; sometimes it is written as a row
x^i	ith entry of the vector x

$x \geq y$	$x^i \geq y^i$ for all i
$x > y$	$x \geq y$ and $x \neq y$
$x \gg y$	$x^i > y^i$ for all i
0	origin of R^n
R_+^n	nonnegative orthant of R^n; that is, $\{x \in R^n : x \geq 0\}$
R_{++}^n	strictly positive orthant of R^n; that is, $\{x \in R^n : x \gg 0\}$
x^T	row vector transpose of x
$+, -$	vector addition and subtraction
αx	scalar multiplication of the vector x by the real α
e_i	ith unit vector; that is, $e_i^i = 1$, $e_i^j = 0$ for $j \neq i$
e	$e^i = 1$ for all i
co A	convex hull of the set A
$x \cdot y$	inner product of the vectors x, y
$A(v, v')$	evaluation of the bilinear form A at v, v'
$\|x\|$	norm of the vector x
S^{n-1}	$(n-1)$ unit sphere; that is, $\{x \in R^n : \|x\| = 1\}$
$[a_{ij}]$	matrix with generic entry a_{ij}
A^T	transpose of the matrix A
I	identity matrix
A^{-1}	inverse of the matrix A
det A, $\|A\|$	determinant of A
C^r, $r \geq 0$	r times continuously differentiable
∂f	derivative of the C^1 funtion $f : U \to R^n$, $U \subset R^n$
$\partial_x f$	derivative with respect to x
$\partial f(x)$	evaluation of the derivative at x, a linear map from R^n into R^m. Also, the $m \times n$ matrix of this map (given a base). In the $m = 1$ case the same symbol is used for the $n \times 1$ gradient vector at x
$\partial^2 f$	second derivative of f
$\partial^2 f(x)$	evaluation of the second derivative of f at x, a bilinear form
IFT	implicit function theorem
$T_x M$	tangent space to the manifold M at x
TM	tangent bundle of M; see H.1
$f \pitchfork Z$	f is tranversal to Z; see I.2
$Y \pitchfork Z$	Y is transversal to Z; see I.2
$f \pitchfork_N Z$	f is transversal to Z on N; see I.2
deg	degree
∎	end-of-proof sign

Economics

We gather here the symbols that have a single (or at least predominant) meaning throughout all the economic chapters. Hence, this is not a complete list of important concepts. A specific economic notion (e.g., the excess utility map) is always denoted by the same symbol [in this case, $h(\lambda)$], but if the concept is particular to a chapter (in this case, Chapter 5), the symbol may be used for a different purpose in another chapter.

ℓ	number of commodities
R^ℓ	commodity space
p	price vector
S	$\{p \in S^{\ell-1} : p \gg 0\}$
X	consumption set; usually it is one of the sets R_+^ℓ, $R_+^\ell \setminus \{0\}$, R_{++}^ℓ
$\succsim$	preference relation; see 2.2.1
$\succ, \sim$	preference and indifference relation derived from $\succsim$
$b(p, w)$	budget set at price vector p and wealth w; see 2.2.1
ω	initial endowment vector
$\varphi(\bullet)$	demand function; the argument of the function may vary according to the context
$f(\bullet)$	excess demand function; it may be individual or aggregate
$g_\succsim(x)$	unit normal to $\{z : z \sim x\}$ at x in the direction of preference; see 2.3
$c(\succsim, x)$	Gaussian curvature of Bdry$\{z : z \succsim x\}$ at x; see 2.5
$S(p, w)$	substitution matrix; see 2.7
$\mathcal{P}_{cl}$	space of continuous, monotone preferences on $R_+^\ell \setminus \{0\}$; see 2.4
$\mathcal{P}_b$	space of continuous, monotone preferences on R_{++}^ℓ with $\{z : z \succsim x\}$ closed in R^ℓ for all x; see 2.4
$\mathcal{P}$	generic symbol for either $\mathcal{P}_{cl}$ or $\mathcal{P}_b$; see 2.4
$\mathcal{P}_c$	$\{\succsim \in \mathcal{P} : \succsim \text{ is convex}\}$; see 2.6
$\mathcal{P}^r, \ r \geq 0$	space of C^r preferences in $\mathcal{P}$; see 2.4
$\mathcal{P}_c^r, \ r \geq 0$	space of C^r, convex preferences in $\mathcal{P}$; see 2.6
$\mathcal{P}_{sm}^r, \ r \geq 0$	space of C^r, strictly monotone (differentiable strictly monotone if $r > 0$) preferences in $\mathcal{P}$; see 2.4

$\mathcal{P}^r_{sc}$, $r \geq 0$	space of C^r, strictly convex (differentiable strictly convex if $r > 1$) preferences in $\mathcal{P}$; see 2.6
Y	production set; see 3.3
Y^*	$\{p \in S : \sup p \cdot Y < \infty\}$; see 3.4
γ_Y	distance function; see 3.4
π_Y	projection function; see 3.4
Γ_Y	normal mainfold; see 3.4
β_Y	profit function; see 3.4
P	set of Pareto optimal allocations; see 4.6
I	set of consumers, either a finite set or $[0,1]$; see 5.2
t	generic element of I
$\mathcal{C}$	generic symbol for a space of characteristics; that is, a product of a space of preferences and an initial endowments set; see 5.2
$\mathcal{E} : I \to \mathcal{C}$	an economy: see 5.2
$\mathfrak{M}$	space of economies; see 5.8
$\mathfrak{M}^*$	space of regular economies; see 5.8
$W(\mathcal{E})$	set of equilibrium prices for the economy $\mathcal{E}$; see 5.8
index p	see 5.3.5

Introduction

1   Modern general equilibrium theory and the calculus

Until the end of World War II mathematical economics was almost synonymous with the application of differential calculus to economics. It was on the strength of this technique that the mathematical approach to economics was initiated by Cournot (1838) and that the theory of general economic equilibrium was created by Walras (1874) and Pareto (1909). Hicks's *Value and Capital* (1939) and Samuelson's *Foundations of Economic Analysis* (1947) represent the culmination of this classical era.

After World War II general equilibrium theory advanced gradually toward the center of economics, but the process was accompanied by a dramatic change of techniques: an almost complete replacement of the calculus by convexity theory and topology. In the fundamental books of the modern tradition, such as Debreu's *Theory of Value* (1959), Arrow and Hahn's *General Competitive Analysis* (1971), Scarf's *Computation of Equilibrium Prices* (1982), and Hildenbrand's *Core and Equilibria of a Large Economy* (1974), derivatives either are entirely absent or play, at most, a peripheral role.

Why did this change occur? Appealing to the combined impact of Leontief's input–output analysis, Dantzig and Koopmans's linear programming, and von Neumann and Morgenstern's theory of games, would be correct but begs the question. Schematizing somewhat (or perhaps a great deal), we could mention two internal weaknesses of the traditional calculus approach that detracted from its rigor and, more importantly, impeded progress.

The first weakness was the custom of settling the problem of existence of an equilibrium by counting equations and unknowns, that is, by verifying that they were the same in number. It became obvious with time, and it never quite escaped the most perceptive authors, that this simply would not do. Eventually, topology came to the rescue and in the form of the fixed-point theory emerged as one of the technical cornerstones of the modern approach.

The second weakness was the inability of the traditional analysis to handle inequalities in a satisfactory manner or even to realize that there was an inequality problem at all. It was here that convexity theory proved to be a decisive tool.

2   The return of the differentiability approach

In 1970 G. Debreu published a pathbreaking paper on economies with a finite set of equilibria. This contribution was at the start of a renewed interest in differentiability techniques. It marked the introduction into economics of the methods of differential topology (particularly of the generic point of view and the theory of transversality of maps) developed by mathematicians, such as R. Thom, during the fifties and early sixties. It would also be difficult to overstress the impact of the delightful little book by Milnor, *Topology from the Differentiable Viewpoint* (1965), on the popularization of the new techniques outside of pure mathematics.

The rebirth of interest in the calculus was born of the perception that the determinateness of equilibrium problem is not exhausted by the existence question but should include matters such as local uniqueness, persistency of equilibria under small perturbations of the data, comparative statics, and stability properties. It had long been recognized (e.g., in the study of stability) that smoothness hypotheses were required to handle some of these issues. The novelty was the realization that the mathematical theory of transversality offered a framework for the rigorous application of the traditional counting-of-the-equations-and-unknowns method to the analysis, not of the existence question, but of other central aspects of the determinateness problem, namely the local uniqueness and the persistency (i.e., the "structural stability") of the equilibria.

Very roughly, the relevance of the transversality theorems to the counting of equations and unknowns could be described as follows. If anything, a count of equations and unknowns must be an appeal to the implicit function theorem (IFT). It is this that allows, locally, the expression of a solution as a differentiable function of exogenous parameters. But the implicit function theorem requires that a "regularity" condition be satisfied: The system of equations should be independent at the solution. To simply assume this independence is not legitimate because solutions are endogenously determined. The transversality theorems offer the way out of the dilemma. They permit us to assert that, in a certain precise sense, the independence condition, while not always satisfied, will typically (or "generically") be so. In ways that would be difficult to summarize in one line, but that are sometimes quite unexpected, the combination of the implicit function theorem and the transversality theorems turns out to be remarkably powerful.

Once the new differential methods had been applied with great success to the solution of basic problems that could not be handled to any degree without them, it is only natural that researchers proceeded to a reexamination of the classical areas of general equilibrium theory from a differentiable perspective. The spell had been broken, so to speak. The gain from this task has been substantial. A general sharpening of the theory has been obtained (e.g., rate of convergence results for limit theorems in economies with many agents) and, occasionally, a fundamentally new insight (e.g., on the topic of computing equilibria).

3   Object and content of the book

The one-line summary of this book is that it gives an account of the theoretical developments just described. Many authors have participated in this work. The pioneering role of G. Debreu has already been mentioned. It is only fair, also, to underline the contributions of S. Smale, E. Dierker, and Y. Balasko.

This is a book of two minds. It is, on the one hand, a book on technique, and technique is, undoubtedly, its raison d'être. Topics and examples have often been chosen for no other reason than their illustrative value for some aspect of the differentiability techniques.

But the book also uses technique as an excuse for a systematic, although not exhaustive, account of some of the central topics of general equilibrium theory. In other words, it is one of the objectives of this book to reexamine the theory of general economic equilibrium from the differentiable point of view.

We give now a brief chapter-by-chapter summary of the content of the book. The "Introduction" section in each of Chapters 2 through 8 contains a more detailed description.

Chapter 1 gathers the mathematics used throughout the book. It covers not only differentiability but also topics such as measure theory, Lipschitzian functions, and convexifying effects of averaging sets. Chapter 1, to put it briefly, is in the nature of a technical appendix.

Chapters 2 and *3* contain the smooth description of our economic agents: consumers and firms, respectively.

Chapter 4 deals with the theory of Pareto optimality. Obviously, issues traditionally associated with the calculus approach – for example, first-

and second-order conditions – are emphasized, but topics such as the manifold structure of the Pareto set or the existence of approximate efficiency prices in noncovex economies are also covered.

Chapter 5 is the longest and most central chapter of this book. It studies Walrasian equilibrium for exchange economies. It covers topics such as the existence of equilibrium, its local uniqueness, the stability of the equilibrium set under perturbation of the data, uniqueness of equilibrium, and the global structure of the equilibrium manifold. The organizing concept of the chapter is the notion of *regular economy* and the central result is an *index theorem* that, in a precise sense, exhausts the implications of the abstract theory of equilibrium.

Chapter 6 studies equilibrium in economies with production. It concentrates on the issues raised by the latter that are interesting and distinct from what is already covered in Chapter 5.

Chapter 7 reexamines in a smooth context some well-known equivalence theorems. These are results for economies with many traders. They focus on properties that single out the Walrasian equilibrium among all possible outcomes of trade. We concentrate on three of these: the core, the anonymity, and the no-surplus properties.

Finally, *Chapter 8* gathers all the applications of the transversality theorems (except for some results in Chapter 5). We have thought that this was the most pedagogical thing to do. Thus, up to Chapter 8 many results are proved for the regular case. What Chapter 8 then does is to establish that *regular* does indeed mean "typical" or "generic."

We note that while the transversality theorems are used mostly in Chapter 8, the other leg of our mathematical treatment, namely the implicit function theorem, is used throughout.

As a last remark, we point out that an effort is made in the different chapters to show that differentiability techniques can handle boundaries. We do this because, as already indicated, boundaries (i.e., inequalities) constituted one of the stumbling blocks for the uses of the calculus in the classical era. To avoid specious generality we choose to make our point by ensuring that the theory covers the case where consumers have as the consumption set the nonnegative orthant of R^{ℓ} and where, therefore, boundary consumption is not ruled out. Allowing this is often just a matter of choosing notation carefully. Sometimes, however, there is a substantial difference between the theory with or without the possibility of boundary consumption; the limit theorems of Chapter 7, Section 4, are a case in point. On a few occasions we have to resort to a calculus (mainly versions of the implicit function theorem) for Lipschitz rather than differentiable functions. In no case does this involve any particular technical complexity.

4   Topics and techniques not covered

There is no better way to be convincing when asserting that this book does not intend to be a treatise than to list what is absent from it.

On the mathematics side, the book contains no (explicit) application of such important differentiability-based topics as singularity theory (see Golubitsky–Guillemin, 1973) or dynamical systems (see Hirsch–Smale, 1974; Arnold, 1973). This book concentrates on the applications of the implicit function and the transversality theorems. And even then, some of the important technical tools associated with the latter (such as jets or the Whitney topology) are never used.

On the economics side, the different areas of general equilibrium theory are covered only selectively or not at all. This is true even of topics where the generic point of view and the smooth approach have been particularly useful – for example, dynamic economic models (e.g., Balasko–Shell, 1980; Millán 1981; Kehoe–Levine, 1982), rational expectations equilibria (e.g., Allen, 1981; Radner, 1979; Jordan, 1982; Jordan–Radner, 1982), or general equilibrium models of monopolistic competition (e.g., Novshek–Sonnenschein, 1978; Roberts, 1980; Mas-Colell, 1982).

5   Reference conventions and sources

In Chapter 2 through Chapter 8 definitions, propositions, and examples are numbered consecutively by means of three digits, the first denoting the chapter and the second the section. There are no subsections in these chapters. Thus, 5.3.2 refers to the statement so numbered in Section 3 of Chapter 5. Such a number can refer to a definition, an example, or a proposition (but not to a figure – these are triple-numbered in a separate sequence). References to the mathematical Chapter 1 follow a different convention. Sections of this chapter are lettered and subsections numbered. Thus, A.3.2 refers to the statement so numbered in Subsection 3 of Section A of Chapter 1. A reference beginning with a letter always refers to Chapter 1.

The references to sources are gathered in a final section in each chapter (except in Chapter 1, where they appear at the end of each section). We would like to emphasize strongly that this book covers the work of many researchers and that the results that have not appeared before are very few. *When consulting this book the presumption should be that there is a* (primary or secondary) *source for each result in the reference section of the corresponding chapter.* I wish to apologize here for any, unintended, misreference.

CHAPTER 1

Mathematics

This chapter gathers a number of mathematical definitions and theorems that, to different extents, will be needed for the economic theory of the following seven chapters. It is not meant to be read systematically before the rest of the book. The chapter is divided into twelve sections. The ordering of the sections is one of convenience and not of intrinsic importance for later developments. This being a book on differentiable techniques, it stands to reason that the central sections are Sections B on linear algebra, C on differential calculus, D on optimization, H on differentiable manifolds, I on transversality theory, and J on degrees of functions and indices of zeros of vector fields.

The economic theory of this book is presented in Chapters 2 through 8 with a fairly strict adherence to the axiomatic method and without presupposing much. No similar claim is made, however, for this chapter. A quick reading of the headings of the different sections will convince the reader that their content cannot be a systematic, complete, or rigorous exposition. It serves to fix terminology and to facilitate reference, but if one wishes to go deeper into the purely mathematical aspects, this chapter is no substitute for the study of the pertinent mathematical sources cited at the end of every section. It should suffice to say that the chapter does not contain any proofs.

The style, the absence of proofs, and the intention that it not be read beforehand all describe this chapter as being in the nature of a series of mathematical appendices. We have not made it so explicitly for two reasons. To be frank, one is to follow tradition. The other is to avoid being guilty of an attempt to disguise the obvious: that this is a text in mathematical economics.

Most of the topics covered are central in mathematics. Others have a long and established tradition in economics (e.g., correspondences, averaging of sets). A few are more special (e.g., measures with compact support, generalized Jacobians of Lipschitzian functions). With rare exceptions, every quoted theorem will be appealed to in the economic chapters, some of them many times, others only once. A minimal background in elementary calculus and set theory is taken for granted. Thus we shall not define terms such as *union, sequence, function, domain, one-to-one, onto,* or *real number.* We refer to the general glossary of terms (pages xiii–xvii) for the set theoretic notation. Once or twice, always far from the mainstream of the exposition, we may mention mathematical techniques not covered in the chapter – for example, differential equations in Section 5.6.

A   Point-set topology and metric spaces

A.1   *Some definitions*

A family $\mathfrak{I}$ of subsets of a set X constitutes a *topology* if the family is closed under arbitrary unions and finite intersections and if it includes both X and the empty set $\varnothing$. The pair $(X, \mathfrak{I})$ is called a *topological space.* If clear from the context, the reference to $\mathfrak{I}$ is omitted. The topology $\mathfrak{I}'$ is *finer* than $\mathfrak{I}$ if $\mathfrak{I}' \supset \mathfrak{I}$. Subsets $X' \subset X$ and products $X \times Y$ of topological spaces inherit, respectively, the *relative* ($\mathfrak{I}' = \{V \cap X' : V \in \mathfrak{I}\}$) and the *product* ($\mathfrak{I}_{X \times Y} = \{V_X \times V_Y : V_X \in \mathfrak{I}_X, V_Y \in \mathfrak{I}_Y\}$) topologies.

Given a topological space $(X, \mathfrak{I})$, the members of the topology are called *open sets.* A *neighborhood* of $x \in X$ is any open set that includes x. The complement of an open set is a *closed set.* Of course, the family of closed sets is closed under arbitrary intersections and finite unions. The smallest closed set (resp. the largest open set) that contains $A \subset X$ (resp. contained in A) is called the *closure* (resp. the *interior*) of A and is denoted $\operatorname{cl} A$ (resp. $\operatorname{Int} A$). The *boundary* of A, denoted ∂A or $\operatorname{Bdry} A$, is the set $\operatorname{cl} A \cap \operatorname{cl}(X \backslash A)$. A countable intersection (resp. union) of open (resp. closed) sets is called a G_δ (resp. F_σ) set.

A set $A \subset X$ is *dense* (resp. *nowhere dense*) if it intersects every nonempty open set (resp. if its closure has empty interior). The topological space X is *separable* if it admits a countable dense set. A *sequence* $x_n \in X$ *converges* to $x \in X$, denoted $x_n \to x$ or $\lim x_n = x$, if for any neighborhood V of x there is N such that $x_n \in V$ for $n > N$. We say that x is a *limit point* of x_n if a subsequence of x_n converges to x.

A function, or map, $f : X \to Y$ between topological spaces is *continuous* if $f^{-1}(V)$ is open for any open $V \subset Y$. The property of continuity is preserved for sums, products, and compositions of continuous functions. The function is *open* if $f(U)$ is open for every open $U \subset X$. Note that, for an open and continuous f, we have $y_n \to y$ if and only if $x_n \to x$ for some $x_n \in f^{-1}(y_n)$, $x \in f^{-1}(y)$.

The continuous function $f: X \to Y$ is a *homeomorphism* if it is onto, one-to-one, and open. It is a *local homeomorphism* at x if the restriction of f to some neighborhood of x is a homeomorphism onto a neighborhood of $f(x)$. The spaces X, Y are *homeomorphic* if there is a homeomorphism $f: X \to Y$. We always have $f(\partial X) = \partial Y$.

Given a topological space X and a function $f: X \to Y$, the *identification* topology in Y is the finest topology that makes f continuous. Equivalently, $V \subset Y$ is open if and only if $f^{-1}(V)$ is open.

We consider only topologies that are separated; that is, if $x \neq y$, then there are open sets U, V such that $x \in U$, $y \in V$, and $U \cap V = \varnothing$.

A.2   *Compactness and connectedness*

A topological space X is *compact* if whenever it is contained in the union of a family of open sets, it is contained in the union of a finite subfamily. Equivalently, X is compact if it has the *finite intersection property;* that is, whenever every finite subfamily of a family of closed sets has nonempty intersection, the entire family has nonempty intersection. A compact subset of a space is closed. Products and closed subsets of compact spaces are compact. A set is *σ-compact* if it is the union of countably many compact sets. It is *locally compact* if every point has a neighborhood with compact closure.

> ***A.2.1.*** *A subset K of R^n is compact if and only if it is closed and bounded (i.e., $|x^i| < s$ for some s and all $x \in K$ and i).*

> ***A.2.2.*** *Let $f: X \to Y$ be continuous. If X is compact, then so is $f(X)$.*

The *one-point compactification* $(X^*, \mathfrak{I}^*)$ of a locally compact space $(X, \mathfrak{I})$ is defined by $X^* = X \cup \{\infty\}$, $\mathfrak{I}^* = \mathfrak{I} \cup \{V \subset X^*: \{\infty\} \subset V, X^* \setminus V \subset X$ is compact in $(X, \mathfrak{I})\}$. As the name suggests, it is a compact space.

A function $f: X \to Y$ is *proper* if $f^{-1}(A)$ is compact whenever $A \subset Y$ is compact.

> ***A.2.3.*** *If $f: R^n \to R^n$ is proper and a local homeomorphism at every $x \in X$, then f is a homeomorphism onto.*

A topological space X is *connected* (resp. *arcwise connected*) if it is not possible to find two open sets U, V such that $X \subset U \cup V$, $U \cap V = \varnothing$, $U \cap X \neq \varnothing$, and $V \cap X \neq \varnothing$ [resp. if for any $x, y \in X$ there is a continuous function $f: [0, 1] \to X$ with $f(0) = x$, $f(1) = y]$. Products of connected spaces are connected. A particular instance of arcwise connected spaces occurs in the contractible spaces. A space X is *contractible* if there is a continuous function $f: X \times [0, 1] \to X$ such that $f \mid (X \times \{0\})$ is the identity and $f \mid (X \times \{1\})$ is a constant.

A.2.4. *Let $f: X \to Y$ be a continuous function. If X is connected, then $f(X)$ is connected.*

A.3 Metric spaces

A function $d: X \times X \to R_+$ is a *metric* on X if, for all $x, y, z \in X$,

  (i) $d(x, y) = 0$ if and only if $x = y$,
  (ii) $d(x, y) = d(y, x)$, and
 (iii) $d(x, y) + d(y, z) \geq d(x, z)$, the triangle inequality.

The pair (X, d) is called a *metric space*. If clear from the context, the reference to d is omitted. The sum of two metrics on X is also a metric on X. The product $X \times Y$ of two metric spaces can be made into a metric space by letting $d_{X \times Y}((x, y), (x', y')) = d_X(x, x') + d_Y(y, y')$.

For $A \subset X$ denote $B_\epsilon(A) = \{y \in X : d(x, y) < \epsilon$ for some $x \in A\}$ and $B_\epsilon(x) = B_\epsilon(\{x\})$. A set $A \subset X$ is *bounded* if $A \subset B_\epsilon(x)$ for some $x \in X$ and $\epsilon > 0$.

A metric d on X induces a topology on X by letting $V \subset X$ be open if and only if for any $x \in V$ there is $\epsilon > 0$ such that $B_\epsilon(x) \subset V$. A topological space whose topology can be induced by some metric is called *metrizable*. If X is metrizable and $f: X \to Y$, then f is continuous if and only if $f(x_n) \to f(x)$ whenever $x_n \to x$. A subset of a separable, metrizable space is separable and metrizable.

A.3.1. *A metric space is compact if and only if every sequence has a convergent subsequence. Any compact metric space is separable.*

A.3.2. *The one-point compactification of a separable, locally compact metric space is metrizable.*

A.3.3. *Suppose that $f: X \to Y$ is continuous function between metric spaces and that X is compact. Then f is uniformly continuous; that is, for any $\epsilon > 0$ there is a $\delta > 0$ such that, for any $z, z' \in X$, $d_X(z, z') < \delta$ implies $d_Y(f(z), f(z')) < \epsilon$.*

A sequence x_n in a metric space X is a *Cauchy sequence* if for any $\epsilon > 0$ there is an N such that $d(x_n, x_m) < \epsilon$ whenever $n, m > N$. The metric space is *complete* if every Cauchy sequence in X converges to a limit in X. A *topological space* that is homeomorphic to a complete metric space is called *complete*.

> **A.3.4.** *Any G_δ subset (i.e., a countable intersection of open sets) of a complete space is complete.*

A.4   *The Baire property*

A topological space X has the *Baire property* if countable intersections of open and dense subsets are dense or, equivalently, if countable unions of closed, nowhere dense subsets (also called first category sets) are nowhere dense (hence strictly smaller than X). A subset $A \subset X$ is called *residual* if it contains a countable intersection of open and dense subsets. So the Baire property can be rephrased as saying that residual subsets must be dense.

> **A.4.1.** *Any complete metric space, hence any complete topological space, has the Baire property.*

A.5   *The space of subsets of a metric space*

Let (X, d) be a fixed reference metric space. Given two nonempty, compact subsets $F, G \subset X$, the *Hausdorff distance* $\rho(F, G)$ is defined as $\rho(F, G) = \mathrm{Min}\{\epsilon : G \subset B_\epsilon(F) \text{ and } F \subset B_\epsilon(G)\}$. It constitutes a metric on $\mathcal{K}(X) = \{F \subset X : F \neq \varnothing \text{ and compact}\}$.

> **A.5.1.** *The Hausdorff distance topology on $\mathcal{K}(X)$ has the following properties:*
>
> (i)   *It only depends on the topology of X and not on the particular metric d.*
>
> (ii) *If $\rho(F_n, F) \to 0$, then $\bigcup_n F_n \cup F$ is compact. If every F_n is connected, then so is F.*
>
> (iii) *If X is separable, then $\mathcal{K}(X)$ is separable.*
>
> (iv) *If X is separable and locally compact, then $\mathcal{K}(X)$ is complete.*
>
> (v)   *If X is compact, then $\mathcal{K}(X)$ is compact.*
>
> (vi) *If X is compact and connected, then $\mathcal{K}(X)$ is arcwise connected.*

An unpleasant fact from the point of view of this book is that the completeness of X does not alone suffice for the completeness of $\mathcal{K}(X)$.

Suppose that (X, d) is separable and locally compact. A separable, locally compact metric $\hat{\rho}$ can then be defined on $\mathcal{C}(X) = \{F \subset X : F \neq \varnothing$ and closed$\}$ as follows. Let d^* be a metric for the one-point compactification of X and denote by ρ^* the corresponding Hausdorff distance on $\mathcal{K}(X^*) = \mathcal{C}(X^*)$. Set then $\hat{\rho}(F, G) = \rho^*(F \cup \{\infty\}, G \cup \{\infty\})$. The induced topology on $\mathcal{C}(X)$ is also called the *closed convergence topology*. This is because the notion of convergence $F_n \to F$ admits a simple description. Let $\operatorname{Ls} F_n = \{x \in X : $ for all $\epsilon > 0$ and N, there is an $n > N$ such that $F_n \cap B_\epsilon(x) \neq \varnothing\}$ and $\operatorname{Li} F_n = \{x \in X : $ for all $\epsilon > 0$ there is an N such that $F_n \cap B_\epsilon(x) \neq \varnothing$ for all $n > N\}$. Then $F_n \to F$ if and only if $\operatorname{Ls} F_n = \operatorname{Li} F_n = F$. *Warning:* For noncompact X the closed convergence topology on $\mathcal{K}(X)$ is distinct from the Hausdorff distance topology. The second is finer.

A.6   *Correspondences*

Given two topological spaces X, Y, a *correspondence* is a rule f which to every $x \in X$ assigns a nonempty subset $f(x) \subset Y$. If, for all x, $f(x)$ is a singleton, then we have a function. Correspondences are much used in economics but will play only a minor role in this book. A correspondence $f : X \to Y$ is called *upper hemicontinuous* (u.h.c.) if the values of f are compact and $\{x \in X : f(x) \subset V\}$ is open for every open $V \subset Y$. Or, for X metric, if $x_n \to x$ implies $\operatorname{Ls} f(x_n) \subset f(x)$. For Y compact this is equivalent to the closedness of Graph $f = \{(y, x) \in Y \times X : Y \in f(x)\}$. For an u.h.c., correspondence A.2.2 holds; that is, if X is compact, then so is $\bigcup_{x \in X} f(x)$.

A.7   *Zorn's lemma*

Let X be a set and $>$ an order relation on X. Technically, $>$ is a subset of $X \times X$ and $x > y$ means $(x, y) \in >$; also, for $>$ to be an order it must be transitive – that is, $x > y$, $y > z$ implies $x > z$ – and *irreflexive* – that is, $x > x$ holds for no x. A subset $A \subset X$ is a *chain* if it is completely ordered; that is, whenever $x, y \in A$, $x \neq y$, we have that either $x > y$ or $y > x$. An element x is an *upper bound* for a chain $A \subset X$ if $x > y$ whenever $y \in A \setminus \{x\}$. Finally, we say that x is *maximal* in X if there is no $y \in X$ such that $y > x$. *Zorn's lemma,* which lies at the axiomatic foundations of set theory, asserts that *if every chain has an upper bound, then there exists a maximal element in X.*

A.8   *Reference notes*

For Sections A.1–A.4 and A.7, most introductions to point-set topology will do (e.g., Dugundji, 1966). For an explicit statement of A.2.3 see, for example, Berger (1977). A convenient source for A.5 and A.6 is W. Hildenbrand (1974, part I). Primary references can be found there. The properties claimed for the Hausdorff distance on $\mathcal{K}(X)$ can all be verified without much difficulty. For A.5.1.vi, see Kuratowski (1961, p. 128).

B   Linear algebra

B.1   *Linear spaces*

A (real) *linear space* is a set M, whose elements are called *vectors,* equipped with a notion of addition of vectors $x + y$ and of multiplication of vectors by real numbers, or scalars, αx. The following familiar axioms must be satisfied for all $x, y, z \in M$ and $\alpha, \beta \in R$: (i) $x + y = y + x$; (ii) $(x + y) + z = x + (y + z)$; (iii) there is an *origin,* or zero vector, $0 \in M$, that is, $x + 0 = x$ for all x; (iv) $\alpha(x + y) = \alpha x + \alpha y$; (v) $(\alpha + \beta)x = \alpha x + \beta x$, (vi) $\alpha(\beta x) = (\alpha\beta)x$; and (vii) $0x = 0$, $1x = x$.

A collection of vectors $\{x_1, \ldots, x_m\} \subset M$ is *linearly independent* if $\alpha_1 x_1 + \cdots + \alpha_m x_m = 0$ implies $\alpha_j = 0$ for all j. The maximum number of linearly independent vectors is an invariant of the space known as the *dimension* of M and is denoted $\dim M$. We shall only deal with spaces of finite dimension. Assume that $\dim M = n$. Any collection $\{x_1, \ldots, x_n\}$ [resp. any *ordered* collection $(x_1, \ldots, x_n)$] of n linearly independent vectors is known as a *base* (resp. an *ordered base*) or *coordinate system* for the space. A base has the property that any vector z can be written in a unique way as $z = \alpha_1 x_1 + \cdots + \alpha_n x_n$. It is then legitimate to identify the vector z with the member of R^n whose jth entry is α_j. With this identification, the jth basic vector becomes the jth unit vector $e_j \in R^n$, and vector addition and scalar multiplication take the familiar component-wise form. It should be emphasized that this representation of M in R^n is dependent on the base chosen. The collection of unit vectors e_j constitute the *standard base* of R^n. As a matter of convenience, we view the members of R^n as *column vectors,* that is, arranged vertically (although to save space we may sometimes describe vectors horizontally). The horizontal arrangement, that is, the *row vector,* associated with a $z \in R^n$ is denoted z^T and called the *transpose* of z. Two vectors x, y are *collinear* if $x = \alpha y$ for some $\alpha \in R$.

For any arbitrary sets $L, N \subset M$ denote $L + N = \{x + y : x \in L, y \in N\}$. If $L, N \subset M$ are closed under the linear operations, then they are called *linear subspaces* of M. Both $L \cap N$ and $L + N$ are then linear subspaces. The subspaces L, N are linearly independent if $\alpha x + \beta y = 0$, $x \in L$, $y \in N$, implies $\alpha = \beta = 0$ or, equivalently, $\dim(L \cap N) = 0$, or $\dim(L + N) = \dim L + \dim N$. If, in addition, $L + N = M$, then L and N are called *com-*

plementary and we say that N is a *complement* of L. Every subspace has a complement. Given a subspace $L \subset M$ the *codimension* of L, denoted codim L, is dim $M -$ dim L, or the largest dimension of a complement. For a $x \in M$ the set $L + \{x\} = \{y + x : y \in L\}$ is called a *translation* of L and, also, an *affine subspace*.

The *rank* of a collection of vectors $A \subset M$ is the dimension of the *linear span* of A, that is, of the smallest linear subspace containing A. The collection is in *general position* if rank $A' = \min\{\#A', \dim M\}$ for all $A' \subset A$. The linear span of any collection of unit vectors in R^n, that is, of members of the standard base, is called a *coordinate subspace*.

B.2   *Linear functions*

A function (or *map,* or *transformation*) $f: M \to N$ between linear spaces is *linear* if $f(\alpha x + \beta y) = \alpha f(x) + \beta f(y)$ for all $\alpha, \beta \in R$ and $x, y \in M$. Linearity is preserved by multiplication with a scalar and by sums and compositions of linear functions. A linear function $f: M \to N$ is uniquely determined by taking any base $\{x_1, \ldots, x_m\}$ for M and specifying as desired the vectors $f(x_j) \in N$.

Two important linear spaces associated with a linear f are Kernel $f = f^{-1}(0) \subset M$ and Range $f = f(M) \subset N$.

B.2.1. *For any linear function* $f: M \to N$ *we have:*

   (i)   dim Kernel $f +$ dim Range $f = $ dim M.
   (ii) *If* $y \in f(M)$, *then* $f^{-1}(y)$ *is a translate of* Kernel f.
   (iii) *There is an inverse* $f^{-1}: f(M) \to M$ *if and only if* Kernel $f = \{0\}$. *If it exists, the inverse is a linear function.*

Suppose that L, N are complementary subspaces in M. Then any $x \in M$ can be written uniquely as $x = y + z$ where $y \in L$, $z \in N$. The function that associates y to x is a linear function from M to L that has L and N as, respectively, Range and Kernel. It is called the *projection of M on L along N*.

B.3   *Matrices*

An $n \times m$ (real) *matrix* A is a rectangular array of real numbers with n rows and m columns. The entry corresponding to the ith row and jth column is denoted a_{ij}. What is left after deleting some rows and columns is called a *submatrix* (*principal* submatrix if $n = m$ and the deleted rows and columns have the same index). The *sum* $A + B$ of two $n \times m$ matrices (resp. the *multiplication by a scalar* αA) is a matrix with generic entry

$a_{ij} + b_{ij}$ (resp. αa_{ij}). The *composition*, or *product,* of an $n \times k$ matrix A and a $k \times m$ matrix B is an $n \times m$ matrix denoted AB and with generic entry $\sum_{h=1}^{k} a_{ih} b_{hj}$. By looking at a vector $x \in R^m$ as an $m \times 1$ matrix, we can apply to it any $n \times m$ matrix A to get the n vector Ax. The *transpose* of an $n \times m$ matrix A, denoted A^T, is the $m \times n$ matrix with generic entry a_{ji}. A matrix is *square* if $n = m$. An example is the *identity* matrix I, which has generic entry $a_{ii} = 1$ and $a_{ij} = 0$ for $i \neq j$. A square matrix A is *nonsingular* if it has an *inverse,* that is, there is a matrix A^{-1} such that $AA^{-1} = I$. The inverse, if it exists, is unique. The inverse exists if and only if the n columns of A, looked upon as vectors in R^n, are linearly independent.

The concept and operations with matrices make sense in light of their relation to linear maps. Suppose that $f: M \to N$ is a linear map between linear spaces of respective dimensions m and n. Suppose that bases have been fixed in M and N and that the vectors in M and N are represented, respectively, by R^m and R^n. Form the $n \times m$ matrix A whose ij entry is $f^i(e_j)$. Then the linear function f can be written as $f(x) = Ax$. In short, for given bases, there is a one-to-one correspondence between linear maps and matrices. However, if the bases change, there must also be a change in the matrix representation of the given linear map. The precise relation is as follows. Let C (resp. D) be the $n \times n$ (resp. $m \times m$) matrix whose columns are intended to be the new basic vectors in N (resp. M). Then the matrix representation after the change is $C^{-1}AD$. If the bases stay fixed in the background, we will often, in order to save notation, identify the linear map with its matrix. But it is important not to lose sight that those are distinct concepts.

The *rank* (or column rank) of an $n \times m$ matrix A is the maximum number of linearly independent columns. It equals, therefore, the dimension of the range of the corresponding linear function $A: R^n \to R^m$ and so we must have rank $A \leq \min\{m, n\}$. When we have equality, we say that A has *full rank.* For a square matrix this is the necessary and sufficient condition for the existence of an inverse.

B.4   *Determinants*

With every $n \times n$ matrix A there is associated a real number called the determinant and denoted $|A|$ or $\det A$. It can be computed recursively as follows. Denote by A_{ij} the submatrix obtained by deleting the ith row and jth column. Then, for any i, the determinant satisfies $|A| = \sum_j a_{ij}(-1)^{i+j}|A_{ij}|$. The determinant of a number is the number itself. The expression $(-1)^{i+j}|A_{ij}|$ is called the ijth *cofactor.* The determinants of submatrices are called *minors.*

As a (continuous) real-valued function on $n \times n$ matrices, the determinant is characterized by three properties: (i) It is linear on every column separately (i.e., it is a *multilinear* map); (ii) if two columns are equal, the determinant is zero; (iii) $|I| = 1$. From these the remaining properties follow.

> **B.4.1.** *If two columns of A are interchanged, then the determinant changes by a sign. The determinant of a matrix is nonzero if and only if the matrix is nonsingular.*

> **B.4.2.** $|-A| = (-1)^n |A|$, $|A| = |A^T|$, *and* $|AB| = |A||B|$.

Consider a linear function $f: L \to N$ between two spaces of dimension n. For some reference (ordered) bases in L and N, the representing matrix is A. Suppose now that new ordered bases are given to L and N represented by, respectively, the columns of the $n \times n$ matrices B and C. Then the new matrix is $C^{-1}AB$. Of course, $|C^{-1}AB| = |A|(|B|/|C|)$. Hence if $L = N$ *and* the same ordered base is used in the domain and the range, then the determinant is an invariant of the function. Whenever we refer to the determinant of a linear function $f: L \to L$ the above qualification on the ordered base has to be kept in mind.

B.5   *Scalar products and orthogonality*

The *scalar,* or *inner, product* of two vectors $x, y \in R^n$ is defined as $x \cdot y = \sum_j x^j y^j = x^T y$. The *Euclidean norm* of $x \in R^n$ is $\|x\| = \sqrt{x \cdot x} \geq 0$. It satisfies the properties of a *norm:*

> **B.5.1.** *For all* $x, y \in R^n$ *and* $\alpha \in R$: $\|x + y\| \leq \|x\| + \|y\|$, $\|\alpha x\| = |\alpha| \|x\|$, *and* $\|x\| = 0$ *if and only if* $x = 0$.

Because of B.5.1 $\|x - y\|$ constitutes a metric on R^n.

For $\bar{x}$ fixed, the expression $f(y) = \bar{x} \cdot y$ defines a linear function $R^n \to R$. Conversely, every linear function $f: R^n \to R$ can be represented in the form $\bar{x} \cdot y$, where $\bar{x}^T$ is the $1 \times n$ matrix of f. The vector $\bar{x}$ is then called the *gradient* of f. A *norm* on $n \times m$ matrices A can be defined by $\|A\| = \max_{\|x\|=1} \|Ax\|$. It satisfies the *Schwarz inequality:* $\|Ax\| \leq \|A\| \|x\|$ for all A and x.

Two vectors x, y are *orthogonal,* or *perpendicular,* or *normal,* if $x \cdot y = 0$. This has the familiar geometric meaning (see Figure B.5.1). Correspondingly, two subspaces $L, M \subset R^n$ are orthogonal if $x \cdot y = 0$ for

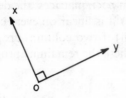

Figure B.5.1

all $x \in L$ and $y \in M$. For any L there is a unique complementary subspace orthogonal to L. It is denoted $L^{\perp}$. The projection of R^n on L along $L^{\perp}$ is called the *orthogonal,* or *perpendicular, projection of R^n on L* and it is sometimes denoted π_L. The vector $\pi_L(x)$ can also be described as the unique minimizer of $\|x - y\|$ for $y \in L$.

Suppose that A and B are, respectively, $n \times n$ and $n \times m$ matrices with rank $B = m$. Let L be the orthogonal complement to Range B, that is, $L = \{x \in R^n : B^T x = 0\} = $ Kernel B^T. Define a linear function $f: L \to L$ by $f(x) = \pi_L A x$. It is often of interest to compute, from A and B, the determinant of f or at least to determine its sign. This can be done by means of a certain $(n+m) \times (n+m)$ bordered matrix.

B.5.2. *The determinant of the linear function $\pi_L A$ from L to L equals*

$$\frac{1}{d} \begin{vmatrix} A & B \\ -B^T & 0 \end{vmatrix}$$

where $d > 0$ is the sum of the squares of all the minors of B corresponding to $m \times m$ submatrices. In particular, if $m = 1$, then $d = \|B\|^2$.

A base $\{x_1, \ldots, x_m\}$ of a linear space $M \subset R^n$ is *orthonormal* if $x_i \cdot x_j = 0$ for $i \neq j$ and $\|x_i\| = 1$ for all i. Every subspace M has an orthonormal base.

B.6   *Eigenvalues and definite matrices*

A (real or complex) number λ is an eigenvalue of the $n \times n$ matrix A if it is a solution of the nth-degree polynomial equation $|A - \lambda I| = 0$. The eigenvalues constitute an invariant of the induced linear map, and their product (taking multiplicity into account) equals the determinant. Note that a real λ is an eigenvalue if and only if $Ax = \lambda x$ for some $x \in R^n$.

In general, the eigenvalues may be complex numbers, but in the important special case where A is *symmetric,* that is, $A = A^T$, they are real.

> **B.6.1.** *For a symmetric matrix A, $\max_{\|x\|=1} x \cdot Ax$ and $\min_{\|x\|=1} x \cdot Ax$ equal, respectively, the largest and the smallest eigenvalue of A.*

A symmetric matrix A is called *positive definite* if all its eigenvalues are strictly positive or, in view of B.6.1, if $x \cdot Ax > 0$ for all $x \neq 0$. The term *definite* is replaced by *semidefinite* if zero eigenvalues are permitted. Hence, a nonsingular semidefinite matrix is automatically definite. An arbitrary matrix A is *quasi-(semi)definite* if the symmetric matrix $A + A^T$ is (semi)definite. As a consequence of B.6.1:

> **B.6.2.** *For symmetric matrices A, B if every eigenvalue of A is larger than every eigenvalue of B, then $A - B$ is positive definite. In particular, if A, B are positive definite and semidefinite, respectively, then $A + B$ is positive definite.*

Also,

> **B.6.3.** *If all the eigenvalues of the symmetric matrix A belong to the interval $(0,1)$ then $A^2 - A = AA - A$ is positive definite.*

The determinant of a positive quasidefinite matrix is positive. Also:

> **B.6.4.** *If A, B are positive semidefinite matrices and L is a subspace, then $|AB + \alpha I| > 0$ and $|A\pi_L + \alpha I| > 0$ for all $\alpha > 0$.*

An $n \times n$ matrix A has a *positive dominant diagonal* if there is some $p \gg 0$ such that $a_{ii} > 0$ and $\sum_j |a_{ij}| p_j > 0$ for all i.

> **B.6.5.** *If the $n \times n$ matrix A has a positive dominant diagonal, then $|A| > 0$. A symmetric A is positive definite if and only if it has a positive dominant diagonal.*

A matrix A is *positive definite on a set* $L \subset R^n$ if: (i) $x \cdot Ay = y \cdot Ax$ for all $x, y \in L$ (symmetry) and (ii) $x \cdot Ax > 0$ for all $x \in L$, $x \neq 0$. For a subspace L, condition (ii) is equivalent to all the eigenvalues of the map $\pi_L A$ from L to L being positive (hence the bordered matrix constructed as in B.5.2 must have a positive determinant). A real λ is an eigenvalue of this map whenever $Ax - \lambda x$ is perpendicular to L for some $x \in L$. Finally, a matrix A is called *negative* (semi, quasi) *definite* on L if $-A$ is positive (semi, quasi) definite on L.

B.7   *Quadratic forms*

A function, or *form*, $f: M \times M \to R$ on a linear space of dimension n is *symmetric* if $f(x, y) = f(y, x)$ for all $x, y \in M$, and *bilinear* if for any fixed $\bar{x} \in M$, $\bar{y} \in M$ the induced functions $f(\bar{x}, \cdot)$, $f(\cdot, \bar{y})$ from M to R are linear. The *quadratic form* $g: M \to R$ corresponding to f is the function $g(x) = f(x, x)$.

By choosing a base we can, without loss of generality, identify M with R^n. If A is an $n \times n$ symmetric matrix, then $f(x, y) = x \cdot Ay$ is a symmetric, bilinear form on R^n. Conversely,

>*B.7.1. Every symmetric bilinear form $f: R^n \times R^n \to R$ can be represented uniquely as $f(x, y) = x \cdot Ay$ for some symmetric matrix A.*

The correspondence between symmetric, bilinear forms and symmetric matrices is an isomorphism in every relevant sense. Therefore, we can apply to forms all the concepts developed for matrices (eigenvalues, definiteness, etc.).

A symmetric, bilinear form defined on a subspace $M \subset R^n$ can always be extended to the entire space.

B.8   *Reference notes*

Everything in this section can be found in, or easily deduced from, most introductions to linear algebra and matrix theory, for example, Lang (1972), Franklin (1968), or Gantmacher (1959). For dominant diagonal matrices (Section B.7), see McKenzie (1960).

C   **Differential calculus**

C.1   *Definitions*

The function $f: U \to R^n$ defined on an open subset of R^m is *differentiable at x* if there is a linear function, denoted $\partial f(x)$, from R^m to R^n such that $\|f(y) - f(x) - \partial f(x)(y - x)\| = o(\|y - x\|)$, where $o(\|y - x\|)$ means that $(1/\|y - x\|)o(\|y - x\|) \to 0$ as $y \to x$. If it exists, the linear function, called the *derivative* at x, is unique. The function is *differentiable* if it is differentiable at every $x \in U$.

Given coordinate systems, the function $\partial f(x)$ can be viewed as an $n \times m$ matrix, called the *Jacobian matrix* (if $n = m$, its determinant is known as the *Jacobian*). The dependence of the $n \times m$ matrix $\partial f(x)$ on x defines a function from U to $R^{n \times m}$. If this function exists and is continuous in a neighborhood of x, we say that f is *continuously differentiable*, or C^1, at x. Correspondingly, f is said to be C^1 if it is C^1 at every $x \in U$. Obviously, the differentiability criterion can in turn be applied to the new function $\partial f: U \to R^{n \times m}$. If the derivative of ∂f exists and is continuous on a neighborhood of x, we say that f is C^2 at x. Reiterating, we can define C^r differentiability for every integer $r \geq 0$. By convention, the 0th derivative is the function itself. The function is C^∞ if it is C^r for every $r \geq 0$. The term *smooth* is used informally to mean "at least C^1."

The generic entry of $\partial f(x)$, denoted $\partial_j f^i(x)$, has the interpretation of a partial derivative; that is,

$$\partial_j f^i(x) = \lim_{\epsilon \to 0} \left[\frac{1}{\epsilon} |f^i(x + \epsilon e_j) - f^i(x)| \right].$$

The existence *and* continuity at x of every partial derivative of f suffices for f to be C^1 at x. A point of notation: $\partial_z f(z, v)$ stands for the derivative of f contemplated as a function of the variables z only; that is, the values of v are kept fixed when computing the derivative.

All the previous definitions are extended to a function on an arbitrary domain U by requiring that an extension of f to some open neighborhood of U exists satisfying the corresponding definition. If U is contained in the closure of its interior, then all the C^r extensions of f have the same rth derivatives at points of U.

C.2   *Basic properties of the derivative*

All the functions in this subsection are assumed to be continuous, and the sets denoted by U and V are always open.

C.2.1. *If $f, g: U \to R^n$, $U \subset R^m$, are differentiable at $x \in U$, then so are $f + g$ and αf, $\alpha \in R$. We have: $\partial(f + g)(x) = \partial f(x) + \partial g(x)$ and $\partial(\alpha f)(x) = \alpha \partial f(x)$.*

C.2.2. Composite function theorem or chain rule. *If $f: U \to R^n$, $U \subset R^m$, and $g: V \to R^s$, $f(U) \subset V \subset R^n$, are differentiable at, respectively, $x \in U$ and $f(x)$, then $g \circ f: U \to R^s$ is differentiable at x and $\partial(g \circ f)(x) = \partial g(f(x)) \circ \partial f(x)$.*

C.2.3. Product rule. *If $f: U \to R^n$, $U \subset R^m$, and $g: U \to R$ are differentiable at $x \in U$, then so is $gf: U \to R^n$ and $\partial(gf)(x) = g(x) \partial f(x) + f(x) \partial g(x)$.*

C.2.4. Mean value theorem. Suppose that $f: U \to R$, $U \subset R^m$, is C^1 and that $\alpha x + (1-\alpha)y \in U$ for all $0 \le \alpha \le 1$. Then there is $\bar{\alpha} \in (0,1)$ such that, setting $z = \bar{\alpha} x + (1-\bar{\alpha})y$, we have $f(y) - f(x) = \partial f(z)(y-x)$.

C.3   Implicit function theorems

The implicit function theorem (IFT) pervades the theory of this monograph. This subsection presents some versions of it. Others will appear in Sections G, H, and I.

The basic problem can be heuristically posed as follows. Suppose that $f: U \times P \to R^n$, $U \subset R^n$, and $f(\bar{x}, \bar{p}) = 0$. That is to say, for the parameters p fixed at $\bar{p}$, the system of n equations with n unknowns $f(\cdot, \bar{p}) = 0$ has a solution $\bar{x}$. To what extent can we now solve x as a function of p? This is the question the IFT is designed to answer. A preparation for it is the inverse function theorem.

C.3.1. Inverse function theorem. Let $U \subset R^n$ be open and $f: U \to R^n$ be C^r, $1 \le r \le \infty$, at x. If $\partial f(x)$ is nonsingular (i.e., a linear homeomorphism), then f is a local homeomorphism at x having a C^r inverse. Precisely, there is an open $V \subset R^n$, $f(x) \in V$, and a C^r function $f^{-1}: V \to R^n$ such that $f^{-1}(f(y)) = y$ on a neighborhood of x. Moreover, $\partial f^{-1}(f(x)) = [\partial f(x)]^{-1}$. A C^1 inverse at $f(x)$ can only exist if $\partial f(x)$ is nonsingular.

C.3.2. Implicit function theorem. Let $U \subset R^n$, $P \subset R^m$ be open and $f: U \times P \to R^n$ be C^r, $1 \le r \le \infty$, at a $(\bar{x}, \bar{p})$ where $f(\bar{x}, \bar{p}) = 0$. If $\partial_x f(\bar{x}, \bar{p})$ is nonsingular, then x can, locally, be solved as a C^r function of p. Precisely, there are open sets $U' \subset U$, $P' \subset P$ and a C^r function $g: P' \to U'$ such that $g(\bar{p}) = \bar{x}$ and $f(x, p) = 0$ holds for $(x, p) \in U' \times P'$ if and only if $x = g(p)$. Moreover, $\partial g(\bar{p}) = -[\partial_x f(\bar{x}, \bar{p})]^{-1} \partial_p f(\bar{x}, \bar{p})$. A C^1 function g exists only if $\partial_x f(\bar{x}, \bar{p})$ is nonsingular.

It is occasionally important to allow the parameters p to be members of an arbitrary topological space. Differentiability of the implicit function is then a meaningless idea, but we may still hope to get its existence and continuity.

C.3.3. Implicit function theorem. Let $U \subset R^n$ be open, P a topological space, and $f: U \times P \to R^n$ a continuous function such *that $\partial_x f(x, p)$ exists and is continuous on $U \times P$. Suppose that $f(\bar{x}, \bar{p}) = 0$. If $\partial_x f(\bar{x}, \bar{p})$ is nonsingular, then x can, locally, be solved as a function of p. Precisely, there are open sets $U' \subset U$, $P' \subset P$ and a continuous function $g: P' \to U'$ such that $g(\bar{p}) = \bar{x}$ and $f(x, p) = 0$ holds for $(x, p) \in U' \times P'$ if and only if $x = g(p)$.*

C.4 Gradients and second derivatives

In this subsection we deal with a real-valued function $f: U \to R$ defined on an open set $U \subset R^n$. If f is C^1, then in matrix form $\partial f(x)$ is a $1 \times n$ matrix. Its transpose is the *gradient* vector of the linear map (see B.5). Abusing notation, we systematically denote the gradient by $\partial f(x)$ instead of the correct $[\partial f(x)]^T$. If f is C^2, then $\partial f(x)$ can be differentiated to yield a linear function, denoted $\partial^2 f(x)$, from R^n to R^n. It can be represented as an $n \times n$ matrix, called the second derivative, or *Hessian*, matrix of f at x. The generic entries are of the form $(\partial^2 f / \partial x_i \, \partial x_j)(x)$ and have the obvious interpretation as (second) partial derivatives. The matrix $\partial^2 f(x)$ turns out to be symmetric. As the first derivative has the interpretation of a linear function, the second derivative can be viewed as a bilinear form. Specifically:

C.4.1. Taylor's formula. *If $f: U \to R$ is C^2 at x, then there are a linear function $\partial f(x): R^n \to R$ and a symmetric bilinear form $\partial^2 f(x): R^n \times R^n \to R$ such that*

$$\|f(y) - f(x) - \partial f(x)(y - x) - \tfrac{1}{2}\partial^2 f(x)(y - x, y - x)\| = o(\|y - x\|^2).$$

Suppose that f is C^2. An x is a *critical point* of f if $\partial f(x) = 0$. It is a *nondegenerate critical point* if, in addition, $\partial^2 f(x)$ is nonsingular. If every critical point of f is nondegenerate, f is called a *Morse function*. A necessary (resp. sufficient) condition for x to be a local maximum of f is that it be a critical point with $\partial^2 f(x)$ negative semidefinite (resp. negative definite). See the next section for further elaboration of this.

C.5 Reference notes

Any introduction to advanced calculus and analysis, for example, Apostol (1957) or Marsden (1974), will do. See also Dieudonné (1960, chap. 8). For the implicit function theorem C.3.3, see Schwartz (1967, chap. 3, sec. 8, theorem 25). For an introduction to the properties of Morse functions, see Hirsch (1976, chap. 6).

D   Smooth optimization

Let the functions $f: R^\ell \to R^n$, $h: R^\ell \to R^m$ be C^1. The components of f are the *objective functions,* whereas $E = \{x \in R^\ell : h(x) \geq 0\}$ is the *constraint set.* A vector $x \in E$ is a *local weak maximum* (resp. *local maximum*) of f subject to h if for some neighborhood of $x \in V$ there is no $x' \in E \cap V$ such that $f(x') \gg f(x)$ [resp. $f(x') > f(x)$].

D.1. First-order necessary conditions. If x is a local weak maximum of f subject to h, then there are $(\lambda, \mu) \in R_+^n \times R_+^m$ such that

  (i) $(\lambda, \mu) \neq 0$.
 (ii)   *If $h_j(x) < 0$, then $\mu_j = 0$.*
(iii) $\sum_{i=1}^n \lambda_i \partial f_i(x) + \sum_{j=1}^m \mu_j \partial h_j(x) = 0$.

D.2. Second-order conditions. Let f and h be C^2. Suppose that $x \in E$ satisfies the first-order necessary conditions with respect to $(\lambda, \mu) \in R_+^n \times R_+^m$. Consider the bilinear form

$$B = \sum_{i=1}^n \lambda_i \partial^2 f_i(x) + \sum_{j=1}^m \mu_j \partial^2 h_j(x)$$

and the cone

$$K = \{v \in R^\ell : \partial f_i(x) \cdot v \geq 0, \quad \lambda_i \partial f_i(x) \cdot v = 0 \text{ for all } i,$$
$$\partial h_j(x) \cdot v \geq 0, \quad \mu_j \partial h_j(x) \cdot v = 0 \text{ for all } j$$
$$\text{with } h_j(x) = 0\}.$$

We have

  (i)   *If x is a local maximum, $\lambda > 0$, and $\operatorname{rank}\{\partial f_i(x), \partial h_j(x): i \leq n, j \leq m, h_j(x) = 0\} = n + \#\{j : h_j(x) = 0\} - 1$, then B is negative semidefinite on K.*
 (ii)   *If B is negative definite on K, then x is a local maximum.*

Observe that in D.2 the cone K reduces to a subspace whenever $\mu_j = 0$ if and only if $h_j(x) \neq 0$. Also, the rank, or nondegeneracy, qualification for the second-order necessary conditions D.2.i can be restated as: The set of gradients of objective functions and binding constraints has the maximal rank consistent with the linear dependence introduced by the first-order conditions.

D.3   Reference notes

This is familiar material in nonlinear programming theory. Some texts are El-Hodiri (1971), Hestenes (1975), Intriligator (1971), Mangasarian

(1969), Simon (1982), and Varaiya (1972). Simon (1982) should be especially helpful for this section.

The second- (and higher-) order conditions can be considerably refined. See, for example, Smale (1973, 1974d, 1975), Wan (1975), van Geldrop (1980), Saari–Simon (1977), and Simon–Titus (1975).

E   Measures and integrals

E.1   *Measures*

A collection $\mathfrak{X}$ of subsets of a topological space X is a *σ-field* if it includes X and is closed under complementation and countable unions and intersections. The *Borel* σ-field is the smallest σ-field including all the open sets. A function $\nu: \mathfrak{X} \to R_+ \cup \{+\infty\}$ is a *(σ-additive) measure* if $\nu(\varnothing) = 0$ and $\nu(\bigcup_{n=1}^{\infty} A_n) = \sum_{n=1}^{\infty} \nu(A_n)$ whenever $\{A_n\}$ is a pairwise disjoint family of subsets. The triple $(X, \mathfrak{X}, \nu)$ is called a *measure space*. If $\nu(X) = 1$, then ν is called a *probability measure* (or *distribution*). A *Borel measure* is defined on the Borel σ-field and gives X a finite value. It is determined by its values on the open sets. In particular, for any Borel distribution ν, Borel set A, and $\epsilon > 0$ there is an open V with $A \subset V$ and $\nu(V) < \nu(A) + \epsilon$. The expression "almost everywhere" (a.e.) means with the exception of the members of a set of measure zero, or *null,* in the relevant measure.

Measures appearing in this book are (i) arbitrary Borel probability measures on separable metric spaces, and (ii) *Lebesgue measure,* denoted λ, on R^n. Lebesgue measure constitutes an extension to a certain σ-field (larger than the Borel σ-field) of the usual notion of volume for rectangular bodies in R^n. In particular, the Lebesgue σ-field is *complete;* that is, all the measure zero (or *null*) sets are in the field. An example of measures of type (i) are the *counting measures* ν. They apply to nonempty, finite sets X and are defined by $\nu(A) = \#A/\#X$ for every subset $A \subset X$.

E.2   *Integrals*

Given a σ-field $\mathfrak{X}$ on X and a topological space Y, the function $f: X \to Y$ is (Borel) *measurable* if $f^{-1}(V) \in \mathfrak{X}$ for every open $V \subset Y$. This is seen to imply $f^{-1}(A) \in \mathfrak{X}$ for every Borel $A \subset Y$ and, therefore, given a ν on $\mathfrak{X}$, a Borel measure on Y, denoted $\nu \circ f^{-1}$, can be defined by setting $(\nu \circ f^{-1})(A) = \nu(f^{-1}(A))$. Interestingly, if Y is separable and complete, any Borel distribution on Y can be generated in this manner for some f and $X = [0, 1]$ with Lebesgue measure.

Measurable functions combine well. Rather than presenting a complete list, let us just say that every operation we wish to perform in this book preserves measurability.

Given a measure ν on $(X, \mathcal{X})$, there is a class of measurable real-valued functions, called the *integrable functions,* with the property that every member of the class can be assigned a number, called the *integral* and denoted $\int f(x)\, d\nu(x)$ [or simply $\int f\, d\nu$, $\int f(x)\, dx$ for $\nu = \lambda$, $\int f$], in a manner compatible with the following three principles:

  (i) $\int \chi_A\, d\nu = \nu(A)$ for all $A \in \mathcal{X}$ [where $\chi_A(x) = 1$ if $x \in A$, $= 0$ otherwise].
  (ii) The integral acts linearly on functions.
  (iii) If $f_n \to 0$ monotonically, that is, $f_{n+1}(x) \le f_n(x)$ and $f_n(x) \to 0$ for all x, then $\int f_n\, d\nu \to 0$.

It turns out that for fixed f the integral also acts linearly on measures. If $\nu(X) < \infty$, then a measurable function f that is bounded [i.e., $|f(x)| < c$ for some c and all x] is integrable. For functions $f: X \to R^n$ the previous definitions apply component-wise. The expression $\int_A f\, d\nu$ means $\int \chi_A f\, d\nu$. Every nonnegative integrable function f defines a new measure ν' by $\nu'(A) = \int_A f\, d\nu$. If $\int f\, d\nu = 1$, then f is called a *density function.*

There is a well-developed theory of integration for correspondences. Naturally, the integral is then also a set. In all generality, given a correspondence $F: X \to R^n$, one defines

$$\int F\, d\nu = \left\{ \int f\, d\nu : f \text{ is integrable and } f(x) \in F(x) \text{ for } \nu\text{-a.e. } x \in X \right\}.$$

> *E.2.1. Let Y be a separable metric space and X either a finite set with a finite measure or $[0,1]$ with Lebesgue measure. Suppose that $g: X \to Y$ is a measurable function and $f: Y \to R_+^n$ a closed graph correspondence. Then $\int (f \circ g)$ is a closed set. If, in addition, $f(Y)$ is bounded, then $\int (f \circ g)$ is a nonempty, compact set.*

E.3   Convergence of measures on a metric space

Consider a fixed, separable metric space X and the set $\mathfrak{M}'(X)$ of Borel measures. It is said that the sequence $\nu_n \in \mathfrak{M}'(X)$ *converges weakly* to $\nu \in \mathfrak{M}'(X)$ if $\int f\, d\nu_n \to \int f\, d\nu$ for every continuous and bounded $f: X \to R$.

> *E.3.1. The weak convergence defines a metrizable and separable topology on $\mathfrak{M}'(X)$. If X is compact or complete, then so is $\mathfrak{M}'(X)$.*

In this book we shall be interested mainly in a set of measures smaller than $\mathfrak{M}'(X)$. The *support* of a measure $\nu \in \mathfrak{M}'(X)$, denoted supp ν, is the smallest closed set $A \subset X$ such that $\nu(A) = \nu(X)$. We are interested in nontrivial [i.e., $\nu(X) > 0$] measures with *compact support*. Let $\mathfrak{M}(X)$ be the set of those. On $\mathfrak{M}(X)$ we wish to consider a finer topology than the weak convergence. Namely, for $\nu_n, \nu \in \mathfrak{M}(X)$ we say that $\nu_n \to \nu$ if:

   (i) ν_n converges weakly to ν, and
   (ii) supp $\nu_n \to$ supp ν in the Hausdorff distance (see A.5 and remember that the topology induced on compact subsets depends only on the topology of X).

It is worth pointing out that the weak convergence implies lim inf $\nu_n(A) \geq \nu(A)$ for any open A and, therefore, supp $\nu \subset$ Li supp ν_n.

> **E.3.2.** *The weak convergence plus Hausdorff convergence of the supports defines a metrizable and separable topology on $\mathfrak{M}(X)$. If X is locally compact, then $\{\nu \in \mathfrak{M}(X) \colon$ supp $\nu \subset E\}$ is complete for any G_δ set $E \subset X$.*

> **E.3.3.** *The measures with finite support are dense in $\mathfrak{M}'(X)$ [resp. $\mathfrak{M}(X)$] for the topology of the weak convergence (resp. of the weak convergence plus Hausdorff convergence of the supports).*

E.4   *Continuity properties*

> **E.4.1.** *Let X be a separable metric space, ν_n, ν Borel measures on X and $f_n, f \colon X \to R$ continuous functions with f bounded. We have:*
>
>   (i)   *If ν_n converges weakly to ν and $f_n \to f$ uniformly (i.e., $\sup_X |f_n(x) - f(x)| \to 0$), then $\int f_n \, d\nu_n \to \int f d\nu$.*
>   (ii) *If $f_n \geq f$ and for ν-a.e. $x \in X$ $f_n(x) \to +\infty$, then $\int f_n \, d\nu \to \infty$.*

> **E.4.2.** *Let X be a compact, metric space, $g_n, g \colon [0,1] \to X$ measurable functions, and $f \colon X \times Q \to R^n$, where Q is a topological space of parameters, an u.h.c. correspondence. For every $p \in Q$ set $F(g, p) = \int f(g(t), p) \, dt$. If the measure $\lambda \circ g_n^{-1}$ converges to $\lambda \circ g^{-1}$ weakly and $p_n \to p$, then Ls $F(g_n, p_n) \subset F(g, p)$.*

E.5   *Integrals and derivatives*

> **E.5.1. Fundamental theorem of calculus.** *Let $f \colon [0,1] \to R$. If f is C^0, then $F(x) = \int_{[0,x]} f(t) \, dt$ is C^1 and $\partial F(x) = f(x)$. Conversely, if f is C^1, then $f(x) - f(0) = \int_{[0,x]} \partial f(t) \, dt$.*

E.5.2. Exchange of derivative and integral. *Let* $f: V \times [0,1] \to R^n$, $V \subset R^m$ *open, be a continuous, bounded function. Suppose that:*

(i)   *There is a* $k > 0$ *such that* $\|f(x,t) - f(x',t)\| \le k\|x-x'\|$ *for all* x, x', *and* t.

(ii)   *For all* $\bar{x} \in V$, $f(x,t)$, *as a function of* x, *is* C^1 *at* $\bar{x}$ *for a.e.* t.

(iii) *For all* x, $f(x, \cdot)$ *and* $\partial_x f(x, \cdot)$ *are (Lebesgue) measurable.*

Then $F(x) = \int f(x,t)\, dt$ *is* C^1 *and* $\partial F(x) = \int \partial_x f(x,t)\, dt$.

E.5.3. Change-of-variable theorem. *Let* $B = \{x \in R^n: \|x\| \le 1\}$ *and* $f: B \to R^n$ *be a* C^1, *one-to-one function with* $\det \partial f(x) \ne 0$ *for all* $x \in B$. *Then for any measurable and bounded* $g: R^n \to R$ *we have* $\int_{f(B)} g\, d\lambda = \int_B (g \circ f)|\det \partial f|\, d\lambda$. *In particular,* $\lambda(f(B)) = \int_B |\det \partial f|\, d\lambda$.

E.6   *Reference notes*

The general mathematical principles for the first four sections are covered, for example, in Royden (1968) and Billingsley (1968). For E.5 see the references for Section C. For the topics of more special interest in economics (e.g., integration of correspondences), consult W. Hildenbrand (1974, part 1).

The last part of E.3.2 requires a hint of a proof. Take the case $E = X$. As an open subset of its one-point compactification, the set X is complete and therefore so is $\mathfrak{M}'(X)$ with the weak convergence topology. Because X is locally compact, the set $\mathcal{K}(X)$ with the Hausdorff distance is also complete. The result follows if one can show that

$$A = \{(\nu, K) \in \mathfrak{M}'(X) \times \mathcal{K}(X): K = \operatorname{supp} \nu\}$$

is a G_δ subset of $\mathfrak{M}'(X) \times \mathcal{K}(X)$. For any n and $(\nu, K) \in \mathfrak{M}'(X) \times \mathcal{K}(X)$ choose $0 < \delta(\nu, K, n) < 1/n$ such that $(\nu', K') \in B_{\delta(\nu, K, n)}(\nu, K)$ implies $\operatorname{supp}\nu \subset B_{1/n}(\operatorname{supp} \nu') \subset X$. It can then be verified without much difficulty that

$$A = \bigcap_n \left[\bigcup_{(\nu, K) \in A} B_{\delta(\nu, K, n)}(\nu, K) \right].$$

It is worth noting that without the local compactness of X, it is still true that $\mathfrak{M}'(X)$ endowed with the weak convergence plus the Hausdorff distance convergence of the supports (the Hausdorff distance is well defined if a bounded metric is adopted for X) is a complete space. However, this is not helpful to us because, first, we want to avoid dependence of the topology on the particular metric on X, and, second, we shall need, in any case, to restrict ourselves to compact supports.

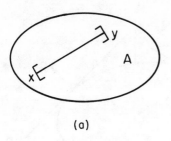
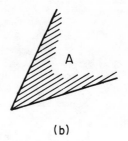

(a)   (b)

Figure F.1.1

F   Convex sets and functions

F.1   *Convex sets*

For $x, y \in R^n$ the *segment* $[x, y]$ is the set $\{\alpha x + (1-\alpha)y : 0 \le \alpha \le 1\}$. A set $A \subset R^n$ is *convex* if $x, y \in A$ implies $[x, y] \subset A$ (see Figure F.1.1a). Intersections, products, sums, closures, and interiors of convex sets are convex. For any $A \subset R^n$ the *convex hull* of A, denoted co A, is the smallest convex set containing A. Equivalently, co $A = \{\sum_{i=1}^{m} \alpha_i x_i : x_i \in A, \ \alpha_i \ge 0, \sum_i \alpha_i = 1,$ some $m\}$. We always have $\text{co}(A+B) = \text{co } A + \text{co } B$. A vector x in the convex set A is an *extreme point* if $x \in [z, y] \subset A$ implies either $z = x$ or $y = x$. Any compact, convex set is the convex hull of its extreme points. The set $\Delta = \text{co}\{e_1, \ldots, e_n\}$ is called the *unit simplex*.

> **F.1.1. Caratheodory's theorem.** *Let $A \subset R^n$, $z \in A$, and $x \in$ co A. Then there are $z_1, \ldots, z_{n+1} \in A$ such that $x = \sum_{i=1}^{n+1} \alpha_i z_i$ for some $\alpha_i \ge 0$, $\sum_{i=1}^{n+1} \alpha_i = 1$. If, in addition, $x \in$ Int co A, we can assume $z_1 = z$ and $\alpha_1 > 0$.*

The dimension of a convex set is the dimension of the smallest affine subspace L containing it. Any two convex sets of the same dimension that are either both compact or both open (relative to the above L) are homeomorphic.

A convex set A is a *convex cone* if $x \in A$ implies $\alpha x \in A$ for every $\alpha \ge 0$ (see Figure F.1.1b). The convex cone *spanned* by a set A is $\{\sum_{i=1}^{m} \alpha_i x_i : \alpha_i \ge 0, x_i \in A,$ some $m\}$. A closed, convex cone A is *pointed* if the origin is an extreme point.

> **F.1.2.** *The convex hull of a compact set is compact. A sufficient condition for the convex hull of a closed set A to be closed is that there exist a closed, pointed cone C such that $A + C \subset A \subset C$.*

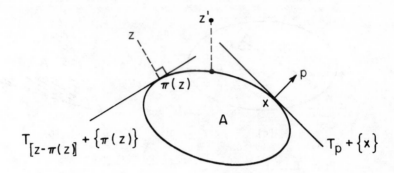

Figure F.2.1

F.2   *Supporting properties*

For any $p \neq 0$ the subspace $T_p = \{v \in R^n : p \cdot v = 0\}$ is called the *hyperplane perpendicular to* p. The convex set $\{v \in R^n : p \cdot v \leq 0\}$ is the *half-space below* T_p. The vector p *supports the convex set* A at $x \in A$ if $A - \{x\}$ is contained in the half-space below T_p, that is, $p \cdot A \leq p \cdot x$ (see Figure F.2.1). Of course, $p \cdot A$ denotes $\{p \cdot y : y \in A\}$. If $p \cdot y < p \cdot x$ for all $y \in A$, $y \neq x$, we say that p *supports strictly*.

> ***F.2.1. Supporting hyperplane theorem.*** *If $A \subset R^n$ is convex and $x \in \partial A$, then A is supported at x by some $p \neq 0$. If A is also a closed, pointed cone and $x = 0$, then the support can be strict.*

> ***F.2.2. Separating hyperplane theorem.*** *If A, B are convex sets with $A \cap B = \varnothing$, then there is $p \neq 0$ and $c \in R$ such that $p \cdot A \geq c \geq p \cdot B$. If the sets are closed and one of the them is nonempty and compact, the inequalities can be taken to be strict.*

> ***F.2.3.*** *A nonempty set $A \in R^n$ is closed and convex if and only if for every $z \in R^n$ there is a unique $\pi(z) \in A$, called the foot of z in A, which is (Euclidean) closest to z, that is, which minimizes $\|z - y\|$ for $y \in A$. Moreoever, $\|\pi(z') - \pi(z)\| \leq \|z - z'\|$ for all $z, z' \in R^n$, and, denoting $p = z - \pi(z)$, $p \cdot A \leq p \cdot \pi(z)$. See Figure F.2.1.*

For every point x in a fixed reference convex set A let $C(x)$ be the smallest closed cone containing $A - \{x\}$. Every $v \in C(x)$, $\|v\| = 1$, is a direction tangent to A at x; that is, there is $x_n \in A$ such that $x_n \to x$ and

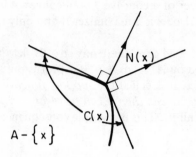

Figure F.2.2

$(1/\|x-x_n\|)(x-x_n) \to v$. Define also the *normal cone* $N(x) = \{p \in R^n: p \cdot A \leq p \cdot x\}$. See Figure F.2.2. The correspondence $N(\cdot)$ has a closed graph on A.

F.2.4. *Given the closed, convex set A and $x \in A$ we have $p \cdot v = 0$, $p \in N(x)$, $v \in C(x)$, $\|v\| = 1$, if and only if there are $x_n \in A$, $p_n \in N(x_n)$ such that $p_n \to p$, $x_n \to x$ and $(1/\|x-x_n\|)(x-x_n) \to v$.*

F.3   *Convex and concave functions*

A function $f: A \to R$ on a convex set A is *concave* if $f(\alpha x + (1-\alpha)y) \geq \alpha f(x) + (1-\alpha)f(y)$ for $x, y \in A$, $0 \leq \alpha \leq 1$. Equivalently, f is concave if and only if $\{(v,s) \in A \times R: s \leq f(v)\}$ is convex. If the defining inequality is strict whenever $x \neq y$, $0 < \alpha < 1$, then the function is *strictly concave*. A function f is *convex* (resp. *strictly convex*) if $-f$ is concave (resp. strictly concave). Functions defined as sums or pointwise minima of concave functions are concave.

A concave function $f: A \to R$ is continuous on Int A. A vector q is a *subgradient* at x of the concave function f if $f(y) - f(x) \leq q \cdot (y-x)$ for all y. The function is differentiable at $x \in$ Int A if and only if it has a unique subgradient at x (which, in this case, coincides with the gradient vector).

F.3.1. *If $A \subset R^n$ is convex and $f: A \to R$ concave, then the map $g: A \to R^n$ that assigns to x the set of subgradient vectors at x is nonempty valued on Int A and it has a closed graph. Moreover, if A is bounded and f is proper, then g is also proper, that is, $\{x \in A: g(x) \cap K \neq \varnothing\}$ is compact for any compact $K \subset R^n$.*

Observe that a local maximizer of a concave f on a convex A is automatically a global maximizer. Also, x is a maximizer if and only if $q = 0$ is a subgradient at x.

Given a nonempty closed set $A \subset R^n$ and any $p \in R^n$ let $h(p) = \sup p \cdot A$. The function h defined on $A^* = \{p : h(p) < \infty\}$ turns out to be a convex function on a convex set. It is called the *support function* of A. Interestingly, if A *is closed and convex then it can be recovered from h* because $A = \{x : p \cdot x \le h(p)$ for all $p\}$. This is a simple consequence of the definition and F.2.2.

> *F.3.2. The support function $h: A^* \to R$ of the nonempty, closed, convex set A is positively homogeneous of degree one [i.e., $h(\lambda p) = \lambda h(p)$ for $\lambda > 0$] and convex. Moreover, x is a subgradient of h at p if and only if $x \in A$ and $p \cdot x = h(p)$.*

There is another interesting convex function $\gamma: R^n \to R$ associated with a nonempty, closed, convex set $A \subset R^n$. For any x, $\gamma(x)$ equals half the squared distance from x to A; that is, $\gamma(x) = \frac{1}{2} \min_{y \in A} \|x - y\|^2$. This "distance" function is always C^1 and it has $x - \pi(x)$ as gradient vector at x.

> *F.3.3. A C^2 function $f: A \to R$ on the open, convex set A is concave if and only if $\partial^2 f(x)$ is negative semidefinite for all x. If $\partial^2 f(x)$ is negative definite for all x, then f is strictly concave.*

A function $g: A \to R^n$ is (negatively) *monotone* (resp. *strictly monotone*) if $[g(y) - g(x)] \cdot (y - x) \le 0$ (resp. < 0 if $y \ne x$) for all $x, y \in A$. The gradient map of a C^1, concave (resp. strictly concave) function is, therefore, monotone (resp. strictly monotone).

> *F.3.4. A C^1 function $g: A \to R^n$ on the open convex set $A \subset R^n$ is (negatively) monotone if and only if $v \cdot \partial g(x) v \le 0$ for all x and v. If the inequality is strict for all x and $v \ne 0$, then g is strictly monotone.*

F.4   *Reference notes*

With the exception of F.2.4, everything in this section is standard. See Rockafellar (1970), Valentine (1964), Eggleston (1958), or Fenchel (1953) for convexity and Ortega–Rheinboldt (1970) or Berger (1977) for monotone functions. Result F.2.4 is from Artzner and Neuefeind (1978, prop. 11, p. 146). The second part of F.1.2 can be proved from F.1.1.

A point of terminology: Strictly speaking, one should use the term *subgradient* for convex functions and *supergradient* for concave. But this is cumbersome. So we use *subgradient* in the sense of "something less than a gradient" and apply it to both kinds of functions.

G   Lipschitzian functions

G.1   *Definitions and basic properties*

A function $f: U \to R^m$, $U \subset R^n$, is *Lipschitzian,* or Lipschitz, *at* $x \in U$ if there is an $\epsilon > 0$ and a k such that $\|f(z) - f(y)\| \leq k\|z - y\|$ whenever $z, y \in B_\epsilon(x)$. The number k is called a *Lipschitz constant* at x. The function is *Lipschitzian* if it is so at every x. On a compact domain the Lipschitz constant can be taken independent of x. Examples are convex functions on open domains and arbitrary C^1 functions (just take $k = \|\partial f(x)\| + 1$ as constant at x). More generally, if $f_j: U \to R^m$, $U \subset R^n$, $j \in J$ is a finite collection of Lipschitzian functions with constants k_j and $f: U \to R^m$ is continuous and satisfies $f(x) \in \bigcup_{j \in J} \{f_j(x)\}$ for every $x \in U$, then f is also Lipschitzian with constant $k = \max_j k_j$. Sums, products, and compositions preserve the Lipschitzian character of the functions.

We have already given some results where Lipschitzian functions played a role (e.g., E.5.2). A fundamental property is:

> **G.1.1.** Let $f: U \to R^m$, $U \subset R^n$ open, be Lipschitzian. Then $\partial f(x)$ exists for a.e. $x \in U$ and, provided $n \leq m$, $f(A)$ is null whenever A is null. Moreover, the fundamental theorem of calculus (E.5.1) holds; that is, if $f: [0,1] \to R$ is Lipschitzian, then $f(x) - f(0) = \int_{[0,x]} \partial f(t) \, dt$.

G.2   *The generalized Jacobian*

Suppose that $f: U \to R^m$, $U \subset R^n$ open, is Lipschitzian and $\partial f(x)$ fails to exist on the set $C \subset U$. Because of G.1.1, C is nowhere dense and therefore, for every $x \in U$, the compact, convex set $\mathrm{co}\{\lim_n \partial f(x_n): x_n \to x, x_n \notin C\}$ is nonempty. This set is called the *generalized Jacobian* at x. In general, even if $\partial f(x)$ exists, the set may include linear functions other than $\partial f(x)$ but this does not happen in any of the few cases where we appeal to the generalized Jacobian concept. Hence, abusing notation somewhat, we denote the set by the same symbol $\partial f(x)$. We remark that the domain of the function must always be clearly specified. For example, if $f: R^2 \to R$, $f(\bar{x}, \bar{y}) = 0$ and $f_{\bar{x}}: R \to R$ is given by $f_{\bar{x}}(y) = f(\bar{x}, y)$, then

$\partial f_{\bar{x}}(\bar{y}) \subset \partial_y f(\bar{x}, \bar{y})$, but the inclusion may be strict. Here $\partial_x f(\bar{x}, \bar{y})$ denotes the projection of the set $\partial f(\bar{x}, \bar{y})$ on the x coordinates. As a correspondence the generalized Jacobian is automatically upper hemicontinuous on compact sets.

> **G.2.1. "Composite function theorem."** If $f: U \to R^n$, $U \subset R^m$, and $g: V \to R^s$, $f(U) \subset V \subset R^n$ are Lipschitzian at, respectively, x and $f(x)$, then $g \circ f: U \to R^s$ is Lipschitzian at x and $\partial(g \circ f)(x) \subset$ $\mathrm{co}\{\partial g(f(x)) \circ \partial f(x)\}$. Equality holds if g is C^1 at $f(x)$.

For our purposes the generalized Jacobian is interesting because it allows a useful generalization of the inverse and implicit function theorems. We say that $\partial f(x)$ is *nonsingular* if every member of $\partial f(x)$ is so. It should be emphasized that this is a very strong condition. While nonsingularity is "almost" necessary for the existence of a local inverse when $\partial f(x)$ is a singleton, this is far from the case when $\partial f(x)$ is a set. In our applications when nonsingularity is assumed at some x, the set $\partial f(x)$ always happens to be a singleton.

> **G.2.2. Inverse function theorem.** Let $U \subset R^n$ be open and $f: U \to R^n$ Lipschitzian. If $\partial f(x)$ is nonsingular, then f is a local homeomorphism at x having a Lipschitzian inverse.

> **G.2.3. Implicit function theorem.** Let $U \subset R^n$ be open, P a topological space, and $f: U \times P \to R^n$ a continuous function that is Lipschitzian in its first variable. Suppose that $\partial f_p(x)$ is an u.h.c. correspondence of p and x. If $f(\bar{x}, \bar{p}) = 0$ and $\partial f_{\bar{p}}(\bar{x})$ are nonsingular, then there are open sets $U' \subset U$, $P' \subset P$ and a continuous function $g: P' \to U'$ such that $g(\bar{p}) = \bar{x}$ and $f(x, p) = 0$ hold for $(x, p) \in U' \times P'$ if and only if $x = g(p)$. Moreover, g is Lipschitzian whenever $P \subset R^m$ and f is Lipschitzian.

G.3   Reference notes

The general properties of Lipschitz functions can be found in most analysis texts, for example, Dieudonné (1960), Lang (1969), Royden (1968), and Apostol (1957). The generalized Jacobian concept and its uses are less standard. See Clarke (1983, 2.6 and 7.1) for the basic concepts and proofs of the inverse function theorem G.2.2 and an implicit function theorem that is not, however, quite the same as G.2.3. Result G.2.3 can be established along the lines of the proof of C.3.3 in Schwartz (1967, 3.8, theorem 25).

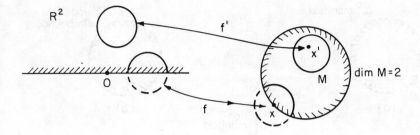

Figure H.1.1

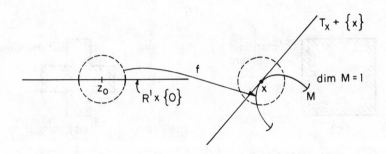

Figure H.1.2

H   Differentiable manifolds

H.1   *Definitions and examples*

To avoid technical complexity we view manifolds as imbedded in some R^s and take full advantage of the properties of the ambient space.

A C^r function $f: U \to R^s$, $U \subset R^s$ open, is a C^r *diffeomorphism*, $r \geq 0$, if it is a homeomorphism with a C^r inverse.

A set $M \subset R^s$ is a C^r n-(dimensional) *manifold* (resp. with *boundary*, resp. *with corners*) if for every $x \in M$ there is a C^r diffeomorphism $f: U \to R^s$, $U \subset R^s$ open, which carries the open set $U \cap (R^n \times \{0\}^{s-n})$ [resp. $U \cap (R^{n-1} \times R_+ \times \{0\}^{s-n})$, resp. $U \cap (R_+^n \times \{0\}^{s-n})$] onto a neighborhood of x on M. See Figure H.1.1. For $z = f^{-1}(x)$, and $r > 0$, the linear subspace $\partial f(z)(R^n \times \{0\}^{s-n})$, which is independent of the particular f, is called the tangent space to M at x and it is denoted $T_x M$. See Figure H.1.2.

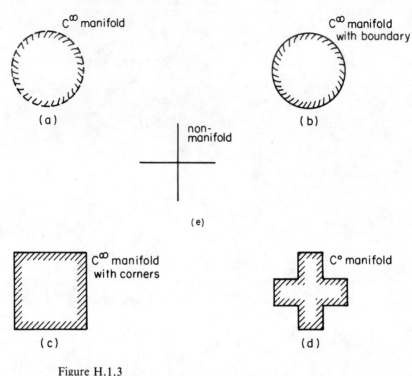

Figure H.1.3

Figures H.1.3a, b, c, d, e represent, respectively, a C^∞ manifold; a C^∞ manifold with boundary; a C^∞ manifold with corners; a set that is a C^0, but not a C^1, manifold with boundary; and a nonmanifold altogether. Beyond an occasional remark, we shall not, in this book, resort to manifolds with corners. So we shall not elaborate any more on them. Manifolds with boundary are, on the other hand, very important. The boundary, ∂M, of a C^r, n-dimensional manifold with boundary, M, is formed by the points $x \in M$ having no neighborhood in M homeomorphic to R^n. In the relative topology of M it coincides with the topological boundary. A fundamental fact is that ∂M is a C^r manifold without boundary of dimension $n-1$. Note that a manifold (which by definition has no boundary) is a particular case of manifold with boundary (because the definition allows the boundary to be empty). But not vice versa. Thus in principle one should be careful to refer to manifolds with boundaries if the latter are not excluded. This is, however, a cumbersome prescription and if no confusion is possible, we often use the term *manifold* in the generic, all-encompassing sense.

Examples of manifolds with (possibly empty) boundary are:

(i) Any affine subspace.

(ii) The unit ball $B^n = \{x \in R^n: \|x\| \leq 1\}$ is a C^∞ manifold with boundary $\partial B^n = S^{n-1} = \{x \in R^n: \|x\| = 1\}$, the $(n-1)$ unit circle. For $p \in S^{n-1}$, $T_p S^{n-1} = \{v \in R^n: p \cdot v = 0\}$. We denote this set simply by T_p.

(iii) To any C^r, $r > 0$, n-manifold $M \subset R^s$ we can associate $TM = \{(x, v) \in R^s \times R^s: v \in T_x M\}$ and $NM = \{(x, v) \in R^s \times R^s: v$ is perpendicular to $T_x M\}$. Those are C^{r-1} manifolds of dimension $2n$ and s, respectively, and are called, respectively, the *tangent bundle* and the *normal bundle* of M.

(iv) The C^∞ two-dimensional manifold $S^1 \times S^1$ is known as the *torus*. Geometrically, it looks like an inner tube.

(v) The graph of a C^r function $f: U \to R^m$, $U \subset R^n$ open, is a C^r n-manifold. As a partial converse we have that if the graph of f is a C^r manifold and f is Lipschitzian, then f is C^r.

(vi) Any compact one-dimensional manifold with boundary is equal, up to a diffeomorphism, to a finite union of circles (i.e., S^1) and closed segments (i.e., $[0, 1]$). Of course, the boundary is formed by the union of the endpoints of the segments and it is thus a finite set of even cardinality.

The ordered bases of a linear space fall into two equivalence classes by the criterion of making two bases equivalent if the sign of the determinant of the matrix that carries one base into the other in an order-preserving way is positive. An *orientation* of a C^r manifold M of dimension $n > 0$ is a consistent C^r assignment of a $+1$ or -1 sign to each of the two equivalence classes of bases on $T_x M$. By consistent, we mean that for every $x \in M$, there is a C^r diffeomorphism $f: U \to R^s$, $U \subset R^s$, mapping $R^n \times \{0\}^{s-n}$ onto a neighborhood of x on M in such a way that, for all $z \in U$, $\partial f(z)$ carries the standard base of R^n into a base of $T_{f(z)} M$ with positive orientation.

A manifold that can be given an orientation is called *orientable*. There are nonorientable manifolds, but they will not appear in this book. Note that every connected C^r manifold admits exactly two orientations. By convention, we agree that this is also the case for connected zero-dimensional manifolds (i.e., for points). A C^1 map $f: M \to N$ between oriented manifolds of the same dimension *preserves* (resp. *reverses*) *orientation* at x if $\partial f(x): T_x M \to T_{f(x)} N$ has a positive (resp. negative) determinant. In Figure H.1.4 the projection map from M to R is orientation-preserving (resp. reversing) at x (resp. x').

The boundary of an oriented C^r manifold with boundary can be given an orientation in a natural manner. For every $x \in \partial M$ let $y_x \in T_x M$ be perpendicular to $T_x \partial M$ and point outward, that is, away from M. See Figure

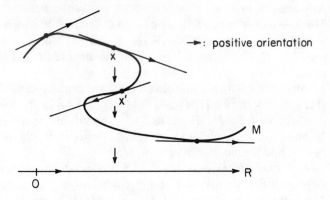

Figure H.1.4

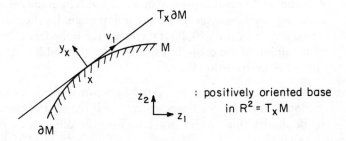

Figure H.1.5

H.1.5. Then we assign to any ordered basis $(v_1, \ldots, v_{n-1}) \in T_x \partial M$ the sign of $(y_x, v_1, \ldots, v_{n-1}) \in T_x M$. In Figure H.1.5, the base v_1 turns out to be negatively oriented.

Any two points x, y of a C^r arcwise connected manifold M can be joined by a C^r *path,* that is, a C^r function $f: [0, 1] \to M$ with $f(0) = x$, $f(1) = y$. Also, if we so wish, we can specify a priori the vector $\partial f(1) \in T_y M$. Alternatively, if x and y are sufficiently close, we can guarantee that, for all t, $\partial f(t)$ points in the direction $y - f(t)$; that is, $\partial f(t)$ is collinear to the projection of $y - f(t)$ on $T_{f(t)} M$.

H.2   *Functions on manifolds*

In this section two C^r, $r > 0$, manifolds with boundary $M, N \subset R^s$ remain fixed.

Let $f: M \to N$ be a C^r function. For any $x \in M$, $\partial f(x)$ takes $T_x M$ into $T_{f(x)} N$. From now on we view $T_x M$ as the domain of the linear function $\partial f(x)$. We say that f is a C^r *immersion* (resp. *submersion*) at x if rank $\partial f(x) = \dim M$ [resp. rank $\partial f(x) = \dim N$]. It is a *diffeomorphism at* x if, restricted to a neighborhood of x, it is a homeomorphism onto a neighborhood of $f(x)$ with a C^r inverse. It is a *diffeomorphism,* or *immersion,* or *submersion,* if it is so at every $x \in M$. It is an *embedding* if it is a one-to-one immersion and proper. Two manifolds are C^r *diffeomorphic* if there is a C^r diffeomorphism between them. From the point of view of differential topology, two diffeomorphic manifolds are indistinguishable.

The following list of results tells us that immersions lead naturally to smooth manifolds.

H.2.1. *For a C^r function $f : M \to N$ we have:*

(i) *(Inverse function theorem) If f is an immersion at $x \in M$ [i.e., rank $\partial f(x) = \dim M$], $x \notin \partial M$, and $\dim M = \dim N$, then f is a diffeomorphism at x.*

(ii) *If f is an immersion at $x \in M$ then there is an open neighborhood of x, $U \subset M$, such that $f(U) \subset N$ is a C^r manifold with boundary and f a diffeomorphism between U and $f(U)$. [This generalizes (i).]*

(iii) *If f is an embedding, then $f(M) \subset N$ is a C^r manifold with boundary and f a diffeomorphism between M and $f(M)$.*

(iv) *(Whitney embedding theorem) Let M be compact, $N = R^n$, and $n \geq 2 \dim M + 1$. Then for every $\epsilon > 0$ there is an embedding $f' : M \to N$ such that $\|f(x) - f'(x)\| < \epsilon$ for all x.*

When $\dim M \geq \dim N$, there cannot be strict immersions $f : M \to N$. It is then submersions that provide a rich source of manifolds. A point $x \in M$ is called a *regular* (resp. *critical* or *singular*) *point* of the C^1 function $f : M \to N$ if $\partial f(x)$ maps onto, that is, if rank $\partial f(x) = \dim N$ (resp. $< \dim N$). A value $y \in N$ is a *critical* (resp. *regular*) *value* if it is (resp. if it is not) the image of a critical point. For example, if $M = R^2$, $N = R$ and $f(x^1, x^2) = (x^1)^2 - (x^2)^2$, then the only critical point is the origin and all values are regular except $y = 0$. Figure H.2.1 represents $f^{-1}(y)$ for $y \in (-\epsilon, \epsilon)$. Note that, except at the critical value, $f^{-1}(y)$ is a one-dimensional manifold. In Figure H.2.2 we describe a map between two-dimensional manifolds. Again, if y is regular, $f^{-1}(y)$ is a manifold, this time of dimension zero. As the next result will show, this is quite general. Observe, parenthetically, that, still with reference to Figure H.2.2, the qualitative features of M near a singular point x depend on rank $\partial f(x)$. Thus, when rank $\partial f(x) = 1$, we get a *fold,* while rank $\partial f(x) = 0$ yields a *cusp.* Singularity theory will not be appealed to in this book, at least not explicitly. A function with no critical point is called *regular*.

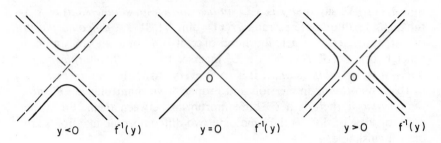

$$y < 0 \qquad f^{-1}(y) \qquad\qquad y = 0 \qquad f^{-1}(y) \qquad\qquad y > 0 \qquad f^{-1}(y)$$

Figure H.2.1

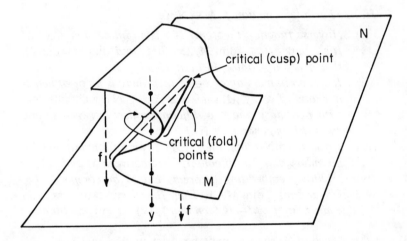

Figure H.2.2

H.2.2. Implicit function theorem. *Let $f: M \to N$ be a C^r function. If $y \in N$ is a regular value of both $f: M \to N$ and $f \mid \partial M: \partial M \to N$, then $f^{-1}(y)$ is a C^r manifold with boundary and $\dim f^{-1}(y) = \dim M - \dim N$; that is, $f^{-1}(y)$ and $\{y\}$ have the same codimension. Moreover, $\partial f^{-1}(y) = f^{-1}(y) \cap \partial M$.*

Informally, H.2.2 can be read as saying that every independent system of equations determines a locally parameterizable solution set with as many degrees of freedom as there as unknowns minus equations. Conversely, it is a trivial consequence of the definitions that if $M \subset N$, $\dim M = m$, $\dim N = n$, and $x \in M$, then there is an open set $x \in U \subset N$ and a C^r $f: U \to R^{n-m}$ such that 0 is a regular value and $f^{-1}(0) = U \cap M$; that is, locally every manifold is the solution set of an independent system of equations.

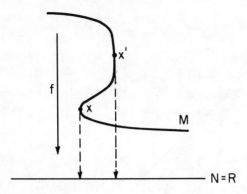

Figure H.2.3

Finally, consider the case where $N = R$. Let $r \geq 2$ and $x \in M$ be a critical point, that is, $\partial f(x) = 0$. As with functions from R^m to R, we call the critical point *nondegenerate* if $\partial^2(f \circ h)(0)$ is nonsingular for any $h: R^m \to M$, $h(0) = x$, which is a C^2 diffeomorphism at 0. If every critical point is nondegenerate, the function is a *Morse function*. In Figure H.2.3, x (resp. x') is a nondegenerate (resp. degenerate) critical point.

H.3   *Curvature*

Consider a closed C^2 n-dimensional manifold with boundary $M \subset R^n$. Then ∂M is a C^2 manifold of codimension 1 and we can define a C^1 function $g: \partial M \to S^{n-1}$, called the *Gauss map,* by associating to every $x \in \partial M$ the unit length vector perpendicular to $T_x \partial M$ and pointing away from M. See Figure H.3.1. Note that, at any $x \in M$, $T_x \partial M = T_{g(x)}$ and, therefore, the linear function $\partial g(x)$ maps $T_{g(x)}$ into itself. The determinant of this linear function, denoted $c_x(\partial M)$, is called the *Gaussian curvature of ∂M at x.* It constitutes a (rough) measure of how flat the manifold is at x. It is usually an easy matter to check if $c_x(\partial M) \neq 0$. For example, if ∂M is parameterized locally in the form $(x^1, \ldots, x^{n-1}, \xi(x^1, \ldots, x^{n-1}))$ then $c_{\bar{x}}(\partial M) = 0$ if and only if $\partial^2 \xi(\bar{x}^1, \ldots, \bar{x}^{n-1})$ is singular.

In Figure H.3.2.a and b, the Gaussian curvature at x is positive whereas in H.3.2.c it is negative. The boundary of a C^2 convex n-manifold with boundary has everywhere nonnegative curvature. A partial converse is: A compact, C^2 n-manifold with everywhere nonnegative (resp. positive) Gaussian curvature is convex (resp. strictly convex).

Given $x \in \partial M$ there is always a sufficiently small $\alpha > 0$ such that the ball of radius α and center $x - \alpha g(x)$ is contained in M. For convex manifolds there is a complement to this: If M is convex and bounded and

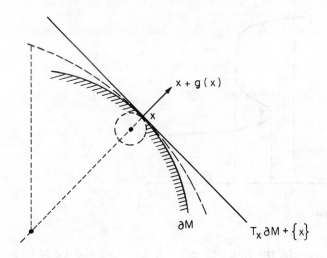

Figure H.3.1

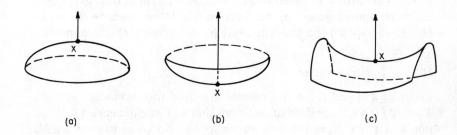

(a)   (b)   (c)

Figure H.3.2

$c_x(\partial M) \neq 0$, then for sufficiently large α the ball of radius α and center $x - \alpha g(x)$ contains M. See Figure H.3.1.

The Gaussian curvature is not invariant to diffeomorphisms. Thus, this is a concept that belongs to differential geometry rather than differential topology.

H.4   *Technical miscellanea*

In this section we put on record the availability of a number of technically useful constructions.

H.4.1. *There is a C^∞ nondecreasing function $f: R \to [0, 1]$ such that $f(x) = 0$ for $x \leq 0$ and $f(x) = 1$ for $x \geq 1$.*

H.4.2. *Let $A \subset R^s$ be a closed set and U an open neighborhood of A. Then there is a C^∞ function $f: R^s \to [0,1]$ such that $f(x) = 0$ for $x \in A$ and $f(x) = 1$ for $x \notin U$.*

An immediate consequence of H.4.2 is:

H.4.3. *For every $\epsilon > 0$ there is a C^∞ function $h_\epsilon: R^n \to R_+$ such that $h(x) = 0$ for $\|x\| \geq \epsilon$ and $\int h_\epsilon(x) \, d\lambda(x) = 1$.*

The next three results provide convenient smoothing techniques. Let $f: U \to R$, $U \subset R^n$, be continuous and $J \subset U$ a domain with $B_\epsilon(J) \subset U$ for some $\epsilon > 0$. With h_ϵ as in H.4.3, we can define $f^*: J \to R$ by $f^*(x) = \int f(z) h_\epsilon(z - x) \, d\lambda(z)$. This f^* is called the *convolution* of f and h_ϵ.

H.4.4. *The convolution function f^* of f and h_ϵ is C^∞. If f is C^1 (and J open), then $\partial f^*(x) = \int \partial f(z) h_\epsilon(z - x) \, d\lambda(z)$, that is, $\partial f^* = (\partial f)^*$. If f is increasing [i.e., $x > y$ implies $f(x) > f(y)$] or concave, then so is f^*.*

H.4.5. *Let $f: U \to R$, $U \subset R^n$ open, be a concave function. Form the set $A = \{(x, f(x), q) \in R^{2n+1}: q$ is a subgradient of f at $x\}$. Then for any open set $V \subset R^{2n+1}$ with $A \subset V$ there is a C^∞ concave function $f': U \to R$ such that $(x, f'(x), \partial f'(x)) \in V$ for all $x \in U$.*

H.4.6. *Let $f: U \to J$ be an u.h.c. convex-valued correspondence. Suppose that J is a convex set and U either a convex set or a C^1 manifold with boundary. Then for any open set $V \subset U \times J$ with $\text{Graph } f \subset V$ there is a C^∞ function $f': U \to J$ such that $\text{Graph } f' \subset V$.*

The last result is on parameterized diffeomorphisms.

H.4.7. *Let $A \subset R^s \times R^n$ be an open set such that, for every $y \in R^n$, $A_y = \{x \in R^s: (x, y) \in A\}$ is convex. Put $V = \{y \in R^n: A_y \neq \varnothing\}$. Then there is a C^∞ diffeomorphism $f: A \to R^s \times V$ such that, for every $y \in V$, f maps A_y onto $R^s \times \{y\}$.*

H.5   Reference notes

Two excellent introductions to differential topology are Hirsch (1976) and Guillemin–Pollack (1974). The short book by Milnor (1965) is strongly recommended. Most of the material in Sections H.1, H.2, and H.4 can be found in chapter 1 of Hirsch (1976) or in chapters 1 and 3 of Guillemin-Pollack (1974). For manifolds with corners, see Nielsen (1981). A topic we have avoided, at some cost, is the theory of singularity of maps, that is, the study of the behavior of functions at or near singular points; see Golubitsky-Guillemin (1973). For Section H.3 (Curvature), see Hicks (1971). For results similar to H.4.6 and H.4.7 see, respectively, Hildenbrand-Kirman (1976) and Schecter (1979). Result H.4.5 follows from H.4.4.

I   Transversality theory

I.1   *The measure of the set of critical values*

In this subsection M, N are C^r, $r > 0$, *manifolds with boundary (of dimension m and n, respectively), and* $f: M \to N$ *is a given* C^r *function.*

The concept of a null or measure zero subset is well defined on a manifold. Indeed, one says that $A \subset N$ is *null* if for any $y \in A$ there is an open neighborhood $y \in U \subset N$ and a C^1 diffeomorphism $h: U \to R^n$ such that $h(U \cap A)$ has Lebesgue measure zero in R^n. This definition is independent of the particular h used. *Note:* The concept of null set applies also to C^0 manifolds. In this case, h is required to be a homeomorphism with a Lipschitzian inverse.

Remember that $y \in N$ is a *regular value* of f if $\partial f(x)$ maps $T_x M$ onto $T_{f(x)} N$ whenever $f(x) = y$. In particular, any $y \notin f(M)$ is regular. A value that is not regular is called *critical*. Regular values are very useful (e.g., H.2.2), but up to now we do not know whether every function has some. The following striking theorem, which is fundamental to the theory of this book, says that regular values abound.

> **I.1.1. Sard's theorem.** *Let* $r > \max\{0, m - n\}$. *Then the set of critical values of the* C^r *function* $f: M \to N$ *has measure zero in* N.

Of course, I.1.1 implies that the set of regular values is dense in N. This set is also easily seen to be a countable intersection of open sets; hence it is a residual set. If f is proper, then the set is in fact open.

We illustrate the power of Sard's theorem by two applications.

The first consists in showing that any C^2 function $f: B^n \to R^n$ that is the identity at $\partial B^n = S^{n-1}$, must have a zero, that is, $f(x) = 0$ for some x. By means of approximation techniques, the result can then be extended to C^0 functions. Suppose, a contrario, that there is no zero. Then we can define a C^2 function $\hat{f}: B^n \to S^{n-1}$ by $\hat{f}(x) = (1/\|f(x)\|)f(x)$. By Sard's theorem there is some $y \in S^{n-1}$ that is a regular value of $\hat{f}: B^n \to S^{n-1}$.

By the implicit function theorem H.2.2, $\hat{f}^{-1}(y)$ is a C^2 one-dimensional manifold with boundary which has $\partial \hat{f}^{-1}(y) = \hat{f}^{-1}(y) \cap S^{n-1}$. We know [Example (vi) in H.1] that $\hat{f}^{-1}(y)$ is then a finite union of segments and circles. Because $\hat{f}$ is the identity on S^{n-1}, we have $y \in \hat{f}^{-1}(y) \cap S^{n-1} \subset \partial \hat{f}^{-1}(y)$ and, therefore, there must be a segment having y as endpoint. Let $z \in \hat{f}^{-1}(y)$ be the other endpoint. Then $z \in \partial \hat{f}^{-1}(y) \subset S^{n-1}$, which constitutes a contradiction because $z \neq y$ but $\hat{f}$ is the identity on S^{n-1}. Note that Sard's theorem has been used just to show that there is some regular value. This is typical.

As the second application we show that any C^2 function $f: R^n \to R$ can be slightly perturbed to a Morse function. More precisely, we prove that $f(x) - q \cdot x$ defines a Morse function for a.e. $q \in R^n$. To this effect, look at $\partial f(x)$ as a C^1 function from R^n to R^n. Then, by Sard's theorem, a.e. $q \in R^n$ is a regular value of this function; that is, if $\partial f(x) = q$, then rank $\partial^2 f(x) = n$. But this is precisely what we wanted.

I.2   Transversality

In this subsection, M, N *are fixed* C^r, $r > 0$, *manifolds with boundary of respective dimensions m and n. Moreover, $\partial N = \varnothing$.*

Let $Z \subset N$ be a C^r manifold of dimension s. We say that a C^r *function* $f: M \to N$ *is transversal to Z on N*, written $f \pitchfork_N Z$, if

$$\partial f(x)(T_x M) + T_{f(x)} Z = T_{f(x)} N.$$

We say that a C^r *manifold with boundary $Y \subset N$ is transversal to Z on N,* written $Y \pitchfork_N Z$ if this is true of the inclusion map or, more symmetrically, if $T_x Y + T_x Z = T_x N$ for all $x \in Y \cap Z$. See Figure I.2.1. If the ambient manifold is clear, we write $\pitchfork$ instead of $\pitchfork_N$.

Note that when $Z = \{z\}$, $f \pitchfork Z$ simply means that z is a regular value. It should therefore come as no surprise that the implicit function theorem can also be formulated in the language of transversality.

> *I.2.1. Implicit function theorem. Let $f: M \to N$ be a C^r function and $Z \subset N$ a boundaryless manifold. If $f \pitchfork_N Z$ and $(f \mid \partial M) \pitchfork_N Z$, that is, both f and $f \mid \partial M$ are transversal to Z, then $f^{-1}(Z)$ is a C^r manifold, $\partial f^{-1}(Z) = f^{-1}(Z) \cap \partial M$ and $\dim f^{-1}(Z) = \dim M - (\dim N - \dim Z)$; that is, $f^{-1}(Z)$ has the same codimension in M as Z in N.*

If M is compact, then $f \pitchfork Z$ is an "open" property in the sense that any perturbation of f that alters only slightly the value and the derivative of the function at any point remains transversal to Z. The next result, the transversality theorem, implies that it is also a "dense" property; that is,

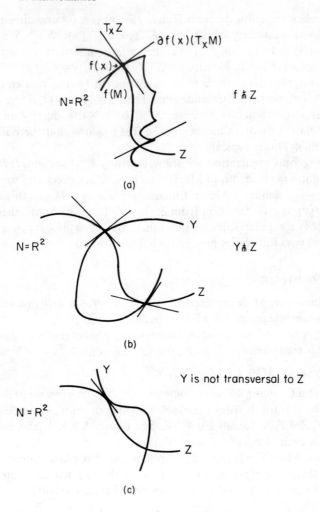

Figure I.2.1

any function can be perturbed slightly to one that is transversal to **Z**. In short, the property, being open and dense, is typical, or *generic*. Genericity theory will be motivated and discussed in more detail in Chapter 8. The transversality theorem is proved by means of Sard's theorem, and it amounts to a different presentation of the latter. In order to get a regular configuration from a given function and value, Sard's theorem perturbs the value, whereas the transversality theorem perturbs the function.

I.2.2. Transversality theorem. Let M, P, N and $Z \subset N$ be C^r manifolds. *(Only M is allowed to have a boundary.)* Suppose that $F: M \times P \to N$ is a C^r function and $r > \max\{0, \dim M + \dim Z - \dim N\}$. Any $p \in P$ induces a F_p: $M \to N$ by $F_p(x) = F(p, x)$. Then $F \pitchfork_N Z$ implies $F_p \pitchfork_N Z$ for a.e. $p \in P$.

I.3   Miscellanea

I.3.1. For X a separable metric space and $Q \subset R^n$ an open set, suppose that $F: X \times Q \to R$ is a continuous function such that $\partial_q F(x, q)$ exists and is continuous for all $x, q \in X \times Q$. If whenever $x \neq x'$ and $F(x, q) = F(x', q)$ we have $\partial_q[F(x, q) - F(x', q)] \neq 0$ then, for a.e. $\bar{q} \in Q$, $F(x, \bar{q})$ has at most one maximizer on X.

I.4   Reference notes

For Sard's theorem and transversality theory, see Guillemin–Pollack (1974, chap. 2), Hirsch (1976, chap. 3), or Milnor (1965). Spivak (1965) has a concise presentation of Sard's theorem. For a very thorough and general discussion of the transversality theorem and its applications to dynamical systems, see Abraham–Robbin (1967). For the philosophy of transversality (on which we shall elaborate a bit in Chapter 8), see Abraham–Marsden (1978), Arnold (1983), or Hirsch (1984). The miscellaneous result I.3.1 is taken from Araujo–Mas-Colell (1978); see also Sondermann (1975).

J   Degrees, indices, and fixed points

J.1   Preliminaries

Let X, Y be arbitrary topological spaces. Two functions $f, f': X \to Y$ are *homotopic* if there is a continuous function $F: X \times [0, 1] \to Y$, called a *homotopy,* such that $F(x, 0) = f(x)$ and $F(x, 1) = f'(x)$ for all $x \in X$, that is to say, if f can be deformed continuously into f'. Many properties of interest turn out to be invariant under homotopy. The case $Y = S^n$ is especially important. Note that any two functions $f, f': X \to S^n$ that are uniformly close to each other are homotopic.

With every compact, nonempty set X there is associated a certain integer $\chi(X)$ called the *Euler characteristic.* It is an extremely useful topological invariant (i.e., a space and its homeomorphic image have the same Euler characteristic). For the moment, it shall suffice to know that

(i) $\chi(B^n) = 1$ for any n, where $B^n = \{x \in R^n : \|x\| \leq 1\}$.

(ii) If X is a compact, boundaryless, oriented manifold of odd dimension, then $\chi(X) = 0$.

(iii) For $n - 1$ even, $\chi(S^{n-1}) = 2$.

J.2   *The degree of a function*

In this section *M, N are two fixed nonempty, oriented, C^1 manifolds of the same dimension n and without boundary. Moreover, M is compact and N connected.*

The *degree of a C^1 function* $f : M \to N$, denoted deg f or degree f, is an integer that, when f is C^2, can be computed as follows. Let $y \in N$ be an arbitrary regular value of f. Because of Sard's theorem (I.1.1), regular values always exist. For any $x \in f^{-1}(y)$, $\partial f(x)$ maps $T_x M$ onto $T_{f(x)} N$, two linear spaces of the same dimension and with prescribed orientations. Therefore, $|\partial f(x)|$ is well defined, and sign$|\partial f(x)| = +1$ or -1 according to whether $\partial f(x)$ preserves or reverses orientation. Because M is compact, $f^{-1}(y)$ is a finite set. Hence deg$(f, y) = \sum_{x \in f^{-1}(y)}$ sign$|\partial f(x)|$ is a well-defined number. Of course, if $f^{-1}(y) = \varnothing$ then deg$(f, y) = 0$. It is a fundamental fact that deg(f, y) is independent of the particular value y. Therefore, a number deg f is unambiguously defined. Sometimes we write deg f for a function $f : M \to R^{n+1}$ such that $0 \notin f(M)$. In this case, what is meant is deg $f = $ deg $\hat{f}$ where $\hat{f} : M \to S^n$ is defined by $\hat{f}(x) = [1/\|f(x)\|]f(x)$ and S^n is oriented as the boundary of B^{n+1}.

What is the degree meant to capture? Roughly speaking, the degree measures how many net times the map f "piles up" M over N. Thus, if $N = S^1$, then deg f indicates how many times M wraps around S^1 in an essential way, that is, cancelling out reversals in the direction of movement. For $N = R^n$ we have deg $f = 0$ [take $y \notin f(X)$], which reflects the fact that the compact set $f(M)$ cannot cover N even once.

J.2.1. *The degree of a function is a homotopy invariant; that is, if f and f' are homotopic, then* deg $f = $ deg f'.

Suppose that $M = N = S^n$ and that S^n is oriented as the boundary of B^{n+1}. Any continuous $f : S^n \to S^n$ is homotopic to some smooth function and so J.2.1 can be used to extend the definition of degree to C^0 functions $f : S^n \to S^n$. It is fairly clear that any outward-pointing function $f : S^n \to S^n$ is homotopic to the identity. Therefore, J.2.1 implies deg $f = +1$ for any such function.

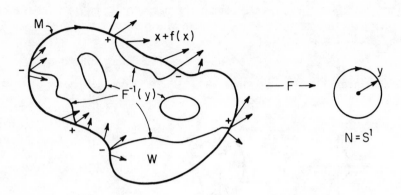

Figure J.2.1

From now on we assume that *M is the boundary of a compact oriented manifold with boundary W and that it has the orientation induced from W.*

> ***J.2.2.*** *Suppose that* $f: M \to N$ *can be extended to a* C^1 *function* $F: W \to N$. *Let* $y \in N$ *be a regular value for* f *and* F *and suppose that* $x, x' \in f^{-1}(y)$ *are endpoints of a segment contained in* $F^{-1}(y)$. *Then* $\text{sign}|\partial f(x)| + \text{sign}|\partial f(x')| = 0$.

Because, for y regular, $F^{-1}(y)$ is a compact one-dimensional manifold (hence, a finite union of circles and segments – H.1.vi), result J.2.2 easily yields:

> ***J.2.3.*** *Suppose that* $f: M \to N$ *can be extended to a* C^1 *function* $F: W \to N$. *Then* $\deg f = 0$. See Figure J.2.1.

For $N = S^n$ and W connected, there is a converse:

> ***J.2.4. Hopf's theorem.*** *If* W *is connected and* $N = S^n$, *then* $f: \partial W \to S^n$ *extends to a function* $F: W \to S^n$ *if and only if* $\deg f = 0$.

J.3   Vector fields and fixed points

Let $N \subset R^s$ be an n-dimensional, C^1 manifold with boundary. A C^r tangent vector field on N is a C^r function $f: N \to R^s$ such that $f(x) \in T_x N$ for

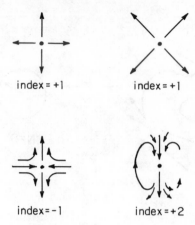

index = +1   index = +1

index = -1   index = +2

Figure J.2.2

every $x \in N$. Whenever $f(x) = 0$ we say that *x is a zero of the vector field*. Note that if $f(x) \neq 0$, then the vector field points in a similar direction for all x' in a neighborhood of x. This is far from the case if x is a zero. It is a remarkable fact that, as we shall see, the topology of N imposes strong global restrictions on the behavior of the vector field near its set of zeros.

Suppose that x is an isolated zero of a vector field $f: N \rightarrow R^s$. Imbedding a neighboorood of x in R^n, we can define, for $\epsilon > 0$ small, a function $h: S^{n-1} \rightarrow S^{n-1}$ by $h(v) = (1/\|f(x + \epsilon v)\|)f(x + \epsilon v)$. The degree of this function is called the index of f at x (S^{n-1} is oriented as the boundary of B^n). Informally, the index measures the number of times that, in an essential way, the vector field points in any particular direction near x. Thus, the larger the index (in absolute value), the more does the vector field "turn around" near x. See Figure J.2.2.

In many cases of practical interest, the index can be easily computed:

J.3.1. If x is a zero of the C^1 vector field f on N, then $\partial f(x)$ maps $T_x N$ into $T_x N$, and if $\partial f(x)$ is nonsingular, the index of f at x equals the sign of the determinant of $\partial f(x): T_x N \rightarrow T_x N$.

The central result is:

***J.3.2. Poincaré–Hopf theorem.** Let N be a compact n-dimensional C^1 manifold with boundary and f a continuous vector field on N. Suppose that:*

(i) *f points outward at ∂N* [when $N \subset R^n$ this means that $f(x) \cdot g(x) > 0$ for all $x \in \partial N$, where g is the Gauss map]; *and*
(ii) *f has a finite number of zeros.*

Then the sum of the indices of f at the different zeros equals the Euler characteristic of N.

Some of the drastic implications of the Poincaré–Hopf theorem are worth explicit mention. For example, if $N = B^n$, then $\chi(B^n) = +1$, and so every vector field $f: B^n \to R^n$ that has 0 as a regular value and points outward at ∂B^n must have an odd (hence nonzero) number of equilibria. For another case, take $N = S^{n-1}$, $n-1$ even. Then $\chi(S^{n-1}) = 2$, and so the vector field must have at least two zeros. The following implicit correspondence theorem is also an easy consequence of J.3.2 (or, even more directly, of J.2.4).

J.3.3. Implicit correspondence theorem. *Let $X \subset R^n$ be an open set, P a topological space of parameters, and $f: X \times P \to R^n$ a continuous function. Suppose that $f(\bar{x}, \bar{p}) = 0$ and for $\bar{p}$ fixed, $\bar{x}$ viewed as a zero of the vector field $f(\cdot, \bar{p})$ is isolated and has a nonzero index (e.g., $f(x, \bar{p})$ is C^1 and $|\partial_x f(\bar{x}, \bar{p})| \neq 0$). Then there is an open set $\bar{p} \in V \subset P$ and an upper hemicontinuous correspondence $h: V \to X$ such that $h(\bar{p}) = \{\bar{x}\}$ and $f(h(p), p) = \{0\}$ for all $p \in V$.*

A *fixed point* of a function or correspondence $f: X \to X$ is a vector x satisfying $x = f(x)$ [or $x \in f(x)$ if f is a correspondence]. Hence the vector $\bar{x}$ is a fixed point of $f: X \to R^n$, $X \subset R^n$, if and only if it is a zero of the vector field, or system of equations, $x - f(x)$. Therefore, given the Poincaré–Hopf theorem, the following familiar fixed point theorems should come as no surprise.

J.3.4. Brouwer fixed-point theorem. *Any continuous function $f: B^n \to B^n$ has a fixed point.*

J.3.5. Kakutani fixed-point theorem. *Any upper hemicontinuous convex-valued correspondence $f: B^n \to B^n$ has a fixed point. More generally, this remains true for any u.h.c. convex-valued correspondence $f: B^n \to R^n$ that points outward at ∂B^n.*

Finally, we remark that J.3.2 and J.3.5 remain valid if $f | \partial B^n$ is, simply, homotopic to an outward-pointing map.

J.4   *Reference notes*

See chapters 4, 5, and 6 of Milnor (1965), chapter 3 of Guillemin–Pollack (1974), or chapter 5 of Hirsch (1976). On the Euler characteristic see, for example, Singer–Thorpe (1967). Result J.3.3 is an easy exercise. Kakutani's fixed-point theorem can be proved by combining Brouwer's theorem with the selection argument H.4.6.

K   **Function spaces**

K.1   *Definitions and basic properties*

We discuss now the properties of some spaces of functions defined on a set $X \subset R^m$. For specificity we consider the case where X is contained in the closure of its interior. With the obvious adaptations everything applies to the case where $X \subset R^m$ is an arbitrary smooth manifold with boundary.

For every $0 \le r \le \infty$, denote by $C^r(X)$ the set of functions $f: X \to R^n$ having, for every $0 \le s < r+1$, an sth derivative that is continuous on X.

Suppose, first, that X is compact. The set $C^r(X)$, $0 \le r < \infty$, is given the topology of *the C^r uniform convergence* by letting $f_n \underset{r}{\to} f$ if and only if every derivative of $f_n - f$, up to the rth order, converges uniformly to zero. Uniform means that for any $\epsilon > 0$ there is an N such that if $n > N$, then every derivative of $f_n - f$ of order r or smaller evaluated at any $x \in X$ is, in norm, smaller than ϵ. Finally, $C^\infty(X)$ is topologized by letting f_n converge to f if and only if it converges in $C^r(X)$ for every $r \ge 0$.

> ***K.1.1.** We have:*
>
> (i) *Every $C^r(X)$, $0 \le r \le \infty$, is metrizable, separable, and complete.*
>
> (ii) *In the following sequence the topologies are increasingly finer and every space is dense in the preceding one:*
> $$C^0(X) \supset \cdots \supset C^r(X) \supset \cdots \supset C^\infty(X).$$

If X is not compact, we give to $C^r(X)$ the topology of the C^r *uniform convergence on compacta* (or compact-open topology). That is to say, $f_n \underset{r}{\to} f$ if for every compact $X' \subset X$, $(f_n \mid X') \underset{r}{\to} (f \mid X')$ in the previously defined sense.

> ***K.1.2.** With the uniform convergence on compacta, K.1.1 holds for noncompact X. Moreover, the evaluation map from $C^0(X) \times X$ to R^n defined by associating $f(x)$ to (f, x) is continuous.*

For noncompact X, the above topology on $C^r(X)$ is sometimes called the weak topology as opposed to the strong, or Whitney, topology. In the latter, for f_n to converge to f we must, in addition, be able to find a compact $K \subset X$ and N such that $f_n(x) = f(x)$ for $n > N$ and $x \notin K$. In this book we shall have no need to use the Whitney topology.

K.2   Compact sets and measures on function spaces

In Chapters 5 and 7 of this book we shall model an economy as a measure with compact support defined on a metric space of functions. It is thus important to know that compact sets abound and to have criteria to recognize them.

A set $\mathfrak{F}$ of functions $f: X \to R^n$, $X \subset R^m$ is *equicontinuous* if for every $\epsilon > 0$ there is a $\delta > 0$ such that $\|x - x'\| < \delta$ and $f \in \mathfrak{F}$ implies $\|f(x) - f(x')\| < \epsilon$.

> **K.2.1.** *Let X be compact and $0 \leq r < \infty$. A set of functions $\mathfrak{F} \subset C^r(X)$ that is closed and bounded (uniformly in x and for every derivative) is compact if and only if the set of rth derivatives is equicontinuous. For arbitrary X, $\mathfrak{F}$ is compact if $\{f \mid X': X' \subset X\}$ is compact for every compact $X' \subset X$. A set is C^∞-compact if it is C^r-compact for every $r < \infty$.*

In particular, the most useful compactness criterion is:

> **K.2.2.** *For every $0 \leq r < \infty$ and $k > 0$ denote by $C_{l,k}^r(X)$ the set of C^r functions such that:*
>
> (i)   *every derivative evaluated at any $x \in X$ is bounded in norm by k, and*
>
> (ii) *the rth derivative is a Lipschitzian function for the uniform Lipschitz constant k.*
>
> *Then $C_{l,k}^r(X)$ is compact.*

As in E.3, we shall want to consider the space $\mathfrak{M}(Y)$ of measures with compact support in the metric space $Y \subset C^r(X)$, $0 \leq r \leq \infty$, topologized by the weak convergence plus the Hausdorff convergence of the supports. Because of E.3.2 we know that if Y is compact, then $\mathfrak{M}(Y)$ is complete. However, if Y is a large subset, for example, open, then $\mathfrak{M}(Y)$ may fail to be complete [the space $C^r(X)$ is locally compact only in the trivial situation where X is finite]. Our interest in completeness derives from the Baire property (A.4). For the purposes of this book, it is interesting to know that $\mathfrak{M}(C^r(X))$ satisfies a somewhat weaker version of the Baire property. The same conclusion obtains, but the hypothesis is slightly stronger.

> **K.2.3.** Let X be compact, $r < \infty$ and $Y \subset C^r(X)$ an open set. Then any countable intersection of subsets of $\mathfrak{M}(Y)$ that are open and dense in $\mathfrak{M}(Y)$ (with Y having the C^r topology) and in $\mathfrak{M}(Y \cap C^{r+1}(X))$ [with $Y \cap C^{r+1}(X)$ having the C^{r+1} topology] is dense in $\mathfrak{M}(Y)$.

K.3   Reference notes

Except for K.2.3, all the material on function spaces is standard. See Dieudonné (1960), Royden (1968), and Hirsch (1976, chap. 2). Function spaces on manifolds are presented in, for example, Abraham–Robbin (1967). Result K.2.3 can be proved from E.3.2 and K.2.2.

L   Averages of sets

This section gathers a miscellaneous collection of results bearing on the theme that the average of several sets tends to be more convex than the sets themselves.

L.1   Sums of sets

> **L.1.1.** (Shapley-Folkman). Given a finite collection of sets $X_j \subset R^m$, $j \in J$, if $x \in \mathrm{co}\, \sum_{j \in J} X_j$, then there are $x_j \in \mathrm{co}\, X_j$, $j \in J$, such that $x = \sum_{j \in J} x_j$ and $\#\{j : x_j \notin X_j\} \le m$.

Given two bounded, closed, nonempty sets $A, E \subset R^n$, denote

$$\rho(A, E) = \inf\{\epsilon : A \subset B_\epsilon(E),\ E \subset B_\epsilon(A)\}.$$

Of course, $\rho(A, E)$ is simply the Euclidean Hausdorff distance between A and E. Suppose now that the finite collection of nonempty sets $X_j \subset R^n$, $j \in J$, is bounded; that is, $\|y\| < c$ for some c and all $y \in X_j$, $j \in J$. Then L.1.1 yields $\rho(\sum_{j \in J} X_j, \mathrm{co}\, \sum_{j \in J} X_j) \le mc$. Note that the bound mc is independent of $\#J$ and, therefore, the distance between the average set and its convex hull is small if $\#J$ is large relative to mc. Interestingly, if the sets being added are smooth, compact, n-dimensional manifolds, then the distance between the sum, not just the average, of the sets and its convex hull may itself be small.

L.1.2. (Howe). *Given $c > 0$ there is a $k > 0$ such that if $X_j \subset R^m$, $j \in J$, is a finite collection of nonempty C^2 compact n-dimensional manifolds with boundary having the properties:*

(i) $\|y\| < c$ *for all $y \in X_j$ and $j \in J$, and*

(ii) *the Gaussian curvature of any ∂X_j at any $y \in \partial X_j$ is less than c in absolute value,*

then for any $x \in$ co $\sum_{j \in J} X_j$ there is $y \in \sum_{j \in J} X_j$ such that $\|x - y\| \le k/\#J$; that is,

$$\rho\left(\sum_{j \in J} X_j, \text{ co} \sum_{j \in J} X_j \right) \le \frac{k}{\#J}.$$

As should be expected, the above results have an exact limit version where the finite average is replaced by the integral sign.

L.1.3. (Lyapunov-Richter). *Let $f : X \to R^m$ be a correspondence from the measure space $(X, \mathfrak{X}, \nu)$. If ν is atomless, that is, $\nu(A) > 0$ implies $0 < \nu(A') < \nu(A)$ for some $A' \subset A$, then $\int f \, d\nu$ is a convex set.*

L.2   Partial sums

Given a finite collection of vectors $x_j \in R^m$, $j \in J$, a *partial sum* is a vector of the form $\sum_{j \in I} x_j$ for some nonempty $I \subset J$. The study of partial sums is logically connected to the topic of the previous section. Indeed, defining $X_j = \{x_j, 0\}$, we have

$$\sum_{j \in J} X_j = \left\{ \sum_{j \in I} x_j : I \subset J, \, I \neq \varnothing \right\} \cup \{0\}.$$

L.2.1. (Steinitz). *If $x_j \in R^m$, $j \in J$, is a finite collection of vectors with $\|x_j\| < c$ for every $j \in J$ and $\sum_{j \in J} x_j = 0$ then, letting $n = \#J$, the vectors can be listed $(x_1, \ldots, x_n)$ in such a way that $\|\sum_{i=1}^{s} x_i\| \le mc$ for every $1 \le s \le n$.*

Under its hypotheses, an implication of L.2.1 is that for every $s \le \#J$ there exists at least one $I \subset J$ with $\#I = s$ and $\|\sum_{i \in I} x_i\| \le mc$. Note that the bound mc is independent of n. If this is weakened, many more $I \subset J$ qualify:

L.2.2. (Chebycheff). *Given c and $\epsilon > 0$ there is a $k > 0$ such that if $x_j \in R^m$, $j \in J$, is a finite collection of vectors with $\|x_j\| < c$ for* every $j \in J$ and $\sum_{j \in J} x_j = 0$, then for every integer $s \leq \#J$ we have:

$$\# \left\{ I \subset J : \#I = s, \left\| \sum_{i \in I} x_i \right\| \leq k\sqrt{s} \right\} \geq (1-\epsilon) \#\{I \subset J : \#I = s\}.$$

The next result obtains a partial sum satisfying an arbitrarily small bound.

L.2.3. *For every $c > 0$ and $\epsilon > 0$ there is an integer N for which the following property holds:*
   Suppose that $x_j \in R^m$, $j \in J$ is a finite collection of vectors with $\|x_j\| < c$ for every $j \in J$ and $\|\sum_{j \in J} x_j\| < c$. Let $C \subset J$, $\#C > N$. Then there is $I \subset J$ such that $\|\sum_{j \in I} x_j\| < \epsilon$ and $I \cap C \neq \varnothing$.

Let $x_j \in R^m$, $j \in J$, be a finite collection of vectors. Denote by Z (resp. Z_+) the set of integers (resp. nonnegative integers). It is logical, after the study of partial sums, to go one step further and allow repetitions, that is, to focus attention on the set

$$G = \left\{ \sum_{j \in J} \alpha_j x_j : \alpha_j \in Z_+ \text{ for all } j \text{ and } \alpha_j > 0 \text{ for some } j \right\}.$$

Although we shall not make this explicit, we point out that the formulation of a limit theory of partial sums leads naturally to the consideration of repetitions. Observe that G is closed under addition; that is, $G + G \subset G$. Our first remark is that there are always points of G arbitrarily close to Z^m.

L.2.4. *Let $x \in R^m$ and $\epsilon > 0$. Then there is an integer $n > 0$ and a vector $y \in Z^m$ such that $\|nx - y\| < \epsilon$.*

Suppose that we also have $\sum_{j \in J} x_j = 0$. Then $-y \in G$ whenever $y \in G$, or $-G \subset G$. This and $G + G \subset G$ are the defining properties of a *subgroup* of R^m. The set G need not be topologically closed, but its closure is again a subgroup; that is, $-\text{cl } G \subset \text{cl } G$ and $\text{cl } G + \text{cl } G \subset \text{cl } G$. It turns out that closed subgroups of R^m have a remarkably simple form. Up to a change of coordinates, they equal $Z^n \times R^{s-n}$ for some $0 \leq n \leq s \leq m$. See the illustration of Figure L.2.1, where it is assumed that $\|x_1\| = \|x_2\|$ and $\|x_3\| / \|x_4\|$ is an irrational number.

L.2.5. *Every closed subgroup $G \subset R^m$ can be expressed as follows: There are $s \leq m$ linearly independent vectors $y_1, \ldots, y_s \in R^m$*

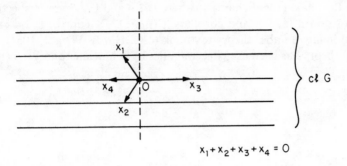

$$x_1 + x_2 + x_3 + x_4 = O$$

Figure L.2.1

and $0 \leq n \leq s$ such that

$$G = \left\{ \sum_{j=1}^{s} \alpha_j y_j : \alpha_j \in Z \text{ for } j \leq n, \; \alpha_j \in R \text{ for } n < j \leq s \right\}.$$

L.3   *Reference notes*

For the original proof of the Shapley–Folkman theorem (L.1.1), see Starr (1969). Cassels (1975) has an interesting proof. For an elegant approach that emphasizes the common structure of Shapley–Folkman's and Lyapunov's theorems (L.1.3), see Arnstein (1980). A result similar to L.1.2 is in Howe (1979).

The original reference for L.2.1 is Steinitz (1913); see also Bourbaki (1966, chap. 7, exercise 3.1). The *mc* bound is taken from Grinberg and Sevastjanov (1980). For much more refined versions of the large numbers result L.2.2, see Hoeffding (1963); that the Chebycheff inequality is what is involved here was shown to me by R. Anderson. By using the pigeonhole principle, result L.2.3 is easily obtained from L.2.1 (as it was shown to me by B. Grodal and S. Hart and as it has been used by Cheng, 1982c). Indeed, let N be larger than the number of balls of diameter less than ϵ needed to cover the ball of radius $(m+1)c$ [note that this number depends exponentially on m]. Then order the vectors as in Steinitz's theorem; note that relaxing the bound from mc to $(m+1)c$, the condition on the sum can also be relaxed to the form in L.2.3. Consider the initial partial sums with last member in C. There are more than N of those. Hence, at least two of them fall into a ball of diameter ϵ. The difference of the two is a partial sum with the desired properties. The results on subgroups are taken from Bourbaki (1966, chap. 7), where L.2.4 and L.2.5 are, respectively, proposition 2 (p. 70) and corollary 1 (p. 72). Of course, L.2.4 can be found in any number theory textbook (e.g., Hardy–Wright, 1954). Subgroup theory has been used in economics by Schmeidler and Vind (1972).

CHAPTER 2

Preferences, utility, and demand

2.1 Introduction

We define and study in this chapter the characteristics of an individual consumer. In particular, we introduce the concepts of *preference relation, utility function,* and *demand function.*

For a considerable part of this book it would suffice to accept the notion of demand function as the definitional characteristic of consumers. It should be emphasized, however, that demand functions are a poor conceptual foundation for economic theory and that the grounding of the latter on preferences goes beyond an aesthetic convenience. Demand functions are good devices for the study of price equilibrium theory but are inadequate for the analysis of welfare issues (see Chapter 4) or theoretical problems that do not emphasize prices (see, for example, Chapter 7).

Our aim in this chapter is not merely to get the existence of demand functions. We want them to be smooth. Mathematically speaking, a demand function exhibits nothing but the parametric dependence of a maximizer element. Therefore, we are, formally, dealing with a problem of the following nature. Suppose that $u(t, p)$ is a function on $t \in R$ depending on a parameter $p \in R$. What does it take to have a smooth function $t(p)$ such that $t(p)$ maximizes $u(\cdot, p)$? Three things are required: (i) u should be smooth; (ii) the maximizer of $u(\cdot, p)$ should be nondegenerate, that is, we must be able to apply the implicit function theorem; and (iii) there should always be a unique maximum, that is, some sort of global concavity is called for. This suggests a program for this chapter: To define first a notion of preferences and smooth preferences (Sections 2.2 and 2.3); to isolate then a concept of critical and regular points of a preference relation (Section 2.5); next, to introduce the notion of smooth, convex preference relations (Section 2.6); and finally, to obtain smooth demand functions (Section 2.7). Sections 2.4 and 2.8 deal with topological properties of smooth and continuous preferences; the basic definitions and facts are in 2.4, while 2.8 concerns itself with approximation issues, that is, with the smoothing of continuous preferences. Finally, Section 2.9 investigates demand theory without preferences by exploring the implications of the so-called weak axiom of revealed preference.

2.2   Definitions

Let $X \subset R^\ell$ be a nonempty set. We interpret ℓ as the number of commodities.

Almost without exception we shall consider sets X that are convex. As a matter of interpretation this implies the perfect divisibility of every commodity.

> **2.2.1. Definition.** *A preference relation on X is a set $\gtrsim \subset X \times X$ that is closed relative to X and satisfies:*
>
> (i)   *$(x, x) \in \gtrsim$ for all $x \in X$ (reflexivity);*
> (ii)   *either $(x, z) \in \gtrsim$ or $(z, x) \in \gtrsim$ for all $(x, z) \in X \times X$ (completeness); and*
> (iii) *$(x, z) \in \gtrsim$ and $(z, v) \in \gtrsim$ implies $(x, v) \in \gtrsim$ (transitivity).*
>
> *The expression $(x, z) \in \gtrsim$ is written $x \gtrsim z$ and read "x is at least as good as z." If $x \gtrsim z$ but not $z \gtrsim x$, then we write $x > z$, which is read "x is preferred to z." If $x \gtrsim z$ and $z \gtrsim x$, then we write $x \sim z$, which is read "x is indifferent to z."*

> **2.2.2. Definition.** *Given $\gtrsim$ on X the function $u: X \to R$ is a utility function for $\gtrsim$ if it is order-preserving; that is, $x \gtrsim z$ if and only if $u(x) \geq u(z)$.*

Of course, utility functions are not uniquely defined. In fact, if $\xi: R \to R$ is increasing and u is a utility for $\gtrsim$, then $\xi \circ u$ is a utility for $\gtrsim$.

> **2.2.3. Definition.** *Let X be convex. The preference relation $\gtrsim$ on X is:*
>
> (i)   *convex if $x \gtrsim z$ implies $\alpha x + (1 - \alpha) z \gtrsim z$ for any $1 \geq \alpha \geq 0$,*
> (ii)   *strictly convex if $x \gtrsim z$, $x \neq z$ implies $\alpha x + (1 - \alpha) z > z$ for any $1 \geq \alpha > 0$.*

The concept of convexity for preferences is central to much of economic theory. It is a restrictive condition that is not in the nature of a regularity hypothesis such as, for example, the closedness or, as it usually is called, continuity, of $\gtrsim$.

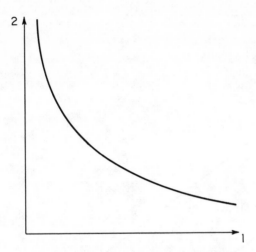

Figure 2.2.1

Let there be two commodities, that is, $\ell = 2$. Suppose that both commodities are desirable; that is, indifference curves are as in Figure 2.2.1. Then the economic meaning of the convexity hypothesis is the following: In order to keep a fixed level of satisfaction, continuous decreases of the amount of one commodity can only be compensated by progressively at least as large increases of the amounts of the other. For the general case the convexity hypothesis means that the previous property must be true when we group the commodities in any manner into two "composite" goods and then restrict preferences to them. For example, let $x, z \in R^\ell$ be mutually orthogonal, L be the two-dimensional space spanned by x, z, and define then the new preference relation by $\gtrsim \cap L \times L$. Another economic interpretation of the convexity hypothesis, more global in nature, goes in terms of a "diversification principle": Given any two bundles of commodities the consumer cannot be hurt by getting half of each. The reader will have no difficulty in finding choice situations that do not fit the principle.

2.2.4. Definition. *The preference relation $\gtrsim$ on X is locally nonsatiated if for all $x \in X$ and $\epsilon > 0$ there is $z \in X$ such that $z > x$ and $\|z - x\| < \epsilon$.*

For the rest of this section, we *let X be bounded below, closed, and convex.*

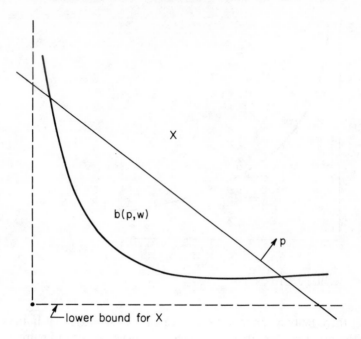

Figure 2.2.2

For $p \in R^{\ell}$, $p \gg 0$, and $w \in R$ let $b(p, w) = \{v \in R^n : p \cdot v \leq w\}$. See Figure 2.2.2. Interpreting p as a vector of prices and w as wealth $b(p, w) \cap X$ is interpreted as the budget set of the consumer.

> **2.2.5. Proposition.** *If $b(p, w) \cap X$ is nonempty, then the set $\varphi(\succsim, p, w) = \{x \in b(p, w) \cap X : x \succsim z$ for every $z \in b(p, w) \cap X\}$ is nonempty. If $\succsim$ is strictly convex, then $\varphi(\succsim, p, w)$ contains a single element. If $\succsim$ is locally nonsatiated, then $p \cdot x = w$ for every $x \in \varphi(\succsim, p, w)$.*

Proof. Note first that because X is bounded below, $b(p, w) \cap X$ is compact and that therefore letting $U_x = \{z \in b(p, w) \cap X : z \succsim x\}$, the collection of sets $\{U_x : z \in b(p, w) \cap X\}$ has the finite intersection property. Indeed, take $x_1, \ldots, x_m$. Without loss of generality it can be assumed that $x_1 \succsim x_j$ for all $j = 1, \ldots, m$. Then $x_1 \in \bigcap_{j=1}^{m} U_{x_j}$. Hence $\bigcap_{x \in b(p, w) \cap X} U_x \neq \varnothing$. But this intersection is contained in $\varphi(\succsim, p, w)$. Suppose there were two distinct maximizers x and z and $\succsim$ is strictly convex. Then $x \sim z$ and by strict convexity $\frac{1}{2}x + \frac{1}{2}z$ is preferred to both. Contradiction. Hence there is at most one maximizer. The property $p \cdot \varphi(p, w) = w$ is an obvious consequence of local nonsatiation. ∎

We call $\varphi(\succsim,p,w)$ the *demand* set. Of course, $\varphi(\succsim,\lambda p,\lambda w) = \varphi(\succsim,p,w)$ for $\lambda > 0$.

2.2.6. Definition. *For $\succsim$ strictly convex, $\varphi(\succsim,\cdot)$, defined as a function on $p \gg 0$, $w > \min\{p\cdot x : x \in X\}$, is called the demand function derived from $\succsim$.*

2.3 Smooth preferences

In developing the concept of smooth preferences we aim at obtaining the differentiability of demand. It is therefore clear that we should restrict ourselves to locally nonsatiated preferences. Except in trivial cases, the demand functions derived from preferences with satiation points will fail to be smooth.

For the rest of this section, $V \subset R^\ell$ *is a fixed, nonempty, open set, and* $\succsim \subset V \times V$ *a locally nonsatiated preference relation on V*.

The closedness and local nonsatiation of $\succsim$ yields a trivial but interesting relation between the topological and order properties of $\succsim$. Remember that $\partial\succsim$ denotes the topological boundary of $\succsim$.

2.3.1. Proposition. $\partial\succsim = \{(x,z) \in V \times V : x \sim z\}$.

Proof. (i) Let $(x,z) \in \partial\succsim$. By the closedness of $\succsim$, $(x,z) \in \succsim$, that is, $x \succsim z$. If $x > z$, then there are open neighborhoods $x \in U_1$, $z \in U_2$ such that $(U_1 \times U_2) \subset \succsim$. So $(x,z) \notin \partial\succsim$. Hence, $x \sim z$.

(ii) Let $x \sim z$. From the local nonsatiation property there is z' arbitrarily close to z such that $z' > z$. Hence $(x,z') \notin \succsim$ and therefore $(x,z) \in \partial\succsim$. ∎

Denote $I = \{(x,z) \in V \times V : x \sim z\}$. The next two examples show that the inclusions $\partial\succsim \subset I$ (resp. $I \subset \partial\succsim$) may fail if the hypothesis of closedness (resp. local nonsatiation) of $\succsim$ is not made.

2.3.2. Example. Let $V = (0,1)$ and $\succsim$ be induced by the utility function:

$$u(t) \begin{cases} = 0 & \text{if } t \text{ is irrational} \\ = \text{minimum number of nonzero terms} & \text{if } t \text{ is rational.} \\ \quad \text{in a binary expansion of } t \end{cases}$$

Then $\succsim$ is not closed but it satisfies the local nonsatiation condition. We have that $\partial\succsim = V \times V$ since for any t, t' with $u(t) \geq u(t')$ we can obviously find a pair (s,s') arbitrarily close to (t,t') and such that $u(s') > u(s)$. But $I \neq V \times V$.

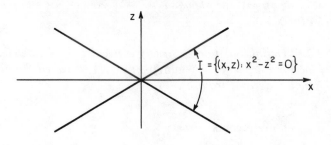

Figure 2.3.1

2.3.3. Example. Let $V = (0,1)$ and $\succsim = V \times V$. Then $\partial \succsim = \varnothing$ and $I = V \times V$. Obviously $\succsim$ is not locally nonsatiated.

The equality of $\partial \succsim$ and I prompts us to focus on the smoothness properties of I.

> **2.3.4. Definition.** *The preference relation $\succsim$ in the nonempty open set V is of class C^r, $r \geq 0$, if it is locally nonsatiated and $\partial \succsim$ is a C^r manifold.*

The most important source of C^r, $r \geq 1$, preferences is given by the next proposition:

> **2.3.5. Proposition.** *If $\succsim$ is representable by a C^r, $r \geq 1$, utility function with no critical point, then $\succsim$ is C^r.*

Proof. Let u be the utility function. Then $I = v^{-1}(0)$, where $v(x,z) = u(x) - u(z)$. Because $\partial u(x) \neq 0$ we have that $\partial v(x,z) \neq 0$ at any x, z. Therefore, by the implicit function theorem (H.2.2), $v^{-1}(0)$ is a C^r manifold. ∎

The requirement that u have no critical point cannot be dispensed with.

2.3.6. Example. $V = R$. The preference relation is represented by the C^∞ utility function x^2. Then I, which is depicted in Figure 2.3.1, fails to be a manifold at $(0,0)$. The origin is, of course, a critical point of the utility function.

In the reverse direction to Proposition 2.3.5, it is of interest to investigate what a concept predicated for preferences implies for utility functions. To this effect, let $\succsim$ be of class C^r. It is easy to verify (see proof

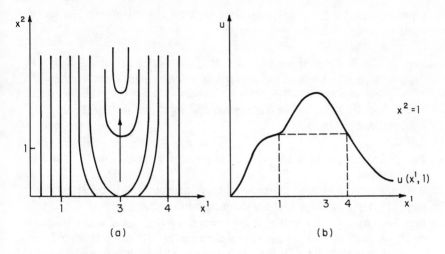

Figure 2.3.2

of Proposition 2.3.9) that $\succsim$ admits a C^r utility function $u: V \to R$. A C^r utility function for $\succsim$ is not, however, very useful if it may have critical points. Unfortunately, it is not in general guaranteed that $\succsim$ possesses a utility representation free of critical points. The next two examples show this.

2.3.7. Example. Let $V = (0, 2) \cup (3, 5)$ and $\succsim$ be represented by $u(t) = t$ if $t \in (0, 2)$ and $u(t) = (t-4)^3 + 1$ if $t \in (3, 5)$. Then any monotonic transformation $\xi: R \to R$ that removes the critical point at $t = 4$ will destroy the differentiability at $t = 1$.

2.3.8. Example. In the previous example V is disconnected. We now quickly describe an example with $V = R_{++}^2$. The indifference curves of $\succsim$ are graphed in Figure 2.3.2a. Figure 2.3.2b gives a utility function for the restriction of $\succsim$ to $(0, \infty) \times \{1\}$. Indeed, as in the previous example the critical point at $(1, 1)$ cannot be removed without destroying differentiability at $(4, 1)$. On the other hand, the property that $\succsim$ is C^∞ is purely local. Obviously, the indifference map of Figure 2.3.2a is compatible with preferences being locally representable by C^∞ utility functions with no critical points. So $\succsim$ may well be C^∞.

In the previous two examples some of the indifference sets $I_x = \{v \in V: v \sim x\}$ are not connected. It turns out that if we require all the indifference sets of $\succsim$ to be connected, then C^r, $r \geq 1$, preferences are representable by C^r utility functions with no critical point. The set V itself may not be connected.

2.3.9. Proposition. *Let $V \subset R^\ell$ be an open set and $\gtrsim \subset V \times V$ a locally nonsatiated preference relation with connected indifference sets $I_x = \{v \in V : v \sim x\}$. Then, for $r \geq 1$, $\gtrsim$ admits a C^r utility function with no critical point if and only if $\partial \gtrsim$ is a C^r manifold.*

Proof. In one direction the proof was given in Proposition 2.3.5 and is quite simple.

In the other direction the proof is more delicate. It will consist of two steps. In step 1 we show that the theorem holds locally; that is, if $\gtrsim$ is C^r, then for any $x \in V$ there is a neighborhood $x \in U \subset V$ and a C^r function $u : U \to R$ with no critical point representing $\gtrsim \cap (U \times U)$. In step 2 the local result is globalized. It is here that connectedness is essential. For the rest of the proof, let "admissible utility" be short for "C^r utility function with no critical point."

Step 1. Let $x \in V$ be fixed. Since $\partial \gtrsim = I$ is a C^r manifold there is an open set $x \in U \subset V$ and a C^r regular funtion $\xi : U \times U \to R$ such that $I \cap (U \times U) = \xi^{-1}(0)$; see H.2. Let $T_{(x,x)}$ be the tangent space to I at (x, x). By reflexivity $(v, v) \in T_{(x,x)}$ for every $v \in R^\ell$. Therefore, we can write $\partial \xi(x, x) = (q, -q)$, $q \neq 0$ for some $q \in R^\ell$.

We can assume that U is convex and sufficiently small for the following to hold "if $(z, z') \in I \cap (U \times U)$, $(v, v') \in U \times U$ and $(v, v') - (z, z') = \lambda(q, -q)$, $\lambda \neq 0$, then $(v, v') \notin I$."

Take $J = \{z \in U : z - x = \lambda q\}$. No two distinct points of J can be indifferent. Indeed, suppose z and z' were. Then, denoting $v = \frac{1}{2}z + \frac{1}{2}z'$, the pair $(v, v), (z, z')$ would contradict the condition of the previous paragraph. So, without loss of generality, we can assume that restricted to J preference is increasing with λ.

On a neighborhood of x, say $U' \subset U$, we can define a function $u : U' \to R$ implicitly by $\xi(v, x + u(v)q) = 0$, where we regard x and q as fixed. Then u is a local utility function because $v \gtrsim v'$ implies $x + u(v)q \gtrsim x + u(v')q$ and thus, by the previous paragraph, $u(v) \geq u(v')$. By the IFT (C.3.2), u is C^r. Also, an immediate computation yields $\partial u(x) = (1/\|q\|^2)q \neq 0$. Hence if U' is small enough, u has no critical point.

Step 2. For every $x \in V$ the nonempty collection of pairs of open sets containing x and admissible utilities is ordered by set inclusion $\subset$ and extension of the functions. By Zorn's lemma (A.7) there is a maximal such set V_x and admissible function $v_x : V_x \to R$.

Take an arbitrary $x \in V$. We first show that whenever $z \in V_x$ we have $I_z \subset V_x$.

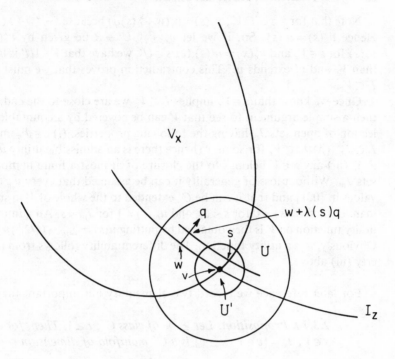

Figure 2.3.3

Indeed, suppose this is not the case. Because I_z is a connected set we can pick v in the closure of $V_x \cap I_z$ but such that $v \notin V_x$. Let U be a neighborhood of v and $u: U \to R$ an admissible utility. Reference to Figure 2.3.3 will be helpful in subsequent arguments.

Pick any $w \in U \cap V_x \cap I_z$ and let $q = \partial u(w)$. On a neighborhood of v we can implicitly define a function $\lambda(s)$ by $u(s) - u(w + \lambda(s)q) = 0$. At $\lambda = 0$, $s = v$ we have $\partial_\lambda[u(v) - u(w + \lambda q)] = -\|q\|^2 \neq 0$. hence, by C.3.2, $\lambda(s)$ is C^r. Because $\partial u(v) - [\partial u(w)q]\partial\lambda(v) = 0$ and $\partial u(v) \neq 0$ we have $\partial\lambda(v) \neq 0$. Summing up, in a neighborhood U' of v, $\lambda(s)$ is C^r and has no critical point. Take U' small enough for $\{w\} + \lambda(U')q \subset V_x$. Finally, let $u': U' \to R$ be defined by $u'(s) = v_x(w + \lambda(s)q)$. Of course, u' is C^r and $\partial u'(v) = [\partial v_x(w)q]\partial\lambda(v) \neq 0$. Also, u' is a utility function on U' because

$$\text{``}s \gtrsim s'\text{''} \Leftrightarrow \text{``}u(s) \geq u(s')\text{''}$$
$$\Leftrightarrow \text{``}u(w + \lambda(s)q) \geq u(w + \lambda(s')q)\text{''}$$
$$\Leftrightarrow \text{``}v_x(w + \lambda(s)q) \geq v_x(w + \lambda(s')q)\text{''}$$
$$\Leftrightarrow \text{``}u'(s) \geq u'(s)\text{''}.$$

Hence, we can assume that u' is an admissible utility on U'.

Note that for $s \in U' \cap V_x$, $v_x(s) = v_x(w + \lambda(s)q)$ because $s \sim (w + \lambda(s)q)$. Hence $v_x(s) = u'(s)$. So, if we let $v_x': V_x \cup U' \to R$ be given by $v_x'(s) = v_x(s)$ for $s \in V_x$ and $v_x'(x) = u'(s)$ for $s \in U'$, we have that $V_x \cup U'$ is larger than V_x and v_x' extends v_x. This contradiction proves that we must have $I_z \subset V_x$.

Once we know that $z \in V_x$ implies $I_z \subset V_x$ we are close to the end. It is then a simple argument to see that V can be covered by a countable collection of open sets J_m having the following properties: (i) $z \in J_m$ implies $I_z \subset J_m$, (ii) $J_m \subset V_x$ for some x (hence there is an admissible utility u_m on J_m), (iii) any $x \in V$ belongs to the closure of at most a finite number of sets J_m. Without loss of generality it can be assumed that every u_m takes values in $[0,1]$ and that it can be C^r extended to the whole of V in such a manner that $u_m(s) = 0$ for $s < J_m$ and $u_m(s) = 1$ for $J_m < s$. An admissible utility function on V is then obtained by putting $u(s) = \sum_{m=1}^{\infty} (1/2^m) u_m(s)$. Obviously, u is a utility function. The differentiability follows from property (iii) above.   ∎

For later reference we record two elementary but important facts.

2.3.10. Proposition. *Let $\gtrsim$ be of class C^r, $r \geq 1$. Then, for every $x \in V$, $I_x = \{v \in V : x \sim v\}$ is a C^r manifold of dimension $\ell - 1$.*

Proof. We saw in step 1 of the previous proof that for every $z \in I_x$ there is an admissible utility $u_z : U \to R$ in some neighborhood of z. But then $I_x \cap U = u_z^{-1}(u(z))$ is an $(\ell - 1)$ C^r manifold (H.2.2) and, therefore, as a matter of definition of manifold, so it is I_x.   ∎

2.3.11. Proposition. *Let $\gtrsim$ be of class C^r, $r \geq 1$, and u, u' two C^r utility functions with no critical point. Then $u = \xi \circ u'$ where $\xi : u'(V) \to R$ is C^r, increasing, and regular, that is, $\partial \xi(t) > 0$ for all $t \in u'(V)$.*

Proof. Take any $t \in u'(v)$. Pick $x \in V$ with $u'(x) = t$ and let $q = \partial u'(x)$. The function $\lambda(s)$ defined locally around t in an implicit manner by $u'(x + \lambda(s)q) - s = 0$, is C^r (C.3.2). Defining $\xi(s) = u(x + \lambda(s)q)$ we see that ξ is as desired. The conclusion $\partial \xi(t) > 0$ follows from $\partial u(x) \neq 0$.   ∎

Given a C^r preference relation $\gtrsim$ on V satisfying the connectedness condition of Proposition 2.3.9, there are many C^r utility representations with no critical point. While at any point the length of the utility gradient vector is essentially arbitrary, its direction depends only on the preference relation. It is useful to define a normalized gradient function.

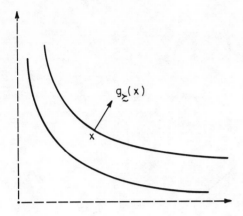

Figure 2.3.4

2.3.12. Definition. *Let $\gtrsim$ be a C^1 preference relation on V representable by some C^1 utility with no critical point. Define $g_{\gtrsim}: V \to S^{\ell-1}$ by $g_{\gtrsim}(x) = (1/\|\partial u(x)\|) \partial u(x)$, where u is any C^1 utility function for $\gtrsim$ with no critical point. See Figure 2.3.4.*

It will be useful to record explicitly an expression for $\partial g_{\gtrsim}(x)$ in terms of the derivatives of u.

2.3.13. Proposition. *With $\gtrsim$, V, u, $g_{\gtrsim}$ as in 2.3.12, take $x \in V$. Suppose that $\gtrsim$ is C^2. Then $\partial g_{\gtrsim}(x): R^{\ell} \to R^{\ell}$ is given by $(1/\|\partial u(x)\|)\pi \circ \partial^2 u(x)$, where π is the perpendicular projection map of R^{ℓ} on $\{v: g_{\gtrsim}(x) \cdot v = 0\}$.*

Proof. Direct computation. ∎

We now state some conditions that we usually impose on preferences. They are restrictive but very convenient. Although in this book we will resort to them permanently, they are not central to the theory being developed.

2.3.14. Definition. *A preference relation $\gtrsim$ on a V satisfying $V + R_{++}^{\ell} \subset V$ is:*

(i) *Monotone if $v \gg x$ implies $v > x$.*
(ii) *Strictly monotone if $v > x$ implies $v > x$.*
(iii) *Differentiably strictly monotone if it is C^1 and $g_{\gtrsim}(x) \gg 0$ for all x.*

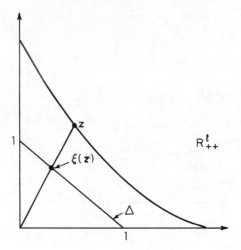

Figure 2.3.5

2.3.15. Proposition. *Let $\succsim$ be a monotone preference relation on R_{++}^{ℓ}. Then every $I_x = \{v \in R_{++}^{\ell} : v \sim x\}$ is homeomorphic to $R^{\ell-1}$, hence connected.*

Proof. $R^{\ell-1}$ is homeomorphic to $\Delta = \{v \in R_{++}^{\ell-1} : v \cdot e = 1\}$. In turn it is simply verified that a homeomorphism $\xi : I_x \to \Delta$ is given by $\xi(z) = [1/(z \cdot e)]z$. See Figure 2.3.5. ∎

A consequence of 2.3.9 and 2.3.15 is that every C^r, $r \geq 1$, monotone preference relation on R_{++}^{ℓ} has a C^r utility representation with no critical point.

2.3.16. Definition. *We say that the preference relation $\succsim$ on V satisfies the boundary condition if, for every $x \in V$, $\{z \in V : z \succsim x\}$ is closed relative to R^{ℓ}. See Figure 2.3.4.*

The economic interpretation of the monotonicity and boundary conditions for preferences on R_{++}^{ℓ} is straightforward. Monotonicity is a desirability hypothesis; that is, commodities are not noxious. The boundary condition is an indispensability hypothesis; that is, some amount of each commodity is required for subsistence.

So far we have dealt with an open V. All the concepts generalize to preferences defined on general X by simply requiring that they hold for some extension of the given preferences to some open V. More formally:

2.3.17. Definition. *Let the preference relation $\gtrsim$ be defined on a nonempty set X. We say that $\gtrsim$ is C^r if Definition 2.3.4 holds for an extension of $\gtrsim$ to some open neighborhood V of X. For any X equaling the closure of its interior and $r \geq 1$, $g_\gtrsim$ is defined as in 2.3.12 with respect to a C^r extension of $\gtrsim$.*

For X with $X + R_{++}^\ell \subset X$, $\gtrsim$ is monotone (resp. strictly monotone, differentiably strictly monotone) if $\gtrsim$ can be extended to an open set V with $V + R_{++}^\ell \subset V$ and still satisfy the definition of monotonicity (resp. strict monotonicity, differentiable strict monotonicity) of 2.3.14.

2.4 Spaces of smooth preferences

The analysis of this book will not strive for utmost generality. Consequently we shall only define spaces of smooth preferences for two possible consumption sets X. Those are $X = R_{++}^\ell$, the simplest open consumption set, and $X = R_+^\ell \setminus \{0\}$, the simplest sort with a nontrivial boundary.

Our two reference spaces of preference relations are:

$$\mathcal{P}_{cl} = \{\gtrsim \subset R_+^\ell \setminus \{0\} \times R_+^\ell \setminus \{0\} : \gtrsim \text{ is monotone}\}$$

$$\mathcal{P}_b = \{\gtrsim \subset R_{++} \times R_{++} : \gtrsim \text{ is monotone and satisfies the}$$
$$\text{boundary condition 2.3.16}\}.$$

From now on *we use $\mathcal{P}$ as a generic symbol for either $\mathcal{P}_{cl}$ or $\mathcal{P}_b$; that is,*

$$\mathcal{P} \in \{\mathcal{P}_{cl}, \mathcal{P}_b\}$$

Similarly *X will stand as the generic symbol for either R_{++}^ℓ or $R_+^\ell \setminus \{0\}$.*

Note that when $X = R_{++}^\ell$ we always assume the boundary condition: "For all x, $\{z \in R_{++}^\ell : z \gtrsim x\}$ is closed in R^ℓ." This guarantees the existence of preferred elements in budget sets; that is, Proposition 2.2.5 applies with no modification of the proof. We exclude the origin from $X = R_+^\ell \setminus \{0\}$ in order to avoid nonessential technicalities. For example, *homothetic preferences* (i.e., those representable by utility functions homogeneous of degree one) could otherwise never qualify as smooth.

Preference spaces of more concrete interest are:

$$\mathcal{P}_{sm} = \{\gtrsim \in \mathcal{P} : \gtrsim \text{ is strictly monotone}\}$$

$$\mathcal{P}^r = \{\gtrsim \subset \mathcal{P} : \gtrsim \text{ is } C^r\}, \qquad r \geq 0$$

$$\mathcal{P}_{sm}^r = \{\gtrsim \subset \mathcal{P} : \gtrsim \text{ is } C^r \text{ and differentiably strictly}$$
$$\text{monotone}\}, \qquad r \geq 1.$$

Except for an explicit warning to the contrary, *it is always understood in the rest of this section that $r \geq 1$.*

It is for many purposes indispensable to have available a notion of closeness for preference relations, that is, to make $\mathcal{P}^r$ into a topological space. The most direct way to accomplish the task is by means of utility representations.

To this effect, let $\mathcal{U}^r$, $r \geq 1$, be the set of increasing functions $u : X \to R$ with no critical point and satisfying the condition "for every $\alpha \in R$, $u^{-1}([\alpha, \infty))$ is closed relative to R^ℓ." We know that every $\succsim \in \mathcal{P}^r$ can be represented by some function $u \in \mathcal{U}^r$ and, conversely, every $u \in \mathcal{U}^r$ represents a $\succsim_u \in \mathcal{U}^r$; see 2.3.9.

Note that $\mathcal{U}^r$ is a subset of $C^r(X)$, the complete, separable metric space of C^r functions on X endowed with the uniform convergence on compacta of the values of the function and the first r derivatives (see K.1). We write $u_n \underset{r}{\to} u$ to denote such convergence. If it is clear by the context the reference to r is dropped.

> **2.4.1. Definition.** *For $\succsim_n, \succsim \in \mathcal{P}^r$ we say that $\succsim_n \underset{r}{\to} \succsim$ if there are representations $u_n, u \in \mathcal{U}^r$ of $\succsim_n, \succsim$, respectively, such that $u_n \underset{r}{\to} u$.*

More formally, the previous is the notion of convergence induced by the following topology. *Let $\Phi_r : \mathcal{U}^r \to \mathcal{P}^r$ be the map that assigns $\succsim_u$ to $u \in \mathcal{U}^r$.* This is not a one-to-one map, but we can still endow $\mathcal{P}^r$ with the identification topology derived from $\mathcal{U}^r$; that is, $V \subset \mathcal{P}^r$ is open if $\Phi_r^{-1}(V)$ is open (see A.1). To verify that this induces the notion of convergence we have adopted, it suffices to check that Φ_r is an open map; see A.1.

> **2.4.2. Proposition.** *With the identification topology on $\mathcal{P}^r$, the map $\Phi_r : \mathcal{U}^r \to \mathcal{P}^r$ is open; that is, images of open sets are open.*

Proof. Let $V \subset \mathcal{U}^r$ be open. We should prove that $\Phi_r(V)$ is open or, equivalently, that $\Phi_r^{-1}(\Phi_r(V))$ is open (see A.1). Let $u \in \Phi_r^{-1}(\Phi_r(V))$. Then $\succsim_u = \Phi_r(u) \in \Phi_r(V)$; that is, $\succsim_u = \succsim_{u'}$ for some $u' \in V$. By 2.3.11 $u' = \xi \circ u$, where $\xi : u(X) \to R$ is C^r, increasing and regular. Let $u_n \to u$. Then $u_n' \to u'$ for $u_n' = \xi \circ u_n$. Since V is open, eventually $u_n' \in V$; hence $\succsim_{u_n'} \in \Phi_r(V)$ and so $u_n \in \Phi_r^{-1}(\Phi_r(V))$. Therefore, $\Phi_r^{-1}(\Phi_r(V))$ is open. ∎

It will be technically convenient to have available a normalized set of utility functions (i.e., only one representative per preference) to be used on occasion in place of $\mathcal{P}^r$.

Let $\mathcal{U}_d^r = \{u \in \mathcal{U}^r : u(\lambda e) = \lambda \text{ for all } \lambda > 0\}$. So $\mathcal{U}_d^r$ is the set of utility functions that assign, to the commodity bundle with equal amounts of every commodity, this common value. The space $\mathcal{U}_d^r$ is endowed with the relative topology of $\mathcal{U}^r$; that is, $u_n \xrightarrow{\mapsto} u$ if and only if the sequence converges C^r uniformly on compacta.

2.4.3. Proposition. $\mathcal{U}_d^r$ and $\mathcal{P}^r$ are homeomorphic under the natural map Φ_r.

Proof. It is rather trivial. One has to verify that Φ_r, restricted to $\mathcal{U}_d^r$, is one-to-one, onto, continuous, and open:

(i) *One-to-one:* Let $u, u' \in \mathcal{U}_d^r$ and $\succsim_u = \succsim_{u'}$. Then $u = \xi \circ u'$ for some $\xi : u'(X) \to R$. But for all $\lambda \in u'(X)$, $\xi(\lambda) = \xi(u'(\lambda e)) = u(\lambda e) = \lambda$. So $u = u'$.

(ii) *Onto:* Let $\succsim \in \mathcal{P}^r$ and $\succsim = \succsim_u$, $u \in \mathcal{U}^r$. Define $u' : X \to R$ implicitly by $u(x) = u(u'(x)e)$. To verify that $u' \in \mathcal{U}_d^r$ we need to check that u' is C^r and has no critical point. That it is C^r follows from the IFT (C.3.2) in the usual manner. That it has no critical point follows from $0 \neq \partial u(x) = (\partial u(u'(x)e)e) \partial u'(x)$.

(iii) *Continuous:* This is simply by Definition 2.4.1.

(iv) *Open:* Mimic the proof of Proposition 2.4.2 or simply notice that the procedure in (ii) above amounts to a C^r continuous construction of the inverse. ∎

Since utility functions are after all only auxiliary concepts, it can be asked if the notion of convergence for preferences can be formulated in terms not involving utility. The answer is yes. The next proposition exhibits a way to do this.

2.4.4. Proposition. Let $\succsim_n, \succsim \in \mathcal{P}^r$. Then $\succsim_n \xrightarrow{\mapsto} \succsim$ if and only if there is a sequence $i_n : X \times X \to X \times X$ of C^r diffeomorphisms such that $i_n(\succsim) = \succsim_n$ and i_n converges to the identity i C^r uniformly on compacta.

Proof. (i) Let $\succsim_n \to \succsim$, that is, $u_n \to u$ for $u_n, u \in \mathcal{U}_d^r$ representing $\succsim_n, \succsim$. For every n, define $\lambda_n : X \to R$ by $u(x) - u_n(\lambda_n(x)x) = 0$. See Figure 2.4.1. By the IFT (C.3.2) λ_n is C^r and, as $n \to \infty$, λ_n converges C^r uniformly on compacta to the constant function equal to 1. We can define a C^r diffeomorphism $i_n : X \times X \to X \times X$ by $i_n(x, z) = (\lambda_n(x)x, \lambda_n(z)z)$. Of course, $i_n \to i$. To see that $i_n(\succsim) = \succsim_n$ note that for any x, we have $\lambda_n(x)x \sim_n u(x)e$ because

$$\lambda_n(x)x \sim_n u(\lambda_n(x)x)e \quad \text{and} \quad u_n(\lambda_n(x)x) = u(x).$$

Therefore, $\lambda_n(x)x \succsim_n \lambda_n(z)z$ if and only if $u(x)e \succsim_n u(z)e$, that is, if and only if $u(x) \geq u(z)$.

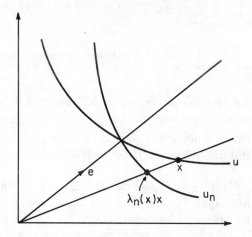

Figure 2.4.1

(ii) Let $i_n \to i$, $i_n(\gtrsim) = \gtrsim_n$. Take $u_n, u \in \mathfrak{U}_d^r$ representing $\gtrsim_n$, $\gtrsim$ respectively. Pick an arbitrary $x \in X$. We will show, and this suffices, that $u_n \to u$ in a neighborhood of x.

Let $V \subset X \times X$ be a neighborhood of $(x, u(x)e)$ and $H : V \to R$ a C^r regular function such that $(\partial \gtrsim) \cap V = H^{-1}(0)$. We show first that $i_n^{-1}(x, u_n(x)e) \to (x, u(x)e)$. Indeed, without loss of generality, we can assume that $u_n(x) \to t$ [the collection $\{u_n(x)\}$ is bounded]. So

$$i_n^{-1}(x, u_n(x)e) \to i^{-1}(x, te) = (x, te).$$

But $(x, te) \in \partial \gtrsim$ because i_n^{-1}, being a homeomorphism between $\gtrsim_n$ and $\gtrsim$, maps $\partial \gtrsim_n$ into $\partial \gtrsim$ (see A.1). Hence, $t = u(x)$. We conclude that, eventually, $i_n^{-1}(x, u_n(x)e) \in V$. An application of the IFT (C.3.2) now gives the result. Indeed, in a neighborhood of x, u_n is implicitly defined by $H(i_n^{-1}(v, u_n(v)e)) = 0$ and, analogously, so is u. Also, by monotonicity, $\partial_u H(x, u(x)e) \neq 0$. Hence, $u_n \to u$ locally. ∎

It is technically important to know if $\mathcal{P}^r$ and $\mathcal{P}_{sm}^r$ are metrizable and topologically complete. Because of 2.4.3, A.3.4, and K.1.1, an affirmative answer is implied by the next proposition. Let $\mathfrak{U}_{d,sm}^r = \{u \in \mathfrak{U}_d^r : \partial u(x) \gg 0, \text{ all } x\}$.

2.4.5. Proposition. $\mathfrak{U}_d^r$ *and* $\mathfrak{U}_{d,sm}^r$ *are* G_δ *subsets of* $C^r(X)$.

Proof. It is clear that our sets are determined by some subset of the following four countable families of conditions, each one of which defines an open subset. The first two families deal with monotonicity, the third with the boundary condition, and the fourth with the normalization. For $\mathcal{P} = \mathcal{P}_b$ they are:

$$\left\{ u \in C^r(X): \partial u(x) \gg -\frac{\alpha}{n}, \; \frac{1}{n}e \leq x \leq ne \right\}, \text{ for } \alpha \in \{0, 1\}$$

$$\left\{ u \in C^r(X): \text{there is } \epsilon > 0 \text{ such that } u\left(\frac{1}{n}e\right) > u(x) \right.$$

$$\left. \text{whenever } x \leq ne \text{ and } x^i = \epsilon \text{ for some } i \right\}$$

$$\left\{ u \in C^r(X): \max_{(1/n) \leq t \leq n} |u(te) - t| < \frac{1}{n} \right\}.$$

For $\mathcal{P} = \mathcal{P}_{cl}$, $(1/n)e \leq x$ should be replaced in the first two families by $1/n \leq e \cdot x$. ∎

The space $\mathcal{U}_d^r$ is a convex subset of the linear space $C^r(X)$. This fact and Proposition 2.4.5 could be resorted to in order to endow $\mathcal{P}^r$ in a natural manner with a linear structure. It would not be, however, a very useful one, because the $C^r(X)$ linear spaces do not behave too well for calculus purposes. Fortunately, we will find no need in this monograph for such an infinite-dimensional linear structure. As a technical tool the use of finite-dimensional parameterizations will prove far more flexible and, at any rate, quite sufficient.

2.4.6. Definition. *A (finite-dimensional) C^r parameterization of preferences is a nonempty, open subset A of some R^s and a C^r map $U: A \times X \rightarrow R$ such that for each $a \in A$, we have $U_a \in \mathcal{U}^r$, where $U_a(x) = U(a, x)$.*

If $U: A \times X \rightarrow R$ is a C^r parameterization, then the map which associates $U_a \in \mathcal{U}^r$ to a is continuous. An equivalent definition of a C^r parameterization is the following (see K.1.2):

2.4.6′. Definition. *A (finite-dimensional) C^r parameterization of preferences is a nonempty, open subset A and a map $\xi: A \rightarrow \mathcal{P}^r$ such that the function $U: A \times X \rightarrow R$ defined by $U(a, x) = u(x)$ for $u \in \mathcal{U}_d^r$, $\succeq_u = \xi(a)$, is C^r. We say that U generates ξ.*

Besides being intuitively reasonable, the criterion of adequacy of a topology is that it be useful. Eventually this will be tantamount to obtaining appropriate continuity properties for the demand function. We now take a technical step in that direction.

In line with Definition 2.3.12 let $g: \mathcal{P}^r \times X \to S = \{v \in R^\ell_{++}: \|v\| = 1\}$ be given by $g(\gtrsim, x) = (1/\|\partial u(x)\|)\, \partial u(x)$, where $u \in \mathcal{U}^r$ represents $\gtrsim$.

2.4.7. Proposition.

  (i) $g: \mathcal{P}^r \times X \to S$ *is jointly continuous.*
  (ii) $\gtrsim_n \underset{r}{\to} \gtrsim$ *implies* $g_{\gtrsim_n} \to g_{\gtrsim}$ C^{r-1}-*uniformly on compacta.*
  (iii) *If* $U: A \times X \to R$ *is a* C^r *parameterization, then the map* $g: A \times X \to S$ *defined by* $g(a, x) = g(\gtrsim_{U_a}, x)$ *is* C^{r-1}.

Proof. Taking into account K.1.2, that is, the continuity of the evaluation map, all these claims are trivial consequences of the definition. ∎

We conclude with a remark on the case $r = 0$. We will have little occasion in this monograph to work with $\mathcal{P}^0$ rather than $\mathcal{P}^r$, $r > 0$. Nevertheless, it is useful to take note of the fact that if we let $\mathcal{U}^0$, Φ^0, $\mathcal{U}^0_d$ have the obvious meaning and topologize $\mathcal{P}^0$ according to Definition 2.4.1 with $r = 0$, then Propositions 2.4.2, 2.4.3, and 2.4.5 remain valid with no modification in the proof of 2.4.2 and 2.4.3. Some slight changes have to be made in the proof of 2.4.5. Furthermore, it is not difficult to check that the topology on $\mathcal{P}^0$ does then coincide with the one induced by the closed convergence on the set of nonempty, closed subsets of $X \times X$ (see A.5). This is the most familiar topology on a space of continuous (i.e., closed) preferences. Therefore, if we view $\mathcal{P}^r$, $r \geq 1$, as a subset of $\mathcal{P}^0$, it is clear that, as it should be, our topologies are strictly finer than the ones in standard use for a continuous (i.e., C^0) framework. We end this section by recording the continuity properties of the demand set $\varphi(\gtrsim, p, w)$ in the domain $\mathcal{P}^0_{sm} \times R_{++} \times R_{++}$.

2.4.8. Proposition. *The set* $G = \{(\gtrsim, p, w, x): x \in \varphi(\gtrsim, p, w)\} \subset$ $\mathcal{P}^0 \times R^\ell_{++} \times R_{++} \times X$ *is closed. Furthermore, if*

$$(\gtrsim_n, p_n, w_n, x_n) \in G, \quad \gtrsim_n \to \gtrsim_0 \in \mathcal{P}^0_{sm},$$

$$p_n \to p \gg 0, \quad and \quad w_n \to w > 0,$$

then $\|x_n\| \to \infty$.

Proof. (i) We prove that G is closed by contradiction. Let $\gtrsim_n \to \gtrsim$, $p_n \to p$, $w_n \to w$, $x_n \in \varphi(\gtrsim_n, p_n, w_n)$. Pick continuous utility functions with $u_n \to u$ (convergence uniform on compacta). Suppose that $z \notin \varphi(\gtrsim, p, w)$. Pick $x \in \varphi(\gtrsim, p, w)$. Assume first that $z \in X$. Then $u(x) > u(z)$ and by continuity of u, $u(x - \delta e_j) > u(z)$ for some j and sufficiently small δ. But then eventually $u_n(x - \delta e_j) > u_n(x_n)$ and $p_n \cdot (x - \delta e_j) < w_n$. The last inequality implies $u_n(x_n) > u_n(x - \delta e_j)$ and we have a contradiction. Therefore, to conclude the proof we should show that $z \in X$. Of course, we only have a problem if $X = R_{++}^{\ell}$. Let $s = \max_j (w/p^j) + 1$. Take $1 > \delta > 0$ small enough so that if $\|x' - x\| \leq \delta$ and $v \leq se$, $v^j = \delta$ for some j, then $u(x') > u(v)$. Such δ exists by the boundary condition. We can assume that, for all n and x', v as above, $u_n(x') > u_n(v)$. Since $(p_n, w_n) \to (p, w)$, eventually we can pick $x'_n \in b(p_n, w_n) \cap R_{++}^{\ell}$ such that $\|x - x'_n\| < \delta$. Then $u_n(x'_n) > u_n(v)$ whenever $v \leq se$ and $v^j = \delta$ for some j. Of course, we also have $u_n(x_n) \geq u_n(x'_n)$. Now suppose that $z \notin R_{++}^{\ell}$. Since $p \cdot z \leq w$ we have $z \leq se - 1$ and so eventually $x_n \leq se$, $x_n^j < \delta$ for some j. Let z_n be defined by $z_n^j = \max\{\delta, x_n^j\}$. Then $u_n(x'_n) > u_n(z_n)$. But $z_n \geq x_n$. So $u_n(z_n) \geq u_n(x_n) \geq u_n(x'_n)$. Contradiction. Hence $z \gg 0$.

(ii) Let $(\succsim_n, p_n, w_n, x_n)$ satisfy the second hypothesis of the proposition. We argue again by contradiction. If the conclusion does not hold, $\{x_n\}$ has a bounded subsequence. So we can assume that $x_n \to z$. But then we can verify as in part (i) that z maximizes $\succsim$ on $b(p, w)$, which is impossible, since if $p^j = 0$, then $z + e_j > z$ and $p \cdot (z + e_j) = p \cdot z \leq w$. ∎

2.5 Regular and critical points

In this section $V \subset R^{\ell}$ is a given open set, $\succsim$ a fixed C^2 preference relation, $u: V \to R$ a C^2 utility function for $\succsim$ with no critical point, $x \in V$ a given point, and $I_x = \{v \in V : v \sim x\}$. By 2.3.10 the indifference set I_x is a C^2 $(\ell - 1)$ manifold. We let T_x denote its tangent space at x; that is, $T_x = \{v \in R^{\ell} : \partial u(x)v = 0\}$. See Figure 2.5.1 for different possibilities. Denote by g the function $g_{\succsim}$ defined in 2.3.12.

Consider the restriction of the utility function u to the affine space $\{x\} + T_x$. Clearly, x is a critical point of this function. In Figure 2.5.1a (resp. 2.5.1b) it is a maximum (resp. a minimum). As this critical point is intimately related to the definition of preferred points in budget sets it is important to have techniques and criteria to establish its degeneracy or nondegeneracy. Remember that a critical point is called degenerate if the Hessian matrix is singular (see H.2). Two facts are intuitively plausible about the degeneracy of the critical point under discussion: (i) It depends solely on the preference relation and not on the utility function, and (ii) it is intimately related to the curvature of the manifold I_x at x. Thus, in Figure 2.5.1d x is a degenerate maxima of $u \mid (\{x\} + T_x)$ because it belongs to an interval of constancy of the function. This is as much as saying that I_x is flat at x, that is, that the curvature of I_x at x is zero. Figure 2.5.1c provides a different example of degeneracy (here x is an inflection point).

Viewing I_x as the boundary of $\{v \in V : v \succsim x\}$ let c_x denote the Gaussian curvature of I_x at x. See H.3 for the definition. It will be useful to have a formula to compute c_x in terms of u.

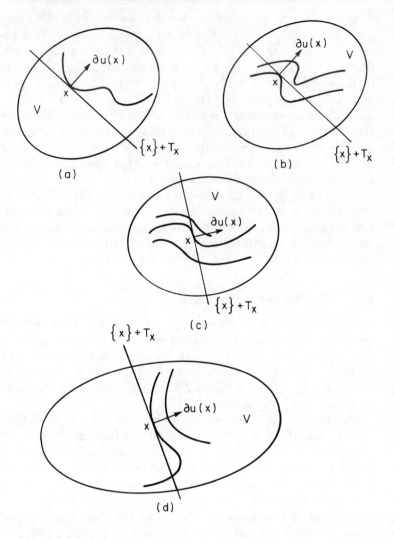

Figure 2.5.1

2.5.1. Proposition. *Denoting by c_x the Gaussian curvature at x of I_x seen as the boundary of $\{v \in V : v \succsim x\}$ we have:*

$$c_x = \begin{vmatrix} -\partial g(x) & g(x) \\ -g(x)^T & 0 \end{vmatrix} = \frac{1}{\|\partial u(x)\|^{\ell+1}} \begin{vmatrix} -\partial^2 u(x) & \partial u(x) \\ -[\partial u(x)]^T & 0 \end{vmatrix}.$$

Proof. By definition (see H.3), c_x is the determinant of the linear map $-\partial g(x) \mid T_x$. Hence

$$c_x = \begin{vmatrix} -\partial g(x) & g(x) \\ -[g(x)]^T & 0 \end{vmatrix}$$

follows from B.5.2 and the fact that $\partial g(x)$ maps onto T_x. The second equality can be obtained from 2.3.13 and B.5.2 or, simply, by direct computation. ∎

We have:

2.5.2. Proposition. *Let* $T_x = \{v \in R^\ell : \partial u(x)v = 0\}$. *Then:*

(i) *x is a critical point of* $u \mid (\{x\} + T_x)$.

(ii) *x is a degenerate critical point of* $u \mid (\{x\} + T_x)$ *if and only if* $c_x = 0$.

(iii) *Let x be a maximum (resp. minimum) point of* $u \mid (\{x\} + T_x)$. *Then x is nondegenerate if and only if the Hessian form of u at x is negative definite (resp. positive definite) on the subspace* T_x.

Proof. (i) This is obvious because $\partial u(x)v = 0$ whenever $v \in T_x$. (ii) The determinant of the Hessian of $u \mid (\{x\} + T_x)$ has the same sign as

$$\begin{vmatrix} \partial^2 u(x) & \partial u(x) \\ -[\partial u(x)]^T & 0 \end{vmatrix}.$$

See B.6. Apply then Proposition 2.5.1. (iii) The restriction to T_x of the Hessian form of u at x is the Hessian form of $u \mid (\{x\} + T_x)$ at x. Hence (iii) follows from D.2; see also B.6. ∎

With the above motivation we conclude this section with a definition.

2.5.3. Definition. *Given a* C^2 *preference relation* $\succsim$ *on an open set V, a point* $x \in V$ *is regular (resp. critical) if the Gaussian curvature at x of* $I_x = \{v \in V : v \sim x\}$, *viewed as the boundary of* $\{v \in V : v \succsim x\}$, *is different from zero (resp. equal to zero). We say that* $\succsim$ *is regular if every point* $x \in V$ *is regular.*

Note that since the computation of the Gaussian curvature is purely local, the latter is defined for any C^2 preference relation (with or without connected indifference sets). The interpretation of the definition is clear from the previous discussion. For a point to be regular the indifference manifold that passes through it should not be, even infinitesimally, flat.

Figure 2.5.2 illustrates the critical set of a preference relation. The figure is in a sense misleading. In higher-dimensional spaces (i.e., for $\ell > 2$) the critical set should not be visualized as a smooth manifold but as a finite union of smooth manifolds of different dimensions (each one corresponding to critical points with different indices of degeneracy, i.e., with different ranks of the Hessian matrix).

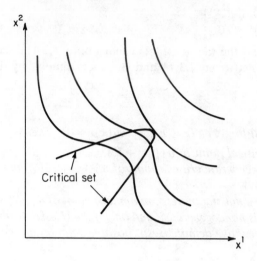

x^2

x^1

Critical set

Figure 2.5.2

2.6   Smooth, convex preferences

Once placed in a differential setting it is natural to strengthen our concept of strictly convex preferences (Definition 2.2.3) to take into account infinitesimal effects, that is, to require that indifference surfaces be not flat even infinitesimally – or, in other words, that the curvature be everywhere nonzero.

> **2.6.1. Definition.** *A C^2 preference relation $\succeq$ on an open, convex set V is differentiably strictly convex if it is strictly convex and every point is regular, that is, $c_x \neq 0$ for all $x \in V$.*

For the rest of this section V *denotes an open, convex set*. If $\succeq$ is a C^2, convex preference relation on V having a C^2 utility function $u: V \to R$ with no critical point, then, for every $x \in V$, x is a maximum of u on $\{x\} + T_x$. Hence $\partial^2 u(x)$ must be negative semidefinite on T_x. Moreover, if $\succeq$ is differentiably strictly convex, then the maximum is nondegenerate, that is, $\partial^2 u(x)$ is in fact negative definite on T_x; see 2.5.2. The converse is also true:

> **2.6.2. Proposition.** *If $\succeq \subset V \times V$ has a C^2 utility representation with no critical point $u: V \to R$, then*
>
> (i) $\succeq$ *is convex if and only if, for every $x \in V$, the form $\partial^2 u(x)$ is negative semidefinite on T_x.*

(ii) $\gtrsim$ is *differentiably strictly convex if and only if, for every*
$x \in V$, *the form* $\partial^2 u(x)$ *is negative definite on* T_x.

Proof. The two "only if" parts as well as the "if" part of (ii) follow from
the definitions, D.2 and 2.5.2.

For the "if" part of (i) consider first a fixed $z \in V$. We show that locally
$\{v : v \gtrsim z\}$ is convex. If this were not so, we could find $v, x \in I_z$, arbitrarily
close to z, and such that $g(v) \cdot (x - v) < 0$. Let then $v(t) \in I_z$, $t \in [0, 1]$ be
a C^1 path with $v(0) = v$, $v(1) = x$ and $\partial v(t)$ collinear to the projection
of $x - v(t)$ on $T_{v(t)} I_z$; see H.1. Define $\xi(t) = g(v(t)) \cdot (x - v(t))$. By the
mean value theorem (C.2.4) there is some $t \in [0, 1]$ with $\partial \xi(t) > 0$. But
taking into account that $\partial v(t) = \alpha_1(x - v(t)) + \alpha_2 g(v(t))$ for some $\alpha_1 > 0$,
$g(v(t)) \cdot \partial g(v(t)) = 0$ and $g(v(t)) \cdot \partial v(t) = 0$, we get

$$0 < \partial \xi(t) = (1/\alpha_1) \partial v(t) \cdot \partial g(v(t)) \partial v(t),$$

which contradicts the negative semidefiniteness of $\partial^2 u(v(t))$ on $T_{v(t)}$; see
2.3.13. Hence, the convexity property must hold locally.

To verify that local implies global note that the convexity property on
$\gtrsim$ is equivalent to the property "$u(tx + (1 - t)v) \geq \min\{u(x), u(v)\}$ for
all $t \in [0, 1]$," called quasiconcavity, on the utility function. Suppose that
the latter is violated for some x and v. Let $\bar{t} > 0$ be the smallest t at which
$u(tx + (1 - t)v)$ attains its minimum on $[0, 1]$. Then the quasiconcavity
of u, hence the convexity of $\gtrsim$, is violated on any neighborhood of $z = \bar{t}x + (1 - \bar{t})v$. Contradiction. ∎

A glance at Figure 2.6.1 suffices to show that the regularity of every
$x \in V$ does not imply the convexity of $\gtrsim$. The next proposition gives a
mildly interesting consequence of the boundary condition 2.3.16.

2.6.3. Proposition. $\gtrsim \in \mathcal{P}_b^2$ *is differentiably strictly convex if
and only if every* $x \in R_{++}^\ell$ *is regular.*

Proof. Let u be a C^2 utility for $\gtrsim$ with no critical point. As is clear from
the definition (or from 2.5.1), c_x equals the product of the eigenvalues of
the form $\partial^2 u(x)$ on T_x. Hence $c_x \neq 0$ everywhere and 2.6.2 yield the conclusion that $\gtrsim$ is differentiably strictly convex if for a single x, $\partial^2 u(x)$ is
negative definite on T_x, or, in other words, if x is a maximum of u on
$\{x\} + T_x$. But the existence of such an x is easily proved. It suffices to let
$e \cdot z < 1$, $X = \{v \in R_{++}^\ell : v \gtrsim z\}$ and apply 2.2.5 to get a maximal element
of $\gtrsim$ on $\{v \in X : e \cdot v \leq 1\}$. Note that by the boundary condition, X is
closed. ∎

If $\gtrsim$ is a convex preference relation on V and $u : V \to R$ a utility function for $\gtrsim$, then the upper level sets of u, that is, $u^{-1}([s, \infty))$, are convex.

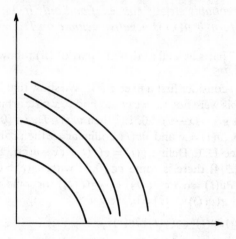

Figure 2.6.1

Of course, this is a property that concave functions have. It would be of considerable technical interest if among the many utility representations for $\succsim$ a concave one could be selected. Unfortunately, for general convex, or strictly convex, preferences, no such utility function needs to exist, not even in compact subsets of V. Figure 2.6.2 illustrates an example. By imagining the three-dimensional representation of the graph of the utility function it is not difficult to persuade oneself that if the straight segments of indifference curves originated in a concave function, then they would have to be parallel.

For differentiably strictly convex preferences the situation is much better.

> **2.6.4. Proposition.** *Let $\succsim$ be a C^2 differentiably strictly convex preference relation on an open convex set V. Suppose that $\succsim$ can be represented by a C^2 utility with no critical point. Then for every compact, convex $K \subset V$ there is a C^2 utility function for $\succsim$ with no critical point such that the restriction to K is differentiably strictly concave; that is, $\partial^2 u(x)$ is negative definite for every $x \in K$.*

Proof. Let $v : V \to R_{++}$ be a C^2 utility function for $\succsim$ with no critical point. Denote by $S^{\ell-1}$ the $(\ell-1)$ unit sphere. Pick an open neighborhood $U \subset K \times S^{\ell-1}$ of $L = \{(x, q) \in K \times S^{\ell-1} : \partial v(x)q = 0\}$ such that

$$\sup\{q \cdot \partial^2 v(x)q : (x, q) \in U\} < 0.$$

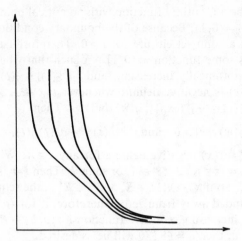

Figure 2.6.2

Such a U exists by continuity, compactness of K, and the hypothesis that $\partial^2 v(x)$ is negative definite on $\{q \in R^\ell : \partial v(x)q = 0\}$. Now let

$$t = \max\left\{ \frac{q \cdot \partial^2 v(x)q}{(\partial v(x)q)^2} : (x, q) \in (K \times S^{\ell-1}) \setminus U \right\}.$$

By compactness and continuity, $t < \infty$. Put $\bar{t} = \max\{1, t\}$. Let $\xi : R_{++} \to R$ be given by $\xi(z) = -(1/\bar{t})\exp(-\bar{t}z)$. Then $\partial \xi(z) = \exp(-\bar{t}z) > 0$ and $\partial^2 \xi(z) = -\bar{t}\partial\xi(z)$. Put $u = \xi \circ v$. Then u is a utility function for $\succeq$ with no critical point and for $x \in K$ and $q \in S^{\ell-1}$,

$$q \cdot \partial^2 u(x)q = q \cdot [\partial \xi(v(x))\partial^2 v(x) + \partial^2 \xi(v(x))[\partial v(x)]^T \partial v(x)]q$$

$$= \xi'(v(x))[q \cdot \partial^2 v(x)q - \bar{t}(\partial v(x)q)^2] < 0.$$

Hence, $\partial^2 u(x)$ is negative definite for every $x \in K$. ∎

The next proposition is a variation of 2.6.4 for preferences defined on R_{++}^ℓ and satisfying the boundary condition.

2.6.5.. Proposition. *Let $\succeq$ be a C^2 differentiably strictly convex monotone preference relation on R_{++}^ℓ. Suppose that $\succeq$ satisfies the boundary·condition (i.e. $\{z : z \succeq x\}$ is closed in R^ℓ for all x). Then for every bounded K there is a C^2 utility function $u : R_{++}^\ell \to R_{++}$ with no critical point such that:*

(i) $\partial u(x)$ is negative definite for every $x \in K$, and

(ii) $x_n \to x$, $x_n \in K$, $x \notin R_{++}^\ell$, implies $\|\partial u(x_n)\| \to \infty$.

Proof. Let $v: R_{++}^\ell \to R$ be a C^2 utility function with no critical point. We can assume that $v(R_{++}^\ell) = (0,1)$. Because of the boundary condition the set $\{z \in K : v(z) \geq t\}$ has a compact closure for $t > 0$. Therefore (see the proof of 2.6.4), there is some function $\eta: (0,1] \to R$ such that whenever $\xi: (0,1) \to R$ is C^2, monotonically increasing, and $|\partial^2 \xi(t)| \leq \eta(t) \partial \xi(t)$ for all t, then $\partial^2(\xi \circ v)(x)$ is negative definite whenever $v(x) \geq t$, $x \in K$. Define $\xi: (0,1) \to R$ by $\xi(t) = -\int_t^1 (\exp\{\int_s^1 \eta(w)\,dw\})\,ds$. Then

$$\partial \xi(t) = \exp\{\int_s^1 \eta(w)\,dw\} > 0 \quad \text{and} \quad \partial^2 \xi(t) = -\partial \xi(t)\eta(t).$$

Therefore, $\xi \circ v$ has $\partial^2(\xi \circ v)(x)$ negative definite for any $x \in K$. Without loss of generality take $K = \{z \in R_{++}^\ell : z \leq ek\}$ for some k. Then $\xi \circ v$ is concave in the convex set K. So if $x_n \to x$, $x_n \in K$, and $x \notin R_{++}^\ell$, the sequence $\partial(\xi \circ v)(x_n)$ remains bounded away from zero. Therefore, if for $(a, b) =$ Range ξ, we take a C^2, increasing, concave function $\xi': (a, b) \to R$ such that $\partial \xi'(s_n) \to \infty$ as $s_n \to a$, then $u = \xi' \circ \xi \circ v$ will be as desired. ∎

So far our definitions have been for an open V. They are extended to general consumption sets in the usual manner:

> **2.6.6. Definition.** *A preference relation $\gtrsim$ in a nonempty, convex X is differentiably strictly convex if $\gtrsim$ can be extended to an open, convex V and satisfy 2.6.1. A C^r, $r \geq 2$, preference relation $\gtrsim$ on a nonempty, convex set X with $X + R_{++}^\ell \subset X$ is monotone and differentiably strictly convex (or differentiably strictly monotone and convex) if those properties are simultaneously satisfied by an extension of $\gtrsim$ to an open V with $V + R_{++}^\ell \subset V$.*

Note that the properties "differentiably strictly convex" and "monotone" automatically imply "differentiably strictly monotone."

Finally, a word on spaces of convex preferences. With $\mathcal{P}^r$ as in Section 2.4, define $\mathcal{P}_c^r = \{\gtrsim \in \mathcal{P}^r : \gtrsim$ is convex$\}$ for all r and:

$$\mathcal{P}_{sc}^r \begin{cases} = \{\gtrsim \in \mathcal{P}_{sm}^r : \gtrsim \text{ is strictly convex}\}, & \text{for } r = 0, 1 \\ = \{\gtrsim \in \mathcal{P}^r : \gtrsim \text{ is differentiably strictly convex}\}, & \text{for } r \geq 2. \end{cases}$$

Then:

> **2.6.7. Proposition.** *For every $r \geq 0$, $\mathcal{P}_{sc}^r$ is a G_δ, contractible subset of $\mathcal{P}^r$.*

Proof. First we exhibit a contraction $H: \mathcal{P}_{sc}^r \times [0,1] \to \mathcal{P}_{sc}^r$; see A.2 for definitions. Pick an arbitrary $\gtrsim \in \mathcal{P}_{sc}^r$ with corresponding utility $\bar{u} \in \mathcal{U}_d^r$. For every $u \in \mathcal{U}_d^r$ and $\alpha \in [0,1]$ we associate a utility function $u_\alpha \in \mathcal{U}_d^r$

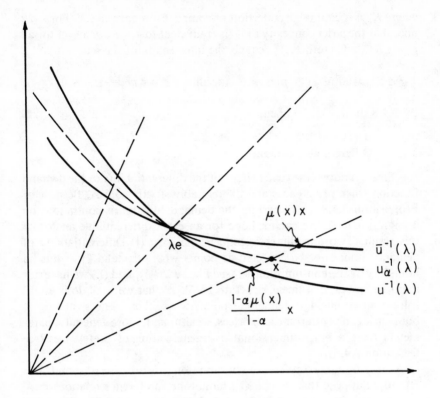

Figure 2.6.3

as follows. For $\alpha = 0, 1$ put $u_0 = u$, $u_1 = \bar{u}$. For $0 < \alpha < 1$ let $0 < \mu(x) < 1/\alpha$ be the unique solution to

$$\bar{u}(\mu(x)x) - u\left(\frac{1 - \alpha\mu(x)}{1 - \alpha}x\right) = 0 \cdot$$

Put then $u_\alpha(x) = \bar{u}(\mu(x)x)$. What u_α does is to assign to every number $\lambda > 0$ an indifference manifold $u_\alpha^{-1}(\lambda)$, which, radially, is the α convex combination of $\bar{u}^{-1}(\lambda)$ and $u^{-1}(\lambda)$. See Figure 2.6.3 and remember that $\bar{u}(\lambda e) = u(\lambda e) = 1$. It is not difficult to verify that $(u, \alpha) \mapsto u_\alpha$ constitutes a contraction of $\mathcal{P}_{sc}^r$; that is, it is continuous and $u_\alpha \in \mathcal{P}_{sc}^r$ whenever $u \in \mathcal{P}_{sc}^r$.

To see that $\mathcal{P}_{sc}^r$ is a G_δ set, that is, a countable intersection of open sets, we distinguish the cases $r < 2$ and $r \geq 2$. For $r \geq 2$ note that, in view of 2.6.4, $\mathcal{P}_{sc}^r$ equals the intersection of the open sets

$\{\gtrsim \in \mathcal{P}^r : \text{for an admissible } u \text{ and all } x \in K_n, \ \partial^2 u(x) \text{ is negative definite}\}$

where K_n is a countable collection of compact sets covering X. For $r < 2$ note that the strict convexity of $\succsim$ is equivalent to $\#\varphi(\succsim, p, w) = 1$ for all $p, w \in R_{++}^{\ell+1}$. Therefore, $\mathcal{P}_{sc}^r$ equals the intersection of the sets

$$\left\{ \succsim \in \mathcal{P}_{sm}^r : \text{radius } \varphi(\succsim, p, w) < \frac{1}{n} \text{ for all } \frac{1}{n} e \leq p \leq ne, \frac{1}{n} \leq w \leq n \right\}.$$

By 2.4.8 these sets are open.   ∎

2.7   Differentiable demand

It is time to address the central issue of the differentiability of the demand function when preferences are differentiably strictly convex. Because of Proposition 2.4.8 we know that the demand function is continuous on $\mathcal{P}_{sc}^2 \times R_{++}^\ell \times R_{++}$. We cannot hope for an exact differentiable analog of this result. Two impediments stand in the way: (i) Differentiability of demand should not be expected at points where demand "just hits" a boundary of the consumption set (see Figure 2.7.1), and (ii) we have not imposed any explicit linear structure on $\mathcal{P}_{sc}^2$. What we shall do is establish the smoothness of demand at points where there is no switching of boundaries and with respect to prices, wealth, and, more generally, parameters from a finite-dimensional parameterization of preferences (see Definition 2.4.6).

As in 2.6 our two reference consumption sets are $X = R_{++}^\ell$ and $X = R_+^\ell \backslash \{0\}$. Suppose that $\succsim$ is a C^1, monotone, preference relation on X and that $x \in \varphi(\succsim, p, w)$, $p \gg 0$, $w > 0$. Let $u : X \to R$ be a C^1 utility function for $\succsim$ with no critical point. Then x maximizes $u(z)$ on $b(p, w) \cap X$. Therefore, applying the first-order conditions D.1, we can find a $\lambda > 0$ such that

$$\begin{cases} \lambda \partial u(x) \leq p \\ [p - \lambda \partial u(x)] \cdot x = 0. \end{cases}$$

In other words, $\lambda \partial_h u(x) \leq p^h$ with equality if $x^h > 0$. We see in Figure 2.7.1 that $x^h = 0$ and $\lambda \partial_h u(x) = p^h$ can occur. We shall denote the situation $(\succsim, p, w, x)$ as regular whenever $\lambda \partial_h u(x) < p^h$ happens if and only if $x^h = 0$. The key fact is that at regular situations demand remains locally in the same coordinate subspace.

> **2.7.1. Definition.** *The point* $(\succsim, p, w) \in \mathcal{P}_{sc}^2 \times R_{++}^\ell \times R_{++}$ *is a regular point of demand if, letting u be a C^2 representation for $\succsim$ with no critical point and denoting $x = \varphi(\succsim, p, w)$ we can find a $\lambda > 0$ such that $\lambda \partial_h u(x) \leq p^h$ for every h with equality if and only if $x^h > 0$.*

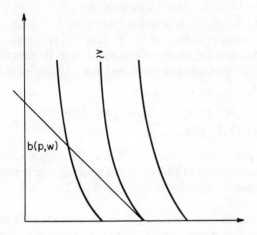

Figure 2.7.1

We then have:

2.7.2. Proposition. *Let* $(\succsim, p, w) \in \mathcal{P}_{sc}^r \times R_{++}^\ell \times R_{++}$ *be a regular point of demand. Then:*

(i)   *The demand function* $\varphi_\succsim : R_{++}^\ell \times (0, \infty) \to R^\ell$ *is* C^{r-1} *at* p, w.

(ii) *If* $\succsim_n \underset{r}{\to} \succsim$, $\succsim_n \in \mathcal{P}_{sc}^r$, *then* $\varphi_\succsim$ *converges to* φ C^{r-1} *uniformly on a neighborhood of* p, w.

(iii) *Given a* C^r *parameterization of preferences* $\xi : A \to \mathcal{P}_{sc}^r$, *with* $\xi(a) = \succsim$, *the demand function* $\varphi : A \times R_{++}^\ell \times (0, \infty) \to R^\ell$ *is* C^{r-1} *at* $(\xi(a), p, w)$.

(iv) *Let* $\xi_n \underset{r}{\to} \xi$, $\xi_n, \xi : A \to \mathcal{P}_{sc}^r$ *mean that* $U_n \underset{r}{\to} U$ *uniformly on compacta, where* $U_n, U : A \times X \to R$ *generate* ξ_n, ξ. *Suppose that* $\xi(a) = \succsim$. *Then* φ_n *converges to* φ C^{r-1} *uniformly on a neighborhood of* (a, p, w).

Proof. Obviously (i) [resp. (ii)] is a particular case of (iii) [resp. (iv)].

To prove (iii) let $x = \varphi(a, p, w)$ and pick a C^r function $U : A \times X \to R$ that generates ξ. Neglecting from the variables x and p the coordinates with null demand we know that $x' = \varphi(a', p', w')$ can be obtained in a neighborhood of (a, p, w) as the solution in the variables x', λ' to the system

$$\begin{cases} \partial_x U(a', x') - \lambda' p' = 0 \\ -p' \cdot x' + w' = 0. \end{cases}$$

Note that $\lambda' \neq 0$. By the IFT (C.3.2) the function that assigns (x', λ') to (a', p', w') will be C^r in a sufficiently small neighborhood of (a, p, w) if and *only if* the Jacobian determinant of the system at (x, λ, a, p, w) is not null. But using 2.5.1 and the observation that if $\gtrsim$ is differentiably strictly convex, then it remains so when restricted to any coordinate subspace, this determinant is

$$\begin{vmatrix} \partial_x^2 U(a, x) & -p \\ -p^T & 0 \end{vmatrix} = \begin{vmatrix} \partial_x^2 U(a, x) & -(1/\lambda)\partial_x U(a, x) \\ -(1/\lambda)[\partial_x U(a, x)]^T & 0 \end{vmatrix} = \alpha c_{a, x} \neq 0$$

where $c_{a, x}$ is the Gaussian curvature and $\alpha \neq 0$ is some constant. Statement (iv) is a simple consequence of (iii) once it is realized that the derivatives of φ can be computed explicitly from ξ. See C.3.2.   ■

The previous proof makes clear that if $\varphi(\gtrsim, p, w) \gg 0$, then the property that $x = \varphi(\gtrsim, p, w)$ is a regular point, that is, $c_x \neq 0$, is a necessary condition for the differentiability of demand.

It is worth putting on record that even if, on account of boundaries, the demand function may fail to be differentiable, it is nevertheless always Lipschitzian.

> **2.7.3. Proposition.** *Given a C^r parameterization of preferences $\xi: A \to \mathcal{P}_{sc}^r$ the demand function $\varphi: A \times R_{++}^\ell \times (0, \infty) \to R^\ell$ is Lipschitzian.*

Proof. It suffices to show this locally. Hence, take a fixed $(\bar{a}, \bar{p}, \bar{w}) \in A \times R_{++}^\ell \times (0, \infty)$ and for every nontrivial coordinate subspace L of R^ℓ that includes $\varphi(\bar{a}, \bar{p}, \bar{w})$, let φ_L be the C^{r-1} function defined as in the proof of 2.7.2; that is, φ_L is the demand function obtained by restricting consumption to L and dropping the remaining nonnegativity constraints. Because φ is continuous (2.4.8) and, locally, $\varphi(a, p, w) \in \bigcup_L \varphi_L(a, p, w)$, we conclude that φ is Lipschitzian (see G.1).   ■

We conclude this section by introducing and discussing three important concepts derived from the demand function: the *indirect utility function,* the *expenditure function,* and the *substitution matrix.*

Consider a fixed preference relation $\gtrsim \in \mathcal{P}_{sc}^2$. To simplify notation, let $\varphi(p, w) = \varphi(\gtrsim, p, w)$, $g = g_\gtrsim$ and pick a fixed C^2 utility representation u for $\gtrsim$ with no critical point.

> **2.7.4. Definition.** *The indirect utility function $v: R_{++}^\ell \times R_{++} \to X$ is defined by $v(p, w) = u(\varphi(p, w))$.*

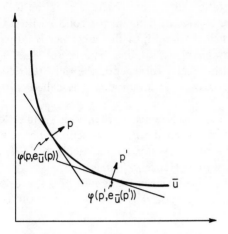

Figure 2.7.2

2.7.5. Definition. *For every $\bar{u} \in u(X)$ the expenditure function $e_{\bar{u}}: R_{++}^{\ell} \to R$ is defined by $e_{\bar{u}}(p) = \min\{p \cdot x : u(x) \geq \bar{u}\}$. See Figure 2.7.2.*

For fixed $\bar{u}$, the expenditure function is nothing but the negative of the support function of the convex set $\{x \in X : u(v) \geq \bar{u}\}$. Hence it provides a complete description of the preference relation $\succsim$ in the sense that if so desired, $\succsim$ can be recovered from the family of functions e_u; see F.3. From the general properties of support functions (see F.3.1, F.3.2) we get:

2.7.6. Proposition. *For fixed $\bar{u}$,*

(i) $e_{\bar{u}}: R_{++}^{\ell} \to R$ *is a concave function.*

(ii) $e_{\bar{u}}: R_{++} \to R$ *is C^1 and $\partial e_{\bar{u}}(p) = x$, where $u(x) \geq \bar{u}$ and $p \cdot x = e_{\bar{u}}(p)$; that is, $\partial e_{\bar{u}}(p) = \varphi(p, e_{\bar{u}}(p))$. See Figure 2.7.2.*

Suppose that $(\succsim, p, e_{\bar{u}}(p))$ is a regular point of demand. Then by 2.7.2 and 2.7.6.ii $e_{\bar{u}}$ is C^2 at p and $\partial^2 e_{\bar{u}}(p) = \partial_p \varphi(p, w) + \partial_w \varphi(p, w) \varphi(p, w)^T$. The remarkable characteristic of this matrix is that it involves only the demand function and not the utility function or any other characteristics of preferences.

2.7.7. Definition. *If the demand function is differentiable at (p, w) the matrix $\partial_p \varphi(p, w) + \partial_w \varphi(p, w) \varphi(p, w)^T$ is denoted $S(p, w)$ and called the substitution matrix.*

The economic interpretation of the matrix $S(p, w)$ is the following: The entry ij measures the change of demand for good i with a change of the price of good j when the wealth of the consumer is adjusted so as to compensate for any change of utility. The vector $\partial_w \varphi(p, w)$ is called the vector of wealth effects. In general, the only restriction on $\partial_w \varphi(p, w)$ is that $p \cdot \partial_w \varphi(p, w) = 1$. Commodity j is called *normal* at p, w if $\partial_w \varphi^j(p, w) > 0$.

Since $S(p, w) = \partial^2 e_{\bar{u}}(p)$ and $e_{\bar{u}}$ is concave, $S(p, w)$ is symmetric, negative semidefinite (F.3.3). It cannot be negative definite because there is a built-in singularity. Indeed, $p \cdot \varphi(p, w) = w$ yields $p \cdot \partial_p \varphi(p, w) = -\varphi(p, w)^T$ and $p \cdot \partial_w \varphi(p, w) = 1$. Hence $p \cdot S(p, w) = 0$.

It makes sense to ask if $S(p, w)$ is negative definite on a space complementary to p, in particular on $T_p = \{v \in R^\ell : p \cdot v = 0\}$, the space into which $S(p, w)$ maps.

2.7.8. Proposition. *The matrix $S(p, w)$ is negative semidefinite and it is negative definite on T_p provided $\varphi(p, w) \gg 0$.*

Proof. The first claim has already been proved. As for the second note that for $q \in S = \{q \in R_{++}^\ell : \|q\| = 1\}$ we have the identity $g(\partial e_{\bar{u}}(q)) = q$, where $\partial e_{\bar{u}}$ is looked at as a map from S to $I_{\bar{u}} = \{x \in X : u(x) = \bar{u}\}$ and g as a map from $I_{\bar{u}}$ to S. Therefore, if we let i be the identity map on T_p, we have $(\partial g \mid T_p) \circ (\partial^2 e_{\bar{u}}(p) \mid T_p) = i$. Observe that $\partial^2 e_{\bar{u}}(p) = S(p, w)$ maps into T_p. Hence, $\partial^2 e_{\bar{u}}(p) \mid T_p$ is nonsingular. In fact, the determinant of $\partial^2 e_{\bar{u}}(p) \mid T_p$ is the inverse of the determinant of $\partial g \mid T_p$, which by definition is $(-1)^{\ell+1} c_{\varphi(p, w)} \neq 0$. ∎

Finally, we state some of the remarkable properties of the indirect utility function.

2.7.9. Proposition. *The indirect utility function v is quasi-convex, that is, $\{(p, w) : v(p, w) \leq \bar{v}\}$ is convex for all v. Moreover, if v is C^1 at $(\bar{p}, \bar{w})$, then:*

(i) $\partial_w v(\bar{p}, \bar{w}) = -(1/w) p \cdot \partial_p v(\bar{p}, \bar{w})$.

(ii) $\varphi(\bar{p}, \bar{w}) = -[1/\partial_w v(\bar{p}, \bar{w})] \partial_p v(\bar{p}, \bar{w})$.

Proof. For quasi-convexity let $v(p, w), v(p', w') \leq \bar{v}$ and take $1 \leq \alpha \leq 1$. Denote $x = \varphi(\alpha p + (1 - \alpha) p', \alpha w + (1 - \alpha) w')$. Because

$$[\alpha p + (1 - \alpha) p'] \cdot x = \alpha w + (1 - \alpha) w',$$

we must have either $p \cdot x \leq w$ or $p' \cdot x \leq w'$. Say that $p \cdot x \leq w$. Then

$$v(\alpha p + (1-\alpha)p', \alpha w + (1-\alpha)w') = u(x) \leq u(\varphi(p,w)) = v(p,w) \leq \bar{v}.$$

Hence v is quasi-convex.

For (i) simply note that $v(\lambda \bar{p}, \lambda \bar{w}) - v(\bar{p}, \bar{w}) = 0$ for all $\lambda > 0$. Hence, (i) follows differentiating with respect to λ and evaluating at $\lambda = 1$. For (ii) differentiate the identity $v(p, e_{\bar{v}}(p)) = \bar{v}$ and take into account $\partial e_{\bar{v}}(\bar{p}) = \varphi(\bar{p}, \bar{w})$. ∎

Clearly, the family of expenditure functions can be recovered from the indirect utility function. Hence, it is always possible to go back from the indirect to the direct utility functions. It is a notable fact, however, that this can be done in a manner that is in exact analogy (i.e., in "duality") to the method used to generate the indirect from the direct utility function. Namely, for every $x \gg 0$ let $p(x)$ be the *minimizer* of $v(p,1)$ on $\{p : p \cdot x \leq 1\}$. Then we always have $u(x) = v(p(x), 1)$.

2.8   Approximation theory

In this section we will deal with a point of technical and conceptual interest. Consider the $\mathcal{P}_{sc}^r$ spaces of preferences. We have $\mathcal{P}_{sc}^\infty \subset \mathcal{P}_{sc}^r \subset \mathcal{P}_{sc}^0$. For $\infty \geq r' > r \geq 0$, $\mathcal{P}_{sc}^{r'}$ is a space of smoother objects than $\mathcal{P}_{sc}^r$ and is correspondingly endowed with a stronger $C^{r'}$-type topology. It should be a basic criterion of adequacy for our topological structures that a "smoothing" notion be defined on $\mathcal{P}_{sc}^r$, that is, that any preference in $\mathcal{P}_{sc}^r$ be approximable by an element of $\mathcal{P}_{sc}^{r'}$, $r' > r$, and, in particular, of $\mathcal{P}_{sc}^\infty$. More precisely: $\mathcal{P}_{sc}^\infty$ should be dense in $\mathcal{P}_{sc}^r$. Of special significance is that $\mathcal{P}_{sc}^\infty$ be dense in $\mathcal{P}_c^0 = \{\succeq \in \mathcal{P}^0 : \succeq \text{ is convex}\}$, and this for two reasons: (i) As it should be, our whole smoothness setup and corresponding differentiable approach can then be interpreted as being in the nature of a regularity hypothesis; and (ii) many of the results to be established in $\mathcal{P}_{sc}^r$ hold true, then, in $\mathcal{P}_c^0$ by continuity. In fact, it is often the case that the shortest way to prove a theorem in a continuity framework is via smoothing and differentiability methods.

In this section we put on record that $\mathcal{P}_{sc}^\infty$ is indeed dense in $\mathcal{P}_c^0$. Our method of proof proceeds by using concave utility representations. One shows first that the approximation problem is trivial for preferences representable by concave utility functions. So the problem reduces to proving (and this is a fact of independent interest) that preferences representable by concave utility functions are dense. For $r \geq 2$ this has almost been established in Proposition 2.6.4. For $r = 0$ we shall prove it. We shall skip the case $r = 1$, not because of any special difficulty, but because it requires a special treatment, and the space $\mathcal{P}^1$ is not important. To be useful, smooth preferences have to be at least of class C^2.

> **2.8.1. Proposition.** *Let $\succsim$ be a preference relation on X that is representable by a utility function $u \colon X \to R$ such that for a given compact, convex set $K \subset X$ and a convex, open neighborhood V of K, u coincides on K with a C^r, $r \geq 0$, concave, increasing function v defined on V. Then there is a sequence $\succsim_n \in \mathcal{P}^\infty_{sc}$ having C^∞, concave, utility representations u_n such that $u_n \,|\, K \to u \,|\, K$.*

Proof. Let $v \colon R^\ell \to R$ be an increasing, concave function such that v equals u on a neighborhood of K. This v could be obtained as follows. Let $K \subset V' \subset V$, where V' is open, convex and $\mathrm{cl}\, V' \subset V$. Take $Q = \{(q,s) \in R^{\ell+1} \colon v(x) \leq q \cdot x + s$ for all $x \in V$ and $v(x) = q \cdot z + s$ for some $z \in V'\}$. Put then $v'(z) = \inf\{q \cdot y + s \colon (q,s) \in Q\}$; see F.3.

Pick a sequence $\xi_n \colon R^\ell \to R$ of C^∞ density functions with support containing the origin and radius $\leq 1/n$. Such a sequence exists by H.4.3. Define $u'_n \colon R^\ell \to R$ by the convolution $u'_n(x) = \int_R v(x-z)\,\xi_n(z)\,dz$. Then u'_n is C^∞ and $u'_n \,|\, K \to u \,|\, K$. Moreover, u'_n is concave and increasing; see H.4.4. To conclude, let $u_n(x) = u'_n(x) + (1/n)[\sum_{h=1}^\ell \ln(x^h + \delta)]$, where $\delta = 0$ or 1 according to whether $\mathcal{P} = \mathcal{P}_b$ or $\mathcal{P}_{cl}$. Of course, $u_n \,|\, K \to u \,|\, K$ and u_n is differentiably strictly concave [because so is $\sum_{h=1}^\ell \ln(x^h + \delta)$ and $u'_n(x)$ is concave], increasing, and, in the case $\mathcal{P} = \mathcal{P}_b$, satisfies the boundary condition. Hence the preferences $\succsim_n$ represented by u_n belong to $\mathcal{P}^\infty_{sc}$. Note that u_n being differentiably strictly concave means that, for all x, $\partial^2 u_n(x)$ is negative definite on R^ℓ, and also, a fortiori, on T_x. ∎

> **2.8.2. Proposition.** *For every $r \geq 2$, $\mathcal{P}^\infty_{sc}$ is dense in $\mathcal{P}^r_{sc}$.*

Proof. Combine Propositions 2.6.4 and 2.8.1. ∎

> **2.8.3. Proposition.** *$\mathcal{P}^\infty_{sc}$ is dense in $\mathcal{P}^0_c$.*

Proof. Let $\succsim \in \mathcal{P}^0_c$ and v be the continuous utility function for $\succsim$ defined by $x \sim v(x)e$. This is, of course, the familiar normalized utility. In general, given any utility u for a monotone preference we denote by $\hat{u}$ the equivalent normalized utility; that is, $\hat{u}(x)$ is defined by $u(x) = u(\hat{u}(x)e)$.

We shall find a sequence of increasing, concave functions $u_n \colon X \to R$ such that $\hat{u}_n \to v$ uniformly on compacta. The conclusion is then a straightforward consequence of Proposition 2.8.1 and the definition of the topology on preferences (see 2.4).

We begin by showing that given any finite set $K = \{x_1, \ldots, x_n\} \subset X$ of points no two of which are indifferent, there is an increasing concave function $u: R^{\ell} \to R$ such that $u \mid K$ is a utility function for $\succsim \cap K \times K$.

Without loss of generality, we can assume $x_n > \cdots > x_2 > x_1$. By convexity and monotonicity of $\succsim$ we can pick $q_1, \ldots, q_n \in R_+^{\ell}$ such that if $z > x_j$, $z \in K$, then $q_j \cdot z > q_j \cdot x_j$. Consider the following induction hypothesis: "There is an increasing concave function $u: R^{\ell} \to R$ such that $u(x_1) < \cdots < u(x_j)$ and $u(x_h) > u(x_j)$ for $h > j$." Clearly, this is true for $j = 1$ [take $u(x) = q_1 \cdot x$]. Let it be true for a given j. Take $\mu \in R$ such that $u(x_j) < \mu < \min_{h > j} u(x_h)$ and for unspecified $\lambda > 0$ define $u_{\lambda}: R^{\ell} \to R$ by $u_{\lambda}(x) = \min\{u(x), \lambda q_{j+1} \cdot (x - x_{j+1}) + \mu\}$. Then u_{λ} is concave and weakly monotone. If λ is sufficiently small, $u(x_h) < \lambda q_{j+1} \cdot (x_h - x_{j+1}) + \mu$ for $h \leq j$. Hence, $u_{\lambda}(x_h) = u(x_h)$ for $h \leq j$ and $u_{\lambda}(x_{j+1}) = \mu > u(x_j)$. On the other hand, if $h > j + 1$, then $x_h > x_{j+1}$, which implies $q_{j+1} \cdot (x_h - x_{j+1}) > 0$; that is, $\lambda q_{j+1} \cdot (x_h - x_{j+1}) + \mu > \mu$ for $h > j + 1$. Therefore, $u_{\lambda}(x_h) > \mu = u(x_{j+1})$ for $h > j + 1$. So the induction hypothesis holds for $j + 1$. We conclude that there is an increasing, concave function u such that $u(x_1) < \cdots < u(x_n)$.

It is now obvious how to proceed. Let K_n be an increasing sequence of sets chosen as above and such that $\bigcup_n K_n$ is dense in X. Take $u_n: X \to R$ to be the function obtained in the previous paragraph for K_n. To verify that $\hat{u}_n \to v$ uniformly on compacta, note that u_n, v are increasing and that the orderings induced by u_n and v on K_n are identical. ■

2.9 Demand theory without preferences

We now abstract from the fact that demand functions come from preferences. In this section *we say that* $\varphi: R_{++}^{\ell} \times R_{++} \to X$ *is a demand function if it is continuous and, for every* (p, w), *it satisfies the conditions:* (i) $p \cdot \varphi(p, w) = w$ and (ii) $\varphi(\lambda p, \lambda w) = \varphi(p, w)$ for $\lambda > 0$. Condition (ii) implies that without loss of generality we could restrict our entire discussion to $w = 1$. We shall do so whenever convenient.

Suppose that φ is C^1. Because the computation of the substitution matrix (2.7.7) at (p, w) involves only the demand function we can still define it, that is $S(p, w) = \partial_p \varphi(p, w) + \partial_w \varphi(p, w) \varphi(p, w)^T$. Even more, it can still be interpreted as a matrix of wealth-compensated demand effects. Indeed, the ij term is simply the effect on the demand of i of a change of the price of j when wealth is adjusted so as to leave the vector $\varphi(p, w)$ just affordable; that is, "real wealth" is kept fixed. Geometrically, the budget hyperplane goes through $\varphi(p, w)$ before and after the change.

2.9.1. Definition. *The matrix $S(p, w)$ is negative quasi-semidefinite, if $v \cdot S(p, w) v \leq 0$ for all $v \in R^{\ell}$. If the inequality is strict for $v \in T_p$, $v \neq 0$, we say that $S(p, w)$ is negative quasi-definite on T_p.*

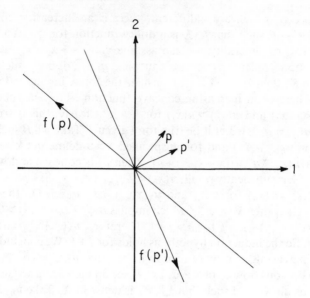

Figure 2.9.1

Except for symmetry these are the definitions of, respectively, negative semidefiniteness and definiteness. We saw that for demand functions originating in preferences the matrix $S(p, w)$ would be (i) symmetric and (ii) negative quasisemidefinite. The first condition is difficult to interpret in economic terms directly from the demand function. The second, however, is straightforward. It is simply a *generalized,* coordinate-free version of the *law of demand:* If a price increases, the corresponding compensated demand decreases. Summarizing: If we wished that the only foundation for our theory of individual demand was this generalized law of demand, then the appropriate class of C^1 demand functions are the ones whose substitution matrices satisfy Definition 2.9.1.

> **2.9.2. Definition.** *Let $J \subset R^\ell_{++} \times R_{++}$ be a nonempty set. We say that the demand function $\varphi : R^\ell_{++} \times (0, \infty) \to X$ satisfies the weak axiom of revealed preference (WA) over J if for any $(p, w), (p', w') \in J$ we cannot have $p' \cdot \varphi(p, w) \leq w'$ whenever $p \cdot \varphi(p', w') \leq w$ and $\varphi(p', w') \neq \varphi(p, w)$.*

The situation ruled out in the above definition is illustrated in Figure 2.9.1. The interpretation of the weak axiom as a consistency of choice condition is clear: If $x = \varphi(p, w)$ is "revealed preferred" to $x' = \varphi(p', w')$, that is, $x \neq x'$ and $p \cdot x' \leq w$, then x' cannot be revealed preferred to x. If φ originates in preferences, then the weak axiom is obviously satisfied. The converse, however, is not true. As it turns out, for C^1 demand functions the weak axiom is closely related to the generalized law of demand. It amounts to the formulation of the latter that uses finite, rather than infinitesimal, price changes, In particular, the weak axiom has no implication whatsoever for the symmetry of substitution matrices. All this is made precise in the next proposition. (*Note:* In the proposition the restriction to a set J is made only for later reference. For present purposes it should read as if $J = R^\ell_{++}$.)

2.9.3. Proposition. *Let* $J \subset R^{\ell+1}_{++}$ *be a* C^1 *manifold and* $\varphi: R^{\ell+1}_{++} \to X$ *be a* C^1 *demand function. For every* $(p, w) \in J$ *denote* $L_{p, w} = \{v \in R^\ell: \text{there is a } C^1 \text{ path } (p(t), w(t)) \in J \text{ with } p(0) = p, \ w(0) = w, \ \partial p(0) = v, \ \partial w(0) = v \cdot \varphi(p, w) \text{ and } w(t) \geq p(t) \cdot \varphi(p, w) \text{ for } t \leq \epsilon, \text{ some } \epsilon > 0\}$. *Note: if* $J = R^{\ell+1}_{++}$, *then* $L_{p, w} = R^\ell$. *We have:*

(i) *If* φ *satisfies the weak axiom over* J, *then, for every* $(p, w) \in J$, $S(p, w)$ *is negative quasi-definite on* $L_{p, w}$; *that is,* $v \cdot S(p, w)v \leq 0$ *for* $v \in L_{p, w}$.

Conversely:

(ii) *Let* J *be convex. If, for every* $(p, w) \in J$, $S(p, w)$ *is negative quasi-definite on* $L_{p, w} \cap T_p$, *that is,* $v \cdot S(p, w)v < 0$ *whenever* $v \in L_{p, w}$, $p \cdot v = 0$ *and* $v \neq 0$, *then* φ *satisfies the weak axiom over* J.

Proof. (i) For given $p(0), w(0) \in J$, $v \in L_{p(0), w(0)}$ and small $\epsilon > 0$, let $p(t), w(t): (-\epsilon, \epsilon) \to J$ be an admissible path. Denote $x(t) = \varphi(p(t), w(t))$. Choose arbitrary $t' < 0$, $t > 0$. By the weak axiom we can assume that $w(t) \leq p(t) \cdot x(t')$. By hypothesis we have $w(t) \geq p(t) \cdot x(0)$. By continuity there is an $s \in [0, t']$ such that $w(t) = p(t) \cdot x(s)$. Because of the weak axiom we must have $w(s) \leq p(s) \cdot x(t)$. Therefore,

$$\frac{1}{(t-s)^2}[p(t) - p(s)] \cdot [x(t) - x(s)] = \frac{1}{(t-s)^2}[w(s) - p(s) \cdot x(t)] \leq 0.$$

Taking limits as $\epsilon \to 0$ we get $v \cdot S(p(0), w(0))v \leq 0$.

(ii) Suppose the weak axiom is violated for the pair $(p, w), (p', w') \in J$. For $t \in [0, 1]$ denote $p(t) = tp + (1-t)p'$, $w(t) = tw + (1-t)w'$, $x(t) = \varphi(p(t), w(t))$. We have $p(t) \cdot x(0) \leq w(t)$, $p(t) \cdot x(1) \leq w(0)$ for all t. If $p(1) \cdot x(t) \neq w(1)$ for some $t < 1$ we must have $p(0) \cdot x(t) < w(0)$ or $p(1) \cdot x(t) < w(1)$. So, relabeling if necessary, we can assume without loss of generality that either $p(1) \cdot x(0) < w(1)$ or $p(1) \cdot x(1) = w(t)$ for all t. In either case $\bar{t} = \sup\{t: p(1) \cdot x(t') \leq w(1) \text{ for } t' \leq t\}$ is strictly positive.

We argue now that $p(\bar{t}) \cdot x(t) \le w(\bar{t})$ and $p(t) \cdot x(\bar{t}) = w(t)$ for $0 < t < \bar{t}$. Indeed, $p(t) \cdot x(t) = w(t)$ and $p(1) \cdot x(t) \le w(1)$ yields $p(0) \cdot x(t) \ge w(0)$. This and $t < \bar{t}$ gives $p(\bar{t}) \cdot x(t) \le w(\bar{t})$. From the definition of $\bar{t}$, $p(1) \cdot x(\bar{t}) = w(1)$. This and $p(\bar{t}) \cdot x(\bar{t}) = w(\bar{t})$ yields $p(0) \cdot x(\bar{t}) = w(0)$. Hence, $p(t) \cdot x(\bar{t}) = w(t)$.

For $t < \bar{t}$ we then have

$$\frac{1}{(\bar{t}-t)^2}[p(t) - p(\bar{t})] \cdot [x(t) - x(\bar{t})] = \frac{1}{(t-t)^2}[w(\bar{t}) - p(\bar{t}) \cdot x(t)] \ge 0.$$

Letting $t \to \bar{t}$ we get $v \cdot S(p(\bar{t}), w(\bar{t}))v \ge 0$ for a $v \in L_{p(\bar{t}), w(\bar{t})}$, which contradicts the negative quasi-definiteness hypothesis.   ∎

2.10   Reference notes

The material covered in this chapter has a long tradition. Classical references are Pareto (1909), Hicks (1939), and Samuelson (1947). General texts are Kartzner (1970), Barten–Böhm (1982), and Diewert (1982). A modern treatment and extensive references can be found in Chipman–Hurwicz–Richter–Sonnenschein (1971), from which, incidentally, the title of the chapter is borrowed.

The most immediate and heavy influence in this chapter is Debreu (1972, 1976a).

Section 2.2. See Debreu (1959, chap. 2), or Arrow and Hahn (1971, chap. 4) for an extensive discussion of the basic concepts.

Section 2.3. The definition of smooth preference (2.3.4), the emphasis on the normalized gradient function (2.3.12), and the boundary condition (2.3.16) are all due to Debreu (1972, 1976a). See also Mas-Colell (1977c). The treatment of utility representation theorems in Debreu (1972) emphasizes an integrability approach that has a classical tradition in economics but that we leave aside.

Section 2.4. Spaces of continuous preferences are discussed extensively in W. Hildenbrand (1974). For the spaces of smooth preferences we rely on Mas-Colell (1974). The normalized utility functions (2.4.3) appeared in Wold (1953) and then in Kannai (1970), where they were already used for the study of topological properties of spaces of preferences.

Section 2.5. The use of bordered Hessians to characterize optima is old; see, for example, Hicks (1939) and Samuelson (1947). The introduction of the Gaussian curvature into consumer theory is due to Debreu (1972).

Section 2.6. The concavifiability problem, that is, the representation of convex preferences by concave functions, has been extensively studied. The earlier references are de Finetti (1949) and Fenchel (1953, 1956).

More recently see Aumann (1975) and the very thorough investigation of Kannai (1977). The contractibility of general spaces of preferences has been studied by Chichilnisky (1976).

Section 2.7. The essence of differentiability proposition 2.7.2, an application of the implicit function theorem, is old. See, for example, Samuelson (1947), where the term *regular optimum* is also used. An example of nondifferentiable demand with smooth, strictly convex (but, of course, not differentiably strictly convex) preferences can be found in Kartzner (1968). For a deeper analysis of the demand function when boundary consumption is possible, see Schecter (1978). For a more extensive exposition on the demand function, the substitution (or Slutsky) matrix, the expenditure function, the indirect utility function, and, more generally, the dual approach to consumer theory, see Diewert (1982). Classical references are Antonelli (1886), Slutsky (1915), Hicks (1939), Hotelling (1935), Roy (1942), and McKenzie (1957).

Section 2.8. The general topic was studied in Mas-Colell (1974). Proposition 2.8.3 appeared in Kannai (1974) and Mas-Colell (1974). A different proof was obtained by Delbaen (private communication – 1972). The key part of Proposition 2.8.1 (the approximability by concavifiable preferences) can also be found in an unpublished paper by Mantel (1969).

Section 2.9. The weak axiom of revealed preference is due to Samuelson (1938, 1948), who also perceived its close relationship with the negative quasi-definiteness of the substitution matrix. The treatment here follows Kihlstrom–Mas-Colell–Sonnenschein (1976).

CHAPTER 3

Production sets

3.1 Introduction

In this chapter we introduce the basic concept of the production set of an economy and discuss some of its properties (Section 3.2). We shall describe how the production set can be viewed as the aggregate of a population of firm-specific technologies (Section 3.3). Associated with each production set we will define a number of derived, but nevertheless important, concepts such as the distance function, the normal manifold, and the profit function (Section 3.4). Finally, smoothness concepts and hypotheses (Sections 3.5 and 3.6), examples (Section 3.7), and a notion of proximity for production sets (Section 3.8) are discussed.

3.2 Production sets and efficient productions

The technological possibilities open to an economy are represented by a set $Y \subset R^\ell$, called the *production set,* of feasible input–output, or production, vectors. If $y \in Y$, then it is understood that it is technologically possible to produce the output vector defined by $\max\{y_i, 0\}$ by using the input vector defined by $\max\{-y_i, 0\}$.

The production vectors of particular interest are those where there is no waste in output production or input use. Formally:

> **3.2.1. Definition.** *The production vector $y \in Y$ is efficient if $y' \geq y$ and $y' \in Y$ implies $y' = y$.*

Throughout most of this book, the production set will be assumed to satisfy four basic properties:

(I) Y is closed.
(II) $Y \cap R^\ell_+ = \{0\}$.
(III) Y is convex.
(IV) $-R^\ell_+ \subset Y$.

96

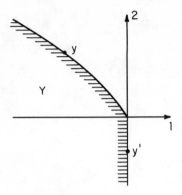

Figure 3.2.1

Of these, (I) is merely technical, but (II), (III) and (IV) have sub-stance. Condition (II) says that inactivity is possible and that it is not feasible to produce a positive amount of some commodity without using any input. Condition (III) has a familiar diversification interpretation: If $y_1, y_2 \in Y$, then it is possible to simultaneously operate y_1 and y_2 at half-level and without interference; that is, $\frac{1}{2}y_1 + \frac{1}{2}y_2 \in Y$. Finally, (IV) is the free disposal of commodities hypothesis. It is strong and by no means es-sential to the theory developed in this book. Still, since no special issues are raised by dispensing with it, we prefer to maintain the ease of exposi-tion and keep it. Figure 3.2.1 illustrates a typical production set. In the figure the production vector y is efficient, whereas y' is not.

Special assumptions that will be made from time to time are:

(V) Y is a pointed cone; that is:
   (i)   if $y \in Y$, then $\alpha y \in Y$ for any $\alpha > 0$, and
   (ii)   if $y \in Y$, $y \neq 0$, then $-y \notin Y$.

By the separating hyperplane theorem, if (III) and (V) are satisfied, then there is a $p \in R^\ell$ such that $p \cdot y < 0$ whenever $y \in Y$, $y \neq 0$ (F.2.1). Of course, (V.i) is the familiar constant returns to scale hypothesis, whereas (V.ii) is usually interpreted as asserting the irreversibility of feasible tech-nologies. It is not a restrictive assumption. A production set satisfying (V) is illustrated in Figure 3.2.2.

(VI) Y is a polyhedral cone.

Hypothesis (VI) asserts that the aggregate production set is formed from a finite number of elementary *activities* $\{a_1, \ldots, a_m\} \subset R$ that can be operated at any nonnegative scale; that is, $Y = \{\sum_{i=1}^m \alpha_i a_i : \alpha_i \geq 0\}$.

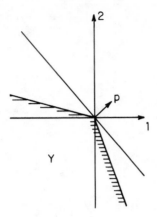

Figure 3.2.2

3.3   From individual to aggregate production sets

The production set can be viewed as a representation of the state of technological knowledge available in the long run. Alternatively, it can be interpreted in more short-run terms as the aggregate input–ouput vectors that are feasible given a population of individual production units. This section is devoted to illustrate the latter viewpoint. No essential use will be made of its content in later developments and it can therefore be skipped without harm.

Suppose we have a population of firms $[0, s]$, $s > 0$. Every firm $t \in [0, s]$ has an individual production set $Y_t \in R^\ell$, that is, a set satisfying properties (I), (II), and (IV) of the previous section. Note that we do not require the convexity of Y_t. Three hypotheses will be made on the assignment $t \mapsto Y_t$. The first is purely technical, the second embodies the existence of a priori technological constraints, and the third limits the capacity of individual firms:

(i) $t \mapsto Y_t$ is a measurable correspondence; that is, it is measurable as a function $t \to \mathcal{C}(R^\ell)$; see A.5 and E.2.

(ii)   There is $q \gg 0$ such that $q \cdot Y_t \leq 0$ for a.e. $t \in [0, s]$.

(iii)   There is an integrable $\xi: [0, s] \to R$ such that $Y_t \leq \xi(t)e$ for a.e. $t \in [0, s]$.

By using the concept of the integral of a correspondence (see E.2.1) we can define the aggregate production set $Y = \int_0^s Y_t\, dt$. The interpretation of Y as the set of mean input–output vectors that are feasible in the aggregate is obvious.

3.3.1. Proposition. *The aggregate production set Y satisfies properties (I), (II), (III), and (IV) of the previous section. In particular, Y is convex.*

Proof. (I) follows from (iii) and E.2.1, (II) from (ii), (III) from L.1.3, and (IV) is obvious. ∎

Observe that in the present setup Y is bounded above and so it can never be precisely a cone. However, Y could be a cone in the relevant region, that is, the region bounded by the total availability of inputs to the economy.

3.4 Some derived constructions

Given a production set Y we will in this section introduce the closely related concepts of *distance function, projection function, normal manifold, profit function,* and *restricted profit function.*

Throughout this section *Y is assumed to be closed and convex.*

The *distance function* $\gamma: R^\ell \to R$ is defined by $\gamma(x) = \frac{1}{2} \min_{y \in Y} \|x - y\|^2$. The convexity of Y implies that for each x the minimum is reached at a single point; that is, there is a unique $\pi(x) \in Y$ such that $\gamma(x) = \frac{1}{2} \|x - \pi(x)\|^2$ (see F.2.3). This defines a new function $\pi: R^\ell \to Y$, which we shall call the *projection function.* It is illustrated in Figure 3.4.1.

3.4.1. Proposition. *The projection function π satisfies*

$$\|\pi(x) - \pi(y)\| \le \|x - y\| \quad \text{for any } x, y \in R^\ell.$$

In particular, π is Lipschitzian. The distance function $\gamma: R^\ell \to R$ is C^1 and convex. Moreover, $\partial \gamma(x) = x - \pi(x)$ at any $x \in R^\ell$.

Proof. These are general convexity facts. The properties of π follow from F.2.3. For the sake of completeness we give a proof for the properties of γ.

First, regarding convexity of γ: Let $x, z \in R^\ell$ and denote $x' = \pi(x)$, $z' = \pi(z)$. Then, for $0 \le t \le 1$,

$$\gamma(tx + (1-t)z) \le \frac{1}{2} \|[tx + (1-t)z] - [tx' + (1-t)z']\|^2$$

$$\le \frac{1}{2} [t\|x - x'\| + (1-t)\|z - z'\|]^2$$

$$\le \frac{1}{2} [t\|x - x'\|^2 + (1-t)\|z - z'\|^2]$$

$$= t\gamma(x) + (1-t)\gamma(z).$$

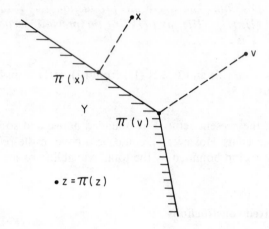

Figure 3.4.1

The first inequality follows by the definition of γ and the convexity of Y, the second by the triangle inequality, and the third by the convexity of the square function.

Once we know that γ is convex and π continuous, the fact that $x - \pi(x)$ is the gradient of γ at x follows if we show that

$$\gamma(x+v) \geq \gamma(x) + [x - \pi(x)] \cdot v \quad \text{for any } v \in R^{\ell}$$

(see F.3). Without loss of generality we can assume $\pi(x) = 0$ and $x \neq 0$. The fact that 0 is the element of Y closest to x implies that Y lies below the hyperplane $H = \{z : x \cdot z = 0\}$ and therefore $\gamma(x+v) \geq \frac{1}{2}\|\alpha x\|^2$, where α is chosen so that $x + v - \alpha x \in H$; see Figure 3.4.2.

Clearly, $\alpha = (x+v) \cdot x / \|x\|^2$ and so

$$\gamma(x+v) \geq \tfrac{1}{2}\|\alpha x\|^2 = \tfrac{1}{2}\frac{(\|x\|^2 + v \cdot x)^2}{\|x\|^2} = \tfrac{1}{2}\|x\|^2 + v \cdot x + \tfrac{1}{2}\frac{(v \cdot x)^2}{\|x\|^2}$$

$$\geq \tfrac{1}{2}\|x\|^2 + v \cdot x = \gamma(x) + v \cdot [x - \pi(x)]. \qquad \blacksquare$$

The *normal manifold* of Y is the subset of $R^{\ell} \times R^{\ell}$ defined by $\Gamma = \{(p, y) \in R^{\ell} \times Y : p \cdot y \geq p \cdot Y\}$.

Some observations are in order:

(i)   If $(p, y) \in \Gamma$, then $(\lambda p, y) \in \Gamma$ for any $\lambda \geq 0$.

(ii) If $y \in \text{Int } Y$, then $(p, y) \in \Gamma$ if and only if $p = 0$.

(iii) If $y \in \partial Y$, then $(p, y) \in \Gamma$ for some $p \neq 0$. This is a consequence of the supporting hyperplane theorem (F.2.1).

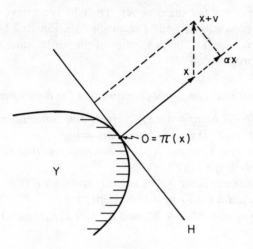

Figure 3.4.2

(iv)   If Y is a cone, then $p \cdot y \geq p \cdot Y$ and $y \in Y$ implies $p \cdot y = 0$. Hence, $p \cdot y = 0$ for all $(p, y) \in \Gamma$, and we can view $\Gamma \cap (S \times \partial Y)$ as a subset of $TS = \{(p, v) \in S \times R^\ell : p \cdot v = 0\}$, the tangent vector bundle of the sphere (see H.1.iii).

The relationship between Γ and the distance and projection functions is clear: (i) $(x - \pi(x), \pi(x)) \in \Gamma$ for all $x \in R^\ell$, and (ii) $y = \pi(y + p)$ for all $(p, y) \in \Gamma$.

The term *manifold* is justified:

> **3.4.2. Proposition.** *If Y is a production set, then Γ is homeomorphic to R^ℓ. Hence, Γ is a topological (that is, C^0) manifold of dimension ℓ.*

Proof. The map $(p, y) \mapsto p + y$ from Γ to R^ℓ is one-to-one. Indeed, let $p + y = p' + y'$ for $(p, y), (p', y') \in \Gamma$. Then

$$0 \geq -\|p - p'\|^2 = p' \cdot (p - p') - p \cdot (p - p') = p' \cdot (y' - y) - p \cdot (y' - y) \geq 0.$$

So $p = p'$ and $y = y'$. In fact, the map is onto and its inverse is

$$x \mapsto (x - \pi(x), \pi(x)).$$

We know from 3.4.1 that $\pi(\cdot)$ is continuous. ∎

We shall now introduce the important concept of the *profit function* associated with a production set Y.

Let $Y^* = \{p \in R^\ell : p \cdot Y < s \text{ for some } s \in R\}$. Then Y^* is a convex cone (see F.3). It is not necessarily closed. The profit function $\beta : Y^* \to R$ is defined by $\beta(p) = \sup_{y \in Y} p \cdot Y$. The properties of the profit function are gathered in the next proposition.

3.4.3. Proposition. *The profit function* $\beta : Y^* \to R$ *satisfies:*

(i) β *is a linear homogeneous, convex, and continuous function. If* $0 \in Y$, *then* β *is also nonnegative.*

(ii)   *The set* $\{y \in Y : p \cdot y = \beta(p)\}$ *is nonempty and compact if and only if* $p \in \text{Int } Y^*$.

(iii)   *The gradient vector* $\partial\beta(p)$ *exists if and only if* $\beta(p) = p \cdot y$ *for a unique* $y \in Y$. *In this case* $\partial\beta(p) = y$.

(iv)   *If* $p_n \to p$, $p_n \in Y^*$, $p \notin Y^*$, *and* $p_n \cdot y_n = \beta(p_n)$, $y_n \in Y$, *then* $\|y_n\| \to \infty$.

Proof. Because the profit function is simply the negative of the support function of $-Y$, the proposition follows from the general properties of support functions. See F.3.1 and F.3.2. ∎

The relationships of β with γ, π, and Γ are obvious:

3.4.4. Proposition. *We have:*

(i) $\beta(x - \pi(x)) = (x - \pi(x)) \cdot \pi(x)$ *for all* x.

(ii)   *If* $p \cdot y = \beta(p)$ *and* $y \in Y$, *then* $y = \pi(p + y)$ *and* $(p, y) \in \Gamma$.

(iii)   *If* $(p, y) \in \Gamma$, *then* $p \in Y^*$ *and* $p \cdot y = \beta(p)$.

It is sometimes of technical interest to consider the profit maximization problem when the production vector is required to satisfy some affine side constraints as, for example, that the output of a certain commodity be equal to one. Denote by $L \subset R^\ell$ the affine space determined by the constraints. Then the *restricted profit function* associated with Y and L is defined to be simply the profit function of the restricted production set $Y \cap L$.

3.5   Some differentiability facts and relations

In this section we put on record some of the relations between the differentiability properties of the distance function γ, the normal manifold Γ, and the profit function β associated with a given closed and convex production set Y.

We know from 3.4.1 that the distance function is C^1, convex, and satisfies $\partial\gamma(x) = x - \pi(x)$ at all x. Therefore, if γ is C^2, $\partial^2\gamma(x)$ is positive semidefinite. Equivalently, all the eigenvalues of $\partial^2\gamma(x)$ are nonnegative real numbers (see B.6). The next proposition tells us that those eigenvalues are, in fact, not larger than one or, in other words, that $I - \partial^2\gamma(x)$ is, again, positive semidefinite (B.6.2). Observe that $I - \partial^2\gamma(x) = \partial\pi(x)$. One implication of this is that, viewed as a matrix, $\partial\pi(x)$ is symmetric.

3.5.1. Proposition. *If γ is C^2 at x, then $\partial^2\gamma(x)$ and $\partial\pi(x) = I - \partial^2\gamma(x)$ are positive semidefinite. Moreover, $\partial\pi(x)v = 0$ and $\partial^2\gamma(x)v = v$ for $v = x - \pi(x)$.*

Proof. The positive semidefiniteness of $\partial^2\gamma(x)$ is a consequence of the convexity of γ (3.4.1, F.3.3).

Let $v \in R^\ell$ be small but otherwise arbitrary. By definition of γ,

$$\gamma(x+v) \le \tfrac{1}{2}\|x+v-\pi(x)\|^2 = \tfrac{1}{2}\|x-\pi(x)\|^2 + [x-\pi(x)]\cdot v + \tfrac{1}{2}\|v\|^2$$
$$= \gamma(x) + \partial\gamma(x)\cdot v + \tfrac{1}{2}\|v\|^2.$$

By Taylor's formula (C.4.1),

$$\gamma(x+v) = \gamma(x) + \partial\gamma(x)\cdot v + \tfrac{1}{2}\partial^2\gamma(x)(v,v) + o(\|v\|^2).$$

Hence $\partial^2\gamma(x)(v,v) + o(\|v\|^2) \le \|v\|^2$, which yields $\partial^2\gamma(x)(v,v) \le \|v\|^2 = v\cdot v$ or $[I - \partial^2\gamma(x)](v,v) \ge 0$.

For v in the direction $x - \pi(x)$ one obviously has $\pi(x+v) = \pi(x)$. Consequently, $\partial\pi(x)v = 0$ and $\partial^2\gamma(x)v = v$. ∎

The differentiability relationships between γ and Γ are gathered in the next proposition.

3.5.2. Proposition. *Given an $x \in R^\ell$ consider $(p, y) = (x - \pi(x), \pi(x))$. The function γ is C^2 at x if and only if Γ is a C^1 manifold at (p, y). Furthermore $T_{(p,y)}\Gamma = \{(I - \partial\pi(x), \partial\pi(x))v : v \in R^\ell\}$. Also, $u \cdot w \ge 0$ for all $(u, w) \in T_{(p,w)}\Gamma$.*

Proof. Let $Q: R^{2\ell} \to R^{2\ell}$ be the nonsingular linear map given by $(v, w) \mapsto (v - w, w)$. By definition Γ is nothing but the image under Q of the graph of the Lipschitzian function $x \mapsto \pi(x)$. Therefore, Γ is a C^1 manifold at $(p, y) = (x - \pi(x), \pi(x))$ if and only if π is C^1 at x (H.1.v). It is then clear that $T_{(p,y)}\Gamma$, if it exists, is given as in the statement of the proposition. Finally, let $(u, w) \in T_{(p,w)}\Gamma$; that is, $u = v - \partial\pi(x)v$, $w = \partial\pi(x)v$ for some

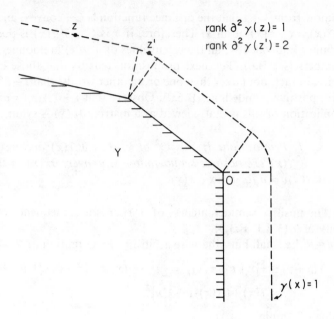

Figure 3.5.1

v. Then $u \cdot w = v \cdot (\partial \pi(x) - [\partial \pi(x)]^2) v \geq 0$ because, being that the eigenvalues of $\partial \pi(x)$ are not greater than one (3.5.1, B.6.2), $\partial \pi(x) - [\partial \pi(x)]^2$ is positive semidefinite (B.6.3). ∎

Suppose that Γ is a C^1 manifold at $(p, y) = (x - \pi(x), x)$. Then 3.5.2 assures us that the projection of $T_{(p, y)}\Gamma$ on the first ℓ coordinates equals the range of $I - \partial \pi(x) = \partial^2 \gamma(x)$. Hence the projection will be onto if and only if rank $\partial^2 \gamma(x) = \ell$, that is, if and only if all the eigenvalues of $\partial \pi(x)$ are strictly less than one. The geometric interpretation of the condition rank $\partial^2 \gamma(x) = \ell$ is clear. It means that γ is (differentiably) strictly convex at x. More specifically it means that in a neighborhood V of x the projection map π is a contraction; that is, for some $k < 1$, $\|\pi(z) - \pi(z')\| \leq k\|z - z'\|$ for $z, z' \in V$. Phrased another way, it says that $\pi(V) \subset \partial Y$ is curved, that is, contains no region that can be first-order-approximated by a segment. See Figure 3.5.1. Note that, in general, rank $\partial^2 \gamma(x) = \ell$ is entirely compatible with the range of π not covering, locally, a neighborhood of $\pi(x)$ on ∂Y and so with rank $\partial \pi(x) < \ell - 1$.

For an arbitrary x denote $p = x - \pi(x)$ and suppose that γ is C^2 at x and rank $\partial^2 \gamma(x) = \ell$. The previous geometric discussion indicates that the set $\{y \in Y : p \cdot y = \beta(p)\}$ is a singleton and that therefore the profit function β is C^1 at $p = x - \pi(x)$; see 3.4.3. In fact, the condition rank $\partial^2\gamma(x) = \ell$ is intimately connected to the twice differentiability of the profit function β at p. We have:

3.5.3. Proposition. *Let $p \in Y^*$, $y \in Y$, and $p \cdot y = \beta(p)$. Suppose that γ is C^2 at $y + p$. Then β is C^2 at p if and only if rank $\partial^2\gamma(y + p) = \ell$. In this case,*

$$\partial^2\beta(p) = [\partial^2\gamma(y+p)]^{-1} - I = [\partial^2\gamma(y+p)]^{-1}\partial\pi(y+p).$$

Proof. Denote the given vectors by $\bar{p}, \bar{y}$. By 3.4.3, β is C^1 at $\bar{p}$ only if the equation $\pi(p+y) - y = 0$ admits in a neighborhood of $\bar{p}$ a unique solution $y(p)$. In this case $\partial\beta(p) = y(p)$. Therefore, β is C^2 at $\bar{p}$ if and only if the equation $\pi(p+y) - y = 0$ admits in a neighborhood of $\bar{p}$ a C^1 solution $y(p)$. By the IFT (C.3.2) this will be the case if and only if rank$[\partial\pi(\bar{p}+\bar{y}) - I] = \ell$. But $\partial\pi(\bar{p}+\bar{y}) - I = -\partial^2\gamma(\bar{p}+\bar{y})$.

By 3.4.3.iii we have $\partial\beta(p) = \pi(p+\partial\beta(p))$ in a neighborhood of $\bar{p}$. Hence $\partial^2\beta(\bar{p}) = \partial\pi(\bar{p}+\bar{y})[I + \partial^2\beta(\bar{p})]$ or

$$\partial^2\beta(\bar{p}) = [I - \partial\pi(\bar{p}+\bar{y})]^{-1}\partial\pi(\bar{p}+\bar{y})$$
$$= [I - \partial\pi(\bar{p}+\bar{y})]^{-1}(I - [I - \partial\pi(\bar{p}+\bar{y})])$$
$$= [I - \partial\pi(\bar{p}+\bar{y})]^{-1} - I = [\partial^2\gamma(\bar{p}+\bar{y})]^{-1} - I. \quad \blacksquare$$

Because β is convex, $\partial^2\beta(p)$ is automatically positive definite (F.3.3). This can also be seen from the previous proposition: The eigenvalues of $\partial^2\gamma(p+y)$ are not greater than one, hence the eigenvalues of $[\partial^2\gamma(p+y)]^{-1}$ are greater or equal to one and so $[\partial^2\gamma(p+y)]^{-1} - I$ is positive definite (B.6.2).

For the remainder of this section *we consider fixed $y \in \partial Y$, $p \in R^\ell$, $p \neq 0$, and $x \in R^\ell$ satisfying $x = y + p$ and $\pi(x) = y$*; see Figure 3.5.2. *Denote $T = \{v \in R^\ell : p \cdot v = 0\}$.*

Suppose that γ is C^2 at x. Because $\partial\pi(x)p = 0$ we have $p \cdot \partial\pi(x)v = 0$ for all $v \in R^\ell$ and we can conclude that the range of $\partial\pi(x)$ is contained in T. Denote by $\partial^2\hat{\gamma}(x), \partial\hat{\pi}(x)$ the restrictions to T of the linear maps $\partial^2\gamma(x), \partial\pi(x)$. Both $\partial\hat{\pi}(x)$ and $\partial^2\hat{\gamma}(x) = I - \partial\hat{\pi}(x)$ are now linear maps from T into T. Of course, rank $\partial\hat{\pi}(x) = $ rank $\partial\pi(x)$ and because $\partial^2\gamma(p)p = p$, rank $\partial^2\gamma(x) = 1 + $ rank $\partial^2\hat{\gamma}(x)$.

Suppose that β is C^2 at p. From the degree one homogeneity of β [i.e., $\beta(\lambda p) = \lambda\beta(p)$ for all $\lambda \geq 0$], we know that $\partial^2\beta(p)p = 0$ and therefore $p \cdot \partial^2\beta(p)v = 0$ for all $v \in R^\ell$. So the range of the linear map $\partial^2\beta(p)$ is contained in T. This can also be seen from the equality $\partial\beta(p) = \pi(p+\partial\beta(p))$. Let $\partial^2\hat{\beta}(p)$ be the restriction of $\partial^2\beta(p)$ to T. This can be looked at as a linear map from T to T. Of course, rank $\partial^2\hat{\beta}(p) = $ rank $\partial^2\beta(p)$.

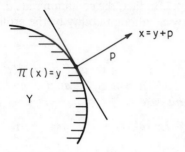

Figure 3.5.2

Suppose that ∂Y is a C^2 manifold at y. Then on a neighborhood $V \subset \partial Y$ of y we can define the Gauss map $g : V \to S$, that is, the map that assigns to every $z \in V$ the outward unit normal to ∂Y at z (see H.3). The linear map $\partial g(y)$ takes T into T and is positive semidefinite (H.3).

The precise relations between the manifold nature of ∂Y at y and the characteristics of γ and β at, respectively, x and p are given in the next proposition.

3.5.4. Proposition. *With the above notational conventions we have:*

    (i)   *If π is C^1 at x and rank $\partial \hat{\pi}(x) = \ell - 1$, then ∂Y is a C^1 manifold at y.*

    (ii) *Let ∂Y be a C^2 manifold at y. Then γ is C^2 at x, rank $\partial \hat{\pi}(x) = \ell - 1$ and $\partial g(y) = [\partial \hat{\pi}(x)]^{-1} \partial^2 \hat{\gamma}(x)$. Further, $\partial^2 \hat{\beta}(p)$ exists if and only if $\partial g(y)$ is nonsingular, that is, if and only if the Gaussian curvature of ∂Y at y is nonzero. In this case $\partial^2 \hat{\beta}(p) = [\partial g(y)]^{-1}$.*

Proof. (i) If rank $\partial \hat{\pi}(x) = \ell - 1$, then π restricted to a neighborhood U of x on $\{x\} + T$ is a C^1 diffeomorphism (H.2.1). So, $\pi(U) \subset \partial Y$ is a C^1 manifold of dimension $\ell - 1$. This implies that $\pi(U)$ covers a neighborhood of y in ∂Y. Therefore, ∂Y is a C^1 manifold at y.

(ii) If ∂Y is a C^2 manifold at y, then for all z in a neighborhood of y, the Gauss map $g(z)$ is well defined and $\pi(g(z) + z) = z$. Moreover, letting I be the identity on T, $\partial g(y) + I$ is positive definite, hence nonsingular. Therefore, $\partial \hat{\pi}(x) = [\partial g(y) + I]^{-1}$, which establishes simultaneously that γ is C^2 at x, rank $\partial \hat{\pi}(x) = \ell - 1$, and

$$\partial g(y) = [\partial \hat{\pi}(x)]^{-1} - I = [\partial \hat{\pi}(x)]^{-1}[I - \partial \hat{\pi}(x)] = [\partial \hat{\pi}(x)]^{-1} \partial^2 \hat{\gamma}(x).$$

Observe that $\partial g(y)$ is nonsingular if and only if rank $\partial^2 \gamma(x) = \ell - 1$, that is to say, if and only if β is C^2 at p (see 3.5.3). In this case, again by 3.5.3, $\partial^2 \hat{\beta}(p) = [\partial^2 \hat{\gamma}(x)]^{-1} \partial \hat{\pi}(x) = [\partial g(y)]^{-1}$. ∎

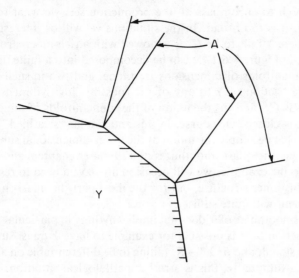

Figure 3.6.1

3.6   Smoothness hypotheses

Given an aggregate production set Y a very convenient smoothness hypothesis would be that the corresponding distance function γ be C^2. Because of its simplicity we shall occasionally postulate this, but it shall not be our main smoothness assumption. It is too strong and it eliminates many interesting production technologies as, for example, all the polyhedral ones. In Figure 3.6.1 γ fails to be C^1 at point in the lines marked by A.

Because γ is convex it is always twice differentiable except on a region $A \subset R^\ell$ of Lebesgue measure zero. This in itself is of no great help. But it turns out that for the purposes of our theory we will be able to get quite far with the hypothesis that Y is such that the region A can be taken to be closed and γ is twice continuously differentiable outside A. This property will be called *quasi-smoothness*. More formally:

> **3.6.1. Definition.** *The production set Y is quasi-smooth if there is a closed region of Lebesgue measure zero $A \subset R^\ell$ such that γ is C^2 on $R^\ell \setminus A$.*

Quasi-smoothness is a weak and natural hypothesis. Examples of production sets that violate it do certainly exist, but they have to be sought with special care. At any rate, the class of quasi-smooth production sets is broad enough to encompass all the production sets we want to consider. In fact, it is too broad. In the situations we will be interested in, the region where γ fails to be C^2 is endowed with a rich inner structure. For example, in Figure 3.6.1 R^2 can be decomposed into a finite disjoint union of submanifolds of dimensions zero, one, and two in such a way that (i) the restriction of γ to any of the (possibly lower-dimensional) submanifolds is C^2, and (ii) the union of the submanifolds of dimension zero and one is closed. Of course, in this and similar "stratified" situations we can let A be simply the union of the lower-dimensional submanifolds and we get the quasi-smoothness of Y. In later chapters and in the context of specific examples we will occasionally have a need to resort to and exploit this inner structure, but for the most part the quasi-smoothness requirement will quite suffice.

The quasi-smoothness of Y does not imply anything in particular about the profit function β. It is possible for example to have Y quasi-smooth, Y^* full-dimensional, and $\beta: Y^* \to R^\ell$ failing to be differentiable on a dense subset of Y^*. Admittedly, this is a rather pathological situation. There would be no loss in requiring β to be C^2 except possibly on a closed, nowhere dense set. But this will also not be needed. The reasons we have chosen to impose our smoothness conditions on γ rather than β are twofold: (i) If we had made our approach via β, a hypothesis such as quasi-smoothness would be too coarse. Consideration of the inner, stratified structure of β would be indispensable (price vectors in the boundary of Y^* cannot be neglected), and (ii) the domain of β depends on Y and this would create awkwardness in the treatment of Section 3.8 on C^2 perturbations of production sets.

The quasi-smoothness of Y has straightforward implications for the corresponding normal manifold Γ. We say that a set $A \subset \Gamma$ is null in Γ if, locally, A is the image of a null set under a Lipschitz function $\xi: R^\ell \to \Gamma$.

3.6.2. Proposition. *The production set Y is quasi-smooth if and only if there is an $A \subset \Gamma$ such that $\Gamma \setminus A$ is a C^1 manifold and A is closed and null in Γ.*

Proof. As in the proof of 3.4.2 let $x \mapsto (x - \pi(x), \pi(x))$ be the homeomorphism between R^ℓ and Γ, denoted ξ. By 3.4.1 ξ is Lipschitzian. Hence if $A' \subset R^\ell$ is null, then $A = \xi(A')$ is null in Γ (I.1). It is straightforward to verify that ξ is proper (i.e., if $\|x_n\| \to \infty$, then $\|\xi(x_n)\| \to \infty$). Hence if $A' \subset R^\ell$ is closed, then so is $A = \xi(A')$. If Y is quasi-smooth, we can choose A' to be closed, null, and such that γ is C^2 on $R^\ell \setminus A'$. Then, by 3.5.2, Γ is a C^1 manifold on $\Gamma \setminus A$. This proves the "only if" part.

The "if" part is proved in an entirely analogous manner. ∎

3.7   Some examples

A type of production set of central importance is the one associated with the linear activity model, namely, the polyhedral cone production technology introduced in 3.2. It is worth noting that these production sets are always quasi-smooth. Indeed, let Y be generated from the elementary activities $\{a_1, \ldots, a_m\} \subset R^\ell$ and π be the corresponding projection function. Then π is piecewise linear in the following sense: π is continuous and there is a finite number of distict linear functions $\eta_j : R^n \to R^n$, $j \in J$ (to be more precise, the η_j functions are the linear projections on the linear spaces spanned by the faces of Y) such that at any $x \in R^\ell$, $\pi(x) \in \bigcup_{j \in J} \{\eta_j(x)\}$. Letting $A = \{x : \eta_j(x) = \eta_{j'}(x), j \ne j'\}$, it follows that π is locally linear at any $x \in R^n \setminus A$. Of course, A is a finite union of linear subspaces of dimension less than ℓ and is therefore closed and null.

The representative elementary activity a_j of the technology described in the previous paragraph only allows for changes of the scale of production, but not for changes of proportions between inputs and outputs. We now present a generalization that permits the latter.

It will be convenient to restrict ourselves to a setting where the free disposal hypothesis is always assumed; that is, we think of the elementary activity a_j as generating the elementary production set

$$Y_j = \{\alpha_j a_j : \alpha_j \ge 0\} - R_+^\ell .$$

The aggregate production set is then $Y = \sum_j Y_j$. The elementary activity a_j could also be equivalently described by the restricted profit function $\beta_j : R_{++}^\ell \to R$ defined by $\beta_j(p) = p \cdot a_j$. Then $\partial \beta_j(p) = a_j$ and, therefore, we can rewrite $Y_j = \{\alpha_j \partial \beta_j(p) : \alpha_j \ge 0, p \gg 0\} - R_+^\ell$. This suggests that an appropriate concept of *generalized linear activity* is obtained by letting the primitive description of the elementary technology (allowing possibly for input and output substitution) be given by the restricted profit function itself. That is to say, a generalized linear activity will be any C^1, linear homogeneous, and convex function $\beta_j : R_{++}^\ell \to R$. It is understood that β_j generates the elementary production set

$$Y_j = \mathrm{cl}\{\alpha_j \partial \beta_j(p) : \alpha_j > 0, p \gg 0\} - R_+^\ell .$$

A generalized linear activity model production set Y is generated by a finite list $\{\beta_1, \ldots, \beta_m\}$ of generalized linear activities.

We now discuss in detail a third example of production sets. We are given a finite index set J and, for each $j \in J$, a C^1 convex function $\eta_j : R^\ell \to R$. Then we put $Y = \{x : \eta_j(x) \le 0 \text{ for all } j\}$. The following is also assumed:

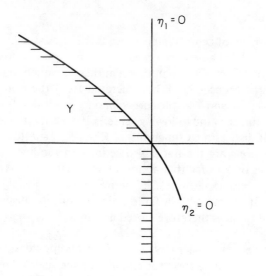

Figure 3.7.1

(i) If we let $J(x) = \{j \in J : \eta_j(x) = 0\}$ then, for all $x \in R^\ell$, the collection of vectors $\{\partial \eta_j(x) : j \in J(x)\}$ is linearly independent.

Of course, (i) implies that $\partial \eta_j(x) \neq 0$ whenever $\eta_j(x) = 0$ and also that for any $J' \subset J$ the set $\{x : \eta_j(x) = 0 \text{ all } j \in J'\}$ is a C^1 manifold of dimension $\ell - \#J'$ (H.2.2). See Figure 3.7.1.

Before analyzing this example in more detail it is worthwhile to compare it with the polyhedral cone example. Essentially, we are requiring now that the production set be "piecewise smooth," with the pieces fitting together nicely. Thus, at first sight we may appear to be discussing a nonlinear generalization of the polyhedral case. But this is not so. For $\ell > 3$ there is no reason for the linear η_j functions naturally arising from a polyhedral technology to satisfy condition (i), although it would be natural to require that they satisfy the weaker:

(ii) For all $x \in R^\ell$, the collection of vectors $\{\partial \eta_j(x) : J(x)\}$ is positively independent; that is, if $0 = \sum_{j \in J(x)} \alpha_j \partial \eta_j(x)$ and $\alpha_j \geq 0$ for all j, then $\alpha_j = 0$ for all j.

At a more fundamental level it is important to realize that the viewpoint of this example differs from the two linear activities examples. Here we view a production set as an intersection of more elementary sets, while in the linear activity case one views it as a convex span from ele-

mentary activities. While the latter would appear to be more economically justified, it is sometimes quite cumbersome technically, and so the
change of perspective is occasionally very expedient.

3.7.1. Proposition. *If condition (i) above is satisfied with respect to a finite collection of C^2 convex functions $\{\eta_j : j \in J\}$, then $Y = \{x : \eta_j(x) \leq 0 \text{ for all } j\}$ is quasi-smooth.*

Proof. We show that the normal manifold Γ is quasi-smooth. By Proposition 3.6.2 this suffices. For any $J' \subset J$ let $M_{J'} = \{x : \eta_j(x) = 0, \ j \in J'\}$.
Define $\Gamma_{J'} = \{(p, x) \in R^\ell \times M_{J'} : p \cdot v = 0 \text{ for all } v \in T_x M_{J'}\}$. Then $\Gamma_{J'}$ is a
C^1 manifold and $\Gamma \subset \bigcup_{J' \in J} \Gamma_{J'}$. Let $A = \{(p, x) \in \Gamma : (p, x) \in \Gamma_{J'} \cap \Gamma_{J''} \text{ for }$
$J' \neq J''\}$. We shall show that A, which is closed, is null. Because Γ is a
topological manifold this means that Γ is a C^1 manifold at any $x \in \Gamma \setminus A$.
  So let $(p, x) \in \Gamma_{J'} \cap \Gamma_{J''}$, $J' \neq J''$. Without loss of generality we can
assume that for some $h \in J$, we have $h \in J'$ but $h \notin J''$. Then $\Gamma_{J'} \cap \Gamma_{J''} \subset$
$\{(p, x) \in J'' : \eta_h(x) = 0\}$. By (i) if $\eta_h(x) = 0$ and $\eta_j(x) = 0$ for all $j \in J'$, then
$\eta_h(x)$ and $\{\partial \eta_j(x) : j \in J''\}$ are linearly independent, which means that if
$\eta_j(x) \cdot v = 0$ for all $j \in J''$ and $v \neq 0$, then $\partial \eta_h(x) v \neq 0$. In other words, η_h
restricted to $M_{J''}$ is a regular function and so is, therefore, $(p, x) \mapsto \eta_h(x)$
from $\Gamma_{J''}$ to R. Hence, by H.2.2, $\{(p, x) \in \Gamma_{J''} : \eta_h(x) = 0\}$ is a C^1 manifold
of codimension one in $\Gamma_{J''}$; that is, it has dimension $\ell - 1$. So $\Gamma_{J'} \cap \Gamma_{J''}$
is contained in a closed C^1 manifold of dimension $\ell - 1$ and is therefore
null. Since the number of pairs $J', J'' \subset J$ is finite, the same property carries to A.   ∎

  It should be clear that 3.7.1 does by no means give the strongest
smoothness property of Y. The comments of Section 3.6 apply with full
force to this example.
  From the proof of Proposition 3.7.1 we see that γ will be C^2, and
therefore π will be C^1, at any $x \in R^\ell$ satisfying the condition: "There is a
neighborhood $x \in V$ such that, for $x' \in V$, $\pi(x') \in \{z \in R^\ell : \eta_j(z) = 0 \text{ for all }$
$j \in J(\pi(x))\}$." So, let $A \in R^\ell$ be the region where the condition is not satisfied. Take a particular $x \in R^\ell \setminus A$, and put $y = \pi(x)$, $p = x - y$. It is of
interest to inquire into the differentiability of the profit function β at p. If
$\#J(y) = 1$, then we know from Proposition 3.5.4 that $\beta(p)$ is C^2 if and
only if the $\ell - 1$ C^2 manifold $\eta_j^{-1}(0)$, where $\{j\} = J(y)$, has nonzero curvature. But what about when $\#J(y) > 1$ and, therefore, the C^2 manifold
$M = \bigcap_{j \in J(y)} \eta_j^{-1}(0) = \{z : \eta_j(z) = 0 \text{ for all } j \in J(y)\}$ has dimension less than
$\ell - 1$? It is intuitive that the smoothness properties of β at p are still related to the curvature properties of M at y since it is clear that what is

involved is the presence or absence of "small" (strictly speaking, infinitesimal) straight segments as subsets of M. The problem is that M is not an $\ell - 1$ manifold and, therefore, we cannot apply to it the definition of Gaussian curvature. This difficulty can be circumvented as follows. Let L be the linear space spanned by p and $T_y M$. It has dimension $m + 1$ [where $m = \dim M = \ell - \#J(y)$] because p is perpendicular to $T_y M$. Let then M' be the perpendicular projection of $M - \{y\}$ into L. Since $M - \{y\}$ is tangent to $T_y M$ at 0, M' is, in a neighborhood of 0, a C^2 submanifold of L of dimension m. Therefore, the curvature in L of M' at 0 is well defined.

It can then be easily shown (essentially as in Proposition 3.5.4) that β is C^2 at p if and only if this curvature is different from zero. Since this fact will not play a role in this book, we will not give a formal proof or elaborate any further. We note, however, an important implication. If for some $j \in J(y)$ $\eta_j^{-1}(0)$ has nonzero curvature in R^ℓ at y [equivalently, if $\partial^2 \eta_j(y)$ is positive definite], then M' has nonzero curvature in L at y. Therefore, if given $x \in R^\ell$, some η_j with $j \in J(\pi(x))$ is differentiably strictly convex at $\pi(x)$, then β is C^2 at $x - \pi(x)$.

3.8   Perturbations of production sets

It shall be important in later chapters to have a notion of proximity for quasi-smooth production sets. Ideally, this calls for a topology in a space of the latter. Although there is no essential difficulty in devising one, we shall rest content with having a notion of convergence.

Let Y be a quasi-smooth production set and $A \subset R^\ell$ a closed, null set such that the corresponding distance function γ is C^2 on $R^\ell \setminus A$. We say that the sequence of quasi-smooth production sets Y_n, with corresponding distance functions γ_n, converges to Y if for every compact $K \subset R^\ell \setminus A$ and $\epsilon > 0$ there is an N such that if $n > N$, then:

(i) γ_n is C^2 in K, and
(ii) $\max_{x \in K}(|\gamma_n(x) - \gamma(x)| + \|\partial \gamma_n(x) - \partial \gamma(x)\|$
$\qquad\qquad + \|\partial^2 \gamma_n(x) - \partial^2 \gamma(x)\|) < \epsilon.$

In words, $Y_n \to Y$ if γ_n converges to γ in the sense of C^2 uniformity on compact subsets of $R^\ell \setminus A$.

The notion is relatively straightforward and sufficient for the purposes of this book. We may note that one of the reasons to introduce explicitly the distance function is that it determines the production set and is defined on the whole of R^ℓ. This permits viewing perturbations of production sets as perturbations of their associated distance functions, which mathematically is very convenient.

3.9   Reference notes

Most of the concepts and constructions of this chapter are very familiar either from the economics literature or from the mathematical theory of convexity. General economic references are Koopmans (1951a), Shephard (1953), Debreu (1959), Fuss–McFadden (1978), and Diewert (1982).

The concepts in 3.2 are discussed in detail in Koopmans (1951b) and Debreu (1959). For the theory of the aggregation of individual production sets, Section 3.3, see Hildenbrand (1981).

The constructions in 3.4 are all standard in convexity theory. See Section F of Chapter 1 and its references.

In economics, the profit and the restricted profit functions have a long tradition; see, for example, McFadden (1978). The distance and projection functions, as well as the normal manifold, are somewhat less standard, although antecedents can be found for all of them (e.g., in Shephard, 1953; see also the reference of Chapter 6). We should point out that we have abused language: What we have called the distance function is, in fact, the square of a true mathematical distance function.

The content of 3.5 is derivative of 3.4. Once the concepts of interest have been identified, there is no essential difficulty in working out its implications.

The term *quasi-smoothness,* Section 3.6, has been coined to denote the departure from full smoothness that was of interest for us. The idea is, of course, completely standard.

As for the examples in 3.7, the linear activity model appeared in Koopmans (1951b). The generalized linear activity model is a straightforward generalization. We take it formally from Mas-Colell (1975), but the idea of describing constant returns technologies by restricted profit functions is old (see, e.g. Shephard, 1953). The third example is formally due to Smale (1974c).

CHAPTER 4

Optimality and price equilibrium

4.1 Introduction

In this chapter we have as initial data a production set Y, a collection of preference relations $\succsim_1, \ldots, \succsim_n$ and a commodity vector $\omega \in R^\ell$. After defining the notion of attainable allocation, we introduce the concepts of optimality in the sense of Pareto and of price equilibrium. This chapter is devoted to the study of the interrelationships of these two concepts. Under general continuity hypotheses, Section 4.2 gathers basic definitions and the well-known facts for the convex preferences case. Under smoothness, but not convexity, assumptions, Sections 4.3 and 4.4 deal, respectively, with local first- and second-order theory, and Section 4.5 contains some results on approximate global supportability of optima by prices. Finally, Section 4.6 investigates the simplest facts about the topological and manifold structure of the set of optimal allocations.

The maintained setting for this chapter is: *There is given a finite collection $\succsim_1, \ldots, \succsim_n$ of continuous, monotone preference relations on R^ℓ_+, a closed and convex production set Y satisfying $Y \cap R^\ell_+ = \{0\}$ and $-R^\ell_+ \subset Y$, and a commodity vector $\omega \in R^\ell$ with the property that $\omega + y \gg 0$ for some $y \in Y$.* Hence, we eliminate from our analysis any commodity that, given ω and Y, cannot be produced. Thus, in the exchange case, that is, $Y = -R^\ell_+$, we are assuming $\omega \gg 0$. *We also let $u_1, \ldots, u_n$ be a family of continuous utility functions for the preferences. We convene that $u_j(0) = 0$ for all j.*

4.2 Optimality and price equilibrium: general theory

We denote a list of n consumption vectors by $x = (x_1, \ldots, x_n) \in R^{\ell n}_+$ and call it an *allocation*.

4.2.1. Definition. The allocation x is attainable if $\sum_{j=1}^{n} x_j - \omega \in Y$.

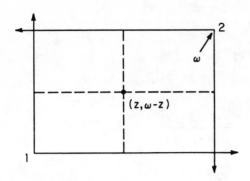

Figure 4.2.1

In other words, x is attainable if, using ω as the input, there is a feasible production plan y that yields $\sum_{j=1}^{n} x_j$ as the output. Observe that in the exchange case, that is, $Y = -R_+^\ell$, attainability means $\sum_{j=1}^{n} x_j \leq \omega$.

4.2.2. Example (the Edgeworth box). Let $n = 2$ and $Y = -R_+^2$. A very convenient device to represent the attainable allocations x with $x_1 + x_2 = \omega$ is the "Edgeworth box," which is defined to be $\{z \in R_+^2 : z \leq \omega\}$. A point z in the box corresponds uniquely to the allocation $x = (z, \omega - z)$. See Figure 4.2.1 for the case $\ell = 2$.

4.2.3. Example. Let $n = 1$. Then the set of attainable allocations is simply $R_+^\ell \cap (Y + \{\omega\})$. See Figure 4.2.2.

A simple fact about attainable allocations is:

> **4.2.4. Proposition.** *The set of attainable allocations is convex, closed, and bounded.*

Proof. The set is the intersection of $R_+^{\ell n}$ with the inverse image of the closed convex set Y under the linear map $\sum_{j=1}^{n} x_j$. So it is closed and convex. For boundedness, let $z_m = \omega + y_m$, $z_m \in R_+^\ell$, $y_m \in Y$, and $\|z_m\| \to \infty$. Define $\hat{z}_m = (1/\|z_m\|)z_m$ and $\hat{y}_m = (1/\|z_m\|)y_m$. Without loss of generality we can assume $\hat{z}_m \to \hat{z}$, $\|\hat{z}\| = 1$, $\hat{z} \geq 0$. Because $\hat{z}_m = (1/\|z_m\|)\omega + \hat{y}_m$, we have $\hat{y}_m \to \hat{z}$. Since Y is closed, $\hat{z} \in Y$. But this contradicts the fact that $Y \cap R_+^\ell = \{0\}$. Therefore, there is some $r > 0$ such that if $z = \omega + y$, $z \geq 0$, $y \in Y$, then $\|z\| \leq r$. So if x is an attainable allocation, then for all i, $\|x_i\| \leq \|\sum_{j=1}^{n} x_j\| \leq r$. ∎

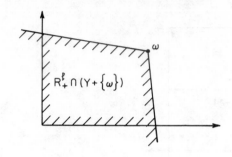

Figure 4.2.2

An attainable allocation x will be called optimal (in the sense of Pareto) if it is not possible to make some agent better off without making some other worse off. This optimality concept is totally unrelated to distributional value judgments. If it had to be named anew, *optimality* would not be the best term for it (*efficiency* would be superior). But the terminology is by now standard.

> **4.2.5. Definition.** *An allocation x is optimal if it is attainable and if there is no other attainable allocation x' such that $x_j' \gtrsim_j x_j$ for all j and $x_j' >_j x_j$ for at least one j.*

A less strict concept is provided by the next definition.

> **4.2.6. Definition.** *An allocation x is weakly optimal if it is attainable and there is no other attainable allocation x' such that $x_j' >_j x_j$ for all j.*

If preferences are strictly monotone, any weakly optimal x is optimal. Indeed, suppose that x, x' are attainable, $x_1' >_1 x_1$, and $x_j' \gtrsim_j x_j$ for all j. Then, at x' agent 1 must be receiving a positive amount of some commodity. Take a small amount of it away from agent 1 and distribute it equally among the remaining agents. This gives a new attainable allocation x''. By continuity of preferences, if small is small enough, we still have $x_1'' >_1 x_1$ and by strict monotonicity $x_j'' >_j x_j$ for all j. Without strict monotonicity, however, this fact need not be true, as Example 4.2.8 will illustrate.

4.2.7. Example. Optimal allocations can be easily visualized in the Edgeworth box. With the convention that a point z represents consumption z

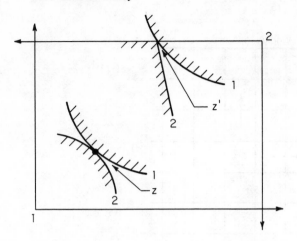

Figure 4.2.3

for agent 1 and consumption $\omega - z$ for agent 2, we can plot the preferences of the two agents in the box, as in Figure 4.2.3. Then a point such as z or z' in Figure 4.2.3 is weakly optimal because the intersection of the set of points preferred by agent 1 and the set of points preferred by agent 2 is empty.

4.2.8. Example. Take $\ell = n = 2$, $Y = -R_+^2$ (i.e., exchange), $\omega = (1, 1)$. Agent 1 (resp. agent 2) cares only about commodity 1 (resp. 2); that is, $\gtrsim_1$ (resp. $\gtrsim_2$) has the form: $x_1 \gtrsim_1 x_1'$ if and only if $x_1^1 \geq x_1'^1$ (resp. $x_2 \gtrsim_2 x_2'$ if and only if $x_2^2 \geq x_2'^2$). Then the only optimal allocation is $x_1 = (1, 0)$, $x_2 = (0, 1)$, but any attainable allocation x with $x_1 + x_2 = \omega$ and $x_1^1 = 1$ or $x_1^2 = 0$ is weakly optimal. Note that preferences are not strictly monotone. See Figure 4.2.4.

4.2.9. Example. Let $n = 1$. In the single agent problem the allocation x is optimal if and only if it maximizes the preferences $\gtrsim$ on the set of attainable allocations. See Figure 4.2.5.

If preferences are convex, the overall optimality of an attainable allocation x is implied by the inexistence at x of potential gains from trade for any group of at most ℓ agents. More precisely:

4.2.10. Proposition. Let preferences $\gtrsim_j$ be convex. Suppose that for the attainable allocation x, there is no other attainable allo-

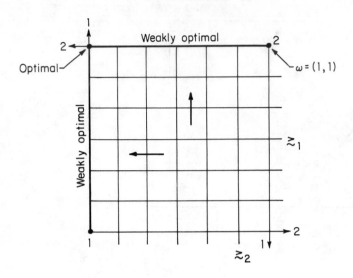

Figure 4.2.4

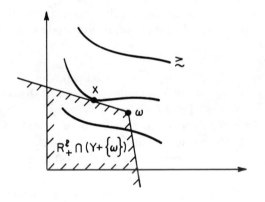

Figure 4.2.5

*cation x' such that: $\#\{j: x'_j \neq x_j\} \leq \ell$, $x'_j \succeq_j x_j$ for all j and $x'_j \succ_j x_j$
for some j. Then x is an optimum.*

Proof. We argue by contradiction. Suppose that x' dominates x. We will
show that x can be dominated by a group of at most ℓ agents. Take
$x'_1 \succ_1 x_1$. Denote $y = \sum_{j=1}^{n} x_j - \omega$, $y' = \sum_{j=1}^{n} x'_j - \omega$, $v_j = x'_j - x_j$, $v_{n+1} =
y - y'$. Then, $0 = \sum_{j=1}^{n+1} v_j$. Call $J = \mathrm{co}\{v_1, \ldots, v_{n+1}\}$ and let $-\lambda e \in \mathrm{Bdry}\, J$.

Remember that e is the vector with all its components equal to 1. By the supporting hyperplane theorem (F.2.1) there is a $q \neq 0$ such that $q \cdot J \geq -\lambda q \cdot e$. Denote by H the $(\ell-1)$-dimensional supporting hyperplane $\{z \in R^\ell : q \cdot z = -\lambda q \cdot e\}$. Of course, $-\lambda e \in \mathrm{co}(J \cap H)$. So by Caratheodory's theorem (F.1.1) we have that $-\lambda e = \sum_{j=1}^{n+1} \alpha_j v_j$, where $\sum_{j=1}^{n+1} \alpha_j = 1$ and $\#\{j : \alpha_j \neq 0\} \leq (\ell-1)+1 = \ell$. Let then the allocation x'' be defined by $x_j'' = x_j + \alpha_j v_j = (1-\alpha_j)x_j + \alpha_j x_j'$. By the convexity of preferences, $x_j'' \succsim_j x_j$ for all j and $x_j'' \succ_j x_j$ whenever $x_j' \succ_j x_j$ and $\alpha_j > 0$. Also,

$$\sum_{j=1}^n x_j'' - \omega = (1-\alpha_{n+1})y + \alpha_{n+1}y' - \lambda e \in Y.$$

If $\lambda > 0$, we are done since then $\sum_{j=1}^n x_j'' - \omega \in \mathrm{Int}\, Y$, which means that an extra amount of each commodity can be given to each agent. So let $\lambda = 0$. Because $0 = \sum_{j=1}^{n+1} v_j$ and $q \cdot v_j \geq 0$ for all j, we must have $J \subset H$. Therefore, in applying Caratheorody's theorem we can make sure that $\alpha_1 > 0$ (F.1.1), which implies $x_1'' \succ_1 x_1$ and ends the proof. ∎

We now introduce the fundamental notion of an attainable allocation being in equilibrium with respect to a price system. Price vectors are denoted $p \in R_+^\ell$.

> **4.2.11. Definition.** *The attainable allocation x is a price equilibrium if there is a price vector $p \geq 0$ such that $p \cdot (\sum_{j=1}^n x_j - \omega) \geq p \cdot y$ for all $y \in Y$ (profit maximization) and, for all j, $p \cdot x_j' > p \cdot x_j$ whenever $x_j' \succ_j x_j$ (preference maximization).*

> **4.2.12. Definition.** *The attainable allocation x is a price quasi-equilibrium if there is a price vector $p > 0$ such that $p \cdot (\sum_{j=1}^n x_j - \omega) \geq p \cdot y$ for all $z \in Y$ (profit maximization) and, for all j, $p \cdot x_j' \geq p \cdot x_j$ whenever $x_j' \succsim x_j$ (cost minimization).*

Because of the monotonicity of preferences a price equilibrium is automatically a price quasi-equilibrium. Figures 4.2.6 and 4.2.7 provide Edgeworth box examples of price equilibria. In Figure 4.2.7 $\succsim_1$ is not monotone and the equilibrium is not a quasi-equilibrium. Figures 4.2.8 and 4.2.9 exhibit two instances of price quasi-equilibria that are not equilibria (agent 1 is not maximizing preferences). Figure 4.2.9 violates the maintained hypothesis $\omega \gg 0$.

When is a quasi-equilibrium an equilibrium? Proposition 4.2.14 will give an answer, while Proposition 4.2.13 states explicitly what constitutes the basic fact.

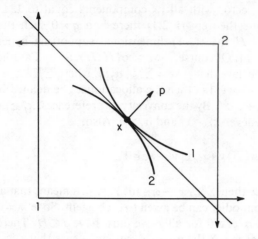

Figure 4.2.6

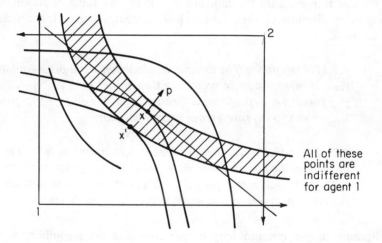

All of these
points are
indifferent
for agent 1

Figure 4.2.7

4.2.13. Proposition. *Let x be an attainable allocation that is a quasi-equilibrium with respect to p. Then, any j with $p \cdot x_j > 0$ satisfies $p \cdot x'_j > p \cdot x_j$ whenever $x'_j >_j x_j$.*

Proof. Let $x'_j >_j x_j$. Then $\alpha x'_j >_j x_j$ for $\alpha < 1$ sufficiently close to 1. By cost minimization $\alpha p \cdot x'_j \geq p \cdot x_j > 0$. So $p \cdot x'_j > 0$, which yields $p \cdot x'_j > \alpha p \cdot x'_j \geq p \cdot x_j$. ∎

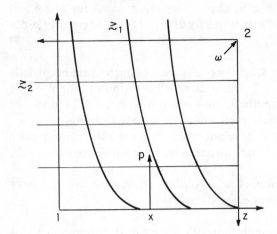

Figure 4.2.8

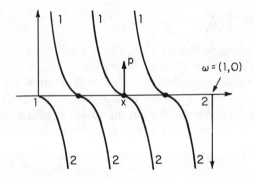

Figure 4.2.9

4.2.14. Proposition. *Let x be an attainable allocation that is a quasi-equilibrium with respect to p. If $p \gg 0$, then x is an equilibrium with respect to p. If preferences are strictly monotone, then $p \gg 0$.*

Proof. Let $p \gg 0$. If $x_j \neq 0$, then $p \cdot x_j > 0$ and preference maximization follows from 4.2.13. If $x_j = 0$, preference maximization is obvious. Now let $p > 0$ and each $\succsim_j$ be strictly monotone. Remember that $\omega + y \gg 0$ for some $y \in Y$. Because of profit maximization, $p \cdot (\sum_{j=1}^{n} x_j) \geq p \cdot (y + \omega) > 0$. Therefore $p \cdot x_j > 0$ for some j. By 4.2.13 agent j is maximizing preferences.

Take any $1 \le h \le \ell$ and let z be the vector with $z^{h'} = x_j^{h'}$ for $h' \neq h$ and $z^h = x_j^h + 1$. Then, by strict monotonicity of $>_j$, $z >_j x_j$. Therefore, $p \cdot z > p \cdot x_j$, which yields $p^h \neq 0$. ∎

Observe that in Figure 4.2.8 the preferences of agent 2 are not strictly monotone, while Figure 4.2.9 illustrates well the kind of pathology we may encounter if the hypothesis "$\omega + y \gg 0$ for some $y \in Y$" does not hold. Note that in the figure preferences are strictly monotone.

We will now investigate the relationships between allocations in price equilibrium and optima. In one direction we have a quite general result.

4.2.15. Proposition. *A price equilibrium is an optimum. A price quasi-equilibrium is a weak optimum.*

Proof. Let x be a price equilibrium with respect to p. Suppose that x' is an allocation such that $x_i' \gtrsim_i x_i$ for all i and $x_j' >_j x_j$ for a j. Then $p \cdot x_j' > p \cdot x_j$. Also, by monotonicity of $\gtrsim_i$, $x_i' + \epsilon e >_i x_i$. Hence, $p \cdot x_i' + \epsilon p \cdot e > p \cdot x_i$ for all i. Letting $\epsilon \to 0$, we get $p \cdot x_i' \ge p \cdot x_i$. Therefore,

$$p \cdot \left(\sum_{i=1}^n x_i' - \omega \right) > p \cdot \left(\sum_{i=1}^n x_i - \omega \right).$$

Because $\sum_{i=1}^n x_i - \omega$ maximizes profits on Y, $\sum_{i=1}^n x_i' - \omega \notin Y$. So x' is not attainable and we conclude that x is optimal. Now suppose that x is only a quasi-equilibrium with respect to p, but that $y + \omega \gg 0$ for some $y \in Y$. As in the proof of 4.2.14, we get $p \cdot x_j > 0$ for some j. Agent j is therefore preference-maximizing (4.2.13). Hence, for any allocation x' with $x_i' >_i x_i$ for all i we get $p \cdot x_i' \ge p \cdot x_i$ for all i and $p \cdot x_j' > p \cdot x_j$, which, as above, leads again to the nonattainability of x'. ∎

Note that in the previous proof, the second conclusion (on price quasi-equilibrium), but not the first (on price equilibrium), depends on the hypothesis "$\omega + y \gg 0$ for some $y \in Y$."

The extreme simplicity of Proposition 4.2.15 (usually called the first fundamental theorem of welfare economics) should not obscure its significance. It is in fact one of the most important theorems of economics, since it is nothing less than a distilled and rigorous formal version of the "invisible hand theorem."

A careful reading of the proof of 4.2.15 will reveal that the only preference hypothesis used is that if x_i is a consumption vector, then we can find a z that is arbitrarily close to x_i and is $\gtrsim_i$-preferred to x_i, or, in other words, the local nonsatiation of preferences. Figure 4.2.7 exhibits an example of price equilibrium that is not optimal on account of the lack of

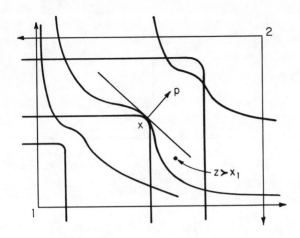

Figure 4.2.10

local nonsatiation in the preferences of agent 1. In the figure, $x_1' \gtrsim_1 x_1$ and $x_2' >_2 x_2$.

We now investigate the converse question, that is, when is an optimum sustainable as a price equilibrium? A glance at allocation x in Figure 4.2.10 makes it clear that a hypothesis of convexity of preferences will be required. But as the optimum allocation z in Figure 4.2.8 illustrates, even with the convexity of preferences an optimum may not be a price equilibrium. However, the next proposition (a form of the so-called second fundamental theorem of welfare economics) asserts that it will always be a price quasi-equilibrium. We have already (Proposition 4.2.14) discussed conditions under which the latter will be price equilibria.

4.2.16. Proposition. *Let preferences be convex and x a weakly optimal allocation. Then x is a price quasi-equilibrium.*

Proof. Let $V = \sum_{j=1}^n \{x_j' \in R_+^\ell : x_j' \gtrsim_j x_j\} - \omega$. Then $\sum_{i=1}^n x_i - \omega \in V \cap Y$. On the other hand, $V \cap \text{Int } Y = \varnothing$ because, otherwise, by the monotonicity of preferences, there would be an attainable x' with $x_j' >_j x_j$ for all j. Therefore, by the separating hyperplane theorem (F.2.2) there is $p \neq 0$ such that $p \cdot (\sum_{i=1}^n x_i - \omega) \geq p \cdot z$ for all $z \in Y$ and $p \cdot z \geq p \cdot (\sum_{i=1}^n x_i - \omega)$ for all $z \in V$. Because $-R_+^\ell \subset Y$ we must have $p > 0$. Suppose that $x_j' \gtrsim_j x_j$. Then, $x_j' + \sum_{i \neq j} x_i - \omega \in V$ and so $p \cdot x_j' \geq p \cdot x_j$. Hence, x is a price quasi-equilibrium. ∎

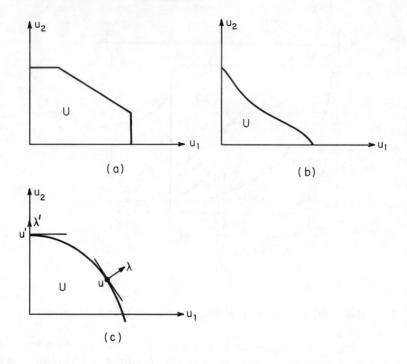

Figure 4.2.11

If x is a price quasi-equilibrium, the corresponding supporting price vector is called an *optimum price vector*. The set of optimum price vectors for a given x is a convex cone.

A deeper analysis of the optimality concept will be possible if we use utility functions.

> **4.2.17. Definition.** *The utility set $U \subset R_+^n$ is the set of utility vectors $u = (u_1, \ldots, u_n)$ which can be reached by attainable allocations; that is, $U = \{u \in R_+^n : for\ an\ attainable\ x,\ u_j(x_j) = u_j\ for\ all\ j\}$.*

See Figure 4.2.11 for some specimens. Abusing notation slightly, we will write $u(x) = (u_1(x_1), \ldots, u_n(x_n))$. Because of Proposition 4.2.4 and the continuity of the u_j functions, U is closed and bounded. Also, by continuity, as well as the free disposal hypothesis on Y, we have "$u \in U$ and $0 \le u' \le u$ implies $u' \in U$."

By definition, an attainable x is a weak optimum if and only if $u(x)$ belongs to the upper boundary of U, that is, if and only if $u' \gg u(x)$ im-

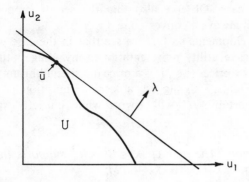

Figure 4.2.12

plies $u' \notin U$ (we call these u *weak utility optima*), whereas x is an optimum if and only if $u' > u(x)$ implies $u' \notin U$ (we call these u *utility optima*). As we know, and Figure 4.2.11a illustrates, both sets need not coincide, although, as in Figure 4.2.11b and c, they will if preferences are strictly monotone.

In analogy with the concept of price equilibrium we will now consider vectors of *utility weights* $\lambda \in R^n_+$ and linear expressions on R^n of the form $\sum_{i=1}^n \lambda_i u_i$.

4.2.18. Definition. *A vector $\bar{u} \in U$ is supported by $\lambda > 0$ if $\bar{u}$ maximizes $\sum_{i=1}^n \lambda_i u_i$ subject to $u \in U$. See Figure 4.2.12.*

It is obvious that any $u \in U$ supported by a $\lambda > 0$ (resp. $\lambda \gg 0$) is a weak utility optimum (resp. a utility optimum). Now assume that each u_j is concave. As we know, this implies the convexity of $\succeq_j$, but it is a somewhat stronger hypothesis (2.6, 2.8). We have:

4.2.19. Proposition. *If each u_j is concave, then U is convex and every weak utility optimum can be supported by a $\lambda > 0$.*

Proof. Let $u, u' \in U$ and $0 \le \alpha \le 1$. Take attainable allocations x, x', with $u(x) = u$, $u(x') = u'$. Then $x'' = \alpha x + (1-\alpha)x'$ is also attainable, that is, $u'' \in U$, and by the concavity of each u_j, $u'' = u(x'') \ge \alpha u + (1-\alpha)u' \ge 0$. Hence, $\alpha u + (1-\alpha)u' \in U$. Knowing that U is convex, the second claim follows immediately from the supporting hyperplane theorem (F.2.1). ∎

The previous proposition is illustrated in Figure 4.2.11c. Note that, as u' in the figure, an optimum may not be supportable by a $\lambda \gg 0$, even in the strictly monotone case. Observe also that the set of supporting weights for a given u is always a convex cone.

Taking stock of developments so far, we see that in the case where preferences admit concave utility representations, any weak optimum can be supported both by prices (i.e., it is a price quasi-equilibrium) and by a vector of utility weights. This suggests a deeper connection between the two notions of supportability. It will be worthwhile to briefly explore the matter.

4.2.20. Definition. *The pair $(p, \lambda) \in R_+^\ell \times R_+^n$ supports the attainable allocation x if $p \neq 0$, $\lambda \neq 0$ and:*

(i) $p \cdot (\sum_{j=1}^n x_j - \omega) \geq p \cdot y$ *for all $y \in Y$*;
(ii) $p \cdot (x_j' - x_j) \geq \lambda_j (u_j(x_j') - u_j(x_j))$ *for all j and $x_j' \in R_+^\ell$*.

If $\lambda_j > 0$, condition (ii) simply says that $(1/\lambda_j)p$ is a subgradient of u_j at x_j (see F.3 for the concept of subgradient). Clearly, the set of pairs (p, λ) supporting x is a convex cone. We have:

4.2.21. Proposition. *If (p, λ) supports the attainable allocation x, then:*

(i) *x is a price quasi-equilibrium with respect to p; and*
(ii) *λ is a vector of supporting utility weights for U at $u(x)$.*

Proof. (i) If $x_j' \succsim_j x_j$, then $u_j(x_j') \geq u_j(x_j)$. So $p \cdot x_j' \geq p \cdot x_j$. (ii) Let x' be attainable. Then $0 \leq p \cdot (\sum_{j=1}^n x_j - \sum_{j=1}^n x_j') \leq \sum_{j=1}^n \lambda_j (u_j(x_j) - u_j(x_j'))$. So $\sum_{j=1}^n \lambda_j u_j(x_j) \geq \sum_{j=1}^n \lambda_j u_j(x_j')$ for all attainable x'. ∎

Suppose that every u_j is concave and let x be a weakly optimal allocation. Because of its instructional value, we shall offer two indirect proofs of the converse of the previous proposition, namely of the existence of a supporting pair (p, λ) for x. Because of 4.2.16 we know that x is a price quasi-equilibrium with respect to some $p > 0$. We will show that for this p we can find $\lambda > 0$ such that (p, λ) is supporting. As a bonus we get an interpretation of the λ vector. By 4.2.19 we also know that U can be supported at $u(x)$ by a $\lambda > 0$. We will show that for this λ we can find $p > 0$ such that (p, λ) is supporting. As a bonus we will get an interpretation of the p vector.

4.2.22. Proposition. *Suppose that every u_j is concave and let x be a quasi-equilibrium with respect to $p > 0$. For each j with $p \cdot x_j > 0$ define $v_j : R_+ \to R_+$ by $v_j(m_j) = \sup\{u_j(z_j) : p \cdot z_j \leq m_j\}$.*

Then:

(i) *Each v_j is well defined, concave, and increasing.*

(ii) *For each j with $p \cdot x_j > 0$, let μ_j be a subgradient of v_j at $p \cdot x_j$; that is, $v_j(p \cdot x_j) + \mu_j(m_j - p \cdot x_j) \geq v_j(m_j)$ for all j and m_j. Put $\lambda_j = 1/\mu_j$ for j with $p \cdot x_j > 0$ and $\lambda_j = 0$ for j with $p \cdot x_j = 0$. Then (p, λ) is a supporting pair for x.*

(iii) *Let λ be such that (p, λ) supports x. If $p \cdot x_j > 0$, then $1/\lambda_j$ is a subgradient of v_j at $p \cdot x_j$.*

Proof. (i) We show that v_j is well defined; that is, $v_j(m) < \infty$ for all m. That v_j is increasing and concave is then immediate. If $p \cdot x_j > 0$, agent j is utility maximizing (4.2.13). Hence, $v_j(m) \leq u_j(x_j)$ for $m \leq p \cdot x_j$. Let $m = \alpha p \cdot x_j$, $\alpha > 1$, $p \cdot x_j' \leq m$. Since $p \cdot [(1/\alpha)x_j'] \leq p \cdot x_j$ and u_j is concave, we have $u_j(x_j) \geq u_j((1/\alpha)x_j') \geq (1/\alpha)u_j(x_j')$. So $u_j(x_j') \leq (m/p \cdot x_j)u_j(x_j)$ for all x_j' with $p \cdot x_j' \leq m$. Therefore, $v_j(m) \leq (m/p \cdot x_j)u_j(x_j)$.

(ii) If $p \cdot x_j = 0$, then $p \cdot (x_j' - x_j) \geq 0$ for all $x_j' \in R_+^\ell$, and so $\lambda_j = 0$ does the trick. Let $p \cdot x_j > 0$ [which implies $u_j(x_j) = v_j(p \cdot x_j)$] and μ_j be a subgradient of v_j at $p \cdot x_j$. Then, for any $x_j' \in R_+^\ell$, $u_j(x_j) + \mu_j p \cdot (x_j' - x_j) = v_j(p \cdot x_j) + \mu_j(p \cdot x_j' - p \cdot x_j) \geq v_j(p \cdot x_j') \geq u_j(x_j')$. So $\lambda_j = 1/\mu_j$ satisfies condition (ii) of Definition 4.2.20. Because $\omega + y \gg 0$ for some $y \in Y$, $p \cdot x_j > 0$ for some j. Hence, $\lambda > 0$.

(iii) If $p \cdot x_j > 0$, then we should have $\lambda_j > 0$. Let $\mu_j = 1/\lambda_j$ and $m \geq 0$. Take any x_j' with $p \cdot x_j' = m$. Then

$$v_j(p \cdot x_j) + \mu_j(m - p \cdot x_j) = u_j(x_j) + \mu_j p \cdot (x_j' - x_j) \geq u_j(x_j').$$

So, $v_j(p \cdot x_j) + \mu_j(m - p \cdot x_j) \geq v_j(m)$ and we conclude that μ_j is a subgradient of v_j at $p \cdot x_j$. ∎

For the given p, $v_j(m_j)$ is the indirect utility of wealth. Hence, for a given supporting pair (p, λ), Proposition 4.2.22 provides an interpretation of $\lambda_j > 0$ as the reciprocal of the marginal utility of wealth.

4.2.23. Proposition. Suppose that every u_j is concave and let $u(x) \in U$ be supported by the utility weights $\lambda > 0$. Define the function $V: R_+^\ell \to R_+$ by letting $V(z)$ be the maximum value of $\sum_{j=1}^n \lambda_j u_j(x_j)$ subject to $\sum_{j=1}^n x_j - z \in Y$. Then:

(i) *V is concave.*

(ii) *If p is a subgradient of V at ω, that is, $V(\omega) + p \cdot (z - \omega) \geq V(z)$ for all $z \in R_+^\ell$, then the pair (p, λ) supports x. Moreover, there is at least one subgradient of V at ω.*

(iii) *If p is such that (p, λ) is a supporting pair for x, then p is a subgradient of V at ω.*

Proof. Let $A = \{z \in R^{\ell} : (z + Y) \cap R_+^{\ell} \neq \varnothing\}$. Note that in the obvious way the function V is defined on the whole convex set A. Because $\omega + y \gg 0$ for some $y \in Y$, we have $\omega \in \text{Int } A$.

To establish the concavity of V note that if the allocation x (resp. x') is attainable for $z \in A$ (resp. $z' \in A$), then $\alpha x + (1 - \alpha)x'$, $0 < \alpha < 1$, is attainable for $\alpha z + (1 - \alpha)z'$. Therefore, by the concavity of the u_j functions, $V(\alpha z + (1 - \alpha)z') \geq \alpha(\sum_{j=1}^n \lambda_j u_j(x_j)) + (1 - \alpha)(\sum_{j=1}^n \lambda_j u_j(x_j'))$. This yields $V(\alpha z + (1 - \alpha)z') \geq \alpha V(z) + (1 - \alpha)V(z')$.

To prove (ii) let p be a subgradient of V at ω. It exists because $\omega \in \text{Int } A$. Since V is increasing, $p \neq 0$. Denote $v = \sum_{j=1}^n x_j - \omega \in Y$. Take any $y \in Y$. Let $z = \omega + v - y$. Since $z + y = \sum_{j=1}^n x_j$, we have $z \in A$ and $V(z) \geq \sum_{j=1}^n \lambda_j u_j(x_j) = V(\omega)$. Therefore, $V(\omega) + p \cdot (v - y) = V(\omega) + p \cdot (z - \omega) \geq V(z) \geq V(\omega)$, which yields $p \cdot v \geq p \cdot y$. So profit maximization holds. Take any j and $x_j' \geq 0$. Put $z = \omega - x_j + x_j' = \sum_{i \neq j} x_i + x_j' - v$. Since $z + v \geq 0$, we have $z \in A$ and

$$V(\omega) + p \cdot (z - \omega) = V(\omega) + p \cdot (x_j' - x_j) \geq V(z) \geq \sum_{i \neq j} \lambda_i u_i(x_i) + \lambda_j u_j(x_j').$$

Subtracting $\sum_{i \neq j} \lambda_i u_i(x_i)$ from both sides, we get $\lambda_j u_j(x_j) + p \cdot (x_j' - x_j) \geq \lambda_j u_j(x_j')$ for all $x_j' \geq 0$. Therefore, condition (ii) of Definition 4.2.20 is satisfied.

Finally, for (iii) put $\sum_{j=1}^n x_j = \omega + v$ and let $\sum_{j=1}^n x_j' = z + v'$ for $x_j', z \geq 0$, and $v' \in Y$. Then

$$V(\omega) + p \cdot (z - \omega) = \sum_{j=1}^n \lambda_j u_j(x_j) + \sum_{j=1}^n p \cdot (x_j' - x_j) + p \cdot (v - v') \geq \sum_{j=1}^n \lambda_j u_j(x_j').$$

Hence, maximizing over x', we get $V(\omega) + p \cdot (z - \omega) \geq V(z)$.   ∎

Thus, given the supporting pair (p, λ), Proposition 4.2.23 tells us that p is a vector of marginal social valuations of resources when social utility is formed by adding the individual utilities weighted according to λ.

As a final remark note that the proof of Proposition 4.2.21 does not make use of the maintained hypothesis "$\omega + y \gg 0$ for some $y \in Y$." Nevertheless, the latter is crucial for the converse (4.2.22, 4.2.23). For example, let $\ell = n = 1$, $Y = -R_+$, $\omega = 0$, $u(x) = \sqrt{x}$, $x = 0$. Then x is optimal and u is concave. But because the slope of $\sqrt{x}$ at 0 is not finite, there is no supporting pair (p, λ).

4.3   First-order necessary conditions for an optimum

The maintained hypotheses of this section are: *x is an attainable allocation, the preference relations are C^2, and $u_1, \ldots, u_n : R_+^{\ell} \to R$ are corresponding C^2 utility representations with no critical point.* The normal manifold of Y (see 3.4) is denoted Γ.

Conditions (i) and (ii) in the following proposition are called the *first-order necessary conditions for optimality*.

> **4.3.1. Proposition.** *If x is a weak optimum, then there are vectors $p \in R^\ell_+$ and $\lambda \in R^n_+$ such that $p \neq 0$, $\lambda \neq 0$, and:*
>
> (i) $\lambda_j \, \partial u_j(x_j) \leq p$, $[p - \lambda_j \, \partial u_j(x_j)] \cdot x_j = 0$ *for all j.*
> (ii) $(\sum_{j=1}^n x_j - \omega, p) \in \Gamma$.

Proof. First consider the case where Y is a polyhedral set, that is, $Y = \{y \in R^\ell : b_i \cdot y \leq c_i, b_i \neq 0, 1 \leq i \leq m\}$. With state space $R^{\ell n}$ we have that, by hypothesis, x is a weak vector maximum of $u = (u_1, \ldots, u_n)$ subject to the constraints:

(i) $x_j^h \geq 0$ for all jh, and
(ii) $b_i \cdot (\sum_{j=1}^n x_j - \omega) \leq c_i$ for all i.

Formally, the functions u_j are regarded as defined on $R^{\ell n}_+$. By D.1 we know there are vectors $\lambda \in R^n_+$, $\alpha \in R^{\ell n}_+$, $q \in R^m_+$, not all zero, such that

$$\lambda_j \, \partial_h u_j(x_j) + \alpha_{jh} - \sum_{i=1}^m q_i b_i^h = 0 \qquad \text{for all } jh$$

$$x_{jh} \alpha_{jh} = 0 \qquad \text{for all } jh$$

and

$$q_i \left(c_i - b_i \cdot \left(\sum_{j=1}^n x_j - \omega \right) \right) = 0 \qquad \text{for all } i.$$

Put $p = \sum_{i=1}^m q_i b_i$. Then the previous expressions can be equivalently rewritten as

$$\lambda_j \, \partial u_j(x_j) \leq p, \qquad [p - \lambda_j \, \partial u_j(x_j)] \cdot x_j = 0 \qquad \text{for all } j$$

and

$$\sum_{j=1}^n x_j - \omega \quad \text{is profit-maximizing for the price vector } p.$$

It only remains to be shown that $\lambda > 0$ and $p > 0$. If $\lambda_j > 0$, then $\lambda_j \, \partial u_j(x_j) > 0$ and so $p > 0$. Suppose, by way of contradiction, that $\lambda = 0$. Then $p \cdot x_j = 0$ for all j and so $p \cdot (\sum_{j=1}^n x_j) = 0$. Because $\sum_{j=1}^n x_j - \omega$ is profit-maximizing for p and $\omega + y \gg 0$ for some $y \in Y$, we get $p = 0$. This yields $\alpha_{jh} = 0$ for all jh and $q_i = 0$ for all i. Therefore, all multipliers are zero and we have a contradiction.

The general case can be proved by continuity. Given Y we can approximate it from the inside by a sequence of polyhedral production sets $Y_m \subset Y$ in such a way that $\sum_{j=1}^n x_j - \omega \in Y_m$ for all m. Then the allocation

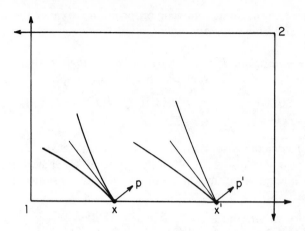

Figure 4.3.1

x is feasible in Y_m and, therefore, still a weak optimum. Let λ_m, p_m satisfy the first-order conditions with respect to x in Y_m. Normalize so that $\|(\lambda_m, p_m)\| = 1$. Without loss of generality we can assume that $(\lambda_m, p_m) \underset{m}{\to} (\lambda, p) \neq 0$. By continuity the first-order conditions and profit maximization will be preserved at the limit (where $Y_m \to Y$ is understood to mean uniform convergence in compacta of the corresponding distance functions). Finally, note that, as in the preceding paragraph, $\lambda > 0$ implies $p > 0$ and $p > 0$ implies $\lambda > 0$.   ∎

The necessary conditions imply that $p^h = \lambda_j \, \partial_h u_j(x_j)$ whenever $x_j^h > 0$. In particular, if $x_j \gg 0$, then p and ∂u_j are collinear. As the optimum allocation x in Figure 4.3.1 shows, it is possible to have $x_j^h = 0$ and $p^h = \lambda_j \, \partial_h u_j(x_j)$. We will call an optimum regular if, for some p, λ, this does not happen (as in the optimum x' in Figure 4.2.1). In Chapter 8 we will see that, typically, most optima are regular.

> **4.3.2. Definition.** *The weak optimum x is regular with respect to $p > 0$ and $\lambda > 0$ if, for all j and h: $\lambda_j \, \partial_h u_j(x_j) \le p^h$ with equality holding if and only if $x_j^h > 0$. We say that x is regular if it is so with respect to some p, λ.*

As is clear enough, and as the notation suggests, there is an intimate connection between the first-order necessary conditions and the concept of supporting prices and utility weights.

4.3.3. Proposition. *We have:*

(i) *If x is a price equilibrium with respect to p, then for some $\lambda > 0$ the first-order necessary conditions are satisfied.*

(ii) *If $u(x)$ is supported by $\lambda > 0$, then for some $p > 0$ the first-order necessary conditions are satisfied.*

(iii) *Let preferences be convex. If the first-order necessary conditions are satisfied with respect to p and λ, then x is a price quasi-equilibrium with respect to p.*

(iv) *Let the utility functions be concave. If the first-order necessary conditions are satisfied with respect to p and λ, then x is supported by (p, λ).*

Proof. (i) By the definition of quasi-equilibrium the price vector p is profit-maximizing; that is, $(\sum_{j=1}^{n} x_j - \omega) \in \Gamma$. Also, for each j, x_j solves the problem: "Miminize $p \cdot z$ subject to $u_j(z) \geq u_j(x_j)$ and $z \geq 0$." The first-order conditions for this problem (see D.1) yield $\alpha_j \geq 0$ and $\lambda_j \geq 0$ such that $\alpha_j p \geq \lambda_j \partial u_j(x_j)$ and $[\alpha_j p - \lambda_j \partial u_j(x_j)] \cdot x_j = 0$. Because not all multipliers can be zero and $\partial u_j(x_j) > 0$, we must have $\alpha_j > 0$. So we can as well take $\alpha_j = 1$. To show that $\lambda = (\lambda_1, \ldots, \lambda_n) > 0$, proceed as in the proof of Proposition 4.3.1.

(ii) For each commodity index h, put $q^h = \max_j \lambda_j \partial_h u_j(x_j)$. Say that maximum is reached for j_h. Because $\partial u_j(x_j) > 0$ for all j and $\lambda_j > 0$ for some j, we have $q > 0$. It is clear that for this q the first-order necessary conditions involving utility are satisfied. Indeed, if $q^h > \lambda_j \partial_h u_j(x_j)$ and $x_j^h > 0$, the λ-weighted sum of utilities could be increased by transferring some amount of commodity h from agent j to agent j_h. Because of the first-order conditions, if $\sum_{j=1}^{n} x_j^h > 0$, we can always assume that $x_{j_h}^h > 0$. Suppose now that $q \cdot (z + \omega) > q \cdot (\sum_{j=1}^{n} x_j)$ and $z + \omega \geq 0$, $z \in Y$. Then, for $\epsilon > 0$ sufficiently small, if for each h we add $\epsilon(z^h + \omega^h - \sum_{j=1}^{n} x_j^h)$ to the consumption of j_h we end up with an attainable allocation that increases the sum of utilities. So $q \cdot (z + \omega) \leq q \cdot (\sum_{j=1}^{n} x_j)$ whenever $z \in Y$ and $z + \omega \geq 0$. This implies $q \cdot (\sum_{j=1}^{n} x_j) > 0$ and also,

$$\text{Int}(Y + \{\omega\}) \cap \{v \in R_+^\ell : q \cdot v \geq q \cdot (\sum_{j=1}^{n} x_j)\} = \varnothing.$$

Let $p > 0$ separate these two convex sets (F.2.2) and normalize p so that $p \cdot (\sum_{j=1}^{n} x_j) = q \cdot (\sum_{j=1}^{n} x_j)$. Then profit maximization is satisfied and it is simply seen that $p \geq q$ with equality holding for any commodity h with $\sum_{j=1}^{n} x_j^h > 0$.

(iii) By the first-order conditions profit maximization holds and

$$\lambda_j \partial u_j(x_j) x_j = p \cdot x_j \quad \text{for all } j.$$

Let $x_j' \succsim_j x_j$. Then, by the first-order conditions and the convexity of $\succsim_j$, we have $p \cdot x_j' \geq \lambda_j \, \partial u_j(x_j) x_j' \geq \lambda_j \, \partial u_j(x_j) x_j = p \cdot x_j$, which is the desired result.

(iv) Profit maximization follows by definition. Also, for all j and x_j', $p \cdot (x_j' - x_j) \geq \lambda_j \, \partial u_j(x_j)(x_j' - x_j) \geq \lambda_j(u_j(x_j') - u_j(x_j))$, where the first inequality follows from the first-order conditions and the second from the concavity of the u_j functions.   ∎

In order to gain some practice on the use of the first-order conditions we shall now explore two topics of theoretical interest. The first is the uniqueness, up to scalar multiplication, of the prices and utility weights generated by the first-order conditions. The corresponding results will turn out to be very useful in later developments. The second concerns the characterization of optimality by the absence of potential gains from trade on the part of any group of two traders.

As for the first topic, Example 4.3.4 illustrates that the prices and utility weights associated with an optimum allocation need to be unique (once normalized) even for commodities that are consumed by some agent or for agents that consume some commodity. Clearly, for commodities that no one consumes or agents that consume no commodities, uniqueness cannot be expected.

4.3.4. Example. Let $\ell = 2$, $n = 2$, $Y = -R_+^2$, $\omega = (1, 1)$, $u_1(x_1) = x_1^1$, $u_2(x_2) = x_2^2$. The allocation $x_1 = (1, 0)$, $x_2 = (0, 1)$ is an optimum and it satisfies the necessary conditions with respect to any p, λ such that $\lambda = p$.

The allocation x of Example 4.3.4 is particular in that the two consumers do not have at x a commodity in common desired by both of them. It naturally suggests the next definition and proposition.

> **4.3.5. Definition.** *The allocation x is linked if:*
>
> (i)   *for each j, $\partial_h u_j(x_j) x_j^h \neq 0$ for some h;*
> (ii) *for each h, $\partial_h u_j(x_j) x_j^h \neq 0$ for some j; and*
> (iii) *the set of agents cannot be partitioned in two groups having no desired commodity in common. More formally, it is not possible to label commodities and agents in such a way that for some $1 < r \leq \ell$, $1 < s \leq r$ we have that $\partial_h u_j(x_j) x_j^h \neq 0$ only if $j \geq s$ and $h \geq r$ or $j < s$ and $h < r$.*

Part (ii) of the previous definition implies $\sum_j x_j \gg 0$, which in a production context is restrictive. We could require part (ii) only for produced commodities. In this case the conclusion of the next proposition would only hold for those commodities. Mutatis mutandis, the same applies to part (i). We have the following strong uniqueness result:

4.3.6. Proposition. *If the allocation x is linked and satisfies the first-order conditions with respect to (p, λ), then $p \gg 0$, $\lambda \gg 0$. Furthermore, there is a neighborhood V of x on $R_+^{\ell n}$ and a C^1 function $\xi: V \to R_{++}^\ell \times R_{++}^n$ such that if $x' \in V$ satisfies the first-order conditions with respect to (p, λ), $\|p\| = 1$, then $(p, \lambda) = \xi(x')$.*

Proof. The proof can be carried out for p and λ separately and in an entirely parallel manner. So to avoid repetition we develop it only for p.

The proof shall be by induction on ℓ and shall require only that x satisfy the first-order conditions involving utility. The result is obviously true for $\ell = 1$. Let it be true for $\ell = m - 1$ and suppose that $\ell = m$. The two key and simple observations are: (i) A commodity can be chosen (say, the ℓth) such that if all the entries x_j^ℓ are deleted from the vector x, then the resulting vector $\hat{x} \in R^{(\ell-1)n}$ still satisfies the definition of linked allocation for the remaining $(\ell-1)$ commodities; and (ii) the vector $\hat{x}$ still satisfies the first-order conditions with respect to λ and $\hat{p} = (p^1, \ldots, p^{\ell-1})$. Therefore, by the induction hypothesis, $\hat{p} \gg 0$ and there is an open set $\hat{x} \in \hat{V} \subset R^{(\ell-1)n}$ and a function $\hat{\xi}: \hat{V} \to R_{++}^{\ell-1}$ satisfying the conclusion of the proposition for the first $(\ell-1)$ commodities.

Because x is linked we have that $\partial_\ell u_j(x_j) x_j^\ell > 0$ for some j and, relabeling commodities if necessary, we can assume that $\partial_{\ell-1} u_j(x_j) x_j^{\ell-1} > 0$. Therefore, $p^\ell / p^{\ell-1} = \partial_\ell u_j(x_j) / \partial_{\ell-1} u_j(x_j)$, which yields $p^\ell > 0$. Now let $V \subset R^{\ell n}$ be an open neighborhood of x such that if $x' \in V$, then $\hat{x}' \in V$ and $\partial_\ell u_j(x_j')$, $\partial_{\ell-1} u_j(x_j')$, $x_j'^\ell$, $x_i'^{\ell-1}$ are strictly positive. Define $\xi': V \to R_{++}^\ell$ by

$$\xi'(x') = \left(\hat{\xi}(\hat{x}'), \frac{\partial_\ell u_j(x_j')}{\partial_{\ell-1} u_j(x_j')} \hat{\xi}^{\ell-1}(\hat{x}') \right).$$

Finally, normalize $\xi(x) = [1/\|\xi'(x)\|] \xi'(x)$. It is then easily verified that ξ is as desired. ∎

As for the second illustrative topic of the use of the first-order conditions, let preferences be convex. By Proposition 4.2.10 we know that if at x there is no group of at most ℓ agents with the ability to improve on their final consumption of commodities by trading among themselves (and making full use of the production set Y), then x is an optimum. Under which conditions can we reach the same conclusion when we test only the groups formed by two traders? As the following example shows, some conditions will be needed.

4.3.7. Example. Let $\ell = n = 3$, $Y = -R_+^3$, $\omega = (2, 2, 2)$, $u_1(x_1) = 2x_1^1 + x_1^2$, $u_2(x_2) = 2x_2^2 + x_2^3$, $u_3(x_3) = x_3^1 + 2x_3^3$. Then the (linked) allocation $\bar{x}_1 = (1, 1, 0)$, $\bar{x}_2 = (0, 1, 1)$, $\bar{x}_3 = (1, 0, 1)$ is not a weak optimum because it is dominated by $x_1' = (2, 0, 0)$, $x_2' = (0, 2, 0)$, $x_3' = (0, 0, 2)$. But no group of two traders can do better alone. The cyclic structure of this example is entirely typical and is readily suggestive of sufficient conditions for pairwise to imply full optimality.

4.3.8. Definition. *The allocation x is a pairwise weak optimum if there are no j, j' and $v, v' \in R^\ell$ such that $x_j + v >_j x_j$, $x_{j'} + v' >_{j'} x_{j'}$ and $\sum_{i=1}^n x_i - \omega + v + v' \in Y$.*

4.3.9. Proposition. *Let preferences be convex and x a pairwise weak optimum. Then x is a weak optimum under any of the following two conditions:*

(i) *There is a j with $x_j \gg 0$.*

(ii) *$Y = -R_+^\ell$ and there is a commodity h such that preferences are strictly monotone with respect to h (i.e., $\partial_h u_j(x_j) > 0$ for all j) and $x_j^h > 0$ for all j.*

Proof. (i) Let $x_1 \gg 0$. Put $\bar{p} = \partial u_1(x_1)$. Since $0 \ll x_1 \in Y + \{\omega\} - \sum_{j=2}^n x_j$, the first-order conditions must be satisfied for any pair (x_1, x_j); that is, $\lambda_1 \partial u_1(x_1) \leq p$, $[p - \lambda_1 \partial u_1(x_1)] \cdot x_1 = 0$, $\lambda_j \partial u_j(x_j) \leq p$, $[p - \lambda_j \partial u_j(x_j)] \cdot x_j = 0$ for some $\lambda_1 \geq 0$, $\lambda_2 \geq 0$ and profit-maximizing $p > 0$. Because $x_1 \gg 0$ we cannot have $\lambda_1 = 0$. Therefore, we can take $\lambda_1 = 1$, which implies $p = \bar{p}$. So $\lambda_j \partial u_j(x_j) \leq \bar{p}$ and $[\bar{p} - \partial u_j(x_j)] \cdot x_j = 0$ for all j. Hence, the first-order conditions are satisfied. Because preferences are convex, x is a quasi-equilibrium (4.3.3) and therefore weakly optimal.

(ii) Let $x_j^1 > 0$ for all j. Put $p^1 = 1$ and for any $2 \leq h \leq \ell$ let $p^h = \max_j [\partial_h u_j(x_j)/\partial_1 u_j(x_j)]$. We show that x satisfies the first-order conditions with respect to p and $\lambda_j = 1/\partial_1 u_j(x_j)$, $1 \leq j \leq n$. As in (i) this will suffice. By construction, $\lambda_j \partial u_j(x_j) \leq p$ for all j. Suppose, by way of contradiction, that $\lambda_j \partial_h u_j(x_j) < p^h$ and $x_j^h > 0$. Take i such that $p^h = \partial_h u_i(x_i)/\partial_1 u_i(x_i)$. Then

$$\partial_h u_j(x_j)/\partial_1 u_j(x_j) < \partial_h u_i(x_i)/\partial_1 u_i(x_i), \quad x_j^h > 0, \quad \text{and} \quad x_i^1 > 0,$$

which, of course, means that there is a favorable exchange of commodity h from j for commodity 1 from i. This is a violation of pairwise optimality. ■

As a final remark on Proposition 4.3.7 we note that the convexity hypothesis on preference plays a key role (see 4.4.5 and the discussion leading to it) and that part (ii) does not hold for general production sets.

4.4   Second-order conditions for an optimum

Besides the maintained hypotheses of Section 4.3 we assume now that *x is a fixed attainable allocation satisfying the first-order necessary conditions with respect to $p > 0$, $\|p\| = 1$, and $\lambda > 0$. Putting*

$$z = (\textstyle\sum_{j=1}^{n} x_j - \omega) + p$$

we also assume that the distance function γ is C^2 at z. Remember (3.4, 3.5) that $\partial\gamma(z) = z - \pi(z)$, where $\pi: R^\ell \to Y$ is the projection function.

The key object for the second-order theory is a certain bilinear form B on a certain cone $K \subset R^{\ell(n+1)}$. Specifically,

$$K = \Big\{ v \in R^{\ell(n+1)}: p \cdot v_j = 0 \text{ for all } 0 \le j \le n+1,$$

$$v_j^h \ge 0 \text{ and } [p_h - \lambda_j \, \partial_h u_j(x_j)] v_j^h = 0 \text{ whenever } x_j^h = 0,$$

$$\sum_{j=1}^{n} v_j = \partial\pi(z) v_{n+1} \Big\}$$

$$B(v, v') = \sum_{j=1}^{n} \lambda_j \, \partial^2 u_j(x_j)(v_j, v_j') - \partial^2 \gamma(z)\Big(\sum_{j=1}^{n} v_j, v_{n+1}' \Big).$$

A few comments on the expressions for K and B are in order:
(i) Clearly, $K \subset T_p^{n+1}$. If x is a regular optimum with respect to p, λ, then K is simply the linear subspace

$$K = \Big\{ v \in R^{\ell(n-1)}: p \cdot v_j = 0 \text{ for all } 1 \le j \le n+1, \ v_j^h = 0 \text{ if } x_j^h = 0,$$

$$\text{and } \sum_{j=1}^{n} v_j = \partial\pi(z) v_{n+1} \Big\}.$$

If, in addition, x is linked, it is easily verified that $\{\sum_{j=1}^{n} v_j : v \in K\} = T_p$.

(ii) The cone K represents the directions on which the form B is to be tested to determine optimality. The entries $v_1, \ldots, v_n$ correspond to the consumption components x_i, whereas v_{n+1} is a displacement direction for the production component z. Informally, all that matters is that $\partial\pi(z) v_{n+1}$ is a direction tangent to the boundary of Y at $\sum_{j=1}^{n} x_j - \omega$. In fact, we could express, if we so wished, the "first-order production constraint" simply as $\sum_{j=1}^{n} v_j \in \text{Range } \partial\pi(z)$, dispensing with the auxiliary variable v_{n+1}. However, the introduction of the latter is most convenient for the expression of the bilinear form B.

Observe that, other things equal, K is smallest when $\sum_{j=1}^{n} x_j - \omega$ is a vertex of Y, in which case, $\partial\pi(z) = 0$, and largest when $\sum_j x_j - \omega$ has a neighborhood in ∂Y that is a C^2 manifold, in which case the range of $\partial\pi(z)$ is the tangent plane to ∂Y at $\sum_{j=1}^{n} x_j - \omega$.

(iii) Concerning B, the last term of the sum (the only one involving the production set) can be rewritten on K, where $\sum_{j=1}^{n} v_j = \partial\pi(z)v_{n+1}$, in several equivalent ways; for example,

$$
\begin{aligned}
-\partial^2\gamma(z)\left(\sum_{j=1}^{n} v_j, v'_{n+1}\right) &= -\partial^2\gamma(z)(\partial\pi(z)v_{n+1}, v'_{n+1}) \\
&= [\partial^2\gamma(z)\partial^2\gamma(z) - \partial^2\gamma(z)](v_{n+1}, v'_{n+1}) \\
&= \partial\pi(z)[\partial\pi(z) - I](v_{n+1}, v'_{n+1}).
\end{aligned}
$$

In particular,

$$
-\partial^2\gamma(z)\left(\sum_{j=1}^{n} v_j, v_{n+1}\right) = \|\partial\pi(z)v_{n+1}\|^2 - \|v_{n+1}\|^2 + \partial^2\gamma(z)(v_{n+1}, v_{n+1}).
$$

Note that because the eigenvalues of $\partial^2\gamma(z)$ are less than or equal to one (3.5.1) the form $\partial^2\gamma(z)\partial^2\gamma(z) - \partial^2\gamma(z) = \partial\pi(z)[\partial\pi(z) - I]$ is negative semidefinite (B.6.2, B.6.3), which is simply a reflection of the convexity hypothesis on Y. Therefore, the presence of the production term will only help to make B negative semidefinite on K. Note also that the form $\partial\pi(z)[\partial\pi(z) - I]$ is null on T_p in the two cases where the vector $\sum_{j=1}^{n} x_j - \omega$ is a vertex of Y [because then $\partial\pi(z) = 0$] or it lies in a flat $(\ell-1)$-dimensional piece of ∂Y [because then $\partial\pi(z) - I = 0$ on T_p].

(iv) At first sight the last term of B may appear a bit puzzling. Let us verify that in a familiar case it coincides with what we would expect. Suppose that in a neighborhood of $\bar{y} = \sum_{j=1}^{n} x_j - \omega$, ∂Y is a C^2 manifold defined by the constraint $\eta(y) \le 0$. We can take $\partial\eta(\bar{y}) = p$. Remember that $\|p\| = 1$. The production contribution to the second-order bilinear form coming out of the mathematical theory (D.2) would then be $-\partial^2\eta(\bar{y})$. Remembering from 3.5 the definition of the function g, we have that, on T_p, $\partial^2\eta(\bar{y}) = \partial g(\bar{y}) = [\partial\hat{\pi}(z)]^{-1}\partial^2\gamma(z)$, where $\hat{\pi}$ is the restriction of π to T_p and for the last equality we appeal to 3.5.4.ii. In order to evaluate $-\partial^2\eta(\bar{y})(w, w)$, put $v_{n+1} = [\partial\hat{\pi}(z)]^{-1}w$. Then

$$
\begin{aligned}
-\partial^2\eta(\bar{y})(w, w) &= -([\partial\hat{\pi}(z)]^{-1}\partial^2\gamma(z))(\partial\hat{\pi}(z)v_{n+1}, \partial\hat{\pi}(z)v_{n+1}) \\
&= [\partial\pi(z) - I](v_{n+1}, \partial\pi(z)v_{n+1}) \\
&= \partial\pi(z)[\partial\pi(z) - I](v_{n+1}, v_{n+1}),
\end{aligned}
$$

which is precisely the expression we are using.

> **4.4.1. Definition.** x *is a local optimum, local weak optimum, local price equilibrium, or local price quasi-equilibrium if it satisfies the corresponding definition when the consumption set of each j is restricted to some open neighborhood of x_j.*

It is obvious that every statement and conclusion of the previous section remains valid if interpreted locally. We are now ready to state:

4.4.2. Proposition (second-order sufficient conditions). Under
the maintained hypotheses and for the given definitions of the
cone $K \subset R^{\ell(n+1)}$ and the bilinear form B, a sufficient condition
for x to be a local optimum is that B be negative definite on K.

The second-order necessary conditions will play a less important role
in this monograph. So, in order to facilitate the application of the general mathematical theory, we shall not hesitate to require that x be linked
(Definition 4.3.5) and that γ be C^3 at z.

4.4.3. Proposition (second-order necessary conditions). Let x be
linked and γ be C^3 at z. Under the maintained hypotheses and
for the given definitions of the cone $K \subset R^{\ell(n+1)}$ and the bilinear
form B, a necessary condition for x to be a weak optimum is that
B be negative semidefinite on K.

Proof of Proposition 4.4.2. The proof shall proceed from first principles
and by contradiction. Suppose that x is not a local optimum. Then we
can find a sequence of attainable allocations x_m such that $x_m \to x$ and, for
all m, $u_j(x_{mj}) \geq u_j(x_j)$ for all j, the inequality being strict for some j.
Therefore, $x_m \neq x$. Let

$$s_m = \left(x_{m1}, \ldots, x_{mn}, \sum_{j=1}^{n} x_{mj} - \omega \right) \in R^{\ell(n+1)}$$

and define s accordingly. Then $s_m \to s$ and $s_m \neq s$. Without loss of gener-
ality we can assume that, for some $w \in R^{\ell(n+1)}$, $(1/\|s_m - s\|)(s_m - s) \to w$.
Of course, $\sum_{j=1}^{n} w_j = w_{n+1}$, which in particular implies $w_j \neq 0$ for some
$j \leq n$. The proof will consist of two steps. In the first, we shall construct a
certain test direction $v \in K$. In the second, we shall show that for this v,
$B(v, v) \geq 0$. Because $v \neq 0$, this will constitute the desired contradiction.

Step 1. Consider a fixed $j \leq n$. Because $u_j(x_{mj}) - u_j(x_j) \geq 0$, Taylor's formula (C.4.1) yields $\partial u_j(x_j)w_j \geq 0$. Because $x_m \geq 0$, we have
$w_j^h \geq 0$ whenever $x_j^h = 0$. By the first-order conditions we get $p \cdot w_j \geq$
$\lambda_j \partial u_j(x_j)w_j \geq 0$.

By profit maximization, $p \cdot (\sum_{j=1}^{n} x_{mj} - \omega) \leq p \cdot (\sum_{j=1}^{n} x_j - \omega)$ for all m.
Therefore, $p \cdot (\sum_{j=1}^{n} w_j) \leq 0$. But from the previous paragraph we have
$p \cdot w_j \geq 0$ for all $j \leq n$. Hence, $p \cdot w_j = 0$ for all j. Let $j \leq n$; if $x_j^h = 0$ and
$w_j^h > 0$, then we must have $p^h = \lambda_j \partial_h u_j(x_j)$. Otherwise, $p^h > \lambda_j \partial_h u_j(x_j)$
and $w_j^h > 0$ yield $\lambda_j \partial u_j(x_j)w_j < p \cdot w_j \leq 0$, which is impossible. Therefore,
if $x_j^h = 0$, then $[p_h - \lambda_j \partial_h u(x_j)]w_j^h = 0$.

Because $w_{n+1} = \sum_{j=1}^{n} w_j$ we have $p \cdot w_{n+1} = 0$; that is, $w_{n+1} \in T_p$. The
vector w_{n+1} is a direction spanned by Y at $y = \sum_{j=1}^{n} x_j - \omega$; that is, if
$w_{n+1} \neq 0$, then

$$\frac{1}{\|w_{n+1}\|} w_{n+1} = \lim_m \frac{1}{\|y_m - y\|} (y_m - y) \qquad \text{for some } y_m \in Y.$$

We could just take $y_m = \sum_{j=1}^n x_{mj} - \omega$. Because p supports Y at y, we have, by F.2.4, that $w_{n+1} \in \text{Range } \partial \pi(z)$; that is, $w_{n+1} = \partial \pi(z) \hat{v}_{n+1}$ for some $\hat{v}_{n+1}$. If $\hat{v}_{n+1} = 0$, put $z_m = 0$. If $\hat{v}_{n+1} \neq 0$, choose any $z_m \to z$ such that

$$\frac{1}{\|z_m - z\|} (z_m - z) \to \hat{v}_{n+1}.$$

Define $\hat{v} \in R^{\ell(n+1)}$ by $\hat{v}_j = w_j$ for $j \leq n$ and take $\hat{v}_{n+1}$ as above, that is, $\sum_{j=1}^n \hat{v}_j = \partial \pi(z) \hat{v}_{n+1}$. Then $\hat{v} \in K$. Finally, take $v = (1/\|\hat{v}\|)\hat{v}$. Then $v \in K$. Note also that if we choose z_m in such a way that $z_m = 0$ if $\hat{v}_{n+1} = 0$ and

$$\frac{1}{\|z_m - z\|} (z_m - z) \to \hat{v}_{n+1} \qquad \text{otherwise}$$

we have

$$\lim_m \frac{1}{\|(x_m, z_m) - (x, z)\|} [(x_m, z_m) - (x, z)] = v.$$

Step 2. Denote by $\bar{x}, \bar{z}$ the given allocation and z vectors. This frees the symbols x, z to be used as generic variables. Define the auxiliary function $\eta(y, z) = \frac{1}{2}\|y - z\|^2 - \gamma(z)$ and note that η is C^2 at any $(y, \bar{z})$. By definition of the γ function we have $\eta(y, z) \geq 0$ for all $y \in Y$ and $z \in R^\ell$. Also, $\eta(\bar{y}, \bar{z}) = 0$ for $\bar{y} = \sum_{j=1}^n \bar{x}_j - \omega$. The derivatives of η are of interest. We have $\partial_y \eta(y, z) = y - z$ and $\partial_z \eta(y, z) = \pi(z) - y$. Hence, $\partial_y \eta(\bar{y}, \bar{z}) = -p$ and $\partial_z \eta(\bar{y}, \bar{z}) = 0$. In matrix form the second derivative is

$$\partial^2 \eta(y, z) = \begin{bmatrix} I & -I \\ -I & \partial \pi(z) \end{bmatrix}.$$

On a neighborhood of $(\bar{x}, \bar{z})$ define the (Lagrangian) function:

$$L(x, z) = \sum_{j=1}^n \lambda_j u_j(x_j) + \eta\left(\sum_{j=1}^n x_j - \omega, z\right).$$

Computing first and second derivatives we get, for any vector $w \in R^{\ell(n+1)}$:

$$\partial L(\bar{x}, \bar{z}) w = \sum_{j=1}^n (\lambda_j \partial u_j(\bar{x}_j) - p) w_j$$

and

$$\partial^2 L(\bar{x}, \bar{z})(w, w) = \sum_{j=1}^n \lambda_j \partial^2 u_j(\bar{x}_j)(w_j, w_j)$$
$$+ \left\|\sum_{j=1}^n w_j\right\|^2 - 2w_{n+1} \cdot \left(\sum_{j=1}^n w_j\right) + \partial \pi(\bar{z})(w_{n+1}, w_{n+1}).$$

Observe that for all m we have $L(x_m, z_m) - L(\bar{x}, \bar{z}) \geq 0$ because

(i) $u_j(x_{mj}) \geq u_j(\bar{x}_j)$ by hypothesis;
(ii) $\sum_{j=1}^{n} x_{mj} - \omega \in Y$ and so $\eta(\sum_{j=1}^{m} x_{mj} - \omega, z) \geq 0$; and
(iii) $\eta(\bar{y}, \bar{z}) = 0$.

Also, $\partial L(\bar{x}, \bar{z})((x_m, z_m) - (\bar{x}, \bar{z})) = \sum_{j=1}^{n} (\lambda_j \partial u_j(\bar{x}_j) - p)(x_{mj} - \bar{x}_j) \leq 0$ because of the first-order conditions. Therefore, by Taylor's formula (C.4.1) we have:

$$0 \leq L(x_m, z_m) - L(\bar{x}, \bar{z}) - \partial L(\bar{x}, \bar{z})((x_m, z_m) - (\bar{x}, \bar{z}))$$

$$= \tfrac{1}{2} \partial^2 L(\bar{x}, \bar{z})((x_m, z_m) - (\bar{x}, \bar{z}), (x_m, z_m) - (\bar{x}, \bar{z})) + o(\|(x_m, z_m) - (\bar{x}, \bar{z})\|^2).$$

So, dividing both sides by $1/\|(x_m, z_m) - (\bar{x}, \bar{z})\|$ and taking limits, we get $\partial^2 L(\bar{x}, \bar{z})(v, v) \geq 0$. We already know that $v \in K$, $v \neq 0$. Hence, the proof will be finished if we show that $\partial^2 L(\bar{x}, \bar{z})(v, v) = B(v, v)$, that is, that

$$\left\| \sum_{j=1}^{n} v_j \right\|^2 - 2v_{n+1} \cdot \left(\sum_{j=1}^{n} v_j \right) + \partial \pi(\bar{z})(v_{n+1}, v_{n+1}) = -\partial^2 \gamma(\bar{z}) \left(\sum_{j=1}^{n} v_j, v_{n+1} \right).$$

But, using $\sum_{j=1}^{n} v_j = \partial \pi(\bar{z}) v_{n+1}$, this is clear enough:

$$\left\| \sum_{j=1}^{n} v_j \right\|^2 - 2v_{n+1} \cdot \left(\sum_{j=1}^{n} v_j \right) + \partial \pi(\bar{z})(v_{n+1}, v_{n+1})$$

$$= \|\partial \pi(\bar{z}) v_{n+1}\|^2 - 2\partial \pi(\bar{z})(v_{n+1}, v_{n+1}) + \partial \pi(\bar{z})(v_{n+1}, v_{n+1})$$

$$= \partial \pi(\bar{z})[\partial \pi(\bar{z}) - I](v_{n+1}, v_{n+1}) = -\partial^2 \gamma(\bar{z})(\partial \pi(\bar{z}) v_{n+1}, v_{n+1})$$

$$= -\partial^2 \gamma(\bar{z}) \left(\sum_{j=1}^{n} v_j, v_{n+1} \right). \qquad \blacksquare$$

Proof of Proposition 4.4.3. Let $\bar{x}$, $\bar{z}$, $\bar{\lambda}$, $\bar{p}$ be the specific values we are considering, thus freeing the symbols x, z, λ, p for use as generic values of the corresponding variables.

In the sequel, it is understood that $u_j(x_j, z) = u_j(x_j)$. We begin by setting up a modified optimization problem in the variable space $(x, z) \in R^{\ell(n+1)}$. Clearly, if $\bar{x}$ is a local weak optimum of $u_1(x_1), \ldots, u_n(x_n)$ subject to $x \geq 0$ and $\sum_{j=1}^{n} x_j - \omega \in Y$, then $(\bar{x}, \bar{z})$ is a local weak optimum of $u_1(x_1, z), \ldots, u_n(x_n, z)$ subject to the constraints (i) $x_j^h \geq 0$ for all j, h and (ii) $\sum_{j=1}^{n} x_j - \omega - \pi(z) \leq 0$. Letting $\lambda \in R_+^n$, $\mu \in R_+^{\ell n}$, $p \in R_+^\ell$ be generic multipliers, the first-order conditions for this problem are (D.1):

(i) $\lambda_j \partial_h u_j(x_j) + \mu_{jh} - p^h = 0$ and $\mu_{jh} x_j^h = 0$ for all j, or, equivalently, $\lambda_j \partial_h u_j(x_j) \leq p^j$ with equality if $x_j^h > 0$.
(ii) $p \partial \pi(z) = 0$ and $p \cdot [\sum_j x_j - \omega - \pi(z)] = 0$.

These first-order conditions are satisfied for the given $\bar{x}$, $\bar{z}$, $\bar{\lambda}$, $\bar{p}$.

In order to apply the general mathematical theorem on second-order necessary conditions (D.2.i) we should verify the rank condition. Here is where the hypothesis that $\bar{x}$ is linked will be of importance. We saw in Proposition 4.3.6 that, subject to the constraints $\lambda \geq 0$, $p \geq 0$, and $\mu_{jh} = 0$ whenever $x_{jh} \neq 0$, the linear system of equations $\lambda_j \partial_h u_j(\bar{x}_j) + \mu_{jh} - p^h = 0$ has a one-dimensional set of solutions λ, p, μ. Further (except for the trivial solution), we have $\lambda \gg 0$ and $p \gg 0$, which means that the uniqueness (up to normalization) of the solutions does not depend on the constraints $\lambda \geq 0$, $p \geq 0$. Summing up: Let A be the matrix whose columns are the gradients at $(\bar{x}, \bar{z})$ of the objective functions and binding constraints. Say that A has m columns. By the uniqueness argument just given, $\dim\{w: Aw = 0\} \leq 1$. Hence, rank $A \geq m - 1$; that is, the rank condition holds.

It remains to verify that the negative semidefiniteness of B on K is precisely the second-order necessary condition one gets from the above optimization problem according to D.2.i. For the test cone K, this is clear enough. Remember that, being x linked, we have $\bar{p} \gg 0$ and so $\sum_{j=1}^n v_j \leq \partial \pi(z) v_{n+1}$, $p \cdot [\partial \pi(\bar{z}) v_{n+1} - \sum_{j=1}^n v_j] = 0$ does in fact imply $\sum_{j=1}^n v_j = \partial \pi(\bar{z}) v_{n+1}$. To find the relevant bilinear form, define the (Lagrangian) function

$$L(x, z) = \sum_{j=1}^n \bar{\lambda}_j u_j(x, z) + \sum_{jh} \mu_{jh} x_j^h - \sum_h \bar{p}^h \left[\sum_{j=1}^n x_j^h - \omega - \pi^h(z) \right].$$

Then by D.2.1 the following form must be negative semidefinite:

$$\partial^2 L(\bar{x}, \bar{z})(v, v) = \sum_{j=1}^n \bar{\lambda}_j \partial^2 u_j(\bar{x}_j)(v_j, v_j) + \sum_h \bar{p}^h \partial^2 \pi^h(\bar{z})(v_{n+1}, v_{n+1}).$$

To check that, on K, $\partial^2 L(\bar{x}, \bar{z})(v, v) = B(v, v)$ we must show that

$$\sum_h p^h \partial^2 \pi^h(\bar{z})(v_{n+1}, v_{n+1}) = -\partial^2 \gamma(\bar{z}) \left(\sum_{j=1}^n v_j, v_{n+1} \right).$$

Differentiating the identity $[z - \pi(z)] \cdot \partial \pi(z) = 0$ at $\bar{z}$ and keeping in mind that $\bar{p} = \bar{z} - \pi(\bar{z})$, we get $\sum_h \bar{p}^h \partial^2 \pi^h(\bar{z}) + [I - \partial \pi(\bar{z})] \partial \pi(\bar{z}) = 0$. So $\sum_h \bar{p}^h \partial^2 \pi^h(\bar{z}) = [\partial \pi(\bar{z}) - I] \partial \pi(\bar{z}) = -\partial^2 \gamma(\bar{z}) \partial \pi(\bar{z})$ and we conclude

$$\sum_h \bar{p}^h \partial^2 \pi^h(\bar{z})(v_{n+1}, v_{n+1}) = -\partial^2 \gamma(\bar{z})(\partial \pi(\bar{z}) v_{n+1}, v_{n+1})$$

$$= -\partial^2 \gamma(\bar{z}) \left(\sum_{j=1}^n v_j, v_{n+1} \right).$$

Note that although the final expression for $\partial^2 L(\bar{x}, \bar{z})$ only involves $\partial^2 \gamma$, we have used in the derivation the thrice differentiability of γ. ∎

The second-order conditions are rich in interesting corollaries. We will discuss now two of them (4.4.4 and 4.4.6). Some more are contained in Section 4.6.

A simple but important fact is that the set of second-order conditions, which can be interpreted as a sort of aggregate curvature property, have implications for the curvature of individual indifference manifolds. For example, suppose that the sufficient conditions are satisfied, $x \gg 0$ and $\sum_{j=1}^{n} x_j - \omega$ lies on a flat $(\ell-1)$-dimensional piece of the surface of Y. Then $\partial \pi(z)w = w$ for $w \in T_p$ and so $K = \{v \in R^{\ell(n+1)} : p \cdot v_j = 0$ for all j and $v_{n+1} = \sum_{j=1}^{n} v_j\}$, $B(v, v) = \sum_{j=1}^{n} \lambda_j \partial^2 u_j(x_j)(v_j, v_j)$. In particular, if we take $v_1 \neq 0$, $p \cdot v_1 = 0$, and $v_j = 0$ for $j > 1$, then $0 > B(v, v) = \lambda_1 \partial^2 u_1(x_1)(v_1, v_1)$. Therefore, the preferences of each j are locally convex at x_j. Geometrically, this is a clear enough fact and certainly not surprising. It is a consequence of the flatness of the production set and one can easily give a direct proof.

The above is also a representative of a whole class of implications of the second-order conditions. To explore the matter further it will be instructive to discuss the situation that, in the relevant sense, is the opposite to the case just considered, namely, the case where $\sum_{j=1}^{n} x_j - \omega$ lies in a vertex of the production set (e.g., $Y = -R_+^{\ell}$). Note that in order to establish individual curvature implications no help will be forthcoming now from the production side.

Let us begin by analyzing a graphical three-commodities, three-agents exchange example. For the utility functions u_1, u_2, u_3 we have an attainable allocation $x = (x_1, x_2, x_3) \in R_{++}^9$ that satisfies the first-order conditions with respect to some $p \gg 0$. In Figure 4.4.1 the plane of the page stands for T_p and the cones K_j, $j = 1, 2, 3$, for directions in T_p of second-order utility improvement for agent j. In particular, $u_j(x_j + \epsilon v_j) > u_j(x_j)$ for $v_j \in K_j$ and ϵ small. If preferences were convex, then those cones would all be empty. In the figure all three are nonempty, but we also see that $v_1 + v_2 + v_3 = 0$ and, therefore, it is possible for the three agents together to improve their situation. Clearly, there is something general here. The example suggests that, if x is to be an optimum, there is a maximum (in this case, $\ell - 1 = 2$) on how many agents can have a nonempty K_j. We now proceed to derive a formal result.

Given an attainable allocation x define $T_{pj} = \{v \in T_p : v^h = 0$ if $x_j^h = 0\}$ for each j. By the first-order necessary conditions the linear space T_{pj} is the tangent space at x_j to the indifference surface through x_j intersected with the coordinate subspace spanned by $\{h : x_j^h > 0\}$. Therefore, we know from 2.6.2 that if $\partial^2 u_j(x_j)$ is negative definite on T_{pj}, then the preferences $\succsim_j$ are, locally and restricted to the relevant coordinate subspace, convex. The second-order conditions yield:

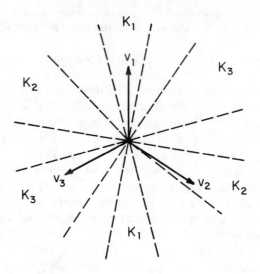

Figure 4.4.1

4.4.4. Proposition. *If B is negative definite (resp. semidefinite) and $\lambda \gg 0$ on K, then except for at most $\ell - 1$ agents, $\partial^2 u_j(x_j)$ is negative definite (resp. semidefinite) on T_{pj}.*

Proof. We argue by contradiction. Suppose there are ℓ agents $(j = 1, \ldots, \ell,$ say) such that for each j there is $v_j \neq 0$, $v_j \in T_{pj}$ with $\partial^2 u_j(x_j)(v_j, v_j) \geq 0$ [resp. $\partial u_j(x_j)(v_j, v_j) > 0$]. Because dim $T_p = \ell - 1$ and $v_1, \ldots, v_\ell \in T_p$ the vectors must be linearly dependent; that is, $\sum_{j=1}^{\ell} \alpha_j v_j = 0$, $\alpha_j \neq 0$ for some j. Define $w \in R^{\ell(n+1)}$ by $w_j = \alpha_j v_j$ for $j \leq \ell$ and $w_j = 0$ for $j > \ell$. Then, $w \in K$. So $B(w, w) < 0$ [resp. $B(w, w) \leq 0$]. But this contradicts

$$B(w, w) = \sum_{j=1}^{\ell} \lambda_j \partial^2 u_j(x_j)(\alpha_j v_j, \alpha_j v_j) = \sum_{j=1}^{\ell} \lambda_j \alpha_j^2 \partial^2 u_j(x_j)(v_j, v_j) \geq 0$$

(resp. > 0 because $\lambda \gg 0$). ∎

Figure 4.4.1 shows that in the previous proposition the bound $\ell - 1$ cannot be improved, while the quite obvious Example 4.4.5 establishes that T_{pj} cannot be replaced by $\{v_j \in R^\ell : \partial u_j(x_j)v_j = 0\}$. Note also that the negative semidefiniteness of $\partial^2 u_j(x_j)$ on T_{pj} does not quite imply the local convexity of (restricted) preferences. Negative definiteness does (2.6.2). The gap is a minor one since if the Gaussian curvature of the restricted indifference manifold is nonzero at x_j, then negative semidefiniteness implies negative definiteness.

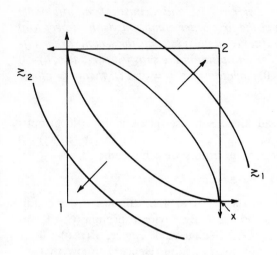

Figure 4.4.2

4.4.5. Example. Let $n = 2r$, $\ell = 2$, $Y = -R_+^2$, $\omega = (r, r)$, $u_j(x_j) = (x_j^1)^2 +$ $(x_j^2)^2$ for all j, $x_j = (0, 1)$ for $1 \le j \le r$, $x_j = (1, 0)$ for $r+1 \le j \le 2r$. The allocation x is an optimum, but $\partial^2 u_j(x_j)$ is positive definite on R^2 for every j. See Figure 4.4.2.

Proposition 4.4.4 has interest when there are more agents than goods. Coupled with $x \gg 0$ and a nonzero curvature assumption on individual preferences at x_j, it tells us, without the benefit of convexity assumptions, that, given any p satisfying the first-order conditions, there are some consumers in local price equilibrium. If n is much larger than ℓ, it also tells us that if x is an optimum, then $V = \{\sum_{j=1}^{n} x_j' : x_j' \succsim_j x_j\}$ must be locally "almost" price-supported. This issue, however, is better studied by more global methods. The next section will be devoted to doing so.

The analog of Proposition 4.3.9 on pairwise optimality does not hold for general smooth, but possibly nonconvex, preferences. We shall not give a formal example, although Figure 4.4.1 makes the fact clear. Note that in the figure no two agents can improve with displacements that remain in T_p. If for each j the negative eigenvalue of the form $\partial^2 u_j(x_j)$ restricted to T_p is chosen large enough, the restriction of the allocation to every pair of agents will satisfy the second-order sufficient conditions. Nonetheless, x is not an optimum. But smoothness is still of some help. It allows for results on the sufficiency of tests involving groups of at most ℓ agents that do not depend (as 4.2.10 does) on convexity hypotheses. As an example:

4.4.6. Proposition. *Let $Y = -R_+^\ell$ and x constitute an attainable allocation satisfying the first-order conditions with respect to p and λ. If for any subset of at most ℓ agents the second-order sufficient conditions for an optimum are satisfied (i.e., $B(v, v) < 0$ for any $v \in K$, $v \neq 0$, such that $\#\{j : v_j \neq 0\} \leq \ell$), then x is a local optimum.*

Proof. We argue by contradiction. Suppose that x is not a local optimum. Then $x_m \to x$, where $x_m \neq x$, $\sum_{j=1}^n x_{mj} = \omega$, and $u_j(x_{mj}) - u_j(x_j) \geq 0$ for all m and j. Without loss of generality we can assume

$$(1/\|x_m - x\|)(x_m - x) \to v \in R^{\ell n}.$$

Of course, $\sum_{j=1}^n v_j = 0$. As in the proof of 4.4.2 the first-order conditions yield $p \cdot v_j = 0$ for all j. So $v \in K$. By Taylor's formula (C.4.1) applied to each u_j we get $\lambda_j \partial^2 u_j(x_j)(v_j, v_j) \geq 0$. Hence, $B(v, v) \geq 0$. If $\#\{j : v_j \neq 0\} \leq \ell - 1$, we have our contradiction. Hence, suppose that we have $v_j \neq 0$ for $j \leq \ell$. The vectors $v_1, \ldots, v_\ell \subset T_p$ are linearly dependent, that is, $\sum_{j=1}^\ell \alpha_j v_j = 0$ and $\alpha_j \neq 0$ for some j. Define $w \in K$ by $w_j = \alpha_j v_j$ for $j \leq \ell$ and $w_j = 0$ for $j > \ell$. Then $w \neq 0$,

$$B(w, w) = \sum_{j=1}^\ell \lambda_j \alpha_j^2 \partial^2 u_j(x_j(v_j, v_j) \geq 0$$

and $w_j \neq 0$ only if $j \leq \ell$. Contradiction. ∎

4.5   General propositions on approximate price supportability

We have seen (Section 4.2, Proposition 4.2.16) that in the case of convex preferences optimum allocations can be price-supported. In this section we will consider the general case and provide estimates for the extent that an arbitrary optimum allocation fails to be price-supportable. The interest of the exercise is that those estimates get better as the agents become more numerous. In other words, under weak conditions to be made precise, if an economy has a large number of agents, then every optimum allocation can be "almost" price-supported. This is a first example of a theme we will encounter repeatedly, namely, that results that hold for economies with convex preferences tend to be approximately true for economies with a large number of agents with not necessarily convex preferences.

To focus on essentials we will only consider the exchange case, that is, $Y = -R_+^\ell$. Remember that we always assume the convexity of the production set so that all the nonconvexities' complications arise in the consumption side. Also, to avoid not very significant technicalities we will assume strict monotonicity of preferences.

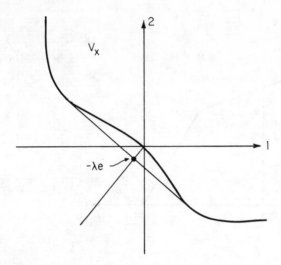

Figure 4.5.1

Maintained hypotheses for the section are: $Y = -R_+^\ell$, *and preferences* $\succsim_1, \ldots, \succsim_n$ *are strictly monotone.*

We consider a fixed optimum allocation $x \in R^{\ell n}$ and center our attention on the set

$$V_x = \sum_{j=1}^{n} (\{z_j : z_j \succsim_j x_j\} - x_j).$$

Because x is an optimum, $0 \in \partial V_x$. Note that x can be price-supported if and only if $p \cdot z \geq 0$ for some $p \in R_+^\ell$ and all $z \in V_x$. Such a p would exist if V_x were convex. In general, V_x is not. But it turns out that, as a sum of sets, the nonconvexities of V_x are bounded. A first result is:

4.5.1. Proposition. *Let x be an optimum allocation. Put $s = \max_j \|x_j\|$. Then there is a $p \gg 0$, $\|p\| = 1$, such that $p \cdot z \geq -(\ell^{3/2} s + 1)$ for all $z \in V_x$.*

Proof. The proof consists of a simple application of the Shapley–Folkman theorem (L.1.1).

Consider co V_x and choose $\lambda \geq 0$ such that $-\lambda e \in \partial(\text{co } V_x)$ (see Figure 4.5.1). This λ exists because co V_x is closed (E.2.1, F.1.2) and bounded below by $-sne$. By the supporting hyperplane theorem (F.2.1) there is $q > 0$ such that $q \cdot z \geq -\lambda q \cdot e$ for all $z \in V_x$. Because V_x is bounded below, we can modify q and get a $p \gg 0$, $\|p\| = 1$, such that $p \cdot z \geq -\lambda p \cdot e - 1$ for all $z \in V_x$. We show that this p is as desired.

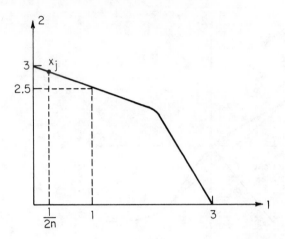

Figure 4.5.2

By the Shapley–Folkman theorem (L.1.1) and the definition of V_x, we have $-\lambda e = v_1 + \cdots + v_n$, where $v_j \geq -x_j$ for all j and, reindexing if necessary, $v_j + x_j \gtrsim_j x_j$ for $j > \ell$. Because x is an optimum we cannot have $\sum_{j=\ell+1}^{n} v_j \ll 0$; that is, $\sum_{j=\ell+1}^{n} v_j^h \geq 0$ for some h. But $v_j^h \geq -s$ for all j. So $\sum_{j=1}^{n} v_j^h \geq -\ell s$ and $-\lambda = \sum_{j=1}^{n} v_j^h \geq -\ell s$. Therefore, $|\lambda p \cdot e| \leq \|p\| \|\lambda e\| \leq \ell^{3/2} s$ and we conclude that $p \cdot z \geq -(\ell^{3/2} s + 1)$ for all $z \in V_x$. ∎

What needs to be emphasized about Proposition 4.5.1 is that as long as s remains bounded, the estimate $-(\ell^{3/2} s + 1)$ is independent of the number of agents n and so, in per-agent terms, the bound to the negative values $p \cdot z$ goes to zero as n increases without limit. Example 4.5.2 shows that if s is not uniformly bounded, $\min p \cdot V_x$ may diverge to $-\infty$ and Example 4.5.3 proves that the order of magnitude of the lower bound $-(\ell^{3/2} s + 1)$ is the right one; that is, $\inf p \cdot V_x$ may remain bounded away from zero as n goes to infinity.

4.5.2. Example. Let $\ell = 2$ and $u_j(z_j) = (z_j^1)^2 + (z_j^2)^2$ for all $1 \leq j \leq n$. Take $\omega = (n, n)$ and consider the allocation $x_1 = (n, n)$, $x_j = (0, 0)$ for all $j \geq 2$. Obviously, x is an optimum, but it is easy to verify that for any $p \gg 0$, $\|p\| = 1$, we have $\min p \cdot V_x \geq n - \sqrt{2}$. Indeed, the best price vector is $p = (1/\sqrt{2}, 1/\sqrt{2})$ and, for this p, $\min p \cdot V_x$ is attained at $(\sqrt{2}n, 0) - (n, n) \in V_x$.

4.5.3. Example. Let $\ell = 2$. The preferences of all n agents will be identical. For present purposes it suffices to specify the single indifference curve plotted in Figure 4.5.2, which is symmetric around the diagonal and a straight line on $[0, 1] \times R$. We take $\omega = (\frac{1}{2}, 3n - \frac{1}{4})$ and consider the allocation $x_j = (1/2n, 3 - 1/4n)$ for all $1 \le j \le n$. Note that x_j is on the indifference curve of Figure 4.5.2.

The allocation x is an optimum. Indeed, because $\{z_j \in [0, 1] \times R: z_j \gtrsim_j x_j\}$ is convex, if an attainable x' were to dominate x, then we would have $x_j'^1 > 1$ for some j. But this is impossible because $\omega^1 = \frac{1}{2}$. The symmetry of the indifference curve yields that the best approximately supporting price with $\|p\| = 1$ will satisfy $p^1 \ge 1/\sqrt{2}$ and $p^2 \le 1/\sqrt{2}$. But $(0, 3) \gtrsim_j x_j$ for all j, which implies $v = (-\frac{1}{2}, \frac{1}{4}) \in V_x$. This yields $p \cdot v \le -1/4\sqrt{2}$. So $\min p \cdot V_x$ does not converge to zero as $n \to \infty$.

Proposition 4.5.1 has a number of interesting corollaries.

4.5.4. Proposition. *Consider a sequence x_n of optimum allocations for economies with n agents. Suppose that for some $r > 0$, $\sum_{j=1}^n \|x_{nj}\| \le rn$. Then, for all $\delta > 0$, there is $p_n \gg 0$ such that $(1/n)\#\{j: p \cdot z_j \le p \cdot x_{nj} - \delta$ for some $z_j \gtrsim_j x_{nj}\}$ goes to zero as n goes to infinity.*

Proof. Let δ be given. Fix $\epsilon > 0$. Denote by N the set of agents in the economy of size n. Let $N' = \{j \in N: \|x_j\| > 2r/\epsilon\}$. Of course, $(1/n)\#N' \le \epsilon/2$. Let $\hat{x}_n$ be the restriction of x_n to $N \backslash N'$. This is still an optimum for the restricted economy and the total endowments $\sum_{j \in N \backslash N'} x_j$. Therefore, by 4.5.1 there is $p_n \gg 0$ such that $p_n \cdot v \ge -[(2r\ell^2/\epsilon) + 1]$ whenever $v \in V_{\hat{x}_n}$. Choose $n > (2/\delta\epsilon)[(2r\ell^2/\epsilon) + 1]$. Denote

$$N'' = \{j \in N \backslash N': p_n \cdot z_j \le p \cdot x_{nj} - \delta \text{ for some } z_j \gtrsim_j x_{nj}\}.$$

Obviously, $\#N'' \le (1/\delta)[(2r\ell^2/\epsilon) + 1]$ and so $\#N''/n \le \epsilon/2$. Therefore, $(1/n)(\#N' + \#N'') \le \epsilon$. Since ϵ is arbitrary, we are done. ∎

For optimum allocations x that are interior, that is, $x_j \gg 0$ for all j, the smoothness hypothesis will allow for substantial improvements on Proposition 4.5.1. Roughly speaking, improvements are possible in two directions. In the first (4.5.5 and 4.5.6) the same conclusion on the degree and manner of approximation as in 4.5.1 is obtained. But the supporting price vector is not chosen arbitrarily: It is the one given by the first-order necessary conditions. In the second direction (4.5.9) there is again complete freedom in choosing the supporting price vector, but the conclusion of 4.5.1 is strengthened to obtain a better degree of approximation.

To the maintained hypothesis so far we now add: *All preferences are C^2 and belong to a set Q that is compact for the topology of uniform C^2 convergence on compacta of associated admissible utility functions* (see 2.4). The interpretation of this compactness hypothesis on characteristics

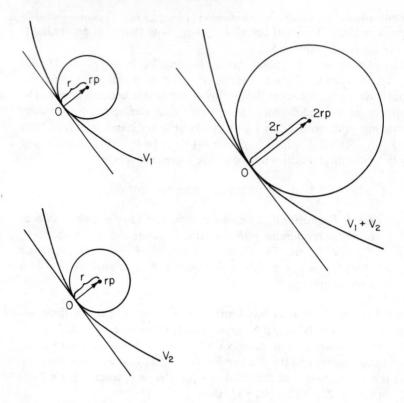

Figure 4.5.3

is that agents, although perhaps very numerous, are not very dissimilar. If x is an interior optimum, let $p_x \gg 0$, $\|p_x\| = 1$, be the price vector given by the first-order conditions.

Informally, the key new fact that smoothness contributes is the tendency of the boundary of V_x at 0 to be almost flat if n is large and x is an interior optimum. For example, let $\min_h x_j^h > \epsilon$, $\|x_j\| \le 1/\epsilon$ for all j and suppose that for all j, p is normal to the indifference manifold of $\gtrsim_j$ through x_j. Then there is $r > 0$ such that, for each j, the set $V_j = \{z_j \in R_+^\ell : z_j \gtrsim_j x_j\} - x_j$ contains a ball S_j of center rp and radius r. So $V_x = \sum_j V_j$ contains a ball of center rnp and radius rn. See Figure 4.5.3.

The next proposition says that for optimum allocations x that are uniformly bounded and uniformly interior, the order of magnitude for the lower bound to $p \cdot V_x$ given by Proposition 4.5.1 remains valid if we take $p = p_x$.

4.5.5. Proposition. *For any $\epsilon > 0$ there is $k > 0$ (depending only on Q and ϵ) such that if x is an optimum with $\epsilon \le x_j^h \le 1/\epsilon$ for all j, h, then $p_x \cdot z \ge -k$ for all $z \in V_x$.*

Proof. It is worth pointing out that the proof does not make use, as the one of 4.3.1 did, of the Shapley-Folkman theorem. Put

$$J = \{z \in R^l : \epsilon \le z^h \le 1/\epsilon \text{ for all } h\}.$$

By the compactness of Q and J the set $g(Q \times J) \subset R_{++}^l$ is compact; remember that $g(\ge, z)$ is the outward unit normal of the indifference surface of $\ge$ through z. For a constant $0 < r < \epsilon, 1$ to be specified, let k be such that $k > \|v\|^2/r$ whenever $v = z - y$, $z \ge 0$, $p \cdot z \le p \cdot y$, $p \in g(Q \times J)$, $y \in J$.

Suppose that x is an optimum allocation satisfying the conditions of the proposition. Then $p_x \in g(Q \times J)$ and $x_j \in J$ for all J. If $n = 1$, the result is clearly true. Let $n \ge 2$. Denote $V_j = \{x_j' \in R_+^l : x_j' \gtrsim_j x_j\} - \{x_j\}$. Then for a sufficiently small r (to be chosen independently of x) the ball B_j of radius r centered at rp_x is contained in V_j (see H.3) and if we consider a group of $n-1$ agents, say $j = 2, ..., n$, then $\sum_{j=2}^n B_j$ ($\subset \sum_{j=2}^n V_j$) is the ball of radius $(n-1)r$ centered at $(n-1)rp_x$. See Figure 4.5.3. Because x is an optimum, if $v_1 \in V_1$ we cannot have $\|-v_1 - (n-1)rp_x\| < (n-1)r$ (otherwise, $-v_1 \in \text{Int} \sum_{j=2}^n V_j$ and so $0 \in \text{Int} V_x$). Henceforth,

$$\|-v_1 - (n-1)rp_x\| \ge (n-1)r.$$

Because $\|-v_1 - (n-1)rp_x\|^2 = (n-1)^2 r^2 + 2(n-1)rp_x \cdot v_1 + \|v_1\|^2$, we have $2(n-1)rp_x \cdot v_1 + \|v_1\|^2 \ge 0$, or $p_x \cdot v_1 \ge -\|v_1\|^2/2(n-1)r$. If $p_x \cdot v_1 \ge 0$, then $p_x \cdot v_1 \ge -k/2(n-1)$. If $p_x \cdot v_1 \le 0$, then $\|v_1\|^2/r < k$ by the way k has been chosen. Hence, $p_x \cdot v_1 \ge -[1/2(n-1)]k$ in either case. Therefore, we conclude that if $v \in V_x = \sum_{j=1}^n V_j$, then $p_x \cdot v \ge -[n/2(n-1)]k \ge -k$. ∎

The proof of Proposition 4.5.5 has not attempted to give the best estimate of k. The order of magnitude, however, is the correct one, as Example 4.5.8 will establish. Note that, if we were to take $p = p_x$ in Example 4.5.3 then $\min p_x V_x$ diverges to $-\infty$ [in fact, $\min p_x V_x = -(3/\sqrt{5})n$]. Therefore, a condition such as $\min_{j,h} x_j^h \ge \epsilon$ is needed in Proposition 4.5.5. Example 4.5.7 shows the same for $\max_{j,h} x_j^h \le 1/\epsilon$.

Under the conditions of Proposition 4.5.5 the analog of Proposition 4.5.4 remains valid for $p = p_x$. Formally:

4.5.6. Proposition. *Consider a sequence of optimum allocations x_n for economies with n agents having preferences in Q. Suppose that for some $\epsilon > 0$ we have $\epsilon \le x_{nj}^h \le 1/\epsilon$ for all n, h, j. Then for all $\delta > 0$, $(1/n)\#\{j : p_{x_n} \cdot (z_j - x_{nj}) \le -\delta \text{ for some } z_j \gtrsim_{nj} x_{nj}\}$ goes to zero as n goes to infinity.*

Proof. Identical to Proposition 4.5.4, but using Proposition 4.5.5 instead of 4.5.1. ∎

4.5.7. Example. Let $\ell = 2$. Total endowments for the economy with n agents are $\omega = (n-1)4e$. Note that average endowments are bounded by $4e$. We consider the allocation x given by $x_1 = 3(n-1)e$ and $x_2 = \cdots = x_n = e$. For the preferences it suffices to specify the indifference curve through x_j. For agent 1 let it be $\{z: \|z\| = 3\sqrt{2}(n-1)\}$, while for agents 2 through n we take $\{z: \|z-4e\| = 3\sqrt{2}\}$. So Q is a two-element set, hence compact. Because $3\sqrt{2} > 4$ the preferences of agents $j \geq 2$ are strictly monotone. The allocation x satisfies the first-order conditions with $p_x = (1/\sqrt{2}, 1/\sqrt{2})$. We claim that x is an optimum. To see this, let us argue by contradiction. Suppose that $\sum_{j=1}^n v_j = 0$ and $x_1 + v_1 \succ_1 x_1$, $x_j + v_j \sim_j x_j$. Because preferences are strictly monotone, this is no loss of generality. We have then $\|4e - (e+v_j)\| = 3\sqrt{2}$ for $j \geq 2$. Therefore,

$$\|3(n-1)e - \textstyle\sum_{j=2}^n v_j\| \leq 3\sqrt{2}(n-1); \quad \text{that is,} \quad \|3(n-1)e + v_1\| \leq 3\sqrt{2}(n-1).$$

But $x_1 + v_1 \succ_1 x_1$ implies $\|x_1 + v_1\| > 3\sqrt{2}(n-1)$, and since $x_1 = 3(n-1)e$, we have a contradiction. Therefore, x is an optimum. Because $(3\sqrt{2}(n-1), 0)$ is in the indifference curve through x_1 of agent 1, we have

$$v = (3(n-1)(\sqrt{2}-1), \ -3(n-1)) \in V_x.$$

Since $p_x \cdot v = 3(1-\sqrt{2})(n-1)$, we see that $\min p_x V_x$ diverges to $-\infty$ with n.

The next example shows that the lower bound found for $p_x V_x$ in 4.5.5 is of the right order of magnitude. The example, however, has a more positive interest. Indeed, we will see that if optimization in the price vector is permitted, then we can improve substantially the lower bound. More specifically, in the example there is $k > 0$ and $p > 0$ such that for the optimum allocations considered x, we have $\min p \cdot V_x \leq k/n$. The first-order price p_x uses information about V_x only on a neighborhood of zero. It is, therefore, not surprising that it does not perform best on the global test $\min p \cdot V_x$. But it is somewhat remarkable that the best "approximately efficient" price vector p improves matters to the point that the lower bound for $p \cdot V_x$ goes to zero as n goes to infinity. In Proposition 4.5.9 we will see that this feature of the example has considerable generality.

4.5.8. Example. Let $\ell = 2$. The n agents have the same preferences. For the example it will suffice to specify the indifference curve J represented in Figure 4.5.4a. The curve J is symmetric around the main diagonal of R_+^2 and on a neighborhood U of $(1,3)$ coincides with the graph of the function $z^2 = \eta(z^1) = \frac{1}{2}(z^1)^2 - 2z^1 + \frac{9}{2}$. Let $v = (1+1/n, \eta(1+1/n))$ and

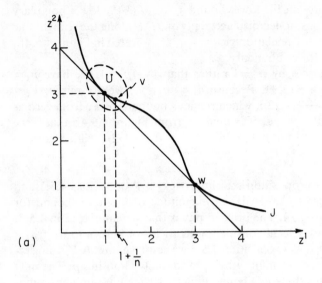

(a)

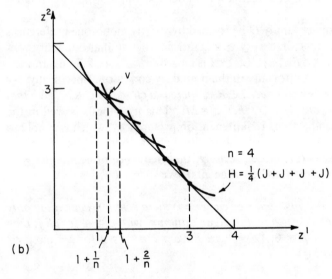

(b)

Figure 4.5.4

suppose that n is large enough for $v \in U$. We take $\omega = nv$ and $x_j = v$ for all j. Then x is an optimum allocation. Rather than by a formal proof we justify this by an informal graphical argument. Put $J_j = J$ and consider $H = (1/n) \sum_{j=1}^{n} J_j$. As shown in Figure 4.5.4b, if we take n sufficiently large, we can represent the lower boundary of H as the lower boundary of $(n+1)$ evenly positioned displacements of $J \cap U$ along the straight line $z^1 + z^2 = 4$. A simple calculation yields that, as indicated in Figure 4.5.4b, v belongs to this lower boundary.

Normalizing prices by $p^2 = 1$ rather than by $\|p\| = 1$, we have $p_x = (1 - 1/n, 1)$. Call $w = (3, 1)$. Because $n(w - v) \in V_x$, we get $\min p_x \cdot V_x \le n(p_x \cdot w - p_x \cdot v) = -2 - 1/2n$, which remains bounded away from zero as $n \to \infty$. On the other hand, it is obvious from Figure 4.5.4b that if we take $p = (1, 1)$, then $\min p \cdot V_x = n(p \cdot w - p \cdot v) = -1/2n$, which goes to zero as $n \to \infty$.

We now give a proposition that improves on Propositions 4.5.1 and 4.5.5 by strengthening the order of magnitude of the lower bound for $p \cdot V_2$ from $-k$ to $-k/n$. The price to pay is that we cannot, as in 4.5.5, obtain p from purely local considerations. It is not known to us if with the same hypothesis as Proposition 4.5.5 we could get $\min p \cdot V_x$ converging to zero as n goes to infinity by appropriately choosing p. The next proposition obtains the $-k/n$ bound under a strong but familiar boundary condition.

Let the compact family Q be formed by strictly monotone preferences on R_{++}. We assume that every $\succeq \in Q$ satisfies the familiar boundary condition: "For all $z \in R_{++}^\ell$, $\{z' : z' \succeq z\}$ is closed in R^ℓ" (see 2.3.16). In fact, we need a certain uniformity in the boundary condition. Specifically, we assume: *"For every compact $J \subset R_{++}^\ell$ there is a closed $M \subset R_{++}^\ell$ such that if $z' \succeq z$, $z \in J$, and $\succeq \in Q$, then $z' \in M$."* This hypothesis is well in the spirit of the compactness requirement on preferences, which is simply to put a bound on the diversity of individual characteristics in an economy with many agents (or, more precisely, on a sequence of economies with an increasingly large number of agents). We then have:

> **4.5.9. Proposition.** *For each $\epsilon > 0$ there is $k > 0$ (depending only on Q and ϵ) such that if x is an optimum with $x_j \ge \epsilon e$ for all j, then for some $p \gg 0$, $\|p\| = 1$, we have $p \cdot z \ge -ks/n$ for $s = \max_j \|x_j\|$ and all $z \in V_x$.*

Proof. The proof is a combination of the two approaches represented by the proofs of 4.5.1 and 4.5.5. As in 4.5.1, we use the Shapley–Folkman theorem to get the right p. As in 4.5.5, we establish the strong degree of approximation by exploiting the expansivity properties of the vector addition of balls.

Notice first that if $z_j \ge 0$, $\sum_j z_j \ge se$, then $\#\{j : z_j \le 2\ell se\} \ge n/2$. Let

$M \subset R_{++}^{\ell}$ be a set closed in R^{ℓ} and such that if $z' \gtrsim z$, $\gtrsim \in Q$, $\epsilon e \le z \le 2\ell se$, then $z' \in M$. Take $J = M \cap \{z \in R^{\ell}: z \le 2\ell se\}$. Then J is compact and so is $g(Q \times J)$. Choose $r > 1$ such that if $y \ge 0$, $p \cdot y \le p \cdot z$, $z \in J$, and $p \in g(Q \times J)$, then $\|y\| < r$. Take also $c > 0$ such that if $z \in M$, $\|z\| \le r$, and $\gtrsim \in Q$, then $\{z': z' \gtrsim z\}$ contains a ball of radius $1/c$ centered at $v + (1/c) g(\gtrsim, z)$. Finally, put $k = 13c\ell^4 r^2$.

The second part of the demonstration could be routed via Howe's theorem (L.1.2), but a direct proof will be simpler. There is no loss of generality in assuming $n > 2\ell$. As in the proof of 4.5.1, let $-\lambda e \in \partial \operatorname{co} V_x$. Pick a $p > 0$, $\|p\| = 1$, supporting co V_x at $-\lambda e$. By the Shapley–Folkman theorem (L.1.1) we have $-\lambda e = \sum_j v_j$, where we can assume $x_j + v_j \gtrsim_j x_j$ for $j > \ell$ and $v_j \in \operatorname{co}\{x_j' - x_j: x_j' \gtrsim_j x_j\}$ for $j \le \ell$. Because p supports co V_x at $-\lambda e$ it also supports $\operatorname{co}(\{x_j' - x_j: x_j' \gtrsim_j x_j\})$ at v_j for every j. Therefore, we must have $p = g_j(x_j + v_j)$ for $j > \ell$. Because $n/2 > \ell$ we have $x_j + v_j \le 2\ell se$ for some $j > \ell$. Therefore, $p \in g(Q \times J)$, which yields $\|x_j + v_j\| \le r$ for all j. Denote $w = \sum_{j=\ell+1}^n v_j$. Then $\|-\lambda e - w\| \le 2\ell r$. Since $w^h \ge 0$ for some h (otherwise, x is not an optimum), this yields $\lambda \le 2\ell r$ and so $\|w\| \le 4\ell^2 r$. For $j \le \ell$ choose v_j' such that $v_j' + x_j \gtrsim_j x_j$ and $p \cdot v_j' = p \cdot v_j$. Clearly, $p = g_j(x_j + v_j')$. Denote $y = \sum_{j=1}^{\ell} v_j' + w$. Then, $y \in V_x$, $p \cdot y = -\lambda p \cdot e$ and $\|y\| \le \ell r + \|w\| \le 5\ell^2 r$.

As in the proof of Proposition 4.5.5 it is clear that V_x contains a ball B of radius n/c and center $y + (n/c)p$. Because $0 \in \partial V_x$ we should have $\|y + (n/c)p\| \ge n/c$; otherwise, $0 \in \operatorname{Int} B \subset \operatorname{Int} V_x$. Because $\|y + (n/c)p\|^2 = \|y\|^2 + (2n/c)p \cdot y + (n/c)^2$, this implies $\|y\|^2 + (2n/c)p \cdot y \ge 0$ or $p \cdot y \ge -(c/2n)\|y\|^2 \ge -(c/2n)25\ell^4 r^2 \ge -k/n$. Since $p \cdot z \ge -\lambda p \cdot e = p \cdot y$ for all $z \in V_x$, this concludes the proof. It should be obvious that our estimate of k is by no means sharp. ∎

4.6 The structure of the set of optimum allocations

So far, we have concerned ourselves with the properties of an optimum allocation considered in isolation. It will be useful if we now devote some attention to the set of optimum allocations and utilities and investigate its topological and differentiable properties both in the local and the global sense. This will be done in three steps. First, we shall study global topological properties under convexity and continuity hypotheses on preferences. Next, we shall assume the smoothness but not the convexity of preferences and analyze the local differentiable structure. Finally, under strong smoothness, boundary, and convexity conditions we shall obtain some global differentiable properties. To keep matters simple we sometimes restrict ourselves to the exchange case.

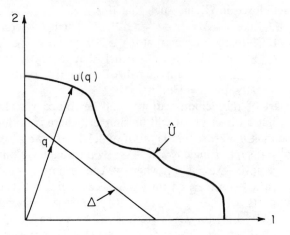

Figure 4.6.1

Recall from Section 4.2 the definition of the utility set, $u = \{u \in R^n:$ $u = u(x) = (u_1(x_1), \ldots, u_n(x_n))$, where $(x_1, \ldots, x_n)$ is an attainable allocation$\}$. We are interested in the weak optimum sets: $\hat{U} = \{u \in U: \text{if } u' \gg u,$ then $u' \notin U\}$, and $P = \{x \in R^{\ell n}: x$ is a weak optimum allocation$\}$. Of course, $\hat{U} = u(P)$. Both sets are compact.

A first, and rather obvious, result is that U is topologically an $n-1$ simplex. Economically, this says that, given the utility functions u_j, the requirement of weak optimality does not impose any restriction on the distribution of utility. Formally:

4.6.1. Proposition. *$\hat{U}$ is homeomorphic to the $(n-1)$ unit simplex.*

Proof. Let Δ be the $(n-1)$ closed unit simplex. By 4.2.4, U is compact. Because "$\omega + y \gg 0$ for some $y \in Y$," $u_j(0) = 0$ for all j, and preferences are monotone, we have that $0 \in \text{Int } U$ and if $0 \leq v' \ll v \in U$, then v' belongs to the interior of U relative to R_+^n. Hence for each $q \in \Delta$, there is a unique $u(q) \in \hat{U}$ such that $q = \alpha u(q)$ for some $\alpha > 0$. See Figure 4.6.1. The compactness of U yields then the continuity of the map $q \mapsto u(q)$, which serves, therefore, as the desired homeomorphism. ∎

Let us emphasize that Proposition 4.6.1 holds for U, the set of weak utility optima, but not for the set of utility optima, which, in general, may fail to be homeomorphically convex or closed.

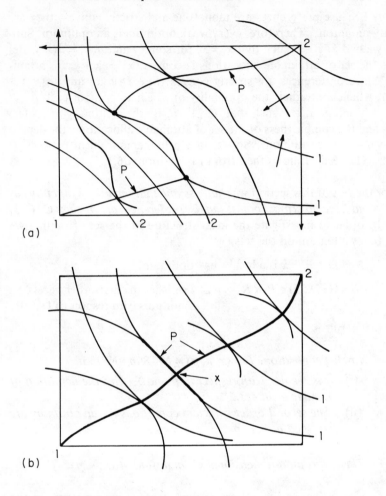

(a)

(b)

Figure 4.6.2

The two Edgeworth boxes in Figures 4.6.2 illustrate the fact that P need not be homeomorphic to a simplex. A common feature of these two examples is that for some $u \in \hat{U}$, there are $x, x' \in P$, $x \neq x'$, such that $u(x) = u(x') = u$. The observation that this occurs only because preferences are not strictly convex suggests the next proposition.

4.6.2. Proposition. *If preferences are strictly convex, then P is homeomorphic to the $(n-1)$ unit simplex.*

Proof. Because preferences are monotone and strictly convex, they are strictly monotone. Therefore, every weak optimum is an optimum. Suppose we had $x, x' \in P$ such that $x_j \neq x'_j$ for some j and $u(x) = u(x')$. Because the set of attainable allocations is convex, $x'' = \frac{1}{2}x + \frac{1}{2}x'$ is attainable. Since preferences are strictly convex, $u(x'') \geq u(x)$ and $u_j(x'') > u_j(x)$, which contradicts the optimality of x. Therefore, for each $u \in \hat{U}$ there is a unique $x_u \in P$ such that $u(x_u) = u$. By the continuity of preferences and the compactness of the set of attainable allocations, the dependence $u \mapsto x_u$ is continuous. So we have a homeomorphism between P and $\hat{U}$. The result follows then from Proposition 4.6.1. ∎

For the rest of this section *we shall assume that the utility functions u_j are C^2 and have no critical point; that is, preferences are of class C^2* (2.3, 2.4). In order to investigate the local structure of the set of optima we shall focus attention on the sets

$$P_l = \{x \in R^{ln}: x \text{ is a local weak optimum}\}$$

$$N_l = \{(x, \lambda, p) \in P_l \times R_+^n \times R_+^\ell : x \text{ satisfies the first-order necessary}$$
$$\text{conditions with respect to } (\lambda, p)\}.$$

A first result is:

4.6.3. Proposition. *Let $(x, \lambda, p) \neq N_l$. Suppose that:*

(i) *x is regular with respect to p and λ (with the definition of regular as in 4.3.2).*

(ii) *The second-order sufficient conditions for an optimum are satisfied at x, λ, p.*

(iii) *The distance function γ is C^3 at $z = \sum_{j=1}^n x_j - \omega + p$.*

Then N_l is an n-dimensional C^1 manifold at (x, λ, p).

Proof. After a few preliminaries we shall proceed in two steps. In the first the problem is set in an equivalent form. In the second it is tackled via the implicit function theorem.

Denote the given (x, λ, p) by $(\bar{x}, \bar{\lambda}, \bar{p})$.

For each j, let L^j (resp. L^j_+) be the coordinate subspace (resp. positive cone) spanned by $\{h: \bar{x}^h_j > 0\}$. For any vector $y \in R^\ell$ we let y^j be the projection on L^j. Put $\ell_j = \dim L^j$ and $r = \sum_{j=1}^n \ell_j$.

Define $\eta: L^1_+ \times \cdots \times L^n_+ \times R^n_+ \times R^\ell \to L^1 \times \cdots \times L^n \times R^\ell$ by $\eta(x, \lambda, z) = (\lambda_1 \partial u_1(x_1) - (z^1 - \pi^1(z)), \ldots, \lambda_n \partial u_n(x_n) - (z^n - \pi^n(z)), \sum_{j=1}^n x_j - \omega - \pi(z))$. This is a C^1 function from a $(r+n+\ell)$-dimensional space into $R^{r+\ell}$. Also, $\eta(\bar{x}, \bar{\lambda}, \bar{z}) = 0$ because of the first-order conditions and $\bar{p} = \bar{z} - \pi(\bar{z})$. Without loss of generality we assume $\|\bar{p}\| = 1$.

Step 1. We show that the one-to-one linear map

$$(x, \lambda, p) \mapsto \left(x, \lambda, \sum_{j=1}^{n} x_j - \omega + p\right)$$

carries a neighborhood of $(\bar{x}, \bar{\lambda}, \bar{p})$ in N_l onto a neighborhood of $(\bar{x}, \bar{\lambda}, \bar{z})$ in $\eta^{-1}(0)$. This is clear enough. Let

$$x_m \to \bar{x}, \quad \lambda_m \to \bar{\lambda}, \quad p_m \to \bar{p}, \quad (x_m, \lambda_m, p_m) \in N_l,$$

and denote $z_m = \sum_{j=1}^{n} x_{mj} - \omega + p_m$. Of course, $p_m = z_m - \pi(z_m)$. Because of the regularity of $\bar{x}$ with respect to $(\bar{\lambda}, \bar{p})$ we must have $x_{mj} \in L^j$ for all j and m sufficiently large. Hence, $\eta(x_m, \lambda_m, z_m) = 0$ by the first-order conditions. Conversely, let $(x_m, \lambda_m, z_m) \to (\bar{x}, \bar{\lambda}, \bar{z})$, $\eta(x_m, \lambda_m, z_m) = 0$. Denote $p_m = z_m - (\sum_{j=1}^{n} x_{mj} - \omega)$. Of course, $p_m \to \bar{p}$. Because of the regularity of $\bar{x}$ with respect to $(\bar{\lambda}, \bar{p})$, all the neglected inequality constraints hold strictly (i.e., with some slack). So if m is sufficiently large, then x_m will satisfy the first-order conditions with respect to (λ_m, p_m) and, therefore, $(x_m, \lambda_m, p_m) \in N_l$. Note also that the test cone for the second-order conditions at $(\bar{x}, \bar{\lambda}, \bar{p})$ is the subspace

$$K = \left\{(v, v_{n+1}) \in R^{\ell n} \times R^n : \partial u_j(\bar{x}_j) v_j = 0 \text{ for all } j \text{ and } \sum_{j=1}^{n} v_j = \partial \pi(\bar{z}) v_{n+1}\right\}.$$

Again by the regularity of $\bar{x}$, if m is large, then the test cone for x_m is the subspace K_m defined accordingly. By continuity, if the second-order sufficient conditions hold at $(\bar{x}, \bar{\lambda}, \bar{p})$, they will hold at $(x_m, \lambda_m, p_m) \in N_l$.

Summing up: It suffices to show that a neighborhood of $(\bar{x}, \bar{\lambda}, \bar{z})$ in $\eta^{-1}(0)$ is an n-dimensional C^1 manifold.

Step 2. By the implicit function theorem (H.2.2), if rank $\partial \eta(\bar{x}, \bar{\lambda}, \bar{z}) = r + \ell$ (i.e., if the rank is maximal), then $\eta^{-1}(0)$ will be a C^1 manifold at $(\bar{x}, \bar{\lambda}, \bar{z})$. Note also that the difference of dimensions between the range and domain spaces of η is precisely n.

The $(r + \ell) \times (r + n + \ell)$ matrix $\partial \eta(\bar{x}, \bar{\lambda}, \bar{z})$ has the form:

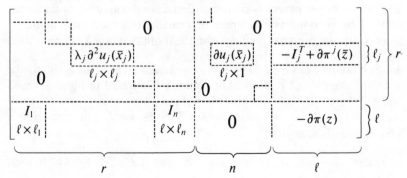

where I_j is the submatrix of the identity formed by the columns spanning L^j.

We wish to show that the rows of this matrix are linearly independent. Let $K \subset R^{r+\ell}$ be the test subspace for the second-order conditions (see step 1). Suppose that with $v \in \prod_j L_j$ and $w \in R^\ell$ we have $(v^T, w^T) \partial \eta(\bar{x}, \bar{\lambda}, \bar{z}) = 0$. Then

$$\lambda_j \partial^2 u_j(\bar{x}_j) v_j + w_j = 0 \quad \text{and} \quad \partial u_j(\bar{x}_j) v_j = 0 \quad \text{for all } j.$$

Also, $\partial \pi(\bar{z})(\sum_{j=1}^n v_j - w) = \sum_{j=1}^n v_j$. Denote $v_{n+1} = \sum_{j=1}^n v_j - w$. Then $(v, v_{n+1}) \in K$ and $w = \sum_{j=1}^n v_j - v_{n+1} = \partial \pi(\bar{z}) v_{n+1} - v_{n+1} = [\partial \pi(\bar{z}) - I] v_{n+1}$. Observe that for all j, $\lambda_j \partial^2 u_j(\bar{x}_j)(v_j, v_j) + v_j \cdot w = 0$. So

$$\sum_{j=1}^n \lambda_j \partial^2 u_j(x_j)(v_j, v_j) + w \cdot \left(\sum_{j=1}^n v_j \right) = 0.$$

But $w \cdot (\sum_{j=1}^n v_j) = w \cdot \partial \pi(\bar{z}) v_{n+1} = [\partial \pi(\bar{z}) - I] \partial \pi(\bar{z})(v_{n+1}, v_{n+1})$. Therefore, by the second-order sufficient conditions we must have $v = 0$ and $v_{n+1} = 0$. Hence, the rows of $\partial \eta(\bar{x}, \bar{\lambda}, \bar{z})$ are linearly independent and we have concluded our proof. ∎

Observe that in Proposition 4.6.3 we get an n rather than $(n-1)$-dimensional manifold because the pairs (λ, p) have not been normalized. The allocation x in the Edgeworth box of Figure 4.6.2b shows that condition (ii) cannot be dispensed with. Example 4.6.4 does the same for the requirement that $\bar{x}$ be regular with respect to (p, λ). Example 4.6.5 illustrates that even if the conditions of the proposition are satisfied, P may not be a C^1 manifold at x.

4.6.4. Example. Let $\ell = 2$, $Y = -R_+^2$, $n = 2$, $\omega = (1, 1)$. The preferences (which are convex) and the set P are represented in the Edgeworth box of Figure 4.6.3. The optimum x is not regular. Clearly, we can take the second-order sufficient conditions to be satisfied at x. Nonetheless, neither $P (= P_l)$ nor N_l is a C^1 manifold at x. The situation is typical. A nonregular optimum will generally correspond to a point where the optimum set moves from a coordinate subspace to a smaller one (because a nonnegativity constraint becomes binding) with the result that it will exhibit a kink.

4.6.5. Example. Let $\ell = 2$, $Y = -R_+^2$, $n = 2$, $\omega = (1, 1)$. This is simply the standard example of nonlinked optimum x illustrated in Figures 4.6.4a and b. Whereas in this example $P (= P_l)$ has a kink at x, N_l is a C^1 manifold at (x, p, λ). See also Example 4.3.4. Note that $\hat{U}$ fails also to be a smooth manifold at $u(x)$.

The problem in the previous example is that x is not linked. In fact, we have:

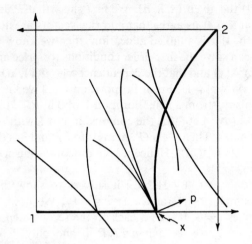

Figure 4.6.3

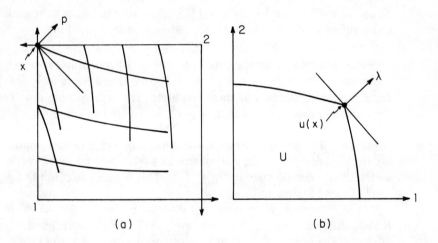

Figure 4.6.4

4.6.6. Proposition. *Let $(x, \lambda, p) \in N_l$ satisfy the conditions of Proposition 4.6.3. Suppose in addition that x is a linked allocation. Then there is an open neighborhood $x \in V \subset R^{ln}$ such that $V \cap P_l$ is a C^1 $(n-1)$-dimensional manifold and $u: V \cap P_l \to R^n$ is a diffeomorphism onto its image.*

Proof. Denote by $(\bar{x}, \bar{\lambda}, \bar{p})$ the given (x, λ, p). We first show that P_l is a $(n-1)$ smooth manifold at $\bar{x}$. Let us agree that all price vectors are normalized to have unit length. If x is a linked allocation, then we know by Proposition 4.3.6 that we can solve the first-order conditions for price and utility weights vectors $p(x), \lambda(x)$ and that the dependence $x \mapsto (p(x), \lambda(x))$ is C^1. Let $\hat{N}_l = \{(x, \lambda, p) \in N_l : \|p\| = 1\}$. From Proposition 4.6.3 we know that there is a diffeomorphism ξ from a neighborhood V of 0 in R^{n-1} to a neighborhood of $(\bar{x}, \bar{\lambda}, \bar{p})$ in $\hat{N}_l$. Let ξ_1 be the composition of ξ with the projection on the x coordinates. Then, ξ_1 is C^1, maps into P_l, and has the C^1 inverse $\xi_1^{-1}(x) = \xi^{-1}(x, \lambda(x), p(x))$. Hence, ξ_1 is a diffeomorphism of V into P_l and we are done.

We now prove the second part. By H.2.1.ii it suffices to show that $\partial u(\bar{x}): T_{\bar{x}} P_l \to R^n$ has maximal $(n-1)$ rank. Let $v \in T_{\bar{x}} P_l$. We need to verify that $\partial u(x) v = 0$ implies $v = 0$. If we go back to the second step of the proof of Proposition 4.6.3, we see that $v \in T_{\bar{x}} P_l$ if and only if for some $s \in R^n$ and $w \in R^l$ we have $\partial \eta(\bar{x}, \bar{\lambda}, \bar{z})(v, s, w) = 0$. Remembering the expression for $\partial \eta(\bar{x}, \bar{\lambda}, \bar{z})$, this implies $\sum_{j=1}^n v_j = \partial \pi(z) w$. Therefore, $(v, w) \in K$, the subspace of test directions for the second-order sufficient conditions. Also, $\lambda_j \partial^2 u_j(\bar{x}_j)(v_j, v_j) - v_j \cdot w + \partial \pi(z)(v_j, w) = 0$ for all j. So $\sum_{j=1}^n \lambda_j \partial^2 u_j(\bar{x}_j)(v_j, v_j) + [\partial \pi(\bar{z}) - I](\sum_{j=1}^n v_j, w) = 0$. Because the second-order sufficient conditions hold, we get $v = 0$ and we are done. $\blacksquare$

Because for linked allocations x the pair (λ, p) is uniquely determined (up to normalization), the conditions of Proposition 4.6.6 involve only x. A geometric implication of these conditions is worth spelling out. Take the exchange case. By letting $x_n = \omega - \sum_{j=1}^{n-1} x_j$, we can represent allocations as members of the space $R^{l(n-1)}$. This is what one does in the Edgeworth box. The proof of Proposition 4.6.6 shows that if the hypotheses are satisfied at x, then K_x, the subspace of second-order test directions, and $T_{\bar{x}} P_l$ are complementary in $R^{l(n-1)}$. This is illustrated in the Edgeworth box of Figure 4.6.5.

The last assertion of Proposition 4.6.6, that is, the fact that $u: V \cap P_l \to R^n$ is a diffeomorphism, does *not* imply that if $x \in P_l$ satisfies the conditions of the proposition, then $\hat{U}$ is a smooth manifold at $u(x)$. In fact, this is false, and the reason there is no contradiction with the proposition is that $u(V)$ may not cover a neighborhood of $u(x)$ in $\hat{U}$. This may be better understood through the discussion of an example.

4.6.7. Example. Let $l = 2$, $Y = -R_2^l$, $n = 2$. The preferences of agent 2 are represented by the utility function $u_2(x_2) = x_2^1 + x_2^2$. The preferences of agent 1 are nonconvex. Some indifference curves are drawn in the Edgeworth box of Figure 4.6.6a, where the sets P and P_l are also indicated.

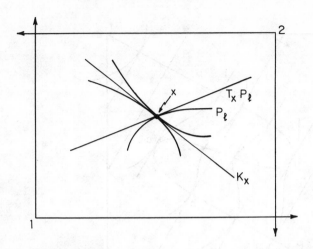

Figure 4.6.5

In the figure the curve from a to f represents the allocations that satisfy the first-order conditions. Of these the segments from a to b and from e to f constitute P (the set of true optima) and the segments from a to c and from d to f form P_l. The points from c to d are not even local optima. Except for $x = c$ and $x = d$ (where the second-order sufficient conditions cannot be satisfied) we can take the hypotheses of Proposition 4.6.6 to hold at each $x \in P_l$. Figure 4.6.6b represents the set U. Note that $\hat{U}$ is not smooth at $u(b) = u(e)$, but that, in agreement with the proposition, $u(V \cap P_l)$ is smooth when V is a small neighborhood around e or b.

Let $\bar{x}$ be an optimum in the interior of an Edgeworth box. From the definition itself we see that $\bar{x}$ is a singularity of the map $x \mapsto u(x)$ from the box to R^2. Otherwise, $u(\bar{x})$ could not belong to the boundary of U. More formally, the first-order conditions imply rank $\partial u(x) < 2$. If the second-order sufficient conditions are satisfied at $\bar{x}$, then Proposition 4.6.6 tells us that as a singularity of u, $\bar{x}$ is of the simplest possible kind, namely, rank $\partial u(\bar{x}) = 1$, or co-rank one. We see from Figure 4.6.6 that in Example 4.6.7, except for $\bar{x} = c, d$, the effect of u at any $\bar{x}$ satisfying the first-order conditions is to merely fold the underlying space. Globally, however, the distortion of the Edgeworth box under the transformation u is more complicated than a fold, and this is reflected on the presence of co-rank 2 singularities (cusps) at $\bar{x} = c$ and $\bar{x} = d$.

In the Edgeworth box of Figure 4.6.6 we have drawn the singularity set as a smooth manifold. In Chapter 8 we shall see that in an appropriate sense this is the typical case for all n.

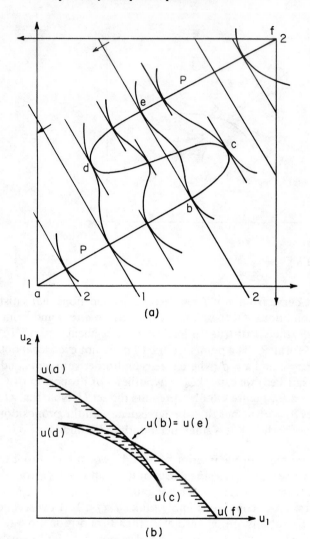

Figure 4.6.6

The looseness of the preceding two paragraphs is indicative of the dilemma that confronts us at this juncture: Either we pursue the general local analysis without convexity hypothesis in its proper mathematical setting – namely, the theory of singularity of maps – or we shy away from this by imposing convexity conditions. We do the second.

From now on *we assume that every agent has convex preferences and that the corresponding indifference manifolds have nonzero Gaussian curvature; that is, preferences are differentiably strictly convex* (2.6.1). Then at any optimum x the second-order sufficient conditions are automatically satisfied. Thus, Propositions 4.6.2 to 4.6.6 yield the following informal picture for P: P is, topologically, an $(n-1)$ simplex that is smooth (C^1) whenever $x \in P$ is regular and linked. So typically, one should expect P to be some sort of piecewise smooth manifold, the fitting of the different pieces taking place at nonregular or nonlinked optima. Nonlinked optima are not troublesome because, if not P, at least N_l is well behaved (4.6.3), and this may be quite enough for practical purposes. One would like to make sure, however, that the set of nonregular optima is small in P (nowhere dense, for example). There is no reason why this should be so (consider Edgeworth box examples), but we shall see in Chapter 8 that typically this is the case. This will constitute our only excursion into the analysis of the finer structure of P.

Under the current hypothesis on preferences, we can without loss of generality assume that U is convex.

4.6.8. Proposition. *If preferences are C^2 and convex, and indifference manifolds have nonzero Gaussian curvature, then there are admissible C^2 utility representations $u_1, \ldots, u_n$ with the property that U is convex.*

Proof. It suffices to choose every u_j to be concave on $R_+^\ell \cap (Y + \{\omega\})$. By 2.6.4 this can be done. ∎

Suppose we are in an exchange economy such that if $u(x) \in \hat{U}$ and $u(x) \gg 0$, then $x_j \gg 0$ for all j. This could be guaranteed by appropriate, and familiar, boundary conditions on preferences; for example, $\{v \in R_{++}^\ell : v \gtrsim_j x_j\}$ is closed in R^ℓ for all j and $x_j \gg 0$. Then we have that every $x \in P$ with $u(x) \gg 0$ is regular, linked, and satisfies the second-order sufficient conditions. So by Proposition 4.6.6, P and $\hat{U}$ are C^1 manifolds at, respectively, x and $u(x)$. As in Proposition 4.6.2, we see that u is a homeomorphism between the smooth manifolds $u^{-1}(\hat{U} \cap R_{++}^n)$ and $\hat{U} \cap R_{++}^n$. By 4.6.6, u is also a local diffeomorphism on $u^{-1}(\hat{U} \cap R_{++}^n)$. Hence, u is in fact a diffeomorphism on this set. We have shown:

4.6.9. Proposition. *In an exchange economy with C^2 convex preferences and nonzero Gaussian curvature of indifference manifolds, suppose that $x \gg 0$ whenever $x \in P$ and $u(x) \gg 0$. Then, $\hat{U} \cap R_{++}^n$ and $\{x \in P : u(x) \gg 0\}$ are C^1 smooth manifolds diffeomorphic under $x \mapsto u(x)$. Also, they are both diffeomorphic to the interior of the $(n-1)$ unit simplex.*

Proof. Only the last statement has not yet been proved, but it is clear enough since if $\hat{U} \cap R_{++}^n$ is a smooth manifold, then it is easily checked that the homeomorphism in the proof of Proposition 4.6.1 is a diffeomorphism. ∎

For later reference we consider in more detail the special case of an exchange economy where preferences are defined on R_{++}^ℓ and the usual boundary condition is satisfied. From 2.6.5 we know that every $\gtrsim_j$ can then be represented by a $u_j = R_{++}^\ell \to R$ such that (i) u_j is C^2; (ii) if $v \leq \omega$, then $\partial^2 u_j(v)$ is negative definite; and (iii) if $v_m \to v$, $0 \leq v_m \leq \omega$, $v_m^h = 0$, then $\|\partial u_j(v_m)\| \to \infty$. To every λ in the interior of the $(n-1)$ simplex we associate the unique $x(\lambda) \in R^{\ell n}$ that maximizes $\sum_{j=1}^n \lambda_j u_j(x_j)$ subject to $\sum_{j=1}^n x_j \leq \omega$. The next proposition tells us that the function $\lambda \mapsto x(\lambda)$ is a diffeomorphism onto the set P of optimal allocations.

> **4.6.10. Proposition.** *Under the above hypotheses and definitions the function $\lambda \mapsto x(\lambda)$ is a C^1 diffeomorphism between the interior of the $(n-1)$ simplex and the set of optimal allocations.*

Proof. It is trivial to verify that the function is a homeomorphism and that its inverse $x \mapsto \lambda(x)$ is C^1 (see 4.3.6). To check that the function is C^1 go back to the proof of 4.6.3 (step 2) and note that, under the hypotheses, the $(\ell + r) \times (\ell + r)$ matrix $\partial_{x, z} \eta(\bar{x}, \bar{\lambda}, \bar{z})$ is nonsingular. Therefore, by the implicit function theorem (C.3.2), x can be solved locally as a differentiable function of λ. But this solution is precisely the function we are concerned with (4.3.3.iv). ∎

4.7   Reference notes

Section 4.2. The setting and results of this section are all standard. The optimum concept originates in V. Pareto (1909, chap. 6). It was refined and tied to the theory of market equilibrium by many authors – among them Hotelling (1938), Lange (1942), and Samuelson (1947, chap. 8). It was not until Arrow (1952) and Debreu (1951) that the "two fundamental theorems of welfare economics" were formulated and proved by means of the mathematical theory of convexity. The content of 4.2 is an account of the resulting convexity-based theory. See also Koopmans (1957, essay 1), Debreu (1959, chap. 7), and Arrow–Hahn (1971, chap. 4). Under the maintained hypotheses, our concept of quasi-equilibrium coincides with the "quasi-equilibrium" of Debreu (1962) and the "compensated equilibrium" of Arrow–Hahn (1971). The concept of utility set (4.2.17) has also a long tradition in welfare economics – see, for example, Samuelson (1950).

Sections 4.3 and 4.4. The calculus approach did, of course, dominate the first period of optimality theory, going roughly from Pareto (1909) until the time when the emphasis on inequalities led to the adoption of convexity methods (see references for 4.2). The work of Lange (1942) and Allais (1943) stressing the Lagrange multiplier technique was a high point of this phase. It was logical that the modern resurgence of interest in differential methods reassume the task of formulating first- and second-order conditions for optima. The modern mathematical literature on smooth vector optimization was reviewed in the references for Section D of Chapter 1. The central results of Sections 4.3 and 4.4 (4.3.1, 4.3.3, 4.4.2 and 4.4.3) represent the specialization to economies of this general, more abstract mathematical theory. Closely related results have been obtained by S. Smale (1974b, 1974d), Y. Wan (1975), van Geldrop (1980), Simon and Titus (1975), and, no doubt, others.

Under the name of "no isolated communities condition" the concept of linked allocations (4.3.5) was introduced by Smale (1974d), to whom 4.3.6 is also due. The pairwise optimality (4.3.8) problem was first studied by Rader (1968), to whom 4.3.9.i is due; 4.3.9.ii is due to Feldman (1973). See also Goldman–Starr (1982). Proposition 4.4.4 is due to Nielsen (1983).

Section 4.5. It is well known that in the limit, that is, for economies with a continuum of consumers, the convexity hypothesis is dispensable in order to establish that optima can be price-supported. See Hildenbrand (1974, chap. 4). Section 4.5 works out the corresponding asymptotic theory.

Section 4.6. Explicitly or implicitly most of the results in this section can be found in Smale (1976a), Schecter (1975, 1977), or Balasko (1976, 1979a). Balasko assumes an open consumption set, thus abstracting from any problem associated with boundaries, whereas Schecter emphasizes precisely those. Thus their analyses complement each other rather well. The observation associated to Figure 4.6.5 is due to Smale (1976a). Results 4.6.1 and 4.6.2 are old; see, for example, Arrow–Hahn (1971).

CHAPTER 5

Exchange economies

5.1 Introduction

In this and the next chapter an extensive account is given of the Walrasian price equilibrium theory of exchange and production. In comparison to the previous chapter, the key new element is that consumers are now characterized not only by their preferences but also by their initial endowments of commodities. To streamline the exposition, the present chapter concentrates on economies without production, whereas the next goes into any distinct issue raised by the latter.

Section 5.2 presents the basic definitions of consumers, exchange economies, and exchange price equilibrium. This is done both for the general and the smooth case. Different systems of equations whose zeroes describe the equilibrium state are presented. One, the excess uitility map, is in the spirit of the previous chapter. We shall nevertheless emphasize an approach via excess demand functions. This is done partly because situations with a continuum of consumers can be accommodated at almost no cost.

Placing ourselves in a smooth framework, Section 5.3 presents the central concept of regular economy. Roughly speaking, an economy is regular if the relevant systems of equations, for example, the excess demand function, is not (first-order) degenerate, that is, singular, at equilibrium. In Section 5.8 and more deeply in chapter 8, we shall argue that, in a precise sense, nonregular economies are pathological. At any rate, it is for regular economies that the full power of the differentiable approach can be displayed. Thus, for example, the equilibria of a regular economy are well determined in the sense of being locally unique and persistent under perturbations of the economy. This is shown in Section 5.4 by an implicit function theorem argument that amounts, in essence, to the verification that the number of equations and unknowns is the same. Regular economies turn out thus to be the proper setting for the rigorous application of this classical technique.

166

Up to Section 5.4 the results obtained are local and depend only on local properties of the excess demand function. Section 5.5 brings into the picture its global, boundary properties. For a regular economy those are seen to imply the finiteness of the set of equilibria and a fundamental index theorem. It turns out that to every equilibrium of a regular economy one can associate in a natural manner an index equal to plus one or minus one, in such a manner that the sum of these indices is one. In particular, this implies that an equilibrium exists because the number of equilibria must be odd. We give the index theorem center stage not so much because of the rather limited strength of its conclusion but because, in a sense that the second part of Section 5.5 makes precise, it is not possible to derive any stronger theorem from the general hypotheses describing an exchange economy. The proof of the index theorem, a purely mathematical but quite instructive affair, is discussed in detail in Section 5.6, where the usefulness of homotopy methods is emphasized.

By placing restrictions on the permissible distributions of preferences and endowments it should be possible to claim stronger properties for the equilibrium set beyond what is allowed by the index theorem. This is illustrated in Section 5.7 with respect to the uniqueness property. Our approach to uniqueness focuses on conditions for the aggregate excess demand to satisfy some appropriate versions of the "law of demand", that is, demand decreases whenever price increases.

Up to Section 5.7 only the properties of the equilibrium set of a fixed regular economy and its local perturbations are considered. Section 5.8 takes a more global point of view and contemplates as central object the complete equilibrium set placed in the cartesian product of the price domain and an a priori given space of economies (which may include nonregular ones). The analysis is particularly fruitful whenever the latter can be parameterized finite-dimensionally.

5.2   Exchange economies and exchange price equilibrium

In this section the basic framework for the chapter is described. We introduce the concepts of *consumer's or agent's characteristics, exchange economy, Walrasian equilibrium allocations,* and *prices.* We show how it is possible to look at equilibria as the zeroes of a certain function to be called the *excess demand function.* Next we note the fundamental fact that Walrasian equilibrium allocations are optima and use it to formulate a dual system of equations whose zeroes are also naturally associated with the Walrasian equilibria. Finally, we introduce the smoothness hypotheses valid for the rest of this chapter and spell out some of its direct implications.

We contemplate a population of agents, also called consumers, described by their *preference relation* and *endowment vector*. The pair of preference relation and endowment vector is called the *characteristics* of an agent. As in Chapter 2, the admissible consumption sets X will be either $X = R_{++}^{\ell}$ or $X = R_{+}^{\ell} \setminus \{0\}$. *Preferences will always be continuous, strictly monotone, and strictly convex.* Therefore, the spaces of admissible preferences are $\mathcal{P}_{sc}$ and $\mathcal{P}_{sc}^{r}$, where, as in 2.4 and 2.8, those are defined by

$$\mathcal{P}_{cl} = \{\succsim \, \subset X \times X : \succsim \text{ is continuous and monotone}\},$$
$$X = R_{+}^{\ell} \setminus \{0\}$$

$$\mathcal{P}_{b} = \{\succsim \, \subset X \times X : \succsim \text{ is continuous and monotone and}$$
$$\text{satisfies the boundary condition } 2.3.16\},$$
$$X = R_{++}^{\ell}$$

$$\mathcal{P} \in \{\mathcal{P}_{cl}, \mathcal{P}_{b}\}$$

$$\mathcal{P}_{sc} = \{\succsim \, \in \mathcal{P} : \succsim \text{ is strictly convex}\}$$

$$\mathcal{P}_{sc}^{r} = \{\succsim \, \in \mathcal{P} : \succsim \text{ is } C^{r} \text{ and differentiably strictly convex}\}, \quad r \geq 2.$$

The space of admissible characteristics is denoted $\mathcal{A}$, its generic element being $a = (\succsim, \omega)$. *The only possibilities that are contemplated in this chapter are $\mathcal{A} = \mathcal{P}_{sc} \times R_{++}^{\ell}$ and $\mathcal{A} = \mathcal{P}_{sc}^{r} \times R_{++}^{\ell}$, $r \geq 2$. By "a space $\mathcal{A}$ of continuous (resp. smooth) characteristics," we always mean the first (resp. second). Note that we always restrict ω to be nonzero. We showed in Chapter 2 (2.6.7, A.3.4) that $\mathcal{P}_{sc}$ and $\mathcal{P}_{sc}^{r}$ when endowed with economically natural topologies become complete metrizable spaces. Thus, letting R^{ℓ} have the Euclidean norm and $\mathcal{A}$ the product topology (i.e., $a_{n} \to a$ if and only if $\succsim_{n} \to \succsim$ and $\omega_{n} \to \omega$) we can give to $\mathcal{A}$ the structure of a complete metric space.

An exchange economy $\mathcal{E}$ is a collection of consumers. Mathematically this is formalized by letting $\mathcal{E}$ be a function from an indexing set I, the set of consumer's names, to the space of characteristics $\mathcal{A}$. The set I is taken to be either finite or the interval $[0, 1]$. The second situation corresponds to an economy with a continuum of agents. In this case we impose two requirements on the map $\mathcal{E} : I \to \mathcal{A}$. The first is purely technical, *namely that it be (Borel) measurable.* The second is substantive, *namely that for some compact $K \subset \mathcal{A}$ we have: "$\mathcal{E}(t) \in K$ for all $t \in I$."* The economic interpretation of the latter condition is that although there is a continuum of agents, the dissimilarities of their characteristics are limited. Note that the two requirements are vacuously satisfied in the case $\#I < \infty$. Because most of the analysis of this chapter applies to $\#I < \infty$ or $I = [0, 1]$ we shall adopt the following terminological convention: Unless otherwise specified, the symbol I stands indistinctly for a finite indexing set or for the interval $[0, 1]$. In the latter case the notation $\sum_{t \in I}$ has to be read as $\int_0^1$. The use of the symbol $\sum$ rather than the mathematically more general $\int$ indicates that for the sake of concreteness we shall emphasize the interpretation of I as a finite set. If the space of characteristics is smooth, we call the economy smooth.

For the rest of this section we let a fixed economy $\mathcal{E}: I \to \mathcal{Q}$ be given.

5.2.1. Definition. *An allocation x is a function from I to X. An allocation $x: I \to R_+^\ell$ is attainable if $\sum_{t \in I} x_t \leq \sum_{t \in I} \omega_t$.*

5.2.2. Definition. *An allocation $x: I \to X$ is a Walrasian price equilibrium (or equilibrium, for short) if it is attainable and there is a vector $p > 0$ called the equilibrium price vector such that, for all t, x_t maximizes $\succeq_t$ on $b(p, p \cdot \omega_t) = \{z \in R_+^\ell : p \cdot z \leq p \cdot \omega_t\}$.*

Given an economy $\mathcal{E}$ there is an obvious incentive for agents to engage in mutually satisfactory exchange of commodities, that is, in trade. The formal notion of Walrasian price equilibrium offers a precise solution concept for the outcome of trade based on organized markets and prices. Two implicit postulates are fundamental to Walrasian theory, namely: (i) Prices are quoted for all commodities, and (ii) they are taken as given (i.e., as independent of their own actions) by economic agents. Since the analytical framework for this and the next chapter is Walrasian theory, we shall not, for the moment, question these postulates. We shall look beyond them in Chapter 7.

The next example gives an Edgeworth box illustration of Walrasian price equilibrium. It also shows that an economy may have several Walrasian equilibrium allocations.

5.2.3. Example. Let $\#I = 2$, $\ell = 2$. The preference $\succeq_1$, $\succeq_2$ and the endowments $\omega = (\omega_1, \omega_2)$ of the two agents are represented in the Edgeworth box of Figure 5.2.1. We see in the figure that the allocation x (resp. x', x'') is Walrasian because we can find a price system p (resp. p', p'') that makes x_1, x_2 preference-maximizing on their respective budget sets.

Because of the strict monotonicity of preferences, if $p^j = 0$, then there is no preference maximizer on $b(p, p \cdot \omega)$. Hence, if x is an equilibrium allocation with equilibrium price vector p, we should have $p \gg 0$.

Because of the strict convexity of preferences there is at most one preference maximizer on a budget set. Therefore, we can speak without ambiguity about equilibrium price vectors. Indeed, a vector $p \gg 0$ is an equilibrium price vector with respect to some attainable allocation x if and only if for all $t \in I$, x_t equals the unique maximizer of $\succeq_t$ on $b(p, p \cdot \omega_t)$.

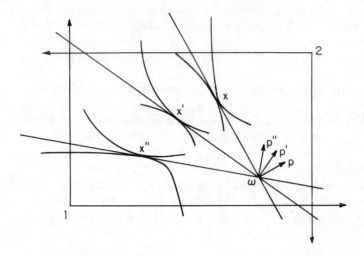

Figure 5.2.1

5.2.4. Definition. *The function* $f_t: R_{++}^\ell \to R^\ell$, *defined by letting* $f_t(p) + \omega_t$ *be the unique maximizer of* $\succsim_t$ *on* $b(p, p \cdot \omega_t)$, *is called the excess demand function of agent t. The negative of excess demand is called excess supply.*

Note that $p \gg 0$ is a price equilibrium vector if and only if the allocation $x_t = f_t(p) + \omega_t$ is attainable, that is, if and only if $\sum_{t \in I} f_t(p) \leq 0$. The excess demand function $f_t(p)$ is obviously equal to $\varphi(\succsim_t, p, p \cdot \omega_t) - \omega_t$, where φ is the demand function. Using the properties of the latter we immediately get: (i) f_t is continuous; (ii) f_t is bounded below; (iii) $p \cdot f_t(p) = 0$ for all $p \in R_{++}^\ell$; (iv) $f_t(\alpha p) = \alpha f_t(p)$ for all $p \in R_{++}^\ell$ and $\alpha > 0$; and (v) if $p_n \to p$ and $p^j = 0$ for some j, then $\|f_t(p_n)\| \to \infty$; see 2.4.8.

The function $f: R_{++}^\ell \to R^\ell$ given by $f(p) = \sum_{t \in I} f_t(p)$ is called the *aggregate excess demand function* (or, simply, the excess demand function). Properties (i)–(v) for single-agent excess demand are inherited by aggregate excess demand. Formally:

5.2.5. Proposition. *Given the economy $\mathcal{E}$ the aggregate excess demand function $f: R_{++}^\ell \to R^\ell$ is well defined and satisfies:*

   (i)   *f is continuous.*

  (ii)   *f is bounded below [i.e., there is $k > 0$ such that $f(p) > -ke$ for all p].*

 (iii) $p \cdot f(p) = 0$ *for all p.*

(iv) $f(\alpha p) = \alpha f(p)$ *for all p and $\alpha > 0$.*

(v) *If $p_n \to p$ and $p^j = 0$ for some j, then $\|f(p_n)\| \to \infty$.*

Proof. For the case $\#I < \infty$ this is obvious because properties (i)–(iv) are preserved under addition and, given (ii), so is (iv). The case $I = [0,1]$ is almost as straightforward once the hypothesis $\mathcal{E}(I) \subset K$, $K \subset \mathcal{Q}$ compact, is taken into account. Indeed, the latter implies that for some $k > 0$, $\omega_t \leq ke$ for all t. Hence, for given $p \gg 0$, the function $t \to f_t(p)$ is bounded and so $f(p) = \int_0^1 f_t(p) \, dt$ exists. Properties (ii), (iii), and (iv) are then obvious. Property (i) follows from the basic results on the exchange of limit and integral sign (E.4.1). For property (v), let $p_n \to p$, $p \in \partial S$, and note that:

(a) $\|f_t(p_n)\| \to \infty$. Because $f_t(p_n) \geq -ke$ this means that
$$\lim \max_j f_t^{\,j}(p_n) = +\infty.$$

(b) $\|\int_0^1 f_t(p_n)\| \geq \max_j [\int_0^1 f_t^{\,j}(p_n)] \geq \max_j [\int_0^1 \max\{f_t^{\,j}(p_n), 0\}] - k$
$$\geq (1/\ell) \int_0^1 \max_j \{f_t^{\,j}(p_n)\} - k.$$

Therefore, we should have $\|\int_0^1 f_t(p_n)\| \to \infty$; see E.4.1. ∎

Observe that $p \gg 0$, $p \cdot f(p) = 0$, and $f(p) \leq 0$ implies $f(p) = 0$. Therefore, we can as well define $p \gg 0$ to be an equilibrium if $f(p) = 0$. By property (iv), if p is a price equilibrium, then so is αp for $\alpha > 0$. To eliminate this degree of freedom it will be convenient on many occasions to *normalize* the domain of f. A particularly interesting normalized price set that treats all commodities symmetrically is the unit $(\ell - 1)$ sphere, that is, $S = \{p \in R_{++}^\ell : \|p\| = 1\}$. Because property (iii) just says that $f(p) \in T_p = \{v \in R^\ell : p \cdot v = 0\}$ for all $p \gg 0$, we have: *Mathematically we can view the (normalized) aggregate excess demand function $f : S \to R^\ell$ as a tangent vector field on the positive portion of the $(\ell - 1)$ unit sphere.* See J.3 and Figure 5.2.2.

Remembering the definition of price equilibrium allocation from Chapter 4 (4.2.11) we see that if x is a Walrasian equilibrium allocation with equilibrium price vector p, then, in particular, it is a price equilibrium allocation with respect to p and, therefore, it is an optimum (Proposition 4.2.15). This is, of course, an extremely important fact that should be recorded as a proposition. Figure 5.2.3 provides an Edgeworth box illustration.

5.2.6. Proposition. *Every Walrasian equilibrium allocation is an optimum.*

Proof. Definitions and Proposition 4.2.15. ∎

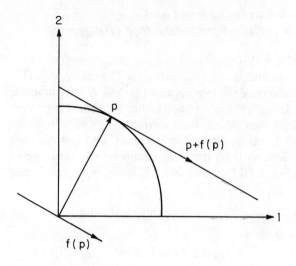

Figure 5.2.2

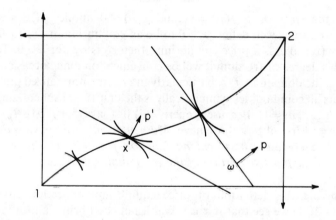

Figure 5.2.3

Denote by P the set of optimum allocations for $\mathcal{E}$. We know from Proposition 4.6.2 that for the case $\#I = n < \infty$ the set P is topologically an $(n-1)$ simplex (strictly speaking, this was shown for the consumption set R_+^ℓ). Proposition 5.2.6 tells us then that the Walrasian allocations are precisely those $x \in P$ that satisfy one further condition, namely that for some supporting $p \gg 0$ and for all $t \in I$ the imputed wealth $p \cdot x_t$ equals the value of t's initial endowments, that is, $p \cdot \omega_t$. More formally: For each $x \in P$, let $h(x) = \{(p \cdot (x_1 - \omega_1), \ldots, p \cdot (x_n - \omega_n)): p \in R_+^\ell$ supports $x\}$; then x is an equilibrium allocation if and only if $0 \in h(x)$. Note that h defines a nonempty, convex-valued map from P into the $(n-1)$-dimensional linear space $T_e = \{z \in R^n: e \cdot z = 0\}$. We could call it the *excess wealth* map. Thus, we have two alternative, dual procedures to identify equilibria with the zeroes of a system of "equations," namely, $0 \in f(p)$ or $0 \in h(x)$. By the first method (excess demand) we construct a function such that preference maximization and the budget constraint are satisfied throughout the domain, and then we search for a point satisfying attainability. The dimensionality of the system of equations is $\ell - 1$, hence independent of the number of agents. By the second method (excess wealth) we construct a map such that preference maximization and attainability are satisfied throughout the domain, and then we search for a point where the budget constraints of all agents are also satisfied. The dimensionality of the system of equations is $n - 1$, hence independent of the number of commodities.

Consider now a space of smooth characteristics $\mathcal{Q}$. For concreteness fix $r = 2$; that is, $\mathcal{Q} = \mathcal{P}_{sc}^2 \times R_{++}^\ell$. If $X = R_{++}^\ell$ and $\mathcal{P} = \mathcal{P}_b$, then for each $t \in I$ the excess demand function of agent t, $f_t: R_{++}^\ell \to R^\ell$ is C^1; see 2.7.2. Because $\mathcal{E}(I) \subset K$, $K \subset \mathcal{Q}$ compact, this carries over to the aggregate excess demand function.

5.2.7. Proposition. *Let* $\mathcal{Q} = \mathcal{P}_{sc}^2 \times R_{++}^\ell$, $\mathcal{P} = \mathcal{P}_b$. *Then* $f: R_{++}^\ell \to R^\ell$ *is* C^1.

Proof. Because $\mathcal{E}(I) \subset K$, $K \subset \mathcal{Q}$ compact, we have $\partial f(p) = \int_0^1 \partial f_t(p) \, dt$ for all p (E.5.2). Of course, the case $\#I < \infty$ is trivial. ■

If $X = R_+^\ell \setminus \{0\}$ the situation is slightly more delicate. We now have to worry about boundaries. The excess demand function of agent $t \in I$ will not be smooth at the price vectors p where $(p, p \cdot \omega_t)$ is not a regular point of demand, that is, where demand does not remain locally in the same coordinate subspace; see Figure 2.7.1. Let $J_t \subset R_{++}$ be the set of these nondifferentiability points. We shall see in Chapter 8, Section 8.4, that typically J_t has closure of Lebesgue measure zero. If $\#I < \infty$, then so does $J = \bigcup_{t \in I} J_t$ and the aggregate excess demand function f is C^1 on $R_{++}^\ell \setminus J$. If $I = [0,1]$, then J may not be small but, in fact, we are now in a better position to formulate conditions for the smoothness of f. Indeed, f will fail to be C^1 at p only if the set of agents that are in their nondifferentiability region is nonnegligible. Intuitively speaking, this is unlikely if characteristics are dispersed across the continuum of agents. Rather than search for a basic concept of disperse preferences we simply state the following smoothing by aggregation result:

5.2.8. Proposition. *Let* $\mathcal{Q} = \mathcal{P}_{sc}^2 \times R_{++}^\ell$, $\mathcal{P} = \mathcal{P}_{cl}$, $I = [0,1]$. *Suppose that, for all* $p \gg 0$, *the set* $\{t \in I : \{j : f_t^j(p) = -\omega_t^j\}$ *is locally constant* $\}$ *has measure one. Then* f *is* C^1.

Proof. Because $\mathcal{E}(I) \subset K$ and $K \subset \mathcal{Q}$ is compact, $f_t(p)$ is Lipschitzian uniformly on t (2.7.3). Also, by hypothesis (and 2.7.2), for each p, $\partial f_t(p)$ is defined for a.e. t. Therefore, by E.5.2, $\partial f(p) = \int_0^1 \partial f_t(p)\, dt$. ∎

Let $\mathcal{P} = \mathcal{P}_b$, $\#I = n < \infty$. Suppose that preferences $\succeq_1, \ldots, \succeq_n$ are represented by C^2 utility functions $u_1, \ldots, u_n$ that satisfy: (i) $\partial^2 u_t(z)$ is negative definite at any $z \leq \sum_{t \in I} \omega_t$; (ii) if $z_m \to z$, $0 \ll z_m \leq \sum_{t \in I} \omega_t$, and $z^h = 0$ for some h, then $\|\partial u_t(z_m)\| \to \infty$. Such utility representations exist (Proposition 2.6.5), and it follows from Proposition 4.6.10 that to each $\lambda \in S^{n-1}$, $\lambda \gg 0$, there corresponds a unique $p(\lambda) \in R_{++}^\ell$ and attainable allocation $x(\lambda)$ such that $\lambda_t \partial u_t(x_t(\lambda)) = p(\lambda)$ for all t. Further, $p(\lambda)$, $x(\lambda)$ are C^1. It is convenient to modify the excess wealth map to *an excess utility map* defined on the variables λ. In other words, to each $\lambda \in S^{n-1}$, $\lambda \gg 0$ we associate

$$h(\lambda) = ((1/\lambda_1)p(\lambda) \cdot (x_1(\lambda) - \omega_1), \ldots, (1/\lambda_n)p(\lambda) \cdot (x_n(\lambda) - \omega_n)) \in T_\lambda.$$

This is a well-defined C^1 tangent vector field on the strictly positive part of S^{n-1}. If we call λ an equilibrium whenever $x(\lambda)$ is a Walrasian allocation, we have that λ is an equilibrium if and only if it is a zero of the excess utility function; that is, $h(\lambda) = 0$. The symmetry with the excess demand approach is complete.

Both the excess demand and the excess utility systems of equations can be viewed as different reductions of the "universal" system of equations on the variables $x, p, \lambda \in R_{++}^{\ell n} \times R_{++}^\ell \times R_{++}^n$ given by:

(i) $\lambda_t \partial u_t(x_t) - p = 0$ for all $t \in I$ (preference maximization).
(ii) $(1/\lambda_t)p \cdot (x_t - \omega_t) = 0$ for all $t \in I$ (budget constraint).
(iii) $\sum_{t \in I}(\omega_t - x_t) = 0$ (attainability).

In forming the excess supply (resp. utility) function, one uses (i) and (ii) [resp. (i) and (iii)] to solve x and λ (resp. x and p) as a function of p (resp. λ) and then substitutes in (iii) [resp. in (ii)]. Still, a third possibility would be to use (i) to solve x as a function of p, λ (this is a decentralized step in the sense that given p and λ each x_t is obtained separately) and then substitute in (ii)–(iii). The end product would be a simultaneous equation system in p and λ.

5.3 Regular exchange equilibrium and regular exchange economies

As a formal theory for the outcome of the process of exchange of commodities among agents, Walrasian theory is deterministic in spirit. It does not merely intend to delineate a broad region of admissible outcomes, but, more ambitiously, it aims at offering a precise prediction of the final consumption of all agents. We will have much to say in this chapter about what *precise* should mean in the present context. For the moment it will suffice to point out that the originators of equilibrium theory (L. Walras, V. Pareto, F. Edgeworth, and many others) sought to verify the determinate character of the theory by applying a counting of equations and unknowns test: A theory would be determinate if its equilibria could be expressed as the zeroes of a system having the same number of equations as of unknowns. This was good heuristics, and the theory of regular economies can be viewed as a rigorous foundation and elaboration of this number-of-equations-and-unknowns approach.

Let us first discuss the purely mathematical situation. Suppose that $f: R^n \to R^m$ is a C^1 function. Even more, let it be linear. Of course, "same number of equations as unknowns" means that $n = m$. In itself this implies little for how well determined the solution to $f(z) = 0$ is. We could even have $f(z) = 0$ for all z. Obviously, if multiplicity of solutions occurs, this is due to the fact that even if formally there are as many equations as unknowns, there are also linear dependencies and so, effectively, the equations are fewer. What one should require is that there be as many linearly independent equations as unknowns or, in other words, that rank $\partial f(z) = n$. Then we indeed have $\#\{z: f(z) = 0\} \leq 1$ (remember f is linear).

For our purposes, the more important nonlinear case is entirely analogous except that the validity of the conclusion is only local. The inverse function theorem tells us: "If $f: R^n \to R^n$ is C^1, $f(z) = 0$ and rank $\partial f(z) = n$, then in some neighborhood of z the equation $f(z') = 0$ has the unique solution $z' = z$"; see Figures 5.3.1a, b. Thus if the notion of determinateness is to imply, at least, the local uniqueness of solutions, full rank (i.e., "regularity") conditions will be required. Before we leave this mathematical remark, a final observation is in order. In the nonlinear case the inverse function theorem says nothing on the existence of a solution to $f(z) = 0$. No set of conditions of a purely local character can be expected to yield the existence of a solution to a general nonlinear system $f(z) = 0$. As presented in this and the next section, the theory of regular economies makes only local hypotheses and so it is mute on existence matters. But in Sections 5.5–5.8 we shall see how once the global restrictions implied by

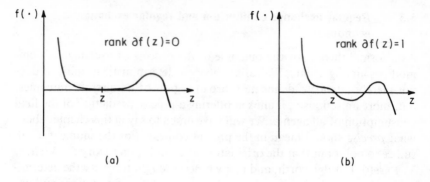

(a)   (b)

Figure 5.3.1

the underlying economies (e.g., the boundary conditions on excess demand) are taken into account, the full rank regularity hypothesis will yield powerful theorems on the existence of solutions.

Back into the economic context, we let $f: R^\ell_{++} \to R^\ell$ be the aggregate excess demand function, assumed to be C^1, for a given smooth economy $\mathcal{E}$. Propositions 5.2.7 and 5.2.8 provide conditions on $\mathcal{E}$ guaranteeing the smoothness of f. The Edgeworth box example of Figure 5.3.2 illustrates the possibility of a continuum of solutions for $f(p) = 0$, $p \in S$. Thus, the considerations of the last paragraphs apply and we are led to the investigation of full-rank-type conditions.

The first thing to observe is that in the definition of the excess demand function f there is a built-in singularity. Indeed, because $f(\alpha p) = f(p)$ for all p and $\alpha > 0$, we have that $\partial f(p)p = 0$ for all p [differentiate $f(\alpha p)$ with respect to α and evaluate at $\alpha = 1$]. Therefore, rank $\partial f(p) \le \ell - 1$ for all p; that is, looked at as an $\ell \times \ell$ matrix, $\partial f(p)$ is always singular. As a consequence, "full rank" will have to mean, in our case, a rank of order $\ell - 1$. With this proviso we can give a formal definition of regular equilibrium. We shall see in the rest of this section (and also in Section 5.8) that the definition admits many equivalent forms.

> **5.3.1. Definition.** *Suppose that the smooth economy $\mathcal{E}$ satisfies the hypothesis of Proposition 5.2.7 or 5.2.8 so that it generates a C^1 excess demand function f. We say that a price equilibrium vector p, that is, $f(p) = 0$, is regular if rank $\partial f(p) = \ell - 1$. We call the economy $\mathcal{E}$ regular if every price equilibrium vector is regular. In other words, $\mathcal{E}$ is regular if $f(p) = 0$ implies rank $\partial f(p) = \ell - 1$.*

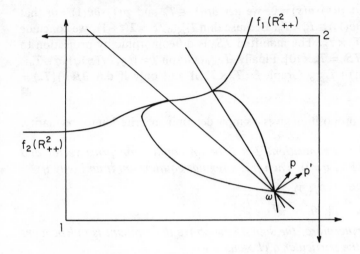

Figure 5.3.2

If so desired, the concept of regular equilibrium can be stated more geometrically as a transversal intersection condition (see I.2 for the concept of transversal manifolds). Take S as a normalized price set. Then, as was pointed out in Section 5.2, f is a vector field on S. Denote by TS the tangent bundle of S; that is, $TS = \{(p, v) \in S \times R^\ell : p \cdot v = 0\}$; see H.1.iii. The set $TS_0 = \{(p, v) \in TS : v = 0\}$ is called the zero section of TS and is naturally diffeomorphic to S. The graph of f is

$$\text{Graph } f = \{(p, v) \in S \times R^\ell : v = f(p)\} \subset TS.$$

Note that $p \in S$ is an equilibrium if and only if $(p, f(p)) \in \text{Graph } f \cap TS_0$. The tangent manifold TS is C^∞ and of dimension $2(\ell - 1)$ (see H.1.iii) while TS_0 and Graph f are C^1 submanifolds of dimension $(\ell - 1)$. Since the dimensions are complementary in TS, it makes sense to require that whenever Graph f and TS_0 intersect the intersection be transversal in TS (i.e., that the sum of the two tangent spaces to the two smaller manifolds be the full tangent space of the larger manifold). We have:

5.3.2. Proposition. *The equilibrium price vector p is regular if and only if at $(p, 0)$ the manifolds TS_0 and Graph f are transversal in TS.*

Proof. First we note that $T_{(p,0)} TS = T_p \times T_p$. Indeed, let $(p(s), v(s)) \in TS$ be a C^1 path with $p(1) = p$, $v(1) = 0$. Since for all $s \in [0, 1]$ we have

$p(s) \in S$ and $p(s) \cdot v(s) = 0$, we get $\partial p(1) \in T_p$ and $p(1) \cdot \partial v(1) = 0$; that is, $(\partial p(1), \partial v(1)) \in T_p \times T_p$. Because $\dim T_{(p,0)} TS = 2(\ell - 1)$, we conclude $T_{(p,0)} TS = T_p \times T_p$. The manifold TS_0 is diffeomorphic by projection to S, so $T_{(p,0)} TS_0 = T_p \times \{0\}$. Finally, $T_{(p,0)}$ Graph $f = \{(q, \partial f(p)q) : q \in T_p\}$. So $(T_p \times \{0\}) + T_{(p,o)}$ Graph $f = T_p \times T_p$ if and only if $\dim \partial f(p)(T_p) = \ell - 1$. ∎

The next proposition gives a simple determinant criterion for regularity.

5.3.3. Proposition. *Let $\bar{p}$ be an equilibrium price vector and $q \in R_+^\ell$, $q \neq 0$. Then $\bar{p}$ is a regular equilibrium if and only if:*

$$\begin{vmatrix} \partial f(\bar{p}) & q \\ q^T & 0 \end{vmatrix} \neq 0.$$

Furthermore, the sign of the above determinant is independent of the particular q chosen.

Proof. Because $\partial f(\bar{p})\bar{p} = 0$ we have that rank $\partial f(\bar{p}) = \ell - 1$ if and only if $\partial f(\bar{p})v = 0$ implies $v = \alpha \bar{p}$ for some $\alpha \in R$. Because $f(\bar{p}) = 0$ the identity $p \cdot f(p) = 0$ yields $\bar{p} \cdot \partial f(\bar{p}) = 0$. Let $q > 0$ and

$$\begin{bmatrix} \partial f(\bar{p}) & q \\ q^T & 0 \end{bmatrix} \begin{bmatrix} v \\ s \end{bmatrix} = 0.$$

Then $q \cdot v = 0$ and $\partial f(\bar{p})v + sq = 0$. Since $\bar{p} \cdot \partial f(\bar{p}) = 0$ and $\bar{p} \cdot q > 0$ we have $s = 0$. Hence $\partial f(\bar{p})v = 0$. If rank $\partial f(\bar{p}) = \ell - 1$, then $v = \alpha \bar{p}$ for some $\alpha \in R$. But $0 = q \cdot v = \alpha q \cdot \bar{p}$, which yields $\alpha = 0$. Therefore, $s = 0$ and $v = 0$, implying that

$$\begin{bmatrix} \partial f(\bar{p}) & q \\ q^T & 0 \end{bmatrix}$$

is nonsingular. Conversely, if this matrix is nonsingular, then $q \cdot v = 0$ has to imply $\partial f(\bar{p})v \neq 0$; that is, $\dim \partial f(\bar{p})(T_q) = \ell - 1$. So rank $\partial f(\bar{p}) = \ell - 1$. We conclude that $\bar{p}$ is a regular equilibrium if and only if

$$\begin{vmatrix} f(\bar{p}) & q \\ q^T & 0 \end{vmatrix} \neq 0.$$

The independence from q of the determinant sign is an obvious consequence of the continuity of the determinant function, the connectedness of R_+^ℓ, and A.2.4. ∎

Particularly interesting cases of Proposition 5.3.3 are obtained by taking $q = \bar{p}$ or $q = e_j$ (where e_j is the jth unit vector). In the latter case the determinant:

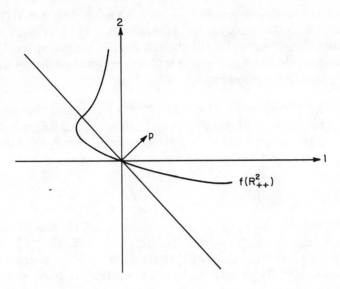

Figure 5.3.3

$$\begin{vmatrix} \partial f(\bar{p}) & e_j \\ e_j^T & 0 \end{vmatrix}$$

equals (-1) times the $(\ell-1)$ principal minor of $\partial f(\bar{p})$ obtained by deleting the jth row and column. Thus, Proposition 5.3.3 tells us that at equilibrium the sign of this $(\ell-1)$ principal minor is independent of the particular commodity index deleted. A warning is in order here: This need not be true at nonequilibrium prices. In Figure 5.3.3 we have an excess demand function where at p the principal minor is negative if the first commodity is deleted, but positive if the second is deleted.

The determinants in Proposition 5.3.3 can be understood in terms of different price normalization conventions. For example, suppose that $f(\bar{p}) = 0$ and we normalize price vectors locally by taking $\xi(p) = 0$, where ξ is C^1 and $\partial \xi(p) > 0$ [e.g., $\xi(p) = \|p\| - 1$, $\xi(p) = q \cdot \bar{p} - 1$, $\xi(p) = p^j - \bar{p}^j$]. We then define $f^*: \xi^{-1}(0) \to R^\ell$ by letting $f^*(p)$ be the perpendicular projection of $f(p)$ on $T_p \xi^{-1}(0)$. Because $p \cdot f(p) = 0$ and $\partial \xi(p) > 0$ we have that $f^*(p) = 0$ if and only $f(p) = 0$. The function f^* is a tangent vector field on $\xi^{-1}(0)$. Therefore, $\partial f^*(\bar{p})$ maps $T_{\bar{p}} \xi^{-1}(0)$ into itself (J.3.1) and so the determinant of $\partial f^*(\bar{p})$ is well defined. By B.5.2 we conclude that

$$\text{sign} |\partial f^*(\bar{p})| = -\text{sign} \begin{vmatrix} \partial f(\bar{p}) & [\partial \xi(\bar{p})]^T \\ \partial \xi(\bar{p}) & 0 \end{vmatrix}.$$

This tells us that we can read Proposition 5.3.3 as asserting that $\bar{p}$ is a regular equilibrium if and only if for some normalization procedure $\partial f^*(\bar{p})$ is nonsingular. Observe that the normalization in the unit sphere has the nice property that $f^* = f$. It will be useful to recapitulate the conclusions for this case in a proposition.

5.3.4. Proposition. *Let* $f: S \to R^\ell$. *If* $\bar{p}$ *is an equilibrium price vector, then* $\partial f(\bar{p})$ *maps* $T_{\bar{p}}$ *into* $T_{\bar{p}}$. *Hence* rank $\partial f(\bar{p}) = \ell - 1$ *(i.e.,* $\bar{p}$ *is regular) if and only if* $\partial f(\bar{p})$ *maps* $T_{\bar{p}}$ *onto* $T_{\bar{p}}$. *The determinant of this linear map is equal to*

$$\begin{vmatrix} \partial f(\bar{p}) & \bar{p} \\ -\bar{p}^T & 0 \end{vmatrix}.$$

Proof. That, whenever $f(\bar{p}) = 0$, $\partial f(\bar{p})$ maps into $T_{\bar{p}}$ is a general property of vector fields (J.3.1). To verify it, one only has to differentiate $p \cdot f(p) = 0$. So $\bar{p}$ is regular if and only if $\partial f(\bar{p})$ maps onto $T_{\bar{p}}$. The determinant of this map is formally identical to the determinant of the linear map on $T_{\bar{p}}$ formed by $\partial f(p)$ composed with the projection on $T_{\bar{p}}$. By B.5.2 we know that this determinant equals

$$\begin{vmatrix} \partial f(\bar{p}) & \bar{p} \\ -\bar{p}^T & 0 \end{vmatrix}. \qquad \blacksquare$$

Proposition 5.3.3 identifies the concept of regularity with the nonnullness of certain determinants. A nonzero number is either positive or negative. For the analysis of this and the next section it shall not matter if an equilibrium is regular by its associated determinants being positive or negative. This will, however, be a crucial piece of information in Sections 5.5–5.8. Thus, for later reference we provide the following definition.

5.3.5. Definition. *Let* p *be a regular price equilibrium. We put* index $p = \pm 1$ *according to whether*

$$\begin{vmatrix} -\partial f(p) & p \\ -p^T & 0 \end{vmatrix} \gtrless 0.$$

The definition of regular equilibrium has assumed that the economy $\mathcal{E}$ generates a C^1 excess demand function f but, clearly, the definition still makes sense if we only have that f is C^1 at the equilibrium p under consideration. This is of interest because, as we know, in the important case where the economy has a finite number of consumers with closed consumption sets we cannot expect f to be C^1 in the entire domain. So we put on record the more general definition:

5.3.6. Definition. *Let p be a price equilibrium vector for the smooth economy $\mathcal{E}$ with excess demand function f. We say that p is a regular equilibrium if (i) for every p' on a neighborhood of p the set of agents $\{t \in I: \{j: f_t^j(p') + \omega_t^j = 0\}$ is not locally constant$\}$ is null, and (ii)* rank $\partial f(p) = \ell - 1$. *The economy $\mathcal{E}$ is regular if every equilibrium p is regular.*

Note that condition (i) guarantees that f is C^1 at p [hence condition (ii) makes sense]. Indeed, if $X = R_{++}^\ell$, this follows from Proposition 5.2.7. If $X = R_+^\ell \setminus \{0\}$ and $I = [0, 1]$ we appeal to Proposition 5.2.8 and its proof, while for the case $\#I < \infty$ we observe that the only null subset of a finite set is the empty set.

It is instructive to investigate the form that the regularity condition takes when equilibrium is approached via the dual excess utility functions. To that effect, let $\mathcal{P} = \mathcal{P}_b$, $\#I = n < \infty$, and u_t be a C^2 utility function with no critical point for agent $t \in I$ that has $\partial^2 u_t(z)$ negative definite for $z \leq \sum_{t \in I} \omega_t$ and satisfies: "$z_m \to z$, $z_m \gg 0$, $z^j = 0$ for some j, implies $\|\partial u_t(z_m)\| \to \infty$." As at the end of Section 5.2 we can define a C^1 excess utility function $h: S_{++}^{n-1} \to R^n$. This yields a tangent vector field on S_{++}^{n-1} with the property that equilibrium price vectors p [i.e., $f(p) = 0$] and equilibrium vectors of utility weights λ [i.e., $h(\lambda) = 0$] correspond to each other in the obvious manner. Because, therefore, excess demand and excess utility functions are different ways to formalize the same theory, it is natural to expect that they generate the same regularity notion. Indeed, we have:

5.3.7. Proposition. *Let $\bar{p}$ and $\bar{\lambda}$ be corresponding price and utility weight equilibria; then* index $\bar{p} = \text{sign} |\partial h(\bar{\lambda})|$.

Proof. Let $\bar{x}$ be the allocation corresponding to $\bar{\lambda}$ and $\bar{p}$. In a neighborhood of $(\bar{x}, \bar{\lambda}, \bar{p})$ we define the functions:

$$\Psi_{1i}(x, \lambda, p) = p - \lambda_i \partial u_i(x_i), \qquad 1 \leq i \leq n$$

$$\Psi_{2i}(x, \lambda, p) = \frac{1}{\lambda_i} p \cdot (x_i - \omega_i), \qquad 1 \leq i \leq n$$

$$\Psi_3(x, \lambda, p) = \sum_{i=1}^{n} (\omega_i - x_i)$$

and $\Psi = (\Psi_{11}, \dots, \Psi_{1n}, \Psi_{21}, \dots, \Psi_{2n}, \Psi_3)$. Then (x, λ, p) is an equilibrium if and only if $\Psi(x, \lambda, p) = 0$. The $(\ell n + n + \ell) \times (\ell n + n + \ell)$ derivative matrix of Ψ at $(\bar{x}, \bar{\lambda}, \bar{p})$, denoted E, has the form

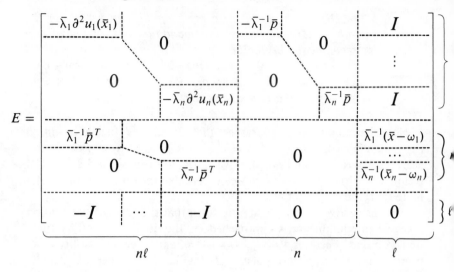

Note that, putting $v = (0, \lambda, p)$, we have $v \cdot E = 0$ and $Ev = 0$. Denote by E_λ (resp. E_p) the matrix obtained from E by deleting the $n\ell + n$ (resp. the $n\ell + n + \ell$) row and column. We wish to show that $\text{sign} |E_\lambda| = \text{sign} |E_p|$. If rank $E < n\ell + n + \ell - 1$, then $|E_\lambda| = |E_p| = 0$. So let rank $E = n\ell + n + \ell - 1$; that is, $Ez = 0$ implies $z = \alpha v$ for some α. For any $q \in R^{\ell n + \ell + n}$ with $q \cdot v > 0$ the matrix

$$\begin{bmatrix} E & q \\ q^T & 0 \end{bmatrix}$$

should be nonsingular. Indeed, suppose that $q \cdot z = 0$ and $Ez = \eta q$. Because $v \cdot Ez = 0$ and $v \cdot q > 0$ we have $\eta = 0$. Therefore, $z = \alpha v$ and so $0 = q \cdot z = \alpha q \cdot v$. Hence $\alpha = 0$; that is, $z = 0$. Let now e_λ (resp. e_p) be a vector of zeroes except for a one in the $\ell n + n$ (resp. $\ell n + n + \ell$) place. Then, for any $1 \le \alpha \le 0$, $[\alpha e_\lambda + (1 - \alpha) e_p] \cdot v > 0$. Therefore,

$$\text{sign} \det \begin{bmatrix} E & e_\lambda \\ e_\lambda^T & 0 \end{bmatrix} = \text{sign} \det \begin{bmatrix} E & e_p \\ e_p^T & 0 \end{bmatrix},$$

that is, $\text{sign} |E_\lambda| = \text{sign} |E_p|$, as we wanted to prove.

Write E_p in the form

$$E_p = \begin{bmatrix} A & B \\ C & 0 \end{bmatrix}$$

where A is the $(\ell n + n) \times (\ell n + n)$ upper left submatrix of E_p. The matrix A is a $\ell n \times \ell n$ positive definite matrix bordered by n independent vectors. Therefore $\text{sign} |A| = +1$; see B.6 and B.5.2.

Observe that if we normalize excess supply by deleting the last row and column, then by the chain rule we have $-\partial f(\bar{p}) = -CA^{-1}B$. [Remember

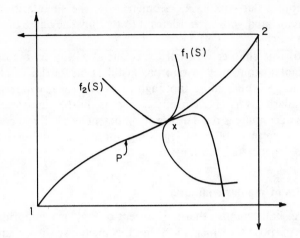

$f_1(S)$

$f_2(S)$

x

P

2

1

Figure 5.3.4

that $-f$ is obtained by putting $\Psi_1(x, \lambda, p) = 0$, $\Psi_2(x, \lambda, p) = 0$, solving for (x, λ), and replacing in Ψ_3.] Because

$$\begin{bmatrix} A & B \\ C & 0 \end{bmatrix} \begin{bmatrix} I & -A^{-1}B \\ 0 & I \end{bmatrix} = \begin{bmatrix} A & 0 \\ C & -CA^{-1}B \end{bmatrix}$$

we have $|E_p| = |A| \, |-\partial f(\bar{p})|$. Therefore,

$$\text{index } \bar{p} = \text{sign} \, |-\partial f(\bar{p})| = \text{sign} \, |E_p|.$$

To compute $|\partial h(\bar{\lambda})|$ we proceed in exactly the same way. We renumber rows and columns and write

$$E_\lambda = \begin{bmatrix} A & B \\ C & 0 \end{bmatrix}$$

where A is the $(n\ell + \ell) \times (n\ell + \ell)$ matrix obtained by bordering the $\ell n \times \ell n$ upper left positive definite submatrix of E with the ℓ independent vectors associated with the p variable (and the Ψ_3 function). Again, and with the obvious normalization, $\partial h(\bar{\lambda}) = -CA^{-1}B$. Therefore, $|\partial h(\bar{\lambda})| = |E_\lambda|$ and so index $\bar{p} = \text{sign} \, |E_p| = \text{sign} \, |E(\lambda)| = \text{sign} \, |\partial h(\bar{\lambda})|$. ∎

What the proof of Proposition 5.3.7 has done is to show that we can define the index of an equilibrium by using the universal system of equations described at the end of Section 5.2 and that this index will be invariant to the different reductions of the universal system.

The Edgeworth box of Figure 5.3.4 provides an illustration of an economy with nonregular equilibria. Geometrically, the singularity of $\partial h(\lambda)$ at the λ associated with x translates into the tangency at x of P, $f_1(S)$, and $f_2(S)$.

For the rest of this chapter we shall focus our attention on regular equilibria and regular economies. A rigorous justification for this will be provided in Section 5.7 and, more thoroughly, in Chaper 8, where we shall see that regularity is a generic property; that is, in the appropriate sense almost every economy is regular. For the moment we shall rest content with the intuitive plausibility of regarding nonregular equilibria as corresponding to degenerate situations.

5.4   Properties of regular equilibria

In this section we shall establish that the concept of regular equilibrium accomplishes the purpose for which it is devised. Namely, we show that a regular equilibrium is locally determinate in the sense of being locally unique, and that, even more importantly, it is persistent under small perturbations of the economy. The latter property is obviously of fundamental importance. An equilibrium such as p in Figure 5.4.1 that disappears with a slight change of the excess demand function is not to be taken seriously as a predicted solution of the theory.

We should, first of all, make a digression on the meaning of an economy $\mathcal{E}'$ being a small perturbation of $\mathcal{E}$. Let $\mathcal{C}$ be the space of characteristics. For all the purposes of this book, an economy $\mathcal{E}: I \to \mathcal{C}$ is completely specified by (i) the number of agents, that is, $\#I$; and (ii) the distribution ν of agents' characteristics; that is, ν is the (Borel) measure defined on $\mathcal{C}$ by $\nu(B) = (1/\#I)\#\{t \in I : \mathcal{E}(t) \in B\}$ in the finite case and $\nu(B) = \lambda(\mathcal{E}^{-1}(B))$ in the continuum case. Saying that only $\#I$ and ν matter is asserting that the name of an agent is irrelevant and that only its characteristics are of importance. It is therefore natural to define $\mathcal{E}': I' \to \mathcal{C}$ to be near $\mathcal{E}: I \to \mathcal{C}$ if $\#I'$ is near $\#I$ and ν' is near ν. By $\#I'$ being near $\#I$ we shall mean that, as real numbers, $1/\#I'$ and $1/\#I$ are close, and by ν' being near ν we mean that (i) the supports of ν and ν' are close, and (ii) ν, ν' are close in the weak convergence for measures. See Section E, Chapter 1 (especially E.3) for all the relevant concepts and Section 5.8 for further discussion. Formally:

> **5.4.1. Definition.** *Let* $\mathcal{E}_n: I_n \to \mathcal{C}$, $\mathcal{E}: I \to \mathcal{C}$ *and corresponding* ν_n, ν *be given. We say that* $\mathcal{E}_n \to \mathcal{E}$ *if:*
>
>   (i) $1/\#I_n \to 1/\#I$.
>   (ii) $\operatorname{supp} \nu_n \to \operatorname{supp} \nu$ *in the Hausdorff distance for sets.*
>   (iii) $\nu_n \to \nu$ *weakly.*

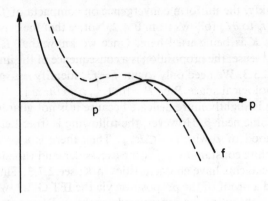

Figure 5.4.1

We postpone until Section 5.8 the formal introduction of a space of economies and a study of its topological and metric properties. Note that condition (i) of the previous definition implies that if $\#I$ is finite, then nearby economies have the same number of agents (but continuum economies can be perturbed to finite ones). So *for the finite number of agents case the definition amounts to saying* that $\mathcal{E}'$ *is near* $\mathcal{E}$ *if* $\mathcal{E}'$ *is obtained from* $\mathcal{E}$ *by a small perturbation of the preferences and endowments of every agent.*

We can now state:

5.4.2. Proposition. *Let $\mathcal{Q}$ be a space of smooth characteristics. Suppose that $\mathcal{E}_n \to \mathcal{E}$ and $\bar{p}$ is a regular price equilibrium vector for $\mathcal{E}$. Then there is $\epsilon > 0$ and N such that if $n > N$, there is a unique price equilibrium vector $\bar{p}_n$ for $\mathcal{E}_n$ satisfying $\|\bar{p}_n - \bar{p}\| \le \epsilon$.*

Proof. This is merely an application of the implicit function theorem. We begin by choosing a compact set of characteristics $K \subset \mathcal{Q}$ such that supp ν_n, supp $\nu \subset K$ for all n. This K exists because supp ν_n and supp ν are compact and supp $\nu_n \to$ supp ν (A.5.1). From now on only the existence of K matters; the condition supp $\nu_n \to$ supp ν plays no additional role.

To illustrate the idea of the proof, consider first the case $\mathcal{P} = \mathcal{P}_b$. Then the excess demand functions f_n and f are C^1 (Proposition 5.2.7). Further, $f_n \to f$ and $\partial f_n \to \partial f$ uniformly on compacta. Indeed, letting $\varphi(p, a)$ maximize $\succsim_a$ on $b(p, p \cdot \omega_a)$, we see

(i) by 2.7.2 the functions $\varphi(p, a)$ and $\partial_p \varphi(p, a)$ are continuous on $R_{++}^\ell \times \mathcal{Q}$; and

(ii) $f_n(p) = \int (\varphi(p, a) - \omega_a)\, d\nu_n(a)$, $f(p) = \int (\varphi(p, a) - \omega_a)\, d\nu$.

Because $v_n \to v$ weakly, the uniform convergence on compacta of f_n to f (and similarly for ∂f_n to ∂f) follows from E.4.2. Notice that the existence of the compact set K is being used here. Once we know that f_n converges to f in the C^1 sense, the proposition is a consequence of the implicit function theorem C.3.3. We need only to put $f = f_\infty$, identify $n \le \infty$ with $1/n$, and let the topological space P be $P = \{0, 1, \frac{1}{2}, \dots, 1/n, \dots\}$.

The general case is slightly more delicate because it is not guaranteed that f_n be differentiable near $\bar{p}$. However, the following is true: Let V be an open neighborhood of $\bar{p}$ with cl $V \subset R^\ell_{++}$. Then there is a constant $d > 0$ that is a Lipschitz constant on V for the excess demand function of any economy whose agents have characteristics in K; see 2.7.3. This can be exploited to yield a proof of the proposition via the IFT G.2.3, which, recall, relies on the concept of the generalized Jacobian. Because of this theorem, it shall suffice to prove that if $p_n \to \hat{p} \in V$ and $\partial f_n(p_n)$ exists, then $\partial f_n(p_n) \to \partial f(\hat{p})$. In particular, the generalized Jacobian matrix of f at $\bar{p}$ is then the single matrix $\partial f(\bar{p})$, which by hypothesis is nonsingular. That $f_n \to f$ uniformly on compacta is proven as in the preceding paragraph.

Let $p_n \to \hat{p}$ and $\partial f_n(p_n)$ exist. Pick an arbitrary $\delta > 0$ and let $A \subset \mathbb{Q}$ satisfy: (i) A is open; (ii) $v(A) < \delta/2$; (iii) if $a \in K \setminus A$, then $\#\{j : \varphi^j(\hat{p}, a) = 0\}$ is locally constant. This A exists because the hypothesis of 5.2.8 holds for $\mathcal{E}$; see also E.1. By 2.7.2 and the compactness of $K \setminus A$ there is an open set $\hat{p} \in U$ such that $\partial_p \varphi(p, a)$ exists and is continuous on $U \times (K \setminus A)$. Without loss of generality we can assume that, for all n, $p_n \in U$ and $v_n(A) < \delta$. Now let $f_n^\delta(p) = \int_{K \setminus A} (\varphi(p, a) - \omega_a) \, dv_n$, and similarly for f^δ. Then $\partial f_n^\delta(p)$ is well defined on U and, as in the second paragraph of the proof, $\partial f_n^\delta \to \partial f^\delta$ uniformly on U. Hence, $\partial f_n^\delta(p_n) \to \partial f^\delta(\hat{p})$. Observe also that $\partial(f_n - f_n^\delta)(p_n) = \partial_p(\int_A [\varphi(p_n, a) - \omega_a] \, dv_n)$ exists and because of the Lipschitz property, $\|\partial f_n(p_n) - \partial f_n^\delta(p_n)\| \le \delta d$. Analogously,

$$\|\partial f(\hat{p}) - \partial f^\delta(\hat{p})\| \le \delta d.$$

Therefore,

$$\|\partial f_n(p_n) - \partial f(\hat{p})\| \le \|\partial f_n(p_n) - \partial f_n^\delta(p_n)\| + \|\partial f_n^\delta(p_n) - \partial f^\delta(\hat{p})\|$$

$$+ \|\partial f^\delta(\hat{p}) - \partial f(\hat{p})\| \le 2\delta d + \|\partial f_n^\delta(p_n) - \partial f^\delta(\hat{p})\|.$$

Because $\|\partial f_n^\delta(p_n) - \partial f^\delta(\hat{p})\| \to 0$ and δ is arbitrary, this yields $\partial f_n(p_n) \to \partial f(\hat{p})$. ∎

By taking $\mathcal{E}_n \equiv \mathcal{E}$ the previous proposition implies the local uniqueness of regular equilibria.

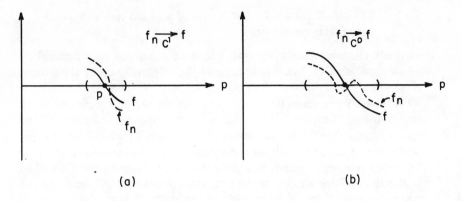

Figure 5.4.2

The perturbations contemplated in Proposition 5.4.2 are C^1 and, indeed, we have seen in the proof that they manage to keep control on the derivatives of aggregate excess demand. It is interesting, and sometimes useful, to point out that the existence, but not the uniqueness, part of the proposition remains valid for C^0 perturbations. The intuitive plausibility of this can be seen from Figure 5.4.2a and b. The rigorous proof requires techniques quite different than the ones used for Proposition 5.4.2.

> **5.4.3. Proposition.** *Let $\mathcal{Q}$ be a space of continuous characteristics. Suppose that $\mathcal{E}_n \to \mathcal{E}$, f is the excess demand function for $\mathcal{E}$, $f(\bar{p}) = 0$, f is C^1, and rank $\partial f(\bar{p}) = \ell - 1$. Then for any $\epsilon > 0$ there is N such that if $n > N$ we can find a price equilibrium vector p_n for $\mathcal{E}_n$ satisfying $\|p_n - \bar{p}\| \le \epsilon$.*

Proof. We could just quote the implicit correspondence theorem (J.3.3), but it may be instructive to give some details. Normalize prices by putting $p^\ell = 1$. The price equilibrium $\bar{p}$ is locally unique. So let $B \subset R^{\ell-1}$ be an arbitrarily small ball centered at $\bar{p}$ and such that $f(p) = 0$, $p \in B$, implies $p = \bar{p}$. Define $F: \partial B \to S^{\ell-2}$ by $F(p) = (1/\|f(p)\|)f(p)$. Then degree $F \ne 0$ because degree $F = \text{sign}\,|\partial f(p)|$. See J.2 and J.3 for the definition and basic facts on the degree of a function. Because $\mathcal{E}_n \to \mathcal{E}$ we have that $f_n \to f$ C^0 uniformly on B. Therefore $F_n(p) = (1/\|f_n(p)\|)f_n(p)$ is eventually well defined on ∂B and homotopic to F. Hence it has the same degree as F, that is, degree $F_n \ne 0$; see J.2.1. By Hopf's theorem (J.2.4) this means F_n cannot be extended to the whole of B. But if $f_n(p) \ne 0$ for all $p \in B$, then it could. Hence $f_n(p_n) = 0$ for some p_n. ∎

5.5   The equilibrium set of an economy and the index theorem for regular economies

In this section we shall investigate the structure of the set of equilibria of an economy $\mathcal{E}: I \to \mathcal{Q}$. For specificity the emphasis will be on equilibrium price vectors (rather than utility weights). We shall go beyond the local analysis prevalent up to now and exploit the global properties of excess demand functions – in particular, the boundary condition 5.2.5.v: "$p_n \to p$, $p^j = 0$ for some j, implies $\|f(p_n)\| \to \infty$." We shall see that the latter can be used to establish the compactness of the equilibrium price set and, in the regular case, a fundamental index theorem. Because of its instructional value we devote the next section to a leisurely discussion of several proofs of the theorem. The index theorem is important for its implications (the existence of an equilibrium price vector, among others) but also because, in a sense which will be made precise, it is not possible to extract more information on the equilibrium price set from our general economic hypotheses than what is contained in it.

The properties of aggregate excess demand were established in 5.2.5. We are here particularly interested in the boundary property 5.2.5.v. It is obvious that the latter may not hold if agents' preferences are not strictly monotone. This is one of the reasons that makes the hypothesis of strict monotonicity of preferences so convenient in this chapter. It should be emphasized, however, that if so desired, the analysis can be adapted to cover general monotone preferences. This would be best done in a context such as the one of Chapter 6, where production is considered explicitly.

A consequence of the boundary property is:

> **5.5.1. Proposition.** *Given an economy* $\mathcal{E}: I \to \mathcal{Q}$ *the set of equilibrium price vectors in S is compact.*

Proof. Let p be an accumulation point of the (bounded) set of equilibrium price vectors in S; that is, $p_n \to p$, $\|p_n\| = 1$, and $f(p_n) = 0$, where f is the excess demand function. By 5.2.5.v we must have $p \gg 0$. By the continuity of f, $f(p) = 0$. Hence p is an equilibrium price vector.   ∎

Let $\mathcal{Q}$ be a space of smooth characteristics and $\mathcal{E}: I \to \mathcal{Q}$ an economy. *For the time being, the economy $\mathcal{E}$ is kept fixed and its set of equilibrium price vectors $p \in S$ is denoted E.*

> **5.5.2. Proposition.** *The set of equilibrium price vectors E of a regular economy $\mathcal{E}$ is finite.*

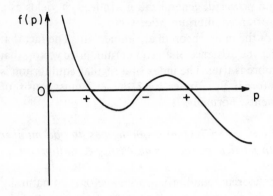

Figure 5.5.1

Proof. By 5.5.1 the set E is compact. If it is not finite, then it has an accumulation point $p \in E$; that is, $p_n \to p$, $p_n \neq p$, and $p_n \in E$. But then p is not a locally unique equilibrium, which contradicts 5.4.2. ■

The index of an equilibrium $p \in E$ of a regular economy, $\mathcal{E}$, denoted index p, has been defined in 5.3.5 as the determinant of the derivative matrix of the excess supply function $-f$ bordered by the price vector. The index, of course, does not depend on the normalization of prices. Because, for a regular economy, E is finite, the expression $\sum_{p \in E}$ index p makes sense (by convention if $E = \varnothing$, the sum equals zero). The index theorem asserts:

5.5.3. Index theorem. *If E is the equilibrium price set of a regular economy $\mathcal{E}$, then $\sum_{p \in E}$ index $p = 1$.*

The index theorem is of central importance. We shall therefore dwell extensively on its proof. Because the latter has a purely mathematical (but very illuminating!) character, we segregate it to the next section in order not to break the flow of our discourse. It should be emphasized that the theorem is not particularly mysterious. In the one-dimensional case, that is, $\ell = 2$, it simply says that if we have a C^1 function $f : (0,1) \to R$ such that $f(t) > 0$ for $t < \epsilon$ and $f(t) < 0$ for $t > 1 - \epsilon$, then, barring tangent crossings of the horizontal axis, the number of downward crossings must exceed by exactly one the number of upward crossings (see Figure 5.5.1). The index theorem amounts to a generalization of this elementary fact.

But it is a nontrivial and powerful generalization. Indeed, it yields as a corollary the existence of an equilibrium price vector.

Some consequences of the index theorem are immediate. The fact that $\sum_{p \in E}$ index $p \neq 0$ implies the existence of an equilibrium price vector, that is, $E \neq \varnothing$, but clearly more is true. The index of a regular equilibrium is always $+1$ or -1. Therefore if $\sum_{p \in E}$ index $p = 1$, the set E must consist of an odd number of elements. Formally,

5.5.4. Proposition. *Every regular economy has an odd number of equilibria. In particular, there is at least one equilibrium.*

In view of the index theorem, equilibrium price vectors can naturally be classified into two types according to whether the determinant of the Jacobian of excess supply is positive or negative. The presumption is that equilibria of the first type (i.e., positive index) are better behaved than equilibria of the second, and we shall find in the next section some contexts (e.g., accessibility by path-following algorithms) where this is indeed the case. Nevertheless, the information provided by the index theorem is rather meager. It is fairly clear that if the only thing we know about an equilibrium is its index, we shall be able to say little about, for example, the direction of price change when some parameter is altered. Thus, it is important to investigate if we can derive on general grounds further restrictions on excess demand near equilibrium. We shall devote the rest of this section to this. As we shall see, the overall conclusions will be very definite but rather negative: To get restrictions on the equilibrium price set beyond the ones yielded by the index theorem it is indispensable to move toward the consideration of special classes of economies. Section 5.7 will undertake this task.

From now on, *it is convenient to restrict* $\mathcal{P} = \mathcal{P}_b$; *that is, $X = R_{++}^{\ell}$ and the boundary condition on preferences is satisfied. Take a $\bar{p} \in S$ and $t \in I$. We have $f_t(p) = \varphi_t(p, p \cdot \omega_t) - \omega_t$, where φ_t is the demand function of $t \in I$. Therefore, $\partial_p f_t(\bar{p}) = \partial_p \varphi_t(\bar{p}, \bar{p} \cdot \omega_t) + \partial_w \varphi_t(\bar{p}, \bar{p} \cdot \omega_t) \omega_t^T$. On the other hand, $\partial_p \varphi_t(\bar{p}, \bar{p} \cdot \omega_t) = S_t(\bar{p}, \bar{p} \cdot \omega_t) - \partial_w \varphi_t(\bar{p}, \bar{p} \cdot \omega_t) \varphi_t^T(\bar{p}, \bar{p} \cdot \omega_t)$, where $S_t(\bar{p}, \bar{p} \cdot \omega_t)$ is the symmetric, negative definite on $T_{\bar{p}}$ substitution matrix; see 2.7.8. Therefore, $\partial f_t(\bar{p}) = S_t(\bar{p}, \bar{p} \cdot \omega_t) - \partial_w \varphi_t(\bar{p}, \bar{p} \cdot \omega_t) f_t^T(\bar{p})$; that is, $\partial f_t(\bar{p})$ can be expressed as the difference of a negative (semi)definite matrix of rank $\ell - 1$ and a matrix of rank one that vanishes on $L_t = \{v \in T_{\bar{p}} : f_t(\bar{p}) \cdot v = 0\}$, the subspace of $T_{\bar{p}}$ orthogonal to $f_t(\bar{p})$. Therefore, $\partial f_t(\bar{p})$ is symmetric, negative definite on L_t; that is, $\partial f_t(\bar{p})(v, u) = \partial f_t(\bar{p})(u, v)$ for $u, v \in L_t$ and $\partial f_t(\bar{p})(v, v) < 0$ for $v \in L_t$, $v \neq 0$. Because the two properties are preserved under sum, the same will be true for the aggregate $\partial f(\bar{p})$ restricted to $L = \bigcap_{t \in I} L_t$. Thus, we have shown:

5.5.5. Proposition. *For any $p \in S$, $\partial f(p)$ is symmetric and negative definite on the subspace $L_p = \{v \in T_p : f_t(p) \cdot v = 0$ for all $t \in I\}$.*

Suppose that we are in an economy with a finite number of agents, that is $\#I = n$. Let $f(p) = 0$. Then the dimension of the space spanned by $\{f_t(p) : t \in I\}$ is less than or equal to $n-1$. Therefore,

$$\dim L_p \geq (\ell - 1) - (n - 1) = \ell - n$$

[if $f(p) \neq 0$, we can only conclude $\dim L_p \geq \ell - n - 1$], and so if $n < \ell$, then L is nontrivial. Thus, if the number of commodities is greater than the number of agents, the matrix $\partial f(p)$ is subject to some restrictions. Explicitly,

5.5.6. Proposition. *Let $\mathcal{E} : I \to \mathcal{Q}$, $\#I = n$. If $f(p) = 0$, then $\dim L_p \geq \ell - n$. If $f(p) \neq 0$, then $\dim L_p \geq \ell - n - 1$.*

The next proposition implies that 5.5.5 and 5.5.6 exhaust all the restrictions that the general properties of substitution matrices impose on the derivative of excess demand at equilibrium.

5.5.7. Proposition. *Let $f(p) = 0$ and $\partial f(p)$ be symmetric, negative definite on a subspace $L \subset T_p$. Denote $n = \ell - \dim L$. Then there are $x_1, \ldots, x_n \in R^\ell$, $c_1, \ldots, c_n \in R^\ell$ and $\ell \times \ell$ matrices $S_1, \ldots, S_n$ such that:*

(i) $\partial f(p) = \sum_{i=1}^n (S_i - c_i x_i^T)$.
(ii) $\sum_i x_i = 0$, $L = \{v \in T_p : x_1 \cdot v = 0$ for all $i\}$.
(iii) *For all i, S_i is symmetric, negative definite on T_p and $p \cdot S_i = 0$.*
(iv) $p \cdot c_i = 1$ *for all i.*

Proof. The solution is far from unique. One way to proceed is to let B be an arbitrary symmetric matrix that satisfies $p \cdot B = 0$, is negative definite on T_p, and, as a linear map, coincides with $\partial f(p)$ on L, that is, $\partial f(p)z = Bz$ for all $z \in L$ (see B.6). Put then $S_i = (1/n)B$ and take an orthonormal system of vectors $x_1, \ldots, x_{n-1} \in T_p$ orthogonal to L. Put $x_n = -\sum_{i=1}^{n-1} x_i$ and $c_i = [B - \partial f(p)]x_i + p$ for $i \leq n-1$. Because $p \cdot \partial f(p) = -f(p) = 0$, $p \cdot B = 0$ and $\|p\| = 1$, we have $p \cdot c_i = 1$. Put $c_n = p$. It remains to verify (i). Let $A = \sum_{i=1}^n (S_i - c_i x_i^T)$. For $z \in L$ we have $Az = Bz = \partial f(p)z$. So it suffices to check that $Ax_i = \partial f(p)x_i$ for each x_i, $i \leq n-1$. (The vectors $x_1, \ldots, x_{n-1}$ constitute a basis for the orthogonal complement of L in T_p.) But, for $i \leq n-1$,

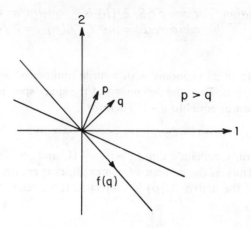

Figure 5.5.2

$$Ax_i = Bx_i - \sum_{j=1}^{n} c_j(x_j \cdot x_i) = Bx_i - c_i - c_n(x_n \cdot x_i)$$

$$= Bx_i - c_i + c_n = Bx_i - [S - \partial f(p)]x_i = \partial f(p)x_i. \qquad \blacksquare$$

We could phrase one of the negative implications of the last propositions as: If $n \geq \ell$, then $\partial f(p)$ is unrestricted. This point can be made in a much stronger form:

> **5.5.8. Proposition.** *Let $f: S \to R^\ell$ be a C^3 vector field satisfying the boundary condition: "$f(S) \geq -ke$ for some k and $p_m \to p \in \partial S$ implies $\|f(p_m)\| \to \infty$." Then for any $\epsilon > 0$ we can find an economy $\mathcal{E}: I \to \mathcal{P}_{b,sc}^2 \times R_+^\ell$ such that $\#I = \ell$, the excess demand function of $\mathcal{E}$ coincides with f on $S_\epsilon = \{p \in S: p > \epsilon e\}$ and p is an equilibrium for $\mathcal{E}$ if and only if $f(p) = 0$ (i.e., no new equilibrium is added). Furthermore, preferences are representable by utility functions homogenous of degree one.*

We shall postpone the proof of this proposition for a little while to gain some insight on why a result along its lines should be true. Let us for a moment identify the notion of a rational agent with that of an excess demand function satisfying a weak form of the so-called strong axiom of revealed preference. Specifically, given a continuous vector field f on S, one defines the relation $>$ on S by $p > q$ if $p \cdot f(q) < 0$; that is to say, p is "revealed preferred" to q if $f(q)$, the "best" commodity vector under q, is below the budget hyperplane under p; see Figure 5.5.2. Then the strong axiom postulates the acyclicity of $>$; that is, if $p_1 > p_2 > \cdots > p_m$, then $p_m > p_1$ cannot occur. Note – and this is the key observation – that by definition, *if $f(p)$ satisfies the strong axiom, then so does $\eta(p)f(p)$, where $\eta(p) > 0$ is any arbitrary function.* Therefore if $f_1, \ldots, f_\ell$ are ℓ continuous vector fields on S that satisfy the strong axiom and have the property that, for all $p \in S$, the strictly positive cone spanned by $\{f_1(p), \ldots, f_\ell(p)\}$ equals T_p, then, given any vector field f, we can always write $f(p)$ in the form $f(p) = \Sigma_{i=1}^{\ell} \eta_i(p) f_i(p)$ with $\eta_i(p) > 0$. So we are done. A family $\{f_1, \ldots, f_\ell\}$ with the desired property is easily found; for example, $f_i(p)$ could be the perpendicular projection of the ith unit vector onto T_p; that is, $f_i(p) = e_i - p^i p$. See Figure 5.5.3a, b for illustrations.

Combined with the next proposition, Proposition 5.5.8 yields as a corollary a sort of converse of the index theorem.

5.5.9. Proposition. *Let $B_1, \ldots, B_m \subset S$ be a family of pairwise disjoint sets that, up to diffeomorphism, are closed balls. Suppose that $S \setminus \bigcup_{i=1}^{m} B_i$ is connected and $f: \bigcup_{i=1}^{m} B_i \to R^\ell$ is a C^2 vector field with the property that if $f(p) = 0$, then rank $\partial f(p) = \ell - 1$. Suppose that $\Sigma_{f(p)=0} (-1)^{\ell-1} \text{sign} |\partial f(p)| = 1$. Then there is a C^2 vector field f' on S such that* (i) $f' | \bigcup_i B_i = f$, (ii) $f'(p) = 0$ *only if* $p \in \bigcup_i B_i$, (iii) $f'(S) \geq ke$ *for some $k \in R$ and $p_n \to p \in \partial S$ implies* $\|f'(p_n)\| \to \infty$.

Proof. This can be handled by standard extension techniques. Let f^* be an arbitrary C^2 excess demand generated by some economy. Let $\bigcup_i B_i \subset S_\epsilon$, $S_\epsilon \setminus \bigcup_i B_i$ be connected and $f^* | \partial S_\epsilon$ be homotopic to the vector field $f_e(p) = (1/p \cdot e)e - p$; see Lemma 5.6.3 in the next section, where an explicit homotopy is exhibited. Then the closure of $S_\epsilon \setminus \bigcup_i B_i$, denoted Λ, is a connected manifold with boundary. We can assume that $f(p) \neq 0$ for $p \in \partial \Lambda$. Let $F: \partial \Lambda \to S^{\ell-2}$ be given by $F(p) = (1/\|f(p)\|)f(p)$ if $p \in \partial B_i$ for some i and $F(p) = (1/\|f^*(p)\|)f^*(p)$ if $p \in \partial S_\epsilon$. See Section J of Chapter 1 for the following concept and arguments. We can identify S_ϵ with its first $\ell - 1$ coordinates and proceed as if S_ϵ had a smooth boundary. Giving $\partial \Lambda$ the induced orientation from Λ, the degree of the map $F: \partial \Lambda \to S^{\ell-2}$ can be easily computed: degree $F = \Sigma_i$ degree$(f | \partial B_i) -$ degree$(f^* | \partial S)$. Because $f^* | S_\epsilon$ is homotopic to $f_e | S_\epsilon$ we get degree$(f^* | \partial S_\epsilon) = (-1)^{\ell-1}$. On the other hand, degree$(f | \partial B_i) = \Sigma_{f(p)=0, p \in B_i} \text{sign} |\partial f(p)|$. Therefore, by hypothesis, degree $F = (-1)^{\ell-1} - (-1)^{\ell-1} = 0$. By Hopf's theorem (J.2.4), $F: \partial \Lambda \to S^{\ell-2}$ can be extended to the whole of Λ. We can then use this extension in the obvious manner to generate an f' such that $f' | \bigcup_i B_i = f$, $f' | S \setminus S_\epsilon = f^*$, and $f'(p) \neq 0$ for $p \notin \bigcup_i B_i$. To complete the construction it may be necessary to smooth out the function f' along $\partial \Lambda$. ∎

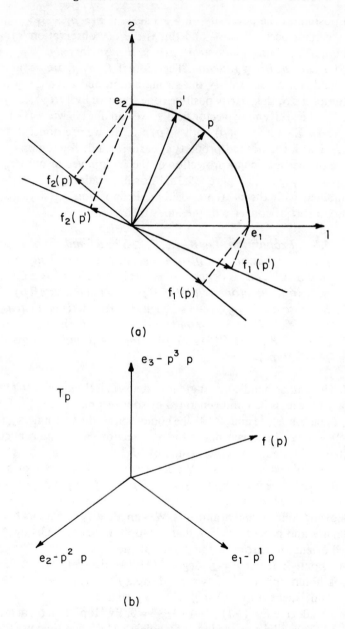

(a)

(b)

Figure 5.5.3

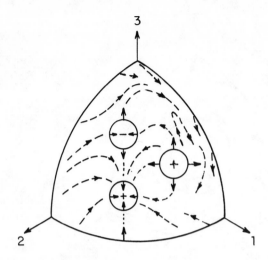

Figure 5.5.4

See Figure 5.5.4 for an illustration of Proposition 5.5.9. Observe also that in the case $\ell = 2$ the hypothesis that the B_i be pairwise disjoint and $S \setminus \bigcup_i B_i$ connected is satisfied only if $m = 1$. This is as it should be. In the one-dimensional case (i.e., $\ell = 2$) the index formula does not exhaust the information on the equilibrium price set. We also know that positive and negative index equilibria must alternate. This is a peculiarity of the real line, and there is nothing of the sort for $\ell > 2$.

Proposition 5.5.8 can also be used to characterize the equilibrium price set in the general, regular or nonregular, case:

> **5.5.10. Proposition.** *Let $K \subset S$ be any nonempty and compact set. Then there is a function $f: S \to R^\ell$ satisfying the hypothesis of 5.5.8 and such that $f(p) = 0$ if and only if $p \in K$.*

Proof. Let $f^*: S \to R^\ell$ be the excess demand of some economy having a unique equilibrium at a $p \in K$. Take a C^∞ function $\alpha: S \to [0, 1]$ such that $K = \alpha^{-1}(0)$ and $\alpha(S \setminus S_\epsilon) = 1$ for $K \subset S_\epsilon$. Such a function exists; see H.4.2. Then let $f(p) = \alpha(p) f^*(p)$. ∎

As a final remark regarding Proposition 5.5.8 we could mention its implications for the problem of actually finding equilibrium prices. Let f be the C^1 excess demand function derived from the economy $\mathcal{E}$. A suggested differential equation system for the computation of equilibrium

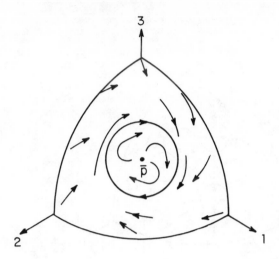

Figure 5.5.5

prices is $\dot{p} = f(p)$. This defines a dynamical system on S (because $\dot{p} \in T_p$), and it is economically natural since it prescribes that the price of a commodity be raised (resp. lowered) if it is in excess demand (resp. supply). Thus, it is a form of the so-called Walrasian tâtonnement. Unfortunately, Proposition 5.5.8 tells us that, except at the boundary, we are dealing with an arbitrary vector field $f(p)$, and a general vector field may exhibit very complicated trajectories. Even if $f(\bar{p}) = 0$ for a unique $\bar{p}$, it is possible for the dynamics $\dot{p} = f(p)$ not to approach $\bar{p}$ from any initial point $p_0 \neq \bar{p}$ (see Figure 5.5.5). In the next section we shall present a differential equation system that converges with probability one to some equilibrium if started at a random point of the boundary. It is of the form $\partial f(p)\dot{p} = \lambda f(p)$. In contrast, $\dot{p} = f(p)$ neglects all the information contained in $\partial f(p)$, and the result is that convergence is not guaranteed.

Suppose that $\#I = n$ and that preferences are endowed with utility functions with respect to which the excess utility function $h: S_+^{n-1} \to R^n$ is well defined (see the last two paragraphs of Section 5.2). As we know, there is a one-to-one correspondence between equilibrium price vectors and equilibrium utility weights. From Proposition 5.3.7 we also know that we can approach the computation of the index using either function. For the excess utility function there is also an analog of Propositions 5.5.5 and 5.5.6. This is the last time we detour to emphasize the parallelism between the excess demand and the excess utility approach.

5.5.11. Proposition. *Let $h(\bar{\lambda}) = 0$. Then $\partial h(\bar{\lambda})$ is symmetric and positive definite on $L = \{y \in T_{\bar{\lambda}} : \partial p(\bar{\lambda})y = 0\}$, the subspace on which prices remain (first-order) constant. We have* $\dim L \geq n - \ell - 1$.

Proof. Let $\bar{\lambda}, \bar{p}, \bar{x}$ be an equilibrium. With $\bar{p}$ fixed let $v_i(w_i)$ be the indirect utility functions with respect to wealth; that is, $v_i(w_i)$ is the maximum value of u_i on $b(\bar{p}, w_i)$. The function v_i is concave; it has nonvanishing first and second derivatives and $\partial v_i(\bar{p} \cdot \bar{x}_i) = 1/\bar{\lambda}_i$; see 4.2.22. Therefore, $\partial v_i(w_i)$ can be inverted to get a decreasing function $w_i(\mu_i)$ satisfying $\partial v_i(w_i(\mu_i)) = \mu_i$ near $1/\bar{\lambda}_i$. Define now

$$H(\lambda) = \left(\frac{1}{\lambda_1}\left(w_1\left(\frac{1}{\lambda_1}\right) - \bar{p} \cdot \omega_1\right), \ldots, \frac{1}{\lambda_n}\left(w_n\left(\frac{1}{\lambda_n}\right) - \bar{p} \cdot \omega_n\right)\right).$$

Observe that $\partial H(\bar{\lambda})$ is a positive diagonal matrix. Hence it is symmetric and positive definite. To conclude the proof note that $H(\lambda) = h(\lambda)$ whenever $p(\lambda) = \bar{p}$. Hence, if $y \in L$, then $\partial h(\bar{\lambda})y = \partial H(\bar{\lambda})y$. Of course, $\dim L \geq n - \ell - 1$ follows from rank $\partial p(\lambda) \leq \ell$; see B.2.1. ∎

It is now time we prove Proposition 5.5.8.

Proof of Proposition 5.5.8. The basic technical tool for this proof is the indirect utility function. We shall proceed in three steps. In the first we present the needed facts on indirect utility functions and reduce the problem to one of finding appropriate indirect utilities. In the second we exhibit ℓ pairs of endowment vectors and preferences satisfying the prescribed properties (except strict monotonicity) and such that the aggregate excess demand function is zero everywhere. In the third we show that by choosing the endowment vectors to be very large it is possible to perturb these preferences so that they become strictly monotone and the economy generates the given excess demand function.

Step 1. In our discussion of the indirect utility function (see 2.7) we always take wealth to equal one. With this convention indirect utility becomes a function $v(p)$ defined on R_{++}^{ℓ}. Remember that if v is a C^1 indirect utility function, then $x(p, 1) = [1/p \cdot \partial v(p)]\partial v(p)$, where $x(p)$ is the demand vector; see 2.7.9. Suppose that v has the property: $v(\lambda p) = v(p) - \ln \lambda$ for all $\lambda > 0$; that is, v is logarithmically homogenous. Then, differentiating $v(\lambda p)$ with respect to λ and evaluating at $\lambda = 1$ we get $p \cdot \partial v(p) = -1$. Hence, $x(p, 1) = -\partial v(p)$. Also, $\partial v(\lambda p) = (1/\lambda)\partial v(p)$ and, therefore, $x(p, w) = x((1/w)p, 1) = -\partial v((1/w)p) = -w\partial v(p)$.

Now let $v: R_{++}^{\ell} \to R$ be an arbitrary function having the properties:

(i) v is C^3 on R_{++}^ℓ.

(ii) At every p, $\partial v(p) \ll 0$ and $\partial^2 v(p)$ is positive definite.

(iii) v is proper; that is, if $p_n \to p$ and $p^j = 0$ for some j, then $v(p_n) \to \infty$, and if $\|p_n\| \to \infty$ and $v(p_n)$ is bounded above, then $v(p_n) \to -\infty$.

We claim that v is the indirect utility function for an admissible C^2 utility function u. This follows from a simple duality argument. We can formally associate with $-v$ an "indirect utility function" $-u: R_{++}^\ell \to R$ by letting $-u(x) = -v(p(x))$ and $p(x)$ maximize $-v$ on the "budget set" $\{p \in R_{++}^\ell : p \cdot x \le 1\}$. By 2.7.2 the "demand function" $p(x)$ is C^2 and so it is $-u$, which also has no critical point. By 2.7.9 $p(x) = [1/x \cdot \partial u(x)] \partial u(x)$ and $\{z : -u(z) \le -u(x)\}$ is convex. Therefore, $p(\bar{x})$ collinear with $\partial u(\bar{x})$ and $p(\bar{x}) \cdot \bar{x} = 1$ implies that any $\bar{x}$ maximizes $u(x)$ on $b(p(\bar{x}), 1)$. By the boundary condition (iii), given $\bar{p}$ we have $\bar{p} = p(\bar{x})$ for some $\bar{x}$. So the indirect utility of $\bar{p}$ derived from u is $v'(\bar{p}) = u(\bar{x}) = v(p(\bar{x})) = v(\bar{p})$. Summing up: The indirect utility function of u is v. Therefore, the demand $x(p, 1)$, which can be obtained from v in the usual way, is a C^2 function defined for all p. The differentiability of demand implies that the C^2 preference relation $\succsim_u$ has every point regular (see 2.7.2). The boundary condition 2.3.16 follows from (iii). Indeed, let $x_n \to x$, $x^j = 0$ for some j. Then, by strict monotonicity of $-v$, $\|p(x_n)\| \to \infty$ and $-v(p(x_n))$ is bounded below. Hence $u(x_n) = v(p(x_n)) \to -\infty$.

Step 2. Agent i has the initial endowment vector $\omega_i = ke_i$, where e_i is the ith unit vector and k a common scale factor to be determined later. For the sake of clarity, in the proof we are violating the condition $\omega_i \gg 0$. This can be easily fixed.

We wish to find logarithmically homogenous, C^∞ indirect utility functions $v_1, \ldots, v_\ell : R_{++}^\ell \to R$ such that (i) $\partial v_i(p) \ll 0$ and $\partial^2 v_i(p)$ is positive definite for all i and p, and (ii) the excess demand function of the economy $\{(v_i, ke_i)\}_{i=1}^\ell$ equals zero at all $p \in R_{++}^\ell$; that is, $\sum_{i=1}^\ell x_i(p, kp \cdot e_i) = ke$. Because $x_i(p, w) = -w \partial v_i(p)$ and $p \cdot e_i = p^i$ we can write this as $-\sum_{i=1}^\ell p^i \partial v_i(p) = e$ or, more compactly, $-\partial V(p)p = e$ for all p, where $V(p) = (v_1(p), \ldots, v_\ell(p))^T$. Take $v_i(p) = -\ln p_i$. Then

$$\partial v_i(p) = (0, \ldots, -1/p_i, \ldots, 0)$$

and, therefore, $-\partial V(p)p = e$. Our problem would be solved except that we only have $\partial v_i(p) < 0$ and $\partial^2 v_i(p)$ positive semidefinite. This can be fixed by "mixing" the functions v_i. Let A be an arbitrary nonsingular matrix with strictly positive entries, row and column sums equal to one, and generic entry a_{ji}. Then $-A^T \partial V(Ap)Ap = A^T e = e$ and, of course, $\partial_p V(Ap) = \partial V(Ap)A$. This suggests that we define $\hat{v}_i(p) = \sum_{j=1}^\ell a_{ji} v_j(Ap)$;

that is, $\hat{V}(p) = A^T V(Ap)$. In this case $\hat{v}_i$ is logarithmically homogenous (because $\sum_{j=1}^{\ell} a_{ji} = 1$), $-\partial \hat{V}(p)p = -A^T \partial V(Ap)Ap = e$, and $\partial \hat{v}_i(p) = \sum_{j=1}^{\ell} a_{ji} \partial v_j(Ap)A \ll 0$. Moreover,

$$\partial^2 \hat{v}_i(p) = \sum_{j=1}^{\ell} a_{ji} A^T \partial^2 v_j(Ap)A$$

is positive definite because $\partial_{jj}^2 v_j(Ap) > 0$ for all j and if we take $z \neq 0$, then $y = Az \neq 0$ and

$$\partial^2 \hat{v}_i(p)(z,z) = \sum_{j=1}^{\ell} a_{ji} \partial^2 v_j(Ap)(y,y) = \sum_{j=1}^{\ell} a_{ji} \partial_{jj}^2 v_j(Ap)y_j^2 > 0.$$

Thus except for the properness condition, the functions $\hat{v}_i$, $i = 1, \ldots, \ell$, are as prescribed.

Step 3. Let f and $\epsilon > 0$ be as in the statement of the proposition. We can assume that $\{p : f(p) = 0\} \subset S_\epsilon$. We first modify f near the boundary to get a new C^2 vector field which satisfies:

 (i) $\hat{f} \mid S_\epsilon = f \mid S_\epsilon$.
 (ii) For some $\mu < \epsilon$, $e \cdot \hat{f}(p) \geq 0$ if $p \in S \setminus S_\mu$ and $\hat{f}(p) = 0$ if $p \in S \setminus S_{\mu/2}$.
 (iii) If $\hat{f}(p) = 0$ and $p \in S_\mu$, then $p \in S_\epsilon$.

To construct $\hat{f}$ let $\alpha, \eta : S \to [0,1]$ be C^3 functions such that $\alpha(S_{2\mu}) = 0$, $\alpha(S \setminus S_\mu) = 1$, $\eta(S_\mu) = 1$, $\eta(S \setminus S_{\mu/2}) = 0$ (see H.4.2) and put

$$\hat{f}(p) = \eta(p)[\alpha(p)f_e(p) + (1 - \alpha(p))f(p)], \quad \text{where } f_e(p) = (1/p \cdot e)e - p.$$

Note that $e \cdot f_e(p) > 0$ whenever $p \neq (1/\|e\|)e$. Properties (i) and (ii) are obviously satisfied for $2\mu < \epsilon$. Property (iii) is also clear for μ small. At any rate, we refer to Lemma 5.6.3 in the next section to verify this. Putting $\hat{f}(p) = \hat{f}((1/\|p\|)p)$, we view $\hat{f}$ as defined on R_{++}^ℓ.

The function $\hat{f}$ is now ready to be introduced as a perturbation into the economy $\{(\hat{v}_i, ke_i)\}_{i=1}^{\ell}$ obtained at the end of step 2. Mathematically, what makes this possible is the great flexibility allowed by logarithmically homogeneous indirect utility functions. Indeed, the convex combination of two such functions, or the sum with a zero homogeneous function, is logarithmically homogenous, and the resulting demand functions are obtained linearly from the original ones.

We need a last preparatory step. Let $u : R_{++}^\ell \to R$ be a C^∞, convex, logarithmically homogeneous function such that:

 (i) $\partial u(p) \ll 0$ for all $p \in R_{++}^\ell$.
 (ii) u is proper.
 (iii) $u(p) = -\ln(p \cdot e)$ if and only if $(1/\|p\|)p \in S_\mu$.
 (iv) $\partial^2 u(p)$ is positive definite at any $(1/\|p\|)p \in S \setminus S_\mu$.

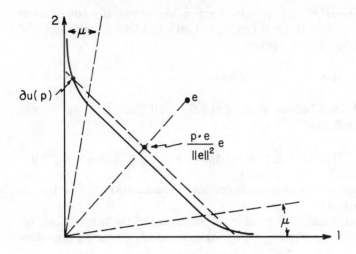

Figure 5.5.6

Such a function does clearly exist. Figure 5.5.6 represents one indifference manifold. The rest can be obtained by radial expansion. Note that if $(1/\|p\|)p \in S \backslash S_\mu$, then

$$\partial u(p) \cdot \left(\frac{p \cdot e}{\|e\|^2} e - p \right) < 0.$$

Consider $u_i(p) = \frac{1}{2} \hat{v}_i(p) + \frac{1}{2} u(p) + (1/k) \hat{f}^i(p)$. The function u_i is C^2 and logarithmically homogenous [remember that $\hat{f}^i(\lambda p) = \hat{f}^i(p)$]. Because $\hat{f}^i(S \backslash S_{\mu/2}) = 0$ and $\hat{f}$ is C^2 there is a sufficiently large k such that $\partial u_i(p) \ll 0$ and $\partial^2 u_i(p)$ remains positive definite for all p. Also, the boundary condition "u_i is proper" is satisfied on account of the term $\frac{1}{2} u(p)$. By step 1 we know that u_i is an indirect utility function for a direct utility that satisfies all of our requirements. Now take the economy $\{(u_i, ke_i)\}_{i=1}^{\ell}$. Its excess demand function is

$$f'(p) = \sum_{i=1}^{\ell} x_i(p, kp^i) - ke$$

$$= \sum_{i=1}^{\ell} kp_i \, \partial u_i(p) - ke$$

$$= -\frac{k}{2} \sum_{i=1}^{\ell} p^i \partial \hat{v}_i(p) - \frac{k}{2}(p \cdot e) \, \partial u(p) - \sum_{i=1}^{\ell} p^i \partial \hat{f}^i(p) - ke$$

$$= -\frac{k}{2} e - \frac{k}{2}(p \cdot e) \, \partial u(p) + \hat{f}(p)$$

where we have used the results of step 2 and the equality $p \cdot \partial \hat{f}(p) = -\hat{f}(p)$
obtained by differentiating $p \cdot \hat{f}(p) = 0$. If $p \in S_\mu$, then $\partial u(p) = -(1/p \cdot e)e$
and, therefore, $f'(p) = f(p)$. If $p \notin S_\mu$ then, letting $z = (p \cdot e/\|e\|^2)e - p$,
we have $z \cdot e = 0$, $-z \cdot \partial u(p) > 0$, and $z \cdot \hat{f}(p) = (p \cdot e/\|e\|^2)e \cdot f(p) \geq 0$.
Therefore, $z \cdot f'(p) > 0$, which implies $f'(p) \neq 0$.

Finally note that if u_i is logarithmically homogenous, then the increasing transformation e^{u_i} is homogeneous of degree zero. ∎

5.6   Proof and discussion of the index theorem

The first thing to point out is that the index theorem is a general mathematical property of a certain class of functions defined by a number of formal conditions. It is because excess demand functions belong to the class that the index theorem holds for them and, therefore, for economies. The next proposition, which is self-contained, restates the index theorem in this general framework:

5.6.1. Proposition. *Let $f : S \to R^\ell$, $S = \{p \in R^\ell_{++} : \|p\| = 1\}$, be a continuous function such that:*

(i)   *f is a vector field on S; that is, $p \cdot f(p) = 0$, or $f(p) \in T_p$, for all $p \in S$.*

(ii)   *f is bounded below; that is, $f(S) \geq ke$ for some $k \in R$.*

(iii)   *If $p_n \in S$ and $p_n \to p \in \partial S$, then $\|f(p_n)\| \to \infty$.*

(iv)   *If $f(p) = 0$, then f is C^1 at p.*

(v)   *If $f(p) = 0$, the linear map $\partial f(p)$ takes T_p onto T_p.*

Then the set $E = \{p \in S : f(p) = 0\}$ is finite and

$$\sum_{p \in E} \text{sign} \,|-\partial f(p)| = 1.$$

We shall pursue two lines of proof for 5.6.1. The first shows that conditions (i)–(v) allow the almost direct application of general index theorems for vector fields. The second stays closer to first principles and elaborates on more constructive approaches. The two directions are not independent. In a sense, what the latter does is to demonstrate the mathematical index theorem used in the first approach.

Suppose that $f : S \to R^\ell$ is a function satisfying conditions (i), (ii), and (iii) of Proposition 5.6.1. Condition (i) says that we are dealing with a tangent vector field on the strictly positive portion of the sphere. Conditions (ii) and (iii) combined give information on the direction of the vector $f(p)$ near ∂S, the boundary of S. Imprecisely speaking, they assert that if p is near ∂S, then $f(p)$ is almost inward-pointing. Precisely,

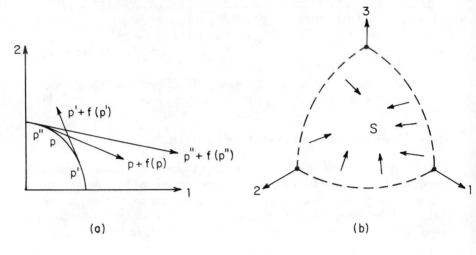

Figure 5.6.1

5.6.2. Lemma. *If $p_n \to p \in \partial S$ and $[1/\|f(p_n)\|]f(p_n) \to z$, then $z > 0$ and $p \cdot z = 0$.*

Proof. For each j the sequence $f^j(p_n)$ is uniformly bounded below [condition (ii)]. Because $\|f(p_n)\| \to \infty$ [condition (iii)], the limit of $f^j(p_n)/\|f(p_n)\|$ must be nonnegative. Hence $z > 0$. If $p^j > 0$, then $f^j(p_n) = (1/p_n^j)[-\sum_{j' \neq j} p^{j'} f^{j'}(p_n)]$ is also uniformly bounded above [again by (ii)] and so z^j must be nonpositive. Hence $p \cdot z = 0$. ∎

Figure 5.6.1a and b illustrate the boundary behavior of the excess demand vector field for the cases $\ell = 2, 3$. Figure 5.6.2 shows that condition (iii) alone does not yield the conclusion of the lemma.

In one respect the conclusion of the lemma is stronger than we shall need. Indeed, it guarantees that $z^j \geq 0$ even for j with $p^j > 0$. However, in another important respect it is slightly weak. We would like to conclude from the lemma that for ϵ sufficiently small, f points inward at the boundary of $S_\epsilon = \{p \in S : p^j > \epsilon, \text{ all } j\}$. This we cannot do because it is not guaranteed that $z^j > 0$ whenever $p^j = 0$. Of course, because $\|z\| = 1$, we must have $z^j > 0$ for some j with $p^j = 0$ but not necessarily for all such j. Thus the situation for $\ell = 2$ is somewhat misleading. See Figure 5.6.3 and keep in mind that if $f^j(p_n) \leq 0$ for all n, then $z^j = 0$. This is why we needed the qualification "almost" in the informal statement before the lemma. Nevertheless, for our purposes it will be enough that, for ϵ small,

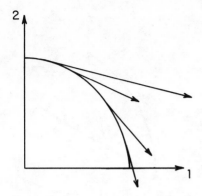

Figure 5.6.2

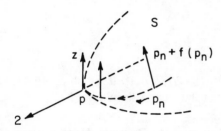

Figure 5.6.3

$f \mid \partial S_\epsilon$ be homotopic to an inward-pointing vector field. For this the conclusion of Lemma 5.6.2 will be quite sufficient.

For any fixed vector $q \gg 0$, define the vector field $f_q : \bar{S} \to R^\ell$ by $f_q(p) =$
$(1/p \cdot q)q - p$; $\bar{S}$ is the closure of S. See Figures 5.6.4a and b. It satisfies
conditions (i), (ii), (iv), and (v) of the statement of Proposition 5.5.6. It
also points inward at the boundary of $\bar{S}$ and, by continuity, at the boundary of S_ϵ for ϵ small. The class f_q of vector fields will play an important
technical role in the proofs of the index theorem.

> **5.6.3. Lemma.** *For ϵ small, f and f_q are homotopic on ∂S. Spe-
> cifically, for ϵ small, $p \in \partial S_\epsilon$ and $0 \leq \alpha \leq 1$, we have*
>
> $$\alpha f(p) + (1 - \alpha) f_q(p) \neq 0.$$

Proof. If $p_n \to p \in \partial \bar{S}$, $p_n \in S$, then for n sufficiently large we have $f_q^j(p_n) >$
0 for all j with $p^j = 0$ and, by Lemma 5.6.2, $f^j(p_n) > 0$ for some j with

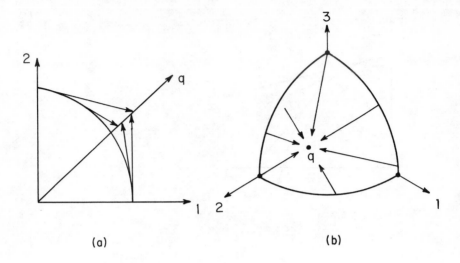

Figure 5.6.4

$p^j = 0$. Therefore, $\alpha f^j(p_n) + (1-\alpha)f_q^j(p_n) > 0$ for all $\alpha \in [0,1]$. Hence, if ϵ is small, the conclusion of the lemma should hold. ∎

We are now in a position to apply the Poincaré–Hopf theorem (J.3.2). Suppose that f also satisfies conditions (iv) and (v) of Proposition 5.6.1. Pick ϵ sufficiently small for $E \subset S_\epsilon$ and the conclusion of Lemma 5.6.3 to hold. Note that if, up to homotopy, f points inward at ∂S_ϵ, $-f$ points outward. Therefore the vector field $-f: S_\epsilon \to R^\ell$ satisfies the hypothesis of the Poincaré–Hopf theorem (J.3.2). Hence, $\sum_{p \in E} \operatorname{sign}|-\partial f(p)| = \chi(S_\epsilon)$. Because the set S_ϵ is homeomorphic to a ball, its Euler characteristic $\chi(S_\epsilon)$ is 1 (see J.1.i), and we have our proof.

It is worth remembering that $f(p)$ being a vector field on the sphere is not an essential characteristic of the previous arguments. There is no difficulty in carrying out the same proof with any of the normalizations discussed in Section 5.2. What is crucial is that the domain of the function be (up to homeomorphism) convex.

In order to gain a more intuitive understanding of the proposition we shall now develop a line of proof that, in essence, amounts to a demonstration of the Poincaré–Hopf theorem. Because a rigorous proof has already been given, we shall allow ourselves a certain informality in what follows.

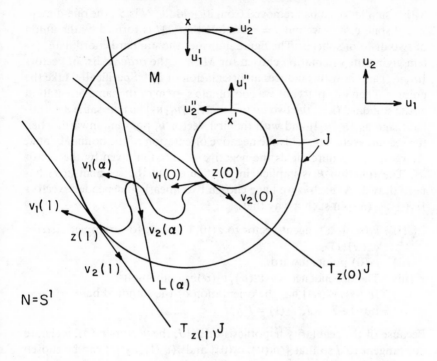

Figure 5.6.5

First, a mathematical preliminary. To fully understand the next lemma, a restatement of J.2.2, it is convenient to gain some familiarity with the notion of orientation. See H.1 for this. A glance at Figure 5.6.5 will also help.

> **5.6.4. Lemma.** *Let M, N be oriented, connected C^1 manifolds with $\dim M = \dim N + 1$. The manifold M has a boundary ∂M with the orientation induced by M. There is also given a manifold $J \subset \partial M$ of the same dimension as N. Suppose that $F: M \to N$ is a smooth function and $y \in N$ is a regular value of F and $F \mid J$ [i.e., if $F(z) = y$, then $\partial F(z): T_z M \to T_y N$ is onto; also, if $F(z) = y$ and $z \in J$, then $\partial F(z): T_z J \to T_y N$ is onto]. Suppose that $z: [0, 1] \to M$ is a C^1 path such that $z(0), z(1) \in J$ and $F(z(\alpha)) = y$ for all $\alpha \in [0, 1]$. Then the determinants of $\partial F(z(0)): T_{z(0)} J \to T_y N$ and $\partial F(z(1)): T_{z(1)} J \to T_y N$ have opposite signs.*

Proof. The lemma will be explained and informally proved with reference to the example in Figure 5.6.5, where M is a two-dimensional ball with a smaller open ball removed from its middle, N is S^1, the one-dimensional sphere, and we put $J = \partial M$. Note that ∂M is formed by the union of two disjoint spheres. The figure indicates the standard coordinate system giving the orientation chosen for M (i.e., the *ordered* list of vectors $\{u_1, u_2\}$) and how this induces an orientation of ∂M. Specifically, take the point x. Then one places at x a coordinate system of the same orientation as the standard (i.e., the two by two matrix $[u'_1, u'_2]$ has the same determinant sign as $[u_1, u_2]$) and with the first vector u'_1 pointing inward. Then the second vector u'_2 yields the negative orientation of the boundary at x. At x' this procedure yields the negative orientation given by the vector u''_2. The function F is implicit in the figure, but the segment $z(\alpha)$ has been drawn. At each α we have chosen two linearly independent vectors $\{v_1(\alpha), v_2(\alpha)\}$ in such a way that:

(i) $v_1(\alpha)$ is a tangent vector to $z([0,1])$ at α; for example, $v_1(\alpha) = \partial z(\alpha)(1)$.

(ii) $v_1(0)$ points inward.

(iii) The dependence $\alpha \mapsto v_1(\alpha), v_2(\alpha)$ is continuous.

(iv) $\{v_1(\alpha), v_2(\alpha)\}$ has the orientation of the standard base.

(v) $v_2(0) \in T_{z(0)} J$, $v_2(1) = T_{z(1)} J$.

Because of the regularity hypothesis on $F \,|\, J$, the vectors $v_1(0), v_1(1)$ are not tangent to J so that $\{(v_1(0), v_2(0)\}$ and $\{(v_1(1), v_2(1)\}$ can be chosen linearly independent. Now let $L(\alpha)$ be the one-dimensional linear space spanned by $v_2(\alpha)$ and denote by $t(\alpha)$ the determinant of the linear map $\partial F(z(\alpha)): L_\alpha \to T_y S^1$ when $v_2(\alpha)$ is chosen to be the basic vector of L_α. We have that, for all α, $\partial F(z(\alpha))(v_1(\alpha)) = 0$. However, the regularity hypothesis on F implies rank $\partial F(z(\alpha)) = 1$ and so $\partial F(z(\alpha))(v_2(\alpha)) \neq 0$ for all α. Therefore, the continuous map $\alpha \mapsto t(\alpha)$ does not take the value 0. Henceforth, sign $t(0) = $ sign $t(1)$. Observe now that $L_0 = T_{z(0)} J$, $L_1 = T_{z(1)} J$ and that whereas $v_2(1)$ has the "correct" orientation (i.e., the same as the one induced on ∂M by the standard bases of M), $v_2(0)$ has the "wrong" one. This is because if $v_1(\alpha)$ points inward at $\alpha = 0$, then it has to point outward at $\alpha = 1$. Consequently,

$$\text{sign det}(\partial F(z(0)): T_{z(0)} J \to T_y S^1) = -\text{sign } t(0)$$

and

$$\text{sign det}(\partial F(z(1)): T_{z(1)} J \to T_y S^1) = \text{sign } t(1)$$

and we have proved the lemma.   ∎

From now on condition (iv) of Proposition 5.6.1 is strengthened to "f is C^2 on S." This is merely a matter of convenience. Also, it is always

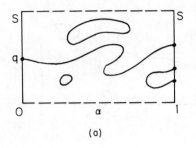 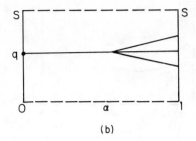

(a)   (b)

Figure 5.6.6

possible to smooth out the function f leaving $\partial f(p)$ unaltered at every $p \in E$.

Given a $q \in S$ we let $f_q: S \to R^\ell$ be the vector field defined in the steps leading to Lemma 5.6.3; that is, $f_q(p) = (1/p \cdot q)q - p$. We shall now consider more explicitly the homotopy $F: S \times [0,1] \to R^\ell$ given by $F(p, \alpha) = \alpha f(p) + (1-\alpha)f_q(p)$. We shall assume that 0 is a regular value of F; that is, rank $\partial F(p, \alpha) = \ell - 1$ whenever $F(p, \alpha) = 0$. We call F a regular homotopy. This is not a restrictive requirement. Indeed, if we regard q as an argument of F, we have that rank $\partial_q F(p, \alpha, q) = \ell - 1$ whenever $\alpha < 1$. Also, $F(p, 1, q) = f(p)$ and by hypothesis f is regular. Therefore, 0 is a regular value of $F: S \times [0,1] \times S \to R^\ell$ and by the transversality theorem (I.2.2) we know there is some q for which 0 is a regular value of $F(\cdot, \cdot, q)$. Transversality arguments will be discussed in more detail in Section 5.8 and in Chapter 8.

Because 0 is a regular value of F, f_q, and f, the set $F^{-1}(0)$ is, by the implicit function theorem (H.2.2), a C^1 one-dimensional manifold with boundary. By Lemma 5.6.3, $F^{-1}(0)$ is compact. Therefore, by the classification theorem for one-dimensional compact smooth manifolds (H.1.vi) the set $F^{-1}(0)$ is, up to diffeomorphism, a finite union of circles and segments. Thus Figure 5.6.6a is permissible whereas 5.6.6b is not. We shall be especially interested in the segments. Denote them by $I_1, \ldots, I_k$. By the IFT (H.2.2), the endpoints of the segments belong to $S \times \{0, 1\}$. Conversely, because f_q and f are regular, we have that $(q, 0)$ and $\{(p, 1): f(p) = 0\}$ are endpoints of segments. Thus, situations such as Figure 5.6.7a and b are ruled out. We are now in a position to apply Lemma 5.6.4. The manifold $S \times [0, 1]$ stands for M and $J = S \times \{0, 1\}$. The key observation is that when $S \times \{0\}$ and $S \times \{1\}$ are oriented as pieces of the boundary of $S \times [0, 1]$ they receive different orientations (see Figure 5.6.8). We can without loss of generality assume that the orientation inherited in

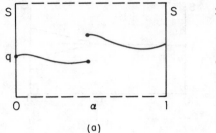
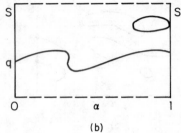

(a)   (b)

Figure 5.6.7

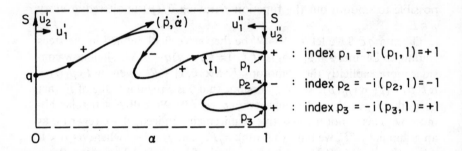

Figure 5.6.8

$S \times \{1\}$ is the standard one in S. If $(p, t) \in S \times \{0, 1\}$ is the endpoint of some segment I_j, $1 \leq j \leq k$, [equivalently, if $(p, t) \in F^{-1}(0) \cap (S \times \{0, 1\})$], we let $i(p, t)$ be the sign of the determinant of $-\partial_p F(p, t): T_p \to T_p$ when the range T_p has the standard orientation and the domain T_p has the orientation corresponding to the piece of the boundary to which (p, t) belongs, that is, the standard one if and only if $t = 1$. Note that if $f(p) = 0$, then index $p = i(p, 1)$. Also, direct computation yields $i(q, 0) = -1$. By Lemma 5.6.4, if (p, t), (p', t') are distinct endpoints of the same segment I_i, then $i(p, t) + i(p', t') = 0$. See Figure 5.6.8. Therefore,

$$\sum_{(p, t) \in F^{-1}(0) \cap (S \times \{0, 1\})} i(p, t) = 0.$$

By construction, f_q has the unique equilibrium q. Hence

$$F^{-1}(0) \cap (S \times \{0\}) = (q, 0).$$

Summing up: $\sum_{f(p)=0} \text{index } p = \sum_{f(p)=0} i(p, 1) = -i(1, 0) = +1$, which is the index formula.

The preceding proof suggests readily a computational procedure for obtaining a $p \in S$ with $f(p) = 0$. Indeed, among the different segments in $F^{-1}(0)$, consider the one, say I_1, having $(q, 0)$ as an endpoint. Because q is the only zero of f_q the other endpoint of I_1 has to be in $S \times \{1\}$; say it is $(p_1, 1)$. Then $f(p_1) = 0$. Therefore, if beginning at $(q, 0)$ we follow I_1 we shall necessarily end up at $(p_1, 1)$. Note that although the resulting deformation from f_q to f will be continuous, it may not be monotone. In order to follow I_1 we may have to backtrack occasionally in the α axis; see Figure 5.6.8.

How do we follow the segment I_1 in practice? This is not the place for even a cursory exposition of algorithmic and numerical analysis methods. Let us simply note that differential equations are a possibility. Suppose that $(p(t), \alpha(t))$ is a solution to the implicit system of differential equations:

(i) $\pi_p \cdot \partial_p F(p, \alpha) \dot{p} = \dot{\alpha} (f_q(p) - f(p))$

(ii) $p \cdot \dot{p} = 0$

(iii) $\|\dot{p}\|^2 + |\dot{\alpha}|^2 = 1$

(iv) $\operatorname{sign} \dot{\alpha} = \operatorname{sign} \det(-\pi_p \cdot \partial_p F(p, \alpha))$

with initial conditions $p(0) = q$, $\alpha(0) = 0$. Here π_p is the orthogonal projection of R^ℓ onto T_p. Then, noting that for $\epsilon > 0$ small, $\|F(p, \alpha)\| < \epsilon$ implies rank $\pi_p \cdot \partial_p F(p, \alpha) = $ rank $\partial_p \partial F(p, \alpha)$, a simple integration yields $F(p(t), \alpha(t)) = 0$ for all t and so $(p(t), \alpha(t)) \in I_1$. In fact, $(p(t), \alpha(t))$ follows I_1 at unit speed [condition (iii)]. Condition (iv) guarantees that we start $\alpha = 0$ in the right direction. There is obviously a unique way to follow I_1 at unit speed, starting at $(q, 0)$ (see Figure 5.6.8), and, therefore, we can conclude that the system of differential equations with initial conditions $p(0) = q$, $\alpha(0) = 0$ has a solution and that the solution is unique and reaches $(p, 1)$ in finite time (note that I_1 has finite length). In a sense this is a remarkable conclusion because, while the system (i)–(iv) is entirely classical at points of the trajectory where rank $\partial_p F(p, \alpha) = \ell - 1$, points where rank $\partial_p F(p, \alpha) = \ell - 2$ cannot be ruled out, and at these (i)–(iv) admits two $(\dot{p}, \dot{\alpha})$ solutions of the form $(v, 0)$, $(-v, 0)$. Nevertheless, the continuity of the trajectory forces a consistent choice of one of the two.

In the procedure above there is no obligation to take $F(\cdot, 0) = f_q$. The only important thing is that the homotopy be constructed from a well-understood f_0 having a unique equilibrium. This allows great flexibility in the f_0 to be chosen. In particular, a priori knowledge of the approximate location of a solution $f(p) = 0$ can be used in choosing f_0, say by taking $f_0 = f_p$, where p is in the likely region. However, there is a severe limitation to the possibilities of computation by this or similar methods. The price vector p obtained as the endpoint $(p, 1)$ of the seg-

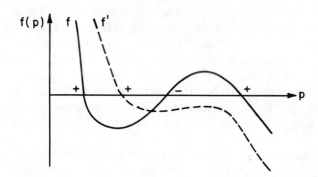

Figure 5.6.9

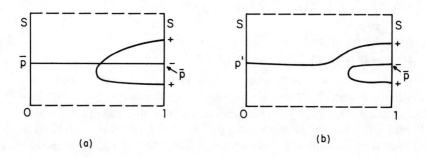

(a)   (b)

Figure 5.6.10

ment that begins at $(q, 0)$ has to have the same index as q in f_q, that is to say, index $p = +1$. The equilibria p with index $p = -1$ are inaccessible. This is no peculiarity of this computation method but a deep fact. In a sense which we shall not make precise, solutions with negative index are removable by homotopy and, therefore, not topological invariants; see Figure 5.6.9. As a further illustration, suppose that $f(\bar{p}) = 0$, index $\bar{p} = -1$. If we take the homotopy

$$F(p, \alpha) = \alpha f(p) + (1 - \alpha) f_{\bar{p}}(p),$$

then $F(\bar{p}, \alpha) = 0$ for all α. So the straight line connecting $(\bar{p}, 0)$ to $(\bar{p}, 1)$ belongs to $F^{-1}(0)$; see Figure 5.6.10a. Therefore, rank $\partial F(\bar{p}, \alpha) =$ rank $\partial_p F(\bar{p}, \alpha)$, and this implies that rank $\partial F(\bar{p}, \bar{\alpha}) < \ell - 1$ for some $\bar{\alpha}$ because sign$|\partial_p F(\bar{p}, 0)| \neq$ sign$|\partial_p F(\bar{p}, 1)|$. Hence, F is not a regular homotopy, and in fact $F^{-1}(0)$ is not a manifold (see Figure 5.6.10a). A small

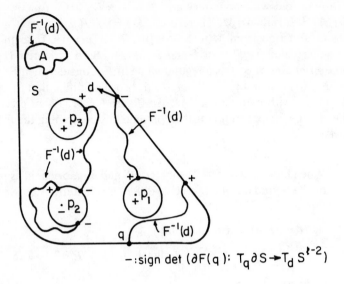

$$-: \text{sign det } (\partial F(q): T_q \partial S \rightarrow T_d S^{\ell-2})$$

Figure 5.6.11

perturbation from $f_{\bar{p}}$ to $f_{p'}$, p' near $\bar{p}$, will make F regular, but then the segment starting at $(p', 0)$ will not end at $(\bar{p}, 1)$; see Figure 5.6.10b.

We have seen that index $p = +1$ is a necessary condition for accessibility of a solution $f(\bar{p}) = 0$. It is not difficult to verify that it is also sufficient in the following formal sense: There is a vector field $f_0: S \rightarrow R^\ell$ such that

(i) $f_0(p) = 0$ has a unique solution $\bar{p}$ (we can take $\bar{\bar{p}} = \bar{p}$) and f_0 points inward near the boundary of S;

(ii) the homotopy $F(p, \alpha) = \alpha f(p) + (1 - \alpha) f_0(p)$ is regular, and the segment in $F^{-1}(0)$ that begins at $(\bar{p}, 0)$ ends at $(\bar{p}, 1)$.

If so desired, the use of a homotopy can be dispensed with in order to prove Proposition 5.6.1 via Lemma 5.6.4. We shall quickly describe how. For the next arguments it shall be convenient to identify S with its first $\ell - 1$ coordinates and accordingly for vector fields on S. We shall also proceed as if S were closed and had a smooth boundary (e.g., S is replaced by the closure of S_ϵ, ϵ small, and the corners of ∂S_ϵ are smoothed out).

For each $p \in E$ remove from S a small open ball B_p centered at p. We can make sure that the closures of the B_p are nonintersecting subsets of S; see Figure 5.6.11. Then $M = S \setminus \bigcup_{p \in E} B_p$ is an $(\ell - 1)$-dimensional smooth manifold with boundary and $f: M \to R^{\ell-1}$, a C^2 function such that $f(p) \neq 0$ for all $p \in M$. Therefore, $F(x) = [1/\|f(p)\|]f(p)$ is a well-defined C^2 function from M to $S^{\ell-2} = \{v \in R^{\ell-1}: \|v\| = 1\}$. Take an arbitrary regular value $d \in S^{\ell-2}$ of F and $F \mid \partial M$. By Sard's theorem (I.1.1), almost every point of $S^{\ell-2}$ is a regular value of F. Consider then $F^{-1}(d)$. Again, $F^{-1}(d)$ is a compact C^1 manifold, hence a finite union of circles and segments with endpoints in M; see Figure 5.6.11. As in preceding arguments, the index formula is then obtained by combining the following facts:

(i)   Lemma 5.6.4.

(ii) When looked at as $(\ell-2)$ spheres, ∂S and ∂B_p, oriented as pieces of the boundary of M, receive different orientations.

(iii) For $p \in E$,

$$\text{sign det } \partial f(p) = \text{degree}(F \mid \partial B_p)$$

$$= \sum_{q \in F^{-1}(d) \cap \partial B_p} \text{sign det}(\partial F(q): T_q \partial B_p \to T_d S^{\ell-2}).$$

See J.2, J.3, J.3.1.

(iv) $F \mid \partial S$ points inward, hence

$$(-1)^{\ell-1} = \text{degree}(F \mid \partial S)$$

$$= \sum_{q \in F^{-1}(d) \cap \partial S} \text{sign det}(\partial F(q): T_q \partial S \to T_d S^{\ell-2}).$$

See J.2.

Note that (i)–(iv) yield $\sum_{p \in E} \text{degree}(F \mid \partial B_p) + \text{degree}(F \mid \partial S) = 0$. Therefore, $\sum_{p \in E} \text{index } p = 1$.

As before, this proof readily suggests a relatively simple argument to show the existence of at least one equilibrium. We see in Figure 5.6.11 that the function F does not need to be one-to-one on ∂S. However, because it points inward we can modify f on a neighborhood of ∂S so that it becomes one-to-one on ∂S and no new equilibrium is added. More precisely, let f_q be as Lemma 5.6.3 and $\eta: S \to [0, 1]$ a C^∞ function such that $\eta(\partial S) = 1$ and $\eta(p) > 0$ only for p in a sufficiently small neighborhood of ∂S. Then $p \mapsto \eta(p)f_q(p) + (1 - \eta(p))f(p)$ will be as desired (Lemma 5.6.3). Hence from now on we assume that $f \mid \partial S$ is one-to-one. This is the analog of the hypothesis in the homotopy proof that $f_0(p) = 0$ has a unique solution. Now suppose, by way of contradiction, that $f(p) \neq 0$ for all $p \in S$. Then $F(p) = [1/\|f(p)\|]f(p)$ is defined on the entire S. Let, as above, $d \in S^{\ell-2}$ be a regular value of F and $F \mid \partial S$. Then $F^{-1}(d)$ is a compact, smooth, one-dimensional manifold whose boundary is a subset of ∂S. Because $F \mid \partial S$ is one-to-one, $F(\partial S)$ contains an open set and so we could have chosen d such that $d \in F(\partial S)$. Let $d = F(z)$, $z \in \partial S$. Then z should be an endpoint of a segment in $F^{-1}(d)$. The other endpoint, call it x, should also belong to ∂S. Hence, we have $x \neq z$ and $F(x) = F(z)$. Contradiction. Therefore, $f(p) = 0$ for some p.

Letting E be the equilibrium set, $F(p) = [1/\|f(p)\|]f(p)$ is defined on $S \setminus E$. Suppose that $F \mid \partial S$ is a one-to-one map with everywhere full $(\ell - 2)$ rank and that for $\bar{p} \in \partial S$, $F(\bar{p}) = d$ is a regular value of F and $F \mid \partial S$ (except for a null set of ∂S every z maps into a regular d). Then (see Figure 5.6.12) $F^{-1}(d)$ contains a half-open segment I, one end of which is $\bar{p}$ and the other end (not included in the segment) is an equilibrium p. Therefore, if starting at $\bar{p}$ we follow the path I, we shall approach an equilibrium arbitrarily closely. Along the path the relative values of f are held constant [i.e., $F(I) = d$], but the norm $\|f\|$ is decreased, perhaps nonmonotonically, to zero. Let $p: [0, a) \to I$ follow the path I at unit speed, that is, $p(0) = 0$, $p([0, a)) = I$, and $\|\partial p(t)\| = 1$ for all $t \in [0, a)$. Then $p(\cdot)$ is a solution to the following system of differential equations:

   (i) $\partial f(p)\dot{p} = \lambda f(p)$
   (ii) $\|\dot{p}\| = 1$
   (iii) $\operatorname{sign} \lambda = (-1)^{\ell} \operatorname{sign} \det(\partial f(p))$

with initial condition $p(0) = \bar{p}$. Conversely, any maximal solution to (i)–(iii) with initial condition $p(0) = \bar{p}$ coincides with $p(\cdot)$. Indeed, there is only one way to follow I at unit speed, and any solution to (i)–(iii) that starts at $\bar{p}$ does precisely this; (i) guarantees that the solution stays in $F^{-1}(f(\bar{p}))$, (ii) imposes unit speed, and (iii) is simply the right choice of sign to guarantee that at $\bar{p}$ we choose the solution to (i)–(ii) that points inward and keeps switching thereafter in a consistent manner. Note that to get started we may initially have to increase, rather than decrease, $\|f(p)\|$ (see Figure 5.6.13a). The solution to (i)–(iii) will reach an equilibrium in finite time. This is not obvious and would require proof. On the other hand, it is clear enough that any neighborhood of equilibria will be reached in finite time.

Let us examine the equation system (i)–(iii) more closely. For integers $s \geq 0$, define $\Lambda_s = \{p \in S : \operatorname{rank} \partial f(p) = \ell - 1 - s\}$. In Figure 5.6.12 we have drawn Λ_1, whereas Λ_2 is the single point $\{v_3\}$ and $\Lambda_0 = S \setminus (\Lambda_1 \cup \Lambda_2)$. Roughly speaking, Λ_s should be thought of as a manifold of codimension s. For $p \in \Lambda_0$, say as v_1 in Figure 5.6.12, $\partial f(p)$ can be inverted, and thus we can solve (i)–(iii) explicitly for $\dot{p}$, that is, we can put $\dot{p} = (1/\|q\|)q$ for $q = (-1)^{\ell} \operatorname{sign} \det(\partial f(p))[\partial f(p)]^{-1}f(p)$. For $p \in \Lambda_1$, say as v_2 in Figure 5.6.12, (i)–(iii) admit two solutions, one being the negative of the other. Thus, whenever we get to one such $p \in \Lambda_1$ there is a single way to exit from it compatible with the continuity of the velocity vector. This is

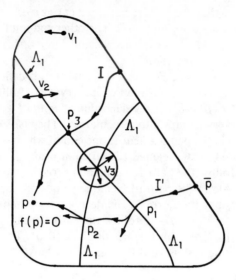

Figure 5.6.12

not the case if we get to $p \in \Lambda_2$ because there the solutions to (i)–(iii) are homeomorphic to S^1. Fortunately, if $p \in \Lambda_2$, then rank $\partial F(p) < \ell - 1$ and so such points are avoided by trajectories, such as I and I' in Figure 5.6.12, that start at a $\bar{p}$ with $F(\bar{p})$ a regular value of F. The points of Λ_1 may not be avoidable [in fact, $p(\bar{t}) \in \Lambda_1$ if and only if $\bar{t}$ is a critical point of $t \mapsto \|f(p(t))\|$; see Figure 5.6.13] but, as we have argued, the trajectories remain well defined. See Figure 5.6.12 for all this. A warning: Although in the figure I and I' cross Λ_1, this is not a crucial aspect; in fact, with the hypothesis made up to now it is entirely possible for $p(t)$ to remain in Λ_1 for a positive length of time. The key point is that $\{v_3\}$ is avoided.

The differential equation system (i)–(iii) offers little room for the use of previous information in the location of solutions $f(p) = 0$. This is because to guarantee convergence the initial condition must be placed at the boundary ∂S. If in Figure 5.6.11 we start in region A, we shall never leave it; that is, the trajectory will eventually cycle. This conclusion has to be contrasted with the homotopy procedure where we argued that initial information could be used to advantage. It seems to be a general heuristic principle that for computational purposes there is much to be gained by adding an extra dimension and proceeding by homotopy.

With this we conclude our discussion of the proposition.

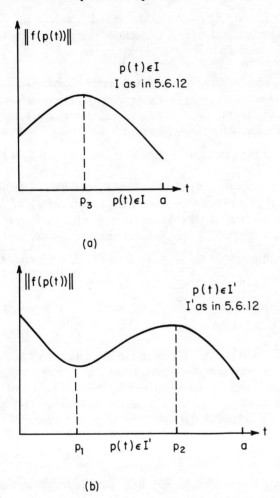

Figure 5.6.13

5.7   Special classes of economies and the uniqueness of equilibria

We saw in Section 5.5 that, with the hypothesis so far made on preferences and endowments, there is no hope of obtaining any stronger conclusion on the nature of the equilibrium price set than the ones contained
in the index theorem. For many purposes those are too general. In this
section we shall go in the reverse direction and discuss some of the eco-

nomically significant restrictions on excess demand functions and underlying economies that guarantee the fulfillment of sharp properties by the
equilibria of the system. To be specific, we concentrate on the uniqueness
property.

We proceed by first focusing on a given C^1 excess demand function f
and abstracting from the economy that generates it. It is convenient to let
the domain of f be the entire R^ℓ_{++}. For a given p three increasingly demanding restrictions on $\partial f(p)$ are of interest:

(I)   If $f(p) = 0$, then the determinant of the map $\partial f(p)\colon T_p \to T_p$ has
sign $(-1)^{\ell-1}$.

(II)   Whenever $p \cdot v = 0$, $f(p) \cdot v = 0$ and $v \neq 0$, we have $v \cdot \partial f(p)v < 0$;
that is, $\partial f(p)$ is negative quasi-definite (n.q.d.) on $T_p \cap T_{f(p)}$.

(III) There is $z > 0$ such that whenever $z \cdot v = 0$, $v \neq 0$, we have
$v \cdot \partial f(p)v < 0$; that is, $\partial f(p)$ is negative quasi-definite on T_z.

If any of the conditions hold for all p, then we say that f itself satisfies
the condition.

5.7.1. Proposition. *Condition (III) implies (II), which in turn implies (I).*

Proof. Suppose that (III) holds with respect to $z > 0$. Take $v \neq 0$ such that
$p \cdot v = 0$ and $v \cdot f(p) = 0$. Let $v_\alpha = v + \alpha p \in T_z$; that is, $\alpha = -(v \cdot z)/(p \cdot z)$.
Then $v_\alpha \cdot \partial f(p)v_\alpha < 0$ and, because $\partial f(p)p = 0$, $p \cdot \partial f(p) + f(p) = 0$, and
$v \cdot f(p) = 0$ we conclude $v \cdot \partial f(p)v = v_\alpha \cdot \partial f(p)v_\alpha < 0$. Hence (II) holds.
That (II) implies (I) is clear. If $f(p) = 0$, then $\partial f(p)$ as a matrix of a map
from T_p to T_p is negative quasi-definite and, therefore, its determinant
has sign $(-1)^{\ell-1}$; see B.6. ∎

Because of the index theorem (5.5.3), to guarantee the uniqueness of
equilibrium for the exchange economies discussed in this chapter it suffices
that f satisfies (I). But for more general purposes (such as establishing
other interesting properties of equilibrium or its uniqueness with production – see 6.6 on this) the stronger condition (II) is more useful. Condition (III) has the advantage over (II) in that it behaves better under addition. If at p two excess demand functions f_1, f_2 satisfy (III) with respect
to the *same* normalizing factor z, then so does $f_1 + f_2$. A warning is in
order here: Without the normalizing vector condition (III), even with
a weak inequality, cannot be satisfied whenever $f(p) \neq 0$. Indeed, let
$q \cdot f(p) < 0$ and put $v_\alpha = p + \alpha q$. Then from $\partial f(p)p = 0$ and $p \cdot \partial f(p) +
f(p) = 0$ we get $v_\alpha \cdot \partial f(p)v_\alpha = -\alpha q \cdot f(p) + \alpha^2 q \cdot \partial f(p)q$, which is positive
for $\alpha > 0$ small enough.

The economic interpretation of conditions (II) and (III) should be clear enough. The conclusion $v \cdot \partial f(p)v < 0$ says, informally, that quantity demanded moves in the opposite direction to price. Thus, this is a generalized law of demand property. It is generalized in the sense of it holding for simple or composite commodities. The difference between (II) and (III) is that in (II) the effect is only required for "compensated" price change, that is, for v that leave real wealth unaltered [equivalently, $v \cdot f(p) = 0$]. We saw in 2.7 that the demand generated by a single consumer will satisfy the generalized law of demand for compensated price changes [condition (II)], but this is not necessarily so for uncompensated ones [condition (III)]. We also saw in 2.9.3 that condition (II) had a corresponding version for finite price moves, the so-called weak axiom of revealed preference. This suggests that the same must be the case for condition (III).

5.7.2. Definition. *Let the excess demand function f be given. Then:*

(i) *f satisfies the weak axiom of revealed preference (WA) if $p \cdot f(q) > 0$ whenever $q \cdot f(p) \leq 0$, $f(p) \neq f(q)$.*

(ii) *f is monotone on T_z, $z > 0$, if $(p - q) \cdot [f(p) - f(q)] < 0$ whenever $p - q \in T_z$, $f(p) \neq f(q)$.*

5.7.3. Proposition

(i) *If f is monotone on some T_z, then it satisfies the weak axiom.*

(ii) *If f satisfies condition (II), then the weak axiom also holds. Conversely, if the weak axiom holds, then $v \cdot \partial f(p)v \leq 0$ for all v and p such that $v \cdot f(p) = 0$.*

(iii) *If f satisfies condition (III) with respect to a given z, then f is monotone on T_z. Conversely, if f is monotone on T_z, then $v \cdot \partial f(p)v \leq 0$ for any $v \in T_z$ and p.*

Proof. (i) Let $q \cdot f(p) \leq 0$, $f(p) \neq f(q)$. Because $p \cdot z > 0$ and $q \cdot z > 0$ there is $\alpha \geq 0$ such that $p - \alpha q \in T_z$. By the monotonicity of f on T_z we then have $-p \cdot f(q) - \alpha q \cdot f(p) = (p - \alpha q) \cdot [f(p) - f(\alpha q)] < 0$. Hence $p \cdot f(q) > -\alpha q \cdot f(p) \geq 0$.

(ii) This was already proved in 2.9.3. It should be obvious how the current case is a particular case of the situation contemplated there.

(iii) Let f be monotone on T_z and consider any p and $v \in T_z$. Define $p(\alpha) = p + \alpha v$. Then

$$\eta(\alpha) = v \cdot [f(p(\alpha)) - f(p)] = (1/\alpha)(p(\alpha) - p) \cdot [f(p(\alpha)) - f(p)] \leq 0$$

for any $\alpha > 0$ and $\eta(0) = 0$. Hence $\partial\eta(\alpha) \le 0$ for some $0 < \alpha \le \epsilon$. But $\partial\eta(\alpha) = v \cdot \partial f(p(\alpha))v$. Letting $\epsilon \to 0$, we get $v \cdot \partial f(p)v \le 0$. Conversely, suppose that the monotonicity property is violated; that is, for some p, $v \in T_z$, $v \ne 0$, and $\eta(\alpha)$ as above, we have

$$0 \le [p(1) - p] \cdot [f(p(1)) - f(p)] = v \cdot [f(p(1)) - f(p)] = \eta(1).$$

Then $0 \le \partial\eta(\alpha) = v \cdot \partial f(p(\alpha))v$ for some $\alpha > 0$ and we obtain a contradiction. ∎

It is worthwhile noting that the previous proposition remains valid if f is merely Lipschitzian and the references to $\partial f(p)$ in the propositions or in conditions (II) or (III) are understood as accompanied by the proviso "if it exists." To see this observe, first, that the proof does not need modification once $\partial f(p)$ is defined for all p in the generalized sense of G.2 and, second, that the relevant negative quasi-definite property of $\partial f(p)$ is preserved under this extension (this is immediate from the definition; see G.2).

To investigate the uniqueness issue with more depth we should bring into the analysis the economy $\mathcal{E} : I \to \mathcal{P}_{sc}^2$, generating the given excess demand function f. For simplicity we take R_{++}^ℓ as the consumption sets. This insures that every individual demand function is C^1. The decomposition of the impact of price changes on individual demand into substitution and wealth effects can now be exploited to yield an instructive decomposition of the aggregate effect. The decomposition is particularly helpful to find sufficient conditions for the negative quasi-definiteness of $\partial f(p)$ on an appropriate subspace, that is, condition (II) or (III).

Take a fixed price vector p and, for every $t \in I$, let

$$x(t) = \varphi(\succsim_t, p, p \cdot \omega(t))$$

$$c(t) = \partial_\omega \varphi(\succsim_t, p, p \cdot \omega(t))$$

$$S(t) = \partial_p \varphi(\succsim_t, p, p \cdot \omega(t)) + c(t)[x(t)]^T.$$

Those are, respectively, the individual demand, wealth effect, and substitution effect. The aggregate, or average, demand, endowment, and substitution terms are

$$\bar{x} = \int x(t)\, dt, \quad \bar{\omega} = \int \omega(t)\, dt, \quad \text{and} \quad \bar{S} = \int S(t)\, dt.$$

Of course, $f(p) = \bar{x} - \bar{\omega}$. For the wealth effects it is more convenient to take a weighted average, the weights being the wealth, or expenditures, shares $\theta(t) = (1/p \cdot \bar{x})p \cdot x(t)$. Specifically, $\bar{c} = \int c(t)\theta(t)\, dt$. Using the same weights $\theta(t)$ we also define the covariances matrices of $c(t)$ with

$[1/\theta(t)]x(t)$ and $[1/\theta(t)]\omega(t)$; that is,

$$C(c,x) = \int [c(t) - \bar{c}][x(t) - \theta(t)\bar{x}]^T dt$$

and

$$C(c,\omega) = \int [c(t) - \bar{c}][\omega(t) - \theta(t)\omega]^T dt.$$

Note that

$$\int [c(t) - \bar{c}][x(t) - \omega(t)]^T dt = C(c,x) - C(c,\omega).$$

Therefore, we can transform

$$\partial f(p) = \int \partial_p \varphi(\succeq_t, p, p \cdot \omega(t)) \, dt = \bar{S} - \int c(t)[x(t) - \omega(t)]^T dt$$

into

$$\partial f(p) = \bar{S} - \bar{c}(\bar{x} - \bar{\omega})^T - C(c,x) + C(c,\omega).$$

Formally:

5.7.4. Proposition. *With the previous notation $\partial f(p)$ admits the following decomposition:*

$$\partial f(p) = \bar{S} - \bar{c}[f(p)]^T - C(c,x) + C(c,\omega).$$

Thus, $\partial f(p)$ decomposes into an average substitution effect, an average wealth effect, an expenditure distribution effect, and an endowment distribution effect. If all consumers were identical, then the two last effects would vanish and, as is the case for a single consumer, condition (II), the negative quasi-definiteness of $\partial f(p)$ on $\{v \in T_p : v \cdot f(p) = 0\}$ would be satisfied. Remember that $\bar{S}$ itself is negative definite on T_p. If consumers are not identical (or, more sharply, if wealth effects are not identical), then the distribution matrices $C(c,x), C(c,\omega)$ come into their own. Roughly speaking, their impact on $\partial f(p)$ will be favorable to negative quasi-semi-definiteness if the association between wealth effects $c(t)$ and normalized expenditures $[1/\theta(t)]x(t)$ (resp. normalized endowments) is nonnegative (resp. nonpositive); that is, relatively high marginal expenditure on a commodity tends to go together with relatively high expenditure on the commodity (resp. relatively low endowments of the commodity). In the contrary case the impact will be unfavorable. Note that $C(c,x)$ or $C(c,\omega)$ will be null whenever, respectively, consumption or endowments are collinear across consumers.

It is quite possible that the decomposition formula 5.7.4 is the most general and enlightening statement that can be hoped for. It will nevertheless be useful to briefly discuss some limit examples where conditions (II) or (III), hence the uniqueness of equilibrium, can be established via the formula. Those will be examples 5.7.5 to 5.7.8. The last one, 5.7.9, illustrates a situation where (II) and (III) may fail but condition (I) still holds. For the purpose of establishing condition (I) above, the decomposition formula is not really useful. So for 5.7.9 the proof will proceed directly.

5.7.5. Example. This is more an observation than an example. The substitution term matrix $\bar{S}$ is negative definite on T_p. Therefore, if the minimum eigenvalue of $\bar{S}$ is sufficiently large, then $\partial f(p)$ will be negative quasidefinite on T_p. Because this property, that is, condition (III), is preserved under addition, the observation can be made at the individual level. If for every agent t the substitution effects are larger than the wealth effects, then condition (III) holds. This is, of course, a vague statement, but note that although there is no upper bound independent of preferences on the magnitude of the substitution effects, that is, indifference manifolds can be arbitrarily flat, there is an important case where an a priori bound dependent on endowments but not on preferences exists for the wealth effect. Indeed, if $c(t) \geq 0$, that is, there is no inferior good at p, then

$$|v \cdot c(t)[x(t) - \omega(t)]^T v| \leq \frac{1}{(\min_j p^j)^2} \|p\| \|\omega(t)\| \quad \text{for } \|v\| = 1.$$

The previous example shows that even if the distribution matrices are badly behaved, not everything is lost. To do real damage they must still overcome the substitution effects. The next three examples make the point that there is no a priori presumption for income and distribution effects to go in the unfavorable direction.

5.7.6. Example. The dispersion across the population of consumptions and endowments matters only to the extent that the wealth effects are themselves disperse. If all of them are the same, that is, $c(t) = \bar{c}$ for all t, then $C(c, x) = C(c, \omega) = 0$ and so condition (II) holds at p. By continuity this remains valid if income effects are very similar.

The next two examples are less obvious. They both concentrate on the consumption distribution term $C(c, x)$ and get $C(c, \omega)$ out of the way by assuming that all $\omega(t)$ are collinear, that is, that the distribution of income is price-independent. This, of course, implies $C(c, \omega) = 0$.

5.7.7. Example. Suppose that the distribution of wealth is price-independent [hence $C(c, x) = 0$] and that every preference relation $\succsim_t$ is homothetic or, equivalently, it is such that demand $\varphi(\succsim_t, p, w)$ is linear in w. Then

$$c(t) = \frac{1}{\theta(t)p \cdot \bar{x}} x(t)$$

and so

$$\bar{c} = \frac{1}{p \cdot \bar{x}} \bar{x}, \qquad C(c, x) = \frac{1}{p \cdot \bar{x}} \int \left[\frac{1}{\theta(t)} x(t) - \bar{x}\right]\left[\frac{1}{\theta(t)} x(t) - \bar{x}\right]^T \theta(t) \, dt.$$

As an average of positive semidefinite matrices $C(c, x)$ is also positive semidefinite. Therefore, condition (II) holds at any p because by the decomposition formula, $v \cdot \partial f(p) v < 0$ whenever $v \in T_p$, $v \neq 0$, and $v \cdot f(p) = 0$.

5.7.8. Example. Let $I = [0, 1]$ be the consumer set and suppose, first, that all preferences are identical and, second, that endowments are uniformly distributed (or, more generally, distributed with a decreasing density) on the segment connecting the origin to $\bar{\omega}$; that is, $\{\alpha\bar{\omega} : 0 \leq \alpha \leq 1\}$. We claim that in this case condition (III) is satisfied with respect to $\bar{\omega}$; that is, $\partial f(p)$ is negative quasi-definite on $T_{\bar{\omega}}$. To see this note that $C(c, \omega) = 0$ and that we can always rewrite $-c[f(p)]^T - C(c, x) = c\bar{\omega}^T - \int c(t)[x(t)]^T \, dt$. In the example, where preferences are identical and the wealth distribution is uniform, we can, without loss of generality, identify t with the consumer having endowments $t\bar{\omega}$. Then $x(t)$ is a differentiable function of t and $c(t) = (1/p \cdot \bar{\omega}) \partial x(t)$. Therefore, for any v,

$$-\int [v \cdot c(t)][x(t) \cdot v] \, dt = -\frac{1}{p \cdot \bar{\omega}} \int [\partial x(t) \cdot v][x(t) \cdot v] \, dt$$

$$= -\frac{1}{2p \cdot \bar{\omega}} \int_0^1 \partial_t [x(t) \cdot v]^2 \, dt$$

$$= -\frac{1}{2p \cdot \bar{\omega}} [x(1) \cdot v]^2 < 0.$$

Hence, $v \cdot \partial f(p) v < 0$ whenever $\bar{\omega} \cdot v = 0$, $v \neq 0$. As a last remark remember that condition (III) will also hold for the union of any two economies satisfying the conditions of the example with respect to the same $\bar{\omega}$.

5.7.9. Example. Suppose now that the $\ell \times \ell$ matrix $\partial f(p)$ displays the so-called gross substitute pattern; that is, diagonal (resp. off-diagonal) entries are negative (resp. positive). In other words, the increase in the price of a commodity decreases its demand and increases the demand of every other commodity. This second part of the condition is very restrictive. If $\ell > 2$, there is no reason why it should be satisfied by, for example, the compensated demand of a single consumer. Nevertheless, it is worthwhile to explore its implications. In general (precisely, for $\ell > 3$) the gross substitution property does not imply that f satisfies condition (II) or, a fortiori, condition (III), for all p. But it turns out that they are satisfied whenever $f(p) = 0$. This makes the property a useful one in the context of exchange economies. For a proof, let A be the $(\ell-1) \times (\ell-1)$ northwest submatrix of $\partial f(p) + [\partial f(p)]^T$. If we show that A is negative definite, then we are done because condition (III) is then satisfied for $z = e_\ell$. By B.6.5 a sufficient condition for A to be negative definite is that its diagonal be negative, which it is, and dominant (see B.6 for definition). Let $\hat{p}$ be the first $\ell-1$ coordinates of p. Because $f(p) = 0$ we have $p \cdot \partial f(p) = 0$, $\partial f(p)p = 0$. This and the gross substitute property imply $A\hat{p} \ll 0$, which, the off-diagonal entries of A being positive, yields the quasi-dominance of the diagonal.

By the above, 5.7.1 and the index theorem, the gross substitute property guarantees the uniqueness of equilibrium in an exchange economy. A direct proof of this is not only possible but straightforward. Let $p_1, p_2 \in R_{++}^\ell$ be equilibrium price vectors. Without loss of generality we can assume $p_1 \geq p_2$ and $p_1^\ell = p_2^\ell$. If $p_1 \neq p_2$, then by decreasing in sequence the prices of the first $\ell-1$ commodities from p_1^j to p_2^j we get $f^\ell(p_2) > f^\ell(p_1)$, which contradicts $f(p_1) = f(p_2) = 0$. Hence $p_1 = p_2$. We cannot resist pointing out that, at least if the standard boundary behavior of f is taken for granted, a straightforward existence proof is also available. Let $\eta(p) = \max_j f^j(p)$ and $\bar{p} \gg 0$ minimize $\eta(p)$ on R_{++}^ℓ. Because of the boundary property on $f(p)$ such a $\bar{p}$ exists and, we claim, constitutes an equilibrium. Suppose not; that is, $\eta(p) > 0$. Then $\bar{p} \cdot f(\bar{p}) = 0$ implies $f^j(\bar{p}) < 0$ for some j. If we decrease the price of j slightly, then the demand for j will remain negative whereas, by gross substitution, the demand of every commodity different from j will decrease. This contradicts the minimization property of $\bar{p}$.

5.8   The equilibrium set: global analysis

In the previous sections we have studied the set of equilibrium of a single economy $\mathcal{E}$. We will now consider entire spaces of economies and investigate the structure of the set-valued equilibrium map.

The hypothesis for this section is: $\mathfrak{M}$ *is the set of economies whose agents have characteristics in a given set* $Q \subset \mathcal{Q}$. *The set* $\mathfrak{M}$ *is endowed with a concept of nearness* (i.e., it is made into a topological space), *as in Section 5.4* (Definition 5.4.1). More precisely, if $\mathcal{E}_n: I_n \to Q$, $\mathcal{E}: I \to Q$, and ν_n, ν are the corresponding distribution of characteristics, then we say that $\mathcal{E}_n \to \mathcal{E}$ if (i) $1/\#I_n \to 1/\#I$, (ii) supp $\nu_n \to$ supp ν (in the Hausdorff distance), and (iii) $\nu_n \to \nu$ weakly. We have:

> **5.8.1. Proposition.** *With the adopted concept of convergence, some of the properties of the space $\mathfrak{M}$ are:*
>
> (i) *$\mathfrak{M}$ is metrizable and separable.*
> (ii) *For each $n \leq \infty$, $\mathfrak{M}_n = \{\mathcal{E} \in \mathfrak{M} : \#(\text{domain } \mathcal{E}) = n\}$ is arcwise connected.*
> (iii) *The set of finite economies is dense in $\mathfrak{M}$.*
> (iv) *If Q is compact, then $\mathfrak{M}$ is compact.*
> (v) *In the continuous case, that is, $\mathcal{Q} = \mathcal{P}_{sc}^0 \times R_{++}^\ell$, $\mathfrak{M}$ is complete.*

Proof. (i) The space $\mathcal{Q}$ can be endowed with a separable metric ρ (2.4.5). Therefore, there is a separable metric ρ' for the weak convergence of the measures on $\mathcal{Q}$ (E.3.1). Let also ρ'' be the Hausdorff distance on the compact subsets of $\mathcal{Q}$ derived from ρ; see A.5.1. Endow then the space $\mathfrak{M}$ with the metric that associates with $\mathcal{E}, \bar{\mathcal{E}} \in \mathfrak{M}$ the distance $\rho'(\nu, \bar{\nu}) + \rho''(\text{supp } \nu, \text{supp } \bar{\nu}) + |1/\#I - 1/\#\bar{I}|$.

(ii) The space $\mathcal{Q}$ is contractible (2.6.7). Let $H: \mathcal{Q} \times [0,1] \mapsto \mathcal{Q}$ be a contraction; that is, H is continuous and for all $a \in \mathcal{Q}$, $H(a, 0) = a$ and $H(a, 1) = \bar{a}$ for some fixed $\bar{a}$. Take any $\mathcal{E} \in \mathfrak{M}$, $\mathcal{E}: I \to \mathcal{Q}$. For $\alpha \in [0, 1]$ put $\mathcal{E}_\alpha(t) = H(\mathcal{E}(t), \alpha)$. Because H is continuous and $\mathcal{E}$ is compactly supported, the function $\alpha \mapsto \mathcal{E}_\alpha$ is continuous. Therefore, we have obtained a continuous path from $\mathcal{E}_0 = \mathcal{E}$ to the constant economy $\mathcal{E}_1(t) = \bar{a}$ for all t. Any two constant economies differ only by their number of traders. Hence any two $\mathcal{E}, \mathcal{E}'$ with #domain $\mathcal{E}$ = #domain $\mathcal{E}'$ can be connected by a path.

(iii) This is a simple consequence of E.3.3.

(iv) See A.5.1.v and E.3.1.

(v) In the continuous case $\mathcal{P}_{sc}^0$ is a G_δ subset of the compact metric space formed by the nonempty closed subset of the one-point compactification of R^ℓ; see A.5, 2.6.7, and the observations preceding 2.4.8. Hence the result follows from E.3.2. ∎

It has seemed to us that in view of the intended applications the adopted formalization of a topological space of economies is the most fruitful. It is not, however, the only possible one. The obvious, weaker alternative is to drop the compact support restriction from the definition of the space and let $\mathfrak{M}'$ be, simply, the space of economies with characteristics in $Q \subset \mathcal{P}_{sc}^r \times [1/k, k]^\ell$ endowed with the notion of convergence:

"$\mathcal{E}_n \to \mathcal{E}$ if $1/\#I_n \to 1/\#I$ and the induced distribution of characteristics converge weakly." The advantage of $\mathfrak{M}'$ over $\mathfrak{M}$ is that, provided Q is G_δ, the space is complete, which would be of some convenience for the analysis of genericity in Chapter 8. Nonetheless, in the context of the smooth approach $\mathfrak{M}'$ is too weak. Thus, for example, properties as basic as 5.2.7 or 5.4.2 will fail if $Q = \mathcal{P}^r_{sc} \times [1/k, k]^\ell$. If Q is compact, they will hold (see observation in the proof of 5.4.2), but the restriction to an a priori given compact set of characteristics is too constraining and, most surely, a serious complication for the analysis of genericity. The possibility remains, of course, that some large but suitably bounded sets Q lead to tractable spaces $\mathfrak{M}'$. But, to repeat, we have thought that on balance (including the needs of the theory of Chapter 7) the richer space was $\mathfrak{M}$ and, to avoid excessive casuistry, we have not pursued alternatives.

The point-to-set equilibrium map $W: \mathfrak{M} \to S$ is defined by letting $W(\mathcal{E})$ be the set of equilibrium price vectors associated with $\mathcal{E}$. We know from Section 5.4 that, for every $\mathcal{E}$, $W(\mathcal{E})$ is compact. This generalizes:

5.8.2. Proposition. *For every compact $K \subset \mathfrak{M}$, the equilibrium set $E = \{(p, \mathcal{E}): p \in W(\mathcal{E}), \mathcal{E} \in K\} \subset S \times K$ is compact.*

Proposition 5.8.2 is a trivial consequence of the following proposition.

5.8.3. Proposition. *Let $f: S \times \mathfrak{M} \to R^{\ell-1}$ be the aggregate excess demand function; that is, $f(\cdot, \mathcal{E})$ is the aggregate excess demand function of the economy $\mathcal{E}$. Then f is continuous and satisfies the boundary condition, "If $p_n \to p \in \partial S$ and $\mathcal{E}_n \to \mathcal{E}$, then $\|f(p_n, \mathcal{E}_n)\| \to \infty$."*

Proof. For continuity see E.4.2 and 5.2.5. For the boundary condition let $\mathcal{E}_n \to \mathcal{E}$ and denote $H = \bigcup_n \operatorname{supp} \nu_n \cup \operatorname{supp} \nu$, where ν_n, ν correspond to $\mathcal{E}_n, \mathcal{E}$. The set H is compact. Choose s such that if $(\succsim, \omega) \in H$, then $\|\omega\| < s$. We argue by contradiction. Suppose that a subsequence of $\|f(p_n, \mathcal{E}_n)\|$ remains finite. Without loss of generality we can assume $\|f(p_n, \mathcal{E}_n)\| \leq (k/\ell^2) - s$ for some k and all n. But this means that $\|f(p_n, a_n)\| \leq k$ for some $a_n = (\succsim_n, \omega_n) \in \operatorname{supp} \nu_n \in H$. Therefore,

$$\varphi(\succsim_n, p_n, p_n \cdot \omega_n) \leq k + \|\omega_n\| \leq k + s.$$

Because H is compact we can assume that $(\succsim_n, \omega_n) \to (\succsim, \omega) \in H$ and we obtain a contradiction to 2.4.8. ∎

Typically the set $\mathfrak{M}$ is quite large. Indeed, if we look at $\mathfrak{M}$ in some natural way as a subset of a linear space, then $\mathfrak{M}$ will be (except whenever Q

is finite) infinite-dimensional. For the investigation of the differentiable properties of W it will be convenient to consider the restrictions of W to smaller (finite-dimensional) subsets of $\mathfrak{M}$.

5.8.4. Definition. *Let B be a subset of some linear space $L \subset R^m$ or, more generally, of some smooth manifold L. A (finite-dimensional) parameterization of economies is a continous function $\eta: B \to \mathfrak{M}$.*

We denote $W(\eta(b))$, $f(p, \eta(b))$ by $W(b)$ and $f(p, b)$. Because $\mathfrak{M}$ is continuous the equilibrium map (resp. the aggregate excess demand function $f: S \times B \to R^\ell$) satisfies Proposition 5.8.2 (resp 5.8.3) with B substituted for $\mathfrak{M}$. We now give several examples of parameterizations. The continuity requirement is, in each case, easily verified.

5.8.5. Example. Take $I_n = \{1, \ldots, n\}$. Let $\succsim_1, \ldots, \succsim_n$ be fixed preference relations. Denote $\Omega = R_{++}^{\ell n}$. Generic elements of Ω are $\omega = (\omega_1, \ldots, \omega_n)$. Each ω defines an economy $\mathcal{E}_\omega: I_n \to \mathcal{Q}$ by $\mathcal{E}_\omega(t) = (\succsim_t, \omega_t)$. Thus, we have a finite-dimensional parameterization with parameter space $B = \Omega$ or, if aggregate endowments are held fixed, with $B = \Omega(\omega) = \{\bar{\omega} \in \Omega : \sum_{t=1}^n \omega_t = \bar{\omega}\}$.

5.8.6. Example. This is a variation of Example 5.8.5 for the continuum case $I = [0, 1]$. Let $0 < \alpha \le 1$ be arbitrary and $\mathcal{E}: I \to \mathcal{Q}$ a fixed reference economy. Then for each $b \in R_{++}^\ell$ we define an economy $\mathcal{E}_b$ by setting $\mathcal{E}_b(t) = (\succsim_t, \omega_t + b)$, [where $(\succsim_t, \omega_t) = \mathcal{E}(t)$] for $t \le \alpha$ and $\mathcal{E}_b(t) = \mathcal{E}(t)$ for $t > \alpha$.

5.8.7. Example. Let v be a strictly concave, increasing, continuous function on the positive (or strictly positive, whichever is appropriate) part of the real line. For each $b \in R_{++}^\ell$ we let $\succsim_b$ be the continuous, convex preference relations represented by the utility function $u_b(z) = \sum_j b_j v(z^j)$. Note that if v is C^2 and has a nondegenerate Hessian everywhere, the same property is inherited by u_b. Take $I_n = \{1, \ldots, n\}$ and let $\succsim_2, \ldots, \succsim_n$, $\omega_1, \ldots, \omega_n$ be arbitrary preferences and (strictly positive) initial endowment vectors. Then for each $b \in R_{++}^\ell$ we have the economy $\mathcal{E}_b: I_n \to \mathcal{Q}$ given by $\mathcal{E}_b(1) = (\succsim_b, \omega_1)$ and $\mathcal{E}_b(t) = (\succsim_t, \omega_t)$ for $t \ge 2$.

5.8.8. Example. The setup is the same as for the previous example except that, given $b \in R_{++}^\ell$, the preferences $\succsim_b$ assigned to agent 1 are formed as follows. There is given an admissible utility function u. Then we let $\succsim_b$ be the preference relation represented by the utility function $u_b(z) = u(b_1 z^1, \ldots, b_\ell z^\ell)$.

5.8.9. Example. This will be an example with a continuum of agents and a finite number of types. Let $Q \subset \mathcal{Q}$ be finite, say $\#Q = m$, and $I = [0, 1]$. Then an economy is completely specified by the relative mass assigned to every type, that is, by a point θ of the $(m-1)$ unit simplex Δ^{m-1}. Thus, taking $B = \text{Int } \Delta^{m-1}$, $L = \{v \in R^m : \sum_{i=1}^m v_i = 0\}$, we have a parameterization.

5.8.10. Example. This is a variation of Example 5.8.9 for economies that do not necessarily have a finite number of types. Let $v_1, \ldots, v_m$ be a finite number of measures on $\mathcal{Q}$ with compact support. With the understanding that there is a continuum of agents we can always specify an economy by one such measure. Thus, for each $b \in \Delta^{m-1}$ we define $\mathcal{E}_b$ by

$$v_b = b_1 v_1 + \cdots + b_m v_m.$$

Taking $B = \text{Int } \Delta^{m-1}$, we get a parameterization.

Except for the last two propositions (5.8.23 and 5.8.24), *we assume from now on that $\mathcal{Q}$ is a space of smooth characteristics and $\mathcal{P} = \mathcal{P}_b$.* On account of boundaries the study of global smoothness properties for the case $\mathcal{P} = \mathcal{P}_{cl}$ is a bit more technical. It will be discussed briefly in Chapter 8, Section 8.8.

       5.8.11. Definition. *We say that the parameterization $\eta: B \to \mathfrak{M}$ is C^r, $r \geq 2$, if $f: S \times B \to R^\ell$ is a C^{r-1} function.*

Each of the parameterizations in Examples 5.8.5–5.8.10 is C^2. For 5.8.9 and 5.8.10 this is obvious (the parameters act linearly on excess demand). For 5.8.5–5.8.8 it follows from 2.7.2, as in 5.2.7. The definition we are adopting is the one indicated for the analysis of equilibria via aggregate excess demand functions, which is the approach we are favoring in this section. It is clear that if we were considering economies of a fixed finite cardinality, we could use the more basic definition of C^r parameterization of preferences 2.4.6, which would imply the C^{r-1} dependence on the parameters of both aggregate excess demand and excess utility (2.7.2).

       5.8.12. Definition. *The C^r parameterization $\eta: B \to \mathfrak{M}$ is regular if the linear map $\partial f(p, b): T_p \times T_b L \to R^\ell$ has rank $\ell - 1$ whenever $f(p, b) = 0$.*

The regularity of a parameterization should not be thought of as a restrictive condition. A typical and important situation is where B is of relatively large dimension. Then, as a matrix $\partial f(p, b)$ has many more columns than rows and so, very informally speaking, the linear independence of as many columns as there are rows is likely. Often the regularity of a parameterization will hold in a strong sense, namely

"rank $\partial_b f(p, b) = \ell - 1$ for all p and b."

We shall now examine the regularity of the parameterizations in Examples 5.8.5–5.8.10.

5.8.5. Example (continued). First consider the case $B = \Omega$. The regularity of η is easily established. It suffices to show that rank $\partial_{\omega_1} f_1(p, \omega_1) = \ell - 1$ for any p and $\omega_1 \gg 0$. Now $f_1(p, \omega_1) = \varphi_1(p, p \cdot \omega_1) - \omega_1$, where φ_1 is the demand function of agent 1. Hence, for any small $v \in T_p$, $f_1(p, \omega_1 + v) = f_1(p, \omega_1) - v$ and so $\partial_{\omega_1} f_1(p, \omega_1) v = -v$ for any $v \in T_p$. In other words, $\partial_{\omega_1} f_1(p, \omega_1)$ is the negative of the identity in T_p. Because dim $T_p = \ell - 1$, we are done.

Observe that, beyond smoothness, the sole property of excess demand functions used in the previous paragraph is that the excess demand f_1 depends on the initial endowments ω_1 only through wealth $p \cdot \omega_1$. As it turns out, this is not sufficient to prove the regularity of the parameterization in the case $B = \Omega(\bar{\omega})$, that is, in the Edgeworth box. It is, of course, understood that $L = \{v \in R^{\ell n}: \Sigma_t \, v_t = 0\}$. The parameterization is in fact regular, but the proof is more delicate and it depends essentially on the properties of excess demand functions derived from preference maximization. Let $(p, \omega) \in S \times \Omega(\bar{\omega})$ be given. Denote by S_t and c_t the substitution matrix and wealth effect vector of agent t at $f_t(p, \omega_t) + \omega_t$; that is, the jh (resp. j) generic entry of S_t (resp. c_t) is

$$\partial_h \varphi_t^j(p, p \cdot \omega_t) + \partial_w \varphi_t^j(p, p \cdot \omega_t) \varphi_t^h(p, p \cdot \omega_t) \quad [\text{resp. } \partial_w \varphi_t^j(p, p \cdot \omega_t)],$$

where φ_t is the demand function of agent t. Direct computation then yields $\partial f_t(p, \omega_t)(z, v_t) = S_t z + [(\omega_t - \varphi_t) \cdot z + p \cdot v_t] c_t$. Therefore, let $v \gg 0$ be arbitrary and for any $z \in T_p$ take $v_t = -(1/p \cdot v)[(\omega_t - \varphi_t) \cdot z] v$. Then $\Sigma_t \, v_t = 0$ because $\Sigma_t \, \varphi_t = \Sigma_t \, \omega_t$. Also, $\partial f(p, \omega)(z, v_1, \ldots, v_n) = (\Sigma_t \, S_t) z$. Because each S_t is negative definite on T_p (see 2.7.7), so is $\Sigma_t \, S_t$. Hence, rank $\partial f(p, \omega) = \ell - 1$.

5.8.6. Example (continued). This parameterization is also regular. The proof is identical to the simple case (i.e., $B = \Omega$) of Example 5.8.5.

5.8.7. Example (continued). The regularity of this parameterization is implied by: rank $\partial_b \varphi_1(p, b) = \ell - 1$ for all p and $b \gg 0$, where φ_1 is the demand function of agent 1. Remember that the demand vector at a fixed p is obtained as the solution in the $\ell + 1$ variables z and λ of the system of

$\ell+1$ equations, $\lambda\partial u_b(z)-p=0$, $p\cdot z-p\cdot\omega_1=0$. Denote by $\Psi(z,\lambda,b)=0$ this equation system. We know from 2.7.2 that the conditions of the implicit function theorem are met, and so whenever $\Psi(\bar z,\bar\lambda,\bar b)=0$ we have $\partial_b(z(\bar b),\lambda(\bar b))=-[\partial_{z,\lambda}\Psi(\bar z,\bar\lambda,\bar b)]^{-1}\partial_b\Psi(\bar z,\bar\lambda,\bar b)$. Because $\partial_b u_b(z)=b_h\partial v(z^h)$, it follows that the $(\ell+1)\times\ell$ matrix $\partial_b\Psi(\bar z,\bar\lambda,\bar b)$ is an $\ell\times\ell$ diagonal matrix supplemented by a last row of zeroes. Hence,

$$\text{rank }\partial_b\Psi(\bar z,\bar\lambda,\bar\ell)=\ell$$

and, therefore, rank $\partial_b(z(\bar b),\lambda(\bar b))=\ell$, which implies rank $\partial_b z(\bar b)\ge\ell-1$. But locally, $z(\bar b)=\varphi_1(p,\bar b)$ and we can conclude that the parameterization is regular.

5.8.8. Example (continued). Perhaps surprisingly at first sight, but quite obviously at second, this parameterization need not be regular. For a simple example, suppose that $\ell=2$ and $u(z)=\sqrt{z^1 z^2}$. Then $u_b(z)=\sqrt{b_1 b_2}\,u(z)$; that is, $u_b(z)$ represents the same preferences as $u(z)$. Hence, aggregate excess demand does not depend on b, and if the economy we start with is not regular, then the parameter b is not going to make it so.

5.8.9. Example (continued). This parameterization is regular. Let f_i be the excess demand function of type i. Then $f(p,\theta)=\sum_{i=1}^m \theta_i f_i(p)$, $\theta_i>0$. Suppose that $f(p,\theta)=0$. Let F be the matrix whose ith column is $f_i(p)$. Then $F\theta=0$. We have $\partial_\theta f(p,\theta)=F$ and so the range of $\partial_\theta f(p,\theta)$ is $\{Fz: z\cdot e=0\}$. Let N be the range of F; that is, $N=\{Fz: z\in R^m\}$. We claim that $N=\{Fz: z\cdot e=0\}$. Indeed, because $e\cdot\theta=0$ and $F\theta=0$, for any z we have $Fz=F(z-(e\cdot z)\theta)$ and $e\cdot(z-(e\cdot z)\theta)=0$. Let $N^\perp\subset T_p$ be the orthogonal complement to N. We shall show that $\partial_p f(p,\theta)(N^\perp)$ is a subspace of T_p complementary to N, or, in other words, that $\partial_p f(p,\theta)v\in T_p\backslash N$ for each $v\in N^\perp$, $v\neq 0$. This will complete the regularity proof. Let S_i be the substitution matrix of type i at $(p,p\cdot\omega_i)$ and remember (5.5.5) that if $f_i(p)\cdot v=0$, then $\partial f_i(p)v=S_i v$. Let $v\in N^\perp$, $v\neq 0$. Then $\partial_p f(p,\theta)v=\sum_i \theta_i S_i v$. Because $p\cdot S_i=0$ for all i, $\sum_i \theta_i S_i v\in T_p$. Suppose that $\sum_i \theta_i S_i v=\sum_i \alpha_i f_i$. Then $\sum_i \theta_i v\cdot S_i v=\sum_i \alpha_i f_i\cdot v=0$ since $v\in N^\perp$. This constitutes a contradiction to the negative definiteness on T_p of each S_i. Therefore, $\sum_i \theta_i S_i v\notin N$, and we are done.

5.8.10. Example (continued). In spite of the similarity with the previous example, this parameterization need not be regular. Too few a priori restrictions on the measures ν_i have been imposed. Let, for example, $\ell=2$, $m=2$, and suppose that $f(\bar p,1)=f(\bar p,0)=0$ and rank $\partial_p f(\bar p,1)=$ rank $\partial_p(\bar p,0)=0$. Then for $f(p,b)=bf(p,1)+(1-b)f(p,0)$, $b\in(0,1)$, we have $f(\bar p,b)=0$ and rank $\partial f(\bar p,b)=0$ for all b.

It is worth noting that the parameterization of Example 5.8.9 would not necessarily be regular if the rank condition was required for all (p, b) and not just for those (p, b) satisfying $f(p, b) = 0$. The first three examples would pass this more stringent test. If the regularity condition is strengthened in the direction of requiring rank $\partial_b f(p, b) = \ell - 1$ whenever $f(p, b) = 0$, then the case $B = \Omega(\bar{\omega})$ of Example 5.8.5 and, again, Example 5.8.9 may fail it.

The importance of the regularity condition for a parameterization derives from the following fundamental fact:

5.8.13. Proposition. *Let $B \subset R^m$ be a C^1 manifold and $\eta : B \to \mathfrak{M}$ a regular parameterization. Then the equilibrium set*

$$E = \{(p, b) \in S \times B : p \in W(b)\}$$

is a C^1 manifold of the same dimension as B.

Proof. Because $E = f^{-1}(0)$, this is a direct application of the implicit function theorem (H.2.2). The only difficulty is that if $f(\bar{p}, \bar{b}) = 0$, the rank of $\partial f(\bar{p}, \bar{b})$ is $\ell - 1$ rather than ℓ. This can be handled in by now familiar ways; for example, if we let $\hat{f}(p, b)$ be the first $\ell - 1$ coordinates of $f(p, b)$, then E can be identified with $\hat{f}^{-1}(0)$ and we have rank $\partial \hat{f}(p, b) = \ell - 1$. ∎

Figure 5.8.1 illustrates the Proposition. For $\ell = 2$ and B two-dimensional, the equilibrium set of Figure 5.8.1a (resp. b) is not (resp. is) consistent with a regular parameterization because it is not (resp. is) a manifold.

In the space $\mathfrak{M}$ we can form the set $\mathfrak{M}^* = \{\mathcal{E} \in \mathfrak{M} : \mathcal{E} \text{ regular}\}$. A simple but very important consequence of Propositions 5.8.2 and 5.4.2 is:

5.8.14. Proposition. *$\mathfrak{M}^*$ is open and at each $\bar{\mathcal{E}} \in \mathfrak{M}^*$ the equilibrium set is stable in the following sense: There is an open neighborhood $V \subset \mathfrak{M}^*$ of $\bar{\mathcal{E}}$ and a finite number of continuous functions $\eta_i : V \to S$, $1 \leq i \leq n$, such that, for each $\mathcal{E} \in V$, $\eta_i(\mathcal{E}) \neq \eta_j(\mathcal{E})$ if $i \neq j$ and $W(\mathcal{E}) = \bigcup_{i=1}^{n} \{\eta_i(\mathcal{E})\}$. In particular, the number of equilibria, that is $\#W(\mathcal{E})$, is locally constant at a regular economy (see Figure 5.8.2).*

Proof. Let $\bar{\mathcal{E}} \in \mathfrak{M}^*$. By hypothesis, rank $\partial f(p, \bar{\mathcal{E}}) = \ell - 1$ for $p \in W(\bar{\mathcal{E}})$. Because $W(\bar{\mathcal{E}})$ is compact and the determinant function is continuous, there are neighborhoods $\bar{\mathcal{E}} \in V_1 \subset \mathfrak{M}$ and $p \in V_2 \subset S$ such that

$$\text{rank } \partial f(p, \mathcal{E}) = \ell - 1 \quad \text{for } p \in V_2, \ \mathcal{E} \in V_1.$$

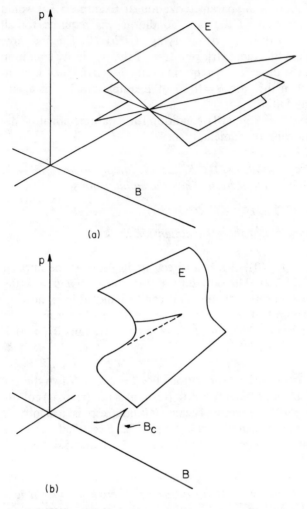

Figure 5.8.1

By 5.8.2 there is an open $V_1' \subset V_1$ such that $W(V_1') \subset V_2$. Therefore, if $\mathcal{E} \in V_1'$, then rank $\partial f(p, \mathcal{E}) = \ell - 1$ for each $p \in W(\mathcal{E})$. Thus $V_1' \subset \mathfrak{M}^*$ and we conclude that $\mathfrak{M}^*$ is open. The stability of the equilibrium set $W(\mathcal{E})$ at regular $\mathcal{E}$ is now a trivial consequence of the openness of $\mathfrak{M}^*$, Proposition 5.8.2, and the persistence of each $p \in W(\mathcal{E})$ (Proposition 5.4.2). ∎

Given a C^2 parameterization $\eta: B \to \mathfrak{M}$ we can also form the set $B^* = \{b \in B : \eta(b) \text{ is a regular economy}\}$. Of course, by the previous proposi-

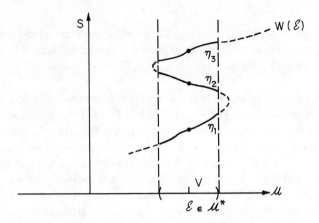

Figure 5.8.2

tion, B^* is open. It is a consequence of Proposition 5.8.13 and Sard's theorem (I.1.1) that if η is regular, then B^* is almost the whole of B. Specifically, the complement of B^* is null (that is, has Lebesgue measure zero) in B. Informally, one says that in a regular parameterization regular economies are generic or that critical economies are rare. Although the subject of genericity will be studied in more detail in Chapter 8, it will be useful to spell out some of the basic results here.

> **5.8.15. Proposition.** *Let B be a C^1 manifold and $\eta\colon B \to \mathfrak{M}$ a regular C^2 parameterization. Then the set B_c of critical economies in B (i.e., $B_c = B \setminus B^*$) is closed and null in B. In particular, regular economies are dense in B.*

Proof. The "closed" part follows from the preceding proposition. For the dense part we could simply quote the tranversality theorem I.2.2, but it will be instructive to give a more direct proof.

Let π be the projection map from the C^1 manifold E to B; that is, $\pi(p, b) = b$. By Sard's theorem (I.1.1) the set of critical values of the smooth map π, denoted B_c, is null in B. We shall show that the critical economies b are precisely the critical values of the projection map π.

By definition of critical value we have that $b \in B_c$ if and only if for some p with $(p, b) \in E$ we have that $T_{(p,b)}E \subset T_p \times T_b B$ does not project onto $T_b B$. Because $T_{(p,b)}E$ and $T_b B$ have the same dimension, this is equivalent to the existence of $v \in T_p$, $v \neq 0$ with $(v, 0) \in T_{(p,b)}E$. But $\partial f(p, b)(T_{(p,b)}E) = 0$ because by definition $f(E) = 0$. Hence,

$$0 = \partial f(p, b)(v, 0) = \partial_p f(p, b)(v).$$

Therefore, rank $\partial_p f(p, b) < \ell - 1$ and b is not a regular economy. Clearly, the converse also holds: If rank $\partial_p f(p, b) < \ell - 1$ we can find $v \neq 0$, $v \in T_p$ with $\partial_p f(p, b)(v) = 0$ and so $(v, 0) \in T_{(p, b)} E$. ∎

The previous proof shows that given a regular parameterization the set of critical economies is easy to visualize. It is formed by those b at which the equilibrium manifold does not project, locally, onto B, that is, at which discontinuous changes of the equilibrium price set are unavoidable. Figures 5.8.1b, 5.8.3, and 5.8.4a illustrate some critical sets of economies. The figures also make clear that the property of a regular parameterization of exhibiting critical economies is very robust. Nonetheless, we shall rest content with knowing there are relatively few of them. In this book we shall not investigate to any extent the structure of critical economies or of the set of critical economies.

A consequence of Proposition 5.8.15 is:

5.8.16. Proposition. *Set* $Q = \mathcal{Q}$. *Then* $\mathfrak{M}^*$ *is dense in* $\mathfrak{M}$.

Proof. Let $\mathcal{E} \in \mathfrak{M}$. Because of Proposition 5.8.15 it suffices to show that there is some regular parameterization $\eta: B \to \mathfrak{M}$ with $\mathcal{E} \in \eta(B)$. That this is the case follows from Examples 5.8.5 (for the finite case) and 5.8.6 (for the continuum case). ∎

We know from Section 5.5 that if $\mathcal{E}$ is regular, then $\#W(\mathcal{E}) < \infty$. Therefore, given a regular parameterization $\eta: B \to \mathfrak{M}$, Proposition 5.8.15 tells us that the set of economies in B with an infinite number of equilibria has measure zero. What about the set of economies with n equilibria or more? Obviously, on a bounded region its measure tends to zero as n goes to infinity. But we should expect more to be true. Intuitively speaking, if B has finite measure, then so will the equilibrium manifold itself. The measure of the part of this manifold over the region with n equilibria must be at least n times the volume of this region. Hence as $n \to \infty$ the measure of the region goes to zero geometrically. This is made formal and rigorous in the next proposition. In the statement λ denotes Lebesgue measure.

5.8.17. Proposition. *Let* $\eta: B \to \mathfrak{M}$ *be a regular parameterization. Form the (open) set* $B_n^* = \{b \in B: \eta(b) \text{ is regular and } \#W(b) \geq n\}$. *Then, for every compact* $K \subset B$, $\sum_{n=1}^{\infty} n\lambda(B_n^* \cap K) < \infty$. *In particular,* $\lim_{n \to \infty} n\lambda(B_n^* \cap K) \to 0$.

Proof. Identify, first, S with an open subset of $R^{\ell-1}$. If $B \subset L$, L a linear space, then E is a manifold in $R^{\ell-1} \times L$. Let π be the perpendicular projection map of $R^{\ell-1} \times L$ onto L.

Let a compact K be given and put it in the interior of another compact $H \subset B$. By 5.8.2, $E \cap (R^{\ell-1} \times H)$ is compact. Because E is a C^1 manifold we can cover $E \cap (R^{\ell-1} \times H)$ by a finite number of open sets $J_h \subset E$, $1 \le h \le m$, such that the closure of each J_h, denoted $\bar{J}_h$, is diffeomorphic to the unit closed ball of L, denoted $\hat{L}$. Let $\xi_h: \bar{J}_h \to L$ be such a diffeomorphism. Of course, $\sum_h \lambda(\xi_h(\bar{J}_h)) = m\lambda(\hat{L}) < \infty$. Take α such that $|\det \pi \circ \partial \xi_h^{-1}(z)| < \alpha$ for all $z \in \hat{L}$ and h.

Fix an n. Then we can find a countable collection of open subsets of B_n^*, $\{B_{nj}^*\}_{j=1}^{\infty}$ with the properties:

(a) $B_{nj}^* \subset \text{Int } H$ for all j.
(b) $B_{nj}^* \cap B_{nj'}^* = \varnothing$ if $j \neq j'$.
(c) $\lambda(B_n^* \setminus \bigcup_j B_{nj}^*) = 0$.
(d) $E \cap (R^{\ell-1} \times B_{nj}^*) = \bigcup_{i=1}^{n} E_{nji}$, where E_{nji} projects diffeomorphically into B_{nj}^*, $E_{nji} \cap E_{nji'} = \varnothing$ if $i \neq i'$, and $E_{nji} \subset J_h$ for some h that we denote $h(nji)$.

The existence of this collection is intuitive enough and can be proved without much difficulty.

Denote $U_{nji} = \xi_{h(nji)}(E_{nji})$. Then $\pi \circ \xi_{h(nji)}^{-1}$ maps U_{nji} diffeomorphically into B_{nj}^*. Henceforth, using E.5.3, $\lambda(B_{nj}^*) = \int_{U_{nji}} |\det \pi \circ \partial \xi_{h(nji)}^{-1}(z)| \, dz \le \alpha\lambda(U_{nji})$.

Because if $(n, j, i) \neq (n', j', i')$, then $E_{nji} \cap E_{n'j'i'} = \varnothing$ we have

$$\sum_{nji} \lambda(U_{nji}) = \sum_{h} \lambda\left(\bigcup_{h(nji)=h} U_{nji}\right) \le m\lambda(\hat{L}) < \infty.$$

Therefore,

$$\infty > \sum_n \left(\sum_j \left[\sum_i \lambda(U_{nji})\right]\right) \ge \frac{1}{\alpha} \sum_n \left[\sum_j n\lambda(B_{nj}^*)\right] = \frac{1}{\alpha} \sum_n [n\lambda(B_n^*)]$$

and we are done. ∎

In most applications we will actually have $B_n^* = \varnothing$ for some n; that is, there is a uniform upper bound on the number of equilibria at regular (and in many cases even nonregular) economies. This is not, however, a general property of regular parameterizations.

If $\bar{\mathcal{E}}$ is regular, the equilibrium map W admits a continuous selection in a neighborhood of $\bar{\mathcal{E}}$, that is, there is an open $V \subset \mathfrak{M}$, $\bar{\mathcal{E}} \in V$, and a continuous map $\xi: V \to S$ such that $\xi(\mathcal{E}) \in W(\mathcal{E})$ for each $\mathcal{E} \in V$ [the value

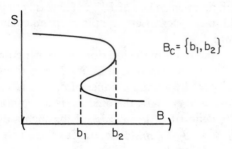

Figure 5.8.3

$\xi(\bar{\mathcal{E}}) \in W(\bar{\mathcal{E}})$ can be predetermined]. This is a consequence of Proposition 5.8.14. It is clear that a continuous selection does not exist on the whole of $\mathfrak{M}$ (consider the typical regular parameterization on a one-dimensional B generating an equilibrium set as in Figure 5.8.3). Interestingly, a continuous selection defined on the whole of the regular set $\mathfrak{M}^*$ does not exist either, but, as the next proposition tells us, it does in a large subset of $\mathfrak{M}^*$. In applications this is sometimes a useful fact to know.

5.8.18. Proposition. *For $Q = \mathcal{C}$ there is an open and dense set $\mathfrak{M}' \subset \mathfrak{M}^*$ and a continuous function $\xi: \mathfrak{M}' \to S$ with $\xi(\mathcal{E}) \in W(\mathcal{E})$ for every $\mathcal{E} \in \mathfrak{M}'$. Similarly, given a regular parameterization $\eta: B \to \mathfrak{M}$ there is an open set $B' \subset B$ with null complement and a continuous function $\xi: B' \to S$ with $\xi(b) \in W(b)$ for each $b \in B'$.*

Proof. We give two quite different proofs. The first is direct and for the second case, whereas the second is purely existential and covers the first.

For the second case we just take a collection of open sets $\{B_m\}_{m=1}^{\infty}$ with the properties (i) $B_m \cap B_{m'} = \varnothing$ if $m \neq m'$; (ii) $\lambda(B \setminus \bigcup_m B_m) = 0$; (iii) for each m there is a continuous $\xi_m: B_m \to S$ with $\xi_m(b) \in W(b)$ for all $b \in B_m$. Such a collection is easily seen to exist. Then, of course, $B' = \bigcup_m B_m$ and $\xi: B' \to S$, given by $\xi(b) = \xi_m(b)$ if $b \in B_m$, satisfy the requirements of the proposition.

The first case can be proved by means of Zorn's lemma (A.7). Let $\mathcal{V}$ be the collection of pairs (V, ξ) such that $V \subset B$ is open and $\xi: V \to S$ is a continuous selection on V. We can define a partial order $\vartriangleright$ on $\mathcal{V}$ by $(V, \xi) \vartriangleright (V', \xi')$ if $V \supset V'$ and $\xi' | V' = \xi$. Clearly, every chain $(V_\alpha, \xi_\alpha)_{\alpha \in J}$ has an upper bound. Just let $V = \bigcup_{\alpha \in J} V_\alpha$ and $\xi: V \to S$ be given by $\xi(b) = \xi_\alpha(b)$ if $b \in V_\alpha$. Therefore, by Zorn's lemma (A.7), there is a maximal element (V, ξ). The set V is open. If we show that it is dense, then we are done. Suppose it is not dense. Then there is an open $U \subset \mathfrak{M}$ with $V \cap U \ne \varnothing$. Because $U \cap \mathfrak{M}^* \ne \varnothing$ (by 5.8.16) there is an open $\hat{U} \subset U$ that admits a continuous selection $\hat{\xi}: \hat{U} \to S$. Then let (V', ξ') be given by $V' = V \cup \hat{U}$ and $\xi' \,|\, V = \xi$, $\xi' \,|\, \hat{U} = \hat{\xi}$. We have $(V', \xi') \in \mathcal{V}$ and $(V', \xi') > (V, \xi)$, which contradicts the maximality of (V, ξ). Hence V is dense. ∎

The central result on the negligibility of critical economies (Proposition 5.8.15) could be phrased as follows: Given a regular parameterization $\eta: B \to \mathfrak{M}$, then, generically, if $B' \subset B$ is zero-dimensional and connected (that is, a point), the restricted parameterization $\eta: B' \to \mathfrak{M}$ is regular. An analogous theory could be worked out for $B' \subset B$ connected and m-dimensional. The case $m = 1$, that is, paths, is especially important and we discuss it in some detail.

> **5.8.19. Definition.** *A path* $\eta: [0, 1] \to \mathfrak{M}$ *is regular if:*
>
> (i) *With* $B = [0, 1]$, η *is a regular* C^2 *parameterization.*
> (ii) $\eta(0)$ *and* $\eta(1)$ *are regular economies (or, in other words,* $\eta: \partial B \to \mathfrak{M}$ *is also regular).*

Regular paths already appeared in Section 5.6. As there, we have:

> **5.8.20. Proposition.** *If* η *is a regular path, then:*
>
> (i) *The equilibrium set* $E = \{(p, b) \in S \times [0, 1]: p \in W(b)\}$ *is, up to diffeomorphism, a finite union of circles and closed segments.*
> (ii) *The set of endpoints of segments coincides with*
>
> $$E \cap (S \times [0, 1]).$$
>
> (iii) *The index of the equilibria at the two endpoints of a segment are the same (resp. different) if and only if the endpoints belong to different (resp. the same) components of the boundary of* $S \times [0, 1]$.
> (iv) *There is a segment with endpoints at different components of the boundary of* $S \times [0, 1]$.

Proof. All this has been shown in Section 5.6, as an application of Lemma 5.6.4, for a special regular path. However, the discussion and proofs were written in such a way that the results are valid for general regular paths. ∎

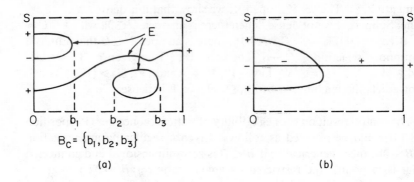

Figure 5.8.4

Figure 5.8.4a illustrates the equilibrium set of a regular path. Figure 5.8.4b is the equilibrium set of a nonregular path. A set E as in Figure 5.8.4b is easily generated; for example, take Example 5.8.5 with $\ell = 2$. Suppose that at $\omega \in \Omega$ we have $\#W(\omega) = 3$. Let x be the Walrasian allocation at the $p \in W(\omega)$ with index $p = -1$. Define then $\eta: [0,1] \to \Omega$ by $\eta(b) = bx + (1-b)\omega$ and note that $W(1) = \{p\}$.

An analog of Proposition 5.8.15 for paths is:

5.8.21. Proposition. *Let B be convex and $\eta: B \to \mathfrak{M}$ a C^3 regular parameterization. Then there is an open set $V \subset B \times B$ with null complement such that for all $(b_1, b_2) \in V$ the path $\alpha \mapsto \eta(\alpha b_1 + (1-\alpha)b_2)$ is regular.*

Proof. Define the C^2 function $F: S \times [0,1] \times B^* \times B^* \to R^\ell$ by

$$F(p, \alpha, b_1, b_2) = f(p, \alpha b_1 + (1-\alpha)b_2).$$

Because η is regular, so is, a fortiori, the function F; that is, whenever $F(p, \alpha, b_1, b_2) = 0$, then rank $F(p, \alpha, b_1, b_2) = \ell - 1$. By identifying, in the usual way, F with its first $(\ell - 1)$ coordinates, we can apply the transversality theorem (I.2.2) to conclude the existence of a set $V \subset B^* \times B^*$ with null complement such that for every $(b_1, b_2) \in V$ we have

$$\text{rank } \partial_{p, \alpha} F(p, \alpha, b_1, b_2) = \ell - 1$$

whenever $F(p, \alpha, b_1, b_2) = 0$. It is in order to apply the transversality theorem that we require that the parameterization η be C^3 [i.e., $f(p, b)$ is

C^2] rather than simply C^2. The openness of V follows from a compactness argument entirely similar to the proof of Proposition 5.8.14. By construction the economies b_1, b_2 are regular. ∎

Finer generic properties of paths will be studied in Chapter 8, Section 8.8.

Given a regular parameterization $\eta: B \to \mathfrak{M}$ the properties of the equilibrium set E discussed so far can all be viewed as consequences of the basic manifold property of E (Proposition 5.8.13). They are, therefore, quite general. More precise properties of E depend on the specific B and η being analyzed. As an example:

5.8.22. Proposition. *Let $B = R_{++}^{\ell n}$ and $\eta: B \to \mathfrak{M}$ be as in Example 5.8.5. Then E is diffeomorphic to $R^{\ell n}$.*

Proof. Let $\hat{E} = \{(p, w, \omega) \in S \times R_{++}^n \times R_{++}^n : w_t = p \cdot \omega_t\}$ for all t. Obviously, E and $\hat{E}$ are diffeomorphic. We carry out the proof for $\hat{E}$. The key observation is that, for each $(p, w) \in S \times R_{++}^n$, $\hat{E}_{(p, w)} = \{\omega : (p, w, \omega) \in \hat{E}\}$ is a convex set of dimension $(\ell-1)(n-1)$. Specifically, $\hat{E}_{(p, w)}$ is the strictly positive solution set to the system of linear equations $p \cdot \omega_t = w_t$, for all t, and $\sum_t \omega_t = \sum_t \varphi_t(p, w_t) \gg 0$.

Define the C^1 function

$$\Psi: S \times R_{++}^n \times R^{(\ell-1)(n-1)} \to S \times R_{++}^n \times R^{\ell n}$$

by $\Psi(p, w, v) = (p, w, \omega(p, w, v))$, where

$$\omega_j(p, w, v) = \frac{w_j}{\sum_t w_t} \sum_t \varphi_t(p, w_t) + \left(v_j, -\frac{1}{p^\ell} \left(\sum_{h=1}^{\ell-1} p^h v_j^h \right) \right)$$

for $j \le n-1$ and

$$\omega_n(p, w, v) = \sum_t \varphi_t(p, w_t) - \sum_{j=1}^{n-1} \omega_j(p, w, v).$$

Then Ψ maps diffeomorphically onto the manifold

$$\{(p, w, \omega) \in S \times R_{++}^n \times R^{\ell n} : p \cdot \omega_t = w_t \text{ for all } i \text{ and } \sum_t \omega_t = \sum_t \varphi(p, w_t)\}.$$

Therefore, it suffices to verify that the set

$$J = \{(p, w, v) \in S \times R_{++}^n \times R^{(\ell-1)(n-1)} : \Psi(p, w, v) \gg 0\}$$

$$\subset S \times R_{++}^n \times R^{(\ell-1)(n-1)}$$

is diffeomorphic to $S \times R_{++}^\ell \times R^{(\ell-1)(n-1)}$ since $\Psi(J) = \hat{E}$.

The set J is open and, for each $(p, w) \in S \times R_{++}^n$, $J_{p,w} = \{v : (p, w, v) \in J\}$ is a nonempty, convex set of dimension $(\ell-1)(n-1)$ that contains the origin in its relative interior. Hence the result follows from H.4.7. ■

The heuristic principle that emerges from examples such as Proposition 5.8.22 is that, given B and a class of η functions, the equilibrium set E (which depends on η) is far from being just any manifold of the right dimension. Usually there will be plenty of additional structure.

Retaining the hypothesis $\mathcal{P} = \mathcal{P}_b$ and setting $Q = \mathcal{Q}$ denote by $\mathfrak{M}_s$ (resp. $\mathfrak{M}_c$) the space of economies with C^2 (resp. continuous) characteristics. The definitions and propositions from 5.8.11 to 5.8.22 have all referred to $\mathfrak{M}_s$. The next proposition puts on record a basic result of the approximation of economies in $\mathfrak{M}_c$ by economies in $\mathfrak{M}_s$.

5.8.23. Proposition. *We have:*

(i)   *$\mathfrak{M}_s$ is dense in $\mathfrak{M}_c$.*

(ii) *Every continuous path $\eta: [0, 1] \to \mathfrak{M}_c$ is the uniform limit of a sequence $\eta_n: [0, 1] \to \mathfrak{M}_s$ of regular C^∞ paths.*

Proof. Note that (i) is a special case of (ii), but because a very simple proof is available, we give it separately.

(i) From 2.8.3 we know that $\mathcal{P}_{sc}^\infty$ is dense in $\mathcal{P}_c^0$. So, given $\mathcal{E} \in \mathfrak{M}_c$, we can first approximate $\mathcal{E}$ by a $\mathcal{E}' \in \mathfrak{M}_c$ having a finite support for its distribution of characteristics (see 5.8.1; of course, if $\mathcal{E}$ is finite, this is a superfluous step), and then approximate each preference relation in $\mathcal{P}$ by one in $\mathcal{P}_{sc}^\infty$.

(ii) The proof shall proceed in three steps. The first contains a technical lemma on the approximation of utility functions. The second approximates the given path η by a sequence of C^∞ paths. Finally, the last step shows how a smooth path can be slightly perturbed to make it regular.

Step 1. In the entire proof, the symbol $u: R_{++}^\ell \to R$ will be reserved for utility functions in the normalized form $u(\lambda e) = \lambda$. Let $\succsim_1, \succsim_2 \in \mathcal{P}$ be represented by, respectively, utility functions $v_1, v_2: R_{++}^\ell \to R$. Take $\alpha \in [0, 1]$ and suppose that the function $v = \alpha v_1 + (1-\alpha) v_2$ represents $\succsim \in \mathcal{P}$. Let $u_1, u_2, u: R_{++}^\ell \to R$ be the normalized utility functions for, respectively, $\succsim_1, \succsim_2$, and $\succsim$. Consider any $z \in R_{++}^\ell$. Suppose, without loss of generality, that $u_1(z) \geq u_2(z)$. Then we claim that $u_1(z) \geq u(z) \geq u_2(z)$. Indeed, by definition we have $v_1(u_1(z)e) = v_1(z)$ and $v_2(u_2(z)e) = v_2(z)$, which implies

$$\alpha v_1(u_1(z)e) + (1-\alpha) v_2(u_2(z)e) = \alpha v_1(z) + (1-\alpha) v_2(z).$$

Also, $v(u(z)e) = v(z)$; that is,

$$\alpha v_1(u(z)e) + (1-\alpha)v_2(u(z)e) = \alpha v_1(z) + (1-\alpha)v_2(z).$$

Therefore,

$$\alpha v_1(u(z)e) + (1-\alpha)v_2(u(z)e) = \alpha v_1(u_1(z)e) + (1-\alpha)v_2(u_2(z)e)$$

which, because v_1 and v_2 are increasing, yields the claim.

The previous claim will be important for the following reason. To avoid repetition we consider only continuum economies. Suppose that $\mathcal{E}_1, \mathcal{E}_2 \in \mathfrak{M}_c$ have the properties (i) $\# \operatorname{supp} \nu_1 = \# \operatorname{supp} \nu_2 = m$, and (ii) for each $(\succsim, \omega) \in \operatorname{supp} \nu_1 \cup \operatorname{supp} \nu_2$, $\succsim$ can be represented by a concave utility function. Take $\{a_1^1, \ldots, a_1^m\} = \operatorname{supp} \nu_1$, $\{a_2^1, \ldots, a_2^m\} = \operatorname{supp} \nu_2$, and let $\theta_i^j > 0$ be the total mass at $1 \le j \le m$ for $i = 1, 2$. Let a third $\mathcal{E} \in \mathfrak{M}_c$ be obtained from $\mathcal{E}_1$ and $\mathcal{E}_2$ as follows. There are m points in $\operatorname{supp} \nu$ and we can list them $\{a^1, \ldots, a^m\}$ in such a way that, for some $0 \le \alpha \le 1$ and all $1 \le j \le m$, $\theta^j = \alpha\theta_1^j + (1-\alpha)\theta_2^j$, $\omega_j = \alpha\omega_1^j + (1-\alpha)\omega_2^j$ and $\succsim^j$ can be represented by $\alpha v_1^j + (1-\alpha)v_2^j$, where v_i^j is a concave utility function for $\succsim_i^j$, $i = 1, 2$. Suppose now that $\mathcal{E}_{1n}, \mathcal{E}_{2n}, \mathcal{E}_n \in \mathfrak{M}_c$ are sequences of economies such that (i) for each n, the triple $\mathcal{E}_{1n}, \mathcal{E}_{2n}, \mathcal{E}_n$ stand in the relation just described (we allow m to depend on n); and (ii) $\mathcal{E}_{1n}, \mathcal{E}_{2n} \to \mathcal{E}$. Then the result of the preceding paragraph together with 2.4.1 allows us to conclude that we also have $\mathcal{E}_n \to \mathcal{E}$.

Step 2. Let $\eta: [0, 1] \to \mathfrak{M}_c$ be the given continuous path. Because in every connected component of $\mathfrak{M}_c$ the number of agents remains unaltered, this is also the case for all the economies in the range of η. We will also preserve cardinality in the approximation. For specificity we take the economies $\eta(t)$ to be continuum economies. For the finite case the construction to follow goes through almost word by word.

Let ρ be a metric on $\mathfrak{M}_c$ (5.8.1). For each n and $1 \le j \le n$, take $\mathcal{E}_{nj} \in \mathfrak{M}_s$ such that $\rho(\mathcal{E}_{nj}, \eta(j/n)) < 1/n$, and agents' preferences are representable by concave utility functions C^∞ on R_{++}^ℓ. Using 2.6.4 and 2.8.1, this can be done as in part (i) of this proposition. For the moment, consider a fixed n. We can also assume that $\# \operatorname{supp} \nu_{nj} = m$ for all $j \le n$. Let $\{a_{nji}, \ldots, a_{njm}\} = \operatorname{supp} \nu_{nj}$ be a listing, θ_{nji} the corresponding weights, and v_{nji} a concave utility function representing $\succsim_{nji}$ and C^∞ on R_{++}^ℓ.

Take a C^∞ function $\alpha: [0, 1] \to [0, 1]$ such that the derivatives of every order vanish at $t = 0, 1$. We construct $\eta_n: [0, 1] \to \mathfrak{M}_s$ by defining $\eta_n(t)$, $j/n \le t \le (j+1)/n$, $0 \le j \le n-1$, to have characteristics $\{a_{n\ell 1}, \ldots, a_{n\ell m}\}$, given by initial endowments

$$\omega_{nti} = \alpha(nt-j)\omega_{n(j+1)i} + [1 - \alpha(nt-j)]\omega_{nji},$$

utility functions

$$v_{nti} = \alpha(nt-j)v_{n(j+1)i} + [1-\alpha(nt-j)]v_{nji},$$

and weights

$$\theta_{nti} = \alpha(nt-j)\theta_{n(j+1)i} + [1-\alpha(nt-j)]\theta_{nji}.$$

It is clear that η_n takes values in $\mathfrak{M}_s$ and yields a C^∞ path (see 2.7.2). To check that $\eta_n \to \eta$ uniformly it suffices to verify that $t_n \to t$ implies $\eta_n(t_n) \to \eta(t)$. This follows from the uniform continuity of η and the conclusion of step 1.

Step 3. The approximation of a C^∞ path η by a regular one is a simple consequence of Proposition 5.8.21. Let $\epsilon > 0$ be small and $B = [0,1] \times (-\epsilon, \epsilon)^\ell$. Construct a regular C^∞ parameterization $\hat{\eta}: B \to R^\ell$ as in Example 5.8.6, namely, $\hat{\eta}(t, z)$ is the economy obtained by adding the vector z to the initial endowments of every agent of the economy $\eta(t)$. We have $\eta(t) = \hat{\eta}(t, 0)$. By Proposition 5.8.21 there are $b_1, b_2 \in B$ arbitrarily close to $(0, 0)$ and $(1, 0)$, respectively, such that $t \to \hat{\eta}(tb_1 + (1-t)b_2)$ is regular (and, of course, C^∞). This path approximates (in the C^∞ sense) the path η as closely as we wish.   ∎

Although this can be proved by more direct means it is, nevertheless, an important implication of Proposition 5.8.23 that the existence results proved for $\mathfrak{M}_s$ will also hold on $\mathfrak{M}_c$. Specifically:

5.8.24. Proposition. *We have:*

(i) $W(\mathcal{E}) \neq \varnothing$ *for all* $\mathcal{E} \in \mathfrak{M}_c$.

(ii) *Given a continuous path* $\eta: [0, 1] \to \mathfrak{M}_c$ *there is a connected component* E' *of the equilibrium set*

$$E = \{(p, b) \in S \times [1, 0]: p \in W(b)\},$$

which projects onto $[0, 1]$; *that is, for every* $b \in [0, 1]$ *there is* $p \in S$ *with* $(p, b) \in E'$.

Proof. (i) Let $\mathcal{E} \in \mathfrak{M}_c$. Then $\mathcal{E}_n \to \mathcal{E}$ for $\mathcal{E}_n \in \mathfrak{M}_s$. By Proposition 5.5.4, $W(\mathcal{E}_n) \neq \varnothing$. Therefore $W(\mathcal{E}) \neq \varnothing$ by 5.8.2.

(ii) Let $\eta_n \to \eta$ uniformly, where η_n is smooth and regular. By Proposition 5.8.20.iv there is a connected, compact subset

$$E'_n \subset E_n = \{(p, t) \in S \times [0, 1]: p \in W(\eta_n(t))\}$$

that projects onto $[0, 1]$. In fact, E'_n can be taken to be diffeomorphic to a segment. Let $E' \subset R^{\ell+1}$ be a Hausdorff distance limit of the sets $\{E'_n\}$; it exists and it is closed and connected (see A.5.1). It is also bounded and therefore compact, which implies that E' must also project onto $[0, 1]$. It only remains to verify that $E' \subset E$, but, again, this is a consequence of Proposition 5.8.2.   ∎

Figure 5.8.5

Part (ii) of Proposition 5.8.24 tells us, for example, that a set E such as the one in Figure 5.8.5 cannot be the equilibrium price set associated with any continuous path $\eta: [0,1] \to \mathfrak{M}_c$.

5.9 Reference notes

This chapter covers a considerable amount of material, and thus references cannot be exhaustive. For an account of the Walrasian model of exchange we simply refer to Debreu (1959), Arrow–Hahn (1971), and the contributions in Arrow–Intriligator (1982). The theory of regular economies was initiated by Debreu (1970). Article-length expositions include Debreu (1976b), E. Dierker (1982), and Smale (1981). For book-length discussions, the very readable text of E. Dierker (1974) is highly recommended.

Section 5.2. For the most part the material of this section is standard in equilibrium theory. See the previous general references. The concept of an economy with a continuum of agents originates in Aumann (1964). A definitive treatment, to which we owe much, is W. Hildenbrand (1974). The first approach to economies with smooth characteristics (Debreu, 1970; Dierker–Dierker, 1972; E. Dierker, 1974; Delbaen, 1971; K. Hildenbrand, 1972) took excess demand functions as primitives. The grounding of the theory on preferences, with results such as 5.2.7, first appeared in H. Dierker (1975a) for the continuum case and in Smale (1974a) for the finite number of agents case.

For a discussion of the boundary property of excess demand functions (5.2.5.v) see Arrow–Hahn (1971) and Debreu (1970). The unit length price normalization and the consideration of the excess demand function as a vector field in the sphere originate, probably, in the study of tâtonnement stability – see Arrow–Hurwicz (1958).

The dual approach to equilibrium theory via the excess wealth or the excess utility map originates in Negishi (1960) and has been pursued by

Mantel (1974), Arrow–Hahn (1971), and many others. I have taken, I believe, the term *excess utility* from Serra (1982).

Section 5.3. The concept of regular economy (5.3.1) is due to Debreu's seminal contribution (1970) that was immediately followed and refined by Smale (1974a) and Dierker–Dierker (1972). I first heard of something like 5.3.7 from Smale in the middle seventies; see also Cheng (1981b).

Section 5.4. As already indicated, the formal consideration of general spaces of economies with smooth preferences originates in H. Dierker (1975a), who also introduced the notion of convergence 5.4.1. Persistency results in the nature of 5.4.2 were proved in increasingly general settings by Debreu (1970), Smale (1974a, c), Dierker–Dierker (1972), Delbaen (1971), K. Hildenbrand (1972, 1974), and H. Dierker (1975a). K. Hildenbrand (1974) introduced into this field the very convenient version of the IFT used in the proof of 5.4.2.

Section 5.5. Proposition 5.5.2 is due to Debreu (1970) and was the initial stimulus for the introduction of the regularity concept. The fulfillment of the index formula by a regular equilibrium price set and the odd number of equilibria corollary was first noticed by E. Dierker (1972). The problem of decomposing arbitrary excess demand function was posed by Sonnenschein (1973, 1974) and solved, in increasing generality, by him, Mantel (1974, 1979), and Debreu (1974). The second part of the section builds on these fundamental contributions. See Mantel (1977) and Shafer–Sonnenschein (1982) for useful surveys. Results 5.5.5 and 5.5.6 were noticed by Diewert (1977). Result 5.5.7 is due to Geanakoplos–Polemarchakis (1980). Except for the homogeneity of degree one utilities of 5.5.8, Propositions 5.5.8, 5.5.9, and 5.5.10 appeared in Mas-Colell (1977b). The key argument after the statement of 5.5.8 is due to Debreu (1974). See also McFadden–Mantel–Mas-Colell–Richter (1974). The proof of 5.5.8 here, which is different from Mas-Colell (1977b), has been modeled closely after Mantel (1979). A resultant parallel to 5.5.8 for excess utility maps has been obtained by Bewley (1980).

Section 5.6. This section has, by design, an entirely mathematical nature. The relevant background and most of its contents can be found in Milnor (1965) and Guillemin–Pollack (1974). See also references for Sections H, I, and J of Chapter 1. There is a close conceptual relation between the material here and the extensive research on practical methods for the computation of fixed points. Scarf (1973) is the classic reference. More recent surveys are Todd (1976) and Scarf (1982). For an early emphasis on the usefulness of homotopy methods and of the adding from extra dimension, see Eaves (1972) and Merrill (1972). The seminal idea of following a solution path by differential equations is due to Kellog–Li–Yorke (1976) and Smale (1976b). In economics Smale (1976b) was fundamental in clarifying the relationship between the combinatorial methods of Scarf (1973), which always converged to a solution, and the more economically motivated, but far from always successful, tâtonnement method. The latter was proposed for Walras (1874), put into a differential equation setting by Samuelson (1947), and developed by Arrow–Hurwicz (1958) and many others. An extensive survey is provided by Hahn (1982).

Section 5.7. For general surveys on uniqueness see Arrow–Hahn (1971, chap. 9) and Kehoe (1985). The treatment here is very much in the spirit of Hicks (1939), except in one respect. As far as possible, we insist on a coordinate-free treatment; that is, a composite is as good as a simple commodity. This is not meant as a criticism of Hicks's approach. We simply follow the modern general equilibrium tradition.

References for the weak axiom and its differential characterization were given in Chapter 2. The concept of monotone map and its differential characterization is standard in nonlinear analysis – see Ortega–Rheinboldt (1970) and Berger (1977). The properties of negative quasi-definite matrices were profusely exploited in Samuelson (1947).

Decomposition formulas similar to 5.7.4 have appeared many times – for example, Arrow–Hahn (1971), Shapiro (1976), Jerison (1982), and Freixas–Mas-Colell (1983). An interesting reference for 5.7.5 is Mitjuschin–Polterovich (1978), where in the case of an homothetic preference relation precise conditions are derived for the monotonicity of the demand map. Example 5.7.6 is due to Hicks (1939) and has been pursued by Gorman (1953). Example 5.7.7 is due to Gale (1960), Eisenberg (1961), and Chipman (1974). The surprising example 5.7.8 is due to Hildenbrand (1983). Example 5.7.9, the gross substitute case, has a long tradition. It originates in Metzler (1945) and has been extensively studied mostly in connection with the theory of tâtonnement stability. See Nikaido (1968) for a very thorough account. Sufficient conditions on preferences yielding gross substitute demand were obtained by Fisher (1972). For $\ell = 3$ gross substitutability implies the weak axiom; see Kehoe–Mas-Colell (1984), but Kehoe (1985) has counterexamples for $\ell \geq 4$. The importance of quasi-dominant diagonal matrices was perceived by McKenzie (1960), who is responsible for its introduction into economics. I learned of the existence argument at the end of the section from J. Greenberg (1977).

See Arrow–Hahn (1971, chap. 10) and Quirk–Saposnik (1968, chap. 6) for surveys of comparative static results, that is, sufficient conditions for interesting restrictions on the displacement of the unique equilibrium with changes in some parameters. This is the next logical step after the study of uniqueness. The available theory, unfortunately, turns out to be quite limited. Section 5.8 considers the dependence of equilibria on parameters, but only at a general, foundational level. Its content stands to the strong restrictions one would like to have as the general properties of regular economies stand to uniqueness.

There are at least two demand aggregation problems that are conceptually distinct from the one studied in Section 5.7 but that are nevertheless intimately connected to it by virtue of the conditions identified as relevant. They all tend to turn up together in the literature. The first studies the "integrability" of aggregate demand, that is, the existence of a "representative" consumer capable of generating it. The key property here is the symmetry of $\partial f(p)$ on $T_{f(p)}$. Note that Examples 5.7.6 and 5.7.7, but not the others, guarantee this. See Jerison (1984) for an account of the state of the art. The second problem studied, among others, by Gorman (1953), Muellbauer (1975, 1976), and Lau (1982), concerns the sufficient conditions for the invariance of aggregate demand to certain redistributions of characteristics – for example, to redistributions of endowments. Deaton–Muellbauer (1980) provide a good background reference for this.

Section 5.8. For the general metric properties of the space of economies with smooth characteristics, see H. Dierker (1975a). The emphasis on the central importance of the equilibrium manifold first appeared in Balasko (1975a) and Smale (1974a). Balasko is responsible for a remarkably deep analysis of the equilibrium manifold in the case where preferences remain fixed and endowments vary. See his thesis (1976) and papers (1975a, 1975b, 1978a, 1978b, 1979b, 1979c, 1980).

Parameterization 5.8.5 in the nonfixed total endowments case was the one used by Debreu and, as indicated, has been extensively studied by Balasko. Something like 5.8.7 has been used by Radner (1979) and Allen (1981) with an interpretation of expected utility. Parameterization 5.8.9 was exploited in Mas-Colell–Neuefeind (1977) for a smoothing-by-aggregation problem.

The approach to regular economies via the study of the projection map from the equilibrium manifold to the space of economies (5.8.13, 5.8.14, 5.8.15) was introduced by Balasko (1975a). Of course, the appeal to Sard's lemma had already been the key technical contribution of the original Debreu article (1970), which also contained, for the parameterization there considered, the persistency and genericity results 5.8.14 and 5.8.15. Propositions 5.8.16 and 5.8.17 are due, respectively, to H. Dierker (1975a) and Balasko (1979c). Result 5.8.18 was motivated by a discussion with R. Anderson. The concept of regular path, its properties, and genericity (5.8.19, 5.8.20, 5.8.21) are practically lifted from Milnor (1965). See also the references in Chapter 8. Proposition 5.8.22 is due to Balasko (1975a), but the proof is in the line of Schecter (1979).

CHAPTER 6

Production economies

6.1 Introduction

In this chapter we study economies with nontrivial production possibilities. The notions of equilibrium and regular equilibrium will be defined and the corresponding index theorem established.

Most of the analysis and results of the previous chapter could be generalized without much difficulty to cover the production case. It would, however, be pointless, not to say dull, to devote this chapter to doing so in detail. Hence, we shall limit ourselves to present the basic concepts and dwell only on those aspects that are specific to the presence of production.

Definitions of production economy, equilibrium, regular equilibrium, and index are presented in Sections 6.2 and 6.3. Section 6.4 is devoted to the special important case of constant returns economies. The index relation for production economies is stated and proved in Section 6.5. Section 6.6. parallels Section 5.7 and spells out the implications of production for the uniqueness of equilibrium. The point will be made that to get the latter the presence of production is helpful and definitely not a complicating factor.

6.2 Production economies

A production economy will be synthetically described by two objects: the production set and the excess demand function. They stand, respectively, for the production and the consumption side of the economy and have to be understood as aggregate entities.

Throughout this chapter the *production set $Y \subset R^\ell$ is closed and convex. It contains $-R_+^\ell$ but no positive vector distinct from the origin.* As in Chapter 3, associated with Y we have some auxiliary concepts:

(i) The *distance function* $\gamma_Y: R^\ell \to R$, defined by

$$\gamma_Y(z) = \tfrac{1}{2} \min_{y \in Y} \|z - y\|^2.$$

(ii) The *projection function* $\pi_Y: R^\ell \to Y$ defined by $\pi_Y(z) \in Y$ and $\|z - \pi_Y(z)\|^2 = 2\gamma_Y(x)$.

(iii) The *normal manifold* $\Gamma_Y = \{(p, y) \in R^\ell \times Y : p \cdot v \le p \cdot y$ for all $v \in Y\}$.

(iv) The *profit function* $\beta_Y: Y^* \to R$ defined by $Y^* = \{p \in R^\ell : p \cdot Y$ is bounded above$\}$ and $\beta_Y(p) = \sup p \cdot Y$.

We refer to Chapter 3 for an analysis of the properties and relationships between these notions.

For the rest of this chapter the production set Y is kept fixed. The subscript Y is dropped, except where this would introduce ambiguity.

The excess demand function is defined analogously to Chapter 5.

6.2.1. Definition. *A Lipschitzian function* $f: S_Y \to R^\ell$, $S_Y = S \cap Y^*$, *qualifies as an excess demand function whenever it satisfies:*

(i) $f(S_Y)$ *is bounded below – that is,* $f(S_Y) > -ke$ *for some* $k \in R$;

(ii) $p \cdot f(p) = \beta(p)$ *for all* $p \in S_Y$, *and*

(iii) *if* $p_n \to p$, $p_n \in S_Y$, *and* $p \notin S$, *that is* $p^j = 0$ *for some j, then* $\|f(p_n)\| \to \infty$.

For the rest of this chapter the excess demand function f is kept fixed.

It is worth emphasizing that the excess demand function cannot in general be specified independently of the production set Y. This is because for any price vector p the demand and supply of a typical consumer depends on profit income and, of course, the latter depends on firms' technologies. Note also that, β being concave, the hypothesis that f is Lipschitzian places no direct restriction on β. In contrast, if f is C^1, then by property (ii) of the previous definition β is also, and, as we know (3.4.3), this has very strong implications for Y.

As it has already been indicated, Y and f are aggregate concepts. A disaggregated presentation of a production economy, which is not required for the purposes of this book, would consist of three ingredients: (i) a collection of firms specified by their production sets (as in, for example, Section 3.3); (ii) a collection of consumers specified by their preferences and endowment vector (as in 5.2); and (iii) a profit distribution rule that determines how every level of profits of every firm is distributed among the different consumers. Clearly, from (i), (ii), or (iii) one could derive corresponding aggregate objects Y and f.

A *production economy ℰ is defined by the pair* (Y, f).

A case of salient interest is when Y *exhibits constant returns to scale;* that is, it is a cone (see 3.2). Then β is identically zero in its domain and, therefore, f satisfies $p \cdot f(p) = 0$ for all $p \in S_Y$. In fact, f is simply the restriction to S_Y of an excess demand function constructed as in the exchange case (see 5.2.4). In turn, the exchange economies of Chapter 5 are simply the particular case of constant returns production economies obtained by having $Y = -R_+^\ell$, that is, by restricting the available techniques to the free disposal of commodities.

6.3 Equilibrium and regular equilibrium

A pair $(p, y) \in S_Y \times Y$ is an equilibrium if demand equals supply and the production vector y maximizes profits. Formally,

> **6.3.1. Definition.** *The pair* $(p, y) \in S_Y \times Y$ *is an equilibrium if:*
>
> (i) $y = f(p)$, *and*
> (ii) $p \cdot y = \beta(p)$.

By part (i), the equilibrium production vector y is uniquely determined by p. Therefore, we can unambiguously refer to equilibrium price vectors. Because $p \cdot f(p) = \beta(p)$ always holds, an equivalent definition is: $p \in S_Y$ *is an equilibrium price vector if and only if* $f(p) \in Y$.

It is of interest to express the equilibrium condition $f(p) \in Y$ as the solution of an equation system. To this effect it is useful to extend the domain of f by letting $f(\lambda p) = f(p)$ for any $p \in S_Y$, $\lambda > 0$. Then we can proceed in a variety of ways. We choose one that we find particularly convenient. Note that $f(p) \in Y$ if and only if, putting $z = p + f(p)$, we have $\pi(z) - f(z - \pi(z)) = 0$; see Figure 6.3.1. Hence, the function $G(z) = f(z - \pi(z))$ is well defined on an open subset of R^ℓ, and whenever the equation system $\pi(z) - G(z) = 0$, $\|z - \pi(z)\| = 1$, is satisfied, the price vector $p = z - \pi(z)$ is an equilibrium.

Let $p \in S_Y$, $y = f(p)$, be an equilibrium. In order to formulate a concept of regularity we need, first of all, the local differentiability of the relevant functions. Thus, we shall require that $\pi(z)$ and the function $G(z) = f(z - \pi(z))$ introduced in the previous paragraph be C^1 at $z = p + y$.

We then have:

> **6.3.2. Proposition.** *If p is an equilibrium and $z = p + f(p)$, then the linear maps $\partial\pi(z)$ and $\partial G(z)$ take values in $T_p = \{v : p \cdot v = 0\}$.*

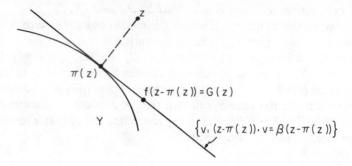

Figure 6.3.1

Proof. For all $v \notin Y$ we have $\frac{1}{2}\|v - G(v)\|^2 - \gamma(v) \geq 0$; see Figure 6.3.1. At $v = z$, $G(z) = \pi(z)$, and so $\frac{1}{2}\|z - G(z)\|^2 - \gamma(z) = 0$. Hence, the function $\frac{1}{2}\|v - G(v)\|^2 - \gamma(v)$ reaches a minimum at $v = z$, which implies $[z - G(z)] \cdot [I - \partial G(z)] - \partial\gamma(z) = 0$. Because $p = z - \pi(z) = z - G(z)$ and, by 3.4.1, $\partial\gamma(z) = z - \pi(z)$, this reduces to $p \cdot \partial G(z) = 0$, and so the range of $\partial G(z)$ is contained in T_p. For $\partial\pi(z)$ see 3.5.4 and the discussion leading to it. ∎

The definition of regularity is now straightforward. Observe first that $\partial\pi(z)p = \partial G(z)p = 0$ and so $\operatorname{rank}(\partial\pi(z) - \partial G(z)) \leq \ell - 1$.

> **6.3.3. Definition.** *The equilibrium p is regular if, putting $z = p + f(p)$, the linear map $\partial\pi(z) - \partial G(z)$ has rank $\ell - 1$ or, equivalently, takes T_p onto T_p. We define:*
>
> $$\text{index } p = \text{sign} \begin{vmatrix} \partial\pi(z) - \partial G(z) & p \\ -p^T & 0 \end{vmatrix}.$$

To help understanding of the index formula it will be useful to discuss two limiting particular cases.

Let p be an equilibrium and put $z = p + f(p)$. Then index p is the sign of the determinant of the linear map $L = \partial\pi(z) - \partial G(z)$ from T_p to T_p. Because $G(x) = f(x - \pi(x))$, f is Lipschitzian, and $\partial^2\gamma(z) = I - \partial\pi(z)$, we have $\partial G(z)v = 0$ whenever $\partial^2\gamma(z)v = 0$; see G.2.1. Therefore, on $M = \{v \in T_p : \partial^2\gamma(z)v = 0\}$, the map $\partial\pi(z) - \partial G(z)$ equals the identity. As we know from Chapter 3, and as it is intuitive enough, M represents the directions on which Y is flat at $f(p)$. Therefore, *if Y is completely flat at y, that is, if $M = T_p$, then L equals the identity on T_p and so index $p = +1$ irrespectively of the form of the excess demand function at p.*

We now consider the opposite case where at $f(p)$, ∂Y has some curvature in every direction, that is to say, where $\partial^2 \gamma(z)$ maps T_p onto T_p and so $M = \{0\}$. Because $\partial^2 \gamma(z)p = p$ this is equivalent to rank $\partial^2 \gamma(z) = \ell$. In the particular case where ∂Y is a C^2 manifold at Y, Proposition 3.5.4 tells us that rank $\partial^2 \gamma(z) = \ell$ if and only if the Gaussian curvature of ∂Y at y is nonzero. From Proposition 3.5.3 we know that if rank $\partial^2 \gamma(z) = \ell$, then the profit function β is C^2 at p and $\partial^2 \beta(p) = [\partial^2 \gamma(z)]^{-1} - I$. Also, by the definition of G, the linear map $\partial G(z)[\partial^2 \gamma(z)]^{-1}$ must equal $\partial f(p)$. This shows, incidentally, that the latter derivative exists. Therefore,

$$\partial \pi(z) - \partial G(z) = [\partial^2 \beta(p) - \partial f(p)] \partial^2 \gamma(z).$$

Because γ is convex (Proposition 3.4.1), $\partial^2 \gamma(z): T_p \to T_p$ has a positive determinant and so index p equals the sign of the determinant of $\partial^2 \beta(p) - \partial f(p)$ from T_p to T_p, or

$$\text{index } p = \text{sign} \begin{vmatrix} \partial^2 \beta(p) - \partial f(p) & p \\ -p^T & 0 \end{vmatrix}.$$

This makes considerable sense. If we write $\partial^2 \beta(p) - \partial f(p)$ as

$$-\partial(f - \partial\beta)(p)$$

and remember (Proposition 3.4.3) that $\partial\beta(q)$ is precisely the vector in Y that maximizes profits at q, that is, the supply vector at q, we see that $f - \partial\beta$ is the total excess demand function inclusive of production. Thus, index p is simply the sign of the Jacobian determinant at p of the negative of the total excess demand function. This is, of course, what we would expect from the analysis of Chapter 5 if the total excess demand function inclusive of production was well defined and C^1 at equilibrium.

6.4   Regular equilibrium in constant returns economies

The index formula will now be specialized to the particular but important situation where the production set displays constant returns to scale. In this case it is natural and convenient to neglect profit income and let the excess demand f be, as in Chapter 5, a C^1 function defined on the entire S and satisfying $p \cdot f(p) = 0$ for all $p \in S$.

For the rest of this section we consider a *fixed regular equilibrium* p, y *and put* $z = p + y$.

Suppose, first, that Y is a polyhedral cone; that is, Y is generated by a finite collection of activities $\{a_j : j \in J\}$, as in 3.7. The distance function γ is then differentiable at z if and only if y belongs to the relative interior of the cone $Y \cap T_p$. Because p is a regular equilibrium, we are in such a case. However, it shall be convenient to strengthen slightly the concept of regularity in the present context. We say that p is *properly regular* if it is regular and, letting $J(p) = \{j \in J : p \cdot a_j = 0\}$, the collection of activities $\{a_j : j \in J(p)\}$ is linearly independent. Proper regularity implies that y can be written in a unique manner as $y = \sum_{j \in J} \alpha_j a_j$ where $\alpha_j \geq 0$ for all $j \in J$ and $\alpha_j > 0$ if and only if $j \in J(p)$. Thus, at a properly regular equilibrium every basic activity that if used would not make losses is in fact used. A sufficient condition for every regular equilibrium to be automatically properly regular is for the collection of basic activities to be in general position; that is, linearly dependent subsets of basic activities have more than ℓ members.

Let us now go back to the index formula, which we defined in the previous section as the determinant of the linear map $L = \partial \pi(z) - \partial G(z) = I - \partial^2 \gamma(z) - \partial f(p) \partial^2 \gamma(z)$ from T_p to T_p. Let $A(p)$ be the $\ell \times k$ matrix, $k < \ell$, whose columns are the activities with indices in $J(p)$. The space $M = \{v \in T_p : \partial^2 \gamma(z)v = 0\}$ is then the k-dimensional range of $A(p)$ and on it, L equals the identity. Denote by N the orthogonal complement of M on T_p. Because Y is polyhedral, if $v \in N$, then $\pi(z + \epsilon v) = \pi(z)$ for ϵ small and so $\partial \pi(z)v = 0$, $\partial^2 \gamma(z)v = v$. Therefore, L equals $-\partial f(p)$ on N. Summing up: In a coordinate system for T_p contained in $M \cup N$ the linear map $L : T_p \to T_p$ has a matrix representation of the form

$$\begin{bmatrix} & 0 \\ -\partial f(p) & \\ & I \\ & {}_{k \times k} \end{bmatrix}.$$

Hence, the determinant of L equals the $\ell - 1 - k$ leading minor of the above matrix, that is to say, the determinant of $-Q \circ \partial f(p) : N \to N$, where Q is the orthogonal projection on N. Taking B.5.2 into account, we have shown:

6.4.1. Proposition. *Let Y be a polyhedral cone and p a properly regular equilibrium for $\mathcal{E} = (Y, f)$. Then:*

$$\text{index } p = \text{sign} \begin{bmatrix} -\partial f(p) & A(p) & p \\ -A^T(p) & & \\ & \mathbf{0} & \\ -p^T & & \end{bmatrix}.$$

Consider next the case where Y is generated by a finite collection J of generalized activities described by C^2 restriction profit functions $\beta_j : R_{++}^\ell \to R$; that is, $Y = \text{closure}\{\sum_{j \in J} \alpha_j \partial \beta_j(p) : \alpha_j \geq 0, p \in S\}$. See Section 3.7 for more details.

As in the polyhedral case, of which this is a generalization, we say that p is a *properly regular equilibrium* if (i) it is regular; (ii) letting $J(p) = \{j \in J : p \cdot \partial \beta_j(p) = 0\}$, the collection of vectors $\{\partial \beta_j(p) : j \in J(p)\}$ is linearly independent. Put then $f(p) = \sum_{j \in J} \alpha_j \partial \beta_j(p)$, where $\alpha_j \geq 0$ for all $j \in J$ and $\alpha_j = 0$ for $j \notin J(p)$. This can be done in a unique manner. At a properly regular equilibrium we further require (iii) $\alpha_j > 0$ for $j \in J(p)$. If we let $A(p)$ be the $\ell \times k$, $k < \ell$ matrix whose columns are the vectors in $\{\partial \beta_j(p) : j \in J(p)\}$ the generalization of Proposition 6.4.1 is:

6.4.2. Proposition. *Let Y be a cone generated by a finite number of generalized activities $\{\beta_j : j \in J\}$ and p a properly regular equilibrium for $\mathcal{E} = (Y, f)$. Then*

$$\text{index } p = \text{sign} \begin{vmatrix} \sum_{j \in J} \alpha_j \partial^2 \beta_j(p) - \partial f(p) & A(p) & p \\ -A^T(p) & & \\ -p^T & & 0 \end{vmatrix}$$

where $f(p) = \sum_{j \in J} \alpha_j \partial \beta_j(p)$, $\alpha_j \geq 0$.

Proof. Let $M \subset T_p$ be the linear space spanned by $A(p)$ and $N \subset T_p$ be its orthogonal complement; that is $N = \{v \in R^\ell : p \cdot v = 0 \text{ and } A^T(p)v = 0\}$. Denote by $Q : T_p \to T_p$ the perpendicular projection on N.

The matrix $B = \sum_{j \in J} \alpha_j \partial^2 \beta_j(p)$ is positive semidefinite and maps T_p into T_p. Therefore, by B.6.4, the linear map $(I + BQ)$ from T_p to T_p has a positive determinant and so index p equals the sign of the determinant of the linear map $L = [\partial \pi(z) - \partial G(p)](I + BQ)$ from T_p to T_p.

We shall establish that (i) L equals the identity map on M and (ii) L equals $B - \partial f(p)$ on N. By B.5.2 this yields, as in the polyhedral cone case, the desired expression for index p.

For property (i) note that if $v \in M$, then $Qv = 0$ and so

$$Lv = \partial \pi(z)v - \partial G(z)v.$$

The proper regularity of p implies that if ϵ is small, then $\pi(z + \epsilon v) = \pi(z) + \epsilon v$. Hence, $\partial \pi(z)v = v$ and so $\partial G(z)v = \partial f(p)[I - \partial \pi(z)]v = 0$. Therefore, $Lv = v$.

For property (ii) observe that by the proper regularity of p, if q is sufficiently near p and $\alpha_j \beta_j(q) = 0$ for all $j \in J$, then $\sum_{j \in J} \alpha_j \partial \beta_j(q) \in Y$ and q supports Y at $\sum_{j \in J} \alpha_j \partial \beta_j(q)$; that is,

$$\pi(q + \sum_{j \in J} \alpha_j \partial \beta_j(q)) = \sum_{j \in J} \alpha_j \partial \beta_j(q).$$

By differentiation of this latest expression we obtain that if $v \in N$, that is, $\alpha_j \partial \beta_j(p)v = 0$ for all $j \in J$, then $\partial \pi(z)(v + Bv) = Bv$. Taking into account that $Qv = v$ and $\partial G(z) = \partial f(p)[I - \partial \pi(z)]$, this yields

$$Lv = [\partial \pi(z) - \partial G(z)](I + BQ)v$$

$$= \partial \pi(z)(v + Bv) - \partial f(p)(v + Bv - \partial \pi(z)(v + Bv)) = Bv - \partial f(p)v$$

and completes our proof. ∎

The plausibility of the index formula of the previous proposition is easily grasped. Let $j = 1, ..., k$ be the indices in $J(p)$. Then locally the equilibrium price vector p and activity levels $\alpha = (\alpha_1, ..., \alpha_k)$ are the solutions in $S \times R^k$ of the equation system

$$\eta(p, \alpha) = \left(\sum_{j=1}^{k} \alpha_j \partial\beta_j(p) - \partial f(p), -\beta_1(p), ..., -\beta_k(p) \right) = 0.$$

We can see that the expression given for index p is nothing but the sign of the determinant of the linear map $\partial\eta(p, \alpha): T_p \times R^k \to T_p \times R^k$ evaluated at the equilibrium p and α.

We end this section with two observations. The first is that the geometric definition of regularity we gave for exchange economies (Section 5.3) has a corresponding version for constant returns economies. Let Γ_1 be the restriction of the normal manifold Γ to the tangent bundle $TS = \{(p, z): p \in S, p \cdot z = 0\}$; that is, $\Gamma_1 = \{(p, z) \in \Gamma: \|p\| = 1\}$. Then both Γ_1 and Graph f are $\ell - 1$ submanifolds of the $2(\ell - 1)$ manifold TS. Moreover, p is an equilibrium if and only if $p \in (\text{Graph } f) \cap \Gamma_1$. Let p be an equilibrium and suppose that Γ_1 is C^1 at p. Then it is a simple matter to verify that p is a regular equilibrium if and only if Graph f and Γ_1, that is to say, the independently given consumption and production sectors, intersect transversally on TS.

The second observation is that the fact that f and Y are described independently facilitates the analysis of the persistence of regular equilibrium. By using implicit function methods as in the preceding chapter we could show, without difficulty, that if f and Y are perturbed slightly in the sense of 5.4 and 3.8, respectively, then we can find near p a (single) equilibrium price vector for the perturbed economy.

6.5   The index theorem

The index theorem of the previous chapter generalizes without difficulty.

> **6.5.1. Definition.** *The production economy* $\mathcal{E} = (Y, f)$ *is called regular if every equilibrium is regular.*

> **6.5.2. Proposition (index theorem).** *Let $E \subset S$ be the set of equilibrium price vectors of the regular production economy* $\mathcal{E} = (Y, f)$. *Then E is finite and $\sum_{p \in E} \text{index } p = 1$.*

Proof. Although the details may seem a bit technical, the idea of the proof is simple enough. We first show that E is compact and then exhibit (steps 2 to 5) a function $\eta: R^\ell \to R^\ell$ with the following three properties:

(a) $\eta(z) = 0$ if and only if $\|z - \pi(z)\| = 1$ and $\pi(z) = G(z)$.
(b)   If $\eta(z) = 0$, then $\partial\eta(z)$ exists, it is nonsingular, and, letting $p(z) = \|z - \pi(z)\|$, $|\partial\eta(z)| = \text{index } p(z)$.
(c)   For r sufficiently large the function $\eta(z)$ restricted to $S_r^{\ell-1} = \{z : \|z\| = r\}$ points outward.

By J.3.2 the combination of the above three properties with the compactness of E yields the desired result.

Step 1. For any $k > 0$ the set $\hat{Y} = \{y \in Y : y \geq -ke\}$ must be bounded. Indeed, suppose that $y_n \in \hat{Y}$ and $\|y_n\| \to \infty$. Without loss of generality we can assume that $(1/\|y_n\|)y_n \to \bar{y}$. Because Y is closed, convex, and $0 \in Y$ we have $\bar{y} \in Y$. From $\|\bar{y}\| = 1$ and $Y \cap R_+^{\ell} = \{0\}$ we deduce that $\bar{y}^i < 0$ for some i. This contradicts the fact that $y_n^i > -k$ for all n.

From now on we let the k above to be such that $f(S) > -ke$. We show that the equilibrium price set E is compact. If $p_n \in E$, then $f(p_n) \in \hat{Y}$. Because $\hat{Y}$ is compact we can assume, extracting a subsequence from p_n if necessary, that $p_n \to p$, $f(p_n) \to y \in \hat{Y}$, and

$$\beta(p_n) = p_n \cdot f(p_n) \to p \cdot y = \beta(p) < \infty.$$

We should also have $p \in S$. Otherwise, $\|f(p_n)\| \to \infty$, and, eventually, $f(p_n)$ would lie outside $\hat{Y}$. Therefore, $p \in S_Y$ and so, by the continuity of f, $f(p) = y$. Hence, $p \in E$ and we conclude that every sequence $p_n \in E$ has a limit point in E; that is, E is compact.

Incidentally, the boundedness of $\hat{Y}$ implies the existence of $q \gg 0$ and $\bar{y} \gg -ke$, $\bar{y} \in Y$, such that q supports $\hat{Y}$ at $\bar{y}$. Simply, let $\bar{y}$ maximize $\sum_i \ln(y^i - k)$ on the compact set $\hat{Y}$ and take $q^i = 1/(\bar{y}^i - k)$.

Step 2. In this step we argue that we can assume, without loss of generality, that S_Y is compact.

For every $\epsilon > 0$ let $S_\epsilon = \{p \in S : p \geq \epsilon e$ and $p \cdot y = \beta(p)$ for some $y \in Y$ such that $y \geq -2ke\}$. The set S_ϵ is compact and, for ϵ small, nonempty (see final remark of step 1). Also, $S_\epsilon \subset S_Y$. Let $Y_\epsilon = \{y \in R^{\ell} : p \cdot y \leq \beta(p)$ for all $p \in S_\epsilon\}$. The construction of Y_ϵ is illustrated in Figure 6.5.1. Note that if $(1/\|z - \pi(z)\|)[z - \pi(z)] \in S_\epsilon$, then $\pi_{Y_\epsilon}(z) = \pi(z)$.

We claim that if ϵ is small enough, we can replace Y by Y_ϵ without altering π, hence G, on a neighborhood of any equilibrium z. This is quite intuitive and it can be formally proved as follows.

Observe first that $\bigcap_{\epsilon > 0} \{y \in Y_\epsilon : y \geq -ke\} = \hat{Y}$, where k and $\hat{Y}$ are as in step 1. Again as in step 1 we can find a $\delta > 0$ such that if p is an equilibrium for any (Y_ϵ, f) then $p > \delta e$. Given this δ, we can then let ϵ be small enough for us to have $(1/\|\bar{z} - \pi(\bar{z})\|)[\bar{z} - \pi(\bar{z})] > \epsilon e$ whenever $\bar{z} = \bar{p} + f(\bar{p})$ and $\bar{p}$ is an equilibrium for (Y_ϵ, f). This ϵ will do. If z is near enough $\bar{z} = \bar{p} + f(\bar{p})$, where $\bar{p}$ is an equilibrium for (Y_ϵ, f), then $(1/\|z - \pi(z)\|)[z - \pi(z)] \in S_\epsilon$. Hence, $\pi_{Y_\epsilon}(z) = \pi(z)$.

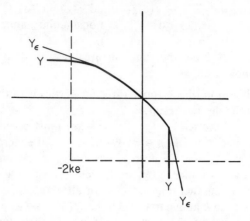

Figure 6.5.1

Summing up: We shall assume from now on that S_Y is compact. One implication of this hypothesis is worth spelling out explicitly: If $z \notin Y$, then $p(z) = (1/\|z - \pi(z)\|)[z - \pi(z)] \gg 0$, that is, $p(z) \in S_Y$.

Step 3. We shall now define a function $\mu: R^\ell \setminus Y \to R^\ell$ that has the properties (a) and (b) described at the beginning of the proof.

For any $z \in R^\ell \setminus Y$ we know (step 2) that $p(z) = (1/\|z - \pi(z)\|)[z - \pi(z)]$ belongs to S_Y, and so the function

$$\mu(z) = z - [f(p(z)) + p(z)] = z - [G(z) + p(z)]$$

is well defined. The construction of μ is illustrated in Figure 6.5.2. From the figure it is clear that property (a) is satisfied. Formally, if $\mu(z) = 0$, then $z - \pi(z) = f(p(z)) - \pi(z) + p(z)$, which, taking into account that $p(z)$ and $f(p(z)) - \pi(z)$ are orthogonal and $p(z)$ is collinear with $z - \pi(z)$, yields $f(p(z)) - \pi(z) = 0$, and $z - \pi(z) = p(z)$. That is to say, $G(z) = \pi(z)$ and $\|z - \pi(z)\| = 1$. The converse, that is, that $G(z) = \pi(z)$ and $\|z - \pi(z)\| = 1$ implies $\mu(z) = 1$, is obvious.

For property (b) note that if $\mu(z) = 0$ then $\partial\mu(z)$ exists because, by the regularity hypothesis, so do $\partial\pi$ and ∂G in a neighborhood of z. If $p(z) \cdot v = 0$, we always have $\partial p(z)v = v - \partial\pi(z)v$. Therefore, if $v \in T_{p(z)}$, then $\partial\mu(z)v = v - \partial p(z)v - \partial G(z)v = \partial\pi(z)v - \partial G(z)v$; that is, on $T_{p(z)}$, $\partial\mu(z)$ coincides with $\partial\pi(z) - \partial G(z)$ and it therefore maps onto $T_{p(z)}$. If v is collinear to $p(z)$, then $\partial\mu(z)v = v$. Hence, $\partial\mu(z)$ is nonsingular and its determinant equals the determinant of $\partial\pi(z) - \partial G(z)$ from $T_{p(z)}$ to $T_{p(z)}$, which is precisely the index of $p(z)$.

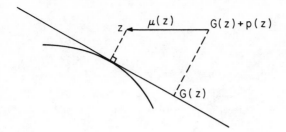

Figure 6.5.2

Step 4. In this step we define a function $\eta: R^\ell \to R^\ell$ such that (i) $\eta(z) = \mu(z)$ whenever $\|z - \pi(z)\| \geq \frac{1}{2}$; and (ii) if $\eta(z) = 0$, then $\|z - \pi(z)\| \geq \frac{1}{2}$. In other words, η modifies and extends μ without either altering a neighborhood of the zeroes of μ nor adding any new zero. Obviously, η will inherit from μ properties (a) and (b).

Let $\alpha: R^\ell \to [0, 1]$ be an arbitrary smooth function such that $\alpha(z) = 1$ if $\|z - \pi(z)\| \geq \frac{1}{2}$ and $\alpha(z) = 0$ if $\|z - \pi(z)\| \leq \frac{1}{4}$. Such a function exists (H.4.2). Pick an arbitrary $\bar{q} \in S_Y$ and denote by $q(z)$ the unit length vector in the direction $\alpha(z)[z - \pi(z)] + [1 - \alpha(z)]\bar{q}$. The vector $q(z)$ is well defined for any $z \in R^\ell$. Also, because the cone spanned by S_Y is convex, we have $q(z) \in S_Y$. Finally, for any $z \in R^\ell$, put $\eta(z) = z - f(q(z)) - q(z)$. Obviously, η satisfies (i). For (ii) notice that because $\|q(z)\| = 1$, the distance from $f(q(z)) + q(z)$ to Y is no less than one for any z. Therefore, we can have $\eta(z) = 0$ only if $\|z - \pi(z)\| \geq 1$.

Step 5. Finally, we verify that η satisfies property (c): $z \cdot \eta(z) > 0$ for any $z \in S_r^{\ell-1}$. For every z, $\eta(z) - z$ belongs to the compact set $f(S_Y) + S_Y$. Pick an $r > 0$ such that $\|\eta(z) - z\| < r$. If $\|z\| > r$, then $\|z \cdot [\eta(z) - z]\| < \|z\|^2$ and so $z \cdot \eta(z) = \|z\|^2 + z \cdot [\eta(z) - z] > 0$, as we wanted. ∎

Figure 6.5.3 illustrates the index theorem in a two-commodity constant returns production economy.

To avoid repetition with Chapter 5 we have given a direct proof of the index theorem. The detailed discussion offered in the exchange case applies with minor adaptations to the production context. There is one aspect, however, where the analysis of the exchange case may lead to a misleadingly simple picture. We refer to the use of path-following methods to find an equilibrium. The general situation, which applies fully to the case of polyhedral production sets, seems to be that many of the natural applications of the path-following idea yield not a smooth but a piecewise smooth path. It is only in the rather special exchange case of Chapter 5

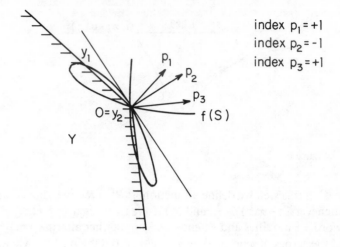

index $p_1 = +1$
index $p_2 = -1$
index $p_3 = +1$

Figure 6.5.3

that there is a single piece and one does not have to worry about the determination of the direction of movement when boundaries between certain subregions (the pieces of differentiability) are reached. The existence of nondifferentiability boundaries is a consequence of the fact that the distance function cannot be assumed, in any generality, to be globally smooth.

6.6   Special classes of economies and the uniqueness of equilibrium

We saw in Chapter 5, section 5.7, that in a regular exchange economy if the excess demand function satisfies the so-called weak axiom of revealed preference, then the equilibrium is unique. This conclusion generalizes straightforwardly to the production case.

> ***6.6.1. Proposition.*** *Suppose that $\mathcal{E} = (Y, f)$ has at least one regular equilibrium and that f satisfies the weak axiom of revealed preference; that is, for all p, p' in the domain of f, $f(p) \neq f(p')$ and $p \cdot f(p') \leq p \cdot f(p)$ imply $p' \cdot f(p) > p' \cdot f(p')$. Then there is a unique equilibrium.*

Proof. We show that the weak axiom implies the convexity of the set of price equilibria. Therefore, if this set is not a single point, there can be no isolated, hence no regular, equilibria.

Let p_1, p_2 be equilibrium price vectors and take any $p_3 = \alpha p_1 + (1-\alpha)p_2$, $0 < \alpha < 1$. By convexity of β, $\beta(p_3) \leq \alpha\beta(p_1) + (1-\alpha)\beta(p_2)$, which, because $\beta(p_3) = p_3 \cdot f(p_3)$, implies that either $p_1 \cdot f(p_3) \leq \beta(p_1)$ or $p_2 \cdot f(p_3) \leq \beta(p_2)$. Say that $p_1 \cdot f(p_3) \leq \beta(p_1) = p_1 \cdot f(p_1)$. If $f(p_3) \neq f(p_1)$, then, by the weak axiom, $p_3 \cdot f(p_1) > p_3 \cdot f(p_3) = \beta(p_3)$, which contradicts $f(p_1) \in Y$. Hence, $f(p_3) = f(p_1) \in Y$ and p_3 is also an equilibrium price vector. ∎

The proof of the previous proposition is direct and does not rely on the index theorem. Appealing to the latter the proposition could also be proved indirectly by showing that any regular equilibrium p has positive index. We illustrate this method by examining the two cases where (i) ∂Y exhibits some curvature at $f(p)$, that is, $\partial^2\beta(p)$ exists, or (ii) p is a properly regular equilibrium of a constant returns economy.

We assume that f satisfies the weak axiom and is C^1 at the regular equilibrium p. Also, p is interior to the domain of definition of f. We can deduce from 2.9.3 that $v \in T_p$ and $\partial f(p)v \in T_p$ imply $v \cdot \partial f(p)v \leq 0$. Therefore, $\partial f(p)$ is negative quasi-semidefinite on $\{v \in T_p : p \cdot \partial f(p)v = 0\}$.

Consider now case (i), that is, $\partial^2\beta(p)$ exists. Then differentiating $0 = p \cdot f(p) - \beta(p)$, we get $0 = f(p) - p \cdot \partial f(p) - \partial\beta(p) = -p \cdot \partial f(p)$. The last equality follows from 3.4.3. Hence, $\partial f(p)$ is negative quasi-semidefinite on T_p and so, remembering that β is convex, $\partial^2\beta(p) + -\partial f(p)$ is positive quasi-semidefinite on T_p. We also know from the last paragraph of 6.3 and from 3.5.4 that

$$\text{index } p = \text{sign} \begin{vmatrix} \partial^2\beta(p) - \partial f(p) & p \\ -p^T & 0 \end{vmatrix}.$$

Because this determinant cannot be negative or null (by hypothesis p is regular) we conclude that index $p = +1$.

As for case (ii), we proceed analogously. Suppose that Y is a cone generated by a finite number of activities and p is properly regular. Remember that in the constant returns case we have convened that f is defined, and therefore satisfies the weak axiom, on the entire S. From $p \cdot f(p) = 0$ we get $p \cdot \partial f(p) + f(p) = 0$. Hence, if $f(p) \cdot v = 0$ then $p \cdot \partial f(p)v = 0$. Therefore, from the weak axiom, we conclude that $\partial f(p)$ is negative quasi-semidefinite on $\{v \in T_p : f(p) \cdot v = 0\}$. If $A(p)$ is the $\ell \times k$ matrix whose columns are the basic activities generating $f(p)$, then $A^T(p)v = 0$ implies $f(p) \cdot v = 0$. Hence, $-\partial f(p)$ is positive quasi-semidefinite on $\{v \in T_p : A^T(p)v = 0\}$. We also know (6.4.1) that

$$\text{index } p = \text{sign} \begin{vmatrix} -f(p) & A(p) & p \\ -A^T(p) & & \\ -p^T & \mathbf{0} & \end{vmatrix}.$$

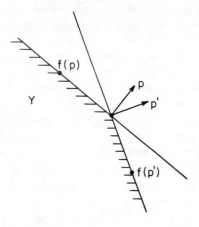

Figure 6.6.1

So we conclude, as before, that index $p = +1$. The generalized activity case is handled in an entirely similar manner.

In the production context the weak axiom property is not only a sufficient condition (with regularity) for the uniqueness of equilibrium but, unless coupled with restrictions on production, also an indispensable one. The following proposition, which is straightforward, and Figure 6.6.1, illustrate this:

> **6.6.2. Proposition.** *Let $f: S \to R^\ell$ be a C^1 excess demand function with $p \cdot f(p) = 0$ for all $p \in S$. If f does not satisfy the weak axiom of revealed preference, then there is a constant returns production set Y such that the economy $\mathcal{E} = (Y, f)$ has several equilibria.*

Proof. This is simple enough. Let $f(p) \neq f(p')$, $p \cdot f(p') \leq p \cdot f(p) = 0$, $p' \cdot f(p) \leq p' \cdot f(p') = 0$. Then we can take

$$Y = \{ y \in R^\ell : p \cdot y \leq 0 \text{ and } p' \cdot y \leq 0 \},$$

and, as in Figure 6.6.1, the price vectors p, p' are distinct equilibria for (Y, f). Observe that if $p \cdot f(p') < p \cdot f(p)$, then p' is in fact a regular equilibrium. Similarly for p if $p' \cdot f(p) < p' \cdot f(p')$.   ∎

Proposition 6.6.2 tells us that the satisfaction of the weak axiom is the most general condition on the consumption side of the economy alone that will guarantee the uniqueness of equilibrium at a regular economy for any production set. Thus, in particular, a condition such as gross substitution that was useful in the exchange case (see 5.7) is now compatible with multiple regular equilibria. As we mentioned in the references for 5.7, the gross substitute property does not imply the weak axiom over the entire domain of the excess demand function.

An important warning is in order. The thrust of Proposition 6.6.2 and the previous paragraph should not be interpreted as asserting that the presence of production makes the sign uniformity of the index, hence the uniqueness of equilibrium, less likely. In fact, rather the contrary is the case. Informally, if p is an equilibrium, then the contribution of the production side to the index tends to make it positive and the more so the flatter is ∂Y at $y = f(p)$. This is of course clear from the general index formula

$$\text{index } p = \text{sign} \begin{vmatrix} \partial \pi(z) - \partial G(z) & p \\ -p^T & 0 \end{vmatrix}, \qquad z = p + f(p),$$

since, as we discussed in Section 6.3, the flatter is ∂Y at y the closer is $\partial \pi(z) - \partial G(z)$ to the identity on T_p. In the limit case where Y is actually flat around y we have

$$\text{index } p = \text{sign} \begin{vmatrix} I & p \\ -p^T & 0 \end{vmatrix} = +1$$

irrespective of the form of f. In the contrasting case where $\partial^2 \beta(p)$ exists, then we found, again in 6.3, that

$$\text{index } p = \text{sign} \begin{vmatrix} \partial^2 \beta(p) - \partial f(p) & p \\ -p^T & 0 \end{vmatrix}.$$

From this expression our claim is seen in a particularly transparent manner. Because $\partial^2 \beta(p)$ is positive semidefinite, if

$$\begin{vmatrix} -\partial f(p) & p \\ -p^T & 0 \end{vmatrix} > 0$$

then

$$\begin{vmatrix} \partial^2 \beta(p) - \partial f(p) & p \\ -p^T & 0 \end{vmatrix} > 0.$$

Also, given $\partial f(p)$, if min $\partial^2 \beta(p)(v, v)$ over $v \in T_p$, $\|v\| = 1$, is large enough, that is, if the curvature of ∂Y at $f(p)$ is small, then $\partial^2 \beta(p) - \partial f(p)$ is positive quasi-semidefinite on T_p and so index $p = +1$.

We can thus assert that in the class of economies we study in this book the source of multiplicity of equilibria lies in the consumption, and not in the production, side of the economy. This can be further clarified by

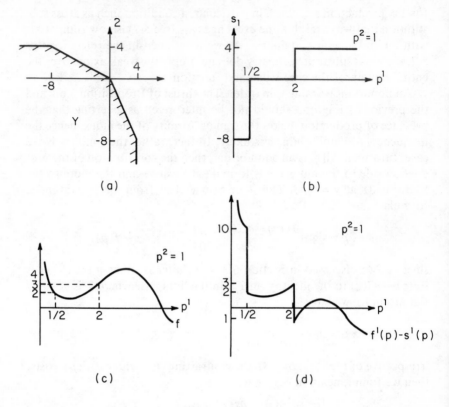

Figure 6.6.2

considering, for every $p \in S_Y$, the supply set $s(p) = \{y \in Y : p \cdot y = \beta(p)\}$. Suppose that $s(\bullet)$ is a function. Then p is an equilibrium if and only if $0 = f(p) - s(p)$. From 5.5 we know that, in general, we cannot make any a priori claim about the local properties of f. We can, however, about $s(p) = \partial \beta(p)$ since we know that, if it exists, $\partial s(p)$ is positive semidefinite. This is, of course, a very strong property. The source of the contrast lies in the wealth effects (see 2.7) that appear in the derivation of f but not of s. Thus, in the total excess demand function $f(p) - s(p)$ the production effects are entirely substitution and, therefore, reinforce the consumption substitution effects. If production effects are very large [production set almost flat at $f(p)$] or, in the limit, of infinite magnitude [production set flat at $f(p)$ and, therefore, $s(\bullet)$ not a function at p], then the consumption wealth effects will be dominated by them and the net effects will be of the substitution type. For a two-commodity case this is illustrated in

Figure 6.6.2, where we see how whenever $s(p)$ is set valued total excess demand $f(\bullet) - s(\bullet)$ decreases at p.

It follows from the preceding discussion that if $\mathcal{E} = (Y, f)$ is a constant returns economy with Y generated by a finite number of activities $A = \{a_1, \ldots, a_n\}$, then a sufficient condition for the uniqueness of equilibrium is: *For every equilibrium* p, $A(p) = \{a_j \in A: p \cdot a_j = 0\}$ *is a linearly independent collection of* $\ell - 1$ *activities and* $f(p)$ *belongs to the strict interior of the cone spanned by the columns of* $A(p)$. If the economy $\mathcal{E}$ is such that (i) the collection A is in general position and for every $a_j \in A$, $a_j^h > 0$ for at most one h (no joint production), and (ii) $f^h(p) > 0$ for all $p \in S_Y$ and $h > 1$ (in the relevant region the first is the only commodity supplied as input by the consumption sector), then the above sufficient condition is automatically satisfied. Indeed, if p is an equilibrium then, by (ii), $f^h(p) > 0$ for $h \geq 2$ and so, by (i) the matrix $A(p)$ must have $\ell - 1$ independent columns. Therefore, $\mathcal{E}$ has a unique equilibrium. Let a finite set of activities A satisfying (i) remain fixed. Suppose that f_1, f_2 satisfy (ii) and $0 = f_1(p_1) = f_2(p_2)$. We shall show that $p_1 = p_2$. Assume, a contrario, that this is not so, that is, $p_1 \neq p_2$. Then we can take a smooth function $\eta: S \rightarrow [0, 1]$ with $\eta(p) = 1$ (resp. $= 0$) for p in a neighborhood of p_1 (resp. p_2) and define $f_3(p) = \eta(p)f_1(p) + [1 - \eta(p)]f_2(p)$. The excess demand function f_3 also satisfies (ii). However, $f_3(p_1) = f_3(p_2) = 0$ and we have obtained a contradiction to the uniqueness of equilibrium for (Y, f_3). Therefore, we must have $p_1 = p_2$. Thus, as long as f satisfies (ii) the unique equilibrium price vector p, and consequently the set of basic activities $A(p)$, is independent of f; hence, it is determined by the production technology alone. This is the so-called nonsubstitution theorem.

6.7 Reference notes

The theory of regular production economies has been developed in a variety of ways by Fuchs (1974, 1977), Kehoe (1980, 1982, 1983, 1985), Mas-Colell (1975, 1977a), and Smale (1974c). The treatment of this chapter follows the general approach of Kehoe and Mas-Colell, and it is much indebted to the work of Kehoe. For the generalized activity production model the concept of regularity was presented in Mas-Colell (1975) and the index theorem for the polyhedral case was stated and proved independently by Kehoe (1980) and Mas-Colell (1977a). The more general case as well as the explicit determinant formulas for the index (Proposition 6.4.2) are essentially due to Kehoe (1982). The line of proof of the index theorem (Proposition 6.5.1) is also directly inspired by Kehoe's demonstration (1982), which, in turn, is indebted to Todd (1979). See also McKenzie (1959, 1961). The proof of the index theorem in Mas-Colell

(1977a), which covers the linear activity case, uses the path-following method and is the natural analog of the proof described in 5.6 for the exchange case. For still another, more abstract, approach see Saigal–Simon (1973).

The content of Propositions 6.6.1 and 6.6.2 is well known. An early reference for 6.6.1 is Wald (1951). Proposition 6.6.2 was first pointed out to me by Scarf. For an example of multiple equilibria with a gross substitute demand system see Kehoe (1985). In Kehoe–Mas-Colell (1984) it is shown that at least four commodities are required for such an example. The nonsubstitution theorem is due to Samuelson (1951); see also Arrow (1951).

CHAPTER 7

Exchange economies with many traders

7.1 Introduction

We saw in Chapter 5 that the Walrasian allocations of an economy are optima or, in more descriptive terms, that they exhaust the gains from trade. The converse is, of course, not true. This raises the following question: Among the optima, which further properties characterize Walrasian equilibria? This chapter is devoted to investigating this problem in the context of exchange economies. Under the hypothesis of a continuum of agents we shall obtain a number of important results. In Walrasian theory individual agents optimize with respect to price vectors given independently of their own actions. Hence, the proper reference framework of the theory is one where single agents lack any macroscopic significance. The continuum hypothesis embodies this requirement, and it is thus natural that it should be an essential ingredient of a characterization of equilibria.

In Section 7.2 we shall offer precise definitions for the following three properties of an allocation x:

(i) No group of traders can allocate their initial endowment vector among themselves in a manner unanimously preferred (core property);

(ii) no individual trader would be better off with the net trade of any other trader (anonymity property); and

(iii) individual agents appropriate all the gains from trade they contribute (no-surplus property).

Sections 7.3, 7.5, and 7.6 will consider continuum economies and state sufficient conditions for the Walrasian to be the only optima that satisfy, respectively, the core, anonymity, and no-surplus properties. For the case of the core, Section 7.4 contains an explicit treatment of the approximation theory corresponding to economies with a finite, to be thought as large, number of traders.

263

Throughout this chapter an exchange economy is defined as in Chapter 5, Section 5.2. It is denoted by $\mathcal{E}: I \to \mathcal{Q}$, where I is the generic symbol for a finite indexing set or the interval $[0, 1]$ and $\mathcal{Q}$ is the generic symbol for any of our space of characteristics with continuous, monotone preferences. Remember that among our maintained hypotheses we have that the support of the distribution of characteristics induced by $\mathcal{E}$, denoted supp $\mathcal{E}$, is compact and also that $\int \omega \gg 0$. As a matter of notation we let $\mathcal{Q}_c$ (respectively $\mathcal{Q}^2$, $\mathcal{Q}_{sc}$) have the same meaning as $\mathcal{Q}$ with the property of convexity (resp. differentiability, strict convexity) of preferences added. With I is associated the counting (if I is finite) or Lebesgue (if $I = [0,1]$) measure. The latter is denoted by λ. Subsets and functions with domain I are always taken measurable. When I is finite the integral sign $\int$ does of course reduce to Σ.

7.2   Properties of Walrasian allocations

The exchange economy $\mathcal{E}: I \to \mathcal{Q}$ is kept fixed throughout this section.

The first property we define can be regarded as a strengthening of the notion of weak optimum.

> **7.2.1. Definition.** *The allocation x has the core property (or is a core allocation) if for every nonnull $G \subset I$ it is not possible to find $x': G \to R_+^\ell$ such that $\int_G x' \le \int_G \omega$ and $x'(t) >_t x(t)$ for a.e. $t \in G$.*

If a group such as G does in fact exist, we say that it improves upon x or blocks x. Taking $G = I$, we see that every core allocation is a weak optimum. Remember that under a strict monotonicity hypothesis on preferences the notions of optimum and weak optimum coincide. The optimality property of Walrasian allocations generalizes straightforwardly. Indeed, the proof of the next proposition makes use only of the definitions and the nonnegativity of prices.

> **7.2.2. Proposition.** *Every Walrasian allocation has the core property.*

Proof. Let $p \ge 0$ be a Walrasian price vector and consider a nonnull $G \subset I$. Suppose that $x': G \to R_+^\ell$ is such that $x'(t) >_t x(t)$ for a.e. $t \in G$. Because p is Walrasian we have $p \cdot x'(t) > p \cdot \omega(t)$ for a.e. $t \in G$. Henceforth, $p \cdot (\int_G x') > p \cdot (\int_G \omega)$ and so, $\int_G x' \le \int_G \omega$ is not possible. ∎

In general, the set of core allocations is larger than the set of Walrasian allocations. Thus, in a two-traders economy the core allocations

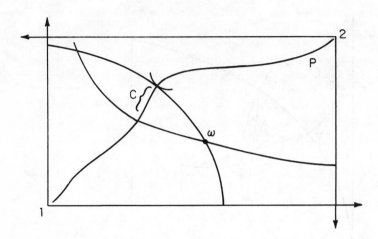

Figure 7.2.1

are the weak optima preferred by the two traders to their initial endowment vectors. In the Edgeworth box of Figure 7.2.1 this corresponds to region C, the so-called *contract curve*.

7.2.3. Definition. *Given an allocation x, $B_x \subset R^\ell$ is the smallest closed set such that $\{t \in I : x(t) - \omega(t) \notin B_x\}$ is null.*

Technically, B_x is the support of the distribution on R^ℓ induced by $x - \omega : I \to R^\ell$. We now introduce a second property:

7.2.4. Definition. *The allocation x is anonymous (or envy-free) if x_t is $\succsim_t$-maximal on $B_x + \omega(t)$ for a.e. $t \in I$.*

In other words, x is envy-free if no trader prefers the net trade of any other trader to his own. The term *anonymous* is suggestive of the following two-step procedure for the practical implementation of x: In the first step every trader is offered the same net trade choice set B_x; in the second step each trader privately chooses a preferred net trade in B_x. An anonymous allocation is one that can be supported in this way. Because all traders face the same price vector, Walrasian allocations are anonymous. Formally,

7.2.5. Proposition. *Every Walrasian allocation is anonymous.*

Proof. Let p be a Walrasian price vector. Each x_t is $\succsim_t$-maximal on $\{y : p \cdot y = p \cdot \omega(t)\}$. But

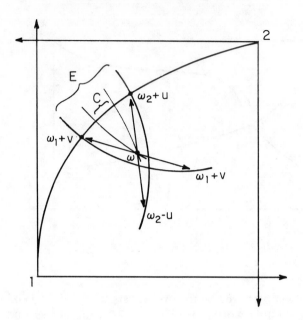

Figure 7.2.2

$$B_x + \omega(t) \subset \{y : p \cdot y = p \cdot \omega(t)\}.$$

Hence the result.   ∎

Walrasian allocations are therefore anonymous optima. In general, however, the set of anonymous optima is larger than the set of Walrasian allocations. For example, if there are only two traders and preferences are strictly convex, the contract curve, that is, the set of core allocations, is a subset of the set of anonymous optima, denoted by E in the Edgeworth box illustration of Figure 7.2.2. This is easy to see. Let $x = (x_1, x_2)$ be an allocation with $x_1 \succsim_1 \omega_1$. We have $\omega_1 = \frac{1}{2}x_1 + \frac{1}{2}(x_2 - \omega_2 + \omega_1)$. Therefore, by the strict convexity of $\succsim_1$, $x_1 \succsim_1 x_2 - \omega_2 + \omega_1$ and so trader 1 does not envy trader 2.

To motivate the definition of the third property, suppose for a moment that our economy is constituted by a finite number of agents with strictly convex preferences. For a Walrasian allocation x with associated price vector p, and any $t \in I$, define $U_t = \sum_{t' \neq t} \{z - \omega(t') : z \succsim_{t'} x(t')\}$. By strict convexity of preferences, $z \succsim_{t'} x(t')$ and $z \neq x(t')$ implies $p \cdot z > p \cdot \omega(t')$. Therefore, $p \cdot v = 0$ and $v \in U_t$ is possible if and only if

$$v = \sum_{t' \neq t} [x(t') - \omega(t')] = -[x(t) - \omega(t)].$$

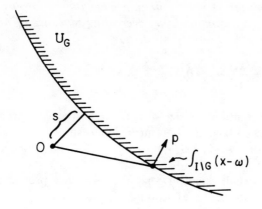

Figure 7.2.3

Hence, $0 \in U_t$ if and only if $x(t) = \omega(t)$. In any case, $0 \notin \text{Int } U_t$ because x has the core property. The economic interpretation of all this is clear. If at the Walrasian allocation x a trader t does actually gain from trade [i.e., $x(t) \neq \omega(t)$], then the rest of the traders also derive a net benefit from his trade in the sense that without it they could not all reach the same level of satisfaction. In other words, in an economy with a finite number of traders, no trader appropriates at a Walrasian allocation all the gains from trade he contributes (if those are positive).

As we shall see in Section 7.6, the situation turns out to be very different in a continuum economy. We need first, however, to give a precise meaning to the idea that a $t \in I$ appropriates all the gains from trade he contributes. Because in a continuum economy every single trader is negligible, some care is needed in the definitioins. *From now on we take $I =$ [0, 1].*

Let x be an allocation and $G \subset I$. Then any element of

$$U_G = \{\textstyle\int_{I \backslash G} (v(t) - \omega(t))\, dt : v(t) \succsim_t x(t)\}$$

represents a vector that if added to the aggregate initial endowments of $I \backslash G$ would allow the traders of $I \backslash G$ to reach by their own means a consumption at least as satisfactory as what they get at x. Therefore, if x is a weak optimum, the magnitude $s(x, G) = \inf_{z \in U_G} \|z\|$ can stand as a rough index of the contribution of G to the welfare of $I \backslash G$; see Figure 7.2.3. For a nonnull G the per trader contribution is measured by $[1/\lambda(G)]s(x, G)$.

The notion of a nonnegligible but arbitrarily small group of traders is captured by the concept of a monotonically decreasing sequence $G_n \subset I$ (that is, $G_n \subset G_{n+1}$) such that $\lambda(G_n) \to 0$.

7.2.6. Definition. *A weak optimum x has the no-surplus property if for every monotonically decreasing sequence of nonnull sets $G_n \subset [0,1]$ with $\lambda(G_n) \to 0$ we have*

$$\lim_n \frac{s(x, G_n)}{\lambda(G_n)} \to 0.$$

In the previous definition the size of a $G \subset I$ has been measured by $\lambda(G)$. We could as well have used an intrinsic measure such as $\|\int_G \omega\|$. Provided that, for some $\epsilon > 0$, $\|\omega(t)\| > \epsilon$ for a.e. $t \in I$, we get an equivalent definition.

In Section 7.6 we shall establish general equivalence properties between Walrasian and no-surplus allocations.

For some of the results of the following sections it is important that any Walrasian allocation x be supported by a single normalized price vector. We know from Chapter 4 that if preferences are C^1 and convex, this will be guaranteed whenever x is linked, that is, whenever $(\int_G x) \cdot (\int_{I \setminus G} x) = 0$ implies that either G or $I \setminus G$ is null. See 4.3.5 and 4.3.6. Although in Chapter 4 we only considered finite economies, it is straightforward to verify that the uniqueness result of 4.3.6 holds also in the continuum case. The next proposition gives a sufficient condition on the economy for the Walrasian allocations to be linked.

7.2.7. Proposition. *Let $\mathcal{E}: I \to \mathcal{Q}_c$ and supp $\mathcal{E}$ be connected. Then every Walrasian allocation x is linked; that is, if $G \subset I$ and $I \setminus G$ are not null, then $(\int_G x) \cdot (\int_{I \setminus G} x) \neq 0$.*

Proof. Let x be Walrasian with associated price vector $p \in S$. Denote by L the set of commodity labels and, for every $J \subset L$, let

$$A(J) = \{a \in \mathcal{Q}_{sc} : \varphi^h(\succsim_a, p, p \cdot \omega_a) > 0 \text{ for some } h \in J\}.$$

By continuity of φ on $\mathcal{P}_{sc} \times (0, \infty)$, $A(J)$ is open. Take any nonnull $G \subset I$ with $I \setminus G$ nonnull and let $J = \{h \in L: \int_G x^h > 0\}$, $J' = \{h \in L: \int_{I \setminus G} x^h > 0\}$. Because supp $\mathcal{E}$ is connected we have $A(J) \cap A(J') \cap \text{supp } \mathcal{E} \neq \varnothing$. Being $A(J) \cap A(J')$ open, this yields the nonnullness of $\{t: \mathcal{E}(t) \in A(J) \cap A(J')\}$, and therefore it implies $(\int_G x) \cdot (\int_{I \setminus G} x) \neq 0$. ∎

The requirement that supp $\mathcal{E}$ be connected is natural for a continuum economy, and it will play an important role in the analysis of Section 7.5 on allocations that are optima and anonymous.

7.3   Core allocations in continuum exchange economies

In this section *we let* $I = [0, 1]$ *and consider a fixed reference exchange economy* $\mathcal{E}: I \to \mathcal{Q}_{sc}$.

We shall first state, prove, and discuss the classical core equivalence theorem, which establishes that, under the continuum hypothesis, only Walrasian allocations have the core property. Then we will proceed to reconsider the theorem and its proof under smoothness hypotheses.

> *7.3.1. Proposition (core equivalence theorem). If the allocation* $x: I \to R_+^\ell$ *has the core property, then it is Walrasian.*

Proof. Let x be the given allocation. A basic construction of core theory, which we will have occasion to encounter repeatedly, is the point-to-set map that assigns to every $t \in I$ the origin and the set of net trades that, from the point of view of t, are at least as desirable as $x(t) - \omega(t)$; that is to say, $V(t) = \{v - \omega(t): v \succsim_t x(t)\} \cup \{0\}$. The key fact is that, by Lyapunov's theorem (L.1.3), the integral $V = \int V(t)\, dt$ is a convex set. Moreover, if $0 \in \text{Int}\, V$, then there is $G \subset I$ and $x': G \to R_+^\ell$ such that $x'(t) \succsim_t x(t)$ for all $t \in G$ and $\int_G x' \ll 0$. Hence G can improve upon x, which contradicts our hypothesis. We conclude that $0 \notin \text{Int}\, V$ and therefore there is $p > 0$ such that $p \cdot z \geq 0$ for all $z \in V$; see F.2.1. By the definition of V this yields that, for a.e. $t \in I$, $v \succsim_t x(t)$ implies $p \cdot v \geq p \cdot \omega(t)$. In particular, $p \cdot x(t) \geq p \cdot \omega(t)$. Because $\int x = \int \omega$ we have $p \cdot x(t) = p \cdot \omega(t)$ for a.e. $t \in I$. Hence, being preferences strictly monotone, x must be Walrasian. ∎

The core equivalence theorem has been refined in a multitude of directions. In particular, much is known about the properties of the groups of agents with the ability to improve upon a given non-Walrasian allocation. Merely as an illustration we record in a proposition that the improving group can be taken to have any predetermined measure or that it can be taken to improve at a Walrasian allocation (i.e., the separate economy can be thought of as Walrasian).

> *7.3.2. Proposition. Suppose that the allocation x is not Walrasian. Then:*
>
> (i)   *For any $r \in (0, 1)$ we can find $G \subset I$ and $x': G \to R_+^\ell$ such that $\lambda(G) = r$, $\int_G (x' - \omega) \leq 0$ and $x'(t) >_t x(t)$ for all $t \in G$.*
>
> (ii) *There is $G \subset I$ and $x': G \to R_+^\ell$ such that $x'(t) >_t x(t)$ for all $t \in G$ and x' is a Walrasian allocation for $\mathcal{E} \mid G$.*

Proof. (i) For each $t \in I$ define $V^*(t) \subset R^{\ell+1}$ by

$$V^*(t) = (\{v - \omega(t): v \gtrsim_t x(t)\} \times \{1\}) \cup \{0\}$$

and let $V^* = \int V^*(t) \, dt \subset R^\ell \times [0,1]$. By L.1.3, V^* is convex. Note that the set V formed in the proof of the previous proposition is the projection of V^* on the first ℓ coordinates. Because $(x(t) - \omega(t), 1) \in V^*(t)$ for all t, we have $(0, 1) \in V^*$. By hypothesis there is $C \subset I$, $x': C \to R^\ell$ such that $x'(t) >_t x(t)$ for a.e. $t \in C$ and $\int_C [x'(t) - \omega(t)] \, dt < 0$. Let $\alpha = \lambda(C)$, $z = \int_C [x'(t) - \omega(t)] \, dt$. Then $(z, \alpha) \in V^*$, and because the segments connecting (z, α) to $(0, 0)$ and to $(0, 1)$ are subsets of V^* we can conclude that, for any $0 < r < 1$, there is $z' < 0$ such that $(z', r) \in V^*$. By the definition of V^* this means there is $G \subset I$ and $x'': G \to R^\ell$ with $\lambda(G) = r$, $x''(t) \gtrsim_t x(t)$ for a.e. $t \in G$ and $\int_G [x''(t) - \omega(t)] \, dt = z' < 0$. Therefore, by the strict monotonicity of preferences, G can improve upon x.

(ii) By hypothesis there is $C \subset I$ and $x': C \to R^\ell$ such that $x'(t) >_t x(t)$ for a.e. $t \in C$ and $z = \int_C [x'(t) - \omega(t)] \, dt \leq 0$. By part (i) we can take C large enough to have $\int_C \omega \gg 0$. Hence, we can assume that $z \ll 0$. We shall see that there is a subset of C with the desired properties. The proof will be a simple application of the standard results on the existence of equilibrium price vectors.

For each $p > 0$ let $C_p = \{t \in C: p \cdot v < p \cdot \omega(t)$ for some $v >_t x'(t)\}$. We have $\lambda(C_p) > 0$. Otherwise, $p \cdot x'(t) \geq p \cdot \omega(t)$ for a.e. $t \in C$, which contradicts $p \cdot z < 0$. Let $f(p, t)$ be the excess demand of $t \in C$ at p. Define $f^*(p, t)$ by:

$$f^*(p,t) = \begin{cases} f(p,t) & \text{if } f(p,t) + \omega(t) >_t x'(t) \\ \{f(p,t), 0\} & \text{if } f(p,t) + \omega(t) \sim_t x'(t) \\ 0 & \text{if } x'(t) >_t f(p,t) + \omega(t). \end{cases}$$

The point-to-set map $p \mapsto f^*(p, t)$ is upper hemicontinuous on S for each $t \in C$. Define $F^*: S \to R_+^\ell$ by $F^*(p) = \int_C f^*(p, t) \, dt$. Then (see E.2.1, E.4.2, L.1.3) F^* is convex valued and has all the properties of an excess demand function including, because $\lambda(C_p) > 0$ for all p, the boundary condition: "If $p_n \to p$, $p_n \in S$, $p \in \partial S$, and $v_n \in F(p_n)$, then $\|v_n\| \to \infty$." Therefore (5.6.2, J.3.5), there is a $p \in S$ with $0 \in F^*(p)$; that is, there is $x'': C \to R^\ell$ such that $\int_C [x''(t) - \omega(t)] \, dt = 0$ and $x''(t) \in f^*(p, t) + \omega(t)$ for a.e. $t \in C$. Let now $G = \{t \in C: f(p, t) + \omega(t) \gtrsim_t x'(t)$ and $x''(t) = f(p, t) + \omega(t)\}$. We have:

(i) $\lambda(G) > 0$ because $C_p \subset G$;
(ii) $\int_G f(p, t) \, dt = 0$ because $x''(t) = \omega(t)$ for $t \notin G$; and
(iii) $f(p, t) + \omega(t) \gtrsim_t x'(t) >_t x(t)$ for a.e. $t \in G$.

Therefore, G and x'' are as we wanted.   ∎

It is of interest to point out that the proof of Propositions 7.3.1 and 7.3.2 do not make use of the convexity hypothesis on preferences.

We now place ourselves in a smooth context, the simplest one being $\mathcal{Q} = \mathcal{O}^2_{b,sc} \times R^\ell_{++}$. Remember that the subscript b means that the consumption set is R^ℓ_{++} and preferences satisfy the boundary condition "$\{v : v \gtrsim z\}$ is R^ℓ-closed for every $z \gg 0$." With this space of characteristics, the core equivalence theorem admits a particularly transparent and elementary proof. Because allocations with the core property are optima we restrict ourselves to those. We are able to exploit the existence of a unique supporting price vector $p \in S$ for an optimum x to show that if x is not Walrasian, then it is always possible to form an improving group by expelling from the economy any small group of traders with high imputed net wealth $p \cdot (x(t) + \omega(t))$.

7.3.3. Proposition. *Let $\mathcal{Q} = \mathcal{O}^2_{b,sc} \times R^\ell_{++}$. Suppose that x is an optimum supported by $p \in S$. If x is not Walrasian, then there is $\epsilon > 0$ and $r > 0$ such that, denoting $C = \{t \in I : p \cdot [x(t) - \omega(t)] \geq r\}$, we have $\lambda(C) > 0$ and for every $G \subset C$ with $0 < \lambda(G) < \epsilon$ the group $I \setminus G$ can improve upon x.*

Proof of Proposition 7.3.3

Denote $z(t) = x(t) - \omega(t)$. For r we can choose any $r > 0$ with

$$\lambda(\{t : p \cdot z(t) \geq r\}) > 0.$$

Because x is not Walrasian the existence of such an r is guaranteed. Choose also a compact $J \subset R^\ell_{++}$ and a $Q \subset I$ with $\lambda(Q) = \alpha > 0$ and $x(t) \in J$ for a.e. $t \in Q$.

We need a lemma that is an obvious enough consequence of the boundedness above of initial endowment vectors.

7.3.4. Lemma. *There is $H > 0$ such that if $t \in C = \{t : p \cdot z(t) \geq r\}$, then $p \cdot z(t) \geq (r/H) \|z(t)\|$.*

Proof. Let $\beta = 1/\min_j p^j$ and ke be an upper bound for $\{\omega(t) : t \in I\}$. Put $H = 2\ell\beta(k\ell + r)$. If $\|z(t)\| \leq H$, there is nothing to prove. Let $\|z(t)\| > H$. Then $|z^j(t)| \geq (1/\ell)\|z(t)\| > H/\ell$ for some j. Because $z^j(t) > -k$ we conclude that $z^j(t) > (1/\ell)\|z(t)\|$. Therefore,

$$p \cdot z(t) > \frac{\|z(t)\|}{\beta\ell} - k\ell = \|z(t)\| \left(\frac{1}{\beta\ell} - \frac{k\ell}{\|z(t)\|} \right).$$

But

$$\frac{1}{\beta\ell} - \frac{k\ell}{\|z(t)\|} > \frac{1}{\beta\ell} - \frac{k\ell}{H} > \frac{1}{\beta\ell} - \frac{1}{2\beta\ell} = \frac{1}{2\beta\ell} > \frac{r}{H}$$

as we wanted.   ∎

Pick now $\rho > 0$ such that if $t \in Q$, $p \cdot v \geq r/H$, $\|v\| = 1$, then $x(t) + \rho v >_t x(t)$. Such a ρ exists by the smoothness of preferences and the compactness of J and supp $\mathcal{E}$. Finally, let $\epsilon > 0$ be such that:

(i) $\epsilon < \min\{\lambda(C), \alpha/2\}$; and

(ii) $\|\int_G z(t) \, dt\| \leq (\alpha/2)\rho$ whenever $\lambda(G) \leq \epsilon$.

To check that ϵ is as desired let $G \subset C$ and $0 < \lambda(G) < \epsilon$. Then $\lambda(Q \setminus G) \geq \alpha - \epsilon \geq \alpha/2$. Denote $\eta = 1/\lambda(Q \setminus G)$ and $z = \int_G z(t) \, dt \neq 0$. We have $\|\eta z\| = \eta \|z\| \leq \rho$. Also,

$$p \cdot z = \int_G p \cdot z(t) \, dt \geq (r/H) \int_G \|z(t)\| \, dt \geq (r/H) \|z\|.$$

Therefore, $x(t) + (\rho/\|z\|)z >_t x(t)$ and so $x(t) + \eta z >_t x(t)$ for every $t \in Q$. Define now $x': I \setminus G \to R^\ell$ by $x'(t) = x(t) - \eta z$ for $t \in Q$ and $x'(t) = x(t)$ for $t \notin Q$. Because $\int_{I \setminus G} x' = \int_{I \setminus G} x + z = \int x - \int_G \omega = \int_{I \setminus G} \omega$ and preferences are strictly monotone, this shows that $I \setminus G$ can improve upon x and concludes the proof. If we could take $Q = I$, then what we have done is simply to eliminate G from the economy and let the remaining members absorb the excess demand vector of G equally. If $Q \subset I$, this absorption is made equally only among the members of Q not in G.

This ends the proof of Proposition 7.3.3.   ∎

The hypothesis $\mathcal{Q} = \mathcal{P}^2_{b,sc} \times R^\ell_{++}$ does, of course, guarantee the existence of a unique $p \in S$ supporting the optimum. But it is much too strong for this. We know from Chapter 4 (4.3.5 and 4.3.6) that with characteristics $\mathcal{Q} = \mathcal{P}^2_{sc} \times R^\ell_+$ an optimum x will have a unique supporting $p \in S$ if it is linked. See also Section 7.2. It is not difficult to verify that Proposition 7.3.3 remains valid under this weaker hypothesis. The existence of a unique supporting price vector cannot, however, be entirely dispensed with. In the next example the conclusion of Proposition 7.3.3 will not be valid for any choice of p.

7.3.5. Example. Let $\ell = 2$. All agents have the same characteristics. Preferences are expressible by the utility function $u(x(t)) = \min\{x^1(t), x^2(t)\}$, and the endowment vector is $\omega = (1,1)$. With these preferences an allocation can be improved upon by a $G \subset I$ if and only if $\int_G (x - \omega) \ll 0$. Consider the allocation x defined by $x(t) = (0,0)$ if $t \leq \frac{1}{2}$, $x(t) = (4,0)$ if $\frac{1}{2} < t \leq \frac{3}{4}$, and $x(t) = (0,4)$ if $\frac{3}{4} < t \leq 1$. It is clearly non-Walrasian and an optimum. Take any $p \in S$ and suppose there is ϵ and r as in the conclusion of 7.3.3. Then the set $\{t \in I : p \cdot [x(t) - \omega(t)] \geq r\}$ has to contain the interval $(\frac{1}{2}, \frac{3}{4}]$ or $(\frac{3}{4}, 1]$ or both. Say that it has $(\frac{3}{4}, 1]$ as a subset and take $\delta = \epsilon/4$. Then $G = [0, 1 - (\epsilon/4)]$ must be able to improve upon x but

$$\int_G (x^1 - \omega^1) = \epsilon/4 > 0,$$

which yields a contradiction. Hence, the conclusion of Proposition 7.3.3 does not hold. The fundamental Proposition 7.3.1 does, of course, apply. With the above x an improving group is, for example,

$$G = [0, \tfrac{1}{2}] \cup [\tfrac{1}{2}, \tfrac{5}{8}] \cup [\tfrac{3}{4}, \tfrac{7}{8}].$$

What happens is that in order to form an improving G the proportions of traders from $[\frac{1}{2}, \frac{3}{4}]$ and $[\frac{3}{4}, 1]$ that are excluded have to be carefully balanced.

7.4 Core allocations in exchange economies with a finite number of traders

From the results of the previous section it stands to reason that there should be some notion of approximation for which the core allocations of economies with a large number of traders are almost Walrasian. However, the analysis in the continuum provides no clue on the manner (mean, uniform, ...) or the rate of convergence. These are matters of importance for the interpretation of any equivalence theorem and justify that some attention be given to the finite and asymptotic analysis. We do this for the core because the theory is more developed than for the other properties but also because doing it once carefully is quite enough to gain a feel for the subject.

The purpose of the section is to illustrate a number of the trade-offs involved in approximation theory. This is done through six propositions. The section is long, and some of the proofs are more involved than one would wish. It will therefore be useful to devote a few lines to discussing the propositions informally. Explicitly or implicitly, each of them proceeds by finding a price system that approximately decentralizes a given core allocation. They differ, among other things, by the meaning of the term *approximately* and also by the possibility of using the supporting prices (remember that a core allocation is an optimum) as approximately decentralizing. Mathematically, every proposition follows from some of the averaging (i.e., convexifying) results reviewed in Section L of Chapter 1. This is not surprising, since the results are approximate versions of the core equivalence theorem in the continuum (7.3.1) that was proved by means of the Lyapunov convexity theorem.

The basic and most general result is Proposition 7.4.1, which is proved simply and elegantly from the Shapley–Folkman theorem. It gives a $1/n$ rate of convergence for an average index of deviation. The price system may not be supporting. In contrast, Proposition 7.4.3 provides a very strong result: The almost decentralizing price system is supporting, and the rate $1/n$ is obtained for a uniform index of deviation. For this, preferences have to be smooth, and the core allocation consumptions must be interior to the consumption set. In other words, we need to assume that the consumption set is R_{++}^ℓ and that the standard boundary condition is satisfied. An averaging result (L.2.1) is still appealed to, but the essence of the proof (Lemma 7.4.8) is remarkably simple and it only uses elementary facts of the calculus. Proposition 7.4.4 is a variation of 7.4.3. It shows how it is possible to trade the strong sense of convergence (uniform) by a weaker one (average) but gain in return the ability to restrict drastically the groups of traders that are permitted to block.

Propositions 7.4.9 and 7.4.12 can be viewed as a group, 7.4.9 being the step toward 7.4.12 summarizing the results that do not essentially depend on smoothness. Proposition 7.4.12 accomplishes the same as 7.4.3 (decentralizing prices are supporting, uniform $1/n$ rate) but for the consumption set is R_+^ℓ. Hence, consumption at the boundary is now permitted. The proof is long and technical. The key argument is in Lemma 7.4.11, which is not difficult to grasp and depends on an averaging result (L.2.3) yielding a finer bound than Shapley–Folkman.

There is a difference between 7.4.1, 7.4.3, 7.4.4 on the one hand and 7.4.9, 7.4.12 on the other. With characteristics restricted to a compact set (i.e., restricted not to be too dissimilar), the first group of results holds for any sufficiently large economy, whereas the second requires the consideration of an increasing sequence of economies with a well-defined continuum limit. The last proposition, 7.4.16, belongs also to this second group. It shows that under the further restriction that the limit economy be regular, one can not only approximately decentralize a core allocation but also claim that there is an exactly decentralized (i.e., Walrasian) allocation in its proximity.

As a matter of definition, an allocation x of an exchange economy $\mathcal{E}: I \to \mathcal{Q}$ is Walrasian if there is a price vector $p \in S$ such that for every $t \in I$ the following two conditions are satisfied:

(i) $p \cdot [x(t) - \omega(t)] = 0$ (budget restriction); and
(ii) $\inf\{p \cdot [v - x(t)]: v \succsim_t x(t)\} = 0$ (preference restriction).

It is therefore natural to measure the departure of a given allocation from being Walrasian by the (mean, maximum, ...) amount by which the best price vector falls short of satisfying (i) and (ii). The next proposition gives the simplest analogue of Proposition 7.3.1, and it is the most basic result of the approximation theory.

7.4.1. Proposition. *Let $\mathcal{E}: I \to \mathcal{P} \times [0, k)^\ell$ be an exchange economy and $\#I = n$. Then there is a constant M (precisely, $M = 2k\ell^{3/2}$) such that for every allocation x with the core property there is a price vector $p \in S$ that satisfies:*

(i) $\quad \dfrac{1}{n}\left(\sum_{t \in I} |p \cdot [x(t) - \omega(t)]| \right) \le \dfrac{M}{n}$

(ii) $\quad \dfrac{1}{n}\left(\sum_{t \in I} |\inf\{p \cdot [v - x(t)]: v \gtrsim_t x(t)\}| \right) \le \dfrac{M}{n}.$

Proof. We shall follow the same steps as in the proof of Proposition 7.3.1 except that the appeal to Lyapunov's theorem will be systematically replaced by the use of its finite analog, the Shapley–Folkman theorem. In a sense, it could be said that 7.4.1 is precisely what one gets if the demonstration of 7.3.1 is applied, mutatis mutandis, to the finite case.

Let $\mathcal{E}$ and x be as in the statement of the proposition. For each $t \in I$, put $V(t) = (\{v: v \gtrsim_t x(t)\} - \{\omega(t)\}) \cup \{0\}$. Let $V = \sum_{t \in I} V(t)$ and denote $\alpha = \sup\{\gamma \in R: -\gamma e \in \operatorname{co} V\} \ge 0$. Of course, the fact that V is bounded below, by $-nke$, implies $\alpha < \infty$ and the closedness of $\operatorname{co} V$ (see E.2.1). Hence, $-\alpha e \in \operatorname{co} V$. See Figure 7.4.1.

We shall now put a bound on α independent of n. The existence of such a bound is plausible because, by the Shapley–Folkman theorem, $-\alpha e$ is not far from V and, because x has the core property, the set V does not intersect $-R^\ell_{++}$. Precisely, by Shapley–Folkman (L.1.1), $-\alpha e = v + y$, where $v \in V$ and $y = y_{t_1} + \cdots + y_{t_\ell}$, $y_{t_i} \in \operatorname{co} V(t_i)$. Hence, $y > -k\ell e$ and so $v = -\alpha e - y \le (k\ell - \alpha)e$. Because $v \ll 0$ cannot happen, we get $\alpha < k\ell$. Therefore, $k\ell$ can serve as our bound.

Let $p > 0$, $\|p\| = 1$, support $\operatorname{co} V$ at $-\alpha e$. We shall show that for this p, (i) and (ii) hold. Denote $z(t) = x(t) - \omega(t)$.

To prove (i), let $I^- = \{t \in I: p \cdot z(t) < 0\}$. Then

$$\sum_{t \in I} |p \cdot z(t)| = -2 \sum_{t \in I^-} p \cdot z(t) = -2p \cdot \left(\sum_{t \in I^-} z(t) \right).$$

Because $\sum_{t \in I^-} z(t) \in V$ we have $p \cdot (\sum_{t \in I^-} z(t)) \ge -\alpha p \cdot e$. Hence,

$$\sum_{t \in I} |p \cdot z(t)| \le 2\alpha p \cdot e \le 2k\ell \|e\| = 2k\ell^{3/2}.$$

To prove (ii), note first that $\inf\{p \cdot [v - x(t)]: v \gtrsim_t x(t)\} \le 0$ for all t. Therefore, it suffices to show that if $v(t) \gtrsim_t x(t)$, then

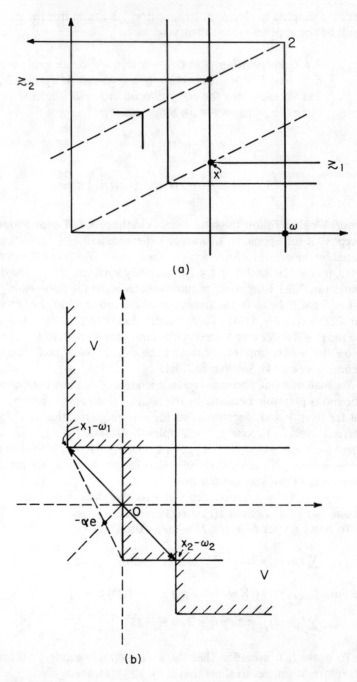

Figure 7.4.1

$$\sum_{t \in I} p \cdot [v(t) - x(t)] \geq -2k\ell^{3/2}.$$

But $\sum_{t \in I} p \cdot [v(t) - x(t)] = \sum_{t \in I} p \cdot [v(t) - \omega(t)]$ and $\sum_{t \in I} [v(t) - \omega(t)] \in V$. Therefore, $\sum_{t \in I} p \cdot [v(t) - x(t)] \geq -\alpha p \cdot e \geq -k\ell^{3/2}$, as we wanted.

Finally, note that if $p > 0$ satisfies (i) and (ii), then by continuity we can take $p \gg 0$. ∎

The next example shows that even with smooth preferences and x linked, we may not be able, in Proposition 7.4.1, to take for p a supporting price vector, that is, with the preference restriction (ii) satisfied exactly. It also shows that the sense of the approximation cannot be improved to the maximum of the individual deviations rather than the mean. The advantage of being able to take a supporting price vector is that this is naturally determined from purely local considerations. A result putting a bound for the maximum deviation is, of course, stronger than one doing so for the average. But the difference is not merely technical; it has economic content. A uniform bound implies the so-called *equal treatment property:* Similar agents get similar consumptions. The converse is also often the case: If the equal treatment property holds, then a bound for the average deviation may yield the automatic existence of a uniform bound (e.g., the proof of 7.4.9 later on).

7.4.2. Example. Let $\ell = 2$. There are three types of agents with preferences represented by, respectively,

$$u_1(x_1) = \tfrac{1}{2} \ln x_1^1 + \tfrac{1}{2} \ln x_1^2, \quad u_2(x_2) = 2x_2^1 + x_2^2, \quad u_3(x_3) = x_3^1 + 2x_3^2.$$

All types have endowment vector $\omega = (1, 2)$. The economy $\mathcal{E}_n$ is formed by taking one agent of type 1, n agents of type 2, and $2n + 1$ agents of type 3. Consider the (linked) allocation x defined by $x(t) = (2, 1), (3, 0), (0, 3)$ if t is, respectively, of type 1, 2, or 3; see Figure 7.4.2a. It is not difficult, and it is a good exercise, to verify that x has the core property (the set V is represented in Figure 7.4.2b). Note that if we take the supporting price vector $\bar{p} = (1, 2)$, then $\sum_{t \in I} |\bar{p} \cdot [x(t) - \omega(t)]| > n$. Also, for the single agent of type 1, there is $\epsilon > 0$ such that, denoting $y = (2, 1)$,

$$|p \cdot (y - \omega)| + |p \cdot (v - y)| \geq \epsilon$$

for all p and v with $u_1(v) \geq u_1(y)$. It is clear that the preferences of this agent can be modified near the boundary so as to make sure that they belong to $\mathcal{P}_{cl}^\infty$.

It turns out, however, that for characteristics in a compact subset of $\mathcal{P}_{b,sc}^2 \times R_{++}$ we can do much better than Proposition 7.4.1. Improvements

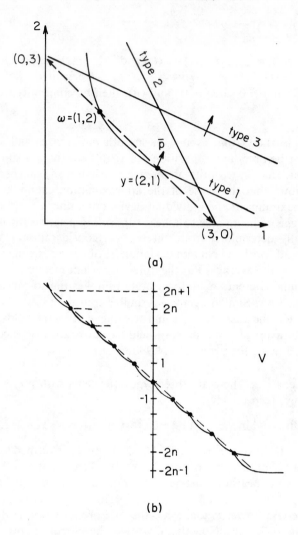

Figure 7.4.2

are possible in the double direction of being able to take for p the supporting price vector and of the conclusion being valid for the maximum of the individual deviations. The interpretation of the compactness of characteristics condition is the usual one: We impose a bound, independent of the number of agents, on how dissimilar individual characteristics can become.

7.4.3. Proposition. *Let $Q \subset \mathcal{P}^2_{b,sc} \times R^{\ell}_{++}$ be compact. Then there is $M > 0$ such that for every economy $\mathcal{E}: I \to Q$, $\#I = n$, and allocation $x: I \to R^{\ell}_{+}$ with the core property, we have*

$$|p \cdot [x(t) - \omega(t)]| \le M/n$$

for all $t \in I$, where $p \in S$ is the supporting price vector for x.

In the setup of the previous proposition, which proof is postponed for a moment, we can obtain a result analogous to Proposition 7.3.3. We impose drastic restrictions on the permissible improving group but are still able to get a M/n approximation bound. We have, however, to go back to the mean, rather than maximum, deviation criterion.

7.4.4. Proposition. *Let $Q \subset \mathcal{P}^2_{b,sc} \times R^{\ell}_{++}$ be compact. Then there is $M > 0$ such that for $\mathcal{E}: I \to Q$, $\#I = n$, and $x: I \to R^{\ell}_{++}$ an optimum allocation with supporting price vector $p \in S$ we have:*

If:

(i) $x(t) \succsim_t \omega(t)$ *for all $t \in I$, and*
(ii) *letting $\bar{t}$ maximize $p \cdot [x(t) - \omega(t)]$, the group $I \setminus \{\bar{t}\}$ cannot improve upon x,*

then

$$\frac{1}{n} \sum_{t \in I} |p \cdot [x(t) - \omega(t)]| \le \frac{M}{n}.$$

In other words, Proposition 7.4.4 says that if x is not almost Walrasian and n is large, then the group formed by all traders, or a single trader, or the group formed by all traders but the one getting the highest transfer of wealth, can improve upon x. The next example shows that condition (i) is required in the proposition; that is, the group formed by single traders cannot be dispensed with. That they be allowable is, however, a very weak requirement.

7.4.5. Example. Let $\ell = 2$. There are three types of traders. Each type has endowment vector $\omega = (1, 1)$. Type 3 has a preference relation representable by $u(z) = \ln z^1 + \ln z^2$. Type 1 (resp. type 2) has a preference relation $\succsim_1$ (resp. $\succsim_2$) in $\mathcal{P}^2_{b,sc}$ with the properties:

(i) For every $n > 2$, the price vector $p = (1, 1)$ supports $\succsim_1$ (resp. $\succsim_2$) at $y_{n1} = (\frac{1}{2}, n - \frac{5}{8})$ [resp. $y_{n2} = (n - \frac{5}{8}, \frac{1}{2})$]; and
(ii) if z is such that $z^2 \le y^2_{n1} - \frac{1}{4}$ (resp. $z^1 \le y^1_{n2} - \frac{1}{4}$), then $y_{n1} \succsim_1 z$ (resp. $y_{n2} \succsim_2 z$).

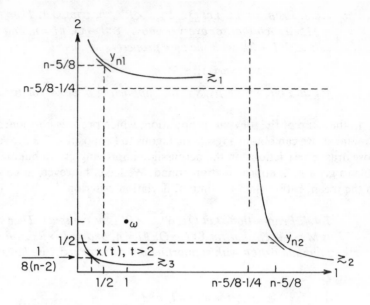

Figure 7.4.3

Such preference relations exist; a particular specimen is represented in Figure 7.4.3.

Define $\mathcal{E}_n$ by letting $\mathcal{E}_n(1)$ be of type 1, $\mathcal{E}_n(2)$ of type 2, and $\mathcal{E}_n(t)$ of type 3 for $2 < t \le n$. Define then x_n by $x_n(1) = y_{n1}$, $x_n(2) = y_{n2}$ and $x(t) = \frac{1}{8}(1/(n-2), 1/(n-2))$ for $t > 2$. Because x_n is supported by $p = (1,1)$ we have an optimum. Evaluating with p, agents 1 and 2 receive a positive transfer of wealth. Consider the group $I \setminus \{1\}$. It has total endowments $(n-1, n-1)$, but in order to guarantee to agent 2 the same level of satisfaction as at y_{n2}, the group would need an amount of the first commodity larger than $n - \frac{5}{8} - \frac{1}{4} > n - 1$. Similarly with group $I \setminus \{2\}$. We have, however, $(1/n) \sum_{t=1}^{n} |p \cdot [x_n(t) - \omega(t)]| > 2$ for $n > 5$. Note that $\omega(t)$ is preferred to $x_n(t)$ for all $t > 2$.

Proofs of Propositions 7.4.3 and 7.4.4

We proceed in three steps. The first contains two preliminary lemmas giving conditions for the uniform boundedness of core allocations. Although the proofs are technical, they have economic content. Indeed, they say that, under the hypotheses, the proportion of the total amount of commodities that a particular agent can receive at an allocation with the core property is of the same order of magnitude as what the agent contributes. Therefore, the proportion will be small if n is large.

The second step contains the central lemma of the demonstration. Its proof is remarkably short and elementary. A good grasp of it will substantially help the understanding of the basic facts of the approximation theory. Finally, step 3 will establish the propositions proper.

Step 1

7.4.6. Lemma. *For any compact $Q \subset \mathcal{P}^2_{b,sc} \times [1/s, s]^\ell$ there is $r > s$ such that if $\mathcal{E}: I \to Q$ and x is an allocation with $x(t) \gtrsim_t \omega(t)$ for all t and $x(\bar{t}) \notin [1/r, r]^\ell$, then the group $I \setminus \{\bar{t}\}$ can improve upon x.*

Proof. Note first that by the compactness of Q there is $\epsilon > 0$ and an integer $r > s$ such that $s/r < \epsilon$ and for any $(\gtrsim, \omega) \in Q$:

(i) if $y \gtrsim \omega$ and $y \leq 3s\ell e$, then $y \geq \epsilon e$; and
(ii) if $\epsilon e \leq y \leq 3s\ell e$, then $y - (s/r)e + e^j > y$ for all j.

It suffices to prove the lemma for $N > 3(r+1)$. Suppose that $\#I > N$ and x satisfies $x(t) \gtrsim_t \omega(t)$ for all t and, for some $\bar{t}$, $x(\bar{t}) \notin [1/r, r]^\ell$, that is, $x^j(\bar{t}) > r$ for some j. Clearly, $\#\{t: \epsilon e \leq x(t) \leq 3s\ell e\} \geq \frac{2}{3}\#I \geq 2(r+1)$ and so we can choose $C \subset I \setminus \{\bar{t}\}$ with $\#C = r$ and $\epsilon e \leq x(t) \leq 3s\ell e$ for each $t \in C$. Define now $x': I \setminus \{\bar{t}\} \to R^\ell$ as follows:

$$x'(t) = x(t) + (1/r)[x(\bar{t}) - \omega(\bar{t})] \gg 0 \quad \text{if } t \in C$$

and $x'(t) = x(t)$ otherwise. Clearly, $\sum_{t \neq \bar{t}} x'(t) = \sum_{t \neq \bar{t}} \omega(t)$ and, because $x'(t) > x(t) - (s/r)e + e^j$, $x'(t) >_t x(t)$ for all $t \in C$. Taking into account the monotonicity of preferences, we conclude that $I \setminus \{\bar{t}\}$ improves upon x. ∎

7.4.7. Lemma. *For any compact $Q \subset \mathcal{P}^2_{b,sc} \times R^\ell_{++}$ there is $r > 0$ such that if $\mathcal{E}: I \to Q$ and x is an optimum with supporting price vector $p \in S$ and such that $x(t) \gtrsim_t \omega(t)$ for all t and $x(t) \notin [1/r, r]^\ell$ for some t then, letting $\bar{t}$ maximize $p \cdot [x(t) - \omega(t)]$, the group $I \setminus \{\bar{t}\}$ can improve upon x.*

Proof. Let $\bar{r}$ be as in Lemma 7.4.6. By the compactness of Q there is $\delta > 0$ such that if $v \leq \bar{r}e$, $(\gtrsim, \omega) \in Q$ and $v \gtrsim \omega$, then $g_\gtrsim(v) > \delta e$. Note that $p \cdot v \leq 2\ell\bar{r}$ and $p > \delta e$ implies $v \leq (2\ell\bar{r}/\delta)e$. Pick $r > 2\ell\bar{r}/\delta$ such that $v \gtrsim \omega$, $v \leq (2\ell\bar{r}/\delta)e$ and $(\gtrsim, \omega) \in Q$ implies $v > (1/r)e$.

Suppose now that x is an optimum supported by a vector $p \in S$, and $x(t) \succsim_t \omega(t)$ for all $t \in I$. Let $\bar{t}$ maximize $p \cdot [x(t) - \omega(t)]$. Suppose that $x(\bar{t}) \le \bar{r}e$. Because $p = g_{\succsim_{\bar{t}}}(x(\bar{t}))$ we have $p > \delta e$. Also, $p \cdot x(\bar{t}) \le \ell\bar{r}$ and, of course, $p \cdot [x(\bar{t}) - \omega(\bar{t})] \le \ell\bar{r}$. Hence, for any $t \in I$,

$$p \cdot x(t) = p \cdot [x(t) - \omega(t)] + p \cdot \omega(t) \le 2\ell\bar{r}$$

and so $(1/r)e \le x(t) \le re$. Therefore, $x(t) \notin [1/r, r]^\ell$ for some t implies $x^j(\bar{t}) > \bar{r}$ for some j in which case, by Lemma 7.4.6, the group $I \setminus \{\bar{t}\}$ can improve upon x. ∎

Step 2

7.4.8. Lemma. *Let $Q \subset \mathcal{P}^2_{b,sc} \times R^\ell_{++}$ be compact and $r > 0$, $k > 0$ given constants. Then there is $M > 0$ such that if x is an optimum for $\mathcal{E}: I \to Q$ satisfying:*

(i)   *$(1/r)e \le x(t) \le re$ for all $t \in I$,*
(ii) *the group $C \subset I$ cannot improve upon x, and*
(iii) *$\|\sum_{t \in C} [x(t) - \omega(t)]\| < k$,*

then

$$\sum_{t \in C} p \cdot [x(t) - \omega(t)] \ge -M/\#C,$$

where p is the supporting price vector for x.

Proof. Because of the smoothness of preferences there is $\theta > 0$ such that if $(1/r)e \le y \le re$ and $(\succsim, \omega) \in Q$, then $\{v: v \succsim y\}$ contains a ball of center $y + \theta g_\succsim(y)$ and radius θ (see H.3). Let k, $\mathcal{E}$, x, C, and p be as in the statement of the lemma. Denote $m = \#C$, $\bar{z} = \sum_{t \in C} [x(t) - \omega(t)]$ and $V(C) = \sum_{t \in C} (\{v: v \succsim_t x(t)\} - \{\omega(t)\})$. By hypothesis:

(i) $V(C)$ contains a ball of center $\bar{z} + m\theta p$ and radius $m\theta$; and
(ii) the origin does not belong to $V(C)$; see Figure 7.4.4.

Therefore, $m^2\theta^2 < \|\bar{z} + m\theta p\|^2 = \|\bar{z}\|^2 + 2m\theta p \cdot \bar{z} + m^2\theta^2$ and so

$$p \cdot \bar{z} \ge -\|\bar{z}\|^2/2m\theta \ge -k^2/m2\theta.$$

We conclude that $M = k^2/2\theta$ will do. ∎

Step 3

We prove first Proposition 7.4.3. With r as in Lemma 7.4.6 and $k = 4\ell^2 r$, let M be as in Lemma 7.4.8. Let x have the core property for $\mathcal{E}: I \to Q$,

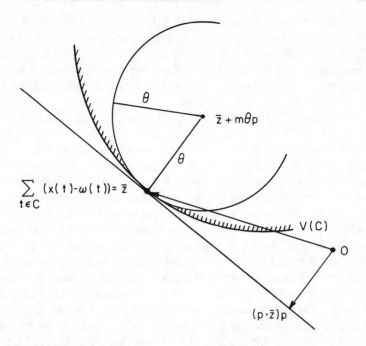

Figure 7.4.4

$\#I = n > 2$. Denote $z = x - \omega$. We shall argue by contradiction. Let p be the supporting price vector and suppose that $|p \cdot z(\bar{t})| > 6M/n$ for some $\bar{t}$. We establish the existence of $C \subset I$ such that $\|\sum_{t \in C} z(t)\| \leq 4\ell^2 r$ and $\sum_{t \in C} p \cdot z(t) < -M/\#C$, thus contradicting Lemma 7.4.8. We distinguish the two cases:

(i) $p \cdot z(\bar{t}) > 6M/n$.

Then $C = I \setminus \{\bar{t}\}$ will obviously do because $\sum_{t \neq \bar{t}} p \cdot z(t) < -6M/n < -M/(n-1)$.

(ii) $p \cdot z(\bar{t}) < -6M/n$.

By Steinitz's theorem (L.2.1) we can find $G \subset I$ such that $n/3 \leq \#G \leq n/2$ and $\|\sum_{t \in G} z(t)\| < 2\ell^2 r$ [remember that, by Lemma 7.4.1, $\|z(t)\| < 2\ell r$ for all t]. If for $C = G$ or $C = I \setminus G$, we have $\sum_{t \in C} p \cdot z(t) < -3M/n$, then because $-3M/n \leq -M/\#C$, we are done. Suppose, therefore, that $|\sum_{t \in G} p \cdot z(t)| \leq 3M/n$. If $\bar{t} \notin G$, we put $C = G \cup \{\bar{t}\}$. Then $\|\sum_{t \in C} z(t)\| \leq 4\ell^2 r$ and $\sum_{t \in C} p \cdot z(t) = \sum_{t \in G} p \cdot z(t) + p \cdot z(\bar{t}) < 3M/n - 6M/n = -3M/n < -M/\#C$. If $\bar{t} \in G$, we put $C = I \setminus G \cup \{\bar{t}\}$ and proceed analogously.

As for the proof of Proposition 7.4.4, let r be as in Lemma 7.4.7 and M as in 7.4.8 for $k = 4\ell r$. As in the preceding proof of 7.4.3, we have that if for the optimum x, $\bar{\imath}$ maximizes $p \cdot z(t)$, then either $I \setminus \{\bar{\imath}\}$ improves upon x or $p \cdot z(\bar{\imath}) \le 6M/n$. In the latter case, putting $I^+ = \{t : p \cdot z(t) \ge 0\}$, we have $\sum_{t \in I} |p \cdot z(t)| = 2 \sum_{t \in I^+} p \cdot z(t) \le 2n \max_{t \in I^+} p \cdot z(t) \le 12M$. Therefore, $12M$ would do as a constant.

This concludes the proofs of Propositions 7.4.3 and 7.4.4.   ∎

The logic of the results so far is to impose restrictions on the permissible characteristics and to obtain as a consequence conclusions valid for any economy that satisfies them. If the economy has a large number of agents, the restrictions on characteristics imply, as a matter of interpretation, that individual agents are almost negligible, whereas the conclusions yield that any allocation with the core property is almost Walrasian. Thus, as claimed, the results provide a finite version of the core equivalence theorem. We shall now become less demanding and adopt an asymptotic point of view; namely, we shall explicitly consider a sequence $\mathcal{E}_n$ *with a well-defined continuum limit* $\mathcal{E}$ and aim at obtaining, via restrictions on $\mathcal{E}_n$ and $\mathcal{E}$, the conclusion that for sufficiently large n the allocations of $\mathcal{E}_n$ with the core property are, in one sense or another, almost Walrasian. For the notion of convergence of economies we are using, see Chapter 5, especially 5.4.1 and Section 5.8. It should be emphasized that the hypothesis $\mathcal{E}_n \to \mathcal{E}$, although natural for the present purposes, adds strength to what has been done so far. It is, indeed, perfectly possible to have $\mathcal{E}_n : I_n \to Q \subset \mathcal{Q}$, $\#I_n = n$, and Q compact without any subsequence of $\mathcal{E}_n$ converging to a limit. Technically, this is because, with ν_n, ν the distribution of characteristics induced by $\mathcal{E}_n$, $\mathcal{E}$, we are defining $\mathcal{E}_n \to \mathcal{E}$ to mean $\nu_n \to \nu$ weakly and supp $\mathcal{E}_n \to$ supp $\mathcal{E}$. It may happen, however, that $\nu_n \to \nu$ (which makes $\mathcal{E}$ the only possible limit of $\mathcal{E}_n$) but no subsequence of supp $\mathcal{E}$ converges to supp $\mathcal{E}$. This will be the case if $\mathcal{E}_n$ is a sequence of economies with isolated characteristics, that is, characteristics for which the fraction of agents having them or similar ones goes to zero. In fact, the isolated characteristic case is the only situation where a sequence $\mathcal{E}_n : Q \to \mathcal{Q}$ with Q compact may fail to have a convergent subsequence.

We shall explore the asymptotic approach in the space of smooth characteristics $\mathcal{Q} = \mathcal{P}^2_{\text{cl}, sc} \times R^\ell_{++}$; that is to say, preferences are smooth in the consumption set $R^\ell_+ \setminus \{0\}$. Remember that whereas under smoothness we were able to improve upon 7.4.1 if the consumption set was R^ℓ_{++} and the boundary condition did hold (Proposition 7.4.3), Example 7.4.2 blocked the way for the consumption set $R^\ell_+ \setminus \{0\}$. To motivate the hope that in the asymptotic context stronger conclusions than Proposition 7.4.1 can be obtained, consider again Example 7.4.2 and observe that the sequence $\mathcal{E}_n$

appearing in it fails to have a limit because the support of the limit distribution of characteristics is formed only by types 2 and 3 whereas the supports of $\mathcal{E}_n$ are formed by types 1, 2 and 3; that is, type 1 is an isolated characteristic for the sequence $\mathcal{E}_n$. This convergence failure turns out to be crucial. Indeed, the next proposition (7.4.9) tells us that if $\mathcal{E}_n$ has a well-defined limit $\mathcal{E}$, then the convergence to zero of the approximation criteria of Proposition 7.4.1 is uniform. An exact analog of 7.4.3 will be obtained immediately after in Proposition 7.4.12. As already mentioned, the proofs of both propositions are rather involved and can be skipped without loss of continuity. Also, to avoid excessive complications we take initial endowments vectors to be strictly positive.

7.4.9. Proposition. *Let* $\mathcal{E}_n: I_n \to \mathcal{P}^2_{cl,sc} \times R^\ell_{++}$, $\#I_n = n$, *be a sequence of exchange economies converging to a continuum economy* $\mathcal{E}$. *Then for every* $\epsilon > 0$ *there is* N *such that if* $n > N$ *and* x *is an allocation for* $\mathcal{E}_n$ *with the core property, we can find a* $p \in S$ *with* $|p \cdot [x(t) - \omega_n(t)]| \leq \epsilon$ *and* $|\inf\{p \cdot [v - x(t)] : v \succsim_{nt} x(t)\}| \leq \epsilon$ *for all* $t \in I_n$.

Proof of Proposition 7.4.9

The first step of the proof is the generalization of the uniform boundedness property of core allocations (4.7.6 and 4.7.7) to the situation where the consumption set is R^ℓ_+.

7.4.10. Lemma. *For any compact* $Q \subset \mathcal{P}^2_{cl,sc} \times [1/k, k]^\ell$ *there is* $r > 0$ *such that if* $\mathcal{E}: I \to Q$ *and* x *is an allocation for* $\mathcal{E}$ *with the core property, then* $x(t) \leq re$ *for all* $t \in I$.

Proof. Although somewhat technical, the idea of the proof is quite simple. One looks for a large constant r such that if an allocation x is not uniformly bounded by re, then an improving group can be formed by excluding from the economy at most ℓ agents. Those are chosen as follows: For each $j \leq \ell$ let t_j maximize $x^j(t)$; if $x^j(t_j) > r$, then t_j is excluded.

We begin by fixing a few constants. Put $\alpha = 1/4(2k^2\ell - 1)$, $s = k\ell/\alpha$. Let $\epsilon > 0$ and $0 < \delta < 1/2k$ be such that if $(\succsim, \omega) \in Q$, $y \leq 2se$, $v \geq -\delta e$, $v \neq 0$, $\max_j v^j \geq (1/\epsilon)|\min_j v^j|$, and $y + v \geq 0$, then $y + v > y$. The constants ϵ and δ exist by the compactness of Q and the strict monotonicity of preferences. We can also assume that both k and $1/\delta$ are integers. Put $m = (\ell + \epsilon)/\epsilon$, $N = k\ell^2/\alpha\delta$, and, finally, $r = mk\ell + Nk$. We shall show that r is as desired.

Let x be an allocation for $\mathcal{E}: I \to \mathcal{P}^2_{\text{cl, sc}} \times [1/k, k]^{\ell}$ with the core property. If $\#I \leq N$, then $x(t) \leq kNe < re$ and we are done. So we assume $\#I = n > N$. Put $L = \{1, \ldots, \ell\}$ and denote $J = \{j \in L: x^j(t) > k\ell$ for some $t\}$, $J' = \{j \in L: x^j(t) > mk\ell$ for some $t\}$. For each $j \in J$ pick a t_j that maximizes $x^j(\bullet)$. Let $y = \sum_{j \in J} [x(t_j) - \omega(t_j)]$ and denote $J'' = \{j \in L: y^j < 0\}$. Notice that $J' \subset J$ and for $j \in J$ [resp. $j \in J'$] we have $y^j > 0$ [resp. $y^j > (m-1)k\ell$]. Hence, $J \cap J'' = \varnothing$. If $J' = \varnothing$, we are done because $mk\ell < r$. We shall prove that if $J' \neq \varnothing$, then $C = I \setminus \bigcup_{j \in J} \{t_j\}$ can improve upon x. For each j, let $C_j = \{t \in C: x^j(t) \geq 1/2k$ and $x(t) \leq se\}$. If $j \notin J$, that is, $x^j(t) \leq k\ell$ for all t, then a simple calculation yields

$$\#\{t \in C: x^j(t) \geq 1/2k\} \geq 3\alpha n.$$

On the other hand, $\#\{t: x^h(t) > s$ for some $h\} < 2\alpha n$. Therefore, $\#C_j \geq \alpha n$ for every $j \in J''$.

Write y in the form $y = y^+ + \sum_{j \in J''} y^j e_j$. Because $J' \neq \varnothing$, $y^+ > 0$. If $J'' = \varnothing$, then obviously C can improve upon x. Suppose that $J'' \neq \varnothing$. For each $j \in J''$ put $v_j = (1/\#J'')y^+ + y^j e_j$. Of course, $\sum_{j \in J''} v_j = y$. Because $\min_h v_j^h \geq -k\ell$ and $\max_h v_j^h \geq [(m-1)/\ell]k\ell$ we have

$$\max_h v_j^h \geq [(m-1)/\ell]|\min_h v_j^h|.$$

By construction $(m-1)/\ell > 1/\epsilon$. Also, $\#C_j \geq \alpha n \geq \alpha N \geq k\ell^2/\delta$ and, therefore, we can take pairwise disjoint sets $G_j \subset C_j$, $j \in J''$, such that $\#G_j \geq k\ell/\delta$. Then, $(1/\#G_j)v_j \geq -\delta e$.

Finally, define $x': C \to R^{\ell}_+$ by letting $x'(t) = x(t) + (1/\#G_j)v_j \geq 0$ if $t \in G_j$ for some $j \in J''$ and $x'(t) = x(t)$ otherwise. Clearly, $\sum_{t \in C} x'(t) = \sum_{t \in C} \omega(t)$ and $x'(t) >_t x(t)$ for $t \in G_j$, $j \in J''$. Therefore, because of the strict monotonicity of preferences, C can improve upon x. ∎

The next step is to establish that under the hypotheses of the proposition, core allocations have approximately the equal treatment property or, in other words, that similar agents get similar consumption vectors. In particular, this implies that as there are no isolated agents, there are no isolated consumptions either.

7.4.11. Lemma. *Let d be a metric on $\mathcal{Q} = \mathcal{P}_{\text{cl, sc}} \to R^{\ell}_{++}$ and $\mathcal{E}_n$: $I_n \to \mathcal{Q}$, $\#I = n$, a sequence of exchange economies converging to a continuum economy $\mathcal{E}$. Then for every $\epsilon > 0$ there are $\delta > 0$ and N such that $\|x(t) - x(t')\| \leq \epsilon$ whenever x is a core allocation for $\mathcal{E}_n$, $n > N$, and $d(\mathcal{E}(t), \mathcal{E}(t')) < \delta$.*

Proof. We argue by contradiction. To this effect suppose the lemma fails for a $\epsilon > 0$.

As usual, we first fix constants. Let r be as in Lemma 7.4.10 for $Q = \bigcup_n \operatorname{supp} \mathcal{E}_n \cup \operatorname{supp} \mathcal{E} \subset \mathcal{P}_{\mathrm{cl},sc}^2 \times [1/k, k]^\ell$. Pick $\alpha > 0$ such that if $a_1, a_2 \in \mathcal{Q}$, $d(a_1, a_2) < \alpha$, $v, v' \le re$, $\|v - v'\| > \epsilon/4$ and some $p \in S$ supports both $\succeq_{a_1}$ and $\succeq_{a_2}$ at, respectively, v and v', then we can assume, relabeling if necessary, that $\|v\| > \alpha$ and $(1 - \alpha)v >_a v'$ for $a = a_1, a_2$. The existence of such a constant follows from the compactness of Q, the bound r, and the strict convexity of preferences. By the same reasons plus the strict monotonicity of preferences, there is $0 < \delta < \alpha/4k$ such that if $v \le re$, $a \in \mathcal{Q}$, $\|v' - v\| < \ell\delta$, then $v' + (\alpha^2/2\ell^2)e_j >_a v$ for any j. Because Q is compact we can choose a finite family of open sets $J_h \subset \mathcal{Q}$, $h = 1, \ldots, m$ covering $\operatorname{supp} \mathcal{E}$ and with the properties that each J_h has radius less than $\frac{1}{2}\delta$ and $J_h \cap \operatorname{supp} \mathcal{E} \ne \varnothing$. The hypothesis $\operatorname{supp} \mathcal{E}_n \to \operatorname{supp} \mathcal{E}$ implies now the existence of some $\mu > 0$ and N_1 such that if $n > N_1$, then $\#\mathcal{E}_n^{-1}(J_h) \ge 2\mu n$ for every h (see E.3 for all this). Finally, given the compact $K = \{z \in R^\ell : -re \le z \le re\}$, we let N_2 be such that the conclusion of the averaging result L.2.3 applies with respect to $\frac{1}{2}\delta$. More precisely, if the vectors $z(t) \in K$, $t \in I_n$, are such that $\sum_{t \in I_n} z(t) \in K$ and $C' \subset I_n$, $\#C' > N_2$, then there is some $C \subset I_n$ with $\|\sum_{t \in C} z(t)\| < \delta$ and $C \cap C' \ne \varnothing$.

By the contradiction hypothesis there is $n > N_1, (1/\mu)N_2$, a core allocation x for $\mathcal{E}_n$ and a J_h such that $\sup\{\|x(t) - x(t')\| : t, t' \in \mathcal{E}_n^{-1}(J_h)\} > \epsilon$. Obviously, there should be some $t_1 \in \mathcal{E}_n^{-1}(J_h)$ such that if we let $C' = \{t \in \mathcal{E}_n^{-1}(J_n) : \|x(t) - x(t_1)\| > \epsilon/2\}$, then $\#C' \ge \mu n > N_2$. Applying L.2.3 to $z(t) = x(t) - \omega_n(t)$, $t \in I_n \setminus \{t_1\}$, we conclude that there is $C \subset I_n \setminus \{t_1\}$ with $\|\sum_{t \in C} z(t)\| < \delta/2$ and $C \cap C' \ne \varnothing$. Summing up: We have succeeded in partitioning I_n into two sets C and $I_n \setminus C$, both with nearly balanced excess demand and such that there are two agents $t_1 \in I_n \setminus C$, $t_2 \in C$ with $d(\mathcal{E}(t_1), \mathcal{E}(t_2)) < \frac{1}{2}\delta$ and $\|x(t_1) - x(t_2)\| > \epsilon/2$.

With n, x, C, t_1, and t_2 as in the previous paragraph we can assume that t_2 is the relatively favored agent; that is, $(1 - \alpha)x(t_2) >_{t_1} x(t_1)$. The idea for obtaining a blocking group is to start with C and replace the relatively favored agent $t_2 \in C$ by $t_1 \notin C$. Because t_1 is willing to give up something for this and the excess demand of C is nearly balanced, it turns out to be possible for t_1 to compensate the other agents and reach an exact balance. Precisely, let $G = C \setminus \{t_2\} \cup \{t_1\}$. Because $\|x(t_2)\| > \alpha$ we can assume $x^1(t_2) > \alpha/\ell$. Denote $L = \{j : x^j(t_2) > \frac{1}{2}\omega_n^j(t_2)\}$ and observe that $(\alpha/2)x^j(t_2) > (\alpha/4)\omega_n^j(t_2) > \alpha/4k > \delta$. Denote

$$L' = \{j : \sum_{t \in C}[x^j(t) - \omega_n^j(t)] + \omega_n^j(t_2) - \omega_n^j(t_1) > 0\}.$$

The indices in L' are the commodities that would be in excess demand if the endowments of t_2 were replaced by the endowments of t_1 but the consumption of t_2 were transferred unaltered to t_1. Those are, therefore, the excess demands that have to be trimmed down to zero. This is not hard to do. For every $j \in L'$ choose $t^j \in C$ with

$$x^j(t^j) - \omega_n^j(t^j) + \omega_n^j(t_2) - \omega_n^j(t_1) > 0.$$

Because $d(\mathcal{E}(t_1), \mathcal{E}(t_2)) < \delta/2$ we can assume $\|\omega_n(t_2) - \omega_n(t_1)\| < \delta/2$. From this and $\omega_n^j(t^j) > 1/k > 2\delta$ we get

$$x^j(t^j) > -\delta/2 + \omega_n^j(t^j) = \tfrac{1}{2}[2\omega_n^j(t^j) - \delta] > \tfrac{1}{2}\omega_n^j(t^j) > 1/2k > \delta.$$

In particular, these inequalities imply that if $j \notin L$, then $t^j \neq t_2$. Finally, define $x': G \to R^\ell$ by $x'(t_1) = (1 - [\alpha/2])x(t_2)$ and

$$x'(t) = x(t) + \sum_{t_j = t,\, j \in L',\, j \notin L} \left(\frac{\alpha^2}{2\ell^2} e_1 - \delta e_j \right).$$

It is now a simple matter to verify that $x'(t) \succsim_t x(t)$ for every $t \in G$ and $\sum_{t \in G} [x'(t) - \omega_n(t)] \leq 0$. Because $x'(t_1) \succ_{t_1} x(t_1)$ and preferences are strictly monotone, the group $G \subset I_n$ can improve upon x, and we have obtained the desired contradiction. ∎

We are now ready for the last step of the proof, which is a straightforward combination of the basic Proposition 7.4.1 with the equal treatment lemma.

Let $\alpha > 0$ be arbitrary, d be a metric on $\mathcal{Q} = \mathcal{P}^2_{\mathrm{cl},\, sc} \times R^\ell_{++}$, and r the bound of Lemma 7.4.10 with respect to $Q = \bigcup_n \operatorname{supp} \mathcal{E}_n \cup \operatorname{supp} \mathcal{E}$. The metric d is taken to have the form of a sum where the constant corresponding to R^ℓ_{++} is the Euclidean metric. It is simply seen that the function $(p, y, a) \mapsto \inf\{p \cdot v : v \succsim_a y\}$ is continuous on

$$\{p \geq 0, \|p\| = 1\} \times [0, r]^\ell \times Q.$$

Therefore, we can find $\epsilon < \alpha/4$ such that if

$$d(a, a') < \epsilon, \quad \|y - y'\| < \epsilon, \quad a, a' \in Q, \quad y, y' \leq re, \quad \text{and} \quad p \in S,$$

then $|\min\{p \cdot v : v \succsim_a y\} - \min\{p \cdot v : v \succsim_{a'} y'\}| < \alpha/4$. With respect to this ϵ let $\delta < \epsilon$ and N_1 be as in Lemma 7.4.11. Because $\operatorname{supp} \mathcal{E}_n \to \operatorname{supp} \mathcal{E}$ we can find $\mu > 0$ and N_2 such that if $n > N_2$, then for any $t \in I_n$, we have $\#\{t' \in I_n : d(\mathcal{E}(t'), \mathcal{E}(t)) < \delta\} > \mu n$. Put $M = 2\ell^{3/2} k$, where k is some bound on initial endowments, and take $N > N_1, N_2$ such that $M/\mu N < \alpha/2$.

Suppose that $n > N$. Let x be an allocation for $\mathcal{E}_n$ with the core property and take $p \in S$ to satisfy the conclusion of Proposition 7.4.1. Then:

(i) For any $t \in I_n$, if $d(\mathcal{E}_n(t'), \mathcal{E}_n(t)) < \delta$, then

$$|p \cdot [x(t) - \omega_n(t)]| \leq |p \cdot [x(t') - \omega_n(t')]| + |p \cdot [x(t) - x(t')]|$$
$$+ |p \cdot [\omega_n(t') - \omega_n(t)]|$$
$$\leq |p \cdot [x(t') - \omega_n(t')]| + \alpha/2.$$

Therefore, for any $t \in I_n$,

$$M \geq \sum_{t' \in I_n} |p \cdot [x(t') - \omega_n(t')]| \geq \mu n \left(|p \cdot [x(t) - \omega_n(t)]| - \frac{\alpha}{2} \right).$$

Hence, $|p \cdot [x(t) - \omega_n(t)]| \leq M/n\mu + \alpha/2 < \alpha$.

(ii) For any $t \in I_n$, let $v_n(t)$ minimize $p \cdot v$ on $\{v : v \succsim_t x(t)\}$. Then, with $\omega_n(t)$ replaced by $v_n(t)$ the proof of the previous paragraph allows us to conclude that $|p \cdot [x(t) - v_n(t)]| < \alpha$ for all $t \in I_n$.

This concludes the proof of Proposition 7.4.9.   ∎

The proof of Proposition 7.4.9 uses the smoothness of preferences only in a minor way. At the cost of a slightly more complex proof of Lemma 7.4.10 it could be seen that the proposition remains true for characteristics in $\mathcal{P}_{\text{cl},sc} \times R_{++}^{\ell}$. However, if we impose the mild condition that the Walrasian allocations of the limit $\mathcal{E}$ be linked (see Proposition 7.2.7), then the full power of the smoothness hypothesis comes into the fore and Proposition 7.4.9 can be strengthened in the usual two directions:

(i)   We can take for p a supporting price vector.
(ii) Once again, we get the bound M/n.

In other words, in the asymptotic framework Proposition 7.4.3 has a natural generalization to the space of characteristics $\mathcal{P}_{\text{cl},sc}^2 \times R_{++}^{\ell}$. Formally:

> **7.4.12. Proposition.** Let $\mathcal{E}_n : I_n \to \mathcal{P}_{\text{cl},sc}^2 \times R_{++}^{\ell}$, $\#I_n = n$, be a sequence of exchange economies converging to a continuum economy $\mathcal{E}$. If all the Walrasian allocations of $\mathcal{E}$ are linked, then there is $M > 0$ such that for all n and allocations x for $\mathcal{E}_n$ with the core property, we have $|p \cdot [x(t) - \omega_n(t)]| \leq M/n$ for all $t \in I_n$, where $p \in S$ is a supporting price vector for x.

Proof of Proposition 7.4.12

The proof will proceed through three lemmas. Although the proof is long, it will not be difficult to recognize that the central lemma, 7.4.14, uses the smoothness of preferences heavily and it amounts to no more than a sophisticated version of 7.4.8.

Denote $L = \{1, \ldots, \ell\}$ and let $J \subset L$ be the generic expression for subsets of L formed by two elements. A collection $\mathcal{J} = \{J_1, \ldots, J_{\ell-1}\}$ will be called *linked* if $L = \bigcup_{h=1}^{\ell-1} J_h$ and it is not possible to partition $\mathcal{J}$ into two nonempty subsets that cover disjoint subsets of L.

> **7.4.13. Lemma.** Under the hypothesis of the proposition there is $\epsilon > 0$, N and a finite number $\mathcal{J}_1, \ldots, \mathcal{J}_m$ of linked collection such

that if x is a core allocation for $\mathcal{E}_n$, $n > N$, then for some $\mathcal{J}_h$ and all $J \in \mathcal{J}_h$ we have:

$$\frac{1}{n}\#\{t \in I_n : x^j(t) > \epsilon \text{ for each } j \in J\} > \epsilon.$$

Proof. Let $\Gamma \subset S$ be the compact set of equilibrium prices of the limit economy. Denoting by φ the demand function, we know by hypothesis that, for every $p \in \Gamma$, the allocation $x(t) = \varphi(\succsim_t, p, p \cdot \omega(t))$ is linked. Clearly, this implies that for each $p \in \Gamma$ we can find a linked collection $\mathcal{J}_p$ and $\epsilon_p > 0$ such that, for every $J \in \mathcal{J}_p$, $\lambda\{t : \varphi^j(\succsim_t, p, p \cdot \omega(t)) > \epsilon_p$ for each $j \in J\} > \epsilon_p$. By the continuity of φ and the compactness of $Q = \bigcup_n \text{supp } \mathcal{E}_n \cup \text{supp } \mathcal{E}$ we can find $\delta > 0$ and a finite collection $p_1, \ldots, p_m \in \Gamma$ such that if $p \in \Gamma$, then $\|p - p_h\| < \delta/2$ for some h and if $\|p - p_h\| < \delta$, then, for all $j \in \mathcal{J}_{p_h}$, $\lambda\{t : \varphi^j(\succsim_t, p, p \cdot \omega(t)) > \frac{1}{2}\epsilon_{p_h}$ for each $j \in J\} > \frac{1}{2}\epsilon_{p_h}$. Put $\epsilon = \min_h \epsilon_{p_h}$, $\mathcal{J}_h = \mathcal{J}_{p_h}$.

Let d be a metric on Q. Without loss of generality, we can assume that if for $(\succsim, \omega), (\succsim', \omega') \in Q$ and $p \in \Gamma$ we have $d((\succsim', \omega'), (\succsim, \omega)) < \delta$, then $\|\varphi(\succsim, p, p \cdot \omega) - \varphi(\succsim', p', p' \cdot \omega')\| < \epsilon/8$. For each $h \leq m$ and $J \in \mathcal{J}_h$, let $U_h(J) = \{(\succsim, \omega) \in \mathcal{P}^2_{\text{cl}, sc} \times R^\ell_{++} : d((\succsim, \omega), (\succsim', \omega')) < \delta$ for some $(\succsim', \omega') \in Q$ with $\varphi^j(\succsim', p_h, p_h \cdot \omega') > \epsilon/2$ for each $j \in J\}$. By definition, $U_h(J)$ is open and, of course, $\lambda(\mathcal{E}^{-1}(U_h(J))) > \epsilon/2$.

We now make use of Proposition 7.4.9 and the continuity properties of φ and preferences to conclude that if N is sufficiently large, $n > N$, x is a core allocation for $\mathcal{E}_n$ and $p \in S$ is as in 7.4.9, then:

(i) $\|p - p_h\| < \delta$ for some h;
(ii) $\|x(t) - \varphi(\succsim_t, p, p \cdot \omega(t))\| < \epsilon/8$ for all $t \in I_n$; and
(iii) $(1/n)\#\{t \in I_n : \mathcal{E}_n(t) \in U_h(J)\} > \epsilon/4$ for all h and $J \in \mathcal{J}_h$.

Property (ii) is the only nonobvious one. The idea is that, denoting $\alpha(t) = \inf\{p \cdot v : v \succsim x(t)\}$, the conclusion of 7.4.9 implies that $\varphi(\succsim_t, p, \alpha(t))$ is, arbitrarily and uniformly, near both $x(t)$ and $\varphi(\succsim_t, p, p \cdot \omega(t))$. This same argument will be used, and explained more carefully, in the proof of 7.4.16 (see Figure 7.4.7).

With this observation the proof of the lemma is complete. Let $n > N$, x be a core allocation for $\mathcal{E}_n$, and $p \in S$ as in 7.4.9. Take h such that $\|p - p_h\| < \delta$ and consider any $J \in \mathcal{J}_h$. We have $(1/n)\#\{t \in I_n : \mathcal{E}_n(t) \in U_h(J)\} > \epsilon/4$, whereas $\mathcal{E}_n(t) \in U_h(J)$ means that, for some $(\succsim', \omega') \in Q$ with $d((\succsim_t, \omega(t)), (\succsim', \omega')) < \delta$ we have that $\varphi^j(\succsim', p_h, p_h \cdot \omega') > \epsilon/2$ for each $j \in J$. Hence, $\varphi^j(\succsim_t, p, p \cdot \omega(t)) > \epsilon/4$ for each $j \in J$, and so $x^j(t) > \epsilon/8$ for each $j \in J$. Therefore, for all $J \in \mathcal{J}_h$, $(1/n)\#\{t \in I_n : x^j(t) > \epsilon/8$ for each $j \in J\} > \epsilon/8$. ∎

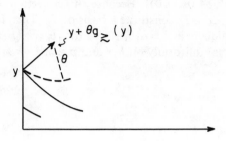

Figure 7.4.5

From now on we let $\mathcal{J}_1, \ldots, \mathcal{J}_m$ be the linked collection obtained in the previous lemma.

Given an allocation x for $\mathcal{E}_n$ and $\delta > 0$, we say that $C \subset I_n$ is δ-*balanced* if $\#C \geq \delta n$ and for some h and all $J \in \mathcal{J}_h$, we have $(1/\#C)\#\{t \in C : x^j(t) > \delta$ for each $j \in J\} > \delta$. With this terminology the previous lemma concludes that for some ϵ and N, if x is a core allocation for $\mathcal{E}_n$, $n > N$, then I_n is ϵ-balanced. Note also that allocations admitting a δ-balanced group are linked.

The next step of the proof is to establish a result analogous to Lemma 7.4.8 for δ-balanced groups.

> **7.4.14. Lemma.** *For any $k > 0$ and $\delta > 0$ there is $N > 0$ and $M > 0$ such that if x has the core property for $\mathcal{E}_n$, $n > N$, and $C \subset I_n$ is a δ-balanced group with $\|\sum_{t \in C} [x(t) - \omega(t)]\| \leq k$, then $\sum_{t \in C} p \cdot [x(t) - \omega(t)] \geq -M/\#C$, where $p \in S$ is the (unique) supporting price vector for x.*

Proof. First we choose a few constants. Let $r > 0$ be as in Lemma 7.4.10 and $Q = \bigcup_n \text{supp } \mathcal{E}_n \cup \text{supp } \mathcal{E}$. By the differentiability of preferences there is $\theta > 0$ such that if $(\succsim, \omega) \in Q$ and $y \leq re$, then $\{v : v \succsim y\}$ contains the nonnegative vectors of the ball of radius θ and center $y + \theta g_\succsim(y)$; see H.3 and Figure 7.4.5. Because of the strict monotonicity of preferences we can pick $\rho > 0$ such that:

(i) $g_\succsim(y) > \rho e$ if $(\succsim, \omega) \in Q$, $y \leq re$; and
(ii) $p > \rho e$ if, for any n, p supports an optimal allocation x for $\mathcal{E}_n$ with $x(t) \leq re$ for all $t \in I_n$.

Consider any $\mathcal{J}_h = (J_1, \ldots, J_{\ell-1})$ and $p \in S$. For every $s \leq \ell - 1$ let $v_s \in T_p$ be a vector such that $\|v_s\| = 1$ and $v_s^j > 0$ only if $j \in J_s$ [e.g., if $J_s = \{1, 2\}$, then v_s is collinear to $(-p^2, p^1, 0, \ldots, 0)$]. Because the collection J_h is linked, the vectors $(v_1, \ldots, v_{\ell-1}) \in T_p$ constitute a basis of T_p. Therefore, any $z \in R^\ell$ can be written uniquely as $z = \alpha_1 v_1 + \cdots + \alpha_{\ell-1} v_{\ell-1} + (p \cdot z)p$. Pick $c > 0$ such that $|\alpha_s| \leq c\|z\|$ uniformly on h, s and $p \geq \rho e$.

Finally, put

$$M > \frac{4\ell^3 (c+1)^2 k^2}{2\delta^4 \theta \rho}$$

and let

$$N > \frac{2\ell}{\delta} \left[\frac{(c+1)k}{\delta^2} + 1 \right].$$

It suffices to prove the lemma for $n > N$.

Let x be a core allocation for $\mathcal{E}_n$, $n > N$ and $C \in I_n$ a δ-balanced group (say that it is balanced with respect to $\mathcal{J}_h$) with $\|\sum_{t \in C} z(t)\| < k$, where $z(t) = x(t) - \omega_n(t)$. Letting $p \in S$ be the unique supporting price vector for x and $(v_1, \ldots, v_{\ell-1}) \in T_p$ as above, we can write

$$\bar{z} = \sum_{t \in C} z(t) = \alpha_1 v_1 + \cdots + \alpha_{\ell-1} v_{\ell-1} + (p \cdot \bar{z})p.$$

Because, by Lemma 7.4.10, $x(t) \leq re$ for all t, we have $p \geq \rho e$ and so $|\alpha_s| \leq c\|\bar{z}\|$ for all s. Put

$$\bar{z}_s = \alpha_s v_s + \frac{1}{\ell-1}(p \cdot \bar{z})p.$$

Then $\bar{z} = \bar{z}_1 + \cdots + \bar{z}_{\ell-1}$ and $\|\bar{z}_s\| \leq (c+1)\|\bar{z}\| \leq (c+1)k$.

Because C is δ-balanced and $n > N$ we can partition C into $\ell - 1$ pairwise disjoint groups $C_1, \ldots, C_{\ell-1}$ such that, for every s:

(i) $\#C_s \geq (\delta^2/2\ell)n$, and
(ii) $x^j(t) > \delta$ for each $j \in J_s$ and $t \in C_s$.

Observe that if $t \in C_s$, then $g_{\geq_t}(x(t)) \cdot v_s = 0$.

We show now that if $p \cdot \bar{z} < -M/\#C$, then C constitutes an improving group, thus obtaining a contradiction. To that effect replace $x(t)$ by $x'(t) = x(t) - (1/\#C_s)\bar{z}_s$ if $t \in C_s$ and note that:

(i) $\sum_{s=1}^{\ell-1} \sum_{t \in C_s} [x'(t) - \omega_n(t)] = 0$;
(ii) $x'(t) \geq 0$ because $\bar{z}_s^j > 0$ only if $j \in J_s$, and in this case

$$\frac{1}{\#C_s} \bar{z}_s^j \leq \frac{2\ell}{\delta^2 n}(c+1)k \leq \delta \leq x^j(t);$$

(iii) $x'(t) >_t x(t)$ because, denoting $q = g_{\geq_t}(x(t))$,

$$\|x(t) + \theta q - x'(t)\|^2 = \left\| \theta q + \frac{1}{\#C_s} \bar{z}_s \right\|^2$$

$$= \theta^2 + \frac{2\theta}{\#C_s} q \cdot \bar{z}_s + \frac{1}{(\#C_s)^2} \|\bar{z}_s\|^2$$

$$\leq \theta^2 - \frac{2\theta(q \cdot p)M}{\#C_s \#C(\ell-1)} + \frac{1}{(\#C_s)^2} \|\bar{z}_s\|^2$$

$$\leq \theta^2 + \frac{1}{n^2} \left[\frac{4(c+1)^2 k^2 \ell^2}{\delta^4} - \frac{2\theta\rho}{\ell-1} M \right] \leq \theta^2. \quad \blacksquare$$

The next result tells us that for small δ, suitable δ-balanced groups abound.

7.4.15. Lemma. *There is $k > 0$, $\delta > 0$, and N such that if x is a core allocation for $\mathcal{E}_n$, $n > N$, then we can find a $C \subset I_n$ with the properties:*

(i) *C and $I \setminus C$ are δ-balanced;*
(ii) *$\|\Sigma_{t \in C} [x(t) - \omega(t)]\| \leq k$; and*
(iii) *$n/3 \leq \#C \leq n/2$.*

Proof. Let $\epsilon < \frac{1}{3}$ and N_1 be as in Lemma 7.4.13. With r as in Lemma 7.4.10, put $k = \ell^2(4r+1)$ and take

$$N > \left\{ N_1, 10\frac{\ell^2}{\epsilon}, \frac{24k(\ell-\epsilon)}{\epsilon} \right\}, \qquad \delta < \frac{1}{3}\frac{\epsilon}{\ell}.$$

Suppose now that x is a core allocation for $\mathcal{E}_n$, $n > N$. By 7.4.13, I_n is ϵ-balanced with respect to, say, $\mathcal{J}_h = (J_1, \ldots, J_{\ell-1})$. Because $n > 10\ell^2/\epsilon$ we can take pairwise disjoint groups $C_1, \ldots, C_{\ell-1} \subset I_n$ such that, for every s:

(i) *if $t \in C_s$, then $x^j(t) > \epsilon$ for each $j \in J_s$; and*
(ii) *$(\epsilon/\ell)n \leq \#C_s \leq (5\epsilon/4\ell)n$.*

For every s put $\eta^s(t) = 1$ if $t \in C_s$ and $\eta^s(t) = -\#C_s/(n - \#C_s)$ otherwise. Note that $|\eta^s(t)| < 1$ and $\Sigma_{t \in I_n} \eta^s(t) = 0$. Define $v: I_n \to R^\ell \times R^{\ell-1}$ by $v(t) = (x^1(t) - \omega_n^1(t), \ldots, x^\ell(t) - \omega_n^\ell(t), \eta^1(t), \ldots, \eta^{\ell-1}(t))$. Note that $\Sigma_{t \in I_n} v(t) = 0$ and $\|v(t)\| \leq 4\ell r + \ell = k/\ell$. As in the proof of Proposition 7.4.3, we now appeal to the averaging result L.2.1 and conclude that there exists $C \subset I_n$ such that $n/3 \leq \#C \leq n/2$ and $\|\Sigma_{t \in C} v(t)\| \leq k$. We shall show that this C has the desired properties. Of course, $\|\Sigma_{t \in C} [x(t) - \omega(t)]\| \leq k$. Therefore, it will be enough to verify that

$$\frac{\#(C \cap C_s)}{\#C} \geq \delta \quad \text{and} \quad \frac{\#((I_n \setminus C) \cap C_s)}{\#(I_n \setminus C)} \geq \delta \quad \text{for every } s.$$

Take an arbitrary s. Then $|\Sigma_{t \in C}\, \eta^s(t)| \le k$, or

$$\left| \#(C \cap C_s) - [\#C - \#(C \cap C_s)] \frac{\#C_s}{n - \#C_s} \right| \le k.$$

Dividing both sides by

$$\#C\left(1 + \frac{\#C_s}{n - \#C_s}\right) \ge \frac{n}{3}\frac{\ell}{\ell - \epsilon}$$

and taking into account that

$$\frac{\#C_s/(n - \#C_s)}{1 + [\#C_s/(n - \#C_s)]} = \frac{\#C_s}{n}$$

we get

$$\left| \frac{\#(C \cap C_s)}{\#C} - \frac{\#C_s}{n} \right| \le \frac{1}{n}\frac{3k(\ell - \epsilon)}{\ell} < \frac{\epsilon}{8\ell}.$$

Therefore,

$$\delta < \frac{7\epsilon}{8\ell} \le \frac{\#C_s}{n} - \frac{\epsilon}{8\ell} \le \frac{\#(C \cap C_s)}{\#C} \le \frac{\#C_s}{n} + \frac{\epsilon}{8\ell} \le \frac{11}{8}\frac{\epsilon}{\ell}.$$

On the other hand, from this follows

$$\frac{\#((I_n \backslash C) \cap C_s)}{\#(I_n \backslash C)} \ge \frac{3}{2}\left(\frac{\#C_s}{n} - \frac{\#C}{n}\frac{\#(C \cap C_s)}{\#C} \right)$$

$$\ge \frac{3}{2}\left(\frac{\epsilon}{\ell} - \frac{1}{2}\frac{11}{8}\frac{\epsilon}{\ell} \right) = \frac{15}{32}\frac{\epsilon}{\ell} > \delta$$

and we are done.   ∎

Using Lemma 7.4.14 instead of 7.4.8, the proposition is now proved in exactly the same manner as Proposition 7.4.3. Given x, one has only to take into account that:

(i)   if $C \subset I_n$ is δ-balanced, then any group differing from C by at most one member is $(\delta/2)$-balanced; and

(ii)   the group G appearing in the proof of Proposition 7.4.3 [case (ii) of step 3] can be taken to be such that both G and $I_n \backslash G$ are δ-balanced (Lemma 7.4.15).

This concludes the proof of Proposition 7.4.12.   ∎

Up to now we have provided estimates implying that a core allocation of a large economy is nearly Walrasian. This, of course, is not the same as asserting that it is near a Walrasian allocation. In fact, this may not be

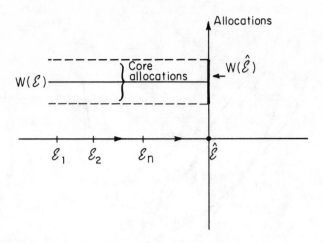

Figure 7.4.6

the case even if we are considering sequences of economies converging to a well-defined limit. Figure 7.4.6 provides a symbolic illustration of what could go wrong and suggests that the problem may be the possible lack of continuity at the limit of the map that assigns Walrasian prices (and allocations) to economies, the equilibrium map $W(\mathcal{E})$. As we are going to see, this is indeed the case.

In the next, and last, proposition we add to the requirement so far the condition that the limit $\mathcal{E}$ be regular. As we know from Chapter 5, regularity yields the continuity of the equilibrium map and eliminates limit situations such as $\hat{\mathcal{E}}$ in Figure 7.4.6. In the proposition, $\mathcal{Q}_{sc}^2$ stands for one of our spaces of smooth, differentiably strictly convex preferences.

> **7.4.16. Proposition.** *Let $\mathcal{E}_n: I_n \to \mathcal{Q}_{sc}^2$ be a sequence of economies converging to a regular limit $\mathcal{E}$. Then there is a constant M such that, for every n and allocation x_n for $\mathcal{E}_n$ with the core property, we can find a Walrasian allocation y_n satisfying*
>
> $(1/n) \sum_{t \in I_n} \|x_n(t) - y_n(t)\| \leq M/\sqrt{n}$ *[case (i)].*
>
> *Moreover, if every Walrasian allocation is linked [and $\omega \gg 0$ whenever $(\gtrsim, \omega) \in \mathrm{supp}\,\mathcal{E}$], we actually have $\|x_n(t) - y_n(t)\| \leq M/n$ for all $t \in I_n$ [case (ii)].*

Proof. Let $Q \subset \mathcal{P}_c^2 \times [0, k]^\ell$ be a compact set of characteristics that contains the supports of $\mathcal{E}_n, \mathcal{E}$. Choose an $M > 2k\ell^2 + 1$ as in Proposition

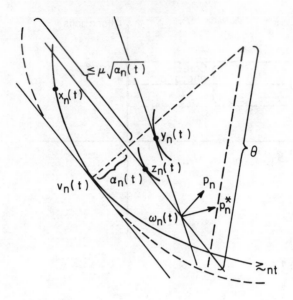

Figure 7.4.7

7.4.1, or as in Propositions 7.4.3, 7.4.12 if we are in case (ii). Let $p_n \in S$ be the price vectors given by those propositions. Denote

$$\alpha_n(t) = |p_n \cdot [x_n(t) - \omega_n(t)]| + |\inf\{p_n \cdot [v - x_n(t)] : v \succsim_t x_n(t)\}|.$$

Then $(1/n) \sum \alpha_n(t) \le 2M/n$ in case (i) and $\max_t \alpha_n(t) \le M/n$ in case (ii). In this proof all the sums are understood to run over $t \in I_n$.

Suppose that p is a limit point of p_n. Because $(1/n) \sum \alpha_n(t) \to 0$ and, by Lemma 7.4.6 or 7.4.10, the allocations x_n are uniformly bounded, the price vector p must be an equilibrium for $\mathcal{E}$. Because the number of equilibria of $\mathcal{E}$ is finite (5.5.2), there shall be no loss of generality if we consider a single one p^* and assume that $p_n \to p^*$.

Denote by f_n, f the excess demand functions of $\mathcal{E}_n, \mathcal{E}$. As in Proposition 5.4.2 and its proof, we know that uniformly on a small neighborhood of $p^* \in U \subset S$, f is C^1, f_n is Lipschitzian, and $f_n \to f$, $\partial f_n \to \partial f$. By the implicit function theorem (G.2.3) there are N, λ, ϵ, and $p_n^* \to p^*$ such that if $n > N$, then $f_n(p_n^*) = 0$ and $\|p - p_n^*\| \le \lambda \|f_n(p)\|$ whenever $\|p - p_n^*\| \le \epsilon$, $\|f_n(p)\| \le \epsilon$. Because $p_n \to p^*$, $p_n^* \to p^*$, $f_n(p_n) \to 0$, this allows us to conclude that $\|p_n - p_n^*\| \le \lambda \|f_n(p_n)\|$. From now on we take $n > N$.

Take $y_n(t) = \varphi(\succsim_{nt}, p_n^*, p_n^* \cdot \omega_n(t))$ and let $z_n(t) = \varphi(\succsim_{nt}, p_n, p_n \cdot \omega_n(t))$ and $v_n(t)$ be such that $p_n \cdot v \ge p_n \cdot v_n(t)$ whenever $v \succsim_{nt} x_n(t)$; see Figure 7.4.7. Of course, in case (ii), $x_n(t) = v_n(t)$.

Pick a $\mu > 0$, which is a Lipschitz constant for the demand function on $Q \times U \times [0, \ell(k+M)]$ and the excess demand function on $Q \times U$. Because the $v_n(t)$ are bounded uniformly on n and t and indifference manifolds have positive Gaussian curvature, we can also assume that μ is large enough for us to have $\|x_n(t) - v_n(t)\| \leq \mu \sqrt{\alpha_n(t)}$ for all $n > N$ and t. See H.3 and Figure 7.4.7, where θ is chosen to be sufficiently large.

We have

$$\|z_n(t) - x_n(t)\| \leq \|z_n(t) - v_n(t)\| + \|v_n(t) - x_n(t)\|$$

$$\leq \mu(\alpha_n(t) + \sqrt{\alpha_n(t)}) \leq \mu(\sqrt{2M} + 1)\sqrt{\alpha_n(t)}$$

in case (i) and $\|z_n(t) - x_n(t)\| \leq \mu \alpha_n(t)$ in case (ii). Therefore,

$$\frac{1}{n} \sum \|z_n(t) - x_n(t)\| \leq \frac{\mu(\sqrt{2M}+1)}{n} \left[\sum \sqrt{\alpha_n(t)} \right]$$

$$\leq \frac{\mu(\sqrt{2M}+1)}{\sqrt{n}} \sqrt{\sum \alpha_n(t)} \leq \frac{\mu(\sqrt{2M}+1)\sqrt{2M}}{\sqrt{n}}$$

in case (i) and

$$\frac{1}{n} \sum \|z_n(t) - x_n(t)\| \leq \frac{\mu M}{n}$$

in case (ii).

Because

$$f_n(p_n) = \frac{1}{n} \sum [z_n(t) - \omega_n(t)] = \frac{1}{n} \sum [z_n(t) - x_n(t)]$$

we have

$$\|p_n - p_n^*\| \leq \lambda \|f_n(p_n)\| \leq \frac{\lambda}{n} \|\sum [z_n(t) - x_n(t)]\| \leq \frac{\lambda}{n} \sum \|z_n(t) - x_n(t)\|.$$

Therefore, in case (i),

$$\frac{1}{n} \sum \|y_n(t) - x_n(t)\| \leq \frac{1}{n} \sum \|y_n(t) - z_n(t)\| + \frac{1}{n} \sum \|z_n(t) - x_n(t)\|$$

$$\leq \mu \|p_n - p_n^*\| + \frac{1}{n} \sum \|z_n(t) - x_n(t)\|$$

$$\leq \frac{(\mu\lambda+1)\mu(\sqrt{2M}+1)\sqrt{2M}}{\sqrt{n}}$$

as we wanted. In case (ii),

$$\|y_n(t) - x_n(t)\| \leq \mu \|p_n - p_n^*\| + \|z_n(t) - x_n(t)\| \leq \frac{\mu^2 \lambda M}{n} + \mu \frac{M}{n}$$

also as we wanted. ∎

Observe that if the limit Walrasian allocation is linked, then a rate of convergence of the order of $1/n$ should be thought of as typical. Otherwise, no assertion of typicality can be made for a rate better than $1/\sqrt{n}$. For the interpretation of the theory the difference between $1/n$ and $1/\sqrt{n}$ is definitely not minor. Therefore, it is important to remember from Proposition 7.2.7 that if supp $\mathcal{E}$ is connected, then every Walrasian allocation is linked. Hence, for continuum economies with connected support, the rate $1/n$ is typical.

7.5   Anonymous optimal allocations in continuum exchange economies

The continuum exchange economy $\mathcal{E}: I \to \mathcal{Q}$ is kept fixed throughout this section. It is always assumed that $\succsim_t$ is strictly convex for a.e. $t \in I$. Warning: This is not assumed for every member of supp $\mathcal{E}$.

We begin by a discussion of the equal treatment property.

Suppose that, with Definitions 7.2.3 and 7.2.4 of Section 7.2, x is an anonymous optimum. If p is a supporting price vector, then

$$x(t) = \varphi(\succsim_t, p, p \cdot x(t)) \quad \text{for a.e. } t \in I.$$

Because $w' > w$ implies $\varphi(\succsim_t, p, w') \succ_t \varphi(\succsim_t, p, w)$, we can conclude that, for a.e. $t \in I$ and $t' \in I$, $\mathcal{E}(t) = \mathcal{E}(t')$ implies $x(t) = x(t')$. That is to say, at an anonymous optimum, identical agents are treated identically. This is the so-called equal treatment property and it is valid in finite or continuum economies indistinctly. In the continuum context, it is natural and important to ask if the property holds continuously; that is, if similar agents are treated similarly. As it turns out, the answer is intimately related to the uniform boundedness of anonymous optimal allocations. Formally, we have the following.

> *7.5.1. Proposition. Let x be an anonymous optimum for $\mathcal{E}: I \to \mathcal{Q}$. Suppose there is $k > 0$ such that $x(t) \leq ke$ for a.e. $t \in I$. Denote by d a metric on supp $\mathcal{E}$. Then if the consumption set is R_{++}^ℓ (i.e., $\mathcal{P} = \mathcal{P}_b$) or if $\omega(t) = \bar{\omega} \gg 0$ for a.e. $t \in I$, we can find, for each $\epsilon > 0$, a $\delta > 0$ such that for a.e. $t \in I$ and $t' \in I$, $d(\mathcal{E}(t), \mathcal{E}(t')) < \delta$ implies $\|x(t) - x(t')\| < \epsilon$.*

Proof. Let x satisfy the hypotheses of the proposition and $p \in S$ be a supporting price vector. Consider the compact set $\Gamma = \text{supp}(\lambda \circ (\mathcal{E}, x)^{-1}) \subset \mathcal{Q} \times [0, k]^\ell$. The projection of Γ on $\mathcal{Q}$ equals supp $\mathcal{E}$. Also, $B_x = \{v - \omega_a : (a, v) \in \Gamma\}$.

By the anonymity property, $x(t)$ is $\succsim_t$-maximal on $B_x + \omega(t)$ for a.e. t. This does not necessarily imply that v is $\succsim_a$-maximal on $B_x + \omega_a$ whenever

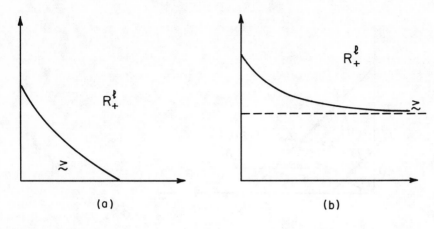

Figure 7.5.1

$(a, v) \in \Gamma$. It is an instructive exercise to verify why this may not be so and also to check that whenever the set of admissible net trades as a function of individual characteristics in supp $\mathcal{E}$ has an open graph (e.g., the consumption set is R_{++}^ℓ) or it is constant (e.g., $\omega_a = \bar{\omega}$ for all $a \in$ supp $\mathcal{E}$), then we indeed have that v is $\succsim_a$-maximal on $B_x + \omega_a$ whenever $(a, v) \in \Gamma$. Obviously, this covers the two cases we are interested in.

Clearly, $v = \varphi(\succsim_a, p, p \cdot v)$ for all $(a, v) \in \Gamma$. Therefore, it is sufficient to show that the closed-graph point-to-set map that assigns

$$\{p \cdot v : (a, v) \in \Gamma\} \subset R$$

to any $a \in$ supp $\mathcal{E}$ is in fact a function (hence, a continuous one). We argue by contradiction. Suppose $(a, v), (a, v') \in \Gamma$ and $p \cdot v' > p \cdot v$. Then $\varphi(\succsim_a, p, p \cdot v') = v' >_a v = \varphi(\succsim_a, p, p \cdot v)$ and $v' - \omega_a \in B_x$, which contradicts the $\succsim_a$-maximality of v on $B_x + \omega_a$. ∎

Given the hypotheses of the previous proposition, when is an anonymous optimum bounded? That it may not always be can be established by examples. Because those are rather complex while very mild (if somewhat ad hoc) strengthenings of the assumptions on preferences yields the desired conclusion (next proposition), it would not be justified to spend time on them. The additional hypotheses are in the nature of desirability conditions and are special for each of the two types of consumption sets we are interested in. If preferences are in $\mathcal{P}_{b,sc}^2$, then demand functions are required to have a strictly positive wealth derivative, and this in a uniform manner. If preferences are in $\mathcal{P}_{cl}$, then indifference manifolds of $\succsim$ are required to intersect the boundary of R_+^ℓ in all directions; that is, they should be as in Figure 7.5.1a. Figure 7.5.1b is the situation ruled out.

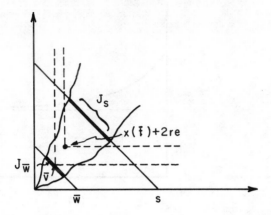

Figure 7.5.2

7.5.2. Proposition. *Let x be an anonymous optimal allocation for $\mathcal{E}: I \to \mathcal{Q}$. Then there is $k > 0$ such that $x(t) \le ke$ for a.e. $t \in I$ if either one of the two following sets of conditions holds:*

(i) *$\mathcal{Q} = \mathcal{P}_{b,sc}^2 \times R_{++}^\ell$. For each $p \in S$ there is $\delta > 0$ such that if $a \in \text{supp } \mathcal{E}$, then $\partial_w \varphi(\gtrsim_a, p, w) \ge \delta e$ for all $w > 0$.*

(ii) *$\mathcal{Q} = \mathcal{P}_{cl} \times R_+^\ell$. For a.e. $t \in I$, $\{v : y \gtrsim_t v\}$ is compact for all y.*

Proof. We can assume $\omega(t) \le re$ for a.e. $t \in I$. We deal with case (i) first. Let p be a supporting price vector for the allocation x under consideration. For any w the set $J_w = \{\varphi(\gtrsim_a, p, w) : a \in \text{supp } \mathcal{E}\} \subset R_{++}^\ell$ is compact. Therefore, because of the uniform hypothesis on wealth derivatives, there is some sufficiently large $s > 0$ such that if $w > s$, then $J_w \gg x(\bar{t}) + 2re$, where $\bar{t}$ has been chosen so that $x(\bar{t})$ is $\gtrsim_{\bar{t}}$-maximal on $B_x + \omega(\bar{t})$ (see Figure 7.5.2). Denote $C = \{t \in I : p \cdot x(t) > s\}$. Because p is a supporting price vector, we have $x(t) = \varphi(\gtrsim_t, p, p \cdot \omega(t))$ for a.e. $t \in C$. Therefore, $x(t) \gg x(\bar{t}) + 2re$ and so $x(t) - \omega(t) + \omega(\bar{t}) \gg x(\bar{t})$ for a.e. $t \in C$. Since $x(\bar{t})$ is $\gtrsim_{\bar{t}}$-maximal on $B_x + \omega(\bar{t})$, we must conclude that C is null.

The proof for case (ii) is even simpler. Pick a $\bar{t} \in I$ such that $x(\bar{t})$ is $\gtrsim_{\bar{t}}$-maximal on $B_x + \omega(\bar{t})$ and $\gtrsim_{\bar{t}}$ satisfies the stated condition on preferences. Then we should have $x(\bar{t}) \gtrsim_t x(t) - \omega(t) + \omega(\bar{t})$ for a.e. $t \in I$. But $\{y \in R_+^\ell : x(\bar{t}) \gtrsim_{\bar{t}} y\}$ is bounded. Hence, the result. ∎

Are anonymous optima of continuum economies Walrasian? The next, trivial example shows that even in the best possible case considered so far, they need not be; that is, when evaluated at supporting price vectors, some transfers of wealth may still be possible.

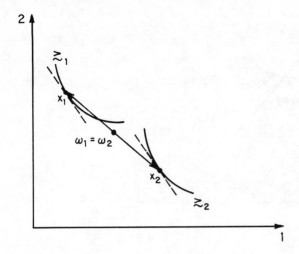

Figure 7.5.3

7.5.3. Example. There are two types of agents receiving equal weights. The preferences and endowment vectors of the two types are described in Figure 7.5.3. Clearly, we can assume that characteristics satisfy either of the conditions of Proposition 7.5.3. With x_1, x_2 as in the figure, we put $x(t) = x_1$ [resp. $x(t) = x_2$] if the characteristics of t are of the first (resp. the second) type. It is obvious from the figure that x is an anonymous optimum but it is not Walrasian.

The previous example makes clear that, in contrast with the core property, the continuum of agents does not now by itself make for any qualitative difference with the finite number of agents case. What will turn out to impose constraints and yield results is not so much that there be many agents but rather the variability of their characteristics. We shall proceed to illustrate this by presenting some representative positive results on the equivalence of Walrasian and anonymous optimal allocations. We shall confine ourselves to economies describable by means of finite-dimensional parameterizations.

For the rest of this section we assume *there is given a C^2 parameterization $h: A \to \mathcal{C}_{sc}^2$ such that $A \subset R^m$ is open (or, more generally, a smooth manifold) and there is a measurable $\eta: I \to A$ with $\mathcal{E} = h \circ \eta$ and $h(A) \subset$ supp $\mathcal{E}$, that is,* supp $\mathcal{E}$ = closure $h(A)$. We denote $h(a) = (\succsim_a, \omega_a)$. It is worth pointing out that we do not require supp $\mathcal{E} \subset \mathcal{C}_{sc}^2$, although, of course, $\mathcal{E}(t) \in \mathcal{C}_{sc}^2$ must hold for a.e. $t \in I$. For the precise definition of parameterization of characteristics see 2.4.6.

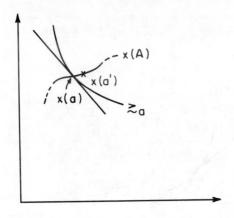

Figure 7.5.4

Suppose for a moment that $A = (0, 1)$, $\omega(a) = \bar{\omega}$, and $\succsim_a \in \mathcal{P}^2_{b, sc}$, for all $a \in A$. Given a bounded, optimal (with supporting price vector p) and anonymous allocation, we can as well, because of the equal treatment property, represent it in the form $x(a)$. Suppose we can show that the function $x(a)$, which by Proposition 7.5.1 we know is continuous, is in fact smooth (or, more generally, Lipschitzian). Then, if at some a we have $p \cdot \partial x(a) \neq 0$, we can find a' near a such that $x(a') >_a x(a)$, which violates anonymity (see Figure 7.5.4). Hence, $p \cdot \partial x(a) = 0$ for all a and, therefore, by integration one deduces that the entire $x(A)$ is contained in a single hyperplane perpendicular to p; that is, the allocation is Walrasian. The proof of the next proposition is nothing but a rigorous and more general version of this simple argument. Note that relative to Example 7.5.3, the key new ingredient is the connectedness of A. It is this hypothesis that allows us to exploit the implications of local anonymity tests to obtain global conclusions, namely, to deduce that the local flatness of $x(A)$ implies its global flatness.

7.5.4. Proposition. *Let A be connected and suppose that either $\mathcal{A} = \mathcal{P}^2_{b, sc} \times R^\ell_{++}$ or* supp $\mathcal{E} \subset \mathcal{P}^2_{sc} \times \{\bar{\omega}\}$ *for some $\bar{\omega}$. Then every bounded, optimal, anonymous allocation for $\mathcal{E}$ is Walrasian.*

Proof. Let x be a bounded, anonymous, optimal allocation. Because $h(A) \subset$ supp $\mathcal{E}$ and x is bounded, it follows from Proposition 7.5.1 that for each $a \in A$ there is a unique $x(a)$ such that

$$(h(a), x(a)) \in \text{supp}(\lambda \circ (\mathcal{E}, x)^{-1}) \subset \mathcal{A} \times R^\ell.$$

Moreover, $x(a)$ is continuous on A. Denote $w(a) = p \cdot [x(a) - \omega(a)]$, where p is a supporting price vector for x. Because $\int w(\eta(t)) \, dt = 0$ it suffices to prove that $w(a_0) = w(a_1)$ for all $a_0, a_1 \in A$.

Let $a_0, a_1 \in A$ be arbitrary. The set A is open and connected. Therefore (see H.4.6), there is a C^2 path $a(s)$ from $[0,1]$ to A with $a(0) = a_0$, $a(1) = a_1$. Denote $K = a([0,1]) \subset A$. We shall show first that $w(a)$ is a Lipschitzian function on K and, second, that if $a_n \to a$, $a_n, a \in K$, $a_n \neq a$, then

$$\limsup_n \frac{w(a_n) - w(a)}{\|a_n - a\|} \le 0.$$

This yields the result because then $s \mapsto w(s) = w(a(s))$ is Lipschitzian, hence it is differentiable a.e. and satisfies $w(1) - w(0) = \int \partial w(s) \, ds$ (see G.1.1). But $\partial w(s) \le 0$ whenever defined. Therefore, $w(1) - w(0) \le 0$. Symmetrically, $w(0) - w(1) \le 0$ and we are done.

Let $U(y, a), \omega(a)$ be a utility function–endowment vector representation of the C^2 parameterization $h : A \to \mathcal{Q}$ (see 2.4.6). To ease the notation we define, whenever they make sense, the symbols

$$v(a, w) = \varphi(\succsim_a, p, p \cdot \omega(a) + w) - \omega(a), \qquad \hat{U}(v, a) = U(v + \omega(a), a).$$

We prove first that $w(a)$ is Lipschitzian at every $\bar{a} \in K$. From now on, we let $J \subset A$ be an open neighborhood of $\bar{a}$ that is sufficiently small for all subsequent arguments to make sense. In particular, under any of the two hypotheses on the preference–endowment distribution, it can always be guaranteed that $x(a) + \omega(a) - \omega(a') \ge 0$ for all $a, a' \in J$. Because U is C^2 parameterization of preferences and φ is Lipschitzian (2.7.3), we can choose a constant c such that:

(i) $|\hat{U}(v(a, w'), a) - \hat{U}(v(a, w), a)| \ge (1/c)|w' - w|$ for all $a \in J$ and w, w' in a neighborhood of $w(\bar{a})$.

(ii) $|U(y, a) - U(y', a)| \le c\|y - y'\|$ for all $a \in J$ and y, y' on a neighborhood of $x(\bar{a})$.

(iii) $\|v(a, w) - v(a', w)\| \le c\|a - a'\|$ for all $a, a' \in J$ and w on a neighborhood of $w(\bar{a})$.

Pick two arbitrary $a, a' \in J$ and let $w(a) \ge w(a')$. Because of the anonymity property on x we should have

$$\hat{U}(v(a, w(a)), a') = U(x(a) - \omega(a) + \omega(a'), a') \le U(x(a'), a')$$
$$= \hat{U}(v(a', w(a')), a').$$

Therefore,

$$(1/c)(w(a) - w(a')) \le \hat{U}(v(a', w(a)), a') - \hat{U}(v(a', w(a')), a')$$
$$\le \hat{U}(v(a', w(a)), a') - \hat{U}(v(a, w(a)), a')$$
$$\le c\|v(a', w(a)) - v(a, w(a))\| \le c^2\|a - a'\|.$$

Hence, $|w(a) - w(a')| \le c^3 \|a - a'\|$ and we conclude that c^3 is a Lipschitz constant for $w(a)$ at $\bar{a}$.

For the second claim of the proof we consider a fixed arbitrary $\bar{a}$ and denote $\bar{w} = w(\bar{a})$, $\bar{v} = v(\bar{a}, \bar{w})$, $\bar{q} = \partial_v \hat{U}(\bar{v}, \bar{a})$. We first establish that for a, w near $\bar{a}, \bar{w}$ we have $\bar{q} \cdot [v(a, w) - v(\bar{a}, w)] = 0$. Indeed, by the first-order conditions, there is α such that $\alpha p \ge \bar{q}$ and $x^j(\bar{a}) = 0$ whenever $\alpha p^j > \bar{q}^j$. Hence, by continuity, if a is near $\bar{a}$, then $x^j(a) = 0$ whenever $\alpha p^j > \bar{q}^j$. So

$$\bar{q} \cdot [v(a, w) - v(\bar{a}, w)] = \alpha p \cdot [\omega(a) - \omega(\bar{a})] - \bar{q} \cdot [\omega(a) - \omega(\bar{a})].$$

If $\mathcal{Q} = \mathcal{P}^2_{b, sc} \times R^\ell_{++}$ [resp. supp $\mathcal{E} \subset \mathcal{P}^2_{sc} \times \{\bar{\omega}\}$], then $\alpha p = \bar{q}$ [resp. $\omega(a) = \bar{\omega} = \omega(\bar{a})$]. In both cases, $\bar{q} \cdot [v(a, w) - v(\bar{a}, w)] = 0$.

Now choose a constant $c > 0$ that satisfies properties (i), (ii), and (iii) above in a neighborhood J of $\bar{a}$. Assume that, in addition:

(iv) $\|v(\bar{a}, w) - \bar{v}\| \le c|w - \bar{w}|$ for w near $\bar{w}$.
(v) $\|\bar{q} + \partial_v \hat{U}(v, \bar{a})\| \le c\|v - \bar{v}\|$ for v near $\bar{v}$.

Suppose that, for a near $\bar{a}$, $w(a) \ge \bar{w}$. Denote $w(a) = w$. As above, we have $(1/c)(w - \bar{w}) \le \hat{U}(v(\bar{a}, w), \bar{a}) - U(v(a, w), \bar{a})$. By Taylor's formula (C.4.1), the latter expression equals

$$-\partial_v \hat{U}(v(\bar{a}, w)\bar{a})(v(a, w) - v(\bar{a}, w)) + o(\|v(a, w) - v(\bar{a}, w)\|^2).$$

Hence, using $\bar{q} \cdot [v(a, w) - v(\bar{a}, w)] = 0$, we get

$$(w - \bar{w}) \le c\|\hat{U}(v(\bar{a}, w), \bar{a}) - \hat{U}(v(a, w), \bar{a})\|$$

$$\le c\|\bar{q} - \partial_v \hat{U}(v(\bar{a}, w), \bar{a})\| \|v(a, w) - v(\bar{a}, w)\| + o(\|a - a\|^2)$$

$$\le c^4 |w - \bar{w}| \|a - \bar{a}\| + o(\|a - \bar{a}\|^2).$$

Therefore, if $a \ne \bar{a}$,

$$\frac{w(a) - \bar{w}}{\|a - \bar{a}\|} \le c^4 |w(a) - \bar{w}| + o(\|a - \bar{a}\|).$$

So, if $a_n \to \bar{a}$, $w(a_n) > \bar{w}$, then

$$\lim_n \frac{w(a_n) - \bar{w}}{\|a_n - \bar{a}\|} = 0$$

which yields

$$\limsup \frac{w(a_n) - \bar{w}}{\|a_n - \bar{a}\|} \le 0 \quad \text{for any } a_n \to \bar{a}, \; a_n \ne \bar{a}. \qquad \blacksquare$$

As already indicated, Example 7.5.3 does not satisfy the hypothesis of Proposition 7.5.4 because of the condition that A be connected; for example, economies with a finite number of types are ruled out. It is known that the assumption that h be a smooth, rather than continuous, parameterization cannot be dispensed with. It is not known to us, however, if the requirement that allocation be bounded is really needed. At any rate, in view of Proposition 7.5.2, this is not a strong hypothesis.

When the consumption set is $R^\ell_+ \backslash \{0\}$ the result of Proposition 7.5.4 is weak because it does not allow for any variation of initial endowments. We now exhibit two examples where endowment vectors vary across agents and there are bounded, linked, optimal, and anonymous allocations that are nonetheless not Walrasian.

7.5.5. Example. Let $\ell = 2$. We take our connected set of parameters to be the interval $A = (0, 1)$. Let $v: R_+ \to R_+$ be an arbitrary C^2 function with $\partial v(r) > 0$, $\partial^2 v(r) < 0$ for all $r \geq 0$. Take $\epsilon > 0$ very small. The characteristics of the economy are described by means of utility functions as follows:

(i) $\omega(a) = (4 - 9a, 4 - 9a)$, $u_a(y) = \bar{u}(y) = \epsilon v(y^1) + (1 - \epsilon)v(y^2)$, for $a \leq \frac{1}{3}$.

(ii) $\omega(a) = (9a - 5, 9a - 5)$, $u_a(y) = \underline{u}(y) = (1 - \epsilon)v(y^1) + \epsilon v(y^2)$, for $a \geq \frac{2}{3}$.

(iii) $\omega(a) = (1, 1)$, $u_a(y) = 3(\frac{2}{3} - a)\bar{u}(y) + 3(a - \frac{1}{3})\underline{u}(y)$, for $\frac{1}{3} \leq a \leq \frac{2}{3}$.

The parameterization fails to be smooth at $a = \frac{1}{3}$ and $a = \frac{2}{3}$. This is inessential; the two corners can be smoothed out without difficulty.

Now let $B \subset R^2$ be the set described in Figure 7.5.5. For each a, let $z(a) \in B$ be such that $z(a) + \omega(a)$ maximizes u_a on $B + \omega(a)$. In the figure the position of the net trades z as functions of a are indicated. Note that every point of B is taken (remember $\epsilon > 0$ is small). Because the origin is interior to the convex hull of B, this means that we can find a map $\eta: [0, 1] \to (0, 1)$ such that supp $\lambda \circ \eta^{-1} = [0, 1]$ and $x(t) = z(a(t)) + \omega(a(t))$ is an allocation; that is, $\int x \leq \int \omega$ for $\mathcal{E} = h \circ \eta$. Obviously, x is bounded and linked. Because in net trade space all agents face the same external constraint set, the allocation is anonymous. To see that it is optimal, note that $p = (0, 1)$ is a supporting price vector. Because B is not contained in a nontrivial hyperplane, the allocation is, however, not Walrasian.

7.5.6. Example. The parameter set will have the product form $A = A_1 \times (0, 1)$, where A_1 indexes preferences and $(0, 1)$ endowments. We let A_1 be open and consider a preference parameterization $h_1: A_1 \to \mathcal{P}^2_{cl, sc}$ such that:

(i) $\succsim_{a_1}$ is a homothetic preference relation for all a_1; and

(ii) the set $\{\varphi(\succsim_{a_1}, e, 1): a_1 \in A_1\}$ equals the boundary of the unit simplex. See Figure 7.5.6a, b.

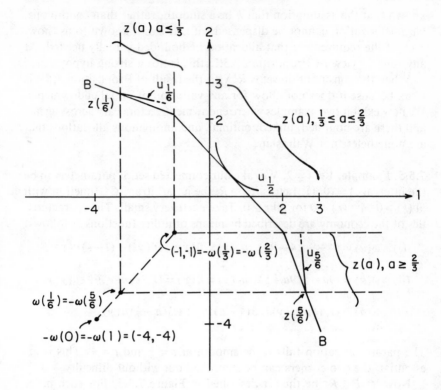

Figure 7.5.5

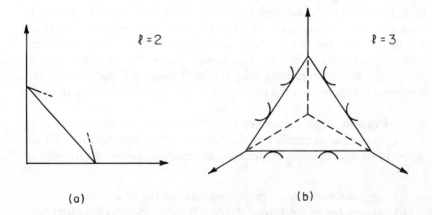

Figure 7.5.6

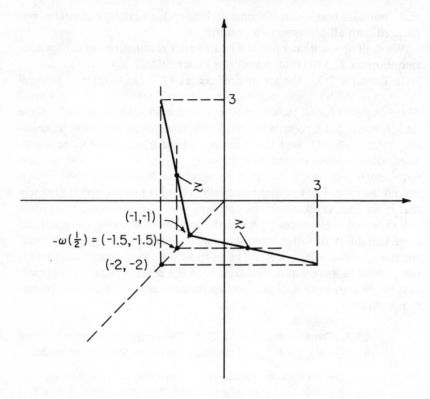

Figure 7.5.7

The key observation is that for $\ell > 2$ (but not for $\ell = 2$) the simplex has a connected boundary, and a parameterization satisfying (i) and (ii) can be constructed for a connected A_1.

The endowment parameterization is $h_2(a_2) = (1 + a_2, 1 + a_2)$. Now for each $a \in A$ let $x(a)$ maximize $\succsim_{a_1}$ on the hyperplane $\{v : e \cdot v = 5a_2\}$. For $\ell = 2$ the set of possible net trades $B = \{x(a) - \omega(a_2) : a \in A\}$ is represented in Figure 7.5.7. We see that, as in the previous example, we can find a suitable $\eta : [0, 1] \to A$ such that $x(t) = x(a(t))$ defines an allocation for $\mathcal{E} = h \circ \eta$. The allocation is obviously not Walrasian, and it is easy to see that it is anonymous and optimal ($p = e$ is a supporting price vector). For $\ell > 2$, which is the interesting case, x is also linked.

The point of the previous example is that with $\ell > 2$ and characteristics in $\mathcal{P}^2_{\mathrm{cl}, sc} \times R^\ell_{++}$ we may get our failure even if individual preferences are very nice and supp $\mathcal{E}$, besides being connected, has the simple structure of a product. We may mention that allowing for less nice preferences (still in

$\mathcal{P}^2_{cl, sc}$ but with nonpositive income derivatives), an example could be constructed with all preferences identical.

We shall now obtain a positive equivalence result allowing for the consumption set $R^\ell_+ \setminus \{0\}$ that generalizes Proposition 7.5.4.

In Example 7.5.5 the set of preferences $Q_\omega = \{\succsim_t : \omega(t) = \omega\}$ is small for most ω. With a slight modification we could make sure that it is actually a singleton for all the ω present in the economy. In Example 7.5.6 the sets Q_ω are much larger, but it is still true that for no ω is there a preference relation $\succsim \in Q_\omega$ such that e supports $\{v : v \succsim y\}$ at y for some $y \gg 0$. These observations suggest that one may be able to exploit the richness requirement on supp $\mathcal{E}$ in order to obtain equivalence results. This is indeed the case. The key idea underlying the next proposition is precisely that if for each ω present in the economy [i.e., $(\succsim, \omega) \in$ supp $\mathcal{E}$ for some $\succsim$], the set of preferences Q_ω is rich in the sense of allowing for small and large variability of tastes across consumers, then we get a positive result for the space $\mathcal{Q} = \mathcal{P}^2_{cl, sc} \times R^\ell_+$. The proposition is very particular, and it has to be seen merely as an illustration of the general principle that richness in the distribution of preferences narrows down the class of anonymous optima.

7.5.7. Proposition. *Let $A_1 \subset R^m$ be open and connected and $h_1 : A_1 \to \mathcal{P}^2_{cl, sc}$ a C^2 parameterization of preferences such that:*

   (i)   *for each $y \in R^\ell_+$ and $q \in R^\ell_{++}$ there is $a_1 \in A_1$ such that q supports $\{v : v \succsim_{a_1} y\}$ at y (variability of preferences); and*

  (ii) *for each $a_1 \in A_1$ the set $\{v : y \succsim_{a_1} v\}$ is compact for all $y \geq 0$ (desirability condition on preferences).*

Let A_2 be a finite set and $h_2 : A_2 \to R^\ell_+$. Suppose that $A = A_1 \times A_2$ and $h(a) = (h_1(a_1), h_2(a_2))$.

   Then every optimal and anonymous allocation x for $\mathcal{E} = h \circ \eta$ is Walrasian.

Proof. Because of the desirability condition and Proposition 7.5.2, x is bounded and, therefore, Proposition 7.5.4 (or, more precisely, the content of its proof) tells us that for a supporting price vector p and each $a_2 \in A_2$ there is $w(a_2)$ such that

$$p \cdot [x(t) - \omega(a_2)] = w(a_2) \quad \text{for a.e. } t \in \eta^{-1}(A_1 \times \{a_2\}).$$

Hence, it will suffice to prove that $w(a'_2) = w(a_2)$ for all $a_2, a'_2 \in A_2$ since then $w(a_2) = 0$ for all $a_2 \in A_2$. This we do in two steps. Denote

$$\Gamma = \text{supp}(\lambda \circ (\mathcal{E}, x)^{-1}) \subset \mathcal{Q} \times R^\ell.$$

Without loss of generality we identify a_2 with $h_2(a_2)$.

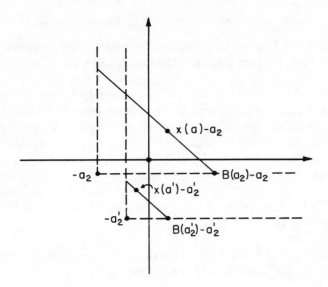

Figure 7.5.8

First, consider an arbitrary $a_2 \in A_2$ and let $B(a_2) = \{y: (\succsim_{a_1}, a_2, y) \in \Gamma$ for some $a_1 \in A_1\}$. It is a consequence of the variability condition on preferences that $B(a_2) = \{y \geq 0: p \cdot y = p \cdot a_2 + w(a_2)\}$. Indeed, let y belong to the latter set. By condition (i) there is $a_1 \in A_1$ such that

$$\varphi(\succsim_{a_1}, p, p \cdot a_2 + w(a_2)) = y \quad \text{and} \quad (\succsim_{a_1}, a_2, x) \in \Gamma \quad \text{for some } x.$$

Then $x \in B(a_2)$; that is, $p \cdot (x - a_2) = w(a_2)$ and, because p is supporting, $x = \varphi(\succsim_{a_1}, p, p \cdot x) = \varphi(\succsim_{a_1}, p, p \cdot a_2 + w(a_2)) = y$.

Next suppose that $w(a_2') \neq w(a_2)$ for some $a_2, a_2' \in A_2$. We can assume $w(a_2') < 0 < w(a_2)$. From the previous paragraph we know there are a_1, a_1' such that $x(a') - a_2' \ll 0 \ll x(a) - a_2$; see Figure 7.5.8. But then

$$x(a) - a_2 + a_2' \gg x(a'),$$

which contradicts the anonymity of x. ∎

Of the hypotheses of Proposition 7.5.7, the key is the one on preferences. The requirement that A_2 be a finite set is made only for simplicity of the proof. An example of an $h_1: A_1 \to \mathcal{P}^2_{\text{cl, sc}}$ satisfying (i) and (ii) is provided by putting $A_1 = R^\ell_{++}$ and letting $h_1(a_1)$ be the preference relation represented by $v(y) = \sum_j a_1^j u(y^j)$, where $u: R_+ \to R$ is a fixed C^2 function with $\partial u(r) > 0$ and $\partial^2 u(r) < 0$ for all $r \geq 0$.

7.6   No-surplus allocations in continuum exchange economies

Throughout this section, $\mathcal{E}: I \to \mathcal{A}_c$ *is a given continuum economy and* $x: I \to R^\ell_+$ *is an optimum allocation.* No-surplus allocations were defined in 7.6.2.

The equivalence results for the no-surplus property have a slightly different flavor than for the core or the anonymity cases. No-surplus allocations turn out to be Walrasian in all generality, and it is the converse proposition (the no-surplus character of Walrasian allocations) that needs an additional hypothesis. The latter is, however, of a weak and familiar sort, namely, that the allocation be linked.

7.6.1. Proposition. *If x has the no-surplus property, then it is Walrasian.*

Proof. Let $p \in R^\ell$, $\|p\| = 1$, support the optimum x. We argue by contradiction. If x is not Walrasian, then for some $\epsilon > 0$ the set

$$G = \{t \in I: p \cdot [x(t) - \omega(t)] \le -\epsilon\}$$

has positive measure. We can pick a decreasing sequence of nonnull $G_n \subset G$ with $\lambda(G_n) \to 0$. If $v \in \int_{I \setminus G_n} \{z - \omega(t): z \succeq_t x(t)\} \, dt$, then

$$\|v\| \ge p \cdot v \ge \int_{I \setminus G_n} p \cdot [x(t) - \omega(t)] \, dt = -\int_{G_n} p \cdot [x(t) - \omega(t)] \, dt \ge \lambda(G_n)\epsilon.$$

Hence, $s(x, I \setminus G_n) \ge \lambda(G_n)\epsilon$, which constitutes a contradiction to the no-surplus hypothesis. ∎

The next example, which has characteristics space $\mathcal{A} = \mathcal{P}^2_{\mathrm{cl}, c} \times R^\ell_+$, shows that a Walrasian allocation need not have the no-surplus property. The interpretation is that, in spite of the agent set being a continuum, very small sets of agents need not be economically powerless (not even approximately) at the Walrasian allocation. In the example, the Walrasian allocation is unique. Hence, because the previous proposition applies, we also get an instance of nonexistence of optimum allocations with the no-surplus property.

7.6.2. Example. The simplest example of nonlinked Walrasian allocation will do. Let $\ell = 2$. There are two types of agents with equal weight and characteristics $u_1(x_1) = x_1^1$, $u_2(x_2) = x_2^2$, $\omega_1 = (0, 2)$, $\omega_2 = (2, 0)$. The Walrasian allocation is obtained by giving $x_1(t) = (2, 0)$ [resp. $x_2(t) = (0, 2)$] to the agents of type 1 (resp. type 2). Obviously, the allocation is not linked. The fact that preferences are not strictly monotone is not an essential feature of the example.

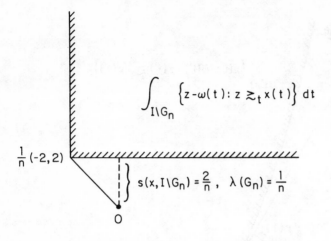

$$\int_{I\backslash G_n} \left\{ z - \omega(t) : z \gtrsim_t x(t) \right\} dt$$

$\frac{1}{n}(-2,2)$

$\left\} \quad s(x, I\backslash G_n) = \frac{2}{n}, \quad \lambda(G_n) = \frac{1}{n}\right.$

O

Figure 7.6.1

Let $G_n \subset I_n$ be composed of agents of type 1 and $\lambda(G_n) = 1/n$. Then,

$$\int_{I\backslash G_n} [x(t) - \omega(t)]\, dt = \frac{1}{n}(-2,2) \quad \text{and} \quad s(x, I\backslash G_n) = \frac{2}{n};$$

see Figure 7.6.1. Therefore, x does not have the no-surplus property.

The previous example has a rather extreme feature. As an optimum, x possesses an open set of supporting price vectors. This turns out to be crucial.

> **7.6.3. Proposition.** *Suppose that preferences are C^1 and strictly monotone and that x is a Walrasian allocation. If x is linked, then it has the no-surplus property.*

Proof. The attentive reader should note that the proof does not depend on the smoothness of preferences. The key fact is that x has a unique supporting price vector.

Let $p \in S$ be an equilibrium price vector and $G_n \subset I$ be an arbitrary monotone sequence of nonnull sets with $\lambda(G_n) \to 0$ and $s(x, I\backslash G_n) > 0$. Denote by v_n the vector in $V_n = \int_{I\backslash G_n} \{y - \omega(t) : y \gtrsim_t x(t)\}\, dt$ with smallest norm. Of course, $s(x, I\backslash G_n) = \|v_n\|$ and $v_n \to 0$. The vector $p_n = (1/\|v_n\|)v_n$ supports V_n at v_n, and so any limit point q of the sequence p_n supports $V = \int \{y - \omega(t) : y \gtrsim_t x(t)\}\, dt$ at the origin. In other words, q is a supporting price vector for the optimum x. Because x is linked, $q = p$ and we conclude that $p_n \to p$.

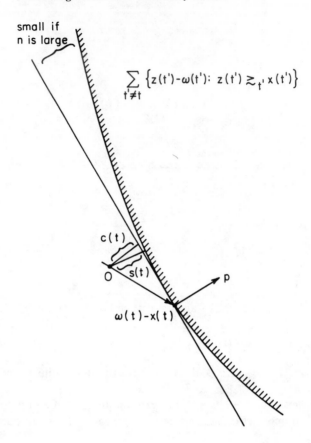

small if
n is large

$$\sum_{t'\neq t}\left\{z(t')-\omega(t'):\ z(t')\succsim_{t'}x(t')\right\}$$

c(t)

O   s(t)   p

$\omega(t)-x(t)$

Figure 7.6.2

Let $z_n=\int_{G_n}[x(t)-\omega(t)]\,dt$. Because $-z_n\in V_n$, $-p_n\cdot z_n\geq p_n\cdot v_n=\|v_n\|=s(x,I\setminus G_n)$. Being $x(t)$ and $\omega(t)$ uniformly bounded above, the sequence $[1/\lambda(G_n)]z_n$ is also bounded. Therefore, $p_n\to p$ and $p\cdot z_n=0$ for all n yields $[1/\lambda(G_n)]s(x,I\setminus G_n)\to 0$, which is the desired conclusion. ∎

We conclude with a brief word on the approximation theory for the finite number of agents case. Let $Q\subset\mathcal{P}^2_{b,sc}\times R^\ell_{++}$ be compact, $\mathcal{E}:I\to Q$, $\#I=n$, and x be an optimum for $\mathcal{E}$ with supporting price vector $p\in S$. For each t denote $c(t)=p\cdot[\omega(t)-x(t)]$ and

$$s(t)=\min\{\|\textstyle\sum_{t'\neq t}[y(t')-\omega(t')]\|:y(t')\succsim_{t'}x(t')\}.$$

Then $s(t)\geq c(t)$; see Figure 7.6.2. It is straightforward to show by the methods of Section 7.4 (especially the proof of Lemma 7.4.8) that there is a constant $H > 0$, depending only on Q, such that, for all t,

$$0 \leq s(t) - c(t) \leq (H/n) \max_t \|x(t)\|;$$

see Figure 7.6.2. Because $\max_t c(t)$ and $\max_t s(t)$ give, respectively, a measure of how far x is from being Walrasian or no-surplus, we get for n large a close relationship between the two properties. *Note:* For the finite economies case, Definition 7.2.6 has to be modified in the obvious way; that is, the optimum x has the no-surplus property if $s(t) = 0$ for all t. Proposition 7.6.1 remains valid. Therefore, no-surplus allocations typically do not exist in finite economies.

7.7 Reference notes

The informal notion that the proper setting for the theoretical study of competition is a model of markets with many traders is as old as economics. Already in the nineteenth century it played an explicit analytical role in the important work of Cournot (1838) and Edgeworth (1881). In the modern era the study of markets with many traders became popular through core theory, especially after the pathbreaking article of Debreu and Scarf (1963).

Section 7.1. The three properties analyzed have been chosen because they are important and simple and do not require much extra apparatus for their definition. Because we are not aiming at exhaustiveness, we have not surveyed some other interesting properties for which equivalence theorems have been proved – for example, being the noncooperative equilibria of certain market mechanisms (see Hurwicz, 1974; Schmeidler, 1980; Dubey–Mas-Colell–Shubik, 1980) or belonging to some solution sets inspired by cooperative game theory such as the Shapley value (see Aumann, 1975; Dubey–Neyman, 1984). We want to emphasize, however, that the driving underlying ideas, both of a technical and of an economic nature, for many equivalence theorems are few in number and that they are fully illustrated by the analysis of our three properties.

Section 7.2. The concept of the core is due to Edgeworth (1881), but it was reinvented in a more abstract setting and named by game theorists (Gillies, 1953). Its introduction into economics is due to Shubik (1959), Scarf (1962), and Debreu–Scarf (1963). The proof that a Walrasian allocation has the core property is implicit in Edgeworth (1881), proved in Debreu–Scarf (1963) and attributed by them to L. Shapley. The concept of envy-free allocation is due to Foley (1967). See Thompson–Varian (1985) for a recent survey. In the continuum the envy-free allocations are intimately related to the equilibria of anonymous market mechanisms (see, for example, Dubey–Mas-Colell–Shubik, 1980, for the anonymity concept). Because our motivation comes more from equilibrium than from ethical analysis, we have preferred the term *anonymous*. The no-surplus concept is due to Ostroy (1980). The classical, distant antecedent is J. B. Clark (1899).

Section 7.3. The literature on the core is very extensive. As general references for this and the next section, see W. Hildenbrand (1974, 1982). Building on Debreu–Scarf (1963), the core equivalence theorem stated in 7.3.1 was proved by Aumann (1964) and Vind (1964). The paper by Vind did first use the Lyapunov theorem. Proposition 7.3.2.i is due to Schmeidler (1972). For the special case where there is only a finite number of types, 7.3.2.ii was first noticed and proved by Townsend (1983). For an approach to core theory based on nonstandard analysis rather than measure theory, see Brown–Robinson (1975).

Section 7.4. Proposition 7.4.1 and its elegant proof are due to Anderson (1978). A similar result was established earlier by E. Dierker (1975) with different techniques. The Shapley–Folkman theorem was first used in economics by Starr (1969) and in core theory by Arrow–Hahn (1971). The various uniform boundedness lemmas of this chapter all go back to a remarkable paper by Bewley (1973). Proposition 7.4.3 appears almost explicitly in Grodal (1975). The two ingredients of its proof – the averaging result used in step 3 and the elementary Lemma 7.4.8 on the flattening out of the sum of smooth preferred sets – are both in her paper. The first ingredient is proved by her via the Shapley–Folkman, rather than Steinitz, theorem. The second had appeared earlier in Debreu (1975), one of the first studies of the core equivalence theorem in a smooth setting. See also Nishino (1971). Something like the proof of 7.4.8 is implicit in some studies of the core equivalence property via the calculus (such as Johansen, 1978, and Schweizer, 1982) and even in the original Edgeworth (1881); see Debreu–Scarf (1972). It could be argued that 7.4.8 is the central fact of the smooth approach to the core equivalence theorem. An antecessor of 7.4.4 is Hansen (1969).

The consideration of sequences of economies with well-defined limits as the central object of the asymptotic theory was proposed and extensively pursued by W. Hildenbrand (see W. Hildenbrand, 1974). Bewley (1973) discovered the need of requiring convergence of the supports in order to obtain uniform convergence. Proposition 7.4.9, which holds without smoothness, is due to Bewley (1973). See also W. Hildenbrand (1974). The proof, however, is different from Bewley's or Hildenbrand's, though it is interesting to point out that both theirs and the one here critically depend on the appeal to averaging results providing deviations from zero of aggregate excess demand that are small in absolute, not just relative (per capita) terms. In our case, this result is L.2.3 (used in the proof of 7.4.11). In theirs it is L.2.4, a number theoretic fact on the absolute approximation of reals by rationals.

Proposition 7.4.12 is due to Cheng (1982c). Case (ii) of Proposition 7.4.16 has been established in increasing generality by Debreu (1975), Grodal (1975), and Cheng (1981a). Examples of slowly convergent cores had been given by Shapley (1975) (see also Aumann, 1979). Debreu (1975) obtained the first positive result by requiring that he limit the regular. Allowing nonlinked allocations, Cheng (1982a) has given examples where the rate $1/n$ is not generic. Case (i) of Proposition 7.4.16 with the general rate $1/\sqrt{n}$ has been obtained by Anderson (1981) and Cheng (1982b). The papers by Cheng only consider the case with a finite number of types.

Section 7.5. Basic references are Varian (1976), Kleinberg (1980), McLennan (1982), and Champsaur–Laroque (1981). For a slightly different point of view see Hammond (1979) and Maskin (1980). The rule of thumb for attribution in this chapter is that all the results, such as 7.5.4, and proofs for the case where no boundary consumption is possible at the anonymous allocation, are contained in some of the above, largely overlapping references. When boundary consumptions are allowed, as in 7.5.7, they are particular instances of Mas-Colell (1983).

The idea that what matters for equivalence is the connectedness of consumptions is due to Varian (1976). The idea that this may be implied by the Lipschitzian connectedness of characteristics seem to first appear in Kleinberg (1980), which is also the reference for the indispensability of this hypothesis.

Section 7.6. All the results of this section are due to Ostroy (1980, 1981, 1984).

CHAPTER 8

Genericity analysis

8.1 Introduction

This chapter has two purposes. The first is to make good on the repeated promise to justify our attention to regular objects by establishing their typicality or, in the terminology of this chapter, their genericity. Hence, we shall argue that whenever a property has been called regular, the term is deserved. The second purpose is to illustrate by reiterated application the uses of transversality theory, an important mathematical technique that can be informally described to economists as a sophisticated version of the old counting of equations and unknowns.

A general introduction to the generic point of view is presented in Section 8.2. Section 8.3 describes the formal setting underlying the mathematical transversality theorems. Those are then applied to an investigation of the generic structure of demand (Section 8.4), production (Section 8.5), optima (Section 8.6), equilibria (Section 8.7), and some aspects of the equilibrium correspondence (Section 8.8). The aim is not to be exhaustive but to discuss a repertoire of typical situations and useful tricks. It is part of the objective of the chapter to make clear that, although they may differ in degree of complexity, most genericity arguments are, at bottom, very similar.

8.2 The generic point of view

It is a reasonable position that in the analysis of a social or physical system, the properties one should first focus on are those that enjoy persistency, that is, stability under perturbations, and are typical – informally, those whose qualitative characteristics do not depend too precisely on the environmental variables (persistency) and that hold but "exceptionally" in all admissible environments (typicality). The underlying justification for both desiderata is the same: In a world that is not observed, or perhaps not even given to us, in a very precise manner, only the persistent and typical have a good chance to be observed.

As indicated, persistence, or stability, means that the qualitative state of the system is not altered by small perturbations of the data. Note that as a matter of definition a persistent property is "open," that is, it holds on an open set of admissible environments. Stability is so basic a desideratum that in most of our analysis we have simply imbedded it at the heart of our modeling. Thus, regularity has usually been defined via full-rank conditions that, by virtue of the implicit function theorem, have been seen to immediately yield persistency. When discussing equilibrium in Chapter 5, we checked this repeatedly and in detail (e.g., Section 5.4). We shall not, therefore, devote much explicit attention in this chapter to verifying the stability of regular properties.

The other desideratum, genericity, cannot be disposed of so quickly. Typicality is no more than a suggestive term. We still need to develop a precise mathematical concept. This we do in two steps.

Suppose first that the universe, that is, the totality of admissible environments, is described by a finite number of parameters. The parameter space could be an open subset B of some R^m, or, more generally, an arbitrary C^1 m-dimensional manifold. It is then natural to denote a property as generic if it only fails to hold in a null set of parameters, that is, on a set of m-dimensional Lebesgue measure zero. Of course, a generic property in this sense is, a fortiori, also dense. Although in many applications stronger properties are known about the nature of exceptional sets – for example, they may be contained in a finite union of lower-dimensional manifolds – we shall rest content with nullness as our standard for the negligibility of sets. Remember also that we have already used and applied this concept in Chapter 5 (e.g., 5.8.15).

Let us now pass on to the more difficult case where the universe cannot be described by a finite number of parameters. The problem is then that Lebesgue measure is not available beyond R^m and, even if the parameter set B is otherwise quite nice, there is no natural measure to appeal to. This is a serious drawback that does not admit a fully satisfactory remedy. A partial one, much used in the mathematical literature, consists in replacing the measure theoretic by a topological approach to the notion of a negligible set.

Say that B, the parameter set, is also a topological space. An acceptable notion of a negligible subset of B should satisfy at least three conditions: (i) Open subsets of B are not negligible, (ii) a subset of a negligible set is negligible, (iii) the union of two negligible sets is negligible. There is an obvious candidate satisfying (i), (ii), and (iii): The nowhere-dense subsets. Hence we shall agree that a property is generic in a topological space if it holds on an open and dense set. For a complete topological space, this definition can be extended in a natural manner. We say in this case that a set is negligible if its complement is a so-called *residual* set, namely, a set that contains a countable intersection of open and dense sets. Because of the Baire property of complete spaces (A.4), residual sets are dense and, therefore, the concept of negligibility satisfies the desiderata (i), (ii), and the countable extension of (iii). Admittedly, the use of the term *residual* to mean "large" is misleading. But, unfortunately, this is a well-established terminological convention.

In our applications, the admissible universe has the structure of a topological space. So we adopt the definition of the previous paragraph, and by a generic property we mean one that holds on an open, dense set or, if the space is complete, on a residual set. We have already encountered some instances of use of this criterion; for example, in Chapter 5 we showed that the property of having a finite number of equilibria holds in an open, dense subset of the space of economies (5.8.14, 5.8.16).

Although the topological notion of genericity discriminates a bit more than merely asserting the density of a given property, it has to be thought of as much less sharp than the measure theoretic concept available in the finite-dimensional case. It is well known, after all, that an open, dense set of a Euclidean space can have an arbitrarily small nonzero measure. It is thus important to emphasize that many of the results of this chapter are in essence finite-dimensional. Indeed, the most common proof technique consists precisely in applying transversality theorems to establish measure theoretic genericity on conveniently chosen finite-dimensional subparameterizations of an infinite-dimensional reference space. Because for clarity of exposition we have chosen to make the genericity claims in the natural universe of admissible parameters, we are forced, however, to use in our formal statements the topological concept of genericity.

We end this section with two observations on the sensible use of the generic point of view.

The first is that when trying to establish the genericity of a property, one should be strict on the definition of the admissible set of parameters. This is clear enough and does not need much elaboration. Any set, for example, R^n, will look small if the universe is large enough, for example, R^{n+1}! Thus, in proving, say, the genericity of regular constant returns economies, we must be careful not to let our universe be such that the property of being constant returns is itself exceptional.

The second observation is that, as a matter of interpretation, focusing on generic objects, for example, economies, does not mean that nongeneric ones are of no interest and can be safely forgotten. Thus, for example, if we consider paths of economies, as we shall in Section 8.8, the property "the path crosses the critical set of economies" is certainly robust. For this situation, what the genericity point of view tells us is only that if the object of analysis is paths, then we should focus first on typical paths.

8.3 The mathematical theory

The mathematical background for this section is in Sections H and I of Chapter 1. The main theorems are directly quoted from there.

Our starting point is a system of equations $F_b(x) = 0$ representing the formal version of a physical or social system. Here $F_b: N \to R^m$, $N \subset R^n$, and b is an exogenous parameter kept fixed for the moment. The equilibria of the system are the vectors x of endogenous variables belonging to the solution set $F_b^{-1}(0)$.

How large is the set of equilibria? For a continuously differentiable F, the implicit function theorem (see H.2.2) makes precise the intuitive notion that with m equations and n unknowns there should be $n - m$ degrees of freedom. Indeed, it tells us that if 0 is a regular value of F_b, then $F_b^{-1}(0)$ is a smooth manifold of dimension $n - m$. The condition that 0 be a regular value of F_b can be paraphrased as saying that the number of distinct constraints on the system be effectively m, that is, that whenever $F_b(x) = 0$, the number of infinitesimally linearly independent equations should be m or, simply put, that rank $\partial F_b(x) = m$. It is worth remembering that the empty set qualifies as a manifold of any dimension, and so the implicit function theorem has in itself no implication whatsoever for the existence of solutions.

Two cases of particular importance in the following pages are $m = n$ and $m > n$. For $m = n$ we get that if 0 is a regular value of F_b, then every solution to $F_b(x) = 0$ is locally unique. When there are more equations than unknowns, that is, $m > n$, and the premise "0 is a regular value of F_b" holds, then we get the logical conclusion that $F_b(x) = 0$ has no solution: $F_b^{-1}(0)$ should be a manifold of dimension $n - m < 0$, and the only such manifold is the empty set. It should be pointed out that this follows directly from the definitions. Indeed, rank $\partial F_b(x) \le n < m$ for all x and so if there was an $\bar{x}$ with $F_b(\bar{x}) = 0$, the definition of regularity could not be satisfied.

We have seen that, provided 0 is a regular value of F_b, the equilibrium set of the system has the natural dimensionality properties we want it to have. But, of course, there is no a priori reason why 0 should be a regular value of F_b; see, for example, Figure 8.3.1. It is at this point that the mathematical transversality theorems come to our rescue. Informally, they allow us to conclude that if there is enough variation on F_b as b ranges

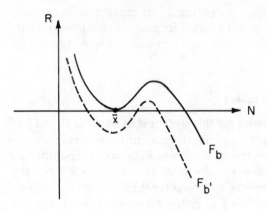

Figure 8.3.1

over its admissible universe – that is, if the universe itself has no built-in singularity – then typical worlds F_b will be nondegenerate, that is, will have 0 as a regular value. The coincidental-looking situation of Figure 8.3.1 will indeed be coincidental.

Precisely, let b take values on some open subset $B \subset R^s$ and $F(x, b) = F_b(x)$ be a C^1 function on $N \times B$. Then the required variability condition is simply that 0 be a regular value of F, that is, that rank $\partial F(x, b) = m$ whenever $F(x, b) = 0$. Obviously, the chances that 0 will be a regular value of F increases over F_b since $\partial F(x, b)$ has the same number of rows as $\partial F_b(x)$, but it has in addition the columns corresponding to $\partial_b F(x, b)$. It often happens that the dependence on b alone is so rich that the stronger condition, "rank $\partial_b F(x, b) = m$ for all (x, b)" does hold.

The following proposition constitutes the basic mathematical tool for this chapter. We quote it from I.2.2 and provide no proof, although for the important case $m = n$ we have already used it in 5.8.15 and shown there how it can be derived from Sard's theorem. The proposition imposes a restriction on the degree of differentiability of F that cannot be dispensed with but that should be taken as purely technical.

> **8.3.1. Proposition.** *Let* $F: N \times B \to R^m$, $N \subset R^n$, $B \subset R^s$ *be* C^r *with* $r > \max\{n - m, 0\}$. *Suppose that* 0 *is a regular value of* F; *that is,* $F(x, b) = 0$ *implies* rank $\partial F(x, b) = m$. *Then, except for a set of* $b \in B$ *of Lebesgue measure zero,* $F_b: N \to R^m$ *has* 0 *as a regular value.*

The above is a remarkable result. Thus, in many applications it allows making almost everywhere inferences about rank $\partial_x F$ from an everywhere

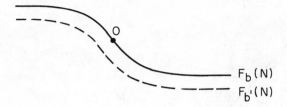

Figure 8.3.2

knowledge about rank $\partial_b F$. The logic of the proposition can perhaps be clarified if we informally discuss two examples corresponding to the cases $m = n$ and $m > n$. For $m = n$ (resp. $m > n$), the proposition says: "If F is C^1, then $F_b^{-1}(0)$ is discrete (resp. empty) for almost every $b \in B$." Take $m = n = 1$ and let F_b be as in Figure 8.3.1. Obviously, 0 is not a regular value of F_b at $\bar{x}$. But the hypothesis of the proposition tells us that $F_b(\bar{x})$ must be sensitive to the perturbations of b [this is what rank $\partial F(\bar{x}, b) = 1$ implies], and so it makes sense that a random displacement of b, to b' say, will lead to an $F_{b'}$ which, as in the illustration, is regular. Similarly, take $n = 1$, $m = 2$ and let $F_b(N) \subset R^2$ be as in Figure 8.3.2. Obviously, 0 is not a regular value of F_b because $0 = F_b(\bar{x})$ for some $\bar{x}$. But the hypothesis, that is, rank $\partial F(\bar{x}, b) = 2$, implies that $F_b(\bar{x})$ is sensitive to the perturbations of b, and so it makes sense that a random displacement of b, to b' say, will put 0 off $F_{b'}(N)$.

We conclude this section by recasting Proposition 8.3.1 in a more geometric setting. Formally, we get a more general result, but it is, in fact, the same one. Take for N and B arbitrary nonempty C^r manifolds of dimensions n and s, respectively. Also, let M be a C^r manifold of dimension m, and let $F: N \times B \to M$ be a C^r function. Suppose that $Q \subset M$ is a C^r manifold of dimension q. All these manifolds are boundaryless. Remember (I.2) that $F_b \pitchfork_M Q$, read "F_b is transversal to Q on M," means that $F_b(N)$ and Q intersect in general position; that is,

$$\partial F_b(T_x N) + T_{F_b(x)} Q = T_{F_b(x)} M \quad \text{whenever } F_b(x) \in Q;$$

see Figure 8.3.3. Similarly for $F \pitchfork_M Q$. If $F_b \pitchfork_M Q$, the implicit function theorem (I.2.1) says that the solution set $\{x : F_b(x) \in Q\}$ has dimension $n - (m - q)$, that is, equal to the number of n unknowns minus the number $m - q$ of restrictions.

The corresponding version of Proposition 3.3.1, to which it specializes for $Q = \{0\}$, is then (see I.2.2):

8.3.2. Proposition. *Let N, B, M be C^r boundaryless manifolds of dimensions n, s, m, respectively. Let $F: N \times B \to M$ be a C^r*

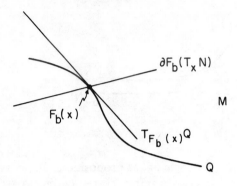

Figure 8.3.3

function and $Q \subset M$ a C^r manifold of dimension q with no boundary. Suppose that $r > \max\{n - (m - q), 0\}$ and $F \pitchfork_M Q$. Then except for $b \in B$ on a null subset of B, we have $F_b \pitchfork_M Q$.

8.4   Generic demand

The aim of this section is to study some of the generic differentiability properties of demand. As usual, our reference consumption sets are $X = R_+^\ell \setminus \{0\}$ and $X = R_{++}^\ell$. We follow the notation of Chapter 2. The space of continuous, monotone preference relations on X satisfying "$\{z \in Z : z \succsim x\}$ is R^ℓ-closed for all x" is denoted $\mathcal{P}_{cl}$ (resp. $\mathcal{P}_b$) if $X = R_+^\ell \setminus \{0\}$ (resp. if $X = R_{++}^\ell$). Then $\mathcal{P}$ is the generic term for either $\mathcal{P}_{cl}$ or $\mathcal{P}_b$. The set $\mathcal{P}^2$ is topologically complete (2.4.5) and therefore the closed subset $\mathcal{P}_c^2 = \{\succsim \in \mathcal{P}^2 : \succsim$ is convex$\}$ is also. Hence, it is meaningful to regard as generic a property on $\mathcal{P}_c^2$ that holds on a residual set, namely, one containing a countable intersection of open, dense sets (see Section 8.2).

We know (see 2.7) that a necessary condition for the demand function $\varphi_\succsim : S \times R_{++}^\ell \to R^\ell$ induced by preferences $\succsim \in \mathcal{P}_c^2$ to be a C^1 function is that $\succsim$ be regular at every $x \in X$, that is, that the Gaussian curvature at x, denoted $c(\succsim, x)$, of the indifference manifold through x be nonzero. The first result of this section should be clear enough. We point out that it is not based on transversality arguments.

8.4.1. Proposition. *The set $\mathcal{P}_{sc}^2 = \{\succsim \in \mathcal{P}_c^2 : c(\succsim, x) \neq 0$ for all $x \in X\}$ is residual in $\mathcal{P}_c^2$. More specifically, for every compact $K \subset X$ the set $\{\succsim \in \mathcal{P}_c^2 : c(\succsim, x) \neq 0$ for every $x \in K\}$ is open and dense.*

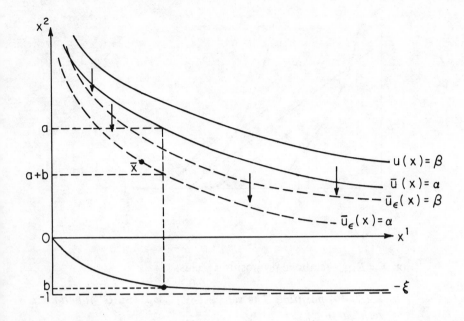

Figure 8.4.1

Proof. Given a compact K the openness property is obvious. So we only need to worry about density, that is, about approaching any $\succeq \in \mathcal{P}_c^2$ by an appropriate $\succeq'$. Let $\succeq$ remain fixed from now on and fix a C^2 utility representation u for $\succeq$ (2.4). Because a countable intersection of open, dense subsets of $\mathcal{P}_c^2$ is nonempty, it suffices to prove that "for every $\bar{x} \in X$ there is a neighborhood V with compact closure $\bar{V}$ in X such that we can find a $\succeq' \in \mathcal{P}_c^2$ arbitrarily close to $\succeq$ with $c(\succeq, x) \neq 0$ for all $x \in \bar{V}$." So let $\bar{x} \in X$ remain fixed and choose the neighborhood V so that, for some j, $\partial_j u(x) \neq 0$ for all $x \in \bar{V}$. Without loss of generality, we put $j = \ell$. Pick an auxiliary C^∞ function $\xi: [0, \infty) \to [0, 1]$ with the properties $\xi'(t) > 0$, $\xi''(t) < 0$ for all t. For every $\epsilon > 0$ we then perturb the given utility function u to $u_\epsilon(x) = u(x^1, \dots, x^{\ell-1}, x^\ell + \epsilon \sum_{j=1}^{\ell-1} \xi(x^j))$. Figure 8.4.1 illustrates the change undergone by the indifference manifolds on a neighborhood of $\bar{x}$. When looked at as graphs of functions $x^\ell = \eta_{\bar{u}}(x^1, \dots, x^{\ell-1})$, the perturbation of u amounts to adding to the indifference functions (which are convex) the convex and regular function $-\epsilon \sum_{j=1}^{\ell-1} \xi(x^j)$. If $X = R_{++}^\ell$, we further approximate u_ϵ by some u_ϵ' representing a $\succeq'$ in $\mathcal{P}_b^2$, that is, satisfying the boundary condition. It is then clear that, if ϵ is small enough, $c(\succeq', x) \neq 0$ for all $x \in \bar{V}$ (see 2.5.1). ∎

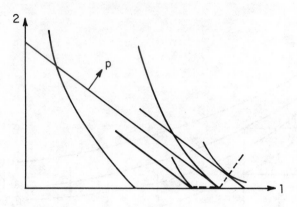

Figure 8.4.2

For $X = R_{++}^{\ell}$ the above proposition yields:

> **8.4.2. Proposition.** *The set* $\{\succsim \in \mathcal{P}_{b,c}^2 : \varphi_{\succsim}$ *is a* C^1 *function$\}$ is residual in* $\mathcal{P}_{b,c}^2$.

Proof. Combine 8.4.1, 2.6.7, and A.3.4.   ∎

When the constraints may bite, that is, for $X = R_+^{\ell} \setminus \{0\}$ and preferences in $\mathcal{P}_{cl,c}^2$, the situation is not so nice. By virtue of 8.4.1 we have, to be sure, a well-defined demand function on a residual set of preferences. Nevertheless, nondifferentiabilities are unavoidable at price–wealth combinations at which demand just passes from a coordinate subspace to a lower-dimensional one. A glance at Figure 8.4.2 should be persuasive enough. The figure, however, also suggests that the points (p, w) at which $\varphi_{\succsim}$ is not differentiably are coincidental, or in other words, that given $\succsim \in \mathcal{P}_{cl,sc}^2$, the property "$\varphi_{\succsim}$ is C^1 at (p, w)" may hold except for a set of price–wealth combinations of null measure. As we shall now see, much more is true. The nondifferentiability region is endowed with a rich inner structure.

> **8.4.3. Proposition.** *Let* $\succsim \in \mathcal{P}_{cl,sc}^2$. *Then* $\varphi_{\succsim}$ *is Lipschitzian and there is a set* $M \subset S \times R$ *that is a finite union of closed, C^1 manifolds of dimension less than* ℓ *and that contains the points where* $\varphi_{\succsim}$ *fails to be* C^1.

Proof. Let $\succsim$ be as in the statement and u a C^2 utility for $\succsim$. Without loss of generality we let u be defined on an open neighborhood V of $R_+^{\ell} \setminus \{0\}$.

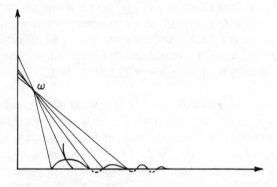

Figure 8.4.3

For each coordinate subspace L and $(p, w) \in S \times R$ consider the maximization of u on $\{u \in L \cap V : p \cdot x \le w\}$. If a solution exists, we denote it by $\varphi_L(p, w)$ and observe that, as with ordinary demand, φ_L is a C^1 function at (p, w) and rank $\partial \varphi_L(p, w) = \dim L$; see 2.7.2. Note that φ_L differs from the usual demand function only in two respects: Its values are restricted to L, and every other nonnegativity constraint is dropped.

Because rank $\partial \varphi_L(p, w) = \dim L$, the implicit function theorem (H.2.2) yields that, for any coordinate subspace $L' \subset L$, $\varphi_L^{-1}(L')$ is a closed, C^1 manifold of dimension $\ell - (\dim L - \dim L')$. Let then the set $M \subset S \times R$ be the union of all $\varphi_L^{-1}(L')$ with $1 \le \dim L' < \dim L$. Consider any (p, w) and denote $x = \varphi_{\succeq}(p, w)$. Then there is $\lambda > 0$ such that $\partial_j u(x) = \lambda p^j$ whenever $x^j > 0$. Let L (resp. L') be the coordinate subspace spanned by the indices j with $\partial_j u(x) = \lambda p^j$ (resp. $x^j > 0$). Then $L' \subset L$, $x \in L'$, and $x = \varphi_L(p, w)$; that is, $(p, w) \in \varphi_L^{-1}(L')$. If $\varphi_{\succeq}$ is not differentiable at (p, w), then there has to be a j with $x^j = 0$ and $\partial_j u(x) = \lambda p^j$. Hence, $\dim L' < \dim L$, and so $(p, w) \in M$. To see that $\varphi_{\succeq}$ is nevertheless Lipschitzian at (p, w), note that, in a neighborhood of (p, w), $\varphi_{\succeq}$ is a continuous selection from $(p', w') \mapsto \bigcup_{L'' \subset L} \{\varphi_{L''}(p', w')\}$ and, therefore, being each $\varphi_{L''}$ Lipschitzian at (p, w), it is itself Lipschitzian (see G.1, 2.7.3). ∎

In many applications, we are interested not so much in the demand as in the excess demand function generated by a given $\succeq$ and initial endowments ω. The result analogous to Proposition 8.4.3 does not then always hold. Figure 8.4.3 indicates how a counterexample could be constructed. Nevertheless, the result does hold generically, that is, for almost every $\omega \in R_{++}^\ell$. This is the content of the next proposition, which constitutes the first application of the transversality theorems in this chapter.

8.4.4. Proposition. *Given* $\succeq \in \mathcal{P}^2_{\text{cl}, sc}$ *there is a null set* $J \subset R_{++}$ *such that if* $\omega \notin J$, *then the excess demand function* $f_\omega(p) = \varphi_\succeq(p, p \cdot \omega) - \omega$ *is Lipschitzian and there is a set* $M_\omega \subset S$ *that is a finite union of closed,* C^1 *manifolds of dimension less than* $\ell - 1$ *and that contains the points where* f_ω *fails to be* C^1.

Proof. By the previous proposition there is $M \subset S \times R$ that contains the nondifferentiability points of $\varphi_\succeq$ and is such that $M = \bigcup_{k=1}^m M^k$, where every M^k is a C^1 manifold of dimension less than ℓ. Because $\varphi_\succeq$ is Lipschitzian, so it is f_ω for any ω. Also, if f_ω is not differentiable at p, then $(p, p \cdot \omega) \in M$; that is, $p \in M_\omega^k = \{p \in S : (p, p \cdot \omega) \in M^k\}$ for some k. We shall show that, generically on ω, M_ω^k is a C^1 manifold of dimension less than $\ell - 1$.

Define $\xi : S \times R^\ell \to S \times R$ by $\xi(p, \omega) = (p, p \cdot \omega)$. Obviously,

$$\text{rank } \partial \xi(p, \omega) = \ell \quad \text{for any } (p, \omega).$$

Hence, $\partial \xi(p, \omega)$ maps onto $T_p \times R$ and so ξ is transversal to any submanifold of $S \times R$. In particular, $\xi \pitchfork M^k$. Therefore, by the transversality theorem (8.3.2), we have $\xi_\omega \pitchfork M^k$ for a.e. ω. But by the implicit function theorem (see I.2.1) $\xi_\omega \pitchfork M^k$ implies that $M_\omega^k = \xi_\omega^{-1}(M^k)$ is a C^1 manifold of the same codimension as M^k, that is, of dimension

$$(\ell - 1) - (\ell - \dim M^k) < (\ell - 1). \qquad \blacksquare$$

We saw in Chapter 5, Section 5.2, that if we deal not with an individual but with the aggregate excess demand function of many, in fact a continuum of consumers, then the nondifferentiabilities due to the boundaries of consumption sets may be naturally smoothed out. In 5.2.8 we stated a condition under which aggregate excess demand function turns out to be C^1. The condition was essentially that for every p only a measure zero set of consumers has a nondifferentiability at p. This can be interpreted as requiring that the underlying distribution of preferences be dispersed. We would like to argue that the differentiability of excess demand is a generic property in continuum economies. Unfortunately, a technical difficulty bars our way. We cannot claim the completeness of the space $\mathfrak{M}$ of continuum economies on $\mathcal{P}^2_{\text{cl}, sc} \times R^\ell_{++}$. See Sections 5.2 and 5.8 for the definition of $\mathfrak{M}$. For what it is worth, we may nevertheless still prove that the excess demand function f_ν is C^1 for a set of $\nu \in \mathfrak{M}$ that is a dense intersection of open subsets.

8.4.5. Proposition. *The set* $\{\nu \in \mathfrak{M} : f_\nu \text{ is } C^1\}$ *contains a dense intersection of open subsets of* $\mathfrak{M}$.

Proof. Denote the set of characteristics by $\mathfrak{A} = \mathcal{P}^2_{cl,\,sc} \times R^\ell_{++}$. Given arbitrary $\succsim, \omega, p$, let u be an admissible utility for $\succsim$ and put $x = \varphi(\succsim, p, p \cdot \omega)$. Utility maximization yields a $\lambda > 0$ such that $\partial_j u(x) \le \lambda p^j$, with equality whenever $x^j > 0$. If, in addition, the condition "$x^j = 0$ implies $\partial_j u(x) < \lambda p^j$" is satisfied, then we know that $\varphi(\succsim, p, p \cdot \omega)$ is C^1 at p (2.7.2). For any p and $\delta \ge 0$ let $A_{p,\delta} \subset \mathfrak{A}$ be the set of characteristics such that if $(\succsim, \omega) \in A_{p,\delta}$ and $\|p' - p\| \le \delta$, then $\succsim, \omega, p'$ satisfy the above condition.

Define $\mathfrak{M}^+ = \{\nu \in \mathfrak{M} : \nu(A_{p,0}) = 1$ for every $p\}$. We saw in 5.2.8 that f_ν is C^1 whenever $\nu \in \mathfrak{M}^+$. The proof is now organized in two steps. The first proves that $\mathfrak{M}^+$ is dense, whereas the second shows that it is also a G_δ set.

Step 1. We want to approximate a given ν by a $\nu' \in \mathfrak{M}^+$. Without loss of generality we can assume that ν is finitely supported (5.8.1). Since we can handle every point in the support separately, it is enough to consider the case where ν is supported by a single $(\succsim, \omega) \in \mathfrak{A}$. Without loss of generality we can also assume (see 2.8) that $\succsim$ is representable by a C^2, concave utility function u.

We proceed by perturbing u linearly. For every $b \in R^\ell_{++}$ define $(\succsim_b, \omega) \in \mathfrak{A}$ by means of the concave utility function $u_b(x) = u(b, x) = u(x) + b \cdot x$. We shall show that, for every p, the set $\{b \in R^\ell_{++} : (\succsim_b, \omega) \notin A_{p,0}\}$ is null. To have the desired result, we than only need to replace the unit mass at $(\succsim, \omega)$ by the measure induced by any distribution on the parameters b that is absolutely continuous with respect to Lebesgue measure and is concentrated near the origin.

The claim is established by a simple transversality argument. Let p be given. If $(\succsim_{\bar{b}}, \omega) \in A_{p,0}$ then, relabeling the axes, there is a solution with $b = \bar{b}$ for a system of $\ell + 2$ equations such as:

$$\xi(x, \lambda, b) = \begin{cases} p \cdot (x - \omega) = 0 \\ \partial_j u(x) + b^j - \lambda p^j = 0, & 1 \le j \le m \\ x^j = 0, & m \le j \le \ell. \end{cases}$$

By noting that $m \ge 2$ it is immediately verified that we always have rank $\partial \xi(x, \lambda, b) = \ell + 2$. Hence, by the transversality theorem (8.3.1), $\xi(x, \lambda, b) = 0$ implies rank $\partial_{x,\lambda} \xi(x, \lambda, b) = \ell + 2$ for a.e. b. But x, λ constitute a set of only $\ell + 1$ variables, and so we must conclude that, for a.e. b, $\xi(x, \lambda, b) = 0$ has no solution. Taking into account that there is only a finite number of ways to relabel the axes, this is precisely the conclusion we wanted.

Step 2. Let $S = \bigcup_n K_n$, where K_n is an increasing sequence of compact sets. Define $\mathfrak{M}_n = \{\nu \in \mathfrak{M} : \nu(A_{p,0}) > 1 - 1/n$ for every $p \in K_n\}$ and note that $\mathfrak{M}^+ = \bigcap_n \mathfrak{M}_n$. We want to show that every $\mathfrak{M}_n$ contains a neighborhood of $\mathfrak{M}^+$. To this effect, let n and $\nu \in \mathfrak{M}^+$ be fixed from now on. We first find a finite collection $\{A_1, \ldots, A_m\}$, $A_k \subset \mathfrak{A}$, such that for any $p \in K_n$ there is some k with $A_{p,0} \supset A_k$ and $\nu(A_k) > 1 - 1/n$ for all k. Obtaining this collection is a simple matter of compactness. Indeed, we have $\nu(A_{p,0}) = 1$ and $\bigcup_{\delta > 0} A_{p,\delta} = A_{p,0}$. Therefore, for any p there is $\delta(p) > 0$ such that $\nu(A_{p,\delta(p)}) > 1 - 1/n$. The sets $\{p' \in S : \|p' - p\| < \delta(p)\}$, $p \in K$, cover K. Hence, there is a finite subcover, and the corresponding $A_{p,\delta(p)}$ constitute then the desired collection.

Note that every element of the collection $\{A_1, \ldots, A_m\}$ is open. Hence, if ν' is near enough ν, we have $\nu'(A_k) > 1 - 1/n$ for all k. Because for any $p \in K_n$ there is k with $A_{p,0} \supset A_k$, this yields $\nu'(A_{p,0}) > 1 - 1/n$ for all $p \in K_n$. Therefore, $\mathfrak{M}_n$ does indeed contain a neighborhood of any $\nu \in \mathfrak{M}^+$. ∎

We remark that the previous proof applies without modification to the set $\mathfrak{M}'$ of all measures on $\mathcal{P}^2_{\text{cl},sc} \times (0, k)^\ell$ endowed with the topology of the weak convergence. In this case $\mathfrak{M}'$ is complete (see comments at the end of 5.8).

Proposition 8.4.5 exemplifies the powerful regularizing effect of aggregation in demand analysis: A certain collection of nonsmooth, individual excess demand functions is aggregated into a smooth function. For the sake of illustration, we discuss another instance of such regularizing effects: The aggregation of a dispersed collection of demand correspondences into a function.

8.4.6. Proposition. Let $\mathfrak{M}$ be the space of continuum economies on $\mathcal{P}_{\text{cl}} \times R^\ell_{++}$, where $\mathcal{P}_{\text{cl}}$ are the continuous, monotone preferences on R^ℓ_+. Then the set $\mathfrak{M}^+ = \{\nu \in \mathfrak{M} : \text{the aggregate excess demand correspondence } f_\nu \text{ is a continuous function}\}$ is residual on the complete space $\mathfrak{M}$.

Proof. For the definition and the completeness of $\mathfrak{M}$, see 5.8.1. The strategy of the proof of 8.4.6 is parallel to that of 8.4.5. Some details will not be repeated.

Step 1. We first show the density of $\mathfrak{M}^+$. Without loss of generality, the problem reduces to the approximation of any given ν that puts unit mass at a single $(\gtrsim, \omega)$. Let u be a continuous utility function for $\gtrsim$. Again, we perturb u linearly. Consider $u(x, b) = u(x) + b \cdot x$, where $b \gg 0$. Given any p, suppose that x_1, x_2 maximize $u(x, b)$ on $\{x \geq 0 : p \cdot x = p \cdot \omega\}$ and $x_1 \neq x_2$. Then $\partial_b(u(x_1, b) - u(x_2, b)) = x_1 - x_2 \neq 0$. Hence, by I.3.1, the set $\{b \in R^\ell_{++} : u_b(x) \text{ has more than one maximizer}\}$ is null. So if we replace the unit mass at $(\succsim, \omega)$ by a measure spread over small values of b, we get a ν' for which $f_{\nu'}$ will be a function. Because, as a correspondence, $f_{\nu'}$ is upper hemicontinuous (5.8.3), it is automatically continuous as a function.

Step 2. Let $K_n \subset S$ be an increasing sequence of compact sets with $\bigcup_n K_n = S$. Define $\mathfrak{M}_n = \{\nu \in \mathfrak{M}: \text{radius } f_\nu(p) < 1/n \text{ for every } p \in K_n\}$. Then $\mathfrak{M}^+ = \bigcap_n \mathfrak{M}_n$. By step 1, every $\mathfrak{M}_n$ is dense. Because, as a correspondence of both ν and p, $f_\nu(p)$ is upper hemicontinuous (see 5.8.3), it is straightforward to verify that every $\mathfrak{M}_n$ is also open. Hence, $\mathfrak{M}^*$ is residual. ∎

Proposition 8.4.6 is an important result. Due to the theory of the integration of correspondences (see E.2), it is well known that price equilibrium theory can handle, to some extent, nonconvex preferences. Indeed, subject to a few boundedness conditions, the aggregation over a continuum of correspondences (demand or otherwise) yields a convex-valued correspondence, and so one gets from this general mathematical principle that f_ν will be a convex-valued correspondence for all $\nu \in \mathfrak{M}$. Therefore, there will always be a price vector p such that $0 \in f_\nu(p)$. However, the interpretation of this p as an equilibrium is a delicate matter because p does not specify completely the state of the economy. It may very well happen that at this p a positive fraction of consumers have more than one preference-maximizing commodity vector. In this case, the consumption of every consumer at equilibrium cannot be determined from the knowledge of the equilibrium price p alone. A careful matching up of consumptions is needed. This seems hardly in the spirit of decentralized resource allocation theory. What Proposition 8.4.6 makes sure for us is that generically this will not happen: At any price, and a fortiori at equilibrium, almost every consumer has a single maximizer in its budget set. From the point of view of this book, an unhappy fact is that Proposition 8.4.6 cannot be strengthened to establish the genericity of C^1 aggregate excess demand. The investigation of dispersion conditions on economies with nonconvex preferences leading to smooth aggregate excess demand is a very subtle affair, and we shall not get into it.

A last remark is that the results of Propositions 8.4.5 and 8.4.6 have no measure theoretic parallel. Generally speaking, their conclusion will not hold as generic statements for finite-dimensional parameterizations. Informally, it is essential for the result that one be able to distort the given economy in infinitely many directions. In light of our comments in Section 8.2, this casts a shadow on the strength of these propositions. But we should not hurry to dismiss them. Keep in mind that at the very least, the density implication of their conclusion is of interest.

8.5   Generic production sets

In this section, which should be read in conjunction with Chapter 3 (especially 3.6 and 3.7), we argue that the property of quasi-smoothness (see 3.6.1) holds generically for production sets. In contrast to what has been done for the consumption side, we have not defined in this book a formal space of production sets. Therefore, we confine our analysis to the discussion of three representative and familiar examples. It is worth pointing out, however, that in each of the examples the notion of convergence for the production sets is in the generic region at least as strong as the one we introduced in Section 3.8 for quasi-smooth sets; that is, a perturbation of a regular production set in the examples is also a perturbation in the sense of Section 3.8.

The first example looks at the production set (perhaps to be thought of as belonging to a single firm) as determined from a finite number of technological constraints. The second contemplates the aggregate production set as derived from the sum of individual production sets. Finally, in the third example, the latter, hence also the aggregate, are restricted to be of the constant returns type. To repeat, the examples are only intended to be representative. Each of them tackles an important phenomenon, but, for the sake of clarity, no effort is made to handle all the complications at once.

8.5.1. Example. As we saw in 3.7.1, a sufficient condition for the quasi-smoothness of Y is that there exists a finite family of C^2, convex functions $\eta_j : R^\ell \to R$, $j \in J$, such that:

  (i) $Y = \{x : \eta_j(x) \le 0 \text{ for all } x\}$; and
  (ii) if we let $J(x) = \{j \in J : \eta_j(x) = 0\}$ then, for all $x \in R^\ell$, the collection of vectors $\{\partial \eta_j(x) : j \in J(x)\}$ is linearly independent.

Denote by $\mathcal{F}_j$ the space of C^2, convex functions on R^ℓ endowed with the topology of the C^2, uniform convergence on compacta. Put $\mathcal{F} = \prod_{j \in J} \mathcal{F}_j$. We identify any $\eta \in \mathcal{F}$ with the production sets defined as in (i) above. To verify that (ii) constitutes then a generic property is trivial enough. First note that, restricted to a compact set $K \in R^\ell$, (ii) is an open property, which means that, unrestricted, it is satisfied on a countable intersection of open sets. Therefore, it suffices to prove its density.

Let $\bar{\eta} \in \mathcal{F}$. Without loss of generality we can assume that $\bar{\eta}$ is C^∞ (H.4.4). Take an arbitrary subset of indices $J' \subset J$. For any $b \in R^j$ define $\eta : R^\ell \times R^J \to R^{J'}$ by $\eta_j(x, b) = \bar{\eta}_j(x) + b_j$. Obviously, rank $\partial \eta(x, b) = \#J'$ at any (x, b). Therefore, by the transversality theorem 8.3.1, $\eta_b(x) = 0$ implies rank $\partial \eta_b(x) = \#J'$ for a.e. b. But this is precisely condition (ii) for

$\bar{\eta}$ perturbed to $\bar{\eta} + b$ and $J(x) = J'$. Because b can be picked to be small and to work for all $J' \subset J$, we have obtained our conclusion. ∎

8.5.2. Example. Suppose now that the aggregate production set is formed as the sum of m individual sets Y_j, $1 \leq j \leq m$. In principle, every Y_j could be as in the previous example, but to focus on essentials we concentrate on the special case where, for every j, there is a C^2, convex function $\eta_j: R^\ell \to R$ and a set of commodity indexes H_j, to be interpreted as inputs, such that $Y_j = \{x: \eta_j(x) \leq 0, x^h \leq 0 \text{ for } h \in H_j\}$. We also assume that $\partial \eta_j(x) \gg 0$ for all x, which implies that $\eta_j^{-1}(0)$ is transversal to any nonzero coordinate subspace.

We shall show that if every η_j is differentiably strictly convex, that is, $\partial^2 \eta_j(x)$ is nonsingular at all x, then $Y = \sum_{j=1}^m Y_j$ is quasi-smooth. At the risk of belaboring the obvious, we mention that this strong convexity condition is generic if we endow a space of convex functions with the C^2 uniform topology on compacta. The proof of quasi-smoothness of Y is quite parallel to the proof of Proposition 8.4.3 for demand functions. This should not be surprising since if we think in terms of supply functions, what we are claiming here is very similar to what we did there.

For specificity, take $m = 2$. Fix two arbitrary nontrivial coordinate subspaces L_1, L_2 and consider the production sets $Y_j = \{x \in L_j: \eta_j(x) \leq 0\}$, $j = 1, 2$. Let $\beta_j: R^\ell \to R$ be the profit function of Y_j and note that $\partial^2 \beta_j$ is positive definite on L_j. Our first observation is a consequence of the implicit function theorem: (a) If $p + \partial \beta_1(p) + \partial \beta_2(p) = z$, then we can solve $p(z)$ in a C^1 manner. Obviously, the function $p(z)$ has rank $\partial p(z) = \ell$, which for the composite function $\xi_j(z) = \partial \beta_j(p(z))$ implies that $\partial \xi_j(z)$ maps onto the tangent space to $\eta_j^{-1}(0) \cap L_j$ at $\partial \beta_j(p(z))$. Because $\eta_j^{-1}(0)$ is transversal to every nonzero coordinate subspace of R^ℓ, it follows that if $L_j' \subset L_j$ is a nonzero coordinate subspace, then $\xi_j \pitchfork_{L_j} L_j'$. This yields our second conclusion: (b) If $L_j' \subset L_j$ is a nonzero coordinate subspace and $L_j' \neq L_j$, then $\{z: \partial \beta_j(p(z)) \in L_j'\}$ is a C^1 manifold of dimension less than ℓ (I.2.1).

The quasi-smoothness property follows from the combination of (a) and (b) above. Let $M \subset R^\ell$ be the union of the sets $\{z: \partial \beta_j(p(z)) \in L_j'\}$ as we run over all L_1, L_2, L_1', L_2'. By (b), M is a finite union of C^1 manifolds of dimension less than ℓ. On the other hand, if $\bar{z} \notin M \cup Y$, then there are L_1, L_2 such that, on a neighborhood of $\bar{z}$, $\pi_Y(z) = z - p(z)$, where $p(z)$ is defined with respect to L_1, L_2 as in the previous paragraph. Therefore, by (a), π_Y is C^1 at $\bar{z}$. Taking $A = M \cup \partial Y$ and remembering that $\Upsilon(z) = \frac{1}{2}\|z - \pi_Y(z)\|^2$, we see that the definition of quasi-smoothness (3.6.1) is satisfied.

8.5.3. Example. In this example the aggregate production set Y is derived from a finite collection of generalized linear activities described by restricted profit functions β_j (see 3.4 and 3.7). We neglect boundary restrictions and take β_j to be as nice as possible; that is, we assume: (i) $\partial^2 \beta_j(p)$ exists and is positive definite on $\{x: \partial\beta(p)x = 0\}$. We first establish the quasi-smoothness of Y under the additional hypothesis: (ii) for all p, the vectors in $A(p) = \{\partial\beta_j(p): \beta_j(p) = 0\}$ are linearly independent. Later we argue the genericity of (ii).

Let J be an arbitrary subset of activity indices. Consider the system of $\ell + \#J$ equations in the $\ell + \#J$ unknowns (p, α):

$$z - p + \sum_{j \in J} \alpha_j \partial\beta_j(p) = 0, \quad \beta_j(p) = 0, \quad j \in J.$$

By conditions (i) and (ii) above, the derivative of this system with respect to p and α has full rank. Therefore, we can locally solve $p(z; J)$ and $\alpha(z; J)$. It is also immediately verified that rank $\partial\alpha(z; J) = \#J$, which, of course, implies $\partial\alpha_j(z; J) \neq 0$ for every $j \in J$. So $M(J) = \bigcup_{j \in J} \alpha_j^{-1}(0; J)$ is a union of manifolds of dimension less than ℓ and, therefore, so is M, the union of the $M(J)$ as we run over the different J. For any $z \notin Y$ let $J(z) = \{j: \beta_j(p) = 0$ for $p = z - \pi_Y(z)\}$. We have $\pi_Y(z) = z - p(z; J(z))$. Since $J(z)$ is locally constant if $z \notin M$, we conclude that π_Y is C^1 on $R^\ell \setminus (\partial Y \cup M)$. Hence, Y is quasi-smooth.

As for the genericity of condition (ii), we show how a set of given restricted profit functions $\bar{\beta}_j$ can be slightly perturbed so as to guarantee its fulfillment. The procedure is very similar to the one used in Example 8.5.1. Suppose, without loss of generality, that every $\bar{\beta}_j$ is C^∞, and let J be an arbitrary subset of activity indices. For each $j \in J$ take a perturbation parameter $b_j \in R$. Then define $\beta: R_{++}^\ell \times R^J \to R^J$ by $\beta_j(p, b) = \bar{\beta}_j(p) + b_j \|p\|$. Because rank $\partial_b \beta(p, b) = \#J$, we have that $\beta_b(p) = 0$ implies rank $\partial\beta_b(p) = \#J$ for a.e. b. Since, for b small, β_b is an admissible profit function, we are done as far as J is concerned. Repeating the process for every J, we get our perturbation.

One observation on the previous paragraph is in order. While the perturbed β_j will satisfy condition (ii), condition (i) may be lost for p near the boundary of S. This could be remedied either by using a more refined nonlinear perturbation or, more directly, by limiting the definition of quasi-smooth production set to the relevant region of the production set.

8.6   Generic optima

An extensive analysis of the optimum concept and the structure of the set of optima is contained in Chapter 4. A notion of regular optimum that proved to be analytically useful was defined there (4.3.2). In this section we argue that for generic economies regularity is a generic property of optima. We limit ourselves to the case of exchange economies.

The economy is specified by a total endowment vector $\omega \in R_{++}^{\ell}$ and by n consumers with C^r, monotone, convex regular preference relations on R_+^{ℓ}. It is convenient to rely explicitly on utility functions, and so, without loss of generality, we shall let the space of economies be $(\mathfrak{U}_{sc}^r)^n \times R_{++}^{\ell}$, where $\mathfrak{U}_{sc}^r$ has the obvious meaning. We assume that $r > n$. This purely technical requirement is needed for the application of the transversality theorems.

Remember from 4.3.1 that given an economy in the above set, an allocation $x \in R_+^{\ell n}$ is an optimum if $\sum_{i=1}^{n} x_i = 0$ and for some $p \in R_+^{\ell}$, $\lambda \in R_+^n$ the following first-order conditions are satisfied for all i:

(a) $\partial u_i(x_i) \leq \lambda_i p$.
(b) $[\lambda_i p - \partial u_i(x_i)] \cdot x_i = 0$.

Equivalently, condition (b) says that in (a) we can have strict inequality only if $x_i^j = 0$. In 4.3.2 we called an optimum regular if, for some p and λ satisfying (a), condition (b) can be strengthened to:

(b') $\partial_j u_i(x_i) < \lambda_i p^j$ if and only if $x_i^j = 0$.

That is to say, over and above (a) and (b) we require strict inequality whenever $x_i^j = 0$. Obviously, the notions of optima and regular optima are independent of the particular admissible utility representation chosen for preferences. It should also be clear from Section 8.4 that there is an intimate relationship – in fact, an exact correspondence – between the property of an optimum x being regular and the existence of a supporting $p \gg 0$ such that every individual demand function is C^1 at p, $p \cdot x_i$.

In the study of optima it is more enlightening to consider triples (x, p, λ) rather than the vector x alone. Let $N \subset R_+^{\ell n} \times R_+^{\ell} \times R_+^n$ (resp. $N_r \subset N$) correspond to the set of optima (resp. regular optima); that is, N is the set of triples (x, p, λ) that satisfy the first-order condition (a) and (b) [resp. (a) and (b')]. It is possible for $N \setminus N_r$ to be a large subset of N. See, for example, Figure 8.6.1, where N is represented by the heavy lines. The next proposition shows that this coincidental-looking situation is indeed exceptional.

8.6.1. Proposition. *On an open and dense subset of economies, the set $N \setminus N_r$ is a disjoint, finite union of C^1 manifolds of dimension less than n, and N_r is a C^1, n-dimensional manifold containing $N \setminus N_r$ in its closure.*

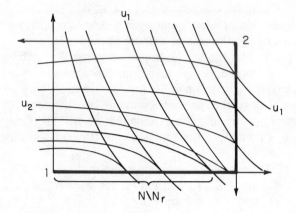

Figure 8.6.1

Proof. We follow the by now familiar procedure of reducing the problem to the study of certain systems of equations on arbitrarily given coordinate subspaces.

Suppose that an economy formed by $\bar{\omega}$ and u_i, $1 \le i \le n$, is given. As we did in the proofs of 8.4.5 and 8.4.6, we shall consider a family of linear perturbations of the utility functions.

Let $L', L \subset R^{\ell n}$ be arbitrary coordinate subspaces with $L' \subset L$. Suppose, to be specific and to facilitate notation, that L (resp. L') is formed by the first $\ell_i \le \ell$ (resp. the first $m_i \le \ell_i$) coordinates of every i. We define a system of functions

$$\Psi : R^{\ell n} \times R^{\ell} \times R^n \times R^{\ell n} \times R^{\ell} \to R^{\ell} \times \prod_i R^{\ell_i} \times \prod_i R^{\ell - m_i}$$

by

$$\Psi(x, p, \lambda, b, \omega) = \begin{cases} \omega - \sum_i x_i \\ \partial_j u_i(x_i) + b_i^j - \lambda_i p^j, & j \le \ell_i, \ \text{all } i \\ x_i^j, & m_i < j \le \ell, \ \text{all } i. \end{cases}$$

Denote by z the $\ell + \ell n + \sum_i (\ell_i - m_i)$ vector of variables formed by ω^j for $1 \le j \le \ell$, b_i^j for $j \le \ell_i$ and all i, x_i^j for $m_i < j$ and all i. Note then that $\partial_z \Psi(x, p, \lambda, b, \omega)$ can be viewed as a triangular matrix with diagonal entries equal to one. Therefore, $\partial \Psi$ is a full-rank matrix. By the transversality theorem 8.3.1, for a.e. b and ω, we have "$\Psi_{b,\omega}(x, p, \lambda) = 0$ implies rank $\partial \Psi_{b,\omega}(x, p, \lambda) = \ell + \ell n + \sum_i (\ell_i - m_i)$." Choose b, ω near $(0, \bar{\omega})$ and such that this implication holds for all L, L'. Replacing the original economy by ω and $u_{ib}(x_i) = u_i(x_i) + b_i \cdot x_i$, we can then conclude that the previous bracketed statement (with $b = 0$, $\omega = \bar{\omega}$) holds for a dense set of economies. For x restricted to some large compact set (chosen to contain the optimal allocations), it also holds on an open neighborhood of this dense set. Let us be in one such economy and for L, L', and Ψ as above define

$$N(L, L') = \{(x, p, \lambda) \in \Psi_{0,\bar{\omega}}^{-1}(0): \partial_j u_i(x_i) - \lambda_i p^j < 0 \text{ for } j > \ell_i, \text{ all } i,$$
$$\text{and } x_i^j > 0 \text{ for } j \leq m_i, \text{ all } i\}.$$

Of course, $N(L, L')$, if nonempty, is a C^1 manifold of dimension at most n, this bound being attained if and only if $\sum_i (\ell_i - m_i) = 0$, that is, if and only if $L' = L$ (see H.2.2). It is also clear from the nature of the system of equations that any point of $N(L, L')$ can be approximated by points of $N(L, L)$; that is, $N(L, L')$ is contained in the closure of $N(L, L)$. Finally, note that if $L_1 \neq L_2$ or $L_1' \neq L_2'$ the sets $N(L_1, L_1')$, $N(L_2, L_2')$ are necessarily disjoint.

The proof is concluded simply by observing that $N \setminus N_r$ (resp. N_r) is the union of the $N(L, L')$ as we run over all L and $L' \subset L$, $L' \neq L$ (resp. over all L and $L' = L$). ∎

Five remarks on the previous proposition are worth making:

(i) The convexity property of preferences is not used in the proof; hence the proposition remains valid without this hypothesis. It must be kept in mind, however, that the satisfaction of the first-order conditions does not then automatically entail optimality.

(ii) The proof yields more about the generic inner structure of $N \setminus N_r$ than is explicit in the statement of the proposition.

(iii) Obviously, the proposition (with or without convexity of preferences) remains valid for the consumption set R_{++}^ℓ. Then $N_r = N$, and so we can conclude that, generically, the set of allocations in $R_{++}^{\ell n}$ that satisfy the first-order conditions for optimality is a C^1 manifold. This substantiates the comment made after Example 4.6.7.

(iv) If we had normalized the p or the λ vector (but not both!), then the proposition remains correct with n replaced throughout by $n - 1$.

(v) Remember from 4.3.5 the concept of linked allocation. It has played an important role in Chapters 4 and 7. Generically, is the set of linked allocations large in N_r? The answer is no: Nonlinkedness is a robust property. There is an open set of economies for which the nonlinked allocations fill an open subset of N_r (see example 4.6.5). There is a moral to this observation: Genericity analysis will not always rule out intuitive implausible situations.

8.7   Genericity of regular economies

The topic of this section was already discussed extensively in Chapter 5 (Section 5.8). There should be little doubt, therefore, that, properly formulated, regular economies are generic. In this section we aim to illustrate some of the finer issues. To this effect, we consider the genericity problem in a general setting that includes production and the possibility of equilibria at the boundary of consumption sets. Nevertheless, and to focus on essentials, we limit ourselves to constant returns economies, even more, to the linear activity model. General production sets can also be incorporated, but the need to keep track of profit income, although technically not difficult, would be notationally cumbersome.

We concentrate on the study of the density problem for regular economies. A few remarks on the openness issue, which as usual is a simpler matter, will be made at the end of the section. Because economies with a finite number of consumers are dense in the set of economies (5.8.1), we pose our problem as one of approximating by a regular economy a given economy with a finite number of consumers and a finite number of linear technologies.

So far (e.g., Chapters 3 and 6) the production side of the economy has been specified by the production set, that, in our case, is defined by m linear activities $\{a_1, \ldots, a_m\} \subset R^\ell$. Presently, we shall require a slightly more general setting. Indeed, we need to consider perturbations of the basic activities and, as we pointed out in Section 8.2, it is then very important to be explicit on the a priori restrictions on individual technologies. This we do by specifying, for every j, a technology set $Z_j \subset R^\ell$. We take it to be a nontrivial coordinate subspace. The interpretation is that any coordinate not included in Z_j is neither an input nor an output of the activity. *The space of permissible production sets is* then some open subset of $Z = Z_1 \times \cdots \times Z_m$. Because our analysis is purely local, there is no loss in taking it to be Z itself. Vectors of activity levels are denoted $\alpha = (\alpha_1, \ldots, \alpha_m) \geq 0$.

As for the consumption side, there are n consumers indexed by i. In principle, every consumer is defined by an initial endowment vector $\omega_i \in R^\ell_+$ and a preference relation $\succsim_i \in \mathcal{P}^2_{sc}$ on R^ℓ_+. We let u_i be a C^2 utility for $\succsim_i$. However, the observation made for the technology side also applies here. Thus, for example, it does not make sense in a reasonably rich model to allow the initial endowment vectors to be perturbed in any direction (implying that for a consumer to have a zero endowment of some commodity is a pathological situation!). As with the production side, what we do is to *assign to every i a nonempty set of permissible initial endow-*

ment vectors $\Omega_i \subset R^\ell$. Again, we take Ω_i to be a coordinate subspace. Because our analysis is local, we have no need to explicitly specify some coordinate subspace as the permissible consumption set for consumer i. This information is embodied in the utility function u_i. Although u_i is formally defined on R_+^ℓ, some commodities may not yield any utility (or very little), and so they will not be consumed at equilibrium.

The framework described so far, with all its explicit and implicit constraints on consumption, endowments, and production sets, is strong enough to yield the generic determinateness of equilibrium productions and allocations, but it is still too general for the generic determinateness (i.e., local uniqueness) of equilibrium prices. There are at least two problems, both obvious enough. For the first, consider the nonpathological situation where some good is, at equilibrium, neither produced nor consumed or owned by any consumer. Clearly, there will typically be a range of equilibrium prices for such a good. This problem is in the nature of things, and so we handle it by means of a sensible amendment of the regularity concept used in Chapter 5. For the second problem, imagine the world economy before Columbus's trip (i.e., complete disjointness between European and American technologies, endowments, and consumption sets). Obviously, the relative price level between Europe and America was indeterminate. We regard this problem as more exotic, and we shall rule it out by means of a convenient indecomposibility condition.

The required modification of the regularity concept consists in restricting the rank condition to hold on the relevant coordinate subspace of commodities and prices. More specifically, we consider an economy where every a_j and ω_i has as many nonzero entries as is permissible. If (p, α) is an equilibrium such that every individual demand function is C^1 at $(p, p \cdot \omega_i)$, then we impose the full rank condition on the smallest coordinate subspace containing every $\alpha_j a_j$, every ω_i, and every consumption. Formally, the following definition generalizes both Definition 5.3.6 and the notion of proper regularity for constant returns economies introduced in Section 6.4.

8.7.1. Definition. *The equilibrium price vector* $\bar{p} \gg 0$ *of an economy* $(a, (\succsim_1, \omega_1), \ldots, (\succsim_n, \omega_n)) \in Z \times \prod_i (\mathcal{P}_{sc}^2 \times \Omega_i)$ *with aggregate excess demand function* $f(p)$ *is regular if:*

(a) *For all* i, $\varphi(\succsim_i, p, w_i)$ *is* C^1 *at* $p = \bar{p}$, $\bar{w}_i = p \cdot \omega_i$.

(b) *There is a unique vector* $\alpha \geq 0$ *such that* $f(\bar{p}) = \sum_j \alpha_j a_j$.

(c) *Denote by* L *the smallest coordinate subspace containing every* $\alpha_j Z_j$, *every* Ω_i *and every* $\varphi_i(\succsim_i, \bar{p}, \bar{p} \cdot \omega_i)$. *Let* $A(\bar{p})$ *be the matrix whose columns are the* a_j *with* $\alpha_j > 0$. *Then:*

$$\text{rank} \begin{bmatrix} \partial f(\bar{p}) & A(\bar{p}) & \bar{p} \\ A^T(\bar{p}) & & \\ p^T & & \mathbf{0} \end{bmatrix} = \dim L - 1.$$

(d) *If $Z_j \subset L$, then $\bar{p} \cdot a_j = 0$ only if $\alpha_j > 0$.*

At a regular equilibrium it is possible to have $\bar{p} \cdot a_j = 0$ and $\alpha_j = 0$. Because of (d), this will occur only if $a_j^h \neq 0$ for some coordinate h not in L (i.e., for a commodity with a naturally indeterminate price). Therefore, by altering slightly the indeterminate price $\bar{p}^h$, we can always, if so desired, perturb $\bar{p}$ to another regular equilibrium $\bar{p}'$ for which the property "$\bar{p}' \cdot a_j < 0$ if and only if $\alpha_j = 0$" holds.

Of course, we say that an economy is *regular* if every equilibrium price vector $p \gg 0$ is regular. It is straightforward to verify that in the present setting, regular economies are as well behaved as in Chapters 5 and 7; for example, equilibrium allocations are locally unique.

For simplicity we shall work with a very crude indecomposability hypothesis.

8.7.2. Definition. *The collection of endowments sets Ω_i, $1 \leq i \leq n$, is indecomposable if there is a coordinate axis contained in all of them.*

The indecomposability concept could be weakened and made more realistic in at least two directions: Indirect rather than direct connections would do, and connections via consumption or production would be as good.

We are ready to state the approximation result:

8.7.3. Proposition. *Let an economy be specified by:*

(i) *a finite collection of activities $a_j \in Z_j \subset R^\ell$, $1 \leq j \leq m$, where Z_j is an a priori given coordinate subspace;*

(ii) *a collection of n consumers $(\succsim_i, \omega_i)$, $1 \leq i \leq n$, with $\succsim_i \in \mathcal{P}^2_{sc}$ and $\omega_i \in \Omega_i$, an a priori given endowment set.*

If the collection Ω_i, $1 \leq i \leq n$, is indecomposable (Definition 8.7.2), then there are $a_j' \in Z_j$ and $(\succsim_i', \omega_i') \in \mathcal{P}^2_{sc} \times \Omega_i$ arbitrarily close to a_j, $(\succsim_i, \omega_i)$ and such that the economy given by a_j', $j \leq m$, and $(\succsim_i', \omega_i')$, $i \leq n$, is regular.

Proof of Proposition 8.7.3

The proof is organized in five steps. The first shows that, in a certain sense, the linear activities can be taken to be in general position. The second spells out the implications of the admissible variation of tastes for an aggregate restricted excess demand function. The third step puts together the previous two and contains the key transversality argument. The fourth iterates the argument in order to take care of properties (a) and (d) of the definition of regularity. The fifth step concludes the proof.

Step 1. Let A be the $\ell \times m$ matrix whose columns are the activities a_j. We can take A to have as many nonzero entries as is possible under the constraints Z. We state as a lemma a general property of matrices:

8.7.4. Lemma. *Let B be an $h \times k$ matrix with a nonzero entry in every row. Then by perturbing only the nonzero entries of B, we can find a nearby matrix B' such that if $B'q = 0$ has a solution $q \gg 0$, then rank $B' = h$.*

Proof. Although this is not the simpler way, we shall get the lemma through a transversality argument. To this effect, let $\bar{B}$ satisfy the hypothesis of the lemma, and let $\mathfrak{B}$ be a (relatively) open neighborhood of $\bar{B}$ constituted by admissible matrices (zero entries of $\bar{B}$ are kept equal to zero). Define $\xi: \mathfrak{B} \times R_{++}^k \to R^h$ by $\xi(B, q) = Bq$. Suppose that $\xi(B, q) = 0$. Because $\partial_{b_{ij}} \xi(B, q) = q^j e_i \neq 0$ and every row has a nonzero entry, we deduce that rank $\partial_B \xi(B, q) = h$. Therefore, by the transversality theorem 8.3.1, there is B' near $\bar{B}$ such that $\xi_{B'}(q) = 0$ implies rank $\partial \xi_{B'}(q) = h$. But $\partial \xi_{B'}(q) = B'$, and so B' is as we wanted. ∎

By virtue of the lemma we can from now on assume that any submatrix of A or A^T with a nonzero entry in each row satisfies the conclusion of the lemma.

Step 2. For every i take a permissible utility function u_i for $\succsim_i$. We assume, without loss of generality, that u_i is defined on the entire R^ℓ and that $\partial^2 u_i(x_i)$ is negative definite everywhere (2.8).

Take a family $J_1, \ldots, J_n \subset R^\ell$ of arbitrary nontrivial coordinate subspaces, one for each consumer. For $b_i \in J_i$ define $\varphi_i(p, w_i, b_i)$ as the maximizer of $u_i(x_i) + b_i \cdot x_i$ on $\{x_i \in J_i : p \cdot x_i \le w_i\}$. We assume that this maximizer exists. It is fairly obvious, and simply checked, that $\partial_{w_i, b_i} \varphi_i(p, w_i, b_i)$ maps onto J_i.

Denote by $\hat{L}$ the smallest coordinate subspace containing every J_i and every Ω_i. Reindexing if necessary, we can assume that $\hat{L}$ is formed by coordinates 1 to k. Define $f: S \times \prod_i \Omega_i \times \prod_i J_i \to \hat{L}$ by

$$f(p, \omega, b) = \Sigma_i \left[\varphi_i(p, p \cdot \omega_i, b_i) - \omega_i \right].$$

We claim that $\partial_{\omega, b} f(p, \omega, b)$ maps onto $\hat{L} \cap T_p$ or, equivalently, that it has rank $k - 1$. By the indecomposability condition, there is a coordinate axis, say the first, in every Ω_i. Take the hth unit vector e_h, $1 < h \le k$. We must have either $e_h \in \Omega_i$ for some i or $e_h \in J_i$ for some i. Suppose that the first possibility holds. Then

$$-\partial_{\omega_i} f(p, \omega, b)(e_h - (p^h/p^1)e_1) = e_h - (p^h/p^1)e_1.$$

Suppose that the second possibility holds. Then there is a vector $(\gamma, v) \in R \times J_i$ such that $\partial_{w_i, b_i} \varphi_i(p, p \cdot \omega_i, b_i)(\gamma, v) = e_h$. Clearly, $\gamma = p^h$ and so $\partial_{\omega_i, b_i} f(p, \omega, b)([\gamma/p^1]e_1, v) = e_h - (p^h/p^1)e_1$. Therefore, our claim is correct. It is also plain that there may be considerable room to choose perturbation parameters and that, therefore, more side constraints could be accommodated.

Step 3. Let u_i, J_i, φ, k, and $\hat{L}$ be as in the previous step. Take an arbitrary $\ell \times s$ submatrix A^* of A. Relabel the commodities with index $h > k$ so that for some $t \ge k$ the row $h > k$ of the matrix A^* is identically zero if and only if $h > t$.

Define $\Psi: \prod_i \Omega_i \times \prod_i J_i \times R_{++}^s \times S \to R^{\ell + s}$ by

$$\Psi(\omega, b, \alpha, p) = (f(p, \omega, b) - A^* \alpha, p \cdot A^*).$$

Note that the coordinates $k < h \le \ell$ (resp. $t < h \le \ell$) of f (resp. Ψ) are identically equal to zero.

Suppose that $\Psi(\bar{\omega}, \bar{b}, \bar{\alpha}, \bar{p}) = 0$. The matrix $\partial \Psi(\bar{\omega}, \bar{b}, \bar{\alpha}, \bar{p})$ has the form

$$\partial\Psi(\bar{\omega}, \bar{b}, \bar{\alpha}, \bar{p}) = \begin{array}{c} \\ k \\ \\ t \\ \\ \ell \\ \ell+s \end{array} \overset{\displaystyle \omega, b \qquad\quad \alpha \qquad\quad p \atop t}{\left[\begin{array}{c:c:c:c} \partial_{\omega, b} f(\bar{p}, \bar{\omega}, \bar{b}) & * & * & 0 \\ \hdashline 0 & A_{k,t}^* & & 0 \\ \hdashline 0 & 0 & & 0 \\ \hdashline 0 & & 0 \;\; A_{1,t}^{*T} & 0 \end{array}\right]}$$

where $A_{k,t}^*$, and similarly for $A_{1,t}^*$, is the submatrix of A^* formed by the rows $k < j \le t$. From step 2 we have that $\partial_{\omega, b} f(\bar{p}, \bar{\omega}, \bar{b})$ maps onto $\hat{L} \cap T_p$. Because the rows of $A_{k,t}^*$ are not identically zero and $A_{k,t}^* \bar{\alpha} = 0$, $\bar{\alpha} \gg 0$, it follows from step 1 that rank $A_{k,t}^* = t - k$. Similarly, $p \cdot A^* = 0$, $p \gg 0$ and the nontriviality of the activities imply, by step 1, that rank $A_{1,t}^* = s$. Therefore, rank $\partial \Psi(\bar{\omega}, \bar{b}, \bar{\alpha}, \bar{p}) = s + t - 1$, and, if we define $\hat{\Psi}$ from Ψ by dropping the equations $t < j \le \ell$, the last $\ell - t$ variables, and, renormalizing, the first equation and the variable p^1, we have that $\partial \hat{\Psi}(\omega, b, \alpha, p)$ has full rank whenever $\Psi(\omega, b, \alpha, p) = 0$. Hence, by the transversality theorem, for a.e. ω and b, the map $\hat{\Psi}_{\omega, b}: R_{++}^s \times R^{t-1} \to R^{t-1} \times R^s$ has zero as a regular value. Note that $\hat{\Psi}_{\omega, b}$ has the same number of equations as of un-knowns. Therefore, $\hat{\Psi}_{\omega, b}(\alpha, p) = 0$ has a discrete set of solutions. In par-ticular, this implies that given ω, b, A^*, and p, the system $f_{\omega, b}(p) = A^*\alpha$ can have at most one solution.

Step 4. Suppose that to the above system of equations $\hat{\Psi}(\omega, b, \alpha, p) = 0$, we add a new equation of any of the two following types:

(i) $p^h - [1/\lambda_i(p, b_i, \omega_i)]\partial_h u_i(\varphi_i(p, p \cdot \omega_i, b_i)) = 0$, where $\lambda_i(\bullet)$ is the marginal utility of wealth, $h \leq t$, and the coordinate h does not belong to J_i.

(ii) $p \cdot a_j = 0$, where a_j is not a column of A^* and $a_j^h = 0$ for $h > t$.

In the expanded equation system there is no additional unknown and 0 is still a regular value. Indeed, with the additional equations, we have new usable perturbation parameters: b_i^h for (i), any $a_j^h \neq 0$ for (ii). Adding those, it is clear that 0 remains a regular value. Therefore, by the trans-versality theorem (8.3.1), for a.e. ω, b and admissible A, the equation system with ω, b, and A fixed and (i) or (ii) added will not have a solution because it will now have $s + t$ equations and $s + t - 1$ unknowns.

Step 5. The proof is now almost complete. Suppose that the economy has been perturbed by means of b, ω, and A belonging to the generic set of any of the (finite in number) arbitrarily choices and relabelings made in the previous steps. Then we only need to notice that at an equilibrium $\bar{p}$, demand functions are differentiable (step 4) and there is an obvious choice of J_i and A^* such that, with L playing the role of the first t coordi-nates, the determinant that appears in part (c) of the definition of regu-larity is precisely (up to normalization and with $b = 0$) the determinant of the map $\partial \hat{\Psi}_{\omega, b}(\bar{p}, \bar{\alpha})$ appearing in step 3. Part (d) of the definition follows from step 4. Part (b) is a consequence of step 3. Indeed, suppose there are two distinct solutions α', $\alpha'' \geq 0$ to $f(\bar{p}) = \sum_j \alpha_j a_j$. If we let A^* be the matrix having as columns the a_j with $\alpha_j' + \alpha_j'' > 0$, then the system $f(\bar{p}) = A^*\alpha$ has more than one solution $\alpha \gg 0$, which contradicts the last state-ment of step 3.

This concludes the proof of 8.7.3. ∎

A careful analysis of the previous proof would show first, that with only minor adjustments we could accommodate the possibility of zero prices at equilibrium, and, second, that there is no essential difficulty in replacing activities by generalized activities.

Finally, a word on the openness of the set of regular economies. It is simply verified that the fulfillment of Definition 8.7.1 on a compact set of prices is an open property with respect to perturbations of $a_j, \succsim_i, \omega_i$. Therefore, in the context of a universe structurally defined by Z, $(\mathcal{P}_{sc}^2)^n$

and $\Omega = \prod_i \Omega$, the regularity property is generic. So far, so good. We may, however, run into some definitional difficulties if we have a continuum of consumers and, as in Chapter 5, our universe is modeled as a set of measures on consumers' characteristics. Then the property that the aggregate excess demand function be C^1 at equilibrium is definitely not open. So if, as in 5.3.6, this is part of the definition of regularity, regular economies cannot be open. Nevertheless, the previous proposition guarantees that they form a dense set, and we saw in 5.4.2 that the equilibrium set has the usual stability property (continuity and local constancy of the set of equilibria) in a neighborhood of any regular economy. Hence, if we defined regularity directly in terms of the persistency of the equilibrium set, the property would then be open and dense. In this sense, therefore, this is not a substantive difficulty.

As in the optimum case, the property that the Walrasian allocation be linked is not generic. Interestingly, Proposition 7.2.7 makes clear that in the continuum of agents situation the property is "almost generic" in the following sense: If the requirement on the convergence of the supports is dropped from the definition of the topology of $\mathfrak{M}$, then every Walrasian allocation is linked for a set of continuum economies that is open and dense for this modified topology.

8.8   Generic properties of the equilibrium manifold

In this section we pursue in a bit more depth the analysis of Chapter 5, Section 5.8. The treatment here will be highly selective. The topics have been chosen not so much for their intrinsic importance but because they lend themselves to the illustration of interesting techniques. Also, we only consider exchange economies with a finite number of consumers.

We have two aims. The first is to verify in some simple instance that allowing consumption sets with boundary (i.e., $R_+^\ell \setminus \{0\}$ instead of R_{++}^ℓ) does not alter the essential generic properties of the equilibrium manifold. It only makes it piecewise rather than fully smooth. Second, we want to analyze in more detail the generic structure of the equilibrium manifold over paths of economies.

As for the first topic, let preferences $\succeq_i$ remain fixed and belong to $\mathcal{P}^2_{\mathrm{cl}, sc}$. The space of parameters is $B = (0, k)^{\ell n}$, a space of initial endowments. Except for the bound k, this is Example 5.8.5. We have, then, an equilibrium set $E \subset S \times B$, and as we saw in the previous section, the set of regular economies B^* is open and dense in B. If preferences were in $\mathcal{P}^2_{b, sc}$ then, by Proposition 5.8.13, E would be a C^1 manifold of dimension ℓn. With preferences in $\mathcal{P}^2_{\mathrm{cl}, sc}$, however, the nonregular economies include, as a

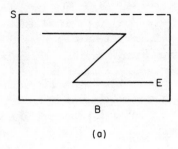 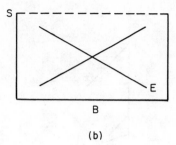

Figure 8.8.1

matter of definition, the economies at which excess demand fails to be differentiable at some equilibrium price. At these nonregular points, kinks are to be expected in the equilibrium set. It is notable, however, that although E may not be a C^1 manifold, it is nevertheless still a manifold of dimension ℓn. This we shall prove formally in the next proposition. Thus, symbolically, the situation of Figure 8.8.1a is admissible, but not the one of Figure 8.8.1b. Of course, because regularity is generic in B, E is smooth at most points.

8.8.1. Proposition. *With the previous hypotheses, the equilibrium set E is a topological manifold of dimension ℓn.*

Proof. We shall, in fact, show much more, namely that E is homeomorphic to $R_{++}^{\ell n}$. This result is parallel to 5.8.22, which obtains a diffeomorphism when preferences are in $\mathcal{P}_b$. The proof, however, needs considerable changes to cover the current case.

Let Δ be the interior of the n-unit simplex and $\bar{B} = (0, nk)^{\ell}$. We shall exhibit an open graph correspondence $\Psi\colon \Delta \times \bar{B} \to R_{++}^{\ell n}$ such that: (i) For all $(s, \bar{\omega}) \in \Delta \times \bar{B}$, $\Psi(s, \bar{\omega})$ is a nonempty convex set of codimension $n + \ell - 1$; and (ii) there is a homeomorphism $\xi\colon \text{graph } \Psi \to E$. This proves the result because, by H.4.7, graph Ψ is homeomorphic to $R^{\ell n}$.

Take a family of C^2 admissible utility functions u_i. Without loss of generality (2.6.4), we can assume that $u_i(ke) < 1/n$ and u_i is concave on $[0, k]^{\ell}$. This is, incidentally, the only step of the proof that would not work with $k = \infty$. For every $\omega \in \bar{B}$ define the set

$$U(\omega) = \{(u_1(x_1), \ldots, u_n(x_n)) \colon \Sigma_i x_i \le \omega\}.$$

It is closed, convex, and lies below the unit simplex. For every $(s, \omega) \in \Delta \times \bar{B}$ let $v(s, \omega)$ be the (unique) point of $U(\omega)$ closest to s, and $p(s, \omega) \in S$

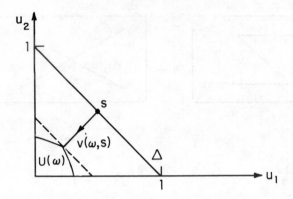

Figure 8.8.2

be the price vector that supports the optimum allocation $x(s, \omega)$ underlying $v(s, \omega)$ and is such that the vector of utility weights (see 4.2) corresponding to $x(s, \omega)$ and $p(s, \omega)$, denoted $\lambda(s, \omega)$, is collinear with $s - v(s, \omega)$; see Figure 8.8.2. Then the correspondence $\Psi: \Delta \times \bar{B} \to R_{++}^{\ell n}$ and the homeomorphism $\xi: \text{graph } \Psi \to E$ are given by

$$\Psi(s, \omega) = \{(\omega_1, \ldots, \omega_n) \in (0, k)^{\ell n}: \Sigma_i \, \omega_i = \omega, \; p(s, \omega) \cdot \omega_i = p(s, \omega) \cdot x_i(s, \omega)$$
$$\text{for all } i\}$$

and $\xi(s, \omega, \omega_1, \ldots, \omega_n) = (p(s, \omega), \omega_1, \ldots, \omega_n)$. $\blacksquare$

For the second topic (paths) we put ourselves in the nicest sort of space of characteristics, namely, $\mathcal{P}_{b,sc}^\infty \times R_{++}^\ell$, and consider exchange economies $\mathcal{E}: I_n \to \mathcal{P}_{b,sc}^\infty \times R_{++}^\ell$. A *path* η assigns to every $t \in [0, 1]$ an admissible economy $\eta(t)$. We shall only consider C^∞ paths, that is, C^∞ parameterizations with parameter space $[0, 1]$. Let $\mathfrak{I}$ be the space of paths so defined. In the obvious way, $\mathfrak{I}$ can be endowed with the C^∞ topology.

For every path $\eta \in \mathfrak{I}$ we have a C^∞ aggregate excess demand function $f_\eta: S \times [0, 1] \to R^\ell$ and so, as in 5.8.19, we can define η as *regular* if $\eta(0)$, $\eta(1)$ are regular economies and $\partial f(p, t): T_p \times R \to R^\ell$ has rank $\ell - 1$ whenever $f(p, t) = 0$. By Proposition 5.8.14, the equilibrium set $E_\eta \subset S \times [0, 1]$ of a regular path η is a C^∞, compact, one-dimensional manifold with a boundary equaling $E_\eta \cap [(S \times \{0\}) \cup (S \times \{1\})]$. Equivalently, E_η is, up to diffeomorphism, a finite disjoint union of circles and segments, the endpoints of the segments being precisely the points of E_η at the boundary of $S \times [0, 1]$ (H.2.2, H.1.vi). Figure 8.3.3 represents a possible E_η for a regular η.

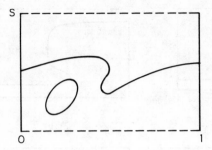

Figure 8.8.3

A first result (analogous to 5.8.21) is:

8.8.2. Proposition. *The set of regular paths $\mathfrak{I}^* \subset \mathfrak{I}$ is open and dense.*

Proof. Openness is obvious. To prove density, let $(\gtrsim_i(t), \omega_i(t))$ be an arbitrary path and define $\xi : S \times [0, 1] \times R^\ell \to R^\ell$ by

$$\xi(p, t, v) = \varphi_1(\gtrsim_1(t), p \cdot [\omega_1(t) + v]) - (\omega_1(t) + v) + \Sigma_{i=2}^n f_i(p, t).$$

Then rank $\partial_v \xi(p, t, v) = \ell - 1$, and so by the transversality theorem 8.3.1, there is $\bar{v}$ near 0 such that $\xi_{\bar{v}}$, $\xi_{\bar{v},0}$, and $\xi_{\bar{v},1}$ have 0 as a regular value (relative to T_p). Replacing $\omega_1(t)$ by $\omega_1(t) + \bar{v}$ for every t, we get our approximating path. ∎

So far, we have not gone beyond the analysis of Chapter 5, Section 5.8. We shall now see that in the generic case substantially more can be said about the structure of E_η.

Observe first that the regularity of η is compatible with some apparent pathology as, for example, $\{t \in [0, 1] : \eta(t)$ is critical$\}$ being infinite or $\{p \in S : (p, t) \in E_\eta\}$ being a continuum for some critical t. See Figures 8.8.4a, b for illustrations of these two possibilities.

Given a regular $\eta \in \mathfrak{I}$, denote by $h_\eta^2 : E_\eta \to R$ the projection map on the second coordinate, that is, $(p, t) \mapsto t$. This is a smooth, real-valued map on a one-dimensional manifold. The critical economies are precisely the images of the critical points (i.e., the critical values) of h_η^2. Thus, for example, in Figures 8.8.4a, b, c, and d, $(\bar{p}, \bar{t})$ is a critical point of h_η^2. Note, however, that it is in all cases a degenerate critical point: an inflection point in Figures 8.8.3a, c and a degenerate maximum in Figures 8.8.4b, d. Therefore, the "pathologies" represented by Figure 8.8.4 cannot

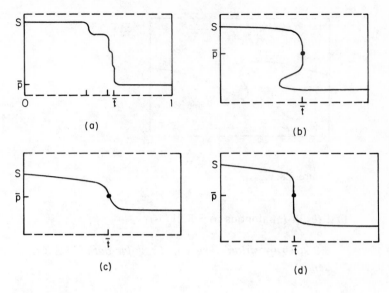

Figure 8.8.4

arise if every critical point of h_η^2 is nondegenerate or, in other words, if h_η^2 is a Morse function (see H.2). The next proposition asserts that, generically, h_η^2 is a Morse function. It is the only instance in this chapter where quadratic, not just linear, perturbations of the utility functions need to be considered. We also point out that more restrictions could be imposed on the projection (e.g., that it be one-to-one on the set of its critical points) without losing genericity.

> **8.8.3. Proposition.** *There is an open and dense set $\mathfrak{I}' \subset \mathfrak{I}$ such that every $\eta \in \mathfrak{I}'$ is regular and the projection of $E_\eta \subset S \times R$ on its second component is a Morse function, that is, it has no degenerate critical point.*

Proof of Proposition 8.8.3

The proof is quite easy once we realize that perturbations of indirect, rather than direct, utility functions have a simple effect on demand.

Let $v: R_{++}^\ell \times R \to R$ be the indirect utility function derived from some admissible direct utility. Denote by $\mathbb{Q}$ a neighborhood of the origin in the linear space of symmetric $\ell \times \ell$ matrices. For every Q define a quadratic perturbation $v_Q: R_{++}^\ell \times R \to R$ by $v_Q(p, w) = v(p, w) + (1/w^2)p \cdot Qp$. For any compact $K \subset R_{++}^\ell \times R$ we can choose $\mathbb{Q}$ small enough for the perturbed

v_Q to be an admissible indirect utility on K. We shall rest content with this. All our later arguments depend only on the values of indirect utility functions on suitably chosen K. It is a trivial matter to use more elaborate perturbations and guarantee that v_b is also admissible outside K.

Denote by $x(p, w, Q)$ the induced demand at (p, w, Q). For every p let $\mathcal{Q}_p = \{Q \in \mathcal{Q}: p \cdot Q = 0\}$. Demand acts in a most simple linear manner over the set $\mathcal{Q}_p$. Precisely:

8.8.4. Lemma. *For every p and $Q \in \mathcal{Q}_p$ we have:*

$$x(p, w, Q) = x(p, w, 0), \qquad \partial_w x(p, w, Q) = \partial_w x(p, w, 0),$$

and

$$\partial_p x(p, w, Q) = \partial_p x(p, w, 0) - \frac{2}{w^2 \partial_w v(p, w, 0)} Q.$$

Proof. Straightforward from the formulas in 2.7.9 and direct computation. ∎

After this digression we go back to the proposition. The first thing to notice is that the desired Morse property can be formulated as a full rank condition. Let $f(p, t)$ be the aggregate excess demand on a given path. Define a new function $\xi: S \times [0, 1] \to R^{\ell+1}$ by $\xi_h(p, t) = f(p, t)$, $1 \le h \le \ell$, and $\xi_{\ell+1}(p, t) = |\pi_p \circ \partial f(p, t)|$, where π_p denotes the projection on T_p [hence $\xi_{\ell+1}(p, t)$ is the determinant of a map from T_p to T_p]. We know that whenever $f(p, t) = 0$ the linear map $\partial \xi(p, t)$ takes $T_p \times R$ into $T_p \times R$ (see 5.3.4). The desired property is then that this map be onto, that is, that rank $\partial \xi(p, t) = \ell$ whenever $\xi(p, t) = 0$. As we move along the one-dimensional equilibrium set of a regular path, this requires that $|\partial_p f(p, t)|$ be transversal to zero, that is, that every nonregular equilibrium be an isolated switch point for regular equilibria with different indexes. This is clearly violated in the examples of Figure 8.8.4.

Once expressed as a transversality condition, the Morse property is obviously open. To establish density we shall perturb the initial endowments $\omega_1(t)$ and the indirect utility v_{1t} of the first consumer (it is trivially verified that we can reparameterize our given path by indirect rather than direct utility). Let $\mathcal{Q}$ be as above, that is, a small neighborhood of symmetric matrices, and $Z \subset R^\ell$ a small neighborhood of zero. Then for every $(z, Q) \in Z \times \mathcal{Q}$ we have a perturbed path of economies by putting

$$\omega_1(t, z) = \omega_1(t) + z, \qquad v_1(p, w, t, Q) = v_1(p, w, t) + (1/w^2) p \cdot Q p.$$

By 8.8.2 we can assume that for every (z, Q) the corresponding path is regular.

The map $\xi: S \times [0,1] \times Z \times \mathbb{Q} \to R^{\ell+1}$ is defined in the obvious way. By the transversality theorem 8.3.1 our proof will be completed if we show that $\partial \xi(p,t,z,Q)$ maps onto $T_p \times R$ whenever $\xi(p,t,z,Q) = 0$. To prove this let $\xi(\bar{p}, \bar{t}, \bar{z}, \bar{Q}) = 0$. Without loss of generality, we can assume that $\bar{z} = 0$ and $\bar{Q} = 0$. As in the proof of 8.8.2, it is clear that $\partial_z \xi(\bar{p}, \bar{t}, 0, 0)$ takes T_p onto $T_p \times \{0\}$. Therefore, it will suffice for us to show that

$$\partial_Q \xi_{\ell+1}(\bar{p}, \bar{t}, 0, 0) \neq 0.$$

Because $|\partial_p f(\bar{p}, \bar{t})| = 0$ and rank $\partial f(\bar{p}, \bar{t}) = \ell - 1$ (remember that the path is regular), we have rank $\partial_p f(\bar{p}, \bar{t}) = \ell - 2$. Let $q \in T_{\bar{p}}$ be a small vector that neither belongs to the range of $\partial_p f(\bar{p}, \bar{t})$ nor is perpendicular to its one-dimensional kernel. Consider then the matrix

$$A(\alpha) = \partial_p f(\bar{p}, \bar{t}) - \alpha q q^T.$$

Of course $|A(0)| = 0$. For any α, $A(\alpha)$ still defines a map from $T_{\bar{p}}$ to $T_{\bar{p}}$ and, because $q q^T$ is a rank one matrix, the basic properties of the determinant (B.4) imply $|A(\alpha)| = \alpha |A(1)| + (1-\alpha)|A(0)| = \alpha |A(1)|$. Also, by the way q has been chosen, we have rank $A(1) = $ rank $A(0) + 1 = \ell - 1$. Hence, $\partial_\alpha |A(\alpha)| = |A(1)| \neq 0$. Finally, it is a consequence of this and 8.8.4 that with $\bar{Q} = q q^T \in \mathbb{Q}_{\bar{p}}$, $\bar{w}_1 = \bar{p} \cdot \omega_1(\bar{t})$, and $c = 2/\bar{w}_1^2 \partial_w v_1(\bar{p}, \bar{w}_1, \bar{t}, 0)$, we have $\partial_Q |\partial_p f(\bar{p}, \bar{t})|(\bar{Q}) = c|A(1)| \neq 0$.

This concludes the proof of Proposition 8.8.3.   ■

We mention two applications of the type of result represented by Proposition 8.8.3. The first is to guarantee the generic existence of *continuous* random selections from the equilibrium manifold [i.e., a function $b \mapsto \mu(b)$, where $\mu(b)$ is a measure on S supported on $\{p: (p, b) \in E\}$]. Note that no such continuous selection exists in Figure 8.8.4d. For the second application, suppose that the equilibrium manifold E only represents the demand side of the economy and that full equilibrium is obtained by intersecting E with the graph of a "supply function" $s(p)$. Something along the lines of Proposition 8.8.3 is then required if one wishes to get the result (very desirable in applications to, for example, monopolistic competition theory) that generically the full equilibrium obtains at an economy that is regular from the demand side point of view. Thus, in Figure 8.8.5 this could not be obtained by perturbations of the $s(p)$ function alone, but we could have it if E is also perturbed to an E' that is generic in the sense of the proposition.

For any $\eta \in \mathcal{J}$ regular, consider now the projection $h_\eta^1: E_\eta \to S$ on the first coordinate $(p, t) \mapsto p$. A property of interest, and obviously not implied by regularity, is that h_η^1 be one-to-one, that is, that any price vector $p \in S$ be an equilibrium for at most one $t \in [0, 1]$. Because h_η^1 is a map from

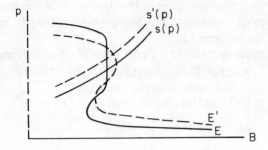

Figure 8.8.5

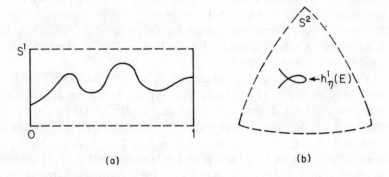

Figure 8.8.6

a one-dimensional to an $(\ell-1)$-dimensional manifold, this is a property
the more likely to hold, the larger ℓ is. It turns out that the key number
is 3. If $\ell-1 \geq 3$, then the next proposition tells us that h_η^1 is, generically, a
homeomorphism; whereas if $\ell-1 < 3$, Figures 8.8.6a and b show that for,
respectively, $\ell-1 = 1, 2$, the homeomorphism property cannot be dense.

8.8.5. Proposition. *Let $\ell-1 \geq 3$. Then there is an open and dense
set $\mathfrak{I}'' \subset \mathfrak{I}$ such that every $\eta \in \mathfrak{I}''$ is regular and the projection of
E_η on its first component is one-to-one.*

Proof. Let η be a given path with associated excess demand for the first
$\ell-1$ commodities $f(p, t)$. For $z = (z_1, z_2) \in R_{++}^{2\ell}$ construct a perturbed path
η_z by replacing $\omega_1(t) + t z_1 + z_2$ for $\omega_1(t)$. Let $f(p, t, z)$ be the corresponding perturbed excess demand. We show that, for a.e. z, η_z satisfies two

transversality conditions. The first implies the denseness of the desired homeomorphism property, whereas the second guarantees that the latter holds stably, that is, on an open set.

For the first condition, let $J = \{(t, t') \in [0, 1]^2 : t \neq t'\}$ and define ξ: $S \times J \times R_{++}^{2\ell} \to R^{2(\ell-1)}$ by $\xi(p, t, t', z) = (f(p, t, z), f(p, t', z))$. The map $\partial_z \xi(p, t, t', z)$ has always full rank. Indeed, given $(a, b) \in R^{2(\ell-1)}$, take $v_1, v_2 \in T_p$ with the first $\ell - 1$ coordinates (denoted $\bar{v}_1, \bar{v}_2$) equal to

$$[1/(t' - t)](b - a), \qquad [1/(t' - t)](t'a - tb),$$

respectively. Then

$$\partial_z \xi(p, t, t', z)(v_1, v_2) = (t\bar{v}_1 + \bar{v}_2, t'\bar{v}_1 + \bar{v}_2) = (a, b).$$

By the transversality theorem we have, therefore, that for a.e. z, the system of $2(\ell - 1)$ equations in $(\ell - 1) + 2$ unknowns $\xi_z(p, t, t') = 0$ has 0 as a regular value. If $\ell - 1 \geq 3$, then the system has more equations than unknowns. Hence, it never has a solution. In other words, for a.e. z, there is no p and $t \neq t'$ such that $(p, t), (p, t') \in E_{\eta_z}$. This is, of course, the desired one-to-one property.

For the second transversality condition, let $\xi : S \times [0, 1] \times R_{++}^{2\ell} \to R^{2(\ell-1)}$ be defined by $\xi(p, t, z) = (f(p, t, z), \partial_p f(p, t, z))$. Again, $\partial_z \xi(p, t, z)$ always has full rank. Indeed, given any $(a, b) \in R^{2(\ell-1)}$ take $v_1, v_2 \in T_p$ with the first $\ell - 1$ coordinates (denoted $\bar{v}_1, \bar{v}_2$) equal to b, $a - tb$, respectively. Then $\partial_z \xi(p, t, z)(v_1, v_2) = (t\bar{v}_1 + \bar{v}_2, \bar{v}_1) = (a, b)$. Hence, for a.e. z, zero is a regular value of ξ_z, which, if $\ell - 1 \geq 2$, means that $\xi_z(p, t) = 0$ has no solution; that is, the projection of E_{η_z} on the p coordinate always has full rank (technically, it is an immersion), and, therefore, it is always locally one-to-one. Note that this is violated in Figure 8.8.5a but is satisfied in Figure 8.8.5b, where $\ell - 1 \geq 2$. Because the full rank condition is open, the local one-to-one property is open and dense. Once this is known, the stability of the global one-to-one property follows from the first transversality condition via a trivial compactness argument.   ∎

As its proof makes clear, the previous proposition amounts to a version of the Whitney embedding theorem (see H.2.1.iv). Thus, there is nothing mysterious about the number 3, since this is just the dimension $2 \dim B + 1$ one gets in the Whitney theorem once we take into account that B is one-dimensional. Presumably, with $\ell - 1 \geq 2 \dim B + 1$, Proposition 8.8.5 extends to parameterizations of any dimensionality. As an example, take the case where B is a compact manifold of zero dimension, that is, a finite set of points. Then the dimensionality condition $\ell - 1 \geq 2 \dim B + 1$ is automatically satisfied (we always assume $\ell - 1 \geq 1$), and so we should generically expect that the equilibrium sets of any b and b' will be disjoint if $b \neq b'$. More formally, let B be a finite set and, with respect to this B, define the space of parameterized economies $\mathfrak{J}_B$ in the same way that $\mathfrak{J}$ has been defined above for $B = [0, 1]$. Then for every $\eta \in \mathfrak{J}_B$ and $b \in B$, we have an economy $\eta(b)$. Note that the concept of regular η is now equivalent to the regularity of $\eta(b)$ for every b, and, therefore, the genericity of regular parameterizations by B is equivalent to the genericity of regular economies. We have then:

> **8.8.6. Proposition.** *For B finite there is an open and dense set $\mathfrak{J}_B'' \subset \mathfrak{J}_B$ such that if $\eta \in \mathfrak{J}_B''$ then:*
>
> (i) $\eta(b)$ *is regular for every* b; *and*
> (ii) $p \neq p'$ *whenever* $(p, b), (p', b') \in E$ *and* $b \neq b'$; *that is, the projection of E_η on the first coordinate is one-to-one.*

Proof. Preferences are kept fixed throughout. Economies are indexed by $\omega \in R_{++}^{\ell n}$. Let $f: S \times R_{++}^{\ell n} \to R^{\ell-1}$ be the aggregate excess demand function. The key and obvious observation is that if $\bar{\omega}$ is regular and $p(\omega)$ is the local C^1 solution to $f(\cdot, \omega) = 0$, then $\partial p(\omega) = -[\partial_p f(p(\bar{\omega}), \bar{\omega})]^{-1} \partial f(p(\bar{\omega}), \bar{\omega})$ has full rank. So we can move the equilibrium price in any direction by perturbing ω. Because a.e. ω yields a regular economy, it suffices now to note that if we have two regular economies ω, ω' with equilibrium sets $W(\omega), W(\omega')$, we can guarantee $p \neq p'$ for every pair $p \in W(\omega)$, $p' \in W(\omega')$ by handling the finite set of such pairs in sequence. ∎

It should be clear from the previous proof that more restrictions could be imposed on η [e.g., general position of the set $h_\eta^1(B)$] without losing genericity.

8.9 Reference notes

For the mathematical and more philosophical aspects of the generic point of view see the references for Section I of Chapter 1.

Section 8.4. For 8.4.1 and 8.4.2 see Mas-Colell (1974). For 8.4.3 and 8.4.4 see Schecter (1978). Proposition 8.4.6 constitutes the only glimpse in this book of the topic of smoothing by aggregation. The literature on this theme is so extensive and the overlap with this text is so small that it would not be practical to attempt a listing of primary sources. Fortunately, we can refer to the excellent survey monograph by Trockel (1984).

Section 8.5. The references for Chapters 3 and 6 are relevant.

Section 8.6. The references for Section 4.6 are relevant.

Section 8.7. The basic references for the genericity of regular economies were given in Chapter 5 (especially the references for Sections 5.3 and 5.4). Proposition 8.7.1 is more general but closely modeled on the main result of Mas-Colell (1975). See also Kehoe (1980, 1982, 1983).

Section 8.8. Proposition 8.8.1 is related to 5.8.22 and, therefore, to Balasko (1975a) and Schecter (1979). The significance of results such as 8.8.3 for the theory of monopolistic competition can be assessed from Roberts (1980) or Mas-Colell (1982). Results analogous to 8.8.5 and 8.8.6 have turned up in the general equilibrium theory of rational expectations (e.g. Radner, 1979; Allen, 1981; Jordan–Radner, 1982) and incomplete markets (e.g., Repullo, 1984).

References

Abbreviation conventions:
A.E.R.   *American Economic Review*
I.E.R.   *International Economic Review*
J.E.T.   *Journal of Economic Theory*
J.M.E.   *Journal of Mathematical Economics*
R.E.S.   *Review of Economic Studies*

Abraham, R., and Marsden, J. 1978. *Foundations of Mechanics,* 2nd ed. Reading, MA: Benjamin/Cummings.

Abraham, R., and Robbin, J. 1967. *Transversal Mappings and Flows.* Reading, MA: Benjamin.

Allais, M., 1943. *A la recherche d'une discipline économique,* vol. 1. Paris: Ateliers Industria. (2nd ed., 1953: *Traité d'économie pure.* Paris: Imprimerie Nationale.)

Allen, B. 1981. Generic existence of completely revealing equilibria for economies with uncertainty when prices convey information. *Econometrica.* 49(5): 1173–99.

Anderson, R. 1978. An elementary core equivalence theorem. *Econometrica.* 46(6): 1483–87.

1981. Core theory with strongly convex preferences. *Econometrica.* 49(6): 1457–68.

Antonelli, G. B. 1886. *Sulla teoria matematica della economia politica.* Pisa: Tipografia del Folchetto. (Translated as chap. 16 in *Preferences, Utility, and Demand,* ed. J. Chipman et al., pp. 336–64. New York: Harcourt Brace Jovanovich, 1971.)

Apostol, T. M. 1957. *Mathematical Analysis.* Reading, MA: Addison-Wesley.

Araujo, A., and Mas-Colell, A. 1978. Notes on the smoothing of aggregate demand. *J.M.E.* 5(2): 113–27.

Arnold, V. I. 1973. *Ordinary Differential Equations.* Cambridge, MA: MIT Press.

1983. *Geometrical Methods in the Theory of Ordinary Differential Equations.* Berlin: Springer-Verlag.

Artstein, Z. 1980. Discrete and continuous bang-bang and facial spaces or: Look for the extreme points. *SIAM Review.* 22(2): 172–85.

Arrow, K. 1951. Alternative proof of the substitution theorem for Leontief models in the general case. In *Activity Analysis of Production and Allocation,* ed. T. Koopmans, pp. 155–64. New York: Wiley.

353

1952. An extension of the basic theorems of classical welfare economics. In *Proceedings of the Second Berkeley Symposium on Mathematical Statistics*, ed. J. Neyman, pp. 507-32. Berkeley: University of California Press.

Arrow, K., and Hahn, F. 1971. *General Competitive Analysis*. San Francisco: Holden-Day.

Arrow, K., and Hurwicz, L. 1958. On the stability of the competitive equilibrium I. *Econometrica.* 26(4): 522-52.

Arrow, K., and Intriligator, M., eds. 1981. *Handbook of Mathematical Economics*, vol. I. New York: North-Holland.

Arrow, K., and Intriligator, M., eds. 1982. *Handbook of Mathematical Economics*, vol. II. New York: North-Holland.

Artzner, P., and Neuefeind, W. 1978. Boundary behavior of supply: A continuity property of the maximizing correspondence. *J.M.E.* 5(2): 133-52.

Aumann, R. 1964. Markets with a continuum of trades. *Econometrica.* 32(1): 39-50.

1975. Values of markets with a continuum of trades. *Econometrica.* 43(4): 611-46.

1979. On the rate of convergence of the core. *I.E.R.* 20(2): 349-57.

Balasko, Y., 1975a. The graph of the Walras correspondence. *Econometrica.* 43(5-6): 907-12.

1975b. Some results on uniqueness and on stability of equilibrium in general equilibrium theory. *J.M.E.* 2(2): 95-118.

1976. *L'équilibre économique du point de vue différentiel*. Doctoral thesis. Université de Paris, IX.

1978a. Economic equilibrium and catastrophe theory: An introduction. *Econometrica.* 46(3): 557-69.

1978b. Equilibrium analysis and envelope theory. *J.M.E.* 5(2): 153-72.

1979a. Budget-constrained Pareto-efficient allocations. *J.E.T.* 21(3): 359-79.

1979b. A geometric approach to equilibrium analysis. *J.M.E.* 6(3): 217-28.

1979c. Economies with a finite but large number of equilibria. *J.M.E.* 6(2): 145-47.

1980. Number and definiteness of economic equilibria. *J.M.E.* 7(3): 215-25.

Balasko, Y., and Shell, K. 1980. The overlapping-generations model, I: The case of pure exchange without money. *J.E.T.* 23(3): 281-306.

Barten, A., and Böhm, V. 1982. Consumer theory. Chap. 9 in *Handbook of Mathematical Economics*, vol. II, ed. K. Arrow and M. Intriligator, pp. 381-429. New York: North-Holland.

Berger, M. 1977. *Nonlinearity and Functional Analysis*. New York: Academic Press.

Bewley, T. 1973. Edgeworth's conjecture. *Econometrica.* 41(3): 425-54.

1980. The permanent income hypothesis and long-run economic stability. *J.E.T.* 22(3): 377-94.

Billingsley, P. 1968. *Convergence of Probability Measures*. New York: Wiley.

Bourbaki, N. 1966. *General Topology,* part 2. Reading, MA: Addison-Wesley.

Brown, D., and Robinson, A. 1972. A limit theorem on the cores of large standard exchange economies. *Proceedings of the National Academy of Sciences of the USA.* 69(5): 1258-60.

1975. Nonstandard exchange economies. *Econometrica.* 43(1): 41-55.

Cassels, J. 1975. Measures of the non-convexity of sets and the Shapley–Folkman–Starr theorem. *Mathematical Proceedings of the Cambridge Philosophical Society.* 78: 433-36.

Champsaur, P. 1975. Cooperation versus competition. *J.E.T.* 11(3): 394–417.

Champsaur, P., and Laroque, G. 1981. Fair allocations in large economies. *J.E.T.* 25(2): 269–82.

Cheng, H. C. 1981a. What is the normal rate of convergence of the core? (Part I). *Econometrica.* 49(1): 73–83.

1981b. On dual regularity and value convergence theorems. *J.M.E.* 8(1): 37–57.

1982a. Generic examples on the rate of convergence of the core. *I.E.R.* 23(2): 309–21.

1982b. What is the normal rate of convergence of the core? (Part II). Typescript.

1982c. A uniform convergence result for non-convex economies. Working Paper No. 8210. Department of Economics, University of Southern California.

Chichilnisky, G. 1976. Manifold of preferences and equilibria. Technical Report No. 27. Project on Efficiency in Decision Making in Economics, Harvard University.

Chipman, J. 1974. Homothetic preferences and aggregation. *J.E.T.* 8(1): 26–38.

Chipman, J., Hurwicz, L., Richter, M., and Sonnenschein, H., eds. 1971. *Preferences, Utility, and Demand.* New York: Harcourt Brace Jovanovich.

Clark, J. B. 1899. *The Distribution of Wealth: A Theory of Wages, Interest, and Profits.* New York: Macmillan.

Clarke, F. 1983. *Optimization and Nonsmooth Analysis.* New York: Wiley.

Cournot, A. 1838. *Recherches sur les principes mathématiques de la théorie des richesses.* Paris: M. Rivière. (Trans. N. Bacon, *Researches into the Mathematical Principles of the Theory of Wealth.* New York: Macmillan, 1897.)

Deaton, A., and Muellbauer, J. 1980. *Economics and Consumer Behaviour.* Cambridge: Cambridge University Press.

Debreu, G. 1951. The coefficient of resource utilization. *Econometrica.* 19(3): 273–92. (Reprinted in G. Debreu, *Mathematical Economics,* pp. 30–49. Cambridge: Cambridge University Press, 1983.)

1959. *Theory of Value.* New York: Wiley.

1962. New concepts and techniques for equilibrium analysis. *I.E.R.* 3(3): 257–73. (Reprinted in G. Debreu, *Mathematical Economics,* pp. 133–50. Cambridge: Cambridge University Press, 1983.)

1970. Economies with a finite set of equilibria. *Econometrica.* 38(3): 387–92. (Reprinted in G. Debreu, *Mathematical Economics,* pp. 179–85. Cambridge: Cambridge University Press, 1983.)

1972. Smooth preferences. *Econometrica.* 40(4): 603–15. (Reprinted in G. Debreu, *Mathematical Economics,* pp. 186–201. Cambridge: Cambridge University Press, 1983.)

1974. Excess demand functions. *J.M.E.* 1(1): 15–21. (Reprinted in G. Debreu, *Mathematical Economics,* pp. 203–209. Cambridge: Cambridge University Press, 1983.)

1975. The rate of convergence of the core of an economy. *J.M.E.* 2(1): 1–7. (Reprinted in G. Debreu, *Mathematical Economics,* pp. 210–16. Cambridge: Cambridge University Press, 1983.)

1976a. Smooth preferences: a corrigendum. *Econometrica.* 44(4): 831–32. (Reprinted in G. Debreu, *Mathematical Economics,* pp. 201–202. Cambridge: Cambridge University Press, 1983.)

1976b. Regular differentiable economies. *A.E.R.* 66(2): 280–87. (Reprinted in G. Debreu, *Mathematical Economics,* pp. 232–41. Cambridge: Cambridge University Press, 1983.)

1983. *Mathematical Economics.* Cambridge: Cambridge University Press.

Debreu, G., and Scarf, H. 1963. A limit theorem on the core of an economy. *I.E.R.* 4(3): 235–46. (Reprinted in G. Debreu, *Mathematical Economics,* pp. 151–62. Cambridge: Cambridge University Press, 1983.)

1972. The limit of the core of an economy. In *Decision and Organization,* ed. C. B. McGuire and R. Radner, pp. 283–95. Amsterdam: North-Holland.

Delbaen, F. 1971. Lower and upper hemicontinuity of the Walras correspondence. Doctoral dissertation. Free University of Brussels.

Dierker, E. 1972. Two remarks on the number of equilibria of an economy. *Econometrica.* 40(5): 951–53.

1974. *Topological Methods in Walrasian Economics.* Lecture notes on Economics and Mathematical Sciences, 92. Berlin: Springer-Verlag.

1975. Gains and losses at core allocations. *J.M.E.* 2(2): 119–28.

1982. Regular economies. Chap. 17 in *Handbook of Mathematical Economics,* vol. II, ed. K. Arrow and M. Intriligator, pp. 795–830. New York: North-Holland.

Dierker, E., and Dierker, H. 1972. The local uniqueness of equilibria. *Econometrica.* 40(5): 867–81.

Dierker, H. 1975a. Smooth preferences and the regularity of equilibria. *J.M.E.* 2(1): 43–62.

1975b. Equilibria and core of large economics. *J.M.E.* 2(2): 155–69.

Dieudonné, J. 1960. *Foundations of Modern Analysis.* New York: Academic Press.

Diewert, W. E. 1977. Generalized Slutsky conditions for aggregate consumer demand functions. *J.E.T.* 15(2): 353–62.

1982. Duality approaches to microeconomic theory. Chap. 12 in *Handbook of Mathematical Economics,* vol. II, ed. K. Arrow and M. Intriligator, pp. 535–99. New York: North-Holland.

Dubey, P., Mas-Colell, A., and Shubik, M. 1980. Efficiency properties of strategic market games: An axiomatic approach. *J.E.T.* 22(2): 339–62.

Dubey, P., and Neyman, A. 1984. Payoffs in nonatomic economies: An axiomatic approach. *Econometrica.* 52(5): 1129–50.

Dugundji, J. 1966. *Topology.* Boston: Allyn & Bacon.

Eaves, B. C. 1972. Homotopies for computation of fixed points. *Mathematical Programming.* 3: 1–22.

Edgeworth, F. Y. 1881. *Mathematical Psychics.* London: Kegan.

Eggleston, H. 1958. *Convexity.* Cambridge: Cambridge University Press.

Eisenberg, B. 1961. Aggregation of utility functions. *Management Science.* 7(3): 337–50.

El-Hodiri, M. 1971. *Constrained Extrema: Introduction to the Differentiable Case with Economic Applications.* New York: Springer-Verlag.

Feldman, A. 1973. Bilateral trading processes, pairwise optimality, and Pareto optimality. *R.E.S.* 40(4): 463–73.

Fenchel, W. 1953. *Convex Cones, Sets, and Functions.* Mimeographed lecture notes. Department of Mathematics, Princeton University.

1956. Ueber konvexe Funktionen mit vorgeschriebenen Niveaumannigfaltigkeiten. *Mathematische Zeitschrift.* 63(5): 496–506.

de Finetti, B. 1949. Sulle stratificazioni convesse. *Annali di Matematica Pura ed Applicata.* 30, serie 4: 173–83.

Fisher, F. 1972. Gross substitutes and the utility function. *J.E.T.* 4(1): 82–87.

Foley, D. 1967. Resource allocation and the public sector. *Yale Economic Essays.* 7(1): 45–98.

Franklin, J. 1968. *Matrix Theory.* Englewood Cliffs, NJ: Prentice-Hall.

Freixas, X., and Mas-Colell, A. 1983. Engel curves leading to the weak axiom in the aggregate. H.I.E.R. D.P. 975, Harvard University.

Fuchs, G. 1974. Private ownership economies with a finite number of equilibria. *J.M.E.* 1(2): 141–58.

1977. Continuity of equilibria for production economies: New results. *Econometrica.* 45(8): 1777–96.

Fuss, M., and McFadden, D., eds. 1978. *Production Economics: A Dual Approach to Theory and Applications,* 2 vols. New York: North-Holland.

Gale, D. 1960. *The Theory of Linear Economic Models.* New York: McGraw-Hill.

Gantmacher, F. R. 1959. *The Theory of Matrices,* vol. 1. New York: Chelsea.

Geanakoplos, J., and Polemarchakis, H. 1980. On the disaggregation of excess demand functions. *Econometrica.* 48(2): 315–31.

Geldrop, J. H. van. 1980. A note on local Pareto optimum. *J.M.E.* 7(1): 51–54.

Gillies, D. B. 1953. *Some Theorems on N-Person Games.* Ph.D. dissertation. Princeton University.

Goldman, S., and Starr, R. 1982. Pairwise, t-wise and Pareto optimalities. *Econometrica.* 50(3): 593–606.

Golubitsky, M., and Guillemin, V. 1973. *Stable Mappings and Their Singularities.* New York: Springer-Verlag.

Gorman, W. 1953. Community preference fields. *Econometrica.* 21(1): 63–80.

Greenberg, J. 1977. An elementary proof of the existence of a competitive equilibrium with weak gross substitutes. *Quarterly Journal of Economics.* 91(4): 513–16.

Grinberg, V. S., and Sevastjanov, S. V. 1980. O velitchine konstanty Steinitza. [In Russian.] *Funktsionzl'vnyi Analiz i Ego Prilozheniia.* 14(2): 56–57.

Grodal, B. 1975. The rate of convergence of the core for a purely competitive sequence of economies. *J.M.E.* 2(2): 171–86.

Guillemin, V., and Pollack, A. 1974. *Differential Topology.* Englewood Cliffs, NJ: Prentice-Hall.

Hahn, F. 1982. Chap. 16 in *Handbook of Mathematical Economies,* vol. II, ed. K. Arrow and M. Intriligator, pp. 745–93. New York: North-Holland.

Hammond, P. 1979. Straightforward individual incentive compatibility in large economies. *R.E.S.* 46(2): 262–82.

Hansen, T. 1969. A note on the limit of the core of an exchange economy. *I.E.R.* 10(3): 479–83.

Hardy, G. H., and Wright, E. M. 1954. *Introduction to the Theory of Numbers,* 3rd ed. Oxford: Oxford University Press.

Hestenes, M. 1975. *Optimization Theory: The Finite Dimensional Case.* New York: Wiley.

Hicks, J. 1939. *Value and Capital.* Oxford: Clarendon Press.

Hicks, J., and Allen, R. G. D. 1934. A reconsideration of the theory of value I, II. *Economica.* N.S. 1: 52–73, 196–219.

Hicks, N. J. 1971. *Notes on Differential Geometry.* London: Van Nostrand Reinhold.

Hildenbrand, K. 1972. Continuity of the equilibrium-set correspondence. *J.E.T.* 5(1): 152–62.

1974. Finiteness of $\Pi(\mathcal{E})$ and continuity of Π. Appendix to chap. 2 of W. Hildenbrand, *Core and Equilibria of a Large Economy.* Princeton: Princeton University Press.

Hildenbrand, W. 1974. *Core and Equilibria of a Large Economy.* Princeton: Princeton University Press.

1981. Short-run production functions based on microdata. *Econometrica.* 49(5): 1095–1125.

1982. Core of an economy. Chap. 18 in *Handbook of Mathematical Economics,* vol. II, ed. K. Arrow and M. Intriligator, pp. 831–77. New York: North-Holland.

1983. On the "Law of Demand." *Econometrica.* 51(4): 997–1020.

Hildenbrand, W., and Kirman, A. 1976. *Introduction to Equilibrium Analysis.* Amsterdam: North-Holland.

Hirsch, M. 1976. *Differential Topology.* New York: Springer-Verlag.

1984. The dynamical systems approach to differential equations. *Bulletin of the American Mathematical Society.* 11(1): 1–64.

Hirsch, M., and Smale, S. 1974. *Differential Equations, Dynamical Systems, and Linear Algebra.* New York: Academic Press.

Hoeffding, W. 1963. Probability inequalities for sums of bounded random variables. *Journal of the American Statistical Association.* 58(301): 13–30.

Hotelling, H. 1935. Demand function with limited budgets. *Econometrica.* 3(1): 66–78.

1938. The general welfare in relation to problems of taxation and of railway and utility rates. *Econometrica.* 6(3): 242–69.

Howe, R. 1979. On the tendency toward convexity of the vector sum of sets. Cowles Foundation Discussion Paper No. 538. Yale University.

Hurwicz, L. 1974. On allocations attainable through Nash equilibria. *J.E.T.* 21(1): 140–65.

Intriligator, M. 1971. *Mathematical Optimization and Economy Theory.* Englewood Cliffs, NJ: Prentice-Hall.

Jerison, M. 1982. The representative consumer and the weak axiom when the distribution of income is fixed. Working Paper No. 150. State University of New York at Albany.

1984. Aggregation and pairwise aggregation of demand when the distribution of income is fixed. *J.E.T.* 33(1): 1–31.

Johansen, L. 1978. A calculus approach to the theory of the core of an exchange economy. *A.E.R.* 68(5): 813–20.

Jordan, J. 1982. The generic existence of rational expectations equilibrium in the higher dimensional case. *J.E.T.* 26(2): 224–43.

Jordan, J., and Radner, R. 1982. Rational expectations in microeconomic models: An overview. *J.E.T.* 26(2): 201–23.

Kannai, Y. 1970. Continuity properties of the core of a market. *Econometrica.* 38(6): 791–815.

1974. Approximation of convex preferences. *J.M.E.* 1(2): 101–106.

1977. Concavifiability and constructions of concave utility functions. *J.M.E.* 4(1): 1–56.

Katzner, D. 1968. A note on the differentiability of consumer demand functions. *Econometrica.* 36(2): 415–18.

1970. *Static Demand Theory.* New York: Macmillan.

Kehoe, T. 1980. An index theorem for general equilibrium models with production. *Econometrica.* 48(5): 1211–32.

1982. Regular production economies. *J.M.E.* 10(2/3): 147–76.

1983. Regularity and index theory for economies with smooth production technologies. *Econometrica.* 51(4): 895–919.

1985. Multiplicity of equilibria and comparative statics. *Quarterly Journal of Economics.* 100(1): 119–48.

Kehoe, T., and Levine, D. 1985. Comparative statics and perfect foresight in infinite horizon economies. *Econometrica.* 53(2): 433–53.

Kehoe, T., and Mas-Colell, A. 1984. An observation on gross substitutability and the weak axiom of revealed preference. *Economic Letters.* 15(3–4): 241–43.

Kellog, B., Li, T. Y., and Yorke, J. 1976. A method of continuation for calculating a Brouwer fixed point. Chap. 3 in *Computing Fixed Points with Applications,* ed. S. Karamardian, pp. 107–20. New York: Academic Press.

Kihlstrom, R., Mas-Colell, A., and Sonnenschein, H. 1976. The demand theory of the weak axiom of revealed preference. *Econometrica.* 44(5): 971–78.

Kleinberg, N. 1980. Fair allocations and equal incomes. *J.E.T.* 23(2): 189–200.

Koopmans, T., ed. 1951a. *Activity Analysis of Production and Allocation.* New York: Wiley.

1951b. Analysis of production as an efficient combination of activities. In *Activity Analysis of Production and Allocation,* ed. T. Koopmans, pp. 33–97. New York: Wiley.

1957. *Three Essays on the State of Economic Science.* New York: McGraw-Hill.

Kuratowski, K. 1961. *Topologie, II.* Warsaw: Panstwowe Wydawnictwo Naukowe.

Lang, S. 1972. *Linear Algebra,* 2nd ed. Reading, MA: Addison-Wesley.

1983. *Real Analysis,* 2nd ed. Reading, MA: Addison-Wesley.

Lange, O. 1942. The foundations of welfare economics. *Econometrica.* 10(2): 215–28.

Lau, L. 1982. A note on the fundamental theorem of exact aggregation. *Economic Letters.* 9(2): 119–26.

McFadden, D. 1978. Cost, revenue, and profit functions. In *Production Economics: A Dual Approach to Theory and Applications,* ed. M. Fuss and D. McFadden, pp. 3–109. New York: North-Holland.

McFadden, D., Mantel, R., Mas-Colell, A., and Richter, M. 1974. A characterization of community excess demand functions. *J.E.T.* 9(4): 361–74.

McKenzie, L. 1957. Demand theory without a utility index. *R.E.S.* 24(3): 185–89.

1959. On the existence of general equilibrium for a competitive market. *Econometrica.* 27(1): 54–71.

1960. Matrices with dominant diagonals and economic theory. In *Mathematical Methods in the Social Sciences, 1959,* ed. K. Arrow, S. Karlin, and P. Suppes, pp. 47–62. Stanford, CA: Stanford University Press.

1961. On the existence of general equilibrium: Some corrections. *Econometrica.* 29(2): 247–48.

McLennan, A. 1982. *Three Essays on Economic Theory.* Ph.D. dissertation. Princeton University.

Mangasarian, O. 1969. *Nonlinear Programming.* New York: McGraw-Hill.

Mantel, R. 1969. On the representation of preferences by concave utility functions. Working Paper No. 66. Instituto Torcuato di Tella, Buenos Aires.

1971. The welfare adjustment process: Its stability properties. *I.E.R.* 12(3): 415–30.

1974. On the characterization of aggregate excess demand. *J.E.T.* 7(3): 348–53.

1976. Homothetic preferences and community excess demand functions. *J.E.T.* 12(2): 197–201.

1977. Implications of microeconomic theory for community excess demand functions. In *Frontiers of Quantitative Economics,* ed. M. Intriligator, vol. IIIA, pp. 111–26. New York: North-Holland.

Marsden, J. 1974. *Elementary Classical Analysis.* San Francisco: Freeman.

Mas-Colell, A. 1974. Continuous and smooth consumers: Approximation theorems. *J.E.T.* 8(3): 305–36.

1975. On the continuity of equilibrium prices in constant-returns production economies. *J.M.E.* 2(1): 21–33.

1977a. An introduction to the differentiable approach in the theory of economic equilibrium. CRMS Working Paper No. 258. University of California, Berkeley. [Forthcoming in *Studies in Mathematical Economics,* ed. S. Reiter. American Mathematical Society Studies in Mathematics Series.]

1977b. On the equilibrium price set of an exchange economy. *J.M.E.* 4(2): 117–26.

1977c. Regular, nonconvex economies. *Econometrica.* 45(6): 1387–407.

1982. The Cournotian foundations of Walrasian equilibrium theory: An exposition of recent theory. Chap. 7 in *Advances in Economic Theory,* ed. W. Hildenbrand, pp. 183–224. Cambridge: Cambridge University Press.

1983. On the second welfare theorem for anonymous net trades in exchange economies with many agents. SEEDS Working Paper No. 8. Bilbao. [Forthcoming in *Information, Incentives and Economic Mechanisms, Essays in Honor of Leonid Hurwicz,* ed. T. Groves, R. Radner, and S. Reiter. Minneapolis: University of Minnesota Press.]

Mas-Colell, A., and Neuefeind, W. 1977. Some generic properties of aggregate excess demand and an application. *Econometrica.* 45(3): 591–99.

Maskin, E. 1980. On first best taxation. In *Income Distribution: The Limit to Redistribution,* ed. D. Collard, R. Lecomber, and M. Slater, pp. 9–22. New York: Wiley.

Merrill, O. H. 1972. *Applications and Extensions of an Algorithm That Computes Fixed Points of Certain Upper Semicontinuous Point-to-Set Mappings.* Ph.D. dissertation. University of Michigan.

Metzler, L. 1945. Stability of multiple markets: The Hicks conditions. *Econometrica.* 13(4): 277–92.

Millán, T. 1981. *Existence of Optimal Equilibria in Overlapping Generation Models.* Ph.D. dissertation. University of Minnesota.

Milnor, J. 1965. *Topology from the Differentiable Viewpoint.* Charlottesville: University Press of Virginia.

Mitjuschin, L. G., and Polterovich, W. M., 1978. Criteria for monotonicity of demand functions. (In Russian.) *Ekonomika i Matematicheskie Metody.* 14: 122–28.

Muellbauer, J. 1975. Aggregation, income distribution, and consumer demand. *R.E.S.* 42(4): 525–43.

1976. Community preferences and the representative consumer. *Econometrica.* 44(5): 979–99.

Negishi, T. 1960. Welfare economics and existence of an equilibrium for a competitive economy. *Metroeconomica.* 12: 92–97.

Nielsen, L. T. 1981. Transversality and the inverse image of a submanifold with corners. *Mathematica Scandinavica.* 49(2): 211–21.

1983. Pareto optima, non-convexities, and regulated market equilibria. *J.M.E.* 11(1): 57–63.

Nikaido, H. 1968. *Convex Structures and Economic Theory.* New York: Academic Press.

Nishino, H. 1971. On the occurrence and the existence of competitive equilibria. *Keio Economic Studies.* 8(2): 33–67.

Novshek, W., and Sonnenschein, H. 1978. Cournot and Walras equilibrium. *J.E.T.* 19(2): 223–66.

Ortega, J. M., and Rheinboldt, W. C. 1970. *Iterative Solution of Nonlinear Equations in Several Variables.* New York: Academic Press.

Ostroy, J. 1980. The no-surplus condition as a characterization of perfectly competitive equilibrium. *J.E.T.* 22(2): 183–207.

1981. Differentiability as convergence to perfectly competitive equilibrium. *J.M.E.* 8(1): 59–73.

1984. A reformulation of the marginal productivity theory of distribution. *Econometrica.* 52(3): 599–630.

Pareto, V. 1909. *Manuel d'economie politique.* Paris: Giard et Brière.

Quirk, J., and Saposnik, R. 1968. *Introduction to General Equilibrium Theory and Welfare Economics.* New York: McGraw-Hill.

Rader, T. 1968. Pairwise optimality and non-competitive behavior. In *Papers in Quantitative Economics,* ed. J. Quirk and A. Zarley, pp. 101–27. Lawrence: University Press of Kansas.

Radner, R. 1979. Rational expectations equilibrium: Generic existence and the information revealed by prices. *Econometrica.* 47(3): 655–78.

Repullo, R. 1984. *Equilibrium and Efficiency in Economies with a Sequence of Markets.* Ph.D. dissertation. University of London.

Roberts, K. 1980. The limit points of monopolistic competition. *J.E.T.* 22(2): 256–78.

Rockafellar, T. 1970. *Convex Analysis.* Princeton: Princeton University Press.

Roy, R. 1942. *De l'utilité: contribution à la théorie des choix.* Paris: Hermann.

Royden, H. 1968. *Real Analysis,* 2nd ed. New York: Macmillan.

Saari, D., and Simon, C. 1977. Singularity theory of utility mappings – I: Degenerate maxima and Pareto optima. *J.M.E.* 4(3): 217–51.

Saigal, R., and Simon, C. 1973. Generic properties of the complementarity problem. *Mathematical Programming.* 4: 324–35.

Samuelson, P. 1938. A note on the pure theory of consumer's behavior. *Economica.* N.S. 5(17): 61–71.

1947. *Foundations of Economic Analysis.* Cambridge: Harvard University Press.

1948. Consumption theory in terms of revealed preference. *Economica.* N.S. 15(60): 243–53.

1950. Evaluation of real national income. *Oxford Economic Papers,* pp. 1–29.

1951. Abstract of a theorem concerning substitutability in open Leontief models. In *Activity Analysis of Production and Allocation,* ed. T. Koopmans, pp. 142–46. New York: Wiley.

Scarf, H. 1962. A mathematical analysis of markets with a large number of participants. *Recent Advances in Game Theory: The Princeton University Conference,* pp. 127–56. Philadelphia: Ivy Curtis Press.

1982. The computation of equilibrium prices. Chap. 21 in *Handbook of Mathematical Economics,* vol. II, ed. K. Arrow and M. Intriligator, pp. 1006–61. New York: North-Holland.

Scarf, H., in collaboration with T. Hansen. 1973. *The Computation of Economic Equilibria.* New Haven: Yale University Press.

Schecter, S. 1975. *Smooth Pareto Economic Systems with Natural Boundary Conditions.* Ph.D. dissertation. University of California, Berkeley.

1977. Accessibility of optima in pure exchange economies. *J.M.E.* 4(3): 197–216.

1978. Structure of the demand function and Pareto optimal set with natural boundary conditions. *J.M.E.* 5(1): 1–21.

1979. On the structure of the equilibrium manifold. *J.M.E.* 6(1): 1–5.

Schmeidler, D. 1972. A remark on the core of an atomless economy. *Econometrica.* 40(3): 579–80.

    1980. Walrasian analysis via strategic outcomes functions. *Econometrica.* 48(7): 1585–93.

Schmeidler, D., and Vind, K. 1972. Fair net trades. *Econometrica.* 40(4): 637–42.

Schwartz, L. 1967. *Cours d'analyse,* vol. I. Paris: Hermann.

Schweizer, U. 1982. A Lagrangian approach to the limit theorem on the core of an economy. *Zeitschrift für Nationalökonomie/Journal of Economics.* 42(1): 23–30.

Serra, P. 1982. The welfare adjustment process: a different approach. Paper presented at the 22nd Latin American Congress of the Econometric Society, Rio de Janeiro, July 1982.

Shafer, W., and Sonnenschein, H. 1982. Market demand and excess demand functions. Chap. 14 in *Handbook of Mathematical Economics,* vol. II, ed. K. Arrow and M. Intriligator, pp. 71–95. New York: North-Holland.

Shapiro, P. 1977. Aggregation and the existence of a social utility function. *J.E.T* 16(2): 475–80.

Shapley, L. 1975. An example of slow-converging core. *I.E.R.* 16(2): 345–51.

Shephard, R. 1953. *Cost and Production Functions.* Princeton: Princeton University Press.

Shubik, M. 1959. Edgeworth market games. In *Contributions to the Theory of Games,* vol. IV, ed. R. D. Luce and A. W. Tucker, pp. 267–78. Princeton: Princeton University Press.

Simon, C. 1982. Scalar and vector maximization: Calculus techniques with economics applications. CREST. University of Michigan. Working Paper No. C48. [Forthcoming in *Studies in Mathematical Economics,* ed. S. Reiter. American Mathematical Association Studies in Mathematics Series.]

Simon, C., and Titus, C. 1975. Characterization of optima in smooth Pareto economic systems. *J.M.E.* 2(2): 297–330.

Singer, I. M., and Thorpe, J. A. 1967. *Lecture Notes on Elementary Topology and Geometry.* Glenview, IL: Scott, Foresman.

Slutsky, E. 1915. Sulla teoria del bilancio del consumatore. *Giornali degli economisti.* 51: 1–26. (Trans. as chap. 2 of *Readings in Price Theory,* ed. G. Stigler and K. Boulding. Chicago: Irwin, 1952.)

Smale, S. 1973. Global analysis and Economics I: Pareto optimum and a generalization of Morse theory. In *Dynamical Systems,* ed. M. Peixoto, pp. 531–44. New York: Academic Press.

    1974a. Global analysis and Economics IIA: Extension of a theorem of Debreu. *J.M.E.* 1(1): 1–14.

    1974b. Global analysis and Economics III: Pareto optima and price equilibria. *J.M.E.* 1(2): 107–17.

    1974c. Global analysis and Economics IV: Finiteness and stability of equilibria with general consumption sets and production. *J.M.E.* 1(2): 119–27.

    1974d. Global analysis and economics V: Pareto theory with constraints. *J.M.E.* 1(3): 213–21.

    1975. Sufficient conditions for an optimum. In *Dynamical Systems – Warwick 1974,* ed. A. Manning, pp. 287–92. New York: Springer-Verlag.

    1976a. Global analysis and Economics VI: Geometric analysis of Pareto optima and price equilibria under classical hypotheses. *J.M.E.* 3(1): 1–14.

    1976b. A convergent process of price adjustment and global Newton methods. *J.M.E.* 3(2): 107–20.

1981. Global analysis and economics. Chap. 8 in *Handbook of Mathematical Economics,* vol. II, ed. K. Arrow and M. Intriligator, pp. 331–70. New York: North-Holland.

Sondermann, D. 1975. Smoothing demand by aggregation. *J.M.E.* 2(2): 201–23.

Sonnenschein, H. 1972. Market excess demand functions. *Econometrica.* 40(3): 549–63.

1973. Do Walras' identity and continuity characterize the class of community excess demand functions? *J.E.T.* 6(4): 345–54.

Spivak, M. 1965. *Calculus on Manifolds.* New York: Benjamin.

Starr, R. 1969. Quasi-equilibria in markets with non-convex preferences. *Econometrica.* 37(1): 25–38.

Steinitz, E. 1913. Bedingt konvergente Reiken und konvexe Systeme. *Journal für die Reine und Angewandte Mathematik.* 143: 128–75.

Thompson, W., and Varian, H. 1985. Theories of justice based on symmetry. In *Social Goals and Social Organization: Essays in Memory of Elisha Pazner,* ed. L. Hurwicz, D. Schmeidler, and H. Sonnenschein, chap. 4. Cambridge: Cambridge University Press.

Todd, M. 1976. *The Computation of Fixed Points and Applications.* Lecture Notes in Economics and Mathematical Systems No. 124. New York: Springer-Verlag.

1979. A note on computing equilibria in economies with activity analysis models of production. *J.M.E.* 6(2): 135–44.

Townsend, R. 1983. Theories of intermediated structures. In *Carnegie–Rochester Conference Series on Public Policy,* vol. 18, ed. K. Brunner and K. Meltzer, pp. 221–72.

Trockel, W. 1984. *Market Demand: An Analysis of Large Economies with Non-convex Preferences.* Lecture Notes in Economics and Mathematical Systems, 223. New York: Springer-Verlag.

Valentine, F. A. 1964. *Convex Sets.* New York: McGraw-Hill.

Varaiya, P. 1972. *Notes on Optimization.* New York: Van Nostrand Reinhold.

Varian, H. 1976. Two problems in the theory of fairness. *Journal of Public Economics.* 5(3, 4): 249–60.

Vind, K. 1964. Edgeworth-allocations in an exchange economy with many traders. *I.E.R.* 5(2): 165–77.

Wald, A. 1951. On some systems of equations in mathematical economics. *Econometrica.* 19(4): 368–403. (Trans. of Ueber einige Gleichungssysteme der mathematischen Oekonomie, *Zeitschrift für Nationalökonomie.* 7(5): 637–70.)

Walras, L. 1874. *Eléments d'économie politique pure.* Lausanne: Corbaz. (Trans. of the definitive 1926 edition by W. Jaffé, *Elements of Pure Economics.* London: Irwin, 1954.)

Wan, Y. H. 1975. On local Pareto optima. *J.M.E.* 2(1): 35–42.

1978. On the structure and stability of local pareto optima in a pure exchange economy. *J.M.E.* 5(3): 255–74.

Wold, H., in collaboration with L. Juréen. 1953. *Demand Analysis.* New York: Wiley.

Name index

Subject index

activity, linear, 97
    generalized linear, 109, 251, 332
aggregation, smoothing by, 174, 326, 329,
    351
allocation, 114
    attainable, 114–15, 169
    attainable and supported by p, λ, 126
    linked, 132–3, 137, 159, 268, 311, 335
    Walrasian, 169, 171
almost everywhere, 23
anonymous allocation, 265
    nearly Walrasian, 302, 308

Baire property, 10, 52
base, for a linear space, 12, 14
    ordered, 12
    orthonormal, 16
    standard, 12
boundary, 7
    of manifold, 33, 34
    of preference relation, 61
boundary condition, 68
bounded set, 9
Brouwer fixed-point theorem, 49
budget set, 60
bundle, normal, 35
bundle, tangent, 35

Caratheodory's theorem, 27
chain, 11
characteristics, space of, 168
closed set, 7
closure, 7
compact space, 8, 9, 10, 24, 27, 51
    locally compact, 8
    σ compact, 8
compactification, one-point, 8, 9
complete space, *see* space, metric;
    space, topological
completeness (of a preference relation), 58
composite function theorem, 19, 32

cone, convex, 27
    pointed, 27
    polyhedral, 97
    spanned by set, 27
cone, normal, 29
connected space, 8, 9, 10
    arcwise connected, 8, 10
constant returns, 97, 249, 336
constraint set, 22
consumption set, 69
contract curve, 265
convergence, weak, 24, 25
convergence of a sequence, 7
convergence of preferences, 70, 71
convergence of production sets, 112
convex hull, 27
convex set, 27
convolution, 41
coordinate system, 12
core allocation, 264
    see also equilibrium for an exchange
        economy
core equivalence theorem, 269
    approximation for economy with
        finitely many traders, 275, 279, 285,
        289, 295
    rate of convergence, 273, 298
correspondence, 11
    upper hemicontinuous, 11
critical point, 21, 37
    nondegenerate, 21, 37
critical value, 37, 42
curvature, Gaussian, 39–40, 106, 142,
    257

degree of a function, 467
demand, 61, 91
    differentiability of, 84–6
    Lipschitzian, 86, 324
    regular point of, 84

369